Everyman's United Nations

Office of Public Information

Everyman's United Nations

A Complete Handbook of the Activities
and Evolution of the United Nations
During its First Twenty Years, 1945-1965

Eighth Edition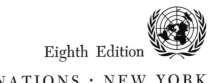

UNITED NATIONS · NEW YORK

1948	First Edition
1950	Second Edition
April 1952	Third Edition
August 1952	*Second Printing*
December 1952	*Third Printing*
August 1953	Fourth Edition
April 1954	*Second Printing*
March 1955	*Third Printing*
September 1956	Fifth Edition
October 1959	Sixth Edition
October 1964	Seventh Edition
March 1968	Eighth Edition

UNITED NATIONS PUBLICATION E.67.I.2

price: $6.00 or equivalent in other currencies

Foreword

When the United Nations was founded in 1945, at the close of the Second World War, it represented the common will of fifty-one nations of the world. Two decades later, the membership of the Organization had increased to one hundred and twenty-two States, many of them countries newly come to nationhood, all of them eager to take their place in the community of nations and to share the common interests and the common aspirations of all mankind in the quest for peace.

This book is a record of that quest. It traces the growth of the United Nations in all the major fields of its activities—the search, through discussion and negotiation, for solutions to the many issues facing the international community, the stationing of peace-keeping forces in troubled areas of the world, the implementation of dynamic programmes of economic and social progress, the adoption of fundamental instruments to ensure basic human rights for all, the active support of colonial peoples in their drive towards independence, and the establishment of justice and the rule of law for all mankind.

It is an open book. Problems and situations brought before the United Nations are set forth and the efforts of the Organization to meet and solve these questions are described. But no attempt has been made to give final answers to the questions or to draw conclusions on the work of the United Nations over its first twenty years. No such attempt could have been made, for that work is continuing, and, in the last analysis, it is for mankind to give the answers.

Nor has any attempt been made to explore all aspects of each question or to give all points of view or even to include every question that has ever been brought before the United Nations. This has been left to the more detailed studies which the Organization produces.

This edition of *Everyman's United Nations*, the eighth in the series, will, it is hoped, provide students, teachers, journalists, government officials and, indeed, men and women in all walks of life an insight into and an understanding of the work of the United Nations in carrying out the purposes of the Charter and in upholding its principles.

AGHA ABDUL HAMID
Assistant Secretary-General
Office of Public Information

Contents

PART THREE

Inter-Governmental Agencies related to the United Nations

Appendices

PART ONE

The United Nations

The United Nations

The deep-felt needs and intentions which inspired the founding of the United Nations are proclaimed in the preamble to the Charter, signed at San Francisco on June 26, 1945:

WE THE PEOPLES OF THE UNITED NATIONS DETERMINED to save succeeding generations from the scourge of war, which twice in our lifetime has brought untold sorrow to mankind, and to reaffirm faith in fundamental human rights, in the dignity and worth of the human person, in the equal rights of men and women and of nations large and small, and to establish conditions under which justice and respect for the obligations arising from treaties and other sources of international law can be maintained, and to promote social progress and better standards of life in larger freedom,

AND FOR THESE ENDS to practice tolerance and live together in peace with one another as good neighbours, and to unite our strength to maintain international peace and security, and to ensure, by the acceptance of principles and the institution of methods, that armed force shall not be used, save in the common interest, and to employ international machinery for the promotion of the economic and social advancement of all peoples,

HAVE RESOLVED TO COMBINE OUR EFFORTS TO ACCOMPLISH THESE AIMS. Accordingly, our respective governments, through representatives assembled in the city of San Francisco, who have exhibited their full powers found to be in good and due form, have agreed to the present Charter of the United Nations and do hereby establish an international organization to be known as the United Nations.

PURPOSES AND PRINCIPLES

The purposes of the United Nations are set forth in Article 1 of the Charter. They are:

1. to maintain international peace and security;
2. to develop friendly relations among nations based on respect for the principle of equal rights and self-determination of peoples;
3. to co-operate in solving international problems of an economic, social, cultural or humanitarian character, and in promoting respect for human rights and fundamental freedoms for all; and
4. to be a centre for harmonizing the actions of nations in attaining these common ends.

To fulfil the purposes for which it was established, the United Nations acts in accordance with the following principles, as set forth in Article 2 of the Charter:

1. the Organization is based on the principle of the sovereign equality of all its members;
2. members are to fulfil in good faith the obligations they have assumed under the Charter;
3. they are to settle their international disputes by peaceful means;
4. they are to refrain in their international relations from the threat or use of force in any manner inconsistent with the purposes of the United Nations;
5. they are to give the United Nations every assistance in any action it takes in accordance with the Charter, and to refrain from giving assistance to any state against which the Organization is taking preventive or enforcement action;
6. the United Nations is to ensure that non-members act in accordance with these principles so far as is necessary for maintaining international peace and security;
7. the Organization is not to intervene in matters essentially within the domestic jurisdiction of any state. This provision does not, however, prejudice the application of enforcement action with respect to threats to the peace, breaches of the peace and acts of aggression.

STEPS TO THE CHARTER

Inter-Allied Declaration

The first of a series of steps which led to the establishment of the United Nations was the Inter-Allied Declaration, which was signed on June 12, 1941, at St. James's Palace, London, by the representatives of Australia, Canada, New Zealand, the Union of South Africa and the United Kingdom, of the exiled Governments of Belgium, Czechoslovakia, Greece, Luxembourg, the Netherlands, Norway, Poland and

Yugoslavia, and of General de Gaulle of France. In the Declaration, the signatories, recognizing that "the only true basis of enduring peace is the willing co-operation of free peoples in a world in which, relieved of the menace of aggression, all may enjoy economic and social security," stated that it was their intention "to work together, and with other free peoples, both in war and peace, to this end."

Atlantic Charter

Two months later, on August 14, 1941, President Franklin D. Roosevelt of the United States and Prime Minister Winston Churchill of the United Kingdom, meeting "somewhere at sea," issued a joint declaration in which they set forth "certain common principles in the national policies of their respective countries" on which they based their hopes for a better future for the world. In the document, known as the Atlantic Charter, the two signatories stated that: "after the final destruction of the Nazi tyranny, they hope to see established a peace which will afford to all nations the means of dwelling in safety within their own boundaries, and which will afford assurance that all the men in all the lands may live out their lives in freedom from fear and want."

They also stated that: "they believe that all of the nations of the world, for realistic as well as spiritual reasons, must come to the abandonment of the use of force. Since no future peace can be maintained if land, sea, or air armaments continue to be employed by nations which threaten, or may threaten, aggression outside of their frontiers, they believe, pending the establishment of a wider and permanent system of general security, that the disarmament of such nations is essential. They will likewise aid and encourage all other practicable measures which will lighten for peace-loving peoples the crushing burden of armaments."

The two statesmen also expressed, in the document, their desire "to bring about the fullest collaboration between all nations in the economic field with the object of securing, for all, improved labour standards, economic advancement and social security."

Declaration by United Nations

On New Year's Day 1942, the representatives of twenty-six nations that were fighting against the Axis aggressors signed at Washington, D.C., the Declaration by United Nations. (This document marked the first formal use of the term "United Nations," which had been suggested by President Roosevelt.)

In the Declaration, the signatory Governments:

"Having subscribed to a common program of purposes and principles embodied in the . . . Atlantic Charter,

"Being convinced that complete victory over their enemies is essential to defend life, liberty, independence and religious freedom, and to preserve human rights and justice in their own lands as well as in other lands, and that they are now engaged in a common struggle against savage and brutal forces seeking to subjugate the world,

"Declare:

"(1) Each Government pledges itself to employ its full resources, military or economic, against those members of the Tripartite Pact and its adherents with which such Government is at war.

"(2) Each Government pledges itself to co-operate with the Governments signatory hereto and not to make a separate armistice or peace with the enemies."

The Declaration was left open for signature by other nations "which are, or may be, rendering material assistance and contributions in the struggle for victory over Hitlerism."

The twenty-six signatories of the Declaration of United Nations were:

United States	Czechoslovakia	Netherlands
United Kingdom	Dominican Republic	New Zealand
USSR	El Salvador	Nicaragua
China	Greece	Norway
Australia	Guatemala	Panama
Belgium	Haiti	Poland
Canada	Honduras	Union of South
Costa Rica	India	Africa
Cuba	Luxembourg	Yugoslavia

Later adherents to the Declaration were (in order of the dates of adherence):

Mexico	Colombia	Venezuela
Philippines	Liberia	Uruguay
Ethiopia	France	Turkey
Iraq	Ecuador	Egypt
Brazil	Peru	Saudi Arabia
Bolivia	Chile	Syria
Iran	Paraguay	Lebanon

(*Note:* France and Denmark were generally regarded as having been identified with the United Nations from the beginning. Free French Forces had fought against the Axis powers and the Danish Minister in Washington had signified the adherence of all free Danes to the Allied cause. Since the Declaration was signed by Governments, they could not at that time, however, formally adhere to it. When the French National Committee was constituted as a Government, France adhered formally to the Declaration. Denmark, which was not liberated until after the opening of the San Francisco Conference, was admitted as one of the United Nations by the Conference.)

Moscow and Teheran Conferences

In a declaration signed in Moscow on October 30, 1943, by V. M. Molotov of the USSR, Anthony Eden of the United Kingdom, Cordell Hull of the United States, and Foo Ping-sheung, the Chinese Ambassador to the Soviet Union, the four Governments proclaimed that: "they recognize the necessity of establishing at the earliest practicable date a general international organization, based on the principle of the sovereign equality of all peace-loving states, and open to membership by all such states, large and small, for the maintenance of international peace and security."

A month later, on December 1, 1943, President Roosevelt, Premier Stalin and Prime Minister Churchill, meeting at Teheran, declared the following:

"We recognize fully the supreme responsibility resting upon us and all the United Nations to make a peace which will command the goodwill of the overwhelming masses of the peoples of the world and banish the scourge and terror of war for many generations."

Dumbarton Oaks and Yalta Conferences

The first concrete step towards the creation of the United Nations was taken in the late summer of 1944 at a mansion known as Dumbarton Oaks in Washington, D.C. In the first phase of the Dumbarton Oaks Conference, from August 21 to September 28, 1944, conversations were held between the representatives of the USSR, the United Kingdom and the United States; in the second phase, from September 29 to October 7, conversations were held between the representatives of China, the United Kingdom and the United States. (This arrangement served to respect USSR neutrality in the war against Japan.) As a result of the conference, the four powers reached a number of agreements which were embodied in proposals for the establishment of a general international organization.

The Dumbarton Oaks proposals were primarily concerned with the purposes and principles of the organization, its membership and principal organs, and arrangements for the maintenance of international peace and security and for international economic and social co-operation. According to the proposals, the key body in the United Nations for preserving world peace was to be the Security Council, on which the "Big Five"—China, France, the USSR, the United Kingdom and the United States—were to be permanently represented. Agreement was not, however, reached on the question of voting procedure in the Security Council.

This question, among others, was discussed by President Roosevelt, Prime Minister Churchill and Premier Stalin at a conference at Yalta in February 1945. On February 11, 1945, following the conference, a report was issued in which the three leaders declared:

"We are resolved upon the earliest possible establishment with our Allies of a general international organization to maintain peace and security. We believe that this is essential, both to prevent aggression and to remove the political, economic and social causes of war through the close and continuing collaboration of all peace-loving peoples.

"The foundations were laid at Dumbarton Oaks. On the important question of voting procedure, however, agreement was not there reached. The present Conference has been able to resolve this difficulty.

"We have agreed that a Conference of United Nations should be called to meet at San Francisco in the United States on the 25th April 1945, to prepare the charter of such an organization, along the lines proposed in the informal conversations of Dumbarton Oaks."

The report further stated that the Government of China and the Provisional Government of France would be invited to sponsor invitations to the Conference jointly with the United States, the United Kingdom and the USSR and that as soon as consultations with China and France had been completed, the text of the proposals on voting procedure would be made public.

The Chinese Government agreed to join in sponsoring the invitations. The French Government agreed to participate in the Conference but decided not to act as a sponsoring nation.

The invitations to the Conference were issued on March 5 to those nations which had declared war on Germany or Japan by March 1 and had signed the Declaration by United Nations. The text of the invitation contained the provisions for voting in the Security Council which were subsequently adopted at San Francisco.

San Francisco Conference

Before the start of the San Francisco Conference, the Dumbarton Oaks proposals were studied and discussed by the nations of the world, both collectively and individually. From February 21 to March 8, 1945, for instance, the representatives of twenty Latin American nations met in Mexico City and adopted a resolution suggesting points to be taken into consideration in the drawing up of the charter of the proposed international organization. From April 4 to 13, 1945, talks were held in London between representatives of the British Commonwealth, and a statement issued at the close of the meetings indicated agreement that the Dumbarton Oaks proposals provided the basis for a charter, while recognizing that clarification, improvement and expansion were called for in certain respects.

On April 25, delegates of fifty nations met in San Francisco for the conference known officially as the United Nations Conference on International Organization. Working on the Dumbarton Oaks proposals, the Yalta Agreement and amendments proposed by various Governments, the delegates, meeting both in plenary sessions and in committees, drew up the 111-article Charter.

The heads of the delegations of the sponsoring countries took turns as chairman of the plenary meetings: Anthony Eden, of the United Kingdom, Edward R. Stettinius, Jr., of the United States, T. V. Soong, of China, and V. M. Molotov, of the Soviet Union. At the later meetings, Lord Halifax deputized for Mr. Eden, V. K. Wellington Koo for Mr. Soong, and A. A. Gromyko for Mr. Molotov.

The Conference formed a Steering Committee, composed of the heads of all the delegations, which decided all matters of major principle and policy. An Executive Committee of fourteen heads of delegations was chosen to prepare recommendations for the Steering Committee.

The proposed Charter was divided into four sections, each of which was considered by a commission. Commission I dealt with the general purposes of the organization, its principles, membership, the secretariat and the subject of amendments to the Charter; Commission II considered the powers and responsibilities of the General Assembly; Commission III took up the Security Council; and Commission IV worked on a draft for the Statute of the International Court of Justice, which had been prepared in Washington in April 1945 by a 44-nation Committee of Jurists.

On June 25, the delegates met in full session in the Opera House in San Francisco and unanimously adopted the Charter, and the next day, they signed it at a ceremony in the auditorium of the Veterans' Memorial Hall.

The Charter came into force on October 24, 1945, when China, France, the USSR, the United Kingdom and the United States and a majority of the other signatories had filed their instruments of ratification.

United Nations Day

On October 31, 1947, the General Assembly decided that October 24, the anniversary of the entry into force of the Charter of the United Nations, should thenceforth be officially called "United Nations Day," and be devoted to informing the peoples of the world of the aims and achievements of the Organization and to obtaining support for its work.

Member governments were invited to co-operate in the observance of the anniversary.

Amendments to the Charter

Amendments to the Charter come into force for all members of the United Nations when they have been adopted by a vote of two-thirds of the members of the General Assembly and ratified by two-thirds of the members of the United Nations, including all the permanent members of the Security Council.

Amendments to Articles 23, 27 and 61, which had been approved by the General Assembly on December 17, 1963, came into force on August 31, 1965. The amendment to Article 23 increases the membership of the Security Council from eleven to fifteen. The amended Article 27 provides that decisions of the Security Council on procedural matters shall be made by an affirmative vote of nine members (formerly seven) and on all other matters by an affirmative vote of nine members (formerly seven), including the concurring votes of the five permanent members. The amendment to Article 61 enlarges the membership of the Economic and Social Council from eighteen to twenty-seven.

Consequent upon the entry into force of these amendments, the General Assembly, at its twentieth session, adopted, on December 20, 1965, an amendment to Article 109 of the Charter to reflect the change in the number of votes (seven to nine) in the Security Council on procedural matters, and called on all member states to ratify the amendment, "in accordance with their respective constitutional processes," at the earliest possible date.

MEMBERSHIP

The original members of the United Nations, numbering fifty-one, are those states which took part in the San Francisco Conference or had previously signed the Declaration by United Nations, and which signed and ratified the Charter. They are:

Argentina	Byelorussian	China	Denmark
Australia	Soviet Socialist	Colombia	Dominican
Belgium	Republic	Costa Rica	Republic
Bolivia	Canada	Cuba	Ecuador
Brazil	Chile	Czechoslovakia	Egypt

El Salvador	Lebanon	Peru	Union of Soviet
Ethiopia	Liberia	Philippines	Socialist Republics
France	Luxembourg	Poland [1]	United Kingdom of
Greece	Mexico	Saudi Arabia	Great Britain and
Guatemala	Netherlands	South Africa	Northern Ireland
Haiti	New Zealand	Syria	United States of
Honduras	Nicaragua	Turkey	America
India	Norway	Ukrainian	Uruguay
Iran	Panama	Soviet Socialist	Venezuela
Iraq	Paraguay	Republic	Yugoslavia

Membership in the United Nations is open to all peace-loving states which accept and, in the judgment of the Organization, are able and willing to carry out the obligations of the Charter. Any state desiring to become a member must submit an application containing a declaration that it accepts the obligations contained in the Charter of the United Nations.

New members are admitted by a two-thirds vote of the General Assembly upon the recommendation of the Security Council. Membership becomes effective on the date the Assembly accepts the application.

The additional members admitted to the United Nations from 1946 to 1966 are listed on the following page by date of admission. At the end of 1966, United Nations membership totalled 122 states.

A member of the United Nations against which preventive or enforcement action has been taken by the Security Council may be suspended from the exercise of the rights and privileges of membership by the General Assembly on the recommendation of the Security Council. The exercise of these rights and privileges may be restored by the Security Council.

A member of the United Nations which has persistently violated the principles of the Charter may be expelled from the Organization by the General Assembly on the recommendation of the Security Council.

There is no provision in the Charter concerning the re-entry into the Organization of an expelled member.

After lengthy debate, it was agreed at the San Francisco Conference not to include any provision in the Charter for the withdrawal of members. It was made clear, however, that it was not the purpose of the Organization to compel a member "to continue its co-operation in the Organization," if that member "because of exceptional circumstances" felt constrained to withdraw.

[1] Poland did not attend the San Francisco Conference because the composition of its new government was not announced until June 28—too late for the Conference. A space, however, was left for the signature of Poland, one of the original signatories of the Declaration by United Nations. Poland signed the Charter on October 15, 1945, thus becoming one of the original members.

Member	Date of Admission	Member	Date of Admission
Afghanistan	November 19, 1946	Congo	
Iceland	November 19, 1946	(Leopold-	
Sweden	November 19, 1946	ville)[2]	September 20, 1960
Thailand	December 16, 1946	Cyprus	September 20, 1960
Pakistan	September 30, 1947	Dahomey	September 20, 1960
Yemen	September 30, 1947	Gabon	September 20, 1960
Burma	April 19, 1948	Ivory Coast	September 20, 1960
Israel	May 11, 1949	Madagascar	September 20, 1960
Indonesia	September 28, 1950	Niger	September 20, 1960
Albania	December 14, 1955	Somalia	September 20, 1960
Austria	December 14, 1955	Togo	September 20, 1960
Bulgaria	December 14, 1955	Upper Volta	September 20, 1960
Cambodia	December 14, 1955	Mali	September 28, 1960
Ceylon	December 14, 1955	Senegal	September 28, 1960
Finland	December 14, 1955	Nigeria	October 7, 1960
Hungary	December 14, 1955	Sierra Leone	September 27, 1961
Ireland	December 14, 1955	Mauritania	October 27, 1961
Italy	December 14, 1955	Mongolia	October 27, 1961
Jordan	December 14, 1955	Tanganyika[3]	December 14, 1961
Laos	December 14, 1955	Burundi	September 18, 1962
Libya	December 14, 1955	Jamaica	September 18, 1962
Nepal	December 14, 1955	Rwanda	September 18, 1962
Portugal	December 14, 1955	Trinidad and	
Romania	December 14, 1955	Tobago	September 18, 1962
Spain	December 14, 1955	Algeria	October 8, 1962
Sudan	November 12, 1956	Uganda	October 25, 1962
Morocco	November 12, 1956	Kuwait	May 14, 1963
Tunisia	November 12, 1956	Kenya	December 16, 1963
Japan	December 18, 1956	Zanzibar[3]	December 16, 1963
Ghana	March 8, 1957	Malawi	December 1, 1964
Federation		Malta	December 1, 1964
of Malaya[1]	September 17, 1957	Zambia	December 1, 1964
Guinea	December 12, 1958	Gambia	September 21, 1965
Cameroon	September 20, 1960	Maldive Islands	September 21, 1965
Central African		Singapore[1]	September 21, 1965
Republic	September 20, 1960	Guyana	September 20, 1966
Chad	September 20, 1960	Botswana	October 17, 1966
Congo		Lesotho	October 17, 1966
(Brazzaville)	September 20, 1960	Barbados	December 9, 1966

[1] The name of the Federation of Malaya was changed to Malaysia following the admission, to the new federation, of Singapore, Sabah (North Borneo) and Sarawak. Singapore became an independent state on August 9, 1965, and a member of the United Nations the following month.

[2] Officially renamed the Democratic Republic of the Congo in July 1964.

[3] Following the ratification on April 24, 1964, of Articles of Union between Tanganyika and Zanzibar, the United Republic of Tanganyika and Zanzibar continued as a single member of the United Nations, later changing its name to United Republic of Tanzania.

Permanent Missions to the United Nations

Since the creation of the United Nations, the practice has developed of establishing permanent missions of member states at the seat of the Organization. The General Assembly sought to regulate the submission of credentials of permanent representatives on December 3, 1948, when it recommended that credentials be issued by the head of the state, by the head of the government, or by the Minister for Foreign Affairs, and be transmitted to the Secretary-General. It was further recommended that the permanent representative, in case of temporary absence, should notify the Secretary-General of the name of his replacement; that member states which wanted their permanent representatives to represent them on one or more organs of the United Nations should specify in their credentials the organs concerned; and finally, that changes of members of permanent missions, other than the permanent representative, should be communicated in writing to the Secretary-General by the head of the mission.

Permanent Observers

The following non-member states maintain offices of permanent observers to the United Nations: Federal Republic of Germany, Holy See, Republic of Korea, Monaco, Switzerland and Republic of Viet-Nam.

THE PRINCIPAL ORGANS

The Charter established six principal organs of the United Nations: the General Assembly, the Security Council, the Economic and Social Council, the Trusteeship Council, the International Court of Justice and the Secretariat.

In all organs of the United Nations other than the International Court of Justice, the official languages are Chinese, English, French, Russian and Spanish, and the working languages are English and French. In the General Assembly and the Economic and Social Council, Spanish is also a working language.

The official languages of the International Court of Justice are English and French.

General Assembly

The General Assembly consists of all the member states of the United Nations, each of which has one vote in the Assembly.

FUNCTIONS AND POWERS.   The General Assembly may discuss any questions or any matters within the scope of the Charter or relating to the powers and functions of any organs provided for in the Charter. It may make recommendations on these questions and matters to the member states or to the Security Council or to both, with one exception—it may not make recommendations on any dispute or situation which the Security Council has under consideration unless the Council so requests.

The Assembly may consider the general principles of co-operation in the maintenance of peace and security, including those governing disarmament and the regulation of armaments.

It may discuss any questions relating to the maintenance of international peace and security brought before it by a member state, by the Security Council or by a non-member state, if that state accepts in advance the obligations of pacific settlement contained in the Charter, and, unless the matter is already being dealt with by the Security Council, may make recommendations on any such question to the state or states concerned or to the Security Council or to both.

Subject to the same exception, the Assembly may recommend measures for the peaceful settlement of any situation, regardless of origin, which it deems likely to impair the general welfare or friendly relations among nations. It may also call to the attention of the Council situations which are likely to endanger international peace and security.

The Assembly initiates studies and makes recommendations for the purpose of: (a) promoting international co-operation in the political field and encouraging the progressive development of international law and its codification; and (b) promoting international co-operation in the economic, social, cultural, educational and health fields and assisting in the realization of human rights and fundamental freedoms for all.

Through the Trusteeship Council, the Assembly supervises the execution of Trusteeship Agreements for all territories except those designated as strategic. It approves the terms of these agreements and any alterations or amendments.

The Assembly receives and considers reports of the other organs of the United Nations. It elects the ten non-permanent members of the Security Council, all twenty-seven members of the Economic and Social Council and those members of the Trusteeship Council which are elected. Voting independently, the Assembly and the Security Council elect the members of the International Court of Justice, and, on the recommendation of the Security Council, the Assembly appoints the Secretary-General.

The finances of the United Nations are controlled by the Assembly, which considers and approves the budget and apportions the expenses among the members. It also examines the administrative budgets of the specialized agencies.

VOTING. Decisions on important questions, such as recommendations on peace and security, election of members to organs, admission, suspension and expulsion of members, trusteeship questions and budgetary matters, are taken by a two-thirds majority of members present and voting. Other questions require a simple majority.

SESSIONS. The Assembly meets once a year in regular session, commencing on the third Tuesday in September. Special sessions may be called at the request of the Security Council, a majority of member states, or one member state with the concurrence of a majority. An emergency special session may be called within twenty-four hours of a request by the Security Council on the vote of any nine of its members, or by a majority of the United Nations members.

STRUCTURE. The Assembly elects its President and Vice-Presidents for each session and adopts its own rules of procedure. At each session, the Assembly distributes most agenda items among its seven Main Committees, on which every member state has the right to be represented. These committees, which prepare recommendations for approval in plenary meetings of the Assembly, are:

First Committee (Political and Security, including the regulation of armaments)

Special Political Committee (shares the work of the First Committee)

Second Committee (Economic and Financial)

Third Committee (Social, Humanitarian and Cultural)

Fourth Committee (Trusteeship, including Non-Self-Governing Territories)

Fifth Committee (Administrative and Budgetary)

Sixth Committee (Legal)

Voting in committees or sub-committees is by simple majority. Agenda items not referred to a Main Committee are dealt with by the Assembly itself, in plenary meetings.

The organization of the work of each session is the responsibility of the General Committee, which is composed of the President of the Assembly, the seventeen Vice-Presidents and the Chairmen of the seven Main Committees. The Credentials Committee, consisting of nine members appointed by the General Assembly on the proposal of the President, reports to the Assembly on the credentials of representatives.

The Assembly is assisted by two standing committees—the twelve-member Advisory Committee on Administrative and Budgetary Questions, and the ten-member Committee on Contributions, which makes recommendations to the General Assembly on the percentage scale for members' contributions to the United Nations. Members of these two committees are selected on the basis of broad geographical representation, personal qualifications and experience.

In addition, the Assembly has, from time to time, set up a number of subsidiary, *ad hoc* and related bodies.

Security Council

The Security Council is composed of five permanent members—China, France, the Union of Soviet Socialist Republics, the United Kingdom and the United States—and ten non-permanent members, elected by the General Assembly for two-year terms and not eligible for immediate re-election.

FUNCTIONS AND POWERS.   Under the Charter, the members of the United Nations confer on the Security Council primary responsibility for the maintenance of international peace and security in accordance with the purposes and principles of the United Nations.

The Council may investigate any dispute or situation which might lead to international friction, and may recommend methods of adjusting such disputes or the terms of settlement. Disputes and situations likely to endanger international peace and security may be brought to the attention of the Council by any member state, by a non-member which accepts in advance the obligations of pacific settlement contained in the Charter, by the General Assembly, or by the Secretary-General.

The Council may determine the existence of any threat to the peace, breach of the peace or act of aggression. It may make recommendations or decide to take enforcement measures to maintain or restore international peace and security. Enforcement action may include a call on members to apply economic sanctions and other measures short of the use of armed force. Should it consider such measures inadequate, the Council may take military action against an aggressor. (Under the Charter, all members have undertaken to make available to the Council on its call, in accordance with special agreements to be negotiated on the Council's initiative, the armed forces, assistance and facilities necessary for maintaining international peace and security.) The Council is also responsible for formulating plans to regulate armaments. In addition, the Security Council exercises the trusteeship functions of the United Nations in those areas classed as strategic.

The Security Council makes annual and special reports to the General Assembly.

The Security Council and the General Assembly, voting independently, elect the judges of the International Court of Justice. On the Security Council's recommendation, the General Assembly appoints the Secretary-General.

VOTING AND PROCEDURE. Voting in the Security Council on all matters other than questions of procedure is by an affirmative vote of nine members, including those of the permanent members. Any member, however, whether permanent or non-permanent, must abstain from voting in a dispute to which it is a party. On questions of procedure, a decision is by an affirmative vote of any nine members.

The Security Council is so organized as to be able to function continuously, and a representative of each of its members must be present at all times at United Nations Headquarters. The Council may meet elsewhere than at Headquarters.

A country which is a member of the United Nations but not of the Council may take part in its discussions when the Council considers that that country's interests are specially affected. Both members and non-members are invited to take part in the Council's discussions when they are parties to disputes being considered; in the case of a non-member, the Council lays down the conditions under which it may participate.

The presidency of the Council is held monthly in turn by members in English alphabetical order. The Council decides its own rules of procedure and may establish subsidiary organs.

There are two standing committees—the Committee of Experts, which studies and advises the Council on rules of procedure and other technical matters, and the Committee on Admission of New Members; each is composed of representatives of all Council members. Over the years, the Council has also established many *ad hoc* bodies.

The Military Staff Committee, composed of the Chiefs of Staff of the five permanent members or their representatives, was established under the Charter to advise and assist the Security Council on such questions as the Council's military requirements for the maintenance of peace, the strategic direction of armed forces placed at its disposal, the regulation of armaments and possible disarmament.

Economic and Social Council

The Economic and Social Council is composed of twenty-seven members, nine of which are elected each year by the General Assembly for a three-year term of office. Retiring members are eligible for immediate re-election.

FUNCTIONS AND POWERS. The Economic and Social Council is the organ responsible, under the authority of the General Assembly, for the economic and social activities of the United Nations. Its functions are: to make or initiate studies, reports and recommendations on international economic, social, cultural, educational, health and related matters; to promote respect for, and observance of, human rights and fundamental freedoms for all; to call international conferences and prepare draft conventions for submission to the General Assembly on matters within its competence; to negotiate agreements with the specialized agencies, defining their relationship with the United Nations, and to co-ordinate the activities of the specialized agencies by means of consultation with them and recommendations to them, and by means of recommendations to the General Assembly and members of the United Nations; to perform services, approved by the Assembly, for members of the United Nations and, upon request, for the specialized agencies; and to consult with non-governmental organizations concerned with matters with which the Council deals.

VOTING.   Voting in the Economic and Social Council is by simple majority; each member has one vote.

SUBSIDIARY BODIES.   The Council works through commissions, committees and various other subsidiary bodies. It has six functional commissions: the Statistical Commission, the Population Commission, the Commission for Social Development, the Commission on Human Rights, the Commission on the Status of Women and the Commission on Narcotic Drugs.

Representatives on the Commission on Narcotic Drugs are appointed directly by their respective Governments. For the other five Commissions, the member countries nominate representatives, after consultation with the Secretary-General, with a view to securing balanced representation in the various fields covered by each Commission; these nominations are in turn confirmed by the Council.

There are also four regional economic commissions: for Europe; for Asia and the Far East; for Latin America; and for Africa, as well as an Economic and Social Office in Beirut.

Other related bodies include the Executive Board of the United Nations Children's Fund; the Governing Council of the United Nations Development Programme; the United Nations/FAO Inter-Governmental Committee on the World Food Programme; the Trade and Development Board of the United Nations Conference on Trade and Development which reports to the General Assembly through the Economic and Social Council; the Permanent Central Opium Board; and the Drug Supervisory Body.

INTER-GOVERNMENTAL AGENCIES.   The inter-governmental agencies are separate, autonomous organizations related to the United Nations by special arrangements. They have their own membership, their own legislative and executive bodies, their own secretariats and their own budgets, but they work with the United Nations and with each other through the co-ordinating machinery of the Economic and Social Council.

The inter-governmental agencies are:

International Atomic Energy Agency (IAEA)
International Labour Organisation (ILO)
Food and Agriculture Organization of the United Nations (FAO)
United Nations Educational, Scientific and Cultural Organization (UNESCO)
World Health Organization (WHO)
International Bank for Reconstruction and Development (World Bank, IBRD)
International Finance Corporation (IFC)
International Development Association (IDA)
International Monetary Fund (Fund, IMF)
International Civil Aviation Organization (ICAO)
Universal Postal Union (UPU)
International Telecommunication Union (ITU)
World Meteorological Organization (WMO)
Inter-Governmental Maritime Consultative Organization (IMCO)

The General Agreement on Tariffs and Trade (GATT) is not a specialized agency but is often listed among them because of its relationship with some of the agencies.

NON-GOVERNMENTAL ORGANIZATIONS. Non-governmental organizations may be consulted by the Economic and Social Council on matters with which they are concerned and which fall within the competence of the Council. The Council recognizes that these organizations should have the opportunity to express their views and that they often possess special experience or technical knowledge which will be of great value to the Council in its work.

Organizations in consultative status are divided into three categories: those with a basic interest in most of the activities of the Council (Category A); those which have a special competence in, and are concerned specifically with, only a few of the Council's fields of activity (Category B); and those which have a significant contribution to make to the work of the Council which may be placed on a register for *ad hoc* consultations. As of December 1965, ten organizations were in Category A, 131 organizations were in Category B and 219 were on the Register.

The non-governmental organizations may designate authorized representatives to sit as observers at public meetings of the Council and its bodies, and they may submit written statements relevant to the work of the Council and its bodies for circulation as United Nations documents. All three categories of consultative non-governmental organizations may consult with the United Nations Secretariat on matters of mutual concern.

Trusteeship Council

The Trusteeship Council is the principal organ of the United Nations responsible for the supervision of territories placed under the International Trusteeship System. The Council consists of member states administering trust territories, permanent members of the Security Council which do not administer trust territories, and enough other non-administering countries elected by the Assembly for three-year terms to ensure that the membership is equally divided between administering and non-administering members.

At the beginning of 1966, the Trusteeship Council was composed of four administering authorities (Australia, New Zealand, the United Kingdom and the United States), and four non-administering members, of whom three (China, France and the USSR) are members by virtue of being permanent members of the Security Council; the fourth, Liberia, was elected by the Assembly in December 1965 for a period of three years.

FUNCTIONS AND POWERS. The Trusteeship Council, under the authority of the General Assembly, carries out the functions of the United Nations with regard to trust territories except in those areas which are designated as strategic. The Security Council exercises the functions of the United Nations in "strategic areas," with the assistance of the Trusteeship Council in political, economic, social and educational matters.

The Trusteeship Council considers reports submitted by the administering authority on the basis of a questionnaire prepared by the Council, and examines petitions in consultation with the administering authority. It provides for periodic visiting missions to trust territories at times agreed upon with the administering authority, and takes other actions in conformity with the terms of the trusteeship agreements.

Three of the original eleven trust territories remain: Nauru, administered by Australia on behalf of Australia, New Zealand and the United Kingdom; New Guinea, administered by Australia; and the Trust Territory of the Pacific Islands, a "strategic" Territory administered by the United States.

VOTING. Voting in the Trusteeship Council is by simple majority; each member has one vote.

The Council meets once a year, usually during June.

International Court of Justice

The International Court of Justice is the principal judicial organ of the United Nations. The Court functions in accordance with its Statute, which is an integral part of the United Nations Charter. The Statute is based upon the Statute of the Permanent Court of International Justice, which functioned under the League of Nations.

The Court is open to the parties to its Statute, which automatically includes all members of the United Nations. A state not belonging to the United Nations may become a party to the Statute on conditions to be determined in each case by the General Assembly on recommendation of the Security Council. Switzerland (1948), Liechtenstein (1950) and San Marino (1954) are the three non-member states which are presently parties to the Statute. The Court is also open to states which are not parties to its Statute on conditions laid down by a Security Council resolution of October 15, 1946. Such states must file with the Registrar of the Court a declaration by which they accept the Court's jurisdiction in accordance with the Charter of the United Nations and the Statute and Rules of the Court, undertaking to comply in good faith with the decision or decisions of the Court and accepting all the obligations of a member of the United Nations under Article 94 of the Charter. Such a declaration may be either particular or general. A particular declaration is one accepting the Court's jurisdiction in respect of a particular dispute or disputes which have already arisen. A general declaration is one accepting the jurisdiction in respect of all disputes, or of a particular class or classes of dispute, which have already arisen or which may arise in the future. General declarations have been filed by the Federal Republic of Germany and the Republic of Viet-Nam under certain treaties. The Court is not open to private individuals.

JURISDICTION. The jurisdiction of the Court comprises all cases which the parties refer to it, and all matters specifically provided for in the Charter or in treaties or conventions in force. In the event of a dispute as to whether the Court has jurisdiction, the matter is settled by the decision of the Court.

To preserve continuity with the work of the Permanent Court of International Justice, the Statute of the International Court of Justice stipulates that whenever a treaty or convention in force provided for reference to the Permanent Court, the matter is referred to the International Court as between the parties to its Statute.

States are not forced to submit cases to the Court. The Charter provides that members of the United Nations may entrust the solution of their differences to other tribunals.

States parties to the Statute may at any time declare that they recognize as compulsory, *ipso facto* and without special agreement, in relation to any state accepting the same obligation, the jurisdiction of the Court in all legal disputes concerning: (a) the interpretation of a treaty; (b) any question of international law; (c) the existence of any fact which, if established, would constitute a breach of an international obligation; and (d) the nature or extent of the reparation to be made for the breach of an international obligation.

ADVISORY OPINIONS. The General Assembly or the Security Council may request the Court to give an advisory opinion on any legal question. Other organs of the United Nations or specialized agencies, when authorized by the Assembly, may also request advisory opinions on legal questions arising within the scope of their activities.

THE LAW APPLIED BY THE COURT. In accordance with Article 38 of the Statute, the Court applies: (a) international treaties and conventions; (b) international custom; (c) the general principles of law recognized by civilized nations; and (d) judicial decisions and the teachings of the most highly qualified publicists as subsidiary means for the determination of the rules of law. Furthermore, the Court may decide a case *ex aequo et bono,* that is, according to the principles of equity, if the parties concerned agree.

The Security Council can be called upon by one of the parties in a case to determine measures to be taken to give effect to a judgment of the Court if the other party fails to perform its obligations under that judgment.

COMPOSITION OF THE COURT. The members of the Court are fifteen independent judges, of different nationalities, elected by the General Assembly and the Security Council from candidates nominated, after consultation with national and international law bodies, by government-appointed national groups of highly reputed international law experts.

The General Assembly and the Security Council hold separate elections independently of one another. They must be satisfied not only that the persons to be elected individually possess the qualifications required in their respective countries for appointment to the highest judicial offices or are recognized authorities on international law, but also that, in the Court as a whole, the result will be the representation of the main forms of civilization and the principal legal systems of the world. To be elected, a candidate must obtain an absolute majority of votes, both in the Assembly and in the Council. The voting in the Council is without distinction as between its permanent and non-permanent members.

The Statute provides for a special joint conference procedure to be applied if, after three meetings, concurring majorities have not been achieved in the two organs for all the vacant seats. Parties to the Statute which are not members of the United Nations may nominate candidates and take part in the elections in the General Assembly.

Judges are elected for terms of nine years and are eligible for reelection. The terms of five of the fifteen judges expire at the end of every three years. The Court itself elects its President and Vice-President for three-year terms.

If there is no judge of their nationality on the bench, the parties to a case are entitled to choose *ad hoc*, or national, judges, to sit only in that particular case. Such judges take part in the decision on terms of complete equality with the other judges. All questions are decided by a majority of the judges present, with nine constituting a quorum. In the event of an equality of votes, the President of the Court has a casting vote.

ADMINISTRATION. The International Court of Justice has its seat at The Hague, Netherlands. Its administration is directed by the President and carried out by a Registrar and Deputy-Registrar elected by the Court, assisted by Registry officials responsible to the Registrar and appointed by the Court.

The Court issues its own publications, which may be obtained wherever United Nations publications are distributed. They include the full texts of the Court's decisions, in the *Reports* series; case documents and speeches, printed after a case is over in the *Pleadings* series; a *Yearbook* of current information on the work of the Court; the instruments governing the Court's operation, in *Acts and Documents*; and an annual *Bibliography*.

The channel of communication with the Court is the Registrar.

Secretariat

The Secretariat is composed of a Secretary-General, appointed by the General Assembly upon the recommendation of the Security Council, and "such staff as the Organization may require."

The Secretary-General's functions are: to be the chief administrative officer of the Organization; to act in his capacity as Secretary-General in all meetings of the General Assembly, the Security Council, the Economic and Social Council and the Trusteeship Council and to perform such other functions as are entrusted to him by these organs; to make an annual report and any supplementary reports necessary to the General Assembly on the work of the United Nations; and to appoint the staff.

Under Article 99 of the Charter, the Secretary-General may bring to the attention of the Security Council any matter which in his opinion may threaten the maintenance of international peace and security.

The first Secretary-General of the United Nations was Trygve Lie, of Norway, who was appointed on February 1, 1946, for a five-year term. On November 1, 1950, he was continued in office for a period of three years. He tendered his resignation on November 10, 1952 and, on April 10, 1953, was succeeded by Dag Hammarskjöld, of Sweden. Mr. Hammarskjöld was appointed on September 26, 1957, for a further five-year term beginning April 10, 1958. Following Mr. Hammarskjöld's death on September 17, 1961, in an airplane crash on his way from Leopoldville in the Congo to Ndola in Northern Rhodesia, the General Assembly, on November 3, 1961, appointed U Thant, of Burma, as Acting Secretary-General for a term of office extending until April 10, 1963. On November 30, 1962, the Assembly, acting on the recommendation of the Security Council, unanimously appointed U Thant Secretary-General for a term of office expiring on November 3, 1966. On November 1, 1966, the General Assembly extended the appointment of U Thant as Secretary-General until the end of the Assembly's twenty-first session and on December 2, 1966, appointed U Thant Secretary-General for another term of office ending December 31, 1971.

The staff of the United Nations is appointed by the Secretary-General under regulations established by the General Assembly. Under the Charter, the "paramount consideration" in employing staff and in determining conditions of service is the necessity of securing the highest standards of efficiency, competence and integrity, with due regard paid to the importance of recruiting on as wide a geographical basis as possible.

Article 100 of the Charter provides that the Secretary-General and the staff, in the performance of their duties, shall not seek or receive instructions from any government or any other authority external to the United Nations. They must also refrain from any action which might reflect on their position as international officials responsible only to the United Nations. For its part, each member of the United Nations is bound by the Charter to respect the exclusively international character of the responsibilities of the Secretary-General and the staff and not to seek to influence them in the discharge of their responsibilities.

The Secretariat is divided into major units, the heads of which are directly responsible to the Secretary-General.

The structure of the United Nations Secretariat is as follows: the Offices of the Secretary-General, consisting of the Executive Office of the Secretary-General, the Offices of the Under-Secretaries for Special Political Affairs, the Office of Legal Affairs, the Office of the Controller and the Office of Personnel; the Department of Political and Security Council Affairs; the Department of Economic and Social Affairs, including the regional economic commissions; the Department of Trusteeship and Non-Self-Governing Territories; the Office of Public Information; the Office of Conference Services; the Office of General

Services; the secretariat of the United Nations Conference on Trade and Development and the United Nations Office at Geneva; and the separate staffs serving the following subsidiary organs established by the General Assembly or the Economic and Social Council: the United Nations Children's Fund (UNICEF), the United Nations Development Programme (UNDP), the Office of the United Nations High Commissioner for Refugees (UNHCR), the United Nations Relief and Works Agency for Palestine Refugees (UNRWA), the United Nations Institute for Training and Research (UNITAR) and the United Nations Industrial Development Organization (UNIDO).

HEADQUARTERS OF THE UNITED NATIONS

Site for Permanent Headquarters

On December 10, 1945, the Congress of the United States unanimously resolved to invite the United Nations to establish its permanent home in the United States. The invitation was accepted by the General Assembly in London on February 14, 1946, after offers and suggestions for permanent sites had also been received from many other parts of the world. At that time, the first part of the first session of the General Assembly was meeting in London's Central Hall, Westminster, while the Secretariat was in nearby Church House.

Early in 1946, the Secretariat was established provisionally at Hunter College in the Bronx, New York, and in the middle of August the United Nations moved to the Sperry Gyroscope plant at Lake Success in Long Island. A few meetings of the Security Council were held at the Henry Hudson Hotel and at 610 Fifth Avenue, New York, prior to the move to Lake Success. Several General Assembly sessions took place in the New York City Building at Flushing Meadow, and on two occasions—in 1948 and 1951—the Assembly met in Paris.

On December 14, 1946, the General Assembly accepted an offer by John D. Rockefeller, Jr., of $8.5 million for the purchase of the present eighteen-acre site between 42nd and 48th streets on Manhattan's East Side, bounded on the west by United Nations Plaza (formerly a part of First Avenue) and on the east by the East River. Concurrently with the Rockefeller gift, the City of New York offered certain lands within and adjacent to the site, together with waterfront rights and easements. The City also undertook a $30 million improvement programme in the immediate area, including the construction of a vehicular tunnel under First Avenue.

Once the site was decided on, the first Secretary-General, Trygve

Lie, appointed the architect Wallace K. Harrison, of the United States, to guide the architectural and development plans in co-operation with an international board of design consultants from ten countries.

The plans prepared by the international board of consultants were unanimously adopted by the General Assembly on November 20, 1947. Demolition of the existing structures on the site had already begun in July. The cornerstone of the buildings was laid on October 24, 1949—United Nations Day—at an open-air plenary meeting of the General Assembly at which the President of the United States, among others, spoke. Occupancy of the Secretariat building began in August 1950 and was completed the following June. The Security Council held its first meetings in its new chamber early in 1952 and in October of the same year the General Assembly convened for the first time in the new Assembly Hall.

The four main structures, all interconnected, that comprise Headquarters, are the thirty-nine-story office building of the Secretariat; the long, low Conference Building paralleling the East River; the General Assembly Hall; and the Dag Hammarskjöld Library.

The official address is United Nations, New York. Telephone: 754-1234.

United States Loan and Total Construction Costs

In approving the plans prepared by the international board, the Assembly also authorized the Secretary-General to negotiate with the United States Government for an interest-free loan of $65 million to finance the cost of construction. An agreement was signed on March 23, 1948, by the Secretary-General and the United States representative to the United Nations providing for repayment of the loan, without interest, over a period of thirty-one years from July 1, 1951, to July 1, 1982, in annual instalments ranging from $1 million to $2.5 million. The agreement was approved by the United States Congress and signed by the President of the United States on August 11, 1948. By the end of 1965, the United Nations had repaid $30 million to the United States Government.

The General Assembly, in February 1952, approved an additional sum of $1.5 million (provided from the United Nations budget) to complete construction of the Headquarters.

Headquarters Agreement

On June 26, 1947, the Secretary-General and the Secretary of State of the United States signed an agreement dealing with the privileges and immunities of the United Nations Headquarters. Under this agreement, which came into force on November 21, 1947, the United Nations has the power to make necessary regulations for the Headquarters district.

Dag Hammarskjöld Library

The Dag Hammarskjöld Library is located at the south-west corner of the Headquarters site, adjoining the Secretariat building. Its construction and furnishing were made possible by a gift from the Ford Foundation in 1959 and, at the Foundation's request, it was named for the late Secretary-General, who met his death just before the Library's dedication in 1961. It was designed to accommodate 400,000 volumes, 175 readers in the principal reading rooms and a staff of upwards of 100 persons.

The Library is highly specialized in the subjects of international law and in political, economic and social affairs and is devoted primarily to providing information, research materials and library services required by delegations and the Secretariat. It includes a collection of documents and publications of the United Nations and the specialized agencies, as well as books, periodicals and pamphlets concerning them. The Woodrow Wilson Memorial Collection, a gift of the Woodrow Wilson Foundation, contains documents of the League of Nations and publications dealing with the League, the peace movements and international relations between the two World Wars. There is also a special collection of maps and geographical reference books.

The services of the main Library are supplemented by two branch collections in the Secretariat building—for Economic and Social Affairs, and for Legal and Security Council Affairs.

Official Seal, Emblem and Flag of the United Nations

The official seal and emblem of the United Nations is a map of the world, as seen from the North Pole, surrounded by a wreath of olive branches. When the General Assembly approved the design in 1946, it also recommended that members should adopt legislation or other appropriate measures to protect the emblem against use not authorized by the Secretary-General. In particular, the Assembly called for prohibition of the use for commercial purposes of the official seal, emblem, name or initials of the world organization.

The United Nations flag was adopted by the General Assembly in 1947. Its design consists of the official emblem in white, centered on a light blue background. In accordance with Assembly directives, the Secretary-General drew up regulations concerning the dimensions of the flag and issued, on December 19, 1947, a Flag Code to govern the use and protect the dignity of the flag. The Code was amended in November 1952 to permit display of the flag by organizations and persons desiring to demonstrate their support of the United Nations.

Among the matters covered by the Flag Code are the protocol to be followed in display of the flag, its use in specified circumstances and its manufacture and sale. Under one of the provisions of the Code, any violation of the Code may be punished in accordance with the law of the country in which such violation occurs.

The text of both the Flag Code and the regulations is contained in a pamphlet, entitled *The United Nations Flag Code and Regulations,* issued by the United Nations.

PART TWO

The Work of the United Nations

Political and Security Questions

DISARMAMENT AND RELATED QUESTIONS

Under the Charter, both the General Assembly and the Security Council have specific responsibilities concerning disarmament and the establishment of a system for the regulation of arms. Article 11 provides that the General Assembly may consider the general principles of co-operation in the maintenance of international peace, including the principles governing disarmament and the regulation of arms. Article 26 makes the Security Council responsible for formulating plans to be submitted to members of the United Nations for the establishment of a system for the regulation of armaments.

When the General Assembly convened for the first time on January 10, 1946, the five permanent members of the Security Council and Canada requested that it consider the problems raised by the discovery of atomic energy and the use of atomic weapons. A draft resolution that was the outcome of the meeting of Heads of Government of Canada, the United Kingdom and the United States in November 1945 and of the Foreign Ministers of the United Kingdom, the USSR and the United States in December 1945, proposed the establishment of a commission under the United Nations to inquire into and make recommendations about all phases of the problem.

By its first resolution, adopted on January 24, 1946, the General Assembly established the Atomic Energy Commission and instructed it to submit proposals to the Security Council for ensuring the use of atomic energy for peaceful purposes only, for the elimination of atomic and other weapons of mass destruction and for a system of safeguards, including inspection, to prevent violations and evasions. The Commission consisted of the members of the Security Council and Canada, when that country was not a member of the Council.

Later in the year, the Assembly also took up the question of the general regulation and reduction of armaments and made a series of recommendations for the early consideration of the Security Council. On February 13, 1947, the Council established the Commission for Conventional Armaments—with the same membership as the Council —to consider measures for the reduction of armaments and armed forces, together with an effective system of guarantees.

When the Atomic Energy Commission opened its meetings on June 14, 1946, the United States proposed the creation of an international atomic development authority to own and manage atomic energy production and the required raw materials. The plan called for the authority to have wide powers of inspection to prevent and detect violations of commitments, and provided for a system of sanctions not subject to the rule of unanimity of the permanent members of the Security Council. The USSR proposed that absolute priority be given to the conclusion of an international agreement prohibiting the production and use of atomic weapons and calling for the destruction of such weapons within three months of the coming into force of the agreement; violations would be punishable under domestic legislation. Subsequent consideration should be given to international control of atomic energy, which would be subject to normal Security Council procedure.

Although the Commission decided that control of atomic energy was scientifically and technically feasible, negotiations reached an impasse. In 1948, the General Assembly recommended the United States plan over the objections of the USSR. Further negotiations failed to change positions, and the Commission suspended work in 1949.

Both sides were also unable to reach agreement on principles to govern the work of the Commission for Conventional Armaments. The Western powers stressed that confidence was required before disarmament measures could be undertaken. They declared that this could be achieved by solution of urgent political problems, such as peace treaties with Germany and Japan and, in the meantime, by disclosure and verification of existing conventional arms and armed forces. The Soviet Union, on the other hand, maintained that immediate practical measures of disarmament would create confidence. It proposed, in 1948, that the permanent members of the Security Council reduce their land, naval and air forces by one-third during the following year, that atomic weapons be prohibited and that the Council establish an international control organ to supervise these measures. The Assembly rejected this proposal but approved a resolution calling for an international control organ to receive, check and publish full information, supplied by member states, on their armed forces.

In October 1949, a French plan for a census and verification of armed forces was discussed in the Council but was not adopted because of a negative vote by the Soviet Union, which proposed, instead, that information be submitted on both conventional and atomic weapons.

In April 1950, the Soviet Union withdrew from the Commission— as it had earlier in the year from the Atomic Energy Commission— over the question of the representation of China. Both Commissions were dissolved in early 1952.

Disarmament Commission and Sub-Committee

On January 11, 1952, the General Assembly created a single Disarmament Commission to carry on the tasks previously assigned to the Atomic Energy Commission and the Commission for Conventional Armaments. The new Commission, which had the same membership as the Security Council plus Canada, was confronted from the beginning by disagreement between the Soviet Union and the Western powers on its terms of reference, as well as on specific plans. On November 1, 1953, the General Assembly suggested that the Disarmament Commission create a Sub-Committee of the powers principally involved to seek in private an acceptable solution.

The Sub-Committee, which was established in April 1954, consisted of Canada, France, the Soviet Union, the United Kingdom and the United States. In the five sessions held between May 1954 and September 1957, many proposals were exchanged and mutual concessions made. The proposals included phased and synchronized general disarmament along with a ban on nuclear weapons and a ceiling on conventional weapons; new forms of inspection against surprise attack, such as ground control posts and the "open skies" or aerial inspection plan, as well as partial or required disarmament measures.

In 1957, the Sub-Committee discussed all aspects of the disarmament problem, including the question of nuclear weapons tests which member states had stressed in General Assembly discussions in 1956. The 1957 meetings of the Sub-Committee marked a transition from emphasis on comprehensive plans to efforts towards securing partial agreements as preliminary steps.

The Soviet Union proposed a cessation of nuclear weapons tests for a period of two or three years and the establishment of an international commission with control posts in the territory of the nuclear powers with adequate equipment to detect tests. The Western powers agreed to a suspension of tests, but made it part of a partial disarmament plan covering both conventional and nuclear weapons, stressing particularly the cessation of future nuclear production and the transfer of existing stocks to peaceful purposes. The Soviet Union, in turn, made a cut-off of production conditional on the complete prohibition and elimination of nuclear weapons.

Under the Western powers' plan, each party to a disarmament agreement would also have undertaken not to transfer out of its control any nuclear weapons or to accept the transfer of such weapons except in situations of individual or collective self-defence against armed attack. The USSR favoured an unconditional prohibition of both the use of nuclear weapons and the stationing of such weapons on the territory of another state.

Discussion of the question of safeguards against surprise attack centred on the different zones for aerial and ground inspection proposed and their context—whether as separate measures or as part of broader disarmament proposals. [In 1958, the Soviet Union and the United States agreed to hold a conference of experts from countries of the North Atlantic Treaty Organization (NATO) and those of the Warsaw Pact to study the problem of safeguards against surprise attack. The Conference, which met in November and December 1958, was suspended for lack of agreement on terms of reference.]

Concessions were made by both sides on the question of the reduction of conventional weapons and armed forces. The United States agreed in principle to further reductions of armed forces to less than 2.5 million, suggesting a second-stage level of 2.1 million and a third-stage level of 1.7 million for the Soviet Union and itself. France and the United Kingdom accepted a second-stage ceiling of 700,000 men and a third-stage level of 650,000 for themselves. The Soviet Union, in turn, accepted these new levels in principle. Regarding the reduction of armaments, the United States proposed that there be an exchange of lists of armaments which the Governments would be willing to withdraw from their national armouries and turn over to internationally supervised depots located in their own territory. The Soviet Union accepted in principle this method of dealing with the armaments during the first stage.

There was no agreement, however, on related technical questions, such as the definition of conventional weapons, or on the conditions for progressing from one stage to the next. For example, the Western powers continued to insist that the second and third stages should be linked to progress towards settlement of political issues, while the Soviet Union urged that they be carried out unconditionally.

The USSR proposed a 15 per cent reduction of defence expenditure. The West, observing that the question of control was extremely complex, proposed, as part of its package plan, the disclosure each year of information on military budgets for the preceding year. Whereas the West maintained that expenditure reduction should be the consequence of the reduction of armed forces and armaments, the Soviet Union maintained that reduction of defence budgets was a simple measure which might serve as a separate first step.

Both sides were in agreement that a control organ to supervise a disarmament treaty should be established under the aegis of the Security Council. While both agreed that there should be moderate or partial controls for partial disarmament, the precise details remained to be elaborated. The West proposed that a committee of experts be set up to elaborate the details of a control system to detect tests before agreement was reached in principle; the Soviet Union insisted on agreement on substance before details of controls were worked out.

With regard to regional disarmament, the Soviet Union proposed as a first step the reduction of forces stationed in the two parts of Germany and in the territory of other members of the North Atlantic and

Warsaw alliances. It also proposed the dismantling of some foreign military bases during the first stage of a partial disarmament plan. The Western powers, on the other hand, contended that regional arms limitation and regulation should be a consequence of general disarmament and not a first step.

The Western powers proposed a technical committee to study how to ensure the peaceful uses of outer space. The Soviet Union proposed that states assume, as a first step, a solemn obligation not to use rocket weapons with nuclear warheads during a first-stage disarmament programme and that during a second stage, simultaneously with the elimination of nuclear weapons, control should be instituted over all types of rockets suitable for use as nuclear weapons. Control over long-range missiles was linked to the liquidation of United States bases in Europe and the Middle East.

After considering the reports of the Sub-Committee on Disarmament, the General Assembly, in 1957, urged that priority be given to reaching a package agreement sponsored by the Western powers which would provide for: immediate suspension of testing of nuclear weapons with prompt installation of effective international control; cessation of production of fissionable materials for weapons purposes under effective international control; reduction of nuclear weapons stockpiles through transfer to peaceful purposes; reduction of armed forces and armaments; progressive establishment of ground and aerial inspection to guard against surprise attack; and joint study of an inspection system designed to ensure that outer space will be used exclusively for peaceful and scientific purposes.

Enlargement of the Disarmament Commission and Establishment of the Ten-Nation Committee

Following efforts by the Soviet Union to change the composition of the Disarmament Commission and its Sub-Committee on the grounds that the membership was weighted in favour of the North Atlantic Treaty powers and had failed to bring about agreement, the Assembly on November 19, 1957, enlarged the membership to twenty-five states. The Soviet Union, however, declared that the imbalance remained and announced that it would not take part in the work of the Commission or its Sub-Committee. It proposed, instead, a meeting of heads of governments.

In 1958, the Assembly decided that the Commission should, for 1959 and on an *ad hoc* basis, include all United Nations member states. The Commission met in September 1959 to consider a communiqué from the Conference of Foreign Ministers of France, the USSR, the United Kingdom and the United States stating that they had agreed on the creation of a new Ten-Nation Disarmament Committee and expressing the hope that the results of the new Committee's meetings would provide a useful basis for the consideration of disarmament measures in the United Nations, in which ultimate responsibility for such measures rested. The Disarmament Commission welcomed the intention of the four powers to resume consultations and to keep the Commission informed of the progress made.

The Ten-Nation Committee, consisting of the representatives of Bulgaria, Canada, Czechoslovakia, France, Italy, Poland, Romania, the USSR, the United Kingdom and the United States, decided to meet following the discussion of disarmament at the fourteenth session of the General Assembly in 1959.

On September 17, 1959, the Secretary of State for Foreign Affairs of the United Kingdom submitted to the Assembly an outline of a comprehensive plan aimed, in three balanced stages, at the abolition of all weapons of mass destruction and the reduction of other weapons and armed forces to levels which would rule out the possibility of aggressive war.

The following day, the Chairman of the Council of Ministers of the Soviet Union submitted to the Assembly a "Declaration of the Soviet Government on General and Complete Disarmament," which proposed a three-stage programme providing for the elimination of all armed forces and armaments within four years. The first stage provided for the reduction of the armed forces of the USSR, the United States and the People's Republic of China to 1.7 million men, and of those of the United Kingdom and France to 650,000 men. The level of forces of other states would be agreed upon at a special session of the General Assembly or at a world conference, and armaments and military equipment would be reduced to correspond to the level fixed for armed forces. The second stage would see the disbandment of remaining armed forces and the elimination of all foreign military bases. The third stage would provide for a series of comprehensive measures, including the destruction of nuclear weapons and missiles, prohibition of military research and development, and discontinuance of military expenditures.

Upon completion of general disarmament, a control organ would be established which would have free access to all objects of control by means of aerial observation and aerial photography. The Soviet Declaration called for violations to be submitted to the Security Council or the General Assembly in accordance with their respective spheres of competence. Finally, it provided for a series of partial measures if the Western powers were not ready to accept complete disarmament proposals.

During the debate in the General Assembly, France suggested that disarmament should start with measures prohibiting first the development and then the manufacture and possession of all vehicles for the delivery of nuclear devices, such as satellites, rockets, supersonic or long-range aircraft, ocean-going submarines, aircraft carriers and launching pads.

On November 20, 1959, the Assembly unanimously adopted a resolution asking governments to achieve a constructive solution of the problem of general and complete disarmament. The Ten-Nation Disarmament Committee received for consideration all the proposals made in the Assembly.

Conference of the Ten-Nation Committee

The Conference of the Ten-Nation Committee convened on March 15, 1960. The new three-stage programme of complete disarmament submitted by the Soviet Union envisaged the elimination of all means of delivering nuclear weapons and the liquidation of all foreign military bases in the very first stage. It was also proposed that a joint study be carried out on the problems of peace and international law in conditions of complete disarmament, so that in the third and final stage, the necessary measures could be taken in accordance with the United Nations Charter to maintain peace in such conditions. These measures could include an undertaking by states to make police units available to the Security Council whenever necessary. The proposal of the Soviet Union further outlined the principles of a control organization.

The United States proposals envisaged, in the first stage, controllable measures which could be taken without delay to halt and reduce weapon stockpiles, as well as the level of armed forces, to the extent possible without jeopardizing security. This first stage would be negotiated and agreed upon by the Ten-Nation Committee, which would then prepare an agreed draft for the second and third stages in accordance with certain principles, including initial and continuing verification. The United States plan provided for an international disarmament control organization "within the framework of the United Nations."

While stating that the new Soviet proposals came closer to their views in various respects, the Western powers held that they were not balanced and progressive and that the elimination of bases in the first stage was particularly unacceptable. The USSR contended that the United States proposals stressed broad measures of control without disarmament. The USSR also stated that the United States plan proposed no reduction of armed forces during the first stage, while seeking to place under foreign control all the armed forces and armaments of the USSR and other states and was, therefore, a screen for espionage activities.

On June 27, 1960, the delegations of Bulgaria, Czechoslovakia, Poland, Romania and the USSR withdrew from the Conference, stating that the Western powers were not interested in general and complete disarmament.

Following the collapse of the ten-nation talks, the Disarmament Commission convened at the request of the United States to review the situation. In the course of the discussion, the United States proposed the reciprocal transfer, by the United States and the USSR, of 30,000 kilogrammes of weapons-grade fissionable material to peaceful purposes, and the reciprocal shutting down of major plants producing enriched uranium and plutonium. The USSR called for a reaffirmation of general and complete disarmament, contending that the United States proposals were not practicable without prohibition of nuclear weapons.

The Disarmament Commission unanimously adopted, on August 18, 1960, a resolution calling for the earliest possible resumption of negotiations.

Joint Statement of Principles

In the first part of its fifteenth session, the General Assembly approved two resolutions—one concerning prevention of the wider dissemination of nuclear weapons and the other concerning a ban on nuclear testing—and was scheduled to resume consideration of disarmament in the second part of the session. However, when the representatives of the Soviet Union and the United States announced on March 30 that their Governments had reached an understanding to hold conversations during June and July 1961, looking forward to the resumption of negotiations in an appropriate body whose composition was to be agreed, the Assembly decided to take up the question at its sixteenth session, later in 1961.

On September 20, 1961, the USSR and the United States issued a Joint Statement in which both Governments agreed to recommend the following principles as a basis for disarmament negotiations.

(a) Disarmament would be general and complete and war would no longer be an instrument for settling international problems. Such disarmament would be accompanied by reliable procedures for peaceful settlement of disputes and arrangements for maintaining peace in accordance with the Charter. States would have only such non-nuclear arms as are agreed to be necessary for internal order and personal security of citizens. States would, further, provide agreed manpower for a United Nations peace force.

(b) The disarmament programme would provide for disbanding of armed forces, dismantling of military establishments, including bases, and cessation of the production of armaments, as well as their liquidation or conversion to peaceful uses; elimination of all stockpiles of nuclear, chemical, bacteriological and other weapons of mass destruction and cessation of the production of such weapons; elimination of all means of delivery of weapons of mass destruction; abolition of the organizations and institutions designed to organize the military effort of states, cessation of military training and closing of all military training institutions, and discontinuance of military expenditures.

(c) The programme would be implemented in agreed sequence, by stages, with verification of the completion of each stage. All disarmament measures would be balanced so that at no stage would any state or group of states gain military advantage. All measures would be implemented under strict international control by an international disarmament organization to be created within the framework of the United Nations. Its inspectors would have unrestricted access, without veto, to all places as necessary for verification.

In an address to the General Assembly on September 25, 1961, President John F. Kennedy submitted a new United States proposal on general and complete disarmament; he described the proposal as an attempt "to bridge the gap between those who insist on a gradual approach and those who talk only of the final and total achievement."

The main elements in the United States proposal as described by the President were: the signing of a test ban treaty by all nations; halting the production of fissionable materials for use in weapons and preventing their transfer to any nation not possessing nuclear weapons; keeping nuclear weapons from seeding new battlegrounds in outer space; gradually destroying existing nuclear weapons and converting their materials to peaceful uses; stopping the unlimited testing and production of strategic nuclear weapons delivery vehicles and gradually destroying them as well; and earmarking, by all nations, of special peace-keeping units in their armed forces which would be on call by the United Nations.

The following day, the USSR submitted a memorandum entitled "Measures to ease international tension, strengthen confidence among states, and contribute to general and complete disarmament." The measures outlined in the memorandum included: freezing of the military budgets of states; renunciation of the use of nuclear weapons; prohibition of war propaganda; conclusion of a non-aggression pact between the countries of NATO and those of the Warsaw Treaty; withdrawal of troops from foreign territory; measures to prevent the further spread of nuclear weapons; establishment of nuclear-free zones; and steps to decrease the danger of surprise attack.

On November 21, the General Assembly unanimously adopted a resolution urging the Governments of the USSR and the United States to reach agreement on the composition of a negotiating body which both they and the rest of the world could regard as satisfactory, and expressing the hope that such negotiations would be started without delay.

Eighteen-Nation Committee on Disarmament

On December 20, the Assembly unanimously endorsed the agreement reached between the Soviet Union and the United States on the composition of a new eighteen-member disarmament committee consisting of Brazil, Bulgaria, Burma, Canada, Czechoslovakia, Ethiopia, France, India, Italy, Mexico, Nigeria, Poland, Romania, Sweden, the USSR, the United Arab Republic, the United Kingdom and the United States. It requested the Eighteen-Nation Disarmament Committee to undertake urgently negotiations on the basis of the Joint Statement of principles by the USSR and the United States, which the Assembly had unanimously welcomed.

The Conference of the Eighteen-Nation Committee—which reports to the General Assembly and the Disarmament Commission—opened in Geneva on March 14, 1962. From the outset, all the members of the Committee have taken part in its work, with the exception of France, which announced that it hoped it might be possible later for the disarmament problem to be discussed among powers that could contribute effectively to its solution. The Co-Chairmen of the Conference are the representatives of the USSR and the United States.

During 1962, the Eighteen-Nation Committee considered draft treaties by the USSR and the United States on general and complete disarmament. These draft treaties, as revised and amended, continue to be the basic documents before the Committee on this question.

Although the two powers agreed on certain elements of general disarmament, both maintained differing views on other essential principles. The USSR sought to remove the threat of nuclear war through the complete elimination of nuclear delivery vehicles by the end of the first stage, and linked this proposal with the liquidation of foreign bases. It viewed the completion of the disarmament process within a fixed short period as essential to ensuring equal security in the course of disarmament.

The United States sought gradual disarmament, accompanied by effective peace-keeping measures and beginning with a halt in the production of nuclear weapons. As confidence developed, it maintained, the military establishment would shrink to zero by progressive reductions. Above all, during the disarmament process, the United States wished to keep the relative military positions as close as possible to what they were at the beginning of the process.

The scope and method of inspection under a system of controls was another point of continuing difference between both nations. Both sides agreed on the need to verify what was being reduced, destroyed or converted to peaceful uses, as well as to control the cessation of production of armaments, but disagreed on the means of verifying retained armaments and armed forces and of ensuring that undisclosed, clandestine forces, weapons or production facilities did not exist.

At the General Assembly session in 1962, the USSR introduced a revised draft treaty whereby, as an exception to the original proposal for the elimination of all nuclear delivery vehicles in the first stage, it provided for the retention by the United States and the USSR, but only on their own territories, of a strictly limited number of inter-continental missiles, anti-missile missiles and anti-aircraft missiles until the second stage of disarmament. The proposal was to be implemented simultaneously with the elimination of foreign military bases carried out under international control. The Soviet Union stressed that the number of missiles would have to be so small as to preclude the waging of nuclear war.

On September 19, 1963, at the eighteenth session of the Assembly, the Foreign Minister of the Soviet Union submitted another modification of the plan to allow for the retention of such missiles until the end of the third and concluding stage of disarmament.

During this period, the United States put forward certain amendments to its draft treaty and suggested, for the first stage, a 30 per cent across-the-board reduction in all major armaments. The United States maintained that percentage reductions would not affect the relative balance of military strength. The USSR plan, it said, would virtually force the United States to terminate its alliances and give tremendous advantage to the USSR and its allies with their preponderance of conventional weapons and contiguous territory with interior lines of communication. At the Assembly's eighteenth session, the United States also reiterated its proposals for a cut-off of production of fissionable material for weapons purposes and for the transfer to peaceful uses of such material in the amount of 60 tons by the United States and 40 tons by the USSR. It stated that it was willing to consider these measures for implementation before the first stage of general and complete disarmament. The Soviet Union did not agree with these proposals, contending that they contributed neither to elimination nor to reduction of the danger of nuclear war.

At the 1963 meetings of the Eighteen-Nation Committee, in which the USSR plan concerning the retention by the United States and the USSR of a strictly limited number of inter-continental, anti-missile and ground-to-air missiles was extensively discussed, the Western powers sought greater clarification of the proposal, particularly on the types of armaments involved and the method of reduction and verification. They also found unacceptable the simultaneous elimination of foreign bases called for in the Soviet proposal. The USSR and the United States each maintained that the other's plan would contradict the principle of balance, giving a military advantage to the other side.

In 1964, the Western powers suggested the establishment of a working group to consider all relevant proposals, including the United States plan for progressive percentage reduction. The Soviet Union was willing to participate in a working group, provided its concept of retention of the limited number of missiles was the basis of consideration. A number of the non-aligned members put forward various intermediate formulae, but because of the divergence of opinion between the two major powers on the question of the elimination of nuclear delivery vehicles, no decision was reached.

Continued negotiations on general disarmament in the Eighteen-Nation Committee were requested by the Disarmament Commission, which reconvened in 1965 at the request of the Soviet Union. The Committee met from July 27 to September 16, 1965, but did not reach specific agreement on either general disarmament or collateral measures. On December 3, 1965, the General Assembly approved a resolution calling on the Eighteen-Nation Committee to continue its efforts towards reaching agreement on general disarmament under effective international control.

Suspension of Nuclear Weapons Tests

In the spring of 1958, an exchange of letters between the President of the United States and the Chairman of the Council of Ministers of the USSR resulted in a decision to convene a conference of experts to study the possibility of detecting violations of a possible agreement on the suspension of nuclear tests, without prejudice to the positions taken on disarmament. The experts met in the summer of 1958 and, on August 21, issued a report which concluded that it was technically feasible to set up, within the capabilities and limitations indicated, a workable and effective control system for the detection of violations of an agreement on world cessation of nuclear weapons tests.

The Geneva Conference on the Discontinuance of Nuclear Weapons Tests, with the USSR, the United Kingdom and the United States participating, convened on October 31, 1958, to draft a treaty on the basis of the experts' report. The conference adopted several articles of a draft treaty, as well as the wording of the preamble and an annex.

At its fourteenth session, in 1959, the General Assembly adopted two resolutions: both urged the states concerned in the Geneva negotiations to continue the *de facto* voluntary discontinuance of the testing of nuclear weapons in effect since November 1958, but one went further and appealed also to "other states to desist from such tests."

The Assembly also considered an item submitted by Morocco concerning French nuclear tests in the Sahara. The Assembly adopted a resolution expressing its grave concern over the intention of France to conduct nuclear tests and requested it to refrain from doing so.

On February 13 and April 1, 1960, atomic devices were exploded by France in the Sahara. Following the first explosion, twenty-two Asian and African states requested the Secretary-General to summon a special session of the General Assembly to consider the French nuclear tests; however, in the absence of a majority in favour of the proposal, the special session was not convened.

At its fifteenth session, in 1960, the General Assembly, recalling its previous resolutions on the cessation of tests, urged the states concerned to seek a solution of the few remaining questions so that the conclusion of an agreement on cessation of tests could be achieved at an early date. It also called for the continuation of voluntary suspension of tests.

Except for French tests in the Sahara, the *de facto* test moratorium was in effect from November 3, 1958 to August 30, 1961, when the USSR announced that, owing to the increasing aggressiveness of NATO, it was compelled to resume nuclear weapons tests. The USSR started its new test series on September 1, 1961.

Two days later, the United States and the United Kingdom jointly proposed to the USSR that the three powers agree before September 9 not to conduct atmospheric nuclear tests and that they rely upon existing means of detection. At the same time, they reaffirmed their desire to conclude a nuclear test ban treaty which would be applicable to other forms of testing as well.

The USSR rejected the proposal, explaining that a ban only on tests in the atmosphere would permit the Western powers to improve their nuclear weapons through testing in other environments while tying the hands of the USSR. The USSR stated that it had held fewer tests than the Western powers and that it had every reason, morally and in the interests of its own security, to equalize the situation. On September 5, the United States announced that because of the resumption of tests by the USSR, it was forced to reconsider its position and, as a result, had resumed underground nuclear testing. On November 3, President Kennedy announced that the United States would conduct atmospheric tests only if it were "deemed necessary to maintain United States responsibilities for free world security."

At its sixteenth session, in 1961, the General Assembly adopted five resolutions on the question of suspension of nuclear weapons tests:

(1) a resolution appealing to the USSR to refrain from its intention to explode a fifty-megaton bomb in the atmosphere;

(2) a resolution expressing the Assembly's deep concern and regret that test explosions had been resumed, urging the powers concerned to refrain from further tests pending the conclusion of binding agreements in regard to tests or general and complete disarmament, and calling for speedy efforts to conclude such agreements;

(3) a resolution, proposed by the United Kingdom and the United States, urging the states negotiating at the Geneva Conference on the Discontinuance of Nuclear Weapons Tests to renew, at once, their efforts to conclude a treaty on the cessation of tests;

(4) a resolution calling on member states not to carry out nuclear tests in Africa;

(5) a resolution, submitted by twelve African-Asian nations, declaring, among other things, that the use of nuclear and thermonuclear weapons was contrary to the spirit, letter and aims of the United Nations and, as such, a direct violation of the Charter of the United Nations.

When the Conference on the Discontinuance of Nuclear Weapons Tests resumed on November 28, 1961, the USSR submitted a draft treaty to ban nuclear tests in the atmosphere, in outer space and under water, relying on national systems of detection for supervision of the agreement. It further proposed a moratorium on underground explosions until a control system had been developed as part of a system of control over general and complete disarmament. On January 16, 1962, the United States and the United Kingdom suggested that the Conference should either resume negotiations on the basis of the 1958 Geneva experts' recommendations or adjourn while the issue was considered by the Eighteen-Nation Disarmament Committee. The Conference adjourned for an indefinite period on January 29, 1962, and responsibility for the matter was transferred, in March 1962, to the three-power sub-committee (the USSR, the United Kingdom and the United States) established by the Eighteen-Nation Disarmament Committee.

In April, eight members of the Committee—Brazil, Burma, Ethiopia, India, Mexico, Nigeria, Sweden and the United Arab Republic —submitted to it a joint memorandum in which they stated that there were possibilities of establishing, by agreement, a system for continuous observation and effective control of a ban on nuclear tests on a purely scientific and non-political basis, and that such a system might be based and built upon already existing national networks of observation posts and institutions or, if more appropriate, on certain existing posts designated by agreement, together with new agreed posts, if necessary.

In addition, the memorandum suggested the possibility of setting up an international commission of a limited number of highly qualified scientists, possibly from non-aligned countries, which would process all data from observation posts. All parties to the treaty should accept the obligation to provide the commission with the facts necessary to establish the nature of any suspicious and significant event. Pursuant to this obligation, the parties "could invite" the commission to visit sites on their territories to check on suspicious events. The commission would report its assessment of the event concerned to all parties to the treaty, who would then be free to determine their action, under the treaty, on the basis of the commission's report.

The USSR expressed its willingness to consider the proposals as a basis for negotiations. The United Kingdom and the United States accepted the eight-power joint memorandum as one of the bases for negotiations.

On November 6, 1962, the General Assembly adopted a two-part resolution. In the first part of the resolution, it condemned all nuclear weapons tests, asked that such tests cease immediately and not later than January 1, 1963, and urged the Governments of the USSR, the United Kingdom and the United States to settle their differences in order to achieve agreement by that date. The Assembly endorsed the eight-power memorandum of April 16, 1962, and recommended it as a basis for negotiations towards removing the outstanding differences on effective control of underground tests. It further recommended that if the parties concerned did not reach agreement on cessation of all tests by January 1, 1963, they should enter into an immediate agreement prohibiting tests in the atmosphere, under water and in outer space, accompanied by an interim arrangement suspending all underground tests, which would include adequate assurances for effective detection and identification of seismic events by an international scientific commission.

In the second part of the resolution, the Assembly urged the Eighteen-Nation Committee to seek the conclusion of a treaty to prohibit nuclear weapons tests for all time and in all environments, under prompt and effective international verification.

Partial Test Ban Treaty

Agreement on a partial nuclear test ban treaty was preceded by an exchange of letters between the Governments of the USSR and the United States in December 1962 and January 1963 and by further deliberations in the Eighteen-Nation Committee on Disarmament, which convened on February 12, 1963.

On June 10, 1963, it was announced that the USSR, the United Kingdom and the United States had agreed to hold talks in Moscow in July on the question of banning nuclear weapons tests. As a result of these talks, which began on July 15, the three powers reached agreement on the text of a Treaty banning nuclear weapons tests in the atmosphere, in outer space and under water. The Treaty was signed by the Foreign Ministers of the three powers on August 5, 1963, and entered into force on October 10, 1963, at which time the original signatories had ratified it and ninety-eight other United Nations members, as well as seven non-members, had signed it.

At the Assembly's eighteenth session, in 1963, virtually all members welcomed the signing of the Treaty as a contribution to improved international relations, as well as a first step towards disarmament. In a resolution adopted by acclamation on November 27, the Assembly called on all states to become parties to the Treaty and to abide by its spirit and provisions. It further requested the Eighteen-Nation Committee on Disarmament to continue its negotiations to achieve the objectives set forth in the Treaty's preamble.

At the 1964 session of the Eighteen-Nation Committee, the eight non-aligned members of the Committee submitted a joint memorandum expressing the hope that all states would adhere to the Treaty and urging the nuclear powers to press on with negotiations to extend the ban to cover underground tests, a step which would be facilitated by an exchange of scientific and other information between the nuclear powers and by the improvement of techniques for the detection of such tests.

At the meetings of the Eighteen-Nation Disarmament Committee in 1965, Sweden submitted a proposal which included a suggestion that states advanced in seismology organize a "detection club." The United Arab Republic proposed a "threshold" ban to cover underground tests above a seismic magnitude of 4.75, accompanied by a moratorium on all other underground tests, pending agreement on an over-all ban. On September 15, the eight non-aligned members of the Committee, in a joint memorandum, called for a suspension forthwith of nuclear weapons tests in all environments. The memorandum stated that an agreement on a comprehensive treaty could be facilitated by the exchange of scientific and other information by the nuclear powers or by the improvement of detection and identification techniques if necessary.

Differences between the nuclear powers on the question of on-site inspection precluded agreement. The USSR maintained that progress in national detection systems had obviated the need for on-site inspection of suspected events. The United States held that the present stage of scientific developments did not as yet justify a modification of its position that on-site inspection was essential.

The urgent need for the suspension of all nuclear tests was again stressed by the General Assembly at its twentieth session, in 1965. In a thirty-five-power resolution approved on December 3, the Assembly noted with regret that, notwithstanding its previous resolutions, nuclear weapons tests continued to take place, and called on the Eighteen-Nation Committee to continue "with a sense of urgency" its work on a comprehensive treaty, taking into account improved possibilities for international co-operation in seismic detection.

Non-Proliferation of Nuclear Weapons

The General Assembly began consideration of the question of preventing the spread of nuclear weapons in 1958 and the following year adopted a resolution recognizing that a danger existed in this connection and that consideration of how to prevent the wider dissemination of nuclear weapons was appropriate within the framework of deliberations on disarmament.

In 1960, the Assembly called upon the governments producing nuclear weapons to prohibit dissemination of such weapons to the countries which did not possess them.

Two further resolutions on the subject were adopted by the Assembly in 1961. One, introduced by Ireland, called on all states, and in particular those possessing nuclear weapons, to use their best endeavours to secure the conclusion of an international treaty under which (a) the nuclear states would undertake not to relinquish control of nuclear weapons or to transmit the information necessary for their manufacture to states not possessing them and (b) states not possessing nuclear weapons would undertake not to manufacture or otherwise acquire control of them.

The other, proposed by Sweden and co-sponsored by Austria, Cambodia, Ceylon, Ethiopia, Liberia, Sudan and Tunisia, asked that an inquiry be made into the conditions under which countries not possessing nuclear weapons might be willing to enter into specific undertakings not to manufacture or acquire them and to refuse to receive nuclear weapons, in the future, in their territories on behalf of any other country. In early 1962, the Secretary-General made such an inquiry of member governments and received replies from sixty-two member states. Among the conditions mentioned by responding governments, reciprocity was most frequently cited. Some singled out specific states or areas as the basis of this condition; others called for universal adherence, especially by non-members.

When the question of non-dissemination of nuclear weapons was taken up by the Eighteen-Nation Committee on Disarmament in 1964, all the members of the Committee expressed the need for early agreement on the question.

The main problem centred on the disagreement between the United States and the Soviet Union on the compatibility of nuclear sharing within an alliance—which the United States and the United Kingdom had proposed for NATO—with the principle of non-dissemination. The United States maintained that such proposals as the Multilateral Nuclear Force did not envisage any transfer of nuclear weapons to national control and were, therefore, fully consistent with the Assembly's resolution. The USSR rejected this view, claiming that a multilateral force would give the Federal Republic of Germany access to nuclear weapons and lead to control over them. It maintained that any agreement on the non-dissemination of nuclear weapons should contain clear provisions excluding any access to nuclear weapons through military alliance.

The question of non-proliferation was discussed by the Disarmament Commission in 1965. By a resolution of June 15, the Commission recommended that the Eighteen-Nation Committee give priority to consideration of a treaty on the question.

On August 17, 1965, the United States introduced in the Eighteen-Nation Committee a draft treaty to prevent the spread of nuclear weapons. The draft spelled out the obligations of nuclear powers and provided for specified corresponding obligations on the part of non-nuclear powers. The United States gave assurance that the proposed NATO nuclear arrangements were not disseminatory. An additional proposal was put forward by Italy in the form of a unilateral non-acquisition declaration, whereby states would unilaterally undertake for an agreed period of time: (1) not to manufacture or acquire national control over nuclear weapons; (2) not to seek or receive assistance from other states in manufacturing such weapons; and (3) to accept application of IAEA or equivalent international safeguards on nuclear activities. Both India and Sweden objected to a concept of "privileged nuclear club members" and maintained that the disarmament process, especially the prevention of proliferation, required non-discriminatory undertakings by both nuclear and non-nuclear powers.

In a joint memorandum of September 15, 1965, the eight non-aligned members expressed the belief that a treaty on non-proliferation was not an end in itself, but only a means to an end, namely, the achievement of general and complete disarmament and, more particularly, nuclear disarmament. They were convinced that measures to prohibit the spread of nuclear weapons should, therefore, be coupled with or followed by tangible steps to halt the nuclear arms race and to limit, reduce and eliminate stocks of nuclear weapons and the means of their delivery.

At its twentieth session, in 1965, the Assembly had before it, in addition to the United States draft treaty, a USSR draft treaty on non-proliferation, the draft unilateral non-acquisition declaration proposed by Italy and the eight-nation joint memorandum. On November 23, the Assembly adopted a proposal submitted by the eight powers who had signed the joint memorandum, in which it called upon the Eighteen-Nation Committee to reconvene as early as possible in order to negotiate an international treaty to prevent the proliferation of nuclear weapons, based on the following main principles: the treaty should be void of any loop-holes which might permit nuclear or non-nuclear powers to proliferate, directly or indirectly, nuclear weapons in any form; it should embody an acceptable balance of mutual responsibilities and obligations of the nuclear and non-nuclear powers; it should be a step towards the achievement of general and complete disarmament and, more particularly, nuclear disarmament; it should contain acceptable and workable provisions to ensure its effectiveness; and nothing in the treaty should adversely affect the right of any group of states to conclude regional treaties in order to ensure the total absence of nuclear weapons in their respective territories.

Question of Nuclear Weapons in Outer Space

The basic draft treaties on general and complete disarmament of both the USSR and the United States provided for a ban on placing weapons of mass destruction into orbit.

In 1963, Mexico submitted a working paper to the Eighteen-Nation Committee containing the outline of a draft treaty to prohibit the orbiting and stationing of nuclear weapons in outer space, and providing for a ban on tests in outer space of all weapons of mass destruction or other warlike devices.

At the Assembly's eighteenth session, the Foreign Minister of the Soviet Union declared, on September 19, 1963, that his Government was prepared to take steps to prevent the spread of the arms race to outer space and considered it necessary to reach agreement with the United States on the question.

In an address to the Assembly the following day, the President of the United States welcomed the Soviet Union's response to the suggestion for an arrangement to keep weapons of mass destruction out of outer space, and suggested that negotiators work out details to attain this goal.

Following private talks between the representatives of both nations, Mexico introduced a draft resolution sponsored by the members of the Eighteen-Nation Committee on Disarmament. The resolution was approved in the General Assembly, by acclamation, on October 17, 1963. In it, the Assembly welcomed the expressions by the United States and the Soviet Union of their intention not to station in outer space any objects carrying nuclear weapons or other kinds of weapons of mass destruction and solemnly called on all states to refrain from (a) placing in orbit around the earth any objects carrying nuclear weapons or any other weapons of mass destruction, installing such weapons on celestial bodies or stationing such weapons in outer space in any other manner, and (b) causing, encouraging or in any way participating in the conduct of such activities.

Collateral Measures

In addition to considering the questions of general and complete disarmament, of banning nuclear weapons tests, of preventing the proliferation of nuclear weapons, and of keeping outer space free from weapons of mass destruction, the General Assembly and the Eighteen-Nation Committee on Disarmament have also discussed collateral measures intended to decrease international tension and build confidence, thus paving the way for an agreement on general and complete disarmament.

QUESTION OF CONVENING A CONFERENCE ON THE PROHIBITION OF THE USE OF NUCLEAR WEAPONS. In 1961, the General Assembly, acting on the initiative of Ethiopia, approved a resolution submitted by twelve Asian and African powers whereby it declared, *inter alia*, that the use of nuclear and thermonuclear weapons was contrary to the spirit, letter and aims of the United Nations and, as such, was a direct violation of the Charter. In accordance with another provision of the resolution, the Assembly asked the Secretary-General to ascertain the views of member states on the possibility of convening a special conference for the purpose of signing a convention on the prohibition of the use of such weapons. Of the sixty-two member states which replied to the Secretary-General in 1962, thirty-three viewed favourably the possibility of such a conference, twenty-six expressed negative views or doubts and three wished to await the results of the meetings of the Eighteen-Nation Committee on Disarmament before submitting their views.

At its eighteenth session, in 1963, the Assembly asked the Eighteen-Nation Committee to study the question of convening such a conference and to report to it on the matter. The United States opposed the holding of such a conference on the grounds that nuclear war could not be prevented by a declaration of intention alone. The USSR held that, although a convention alone could not prevent nuclear war, it could reduce the possibility of such a war.

REDUCING THE POSSIBILITY OF WAR BY ACCIDENT. The question of reducing the possibility of war by accident was dealt with in both the USSR and United States draft treaties on general disarmament in 1962. Both Governments agreed in principle on the usefulness of advance notification of military movements, on exchange of military missions and on the establishment of rapid communications between heads of states. In addition, the USSR proposed a ban on joint manœuvres of two or more states in the first stage of disarmament. The United States proposed, as a complement to first-stage measures, a system of fixed observation posts, additional observation arrangements and the establishment of an international commission to study the problems involved in the reduction of the risks of war by accident.

The measure to establish a direct communications link or "hot line" between the United States and the USSR for use in time of emergency had its origin in a working paper which the United States submitted to the Eighteen-Nation Committee in 1962. On April 5, 1963, the USSR announced its readiness to accept the proposal.

Following a number of meetings on the question between representatives of the two Governments, agreement was reached on June 20, 1963, and the communications link was established on August 30.

QUESTION OF A NON-AGGRESSION PACT. On February 20, 1963, the USSR submitted to the Eighteen-Nation Committee a draft non-aggression pact whereby the states parties to the Warsaw Treaty and the states parties to NATO would undertake to refrain from aggression, and from the threat or use of force in any manner inconsistent with the purposes and principles of the Charter, against one another or in their international relations in general. They would further undertake to resolve by peaceful means only, through negotiations between them or by the means provided by the Charter, all disputes that might arise.

The Western powers opposed the consideration of this proposal, maintaining that it not only had a predominantly political character but was also related to European regional security matters and that many of the countries directly concerned were not represented at the Conference.

VERIFIED FREEZE ON STRATEGIC NUCLEAR DELIVERY VEHI-CLES.   In 1964, the United States proposed a freeze on the number and characteristics of strategic nuclear delivery vehicles. In making its proposal, the United States declared that its objective was to maintain at constant levels the quantities of such vehicles held by the East and the West and to prevent the development and deployment of strategic delivery vehicles of a significantly new type. The United States explained in detail the vehicles which should be included and elaborated criteria for a proposed inspection system.

The Soviet Union did not agree with this proposal, arguing that it was not a disarmament measure since under it all existing means of delivery would be retained and the present over-kill capacity of the United States and its NATO allies would be maintained.

During the Assembly's twentieth session, in 1965, the United States announced that if progress were made on a freeze, it would be willing to explore the possibility of significant reductions in the number of nuclear delivery vehicles.

REDUCTION OF MILITARY BUDGETS.   In 1964, the Soviet Union introduced in the Eighteen-Nation Committee a proposal that states reduce their military budgets by between 10 and 15 per cent. It maintained that this was feasible because of the favourable conditions created by the unilateral reduction of military expenditures for 1964 which had been announced by the USSR and the United States.

The United States stated that the Committee would require more information about military expenditures and how they could be verified. Canada and the United Kingdom also expressed concern about verification and, together with Sweden, stressed the need to consider, through a technical working group, the comparability of budget components of various countries and the question of verifying expenditures. The Soviet Union was willing to consider a detailed study, however, only after the principle of reducing military budgets by between 10 and 15 per cent had been agreed upon.

CUT-OFF IN PRODUCTION OF FISSIONABLE MATERIALS FOR
WEAPONS PURPOSES.   On April 20, 1964, the United States
and the USSR unilaterally announced decisions to reduce the production of fissionable materials for use in manufacturing weapons. Both nations specified in the Eighteen-Nation Committee the extent of their planned reductions. The United Kingdom stated that it had earlier announced it had ceased production of uranium-235 and was gradually ending production of plutonium.

In a subsequent detailed proposal, the United States declared it was prepared to advance from its announced cut-backs, through verified plant-by-plant shutdowns to a complete cut-off of production with verification. On June 25, it submitted a working paper specifying three kinds of required inspection and the types of plants to be inspected. It also reaffirmed its readiness to transfer for peaceful uses larger amounts of fissionable materials than the USSR—for instance, 60,000 kilogrammes as against 40,000 kilogrammes.

The USSR held that the United States plan amounted to control without disarmament. It contended that the proposed inspection system, particularly the requirement that parties submit data on location and output of all plants producing uranium-235 and plutonium, would disclose the volume and sources of existing stocks and the complete technology of the production of fissionable materials on which a nation's security was based. The Soviet Union doubted whether such an agreement was possible outside of general disarmament.

In a further proposal made during the twentieth session of the General Assembly, the United States suggested the demonstrated destruction of a substantial number of nuclear weapons from the respective stocks of the United States and the USSR for the purpose of transferring weapons-grade fissionable material to peaceful uses.

DESTRUCTION OF BOMBER AIRCRAFT.   Both the USSR and the United States submitted proposals on the destruction of bomber aircraft to the Eighteen-Nation Committee in 1964. The USSR proposed that all bomber aircraft be eliminated; the United States proposed that it and the Soviet Union destroy their B-47 and TU-16 aircraft, respectively, at the rate of twenty aircraft a month over a two-year period.

The United States opposed the Soviet proposal, except as a part of general disarmament, stating that it would weigh heavily on one type of armaments and would, therefore, disturb the military balance. Its own proposal, the United States said, would provide a tangible reduction in an important category of weapons and, in relation to a freeze on the production of strategic delivery vehicles, would mean freezing such vehicles at an even lower level. The USSR, on the other hand, maintained that the United States plan would not lead to a measure of disarmament, since it was designed to replace obsolete weapons already being phased out by new types, and would thus result in an acceleration of the arms race.

Burma, India, Mexico, Nigeria and the United Arab Republic expressed the belief that the two proposals could be linked by enlarging on types and number of bombers to be immediately involved, by differentiating as to the countries to be affected and by including some missiles in the process.

WITHDRAWAL OF FOREIGN TROOPS FROM THE TERRITORIES OF OTHER COUNTRIES AND THE ELIMINATION OF FOREIGN MILITARY BASES. In 1963, the USSR submitted to the Eighteen-Nation Committee a draft declaration renouncing the use of foreign territories for stationing strategic delivery systems. The USSR maintained that the declaration, if adopted, would be a first step towards the elimination of all military bases on foreign territories and the prevention of the proliferation of nuclear weapons. The Western powers rejected the Soviet proposal as one-sided; the elimination of military bases, they argued, could be achieved only through general and complete disarmament.

In 1964, the USSR proposed that the number of armed forces in foreign territories be reduced on a basis of reciprocity, the long-range objective being the complete withdrawal of foreign troops. The USSR was prepared to start by reducing its troops in the territory of the German Democratic Republic and other European states, if the Western powers would reduce the number of their troops in the Federal Republic of Germany and other countries.

A Soviet draft resolution before the Disarmament Commission in 1965 proposed that the Commission call upon all states maintaining military bases in other countries to liquidate them forthwith and refrain henceforth from establishing new ones. The draft resolution, which would also have called upon the states to agree on the withdrawal of all foreign troops, was not put to the vote.

The United States and its allies opposed these Soviet proposals on the grounds that military bases and armed forces abroad are part of security arrangements voluntarily entered into by sovereign states for collective self-defence, that their liquidation would upset the existing military balance to the advantage of the USSR and that, hence, these problems could only be solved in the context of general and complete disarmament.

Denuclearization of Africa

At the Assembly's fifteenth session, in 1960, several African nations launched the effort to have their continent considered a denuclearized zone. The basic resolution on the question—sponsored by the Congo

(Leopoldville), Ethiopia, Ghana, Guinea, Liberia, Mali, Morocco, Nigeria, Sierra Leone, Somalia, Sudan, Togo, Tunisia and the United Arab Republic—was approved by the Assembly on November 16, 1961. In it, the Assembly called upon member states to refrain from carrying out or continuing to carry out nuclear tests in Africa; to refrain from using the territory, territorial waters or air space of Africa for testing, storing or transporting nuclear weapons; and, finally, to consider and respect the continent of Africa as a denuclearized zone.

In August 1964, thirty-three African states asked the Assembly to approve a declaration on the denuclearization of Africa which had been adopted by the Assembly of the Heads of State and Government of the Organization of African Unity (OAU) at Cairo in July 1964. The OAU Conference had solemnly declared that the respective states were ready to undertake, through an international agreement to be concluded under United Nations auspices, not to manufacture or acquire control of atomic weapons, and had appealed to all peace-loving nations to accept the same declaration, and to all the nuclear powers, in particular, to respect the declaration and conform to it.

On December 3, 1965, the Assembly approved a declaration by which it reaffirmed its call upon all states to respect the African continent as a nuclear-free zone; endorsed the OAU declaration on the subject; called upon all states to refrain from testing, manufacturing, using or deploying nuclear weapons on the continent of Africa, and from acquiring such weapons or taking any action which would compel African states to take similar action. The Assembly also urged those states possessing nuclear weapons and capability not to transfer such weapons, scientific data or technological assistance to the national control of any state, either directly or indirectly, in any form which might be used to assist such states in the manufacture or use of nuclear weapons in Africa.

Denuclearization of Latin America

In May 1963, Brazil and Mexico submitted to the United Nations a joint declaration which had been issued on April 29 by the Presidents of Bolivia, Brazil, Chile, Ecuador and Mexico on the denuclearization of Latin America. The Presidents announced that their Governments were prepared to sign a multilateral agreement whereby countries would undertake not to manufacture, receive, store or test nuclear weapons or nuclear launching devices, and brought the declaration to the attention of heads of state of the other Latin American republics with an invitation to accede to it.

At the request of Brazil, the question was discussed at the Assembly's eighteenth session. The Assembly noted with satisfaction the initiative for the denuclearization of Latin America taken in the joint declaration of April 29, 1963, and expressed the hope that the Latin American states would initiate studies, as they deemed appropriate, in the light of the principles of the United Nations and of regional arrangements, concerning the measures that should be agreed upon in order to achieve the aims of the declaration.

The text of the Final Act of the preliminary meeting of Latin American states on this question was submitted to the Assembly in 1964. According to the document, the seventeen participating states, which had met in Mexico City in November 1964, had decided to establish a Preparatory Commission for the Denuclearization of Latin America.

During the Assembly's twentieth session, in 1965, Mexico stated that the efforts of the Preparatory Commission had resulted in a preliminary draft treaty of fourteen articles defining obligations, as well as a system of verification based on International Atomic Energy Agency safeguards. Two prerequisites remained to be resolved: (a) agreement on the geographical demarcation of the zone under the treaty; and (b) assurances from all nuclear powers to respect in all aspects the juridical status of the zone.

Proposals for Other Denuclearized Zones

On May 27, 1963, the Soviet Union transmitted to the Eighteen-Nation Disarmament Committee the text of a note it had addressed to the United States Government on the denuclearization of the Mediterranean area. The note stated that the United States and its allies were creating a "concentrated NATO nuclear force and taking the course of" spreading nuclear missile weapons to other continents and seas." The USSR proposed that the Mediterranean Sea area be declared a zone free of nuclear missile weapons and stated that it was prepared to assume an obligation not to deploy any weapons or their means of delivery in the waters of the area, provided that similar obligations were assumed by other powers.

The Western powers regarded the proposal as one-sided and, therefore, unacceptable. Reflecting the Western view, the United Kingdom opposed denuclearized zones in areas where there was a military confrontation of the great powers or a complex system of defensive arrangements or where nuclear weapons already existed, as in Central Europe or the Mediterranean.

In 1964, the USSR and the East European members of the Eighteen-Nation Committee suggested that proposals be formulated envisaging the establishment of nuclear-free zones, particularly where there was the greatest danger of nuclear conflict, such as Central Europe. In this connection, the Committee's attention was drawn to a Polish proposal for a freeze on nuclear armaments in Central Europe which, in Poland's view, would help to halt the arms race, prevent the further spread of nuclear weapons in the area and prevent the production of such weapons by powers not possessing them.

Proposal for World Disarmament Conference

The Second Conference of Heads of State or Government of Non-Aligned Countries, held in Cairo from October 5 to 10, 1964, submitted to the General Assembly its "Programme for Peace and International Co-operation," containing a proposal for the convening of a world disarmament conference, under United Nations auspices, to which all countries would be invited.

During 1965, the Disarmament Commission considered the question of a world disarmament conference and recommended that the General Assembly give the proposal urgent consideration. The basis of the Assembly's consideration at its twentieth session, in 1965, was a 43-power draft resolution endorsing the proposal and urging that the necessary consultations be concluded with all countries for the purpose of establishing a widely representative preparatory committee which would take appropriate steps for the convening of a world disarmament conference not later than 1967.

The question of the participation of all countries, and, especially, important military powers, was stressed by several member states. In particular, the presence of the People's Republic of China was considered indispensable by a number of member states.

In order to insure universality, some states said that the conference must not be convened under the aegis of the United Nations. It was pointed out that a dilemma existed, namely, how to associate the United Nations with the world conference and yet avoid any firm link between the two, so as not to alienate non-member states. Some states stressed the continuing responsibility of the United Nations in this field. Others viewed the world conference as a complementary mechanism. In the preamble, the resolution recognized the "continuing interest and responsibility of the United Nations in connection with the solution of the disarmament problem."

The General Assembly adopted the resolution on November 29, 1965, by 112 votes to none, with one abstention (France).

Economic and Social Consequences of Disarmament

In response to a request of the General Assembly at its fifteenth session, a report on the economic and social consequences of disarmament was submitted by the Secretary-General to the Economic and Social Council in mid-1962.

The report was prepared by a group of expert consultants consisting of ten members drawn from countries with different economic systems and in different stages of economic development. The consultative group reached the conclusion that "the achievement of general and complete disarmament would be an unqualified blessing to all mankind"; that the improvement of world economic and social conditions that disarmament would make possible could be achieved without raising any insoluble problems of transition; and that "all the problems and difficulties of transition connected with disarmament could be met by appropriate national and international measures."

In reviewing the resources devoted to military purposes, the experts found that world military expenditure constituted not only a grave political danger but also a heavy economic and social burden on most countries. They noted that it was generally agreed that the world was spending roughly $120 thousand million annually on military account, a figure close to the value of the world's annual exports of all commodities and corresponding to about one-half of the total gross capital formation throughout the world or to two-thirds of—or perhaps the whole of—the entire national income of all the underdeveloped countries.

In a resolution on the subject, the Council, besides endorsing the consultative group's report and appealing to all states to take the findings of the report into consideration, urged United Nations members, particularly those involved in current military programmes, to devote further attention to the detailed aspects of the economic and social consequences of disarmament. The Council requested that the Secretary-General report to it on any studies on this subject that member states had made. The Secretary-General was also requested to transmit the consultative group's report, together with the comments made in the Council, to the Assembly at its seventeenth session and to submit it to the Conference of the Eighteen-Nation Committee on Disarmament.

The Assembly, at its seventeenth session, adopted a resolution entitled "Declaration on the conversion to peaceful needs of the resources released by disarmament," in which it expressed its appreciation of, and endorsed, the consultative group's report. It invited the Secretary-General and the governments of the developing countries to intensify their efforts to establish and implement soundly conceived projects and well-integrated development plans for implementation at such time as additional resources were released following an agreement on general and complete disarmament.

A report by the Secretary-General, which was submitted to the Economic and Social Council in 1964, reviewed national and international studies and activities in relation to: (1) the over-all planning of conversion of military expenditures to peaceful uses; (2) the promotion of necessary economic and social readjustments during the period of conversion; and (3) the longer-term uses of liberated resources for accelerating economic and social development within national economies and for expanding the total flow and improving the effectiveness of financial aid and technical assistance to developing countries.

In 1965, the Council recommended that member states, particularly those countries significantly involved, continue and attempt to develop national studies regarding economic and social aspects of disarmament and to transmit them to the Secretary-General as feasible. The Council also requested the Secretary-General to continue to inform it of the national, international and non-governmental studies he receives concerning the economic and social consequences of disarmament.

PEACEFUL USES OF ATOMIC ENERGY

On December 8, 1953, the President of the United States, addressing the eighth session of the General Assembly, proposed that governments jointly contribute normal uranium and fissionable materials to an international atomic energy agency to be set up under the aegis of the United Nations.

At its ninth session, the General Assembly adopted, on December 4, 1954, a resolution expressing the hope that an international atomic energy agency would be established without delay, and suggested that it should then negotiate an appropriate form of agreement with the United Nations.

The resolution provided that an international technical conference be held under the auspices of the United Nations to explore means of developing the peaceful uses of atomic energy through international co-operation and, in particular, to study the development of atomic power and to consider other technical areas, such as biology, medicine and protection from radiation, most suitable for effective international co-operation.

The United Nations International Conference on the Peaceful Uses of Atomic Energy met in Geneva from August 8 to 20, 1955. A draft statute for the establishment of the agency was drawn up and was circulated to governments, other than those at the Conference, at the end of August 1955 for their consideration and comment. The statute, after further elaboration, was submitted for approval to a conference of eighty-one nations at United Nations Headquarters in September 1956. After a series of amendments, the statute was unanimously approved on October 26, 1956, and was signed by the representatives of seventy nations. A further ten nations signed it in the subsequent ninety-day period during which it was open for signature.

At its tenth session, the General Assembly noted the impressive results achieved by the Conference in facilitating the free flow of scientific knowledge on the peaceful uses of atomic energy, and recommended that a second conference be held in two or three years' time.

The second United Nations International Conference on the Peaceful Uses of Atomic Energy was held from September 1 to 13, 1958, in Geneva. The agenda of the Conference was wider in scope than that of the first Conference since it covered a new field—the possibility of controlled fusion.

After considering a report by the Secretary-General on the second Conference, the Assembly, on December 13, 1958, unanimously approved a resolution in which it decided that the advisory committee established by the ninth session of the Assembly to assist the Secretary-General in the organization and convening of both conferences be extended, as constituted, as the United Nations Scientific Advisory Committee and that this Committee was to advise and assist the Secretary-General, at his request, on all matters relating to the peaceful uses of atomic energy with which the United Nations might be concerned.

The Secretary-General and the Scientific Advisory Committee, in consultation with the International Atomic Energy Agency and the interested specialized agencies, were requested to undertake a thorough evaluation of the second Conference in relation to the need, nature and timing of similar conferences in this field.

In 1960, in his report to the General Assembly at its fifteenth session, the Secretary-General recommended that a third conference be held in two or three years' time.

The Third International Conference on the Peaceful Uses of Atomic Energy was held in Geneva from August 31 to September 9, 1964. It differed from the two previous conferences in that it concentrated on one major aspect of the development of atomic energy, the technology of nuclear power. Participation in the Conference was substantially larger than in 1955, in spite of the narrower scope of the agenda. Seventy-seven states, ten specialized agencies and the International Atomic Energy Agency were represented. (*See also page* 488.)

EFFECTS OF ATOMIC RADIATION

The Scientific Committee on the Effects of Atomic Radiation was established by the General Assembly on December 3, 1955. The Committee, composed of Argentina, Australia, Belgium, Brazil, Canada, Czechoslovakia, France, India, Japan, Mexico, Sweden, USSR, United Arab Republic, United Kingdom and United States, was requested: (a) to receive and assemble information, furnished by members of the United Nations or of the specialized agencies, on observed levels of ionizing radiation and radioactivity in the environment, and on effects of ionizing radiation upon man and his environment; (b) to recommend uniform standards with respect to procedures for sample collection and analyses; (c) to compile and assemble, in an integrated manner, the information received on observed radiation levels; (d) to review and collate national reports; (e) to make yearly progress reports and to develop a summary and evaluation of the reports received on radiation levels and effects; and (f) to transmit from time to time those reports and evaluations to the Secretary-General for publication.

The Committee carries out its task by analysing and evaluating, in the light of current scientific knowledge, the reports submitted to it, as well as the relevant information that is generally available to the scientific community. In its activity, the Committee is assisted by a scientific staff, provided by the Secretary-General, which is responsible for securing the requisite information and for carrying out preliminary work of review, analysis and evaluation. The Committee reports yearly to the General Assembly by means of documents of a largely formal nature.

The first substantive report of the Committee, which was submitted to the General Assembly in 1958, constituted a broad and comprehensive evaluation of existing knowledge of the levels of ionizing radiation to which human beings are exposed and of the effects which these radiations may have. The report also cited research projects of interest. After discussing the report, the General Assembly unanimously decided to request that the Committee continue its useful work and further report to the General Assembly as appropriate.

As a result of its further work, the Committee issued a new comprehensive report to the General Assembly in 1962. In this report, the Committee examined the same topics that it had reviewed in its first comprehensive report in the light of the new information that had since become available. The report consisted of a main text and of technical annexes in which the information used by the Committee was examined and assessed in detail.

The salient results of the Committee's discussion were the following.

(1) Average doses of radiation from natural sources had been more accurately estimated than had been possible in the Committee's first comprehensive report. Estimates were slightly higher, but the Committee emphasized that they were subject to considerable geographical variation.

(2) New data on irradiation for medical purposes, obtained in

a number of countries with advanced medical facilities, indicated that the use of appropriate radiological methods and equipment could lead to a substantial reduction of the doses. However, even in those countries in which the dose contribution of all medical sources was the lowest, it was still the major man-made source contributing to the exposure of human populations.

(3) The doses received by the great majority of workers directly engaged in radiation work, and therefore the contribution of these doses to the over-all exposure of the population, were very low when proper radiation protection methods were applied. Doses from the radioactive wastes that were inevitably produced by peaceful uses of atomic energy and released into the environment in a controlled fashion still gave rise to very small contributions to the exposure of populations.

(4) Knowledge of the mechanisms by which radioactive debris from atmospheric nuclear tests were distributed over the surface of the earth and of the mechanisms controlling the transfer of radioactive nuclides—particularly strontium-90 and caesium-137—to body tissues through the food chain had greatly increased since the previous report. The evaluation of the resulting doses had thus been based on firmer grounds. The Committee had also been able for the first time to assess the contribution of such radioactive nuclides of biological importance as carbon-14 and iodine-131.

(5) The Committee considered it to be clearly established that exposure to radiation, even in doses substantially lower than those producing acute effects, might occasionally give rise to a wide variety of harmful effects, including cancer, leukaemia and inherited abnormalities, which in some cases might not be easily distinguishable from naturally occurring conditions or indentifiable as due to radiation. Because of the available evidence that genetic damage occurred at the lowest levels as yet experimentally tested, it was prudent to assume that some genetic damage might follow any dose of radiation, however small.

(6) The Committee emphasized that all forms of unnecessary radiation exposure should be minimized or avoided entirely, particularly when the exposure of large populations was entailed, and that every procedure involving the peaceful uses of ionizing radiation should be subject to appropriate immediate and continuing scrutiny to ensure that the resulting exposure was kept to the minimum practicable level and that this level was consistent with the necessity or the value of the procedure. The Committee added that as there were no effective measures to prevent the occurrence of harmful effects of global radioactive contamination from nuclear explosions, the achievement of a final cessation of nuclear tests would benefit present and future generations of mankind.

The General Assembly considered the second comprehensive report of the Scientific Committee at its seventeenth session. In commending the Committee for its work and its valuable report, the Assembly requested the Committee to continue its assessment of radiation risks. The Assembly also authorized implementation of a scheme proposed by the World Meteorological Organization (WMO) for worldwide monitoring and reporting on levels of atmospheric radioactivity.

The Committee pursued its activity through 1963 and 1964 and submitted a further report to the General Assembly's nineteenth session. The new report dealt only with radioactive contamination of the environment by nuclear tests—a subject that was in need of review as a consequence of the resumption of large-scale atmospheric nuclear testing at the end of 1961—and discussed risks of induction of malignancies by radiation in man on the basis of recently obtained epidemiological data. The main conclusions arrived at by the Committee in the report were the following.

(1) The radioactive contamination of the environment due to tests carried out in 1961-1962 had roughly doubled the total dose of radiation from radioactive debris that the world population would receive by the end of the twentieth century.

(2) Those small populations which live in sub-arctic regions showed body levels of caesium-137 that sometimes exceeded the world average by a factor of more than 100 as a consequence of their very high consumption of caribou and reindeer meat. Because of their feeding habits, these animals are heavily contaminated with radioactive material deposited on the local vegetation.

(3) The total doses of radiation to be received from all tests that had been carried out were evaluated with regard to the reproductive organs, irradiation of which may give rise to genetic effects, to the bone marrow from which leukaemias arise and to those cells in which bone tumours may be induced. The total doses to be received by the end of the century were estimated to be equivalent to those received from natural sources during nine, thirty and twenty months, respectively.

(4) Iodine-131, a short-lived nuclide that is easily absorbed from milk, particularly by infants, and irradiates the thyroid gland, had been widely measured in the environment since the atmospheric nuclear tests had been resumed in 1961. In the northern hemisphere, average radiation doses to the thyroids of infants fed with fresh milk were about equal to those received in one year from natural sources.

(5) A re-examination of the data obtained from the survivors of Hiroshima and Nagasaki, on the basis of dosimetric information not available when the 1962 report was prepared, led the Committee to estimate that the rate of induction of leukaemia was between one and two cases per year per rad per million individuals exposed at acute doses between 100 and 900 rads. These doses are of the order of 1,000 and 9,000 times higher than those received continuously from natural

sources in one year. The Committee emphasized that the estimate of the rate of induction that it had obtained could not be applied without serious reservations in predicting the effects of acute irradiation in other populations and under different conditions of exposure. Though the Committee did not give risk estimates applying at low doses, it noted that estimates per unit dose valid above 100 rads were likely to represent an upper limit to values obtaining at very low doses. The Committee also noted that the risk of leukaemia per unit dose for children irradiated *in utero* might be several times higher than in adults.

(6) Recent results had made it possible for the Committee to obtain an estimate of the risk of induction of cancer of the thyroid in children who had been irradiated for therapeutic reasons. The estimate, valid for doses between 100 and 300 rads, amounted to about one case per year per rad per million exposed individuals. With regard to this estimate also, it was necessary to exercise caution in applying it to the general population of children and to different conditions of exposure.

The third report of the Scientific Committee was noted by the General Assembly at its nineteenth session and considered at its twentieth session, together with the Committee's yearly progress report for 1965. The General Assembly unanimously approved a resolution by which it commended the Scientific Committee for its valuable contribution to wider knowledge and understanding of the effects and levels of atomic radiation and asked it to continue its programme.

PEACEFUL USES OF OUTER SPACE

The question of the peaceful uses of outer space was first considered by the United Nations in 1958. A USSR proposal recommending "the establishment within the framework of the United Nations of an international committee for co-operation in the study of cosmic space for peaceful purposes" and a United States proposal "to obtain fullest information on the many problems relating to outer space before recommending specific programmes of international co-operation in this field by an *Ad Hoc* Committee of the United Nations" resulted in the Assembly's decision at its thirteenth session, in 1958, to include both items under the title "Question of peaceful uses of outer space."

After considering various proposals on the subject, the Assembly created an *Ad Hoc* Committee, consisting of eighteen nations, to report to the Assembly on the activities and resources of the United Nations and its agencies in the area of international co-operation in the peaceful uses of outer space, the future organizational arrangements and the nature of legal problems which might arise in carrying out programmes to explore outer space.

In December 1959, the General Assembly, recognizing the need for a special organ to further international co-operation in this area, established a twenty-four-member committee (later increased to twenty-eight) to review, as appropriate, the area of international co-operation and to study practical and feasible means for giving effect to programmes in the peaceful uses of outer space which could appropriately be undertaken under United Nations auspices, and also to study the legal problems which may arise from the exploration and use of outer space. The members of the Committee are: Albania, Argentina, Australia, Austria, Belgium, Brazil, Bulgaria, Canada, Chad, Czechoslovakia, France, Hungary, India, Iran, Italy, Japan, Lebanon, Mexico, Mongolia, Morocco, Poland, Romania, Sierra Leone, Sweden, the USSR, the United Arab Republic, the United Kingdom and the United States.

The Committee on the Peaceful Uses of Outer Space—with its legal and scientific sub-committees, which have the same membership as the Committee—provides a forum for consideration of the political and legal issues arising in the peaceful exploration of outer space. It also furnishes the focal point for international co-operation in the peaceful uses of outer space, a broad field in which a great many organizations are engaged in a variety of activities ranging from purely scientific investigations to the development of applications of space technology having far-reaching social and economic implications.

Scientific and Technical Aspects

Through the work of its Scientific and Technical Sub-Committee, the Committee on the Peaceful Uses of Outer Space has made notable progress towards the goal of expanded international co-operation in the scientific and technical aspects of outer space.

On the basis of the reports of the Sub-Committee, the Committee has presented a series of agreed recommendations on exchange of information, encouragement of international programmes, creation of sounding rocket facilities, potentially harmful effects of space experiments, and education and training which have laid the groundwork for further practical action in the development of international co-operation.

EXCHANGE OF INFORMATION.   In each of its successive resolutions on international co-operation in the peaceful uses of outer space, the General Assembly has included provisions relating to the exchange and dissemination of information on outer space matters. In a resolution adopted at its sixteenth session, in 1961, the Assembly—after affirming its belief that the United Nations should provide a focal point for international co-operation in the peaceful exploration and use of outer space—recommended two measures to promote this objective: (1) the maintenance of a public registry of data furnished to the Committee on the Peaceful Uses of Outer Space by states launching objects into outer space; and (2) the organization of the exchange of such information "as Governments may supply on a voluntary basis relating to outer space activities, supplementing but not duplicating existing technical and scientific exchanges."

In accordance with the Assembly's resolution, a public registry of launching data has been established, and the launching data furnished by the United States, the USSR, Italy and France have been recorded in it. With regard to the exchange of information, the Secretariat, on the basis of information obtained from member states, has from time to time prepared documents designed to provide a consolidated world-wide picture of international co-operation. These documents have included a review of national and co-operative international programmes in the field of outer space; a review of the activities and resources of the United Nations, its specialized agencies and other international bodies relating to the peaceful uses of outer space; and a report on material to ensure popular understanding of the purposes and potentialities of space activities.

ENCOURAGEMENT OF INTERNATIONAL PROGRAMMES. In the Committee's opinion, mutual benefits may be derived by developing countries and by those not yet advanced in space activities when they can participate in well-planned space programmes, and such participation may contribute to the general welfare of mankind.

At present, there is international collaboration mainly in satellite meteorology and space communications, though other programmes are in progress, such as the International Years of Quiet Sun, the International Indian Ocean Expedition and the World Magnetic Survey.

In space meteorology, particular emphasis has been placed on the need to establish a World Weather Watch, using information from meteorological observation of all kinds. Under the plan, there will ultimately be a world weather service, integrating national and international meteorological activities. The plan will involve a co-ordinated programme of weather observations, and the communication of these observations to national, regional and world centres for providing meteorological analyses and for their subsequent distribution to national services which desire them. The use of satellites for this purpose will not only result in increasing the coverage of the surface which is simultaneously under observation, and in fast transmission of meteorological data to centres, but will also help to cover the vast gaps over oceanic and equatorial areas in the world-wide network of conventional observations.

The Committee has recognized that international space communications should be available for the use of all countries on a global and non-discriminatory basis so that all member states would be able to benefit from them. The Sub-Committee has stressed the importance of space communications and space meteorology in connection with the problems of growing population and the need to provide food for it in many parts of the world, and has recognized that development in these fields might help to alleviate these problems.

In its reports and recommendations, the Committee has drawn the attention of member states and specialized agencies to these programmes and invited them to support the activities of international organizations in these areas. The Committee has also expressed appreciation of the role of WMO and ITU in these fields.

The Sub-Committee has also discussed the possibility of establishing a world civil navigation system, which, in the Sub-Committee's opinion, could be a very useful practical consequence of the exploration of outer space, and has recommended the establishment of a working group to consider the need, feasibility and implementation of such a system.

EDUCATION AND TRAINING.   Recognizing the importance, especially for developing countries, of scholarships, fellowships and other training opportunities in fields related to the exploration and peaceful uses of outer space, the Committee has invited member states to make their specific interests and needs known to the Secretary-General and to inform him of facilities for education and training in these fields. Arrangements have been made for the dissemination of this information on a continuing basis and for the publication of a biennial review of space education and training facilities. The Committee has also invited the attention of member states to the need to give favourable consideration to requests of countries wishing to participate in the peaceful exploration of outer space for training and technical assistance. On the recommendation of the Committee, the Secretariat is preparing a directory of available space education and training facilities and fellowships. Under a General Assembly resolution adopted in December 1965, the Committee has been requested to consider and prepare suggestions for programmes of education and training of specialists in the peaceful uses of outer space.

INTERNATIONAL SOUNDING ROCKET LAUNCHING FACILITIES. It has been recognized that sounding rockets provide a very useful tool for the experimental study of the upper atmosphere and the earth's magnetic fields but that there are major gaps in the world coverage of sounding rocket launching sites, particularly in the equatorial region and the southern hemisphere.

For this reason, the Committee, noting that the creation and use of sounding rocket launching facilities, especially in the equatorial region and the southern hemisphere, under United Nations sponsorship would further international collaboration in space research, and that such facilities would open possibilities for nations wishing to enter the field of space research but unable to do so because of economic, technological or other factors, suggested in 1962 the basic principles for creation of such international facilities on the understanding that it would be a United Nations project in which the principal powers concerned would co-operate. In the same year, the General Assembly accepted the suggestion of the Committee that an international equatorial sounding rocket launching facility be established under the auspices of the United Nations.

The Sub-Committee commended the initiative taken by the Government of India in establishing the equatorial sounding rocket launching site at Thumba and recommended that the Committee approve the establishment of a group of scientists to visit the station and to advise the Committee on its eligibility for United Nations sponsorship. In a resolution adopted in 1965, the General Assembly accorded United Nations sponsorship to India for the continuing operation of the Thumba Equatorial Rocket Launching Station (TERLS) under the basic principles endorsed by the Assembly in 1962.

In forwarding its recommendation to the Assembly, the Committee urged that due attention should be paid by the United Nations, the specialized agencies and member states to requests for assistance to increase the utility of TERLS as a place for international collaboration in sounding rocket experiments.

TERLS, the first rocket launching station to enjoy such sponsorship, has instituted a programme to create special facilities in the way of workshops, classrooms and living accommodations for scientists, technicians and trainees so as to increase the potential of TERLS as an international training centre. An international seminar on sounding rocket techniques and experiments was held at TERLS in 1965 with the financial assistance of UNESCO.

In addition, the Committee has invited COSPAR to review the geographic distribution of sounding rocket launching facilities and their capabilities and to advise the Scientific and Technical Sub-Committee from time to time on desirable locations and important topics of research.

POTENTIALLY HARMFUL EFFECTS OF SPACE EXPLORATION. In its report to the General Assembly in 1963, the Committee recognized the importance of the problem of preventing potentially harmful interference with peaceful uses of outer space. Later, in 1964, the Committee, having before it the resolution adopted by the Executive Council of COSPAR on the basis of the report of its Consultative Group, in which COSPAR made specific proposals concerning space experiments, requested the Secretary-General to circulate to member states the

COSPAR resolution and the Consultative Group's report and its appendices. The Committee has also urged that member states proposing to carry out experiments in space should give consideration to the problem of possible interference with other peaceful uses of outer space, as well as possible harmful changes in the natural environment caused by space activities and, where member states consider it appropriate, should seek a scientific analysis of the qualitative and quantitative aspects of the experiments from the COSPAR Consultative Group.

INTERNATIONAL CONFERENCE ON PEACEFUL USES OF OUTER SPACE. On the recommendation of the Committee, the General Assembly unanimously decided in 1965 to establish a working group to examine the desirability, organization and objectives of an international conference or meeting on peaceful uses of outer space, under United Nations auspices, to be held in 1967.

At the meetings of the working group in January 1966, recommendations were made that the conference should examine the practical benefits to be derived from space research and exploration on the basis of technical and scientific achievements, and the extent to which non-space powers, especially the developing countries, may enjoy these benefits. It was also recommended that the conference examine the opportunities available to non-space powers for international co-operation in space activities, taking into account the extent to which the United Nations may play a role.

Legal Aspects

The General Assembly, on December 20, 1961, adopted a resolution by which, among other things, it invited the Committee on the Peaceful Uses of Outer Space to study and report on the legal problems which might arise from the exploration and use of outer space.

The consideration of such problems has taken place primarily in the Committee's Legal Sub-Committee, which, since its establishment in 1962, has discussed the following issues: (a) a declaration of legal principles governing the activities of states in outer space; (b) assistance to and return of astronauts and space vehicles; (c) liability for damage caused by objects launched into outer space; and (d) a draft treaty governing the exploration and use of outer space, including the moon and other celestial bodies.

DECLARATION OF LEGAL PRINCIPLES. The question of the elaboration of a declaration of legal principles governing the activities of states in outer space was first raised at the 1962 session of the Legal Sub-Committee, when the USSR submitted a draft declaration on the subject. During 1962, three other proposals relating to this issue were submitted by the United Arab Republic, the United Kingdom and the United States, respectively.

Discussion of the question was continued in 1963 in the United Nations organs concerned and, on December 13, 1963, the General Assembly unanimously adopted a Declaration of Legal Principles Governing the Activities of States in the Exploration and Use of Outer Space. The nine principles contained in the Declaration covered the following points:

(1) the use of outer space for the benefit of all mankind;

(2) freedom of exploration and use of outer space and celestial bodies by all states in accordance with international law;

(3) prohibition of national appropriation of outer space and celestial bodies;

(4) the carrying out of activities of states in the exploration and use of outer space in accordance with international law, including the United Nations Charter, and in the interest of maintaining international peace and security and promoting international co-operation and understanding;

(5) international responsibility of states for activities in outer space by their governmental agencies or by non-governmental entities, and responsibility of an international organization and the states participating in it for activities in outer space by that international organization;

(6) observance of corresponding interests of other states in outer space and conduct of appropriate international consultations if an outer space activity or experiment planned by a state or its nationals would cause potentially harmful interference with activities of other states;

(7) retention of ownership of objects launched into outer space and of jurisdiction and control by the state of registry over such objects, and personnel thereon, while in outer space; and return of such objects found outside the state of registry to that state and the furnishing by that state of identifying data upon request prior to return;

(8) international liability of states for damage caused by objects launched into outer space; and

(9) rendering of all possible assistance to, and return of, astronauts in the event of accident, distress or emergency landing.

The General Assembly also adopted on December 13, 1963, another resolution recommending that consideration be given to incorporating in international agreement form, in the future as appropriate, legal principles governing the activities of states in outer space.

ASSISTANCE TO AND RETURN OF ASTRONAUTS AND SPACE VEHICLES.   Consideration of the question of assistance to and return of astronauts and space vehicles began at the first session of the Legal

Sub-Committee when the USSR and the United States submitted proposals drafted in the form of an international agreement and of a General Assembly resolution, respectively. In the course of discussions at later sessions of the Sub-Committee, both the USSR and the United States revised their proposals on several occasions. In 1964, the United States proposal was submitted in the form of an international agreement, and Australia and Canada submitted the text of a draft agreement based on the discussion of the draft agreements of the USSR and the United States and aimed at finding a mutually acceptable text. In the course of the Sub-Committee's consideration of the draft texts, a number of amendments were proposed, and Australia and Canada submitted a revised text of their proposal.

The following matters, among others, have been considered by the Sub-Committee: control over assistance and rescue operations on the territory of a contracting state and on the high seas or in any area not under the jurisdiction or control of any state; notification to the launching state and the Secretary-General concerning the emergency landings of astronauts and the return to earth of space objects; identification of space objects and registration of launchings with the Secretary-General; obligations with respect to the return of the personnel of a spacecraft to the launching state; relevance of a reference to the launching being made in accordance with the Declaration of Legal Principles of December 13, 1963, as a criterion for co-operation in salvaging space objects and the return of astronauts and space objects; removal by the launching state of hazardous space objects from the territory of the state into which they have fallen; reimbursement by the launching state of expenses incurred by a state rendering assistance; inclusion in the agreement of provisions on the payment of compensation for damage caused by a space object; the designation by the Secretary-General, at the request of a state concerned, of experts to give an advisory opinion as to the origin of the space object in cases where differences arose as to its identification; and procedures for the settlement of disputes concerning the application and interpretation of the agreement.

Towards the end of the Legal Sub-Committee's 1964 session, in an informal working party of the Sub-Committee, preliminary agreement was reached on the preamble and certain articles of a draft agreement. At the Sub-Committee's 1965 session, further clarification of positions was made on certain other provisions of the draft agreement. However, although there was rapprochement of views on some points, substantial difference of views remained on other points, and the Sub-Committee did not add any further provisions to those preliminarily agreed on in 1964.

LIABILITY FOR DAMAGE CAUSED FROM OUTER SPACE.   Consideration of the question of liability for damage caused by objects launched into outer space also began at the 1962 session of the Legal Sub-Committee, when the United States proposed the setting up of an advisory panel to prepare a draft international agreement on liability for space vehicle accidents, and suggested a set of principles for the guidance of the panel. At its subsequent sessions, the Legal Sub-Committee started substantive work on the subject of liability on the basis of a working paper by Belgium, later revised to take the form of a draft convention, on the unification of certain rules governing liability for damage caused by space vehicles, and draft conventions concerning liability for damage caused by the launching of objects into outer space proposed by the United States and Hungary, respectively.

The following matters, among others, were considered by the Sub-Committee: the question whether damage caused to nationals of the launching state should be excluded from the scope of the convention, whether both damage caused to nationals of the launching state and damage caused on the territory of the launching state should be excluded, or whether damage caused on the territory of the launching state should alone be excluded; the states which should be made liable for damage caused by a space object; the procedure by which the convention might apply to international organizations engaging in space activities; the question of the liability of such organizations and the liability of their constituent members; the nature of liability in cases where more than one party was liable; the question of absolute liability for damage caused by space objects; and the question whether exoneration from liability should be permitted in certain circumstances and, if so, what those circumstances should be; the question whether the convention should be applied to damage caused by space objects on earth, in air space and in outer space; the kinds of damage for which there should be liability for compensation; the question whether there should be a limitation imposed on the amount of liability; the time limits for the presentation of claims and the procedure for the settlement of claims for compensation; the inclusion in the convention of provisions requiring launching states to take measures to prevent damage being caused by their space objects; and the procedure for the settlement of disputes concerning the application and interpretation of the convention.

As the result of the work of the Legal Sub-Committee in 1965, agreements of a preliminary character were reached on some of the issues of the draft agreement.

DRAFT TREATY GOVERNING THE EXPLORATION AND USE OF OUTER SPACE, INCLUDING THE MOON AND OTHER CELESTIAL BODIES. At its fifth session, in 1966, the Legal Sub-Committee began consideration of the question of a treaty governing the exploration and use of outer space, the moon and other celestial bodies. It had before it two draft treaties submitted by the USSR and the United

States, respectively. As a result of the Sub-Committee's consideration, agreement was reached on a series of articles applicable to outer space, including the moon and other celestial bodies. There was, however, no agreement on some other draft articles and proposals. The agreed articles concerned the following matters:

(a) jurisdiction over, and ownership of, objects launched into outer space and their return to the launching state;

(b) liability for damage caused by objects launched into outer space;

(c) freedom of exploration and use of, and scientific investigation in, outer space;

(d) prohibition to station nuclear weapons in outer space and reservation of the moon and other celestial bodies exclusively for peaceful purposes;

(e) rendering of assistance to, and return of, astronauts and provision of information on any phenomena discovered in outer space dangerous to the life or health of astronauts;

(f) responsibility for national activities in outer space and for activities of international organizations;

(g) prohibition of national appropriation in outer space;

(h) conduct of outer space activities in accordance with international law, including the Charter of the United Nations; and

(i) observance of corresponding interests of other states, avoidance of harmful contamination of outer space and adverse changes in the environment of the earth, and conduct of international consultations to avoid potentially harmful interference with outer space activities of other states.

MEASURES TO STRENGTHEN PEACE
AND REDUCE TENSIONS

Since its second session, in 1947, the General Assembly has adopted a number of resolutions containing general recommendations aimed at reducing international tensions and strengthening peace and friendship among nations.

In 1947, the Assembly condemned all warlike propaganda and asked states to encourage dissemination of information expressing the desire of all peoples for peace. The Assembly again condemned propaganda against peace in 1950, and declared that such propaganda included incitements to conflicts or aggression, measures to isolate people from contact with the outside world, and measures tending to silence or distort the activities of the United Nations or to prevent people from knowing the views of member states. Recalling these resolutions in 1954, the Assembly repeated its call to states to remove the barriers denying people the free exchange of information and ideas.

In addition to condemning propaganda against peace, the General Assembly has set forth further essentials for the maintenance of peace. In 1949, the Assembly called on nations to refrain from the threat or use of force contrary to the Charter and from any threat or act aimed at impairing the independence of any state or at fomenting civil strife. All nations were asked to co-operate fully with the United Nations. Permanent members of the Security Council were requested to broaden their co-operation and to exercise restraint in the use of the "veto." The Assembly also called for co-operation to attain international regulation of armaments and the control of atomic energy.

On November 17, 1950, in a resolution entitled "Peace through deeds," the Assembly condemned intervention by a state in the internal affairs of another in order to change its legally established government by the threat or use of force. The Assembly reaffirmed that whatever the weapons used, aggression, whether committed openly or by fomenting civil strife in the interest of a foreign power or by other means, was the gravest of all crimes against peace and security. The Assembly determined that for lasting peace it was indispensable that prompt united action be taken to meet aggression and that every nation agree to accept effective international control of atomic energy, to strive for control and elimination of weapons of mass destruction, to regulate armaments and armed forces and to reduce to a minimum the diversion of human and economic resources for armaments. These resources, the Assembly stated, should be developed for the general welfare with due regard to the needs of the under-developed areas of the world.

Measures to promote peaceful and neighbourly relations among states were the subject of resolutions adopted by the Assembly in 1957, 1958 and 1965. In 1957, the Assembly called upon all states to make every effort to strengthen international peace, to develop friendly and co-operative relations and to settle disputes by peaceful means as enjoined by the Charter. The Assembly recognized the need to broaden international co-operation, reduce tensions and settle disputes by peaceful means.

A year later, the Assembly again asked member states to live together within the letter and spirit of the Charter. Member states were urged, while making full use of Article 33 of the Charter, to resort to the Organization for the peaceful solution of problems which interfere with friendly relations among states or threaten international peace. The Assembly also recommended that members foster open, free and friendly co-operation and understanding in the fields of economy, culture, science, technology and communications. Finally, the Assembly welcomed the agreements between member states which work towards the aims envisaged in the resolution.

In 1965, the Assembly welcomed the growing interest among European states having different social and political systems in developing good neighbourly relations and co-operation. The Assembly requested these states to intensify their efforts in order to create an atmosphere of confidence which would be conducive to an effective consideration of problems still hampering relaxation of tension in Europe and throughout the world. The Assembly decided to give continuing attention to the matter.

Declaration on the Inadmissibility of Intervention in the Domestic Affairs of States and the Protection of Their Independence and Sovereignty

Any form of intervention in the domestic affairs of other states was condemned by the General Assembly in an eight-point declaration adopted on December 21, 1965. In it, the Assembly declared that no state has the right to intervene, directly or indirectly, for any reason whatever, in the internal or external affairs of any other state; that no state may use or encourage the use of economic, political or any other type of measures to coerce another state in order to subordinate the exercise of its sovereign rights or to secure from it advantages of any kind; and that no state shall organize, assist, foment, finance, incite or tolerate subversive, terrorist or armed activities directed towards the violent overthrow of the régime of another state, or interfere in civil strife in another state.

The Assembly further affirmed that every state has an inalienable right to choose its political, economic, social and cultural systems, without interference in any form by another state, and that all states shall respect the right of self-determination and independence of peoples and nations, to be freely exercised without any foreign pressure, and with absolute respect for human rights and fundamental freedoms. Consequently, the Assembly declared, all states shall contribute to the complete elimination of racial discrimination and colonialism in all its forms and manifestations.

Specific Measures and Procedures Proposed

As well as making general recommendations to strengthen international peace and reduce tensions, the General Assembly has proposed specific measures and procedures from time to time for dealing with threats to the peace and for the pacific settlement of disputes.

In 1948, the Interim Committee of the General Assembly (*see page* 204) recommended the establishment of a panel for inquiry and conciliation to be available to any states involved in controversies and to the organs of the United Nations. The Assembly, in April 1949, decided to invite each member state to designate from one to five persons who, by reason of their training, experience, character and standing, were deemed to be well fitted to serve as members of commissions of inquiry or of conciliation and who would be disposed to serve in that capacity for a term of five years.

In accordance with the resolution, the Secretary-General has from time to time communicated lists of persons nominated by member governments for inclusion in the panel.

The Interim Committee also recommended, in its 1948 report, the establishment of a procedure whereby parties to a dispute before the Security Council would attempt to agree upon a representative of the Council to act as rapporteur or conciliator in an effort to conciliate the situation. The Assembly accepted the suggestion and made a specific recommendation to the Security Council on the matter. In 1950, the Security Council adopted a resolution stating that the Council had decided to base itself, should an appropriate occasion arise, on the principles set forth in the Assembly resolution. The resolution was adopted unanimously, with one member (USSR) absent.

"Uniting for Peace" Resolution

At its fifth session, in 1950, the General Assembly considered proposals to enable the Assembly to perform more effectively the functions entrusted to it by the Charter in the field of international peace and security.

Under the title "Uniting for Peace," the Assembly, on November 3, 1950, adopted a resolution which provided, among other things, that if the Security Council, because of the lack of unanimity of its permanent members, fails to exercise its primary responsibility in the maintenance of peace, in a case where there appears to be a threat to the peace, breach of the peace or act of aggression, the Assembly shall consider the matter immediately with a view to making recommendations to members for collective measures, including, in the case of a breach of the peace or act of aggression, the use of armed force when necessary to maintain international peace and security. If not in session, the Assembly shall meet in emergency special session within twenty-four hours of a request for such a session by the Security Council on a vote of any seven of its members* or by a majority of the members of the United Nations.

---

* Under the amendment to Article 27 of the Charter, which came into force in 1965, decisions of the Security Council on procedural matters shall be made on the affirmative vote of any nine of its members.

The resolution also established a Peace Observation Commission of fourteen members, including the five permanent members of the Security Council, to observe and report on the situation in areas where peace was threatened. Further, a Collective Measures Committee of fourteen members was established to report on methods which might be used collectively to maintain peace.

International Co-operation Year

The year 1965, the twentieth year of the United Nations, was designated as International Co-operation Year by the General Assembly on November 21, 1963. The purpose of the Year was to draw attention to the existing co-operation among states in the hope that increased awareness of it would gradually lead to intensified co-operation and accelerate joint efforts to further the common interests of mankind. A twelve-member Committee for the International Co-operation Year, appointed by the President of the General Assembly in 1963, prepared and co-ordinated plans to be undertaken by the United Nations.

International Co-operation Year was inaugurated at United Nations Headquarters by a series of seven lectures given by distinguished scholars on the general theme of international co-operation in the contemporary world.

As in 1955—the tenth year of the United Nations—a commemorative meeting of the United Nations was held at San Francisco in the Opera House, where the United Nations Charter was approved. At the meeting, which was held on June 25-26, 1965, statements were made by the President of the United States, the Secretary-General, the President of the nineteenth session of the General Assembly, a representative group of permanent delegates, speaking on the diverse aspects of United Nations activities, and the Director-General of the World Health Organization, speaking on behalf of the specialized agencies.

Two versions of a medallion commemorating International Co-operation Year and the Twentieth Anniversary of the United Nations were struck, the larger version being used for official United Nations purposes. In addition, the United Nations and a large number of member states issued International Co-operation Year stamps using the same basic design.

The Committee for the International Co-operation Year noted that there had been a gratifying response from United Nations member states to the suggestion for an early ratification of a number of multilateral treaties and conventions of which the Secretary-General is the depositary. In connection with International Co-operation Year, the Economic and Social Council and, subsequently, the General Assembly adopted resolutions concerning the promotion of town-twinning. Extensive efforts were also made to inform the public in various parts of the world about the scope of United Nations activities in the political, economic, social and humanitarian fields.

In its final report to the General Assembly, the Committee for the International Co-operation Year concluded that the main objectives of the year had been achieved to an unexpected extent.

PEACE-KEEPING OPERATIONS
AND RELATED MATTERS

The nature of the peace-keeping operations of the United Nations and the manner in which they should be financed have been the subject of considerable debate since the establishment of the United Nations Emergency Force (UNEF) and the United Nations Operation in the Congo (ONUC), and divergent positions have been taken by member states.

In 1961, the General Assembly, having been informed of substantial arrears in the payment of assessments, mainly for ONUC and UNEF, adopted, on December 20, a resolution recognizing the need "for authoritative legal guidance as to obligations" of member states under the Charter in the matter of financing the United Nations operations in the Congo and in the Middle East. In this resolution, the Assembly asked the International Court of Justice to give an advisory opinion as to whether the expenditures in the Congo, undertaken in response to Security Council and Assembly decisions, and expenditures authorized in resolutions relating to operations of UNEF constituted "expenses of the Organization" within the meaning of Article 17, paragraph 2, of the Charter, which states: "The expenses of the Organization shall be borne by the members as apportioned by the General Assembly."

On December 19, 1962, the Assembly voted to accept the advisory opinion of the International Court to the effect that the expenditures for these operations constitute "expenses of the Organization" within the meaning of Article 17, paragraph 2, of the Charter (*see page* 450).

The Assembly also set up a twenty-one-member working group to study special methods for financing peace-keeping operations of the United Nations involving heavy expenditures, such as those for the Congo and the Middle East, including a possible special scale of assessments for such operations. The group, known as the Working Group on the Examination of the Administrative and Budgetary Procedures of the United Nations, was requested to examine the situation arising from the arrears of some member states in the payment of contributions for the financing of the peace-keeping operations, and to recommend, within the letter and spirit of the Charter, arrangements designed to bring such payments up to date, bearing in mind the relative economic positions of such member states.

The Assembly further decided to convene, in 1963, a special session to consider the financial situation of the Organization.

The Fourth Special Session of the Assembly met from May 14 to June 17, 1963. It had before it, among other documents, a report by the Working Group and a report by the Secretary-General on the financial position of the Organization.

The report of the Working Group indicated that in the time at its disposal, the Group had not been able to arrive at any generally agreed recommendation on a special method of financing but had managed to identify the views of member states as regards principles for the financing of future peace-keeping operations and possible *ad hoc* approaches to the financing of current peace-keeping operations.

The Secretary-General's report stated that the deficit had increased to $93.9 million on March 31, 1963, and might be expected to attain the $140 million mark by December 31. The Secretary-General urged the Special Session to ensure that the Organization had the necessary cash resources to defray peace-keeping costs either by assessing the costs among members or by other methods.

At the conclusion of the Special Session, the Assembly decided on an *ad hoc* formula for the financing of UNEF and ONUC for the period July 1 to December 31, 1963. No appropriation or apportionment action was taken in respect of the expenditures incurred during the period July 1, 1962 to June 30, 1963, the understanding being that the proceeds of the United Nations bond issue would help in discharging the Organization's financial commitments.

At the same time, the Assembly decided that the Working Group should continue to seek a permanent solution to the problem, reporting to the Assembly not later than at its 1964 session. The Assembly also adopted certain related resolutions, one laying down general guiding principles governing the financing of future peace-keeping operations, one concerning the payment of arrears of assessments for UNEF and ONUC expenses, one dealing with the possible establishment of a peace fund, and one extending the period during which United Nations bonds might be sold.

Later in 1963, at its eighteenth session, the Assembly, among other things, approved appropriations for ONUC for the period January 1 to June 30, 1964, and for UNEF for the period January 1 to December 31, 1964. The costs involved were again apportioned according to an *ad hoc* formula, pending consideration at the Assembly's nineteenth session in 1964 of a more permanent method of financing peace-keeping operations in the light of the further report of the Working Group.

Special Committee on Peace-keeping Operations

The Working Group on the Examination of the Administrative and Budgetary Procedures of the United Nations adjourned on the eve of the nineteenth session of the General Assembly without adopting any recommendation or submitting a report to the General Assembly. In the special circumstances which prevailed during the nineteenth session of the Assembly,* it became clear that a far more comprehensive study of all aspects of the question of peace-keeping operations was necessary than had been contemplated in the resolution which established the Working Group.

In a resolution adopted on February 18, 1965, the General Assembly authorized the President to establish a Special Committee on Peace-keeping Operations under his chairmanship and with the collaboration of the Secretary-General. It instructed the Committee to undertake a comprehensive review of the peace-keeping operations, including ways of overcoming the financial difficulties of the Organization, and to submit a report to the Assembly not later than June 15, 1965.

On February 26, the President of the Assembly announced that the following members had agreed to serve on the Special Committee: Afghanistan, Algeria, Argentina, Australia, Austria, Brazil, Canada, Czechoslovakia, El Salvador, Ethiopia, France, Hungary, India, Iraq, Italy, Japan, Mauritania, Mexico, Netherlands, Nigeria, Pakistan, Poland, Romania, Sierra Leone, Spain, Sweden, Thailand, USSR, United Arab Republic, United Kingdom, United States, Venezuela and Yugoslavia.

The Committee held fourteen meetings during the period from March 26 to June 15. After the first meeting, the President of the General Assembly and the Secretary-General held consultations on a broad basis, not restricted to the members of the Committee, and on May 31, they issued a report in which they placed before the members of the Committee an account of the views and suggestions that had been made both during the informal consultations and the formal meetings of the Committee.

In section I of the report, it was stated that there did not appear to exist a general consensus as to what constituted a "peace-keeping operation" and that the concept of peace-keeping could not be accurately defined to the satisfaction of all member states. United Nations peace-keeping operations had been organized in Greece, Palestine,

---

* In response to requests of the majority of members, the opening of the nineteenth session of the General Assembly (which normally meets in September) was postponed to December 1, 1964 and, in order to avoid a confrontation among the powers over the question of the applicability of Article 19, it was decided to follow a procedure by which only those questions would be taken up which could be disposed of without objection. (Article 19 states that a member of the United Nations which is in arrears in the payment of its financial contributions to the Organization shall have no vote in the General Assembly if the amount of its arrears equals or exceeds the amount of the contributions due from it for the preceding two full years.)

Kashmir, Suez and Gaza, Lebanon, Jordan, the Congo, West Irian, Yemen and Cyprus, but only in the cases of Suez and Gaza and of West Irian had the initiative for setting up those missions come from the Assembly.

Generally speaking, the report stated, United Nations operations could be divided into two main categories, namely, observer operations and operations involving the deployment of armed forces. The methods of financing had varied widely: some were charged to the regular budget and some were charged to a special account outside the regular budget; others were financed on an *ad hoc* basis and a combination of assessed and voluntary contributions; still others had been financed on the basis of a sharing of costs by the governments principally concerned, or by voluntary contributions.

In section II of the report, it was stated that it had frequently been asserted that all enforcement actions were the exclusive prerogative of the Security Council under the provisions of the Charter. However, a serious difference of view existed as to what constituted enforcement action. It seemed to be the general opinion that any question which involved peace-keeping operations should be examined in the first place by the Security Council and that, if the Council was unable for any reason whatever to adopt decisions, there was nothing to prevent the General Assembly from considering the matter immediately and making appropriate recommendations. There appeared to be considerable support for the view that the Assembly should, in the first instance, address its recommendations back to the Council. If the General Assembly resolved, by the required two-thirds majority, to make recommendations to the Security Council, the weight of such recommendations would have a very significant effect upon the subsequent action of the Council. It was apparent that there was a difference of opinion concerning the scope and nature of the recommendations which the Assembly was authorized to make.

Some members held the view, the report stated, that if the Security Council was unable to act in spite of a strong recommendation of the General Assembly, it would be realistic to accept the inability of the Organization to intervene in the given situation. That view, however, did not appear to be supported by the majority of member states. There were some who wished to see the Assembly empowered in such a situation to authorize the peace-keeping operation, whereas others would prefer that it make appropriate recommendations for measures possibly not involving the establishment of a peace-keeping operation to deal with the situation.

In section III, the report stated that it was widely accepted that the immediate task of the Special Committee was the restoration of the solvency of the Organization and that that should be achieved through voluntary contributions by member states. Views on the question of financing of future peace-keeping operations differed widely.

There were different proposals for the establishment of a finance committee, which would make recommendations to the General Assembly or the Security Council, or to both, as to how the expenses of a peace-keeping operation should be apportioned. Another proposal aimed at the creation of a fund made up of voluntary contributions from which appropriations would be made by the Assembly to meet the costs of a given peace-keeping operation. It had been suggested further that any resolution involving expenditure on a peace-keeping operation should as far as possible include an indication as to how the required financing was to be provided.

Section IV of the report dealt with organizational questions, including those related to Article 43 of the Charter and the Military Staff Committee.

In the final section of the report, the Secretary-General and the President of the General Assembly presented some observations and conclusions and suggested certain broad guidelines which could apply to future peace-keeping operations.

In its first report to the Assembly on June 15, 1965, the Special Committee pointed to the need for more time to consider the question. The Committee resumed its meetings on August 16, at which time it heard statements from the representatives of the United States, the United Kingdom and the USSR.

The representative of the United States reiterated that his Government was not prepared to abandon positions which it believed to be constitutionally, legally, procedurally and administratively correct. Nor was it prepared to undo or revise the precedents established by the Assembly itself by overwhelming majorities. Those precedents included the Assembly resolutions levying assessments to finance UNEF and ONUC, the 1961 decision to request the International Court's advisory opinion on whether those assessments constituted "expenses of the Organization" within the meaning of Article 17, the authorization in that same year of the United Nations bond issue, the acceptance in 1962 of the Court's advisory opinion, the reaffirmation of the collective financial responsibility of all member states at the fourth special session in 1963 and the appeal to all delinquent states to pay their arrears.

On the other hand, on the basis of the entire history of the problem of financing peace-keeping operations, the United States had regretfully concluded that, at the present stage, the General Assembly was not prepared to carry out the relevant provisions of the Charter, that is, to apply the loss-of-vote sanction provided in Article 19. The intransigence of a few member states and their unwillingness to abide by the rule of law had created that state of affairs, and while the United States continued to maintain that Article 19 was applicable in present circumstances, it recognized that the consensus in the Assembly was against application of the Article and in favour of having the Assembly proceed normally. The United States would not seek to frus-

trate that consensus, since it was not in the interest of the world to
have the Assembly's work immobilized. It agreed that the Assembly
must proceed with its work. At the same time, if any member state
could make an exception to the principle of collective financial responsibility with respect to certain United Nations activities, the United
States reserved the same option to make exceptions if there were compelling reasons to do so.

The representative of the United Kingdom recalled that his country and others had taken the lead in the co-operative effort to end the
financial crisis by making voluntary and unconditional contributions
amounting to some $18 million. He was confident that those who had
voted unanimously in favour of a co-operative effort would soon demonstrate that theirs was no empty vote. Although remaining convinced
that the stand it had taken was in the best interest of the United Nations, the United Kingdom had to recognize that there were differences
of views among members about the assessments for the United Nations
operations in the Congo and the Middle East. Since it also recognized
that it was of overriding importance that the work of the General Assembly should continue, it had decided that the Assembly should resume its business in the normal manner without the United Kingdom
insisting on a resolution of the controversy on that issue.

The representative of the USSR declared that the majority of
member states called for removal of the artificial obstacles raised in the
General Assembly's path at the nineteenth session and an unconditional
return to normal procedures. He recalled that the Soviet Government,
in a memorandum submitted on July 10, 1964, had set out a constructive programme aimed at strengthening the effectiveness of the United
Nations in its work of ensuring international peace and security. The
peace-keeping effectiveness of the United Nations could only be ensured by strict compliance with the provisions of the Charter. The
African-Asian plan of December 30, 1964, which provided that the
Organization's financial difficulties should be resolved by means of voluntary contributions from all member states, had as its key feature the
inseparable link between the question of voluntary contributions and
the non-applicability of Article 19 in connection with the unlawful expenses of the United Nations military operations in the Congo and in
the Middle East. The Soviet Union, which had demonstrated the maximum goodwill by adopting that plan and agreeing to make a substantial contribution, even though it bore no responsibility for those difficulties, must not be expected to make any voluntary contribution in
the absence of a firm guarantee that the question of the application of
Article 19 would not be raised again. He welcomed the extent of agreement in the Committee that every effort must be made to carry out the
unanimous decision that the work of the Assembly must proceed normally at the twentieth session.

At subsequent meetings of the Committee, several speakers, and in particular the representatives of Canada, Japan, Mexico and Nigeria, stressed the importance of the step taken by the United States and the need for contributions to meet the financial difficulties of the Organization. The representatives of Nigeria and Canada referred in that connection to voluntary unconditional contributions made by their Governments. Members of the Committee generally welcomed the prospect that the General Assembly would resume its work normally. Several of them emphasized that the agreement reached in respect of Article 19 in relation to debts arising out of emergency operations in the Middle East and the Congo should not be allowed to undermine the indisputable obligation of all member states to contribute to the regular budget approved by the General Assembly.

On August 31, the representative of France noted with satisfaction that the Assembly would be able to begin its work on the scheduled date and that the question of Article 19 would no longer be at issue. Along with the other members of the Special Committee, he noted that the problem of the procedure to be followed with regard to possible future peace-keeping operations remained. As far as voluntary contributions for the purpose of solving the Organization's financial difficulties were concerned, the French Government had as yet made no commitment, for it considered it necessary that the question should be studied in the broader context of the general financial policy of the United Nations and its specialized agencies and thought that a solution should be sought within the framework of general reform.

On the same day, the Committee formally approved without objection the inclusion in its second report to the General Assembly of a statement, which represented the consensus of the Committee, that (1) the Assembly would carry on its work normally in accordance with its rules of procedure; (2) the question of the applicability of Article 19 would not be raised with regard to the United Nations Emergency Force and the United Nations Operation in the Congo; and (3) the financial difficulties of the Organization should be solved through voluntary contributions by member states, with the highly developed countries making substantial contributions.

On September 1, 1965, at the close of the nineteenth session, the General Assembly adopted the two reports of the Special Committee and decided that the modalities for the continuance of the Committee's work should be determined at the twentieth session.

At the twentieth session, the Assembly's Special Political Committee took up the question. In the course of the Committee's discussions, Ireland introduced a draft resolution containing a number of specific proposals designed, among other things: (a) to ensure that future peace-keeping operations recommended by the Assembly under the "Uniting for Peace" resolution of 1950 would be reliably financed by mandatory assessments under Article 17 (2) of the Charter; (b) to prevent a confrontation between the Assembly and a permanent member of the Security Council when that member votes against or fails to vote in favour of a peace-keeping operation; (c) to enable members of the Assembly as a last resort to assert their inherent right to recommend the establishment of a peace-keeping operation when a majority of them determines they have sufficient strength and adequate support to give effective assistance to a small state which appeals to the Security Council; and (d) to make it impossible for a situation to arise in which a small state seeking assistance must be turned away because of opposition by one or two members of the Organization.

The Irish draft resolution, subsequently co-sponsored by Ceylon, Costa Rica, Ghana, Ivory Coast, Liberia, Nepal, Philippines and Somalia, further specified that until permanent arrangements were agreed upon, there should be a financial arrangement to deal with expenses of peace-keeping operations, to be included within the regular budget, the cost of which would be apportioned as follows: 5 per cent among the less developed members; 25 per cent among developed members other than permanent members of the Security Council; and 70 per cent among permanent members which vote in favour of a peace-keeping operation, provided that no member shall be assessed more than 50 per cent of the operation's net cost.

The Special Political Committee finally adopted two resolutions which it recommended to the General Assembly and which the Assembly adopted on December 15, 1965. The first resolution requested the Special Committee on Peace-Keeping Operations to continue and complete its work as soon as possible, transmitted the records of debate to that Committee and called on all members to make voluntary contributions.

The second resolution adopted by the Special Political Committee referred the Irish draft proposals to the Special Committee on Peace-keeping Operations for its careful consideration.

THE QUESTION OF CYPRUS

The question of Cyprus first came before the United Nations in 1954, when Greece requested the General Assembly to consider the application of the principle of self-determination to the people of Cyprus, which was then under British sovereignty. No action was taken, however, and Greece again requested in 1956 that the question of Cyprus be considered by the General Assembly. The United Kingdom also placed on the Assembly's agenda in 1956 the question of support from Greece for terrorism in Cyprus.

On February 26, 1957, the Assembly adopted a resolution expressing the earnest desire that a peaceful, democratic and just solution would be found and that negotiations to that end would continue between the parties concerned.

In July 1957, Greece again requested that the question of self-determination in Cyprus be considered by the Assembly. A draft resolution proposed by Greece asking that the people of Cyprus be given the opportunity to decide their own future was not adopted because it failed to receive the required two-thirds majority. In 1958, the General Assembly again expressed confidence that the parties concerned would continue their efforts to reach a peaceful, democratic and just solution.

Following discussions in Zurich between the Foreign Ministers of Greece and Turkey, an agreement was signed in London on February 19, 1959, by the Prime Ministers of the United Kingdom, Greece and Turkey and was declared acceptable by the representatives of the Greek Cypriot and Turkish Cypriot peoples. The agreement was implemented on August 16, 1960, when Cyprus became an independent republic, under special constitutional and treaty arrangements. These included a Constitution designed to preserve a legal distinction between the Greek Cypriot and Turkish Cypriot communities and to maintain a certain balance between their rights and interests; multilateral guarantees—a Treaty of Alliance and Treaty of Guarantee—of the maintenance of the state of affairs established by the Constitution, including the right of Greece, Turkey and the United Kingdom to intervene jointly or separately; the prohibition of the union of Cyprus with any other state, or its partitioning; the stationing of Greek and Turkish national contingents in Cyprus; and the retention by the United Kingdom of sovereignty over two areas on the island to be maintained as military bases.

The Republic of Cyprus became a member of the United Nations on September 20, 1960, and relative calm prevailed in the post-independence period until the end of 1963, when the situation gradually deteriorated, with disturbances and fighting between the Greek Cypriot and Turkish Cypriot groups, after President Makarios submitted thirteen amendments to the Constitution for the consideration of the Turkish Cypriot community's leadership.

On December 26, 1963, Cyprus called for an urgent meeting of the Security Council to consider charges that Turkey had committed aggression and had intervened in the internal affairs of Cyprus by the threat and use of force against its territorial integrity and political independence. Cyprus stated that Turkey had violated the air space and territorial waters of Cyprus, that the Prime Minister of Turkey had threatened to use force and that Turkish troops stationed on the island under the Treaty of Alliance had moved into Nicosia to fight alongside Turkish Cypriots.

At a meeting of the Security Council on December 27, Turkey

denied the charges, which, Turkey said, had been invented to hide the crimes committed against the Turkish community in Cyprus and the attempts made by the Greek Cypriots to annihilate the Turkish community.

On January 13, 1964, the Secretary-General informed the Council that the Government of Cyprus, in conjunction with the United Kingdom, Greece and Turkey, had requested him to appoint a Personal Representative to observe the situation on the island. On January 16, he appointed Lieutenant-General P. S. Gyani, of India, to observe the operation undertaken in Cyprus by the United Kingdom, Greece and Turkey to secure and maintain a cease-fire for an initial period extending to the end of February 1964.

In the meantime, a conference held in London in January, with the participation of Cyprus, Greece, Turkey and the United Kingdom, produced no agreement, and on February 15, the United Kingdom requested an early meeting of the Security Council to take appropriate steps to ensure that the dangerous situation in Cyprus could be resolved with full regard to the rights and responsibilities of both Cypriot communities, as well as those of the Government of Cyprus and of the signatories to the Treaty of Guarantee.

On the same day, Cyprus urgently requested an emergency meeting of the Security Council to consider the increasing threat from war preparations and declarations of the Turkish Government, which had made the danger of the invasion of Cyprus imminent.

United Nations Peace-keeping Force

The Council considered the matter between February 17 and March 4 and, on the latter date, unanimously recommended the creation of a United Nations peace-keeping force in Cyprus and the appointment of a United Nations mediator to promote a peaceful solution to the Cyprus problem. The Force was to be stationed initially for three months, with all costs to be met by the governments providing the contingents and by the Government of Cyprus. The Secretary-General was authorized to accept, also, voluntary contributions. The Force was to use its best efforts to prevent the recurrence of fighting and, as necessary, to contribute to the maintenance and restoration of law and order and a return to normal conditions. The Council recommended that the Secretary-General designate the mediator in agreement with the Government of Cyprus and the Governments of Greece, Turkey and the United Kingdom.

In its resolution, the Council also called on all member states to refrain from any action or threat of action likely to worsen the situation in Cyprus or to endanger international peace. It asked the Government of Cyprus to take all additional measures necessary to stop violence and bloodshed in Cyprus and called on the communities in Cyprus and their leaders to act with the utmost restraint.

Czechoslovakia and the Soviet Union abstained in the vote on the paragraph of the resolution which concerned the role of the Secretary-General because they felt it amounted to circumvention of the Security Council. France also abstained in the vote on that paragraph because France felt it gave too much power to one individual. The resolution as a whole was adopted unanimously.

When the Security Council met again on March 13 at the request of Cyprus, which alleged that it faced imminent invasion by Turkish forces, it adopted another resolution reaffirming its call to all member states to refrain from any action likely to worsen the situation in Cyprus and calling on the Secretary-General to continue his efforts regarding the creation of a peace-keeping force and the appointment of a mediator.

On March 25, the Secretary-General designated Sakari S. Tuomioja, of Finland, as the United Nations Mediator in Cyprus, and Lieutenant-General Gyani as Commander of the United Nations Force in Cyprus (UNFICYP). General Gyani took command of UNFICYP on March 27, the day it became operational. On May 11, the Secretary-General announced the appointment of Galo Plaza, of Ecuador, as his Special Representative in Cyprus with the task of carrying out the short-term goals set by the Security Council to restore the country to normalcy and to create a climate for a long-term political solution of the problem.

The composition of UNFICYP in June 1964 included 6,238 military personnel from Austria, Canada, Denmark, Finland, Ireland, Sweden and the United Kingdom, and 173 civilian police from Austria, Australia, Denmark, New Zealand and Sweden, making a total of 6,411 persons.

In his first comprehensive report on Cyprus, made on June 15, 1964, the Secretary-General stated that UNFICYP had served to prevent a recurrence of fighting on the island but that there had been no substantial lessening of tensions. He recommended extension of the term of UNFICYP for another three months.

On June 20, the Council voted unanimously to extend UNFICYP for another three-month period, from June 27 to September 26, 1964. On the same day, the Secretary-General appointed General Kodendra Subayya Timayya, of India, as Commander of UNFICYP, replacing General Gyani, who had resigned.

On July 16, the Secretary-General made identical appeals to the President and Vice-President of Cyprus, the Prime Minister of Greece and the Prime Minister of Turkey calling attention to the reported arms build-up by the two opposing sides in Cyprus and appealing to all parties to fully observe both the letter and the spirit of the Security Council resolution of March 4, 1964.

Early in August, fighting between the two communities in Cyprus broke out again, and air and naval action was taken against Cyprus by Turkey. On August 8, the Security Council convened at the request of both Cyprus and Turkey, and on August 9 it called for an immediate cease-fire in Cyprus by all concerned and asked them to co-operate with UNFICYP in restoring peace. It also authorized the President of the Council to make an urgent appeal to Turkey to cease instantly the bombardment and the use of military force of any kind against Cyprus, and to the Government of Cyprus to order its armed forces to cease firing immediately.

The Security Council met again on August 11 to consider a complaint by Cyprus that Turkey had made another air attack on the island. The Council reached a consensus on an appeal for full compliance with its resolution of August 9 on Cyprus, the suspension of overflights over the island and supervision of the cease-fire by UNFICYP.

On the recommendation of the Secretary-General, the Security Council, on September 25, extended the mandate of UNFICYP for a further three months, ending December 26. Carlos Alfredo Bernardes, of Brazil, was appointed Special Representative of the Secretary-General in Cyprus, replacing Mr. Plaza, who became the new United Nations Mediator, following the death in Helsinki on September 9 of Mr. Tuomioja.

In December, the Secretary-General, in his third report on Cyprus, observed that the general situation in Cyprus was slightly improving, owing to United Nations presence on the island. The Council extended the mandate of UNFICYP for a further three-month period. Subsequently, in 1965, the Force's mandate was extended by the Council on March 17 for a three-month period and on June 15 for a six-month period.

The United Nations Mediator reported on Cyprus to the Secretary-General on March 30, 1965, in accordance with the Security Council resolution of March 4, 1964. He recommended that talks on the Cyprus problem be held between the two communities (Greek and Turkish Cypriots) as soon as possible. Such talks, he said, were most likely to produce results, though any agreement emerging from them would require the endorsement of the other parties concerned. In his view, the Cyprus Government should not give the population the opportunity to opt for *enosis* (union with Greece), but should maintain the independence of the State.

On the question of demilitarization of the island, the Mediator stated that President Makarios had expressed willingness to take such a step with United Nations assistance and that Turkey favoured it within the context of a settlement guaranteeing the independence of Cyprus.

With regard to the British bases in Cyprus, which the United Kingdom had maintained did not form part of the dispute since they lay outside the territory of the Republic, the Mediator felt that should this question become vital to settlement, it could be constructively discussed by the parties to the agreement concerning the base areas.

The Mediator expressed fear that the geographical separation which the Turkish Cypriot proposals for a federal state involved would inevitably lead to partition and thus risk creating a new frontier of a "highly provocative nature" between Greece and Turkey. However, he supported the principle that the Turkish Cypriot community should be protected adequately and felt that everything possible should be done, including the provision of safeguards of an exceptional kind, to ensure this.

The Mediator stated that President Makarios had indicated a willingness to apply specific measures to ensure members of the minority community a proper voice in their traditional communal affairs and an equitable part in the public life of the country as a whole.

The Mediator's report was forwarded on March 30 to all the parties concerned, to the members of the Security Council and to all member states of the United Nations.

In its response to the report, Turkey said that the report contained sections which went beyond the Mediator's terms of references as specified in the Security Council resolution of March 4, 1964, and that these sections could not be entertained as a mediation effort and could not constitute a basis for future efforts. Turkey added, however, that it continued to support the mediation effort and attached great importance to it.

In its response to the report, Cyprus expressed appreciation for the efforts of the Mediator and the conviction that those efforts would prove constructive.

The Security Council met on August 3 and 10, 1965, to consider fresh complaints by Cyprus and Turkey. Turkey charged that the Greek Cypriot Government had committed provocative acts by attempting to amend the electoral laws, contrary to the Constitution of the island. Cyprus alleged that Turkey had interfered in the internal affairs of Cyprus and had threatened to use force. The Council then called on all parties concerned in the recent developments in Cyprus to avoid, in conformity with the March 4, 1964 resolution, any action likely to worsen the situation.

The Council met again on November 5 on an urgent request from Turkey and on the basis of a report by the Secretary-General concerning armed clashes in the Famagusta area. The Council expressed regret over the incidents and appreciation of the efforts of the United Nations representatives there to achieve a cease-fire and a relaxation of tension.

At its twentieth session, in 1965, the General Assembly considered the "Question of Cyprus" on the basis of requests by both Turkey and Cyprus. The Turkish request stated that it was essential "to safeguard and maintain the Turkish Cypriot community's right to live by consolidating its rights emanating from valid international treaties solemnly concluded" and that the "persistence by Greece in a policy of annexation" would "lead to an outbreak of war between the two countries" and would consequently endanger the peace and stability of the area.

Cyprus, in its memorandum, stated that the problem stemmed from a virtual denial to the people of Cyprus of their fundamental right to self-determination and from the effort to deprive Cyprus of the substance of its sovereignty and independence. The memorandum added that Cyprus looked to the Assembly to uphold the island's unrestricted and unfettered sovereignty and independence, thereby allowing its people to determine freely, and without foreign intervention or interference, the political future of the country in accordance with the United Nations Charter.

On December 17, the Assembly adopted a resolution by which it took note of the Declaration of Intent and Memorandum of the Government of Cyprus regarding human rights, ensuring of minority rights, and safeguarding of those rights; recognized that Cyprus should enjoy full sovereignty and complete independence without any foreign intervention or interference; called upon all states to respect the sovereignty, unity, independence and territorial integrity of Cyprus; and recommended to the Security Council the continuation of United Nations mediation work, in conformity with the Council's resolution of March 4, 1964.

On the same day, the Security Council met to consider the Secretary-General's report on the United Nations operation in Cyprus for the period June 11 to December 8, 1965. In his report, the Secretary-General stated that there was still a need for the Force in Cyprus. He observed that the presence and functioning of the Force had provided a climate of relative quiet in which a peaceful solution might be sought.

The Council extended the Force's mandate until March 26, 1966 and subsequently until June 26, 1966. In June the Council again extended the mandate of the Force for six months, until December 26, 1966, and expressed the hope that by the end of that period substantial progress towards a solution would have been achieved so as to render possible a withdrawal or a substantial reduction of the Force.

The United Nations Mediator in Cyprus, Mr. Galo Plaza, resigned on December 22, 1965. On March 4, 1966, the Secretary-General informed the Security Council that after having informed the parties directly concerned, he had broadened the responsibilities of his Special Representative in Cyprus, Mr. Bernardes, and that without prejudice to the mediation function as envisaged in the Council's resolution of March 4, 1964, Mr. Bernardes was authorized to employ his good offices and make such approaches to the parties as might in the first instance achieve discussions at any level of local or broader problems.

QUESTIONS RELATING TO THE MIDDLE EAST

Palestine Question

The question of Palestine was first brought before the United Nations early in 1947 when, in a letter to the Secretary-General dated April 2, the United Kingdom requested that the question be placed on the agenda of the next regular session of the General Assembly, at which time the United Kingdom would submit an account of its administration of the League of Nations mandate over Palestine. Stressing the desirability of an early settlement in Palestine, the United Kingdom also requested the early convening of a special session which would appoint and instruct a special committee to make a study of the question preparatory to the convening of the regular session.

After a majority of the member states had approved the proposal to hold a special session, the session met in New York between April 28 and May 15, 1947. The only item on its agenda was the one proposed by the United Kingdom for constituting and instructing a special committee to make a preliminary study of the Palestine question. Egypt, Iraq, Lebanon, Saudi Arabia and Syria requested the inclusion of an additional item—the termination of the mandate over Palestine and the declaration of its independence, but this item was rejected by the Assembly.

On May 15, at the close of the special session, the Assembly established the United Nations Special Committee on Palestine, consisting of eleven members—Australia, Canada, Czechoslovakia, Guatemala, India, Iran, the Netherlands, Peru, Sweden, Uruguay and Yugoslavia. The Committee was given full powers to investigate all questions relating to the Palestine problem and to make recommendations. It was authorized to conduct investigations in Palestine and wherever else it deemed useful.

The Special Committee's terms of reference were challenged by the Arab states, which objected to the fact that the independence of Palestine or the principles of the Charter were not mentioned and that no reference was made to the interests of inhabitants of Palestine. Provision for the Committee's power to conduct investigations wherever it wished had been expressly intended, the Arab states said, to enable the Committee to visit displaced persons' camps in order to link the Palestine question with the question of refugees in Europe. They warned that the Committee's terms of reference would not aid peace in the Middle East.

In response to a request from the Special Committee, the Government of Palestine and the Jewish Agency for Palestine appointed liaison officers. The Arab Higher Committee, however, resolved that

Palestine Arabs should not collaborate with the Committee or appear before it.

During the course of its investigations, the Committee visited Palestine, Lebanon, Syria and Transjordan and also made a tour of displaced persons' camps in Germany and Austria. Its report, which was submitted to the Assembly on August 31, 1947, contained two sets of proposals.

The majority proposal, to which Canada, Czechoslovakia, Guatemala, the Netherlands, Peru, Sweden and Uruguay had subscribed, recommended the partition of Palestine into two independent states—a Jewish state and an Arab state. The city of Jerusalem was to be placed under the International Trusteeship System with the United Nations as the Administering Authority. The three entities were to be linked in an economic union.

The minority plan, submitted by India, Iran and Yugoslavia, proposed an independent federal state, consisting of an Arab state and a Jewish state, with Jerusalem as its federal capital.

Australia abstained from voting on either plan on the ground that the recommendations exceeded the Committee's terms of reference.

During its second regular session, the General Assembly, on September 23, 1947, established an *ad hoc* Committee on the Palestine Question, composed of all member states. During its deliberations, the *ad hoc* Committee heard the views of the three parties—the United Kingdom as the mandatory power, the Arab Higher Committee and the Jewish Agency for Palestine.

The United Kingdom maintained that it could not undertake the task of imposing a policy in Palestine by force of arms. In the absence of a settlement, it must plan to withdraw its forces and administration from Palestine at an early date.

The representative of the Arab Higher Committee stated that the Arabs of Palestine were solidly determined to oppose, with all the means they had, any scheme which involved the dissection, segregation or partition of their country or which gave a minority any special or preferential status.

The representative of the Jewish Agency for Palestine stated that if acceptance of the majority plan of the Special Committee would make possible the immediate re-establishment of the Jewish state with sovereign control of its own immigration, then the Jewish Agency would recommend the acceptance of the partition solution, subject to further discussion of constitutional and territorial provisions.

After further discussion, the *ad hoc* Committee on the Palestine Question recommended the majority plan to the General Assembly, which adopted it on November 29, 1947, by a vote of 33 in favour to 13 against, with 10 abstentions.

The Assembly resolution provided that the British mandate over Palestine would terminate and the British armed forces be withdrawn as soon as possible, and not later than August 1, 1948, and that the Trusteeship Council would prepare and approve a detailed Statute of the City of Jerusalem. Also under the resolution, the Assembly established the United Nations Palestine Commission to carry out its recommendations. The Security Council was requested to take the necessary measures to implement the plan and, if necessary, to consider whether the situation in Palestine constituted a threat to peace and, further, to determine if any attempt to alter by force the settlement envisaged by the Assembly's resolution was a threat to the peace under Article 39 of the Charter.

The reports of the Palestine Commission having revealed a steady deterioration of the situation in Palestine, the Security Council, after studying suggestions for ending violence presented by its permanent members, adopted a proposal calling for a new special session of the Assembly.

At the session, held in New York from April 16 to May 14, 1948, the Assembly approved recommendations, which it had requested the Trusteeship Council to present, for the protection of the City of Jerusalem and its inhabitants, and decided to appoint a United Nations Mediator for Palestine and to relieve the Palestine Commission of its responsibilities. The Mediator was to use his good offices to assure the protection of the Holy Places and to promote a peaceful adjustment. He was also requested to co-operate with the Truce Commission for Palestine. On May 20, 1948, the Assembly's Special Committee chose as Mediator Count Folke Bernadotte, President of the Swedish Red Cross.

Meanwhile, on April 17, the Security Council adopted a resolution calling for a truce between the Arab and Jewish communities in Palestine, and on April 23 it established a Truce Commission for Palestine composed of representatives of those members of the Council which had career consular officers in Jerusalem—Belgium, France and the United States. (Syria, which also had a consular officer in Jerusalem, informed the Council that it would not appoint a representative to the Commission.) The Commission was to assist the Security Council in supervising the truce called for in the Council's April 17 resolution.

On May 14, the mandate of the United Kingdom over Palestine expired, and a Jewish state was proclaimed under the name of Israel. On the following day, the Arab states instituted armed action in Palestine.

The Security Council, on May 22, called on all governments and authorities to abstain from any hostile military action in Palestine, and a week later it requested the observance of a four-week truce. The truce became effective on June 11, 1948. On July 7, the Security Council urgently appealed to the interested parties to accept the prolongation of the truce for such period as might be decided on in consultation with the Mediator. The Provisional Government of Israel agreed to extend the truce, but the Arab states refused and hostilities broke out anew.

On July 15, the Council, invoking Chapter VII of the Charter, ordered all authorities and governments concerned to desist from further military action and to issue cease-fire orders. The Council's resolution declared that failure to comply with this order would be construed as a breach of the peace which would require immediate consideration of enforcement measures to be taken under the Charter. In response to an appeal from the Mediator, Count Bernadotte, the Council, on August 19, warned that both Arab and Jewish authorities would be held responsible for any violation of the truce.

On September 17, 1948, Count Bernadotte and the Chief of the French observers, Colonel André Sérot, were shot and killed in the Israel-held sector of Jerusalem.

In October, large-scale fighting broke out in the Negev area and hostilities were renewed in November and December. The Security Council, in resolutions adopted on October 19, November 4 and 16 and December 29, called upon the parties to order a cease-fire and to seek an agreement.

Following negotiations with the Acting Mediator, Ralph J. Bunche, who succeeded Count Bernadotte, Egypt and Israel signed a General Armistice Agreement at Rhodes on February 24, 1949; Lebanon and Israel at Ras en Naqoura on March 23; the Hashemite Kingdom of Jordan (including former Transjordan) and Israel at Rhodes on April 3; and Syria and Israel at Manhanayim on July 20. The armistice agreements instituted Mixed Armistice Commissions to supervise the implementation of the agreements.

On August 11, the Security Council adopted a resolution which, *inter alia*, urged the parties concerned to negotiate a final peace settlement, either directly or through the Palestine Conciliation Commission (*see below*); relieved the Acting Mediator of any further responsibility under Security Council resolutions; and provided for the continued service of such United Nations observers as might be necessary to observe the cease-fire and to help in the implementation of the armistice agreements.

Since 1949, the Security Council has been assisted in its consideration of a series of complaints relating to the Palestine question by the United Nations Truce Supervision Organization (UNTSO), an organ composed of international observers and headed by a Chief of Staff who supervises, as Chairman of the four Mixed Armistice Commissions, the implementation of the armistice agreements and also reports to the Security Council as the need arises.

Since 1951, the Security Council has been seized of a series of disputes and controversies arising from the unsettled situation in the area and from complaints and protests presented to it by the parties concerning developments along the established Armistice Demarcation Lines and the various demilitarized zones.

PALESTINE CONCILIATION COMMISSION. On December 11, 1948, the Assembly, following the suggestions in a report which Count Bernadotte had prepared before his death, adopted a resolution which, *inter alia*, provided for: (*a*) the establishment of a Conciliation Commission of three members (France, Turkey and the United States) to take steps to assist the parties concerned to achieve a final settlement of all questions; (*b*) the protection of the Holy Places in Jerusalem and free access to them through arrangements under United Nations supervision; and (*c*) further steps to be taken by the Security Council to ensure Jerusalem's demilitarization, and instructions to the Conciliation Commission to present detailed proposals for a permanent international régime and to facilitate the repatriation, resettlement and economic and social rehabilitation of the refugees and the payment of compensation. (*See* United Nations Assistance to Palestine Refugees, *below.*)

In periodic reports submitted to the General Assembly since 1951, the Palestine Conciliation Commission, whose mandate has been renewed annually by the General Assembly, has repeatedly drawn attention to the unwillingness of the parties to implement the Assembly resolutions under which the Commission is operating. Since 1958, the Commission has, however, made efforts to secure the release of Arab refugee bank accounts blocked in Israel and to undertake the identification and evaluation of Arab refugee property.

JERUSALEM. The General Assembly adopted, on December 9, 1949, a resolution restating its intention that Jerusalem should be placed under a permanent international régime as a *corpus separatum* to be administered by the United Nations, and providing appropriate safeguards for the Holy Places. In the resolution, the Trusteeship Council was designated to discharge the responsibility of administering authority.

The President of the Trusteeship Council reported in June 1950 that the Governments of Israel and Jordan had, in effect, refused to co-operate in carrying out the projected statute. The Council reported this position to the Assembly, which in 1950, at its fifth session, failed to reach a decision.

United Nations Assistance to Palestine Refugees

United Nations aid to Palestine refugees began in November 1948, when the General Assembly authorized the advance of $5 million for relief, urged all countries to contribute to a special fund and appealed to the World Health Organization (WHO), the International Refugee Organization (IRO), the Food and Agriculture Organization (FAO), the United Nations Children's Fund (UNICEF) and the United Nations Educational, Scientific and Cultural Organization (UNESCO) to accord their full co-operation in the field of relief.

United Nations Relief for Palestine Refugees (UNRPR) was established on December 1, 1948, and received voluntary contributions of $35 million from thirty-three governments.

On December 8, 1949, the Assembly established the United Nations Relief and Works Agency for Palestine Refugees in the Near East (UNRWA), to be financed by voluntary contributions. It also set up an Advisory Commission to advise and assist the Director (in 1962 retitled the Commissioner-General) of the Agency.

Under the founding resolution, UNRWA's functions were primarily to carry out relief and works programmes in collaboration with local governments and also to consult with the interested Near Eastern governments concerning the measures they should take against the time when international aid for such programmes would cease to be available. On May 1, 1950, the new Agency took over the assets, liabilities and responsibilities of UNRPR and set up its headquarters in Beirut, Lebanon.

Since then, the question of assistance to the Palestine refugees has been considered by the General Assembly at every session on the basis of an annual report in which the head of the Agency reviews its activities and makes recommendations for programmes and budgets. At each of its sessions the Assembly has adopted resolutions pertaining to the work of the Agency and has noted that repatriation or compensation of the refugees, as provided for in its resolution of December 11, 1948, has not been effected and that their situation continues to be a matter of serious concern. The intractability of the refugee problem has prompted the Assembly to extend the Agency's mandate on six occasions, most recently until June 30, 1969.

In 1956, the Assembly, faced with a serious financial crisis in refugee relief, recommended that a special pledging conference be held. Accordingly, the General Assembly met on October 4, 1957, as an *Ad Hoc* Committee of the Whole so that pledges of voluntary contributions to United Nations refugee programmes might be announced. A pledging conference of this kind is now established as an annual procedure.

UNRWA's funds permit an average daily expenditure of about 10 cents per refugee. Thus the Agency's programmes for 1966 provide for expenditure of $38.6 million on some 1,300,000 refugees living in Jordan, the Gaza Strip, Lebanon and the Syrian Arab Republic.

The relief offered eligible refugees comprises food rations distributed to some 873,000 persons, ensuring 1,500 calories a day in summer and 1,600 in winter; supplementary feeding for needy categories of persons; shelter for some 500,000 persons in camps; and welfare services. The Agency also provides medical care and education with the help of staff seconded from, respectively, WHO and UNESCO.

Since 1960, the *per capita* level of expenditure on relief has remained approximately the same. The Agency has, however, embarked on an expansion of education. With half of the refugees under eighteen years of age, it is believed that education and training offer the best hope of enabling the younger generation to escape the economic handicaps of their refugee condition. UNRWA now runs a school system comparable to those of the local governments, making six years of elementary instruction available to all refugee children and a further three years to those who qualify. A limited number of children are helped to obtain secondary or higher education. To equip young refugee men and women for employment, ten vocational training centres have been established, in part with funds derived from World Refugee Year. Together with other institutions where refugees receive training at UNRWA's expense, these provide 3,500 places and graduate some 1,700 technicians and teachers per year. Education and training account for 41 per cent of the Agency's total expenditure.

In his report to the twentieth session of the General Assembly, in 1965, the Commissioner-General stated that unless progress was made towards a political solution of the problem, the plight of the refugees was likely to demand the sympathy and support of the international community for an indefinite period. He noted that the permanent needs for education and health services, applying to almost the entire refugee community, were increasing on account of population growth and that it would remain necessary for many years to maintain relief and welfare services at current levels. The injustice of which the refugees felt themselves victims still rankled, he said, and their desire to return home was unabated; thus their problem still constituted a danger to the peace and stability of the Near East.

The Commissioner-General pointed out that, at the end of 1963, UNRWA had a budgetary deficit of $0.5 million and that despite stringent economy, this gap between income and expenditure had steadily widened until a deficit of $4.2 million, which would mean reductions in essential services to the refugees, appeared likely for 1966. The Commissioner-General concluded his report to the twentieth session by seeking the guidance of the Assembly in ensuring the future effectiveness of the Agency and by recommending that funds be provided to enable existing services to be maintained.

In a resolution adopted on December 15, 1965, the General Assembly called upon all governments, as a matter of urgency, to make the most generous efforts possible to meet the needs of UNRWA and directed the Commissioner-General to ensure, in co-operation with the governments concerned, the most equitable distribution of relief based on need.

Iranian Question

The first meeting of the Security Council was held on January 19, 1946, to consider a complaint by Iran that Soviet officials and armed forces present under the Tripartite Treaty of Alliance of 1942 (between Iran, the United Kingdom and the USSR) had interfered in Iran's internal affairs by preventing the entry of Iranian troops into Azerbaijan to suppress local disorders. The USSR, Iran said, had supported a separatist movement in that province.

The USSR maintained that the disorders were not connected with the presence of Soviet troops but had been caused by the failure of the Iranian Government to satisfy legitimate demands for regional autonomy. The USSR contended that there was no threat to the peace and that the matter should be settled by bilateral negotiations.

The Council, on January 30, noted the readiness of the parties to resume negotiations. In May, Iran reported to the Security Council the withdrawal of Soviet troops.

Syrian-Lebanese Complaint

A similar complaint was addressed to the Security Council in February 1946 by Syria and Lebanon, which stated that France and the United Kingdom had refused to withdraw their troops from those countries even though the war with Germany and Japan had ended. France and the United Kingdom stated that the presence of their troops was a "heritage" of the war and would not be continued indefinitely.

A resolution expressing "confidence" that the troops would be withdrawn as soon as practical received seven votes in the Council but was not adopted because of the negative vote of the USSR, a permanent member. The USSR had favoured a "recommendation" by the Council that the troops be withdrawn as "soon as possible." France and the United Kingdom stated that they would comply with the majority view.

The withdrawal of French and British troops from Syria was completed during the first two weeks of April 1946. On May 9, Lebanon reported French agreement to withdraw all but a small group of its forces by August 31 and the United Kingdom its entire strength, except a small liquidation party, by June 30, 1946.

Suez Canal Question

On July 26, 1956, Egypt proclaimed the nationalization of the Suez Canal Company and placed the management of the Canal in the hands of an Egyptian operating authority. The decree provided for compensation to the stockholders in the Canal Company on the basis of the market value of the shares.

At a meeting of the Security Council on October 13, a resolution was unanimously adopted by which it was agreed that any settlement of the Suez question should meet six requirements which had previously been agreed to in the course of private meetings between the Ministers for Foreign Affairs of Egypt, France and the United Kingdom. The requirements were: (1) there should be free and open transit through the Canal without discrimination; (2) the sovereignty of Egypt should be respected; (3) the operation of the Canal should be insulated from the politics of any country; (4) the manner of fixing tolls and charges should be decided by agreement between Egypt and the users; (5) a fair proportion of the dues should be allotted to development; and (6) in case of disputes, unresolved affairs between the Suez Canal Company and the Egyptian Government should be settled by arbitration with suitable terms of reference and suitable provisions for the payment of sums found to be due.

Between October 13 and 19, the Secretary-General held private meetings with the Minister for Foreign Affairs of Egypt to study arrangements for the resumption of exploratory talks among the three Governments directly concerned. Further negotiations, however, were interrupted by the military action in Egypt of Israeli and Anglo-French forces and by the blocking of the Canal.

On October 29, the United States informed the Security Council by letter that armed forces of Israel had penetrated deeply into Egyptian territory in violation of the Armistice Agreement between Israel and Egypt, and requested an immediate meeting of the Council to consider "The Palestine question: steps for the immediate cessation of the military action of Israel in Egypt." The Council considered the question at four meetings between October 30 and November 1.

On October 30, the representative of the United Kingdom stated that unless hostilities between Egypt and Israel could quickly be stopped, free passage through the Suez Canal would be jeopardized. He informed the Council that the United Kingdom and French Governments had called upon Egypt and Israel to withdraw their armed forces to a distance of ten miles from the Suez Canal. If, on the expiration of twelve hours, either or both Governments had not undertaken to comply with these requirements, British and French forces would intervene in whatever strength might be necessary to secure compliance.

Two draft resolutions before the Council, one by the United States and the other by the USSR, calling upon Israel to withdraw immediately behind the established Armistice Line, failed of adoption on October 30 because of the negative votes of two permanent members, France and the United Kingdom.

On October 31, reports were received that French and British aircraft had begun air attacks against military targets in Egypt. The representatives of France and the United Kingdom stated that the Egyptian Government had rejected the Franco-British communication of October 30 and, as a consequence, the United Kingdom and French Governments had intervened; the intervention had as its overriding purpose the safeguarding of the Suez Canal and the restoration of peaceful conditions in the Middle East. The Suez Canal was subsequently blocked when Egypt sank ships in the Canal, closing it to navigation.

Also on October 31, Yugoslavia submitted a draft resolution whereby the Security Council, since it lacked the unanimity of its permanent members and was prevented from exercising its primary responsibility for the maintenance of international peace and security, would decide to call an emergency special session of the General Assembly, as provided in the Assembly's "Uniting for Peace" resolution. The Yugoslav resolution was adopted by a procedural vote of 7 to 2 (France and United Kingdom), with 2 abstentions.

The Assembly met in emergency special session from November 1 to 10, 1956. On November 2, it adopted a United States resolution which: (1) urged that all parties involved in hostilities in the area agree to an immediate cease-fire; (2) urged the parties to the armistice agreements promptly to withdraw all forces behind the armistice line; (3) recommended that all member states refrain from any acts which would delay or prevent the implementation of the resolution; (4) urged that, upon the cease-fire being effective, steps be taken to reopen the Suez Canal; and (5) requested the Secretary-General to observe and report promptly on compliance to the Security Council and to the General Assembly.

By November 2, 1956, however, Israel had established control over virtually the whole Sinai Peninsula and had occupied Gaza, and, by November 5, it controlled the entrance to the Gulf of Aqaba. On the morning of November 2, Anglo-French landings had taken place in the Port Said area. On November 3, the Secretary-General reported that Egypt had accepted the resolution but had stated that it could not implement it if aggression on its soil continued. The Secretary-General also reported that France and the United Kingdom continued to maintain that the "police action" must be carried through to stop hostilities which threatened the Suez Canal. They would stop military action if, among other things, Egypt and Israel would accept a United Nations force which would be maintained until an Arab-Israel peace settlement was reached and satisfactory arrangements were agreed upon concerning the Suez Canal.

On November 4, the Assembly adopted two resolutions designed to bring about the implementation of its November 2 resolution. In the first resolution, submitted by India together with eighteen African countries, the Assembly reaffirmed its November 2 resolution and authorized the Secretary-General to arrange for its implementation. In the second resolution, submitted by Canada, the Assembly asked the Secretary-General to submit within forty-eight hours a plan for a United Nations emergency force to secure and supervise the cessation of hostilities. In a report submitted the same day, the Secretary-General suggested that a United Nations Command for an emergency force be established and that Major-General E. L. M. Burns, of Canada, then Chief of Staff of the United Nations Truce Supervision Organization (UNTSO), be appointed Chief of the Command. The Secretary-General recommended that, as a matter of principle, troops should not be drawn from permanent members of the Security Council. The Assembly established the Command on November 5 and two days later adopted a resolution expressing approval of the guiding principles for its organization and functioning set forth in the Secretary-General's report (see United Nations Emergency Force, below).

At its eleventh session, in 1956, the General Assembly decided to include in its agenda the question of the Middle East and of the intervention by Israel and by France and the United Kingdom in Egypt. On November 24, it reiterated its call to France, Israel and the United Kingdom to comply forthwith with its previous resolutions on the withdrawal of their forces from Egypt.

The Secretary-General, in an oral report to the Assembly on December 21, stated that the representative of Israel had presented that day a schedule of withdrawals in two phases, the second of which would complete the withdrawal of all its forces. It was understood that the forces would be withdrawn behind the Armistice line. However, the date of the withdrawals was not specified.

The Anglo-French forces completed their withdrawal on December 22, with contingents of the United Nations Emergency Force (UNEF) moving in and taking up positions.

In January 1957, the Secretary-General reported to the Assembly on the status of compliance with the Assembly resolutions. The Assembly, in two resolutions on January 19 and February 2, noted the non-compliance of Israel.

On March 1, Israel announced to the Assembly that it was prepared to withdraw its forces from the Gulf of Aqaba and the Straits of Tiran in the confidence that there would be continued freedom of navigation there for international and Israeli shipping, and that it was also making a complete withdrawal from the Gaza Strip on certain assumptions, particularly that UNEF would take over.

On March 4, the Secretary-General informed the Assembly that the Commander of UNEF had reached agreement with Israel's Commander-in-Chief on technical arrangements for the withdrawal. Four days later, the Secretary-General reported full compliance by Israel with the Assembly resolution of February 2.

CLEARANCE OF SUEZ CANAL.   Meanwhile, the Secretary-General had proposed, on November 20, 1956, in response to the Assembly's November 2 resolution urging that, "upon the cease-fire being effective, steps be taken to reopen the Suez Canal," that the Assembly authorize him to negotiate agreements for clearing operations with firms of countries outside the existing conflict.

On November 24, the Assembly adopted a resolution noting with approval the progress made by the Secretary-General in connection with arrangements for clearing the Suez Canal and authorized him to proceed with the exploration of practical arrangements. Clearance of the Canal was started on December 27, 1956, and was completed on April 10, 1957. On April 12, the Secretary-General announced receipt of loans for the Canal clearance operation totalling nearly $11 million from Canada, Sweden, Liberia, Ceylon, Australia, the United States, the Federal Republic of Germany, Norway, Denmark and the Netherlands and a pledge from Italy which was subsequently paid. It was estimated that the advances would be sufficient to cover the costs.

On April 24, 1957, Egypt informed the Secretary-General that the Canal was open again for normal traffic and transmitted a Declaration on the Suez Canal and the arrangements for its operation. In the Declaration, the Government of Egypt stated its determination to continue to observe the Constantinople Convention of 1888 and expressed its confidence that the other signatories and all others concerned would do the same. Free navigation for all nations would be maintained within the limits of that Convention, and complaints of discrimination or violation would be referred first to the Canal Authority and, if not resolved, to an arbitration tribunal. Egypt stated that the Declaration, with the obligations therein, constituted an international instrument and that it would be deposited and registered with the United Nations Secretariat. On July 18, Egypt supplemented its Declaration of April 24 by accepting as compulsory the jurisdiction of the International Court of Justice in all legal disputes that might arise between the parties to the Constantinople Convention regarding the interpretation or applicability of its provisions.

On December 14, 1957, the General Assembly approved a report of the Secretary-General which stated that the expenditure and obligations incurred by the United Nations had totalled $8.4 million. The amount of $11 million advanced by the eleven contributing countries was to be repaid by means of a surcharge on Canal traffic.

Under the good offices of the International Bank for Reconstruction and Development, the United Arab Republic and the Suez stockholders negotiated a preliminary accord entitled a Heads of Agreement, which was signed by the two parties on April 29, 1958. By this Agreement, the United Arab Republic undertook to pay £E28.3 million (equivalent of more than $81 million) as compensation and to leave all the external assets to the stockholders. The Final Agreement, which confirmed the Heads of Agreement, was signed at Geneva on July 13, 1958.

In a report to the General Assembly dated August 1, 1958, the Secretary-General stated that the arrangements for the collection of a 3 per cent surcharge on Canal traffic—to be paid by all shipping and trade using the Canal—would go into effect on September 15, 1958, in order to repay loans made for clearance of the Canal. The Secretary-General had signed an agreement with the Banque de la Société Générale de Belgique, Brussels, appointing the Bank as agent of the United Nations for the collection of the surcharge. The amount to be recovered, subject to necessary adjustments, was approximately $8.2 million.

UNITED NATIONS EMERGENCY FORCE.   Following the Assembly's resolutions of November 5 and 7, 1956, Egypt agreed to the arrival of the United Nations Emergency Force (UNEF) on its territory. Twenty-four member states offered to participate in the Force. Offers of troop units were accepted from ten states: Brazil, Canada, Colombia, Denmark, Finland, India, Indonesia, Norway, Sweden and Yugoslavia. Those of fourteen other states remained outstanding and available for activation should the need arise.

The first UNEF unit to reach Egypt arrived on November 15, 1956. By early February 1957, UNEF had been virtually brought to its full complement of some 6,000 officers and men from ten member states.

Beginning in 1957, UNEF served as a stabilizing influence in the Gaza/Sinai area, observing and patrolling the 59-kilometre Demarcation Line in the Gaza Strip and the 209-kilometre frontier between the United Arab Republic and Israel and also observing shipping going through the Straits of Tiran at the southern tip of the Sinai Peninsula.

By the end of 1965, UNEF had a strength of about 4,000, consisting of contingents from Brazil, Canada, Denmark, India, Norway, Sweden and Yugoslavia.

Financing of UNEF. In accordance with a resolution adopted by the General Assembly on November 26, 1956, a Special Account for the United Nations Emergency Force was established in an initial amount of $10 million apportioned among all member states. During the discussion of the question, the Secretary-General maintained that the expenses of UNEF were "expenses of the Organization" within the meaning of Article 17, paragraph 2, of the Charter, which states that "the expenses of the Organization shall be borne by the members as apportioned by the General Assembly." The representatives of Albania, Bulgaria, Byelorussian SSR, Czechoslovakia, Hungary, Poland, Romania, Ukrainian SSR and USSR, however, declared that they would not participate in the financing of the Force since it had been established in violation of the Charter provision under which the establishment of United Nations armed forces was within the exclusive competence of the Security Council. Doubts were also expressed on the question by some other members who, nevertheless, favoured the establishment of the Force and its financing. In subsequent years, a number of developing countries, though approving the Force, have considered assessments in respect of the Force to be inequitable and burdensome.

In 1962, the General Assembly asked the Secretary-General to request an advisory opinion from the International Court of Justice on the question of whether expenditures authorized in relation to UNEF and also the Congo operations constitute "expenses of the Organization within the meaning of Article 17, paragraph 2, of the Charter." The Court, on July 20, 1962, delivered an advisory opinion (*see page* 450) in which it stated that the expenditures were expenses of the Organization within the meaning of Article 17.

The Assembly recognized, however, that the extraordinary expenses of peace-keeping operations placed a financial burden on some governments having the least capacity to pay. Accordingly, a special temporary formula was approved whereby developing nations were given a substantial reduction on their assessments, with the difference to be made up by voluntary contributions from the developed countries.

Total expenditures authorized for UNEF through September 30, 1965, amounted to $186.9 million. The annual breakdown was as follows: 1957, $30 million; 1958, $25 million; 1959, $19 million; 1960, $21.1 million; 1961, $19.2 million; 1962, $19.5 million; 1963, $19 million; 1964, $17.8 million; 1965 (to Sept. 30), $16.3 million.

A financial report issued by the Secretary-General in January 1966 showed that the actual cash expenses incurred by UNEF through September 30, 1965 totalled $170.1 million, with unliquidated obligations amounting to $16.6 million.

The funds obtained to meet cash expenditures totalled $174.2 million. Of this sum, $96.7 million was the total amount collected from member states in assessed contributions for UNEF; voluntary contributions to the UNEF Account totalled $27.8 million; the amount met from the proceeds of the United Nations Bond Issue was $29.9 million; and from other sources, $19.8 million.

Complaints by Lebanon and Jordan

On May 22, 1958, Lebanon submitted a complaint to the Security Council charging intervention by the United Arab Republic in its internal affairs. The United Arab Republic, Lebanon stated, had infiltrated armed bands from Syria into Lebanon; its nationals had participated in acts of terrorism and rebellion against the established authority in Lebanon and had supplied arms to rebellious groups and to individuals; and it had carried on a violent radio and press campaign inciting the overthrow of the Lebanese government.

The United Arab Republic rejected the charges, stating that the disturbances in Lebanon were purely internal and were mainly directed against the Lebanese president who wished to alter the constitution to permit his candidacy for a second term.

The Council decided on June 11, 1958, to dispatch an observation group to Lebanon so as to ensure that there was no illegal infiltration of personnel or supply of arms or other material across the Lebanese borders. The United Nations Observation Group consisted of Galo Plaza, of Ecuador, Chairman; Major-General Odd Bull, of Norway, executive member and chief-of-staff in charge of military observers; Rajeshwar Dayal, of India, and a staff of observers.

On July 15, the United States informed the Council that in response to a request by Lebanon for the help of friendly governments so as to preserve the country's integrity and independence, it had dispatched forces to Lebanon, not to engage in hostilities of any kind, but in order to help Lebanon in its efforts to stabilize the situation; that the United States forces would be withdrawn as soon as the United Nations could take over; and that they had been instructed to co-operate with the United Nations Observation Group.

The USSR asked the Council to call upon the United States to cease armed intervention in the domestic affairs of the Arab states and to remove its troops from Lebanon immediately.

The United States proposed that the Council invite the Observation Group to continue and develop its activities.

On July 17, Jordan complained to the Council of interference in its domestic affairs by the United Arab Republic and stated that, following its requests to the United Kingdom and the United States for immediate aid, British troops had landed in Jordan.

The United Arab Republic denied the existence of any threat against Jordan. Sharing that view, the USSR proposed that the Council call on the United States and the United Kingdom to remove their troops from Lebanon and Jordan. Sweden, considering that the United States action in Lebanon had substantially altered the conditions under which the Council had decided to send observers, proposed that the activities of the Observation Group be suspended until further notice. The Council rejected the USSR and Swedish proposals; that of the United States was not adopted because of the negative vote of a permanent member of the Council (USSR).

Early in August 1958, the Council decided unanimously to call an emergency special session of the General Assembly. At the session, ten Arab states—Iraq, Jordan, Lebanon, Libya, Morocco, Saudi Arabia, the Sudan, Tunisia, the United Arab Republic and Yemen—proposed that the General Assembly should, *inter alia:* (1) (a) welcome the renewed assurances given by the Arab states to observe the provision of the Pact of the League of Arab States that each member state would respect the systems of government established in other member states and regard them as exclusive concerns of those states, and that each would pledge to abstain from any action calculated to change established systems of government; (b) call upon all member states of the United Nations to act strictly in accordance with the principles of mutual respect for each other's territorial integrity and sovereignty, of non-aggression, of strict non-interference in each other's internal affairs and of equal and mutual benefit, and to ensure that their conduct conformed to those principles; (2) request the Secretary-General to make such practical arrangements as would adequately help to uphold the purposes and principles of the Charter in relation to Lebanon and Jordan in the existing circumstances, and thereby facilitate the early withdrawal of the foreign troops from the two countries; and (3) invite the Secretary-General to continue his studies and consult with the Arab countries of the Near East with a view to possible assistance regarding an Arab development institution designed to further economic growth in those countries. The Arab draft resolution was adopted unanimously by the Assembly on August 21, 1958.

At the end of September, the Secretary-General reported that the work of the Observation Group in Lebanon had had to be re-evaluated with a view to determining its possible role when the Assembly resolution of August 21 was implemented. In regard to Jordan, Pier P. Spinelli, the Under-Secretary in charge of the United Nations Office in Geneva, had been appointed Special Representative of the Secretary-General to assist in the implementation of the resolution.

The withdrawal of United States troops from Lebanon was completed on October 25, 1958, and the withdrawal of British troops from Jordan on November 2. On November 17, Lebanon informed the Security Council that cordial and close relations between Lebanon and the United Arab Republic had been resumed. The United Nations Observation Group in Lebanon ceased its operation on December 9, 1958.

Question Relating to the Case of Adolf Eichmann

On June 15, 1960, Argentina requested an urgent meeting of the Security Council to consider "the violation of the sovereign rights of the Argentine Republic resulting from the illicit and clandestine transfer of Adolf Eichmann" from Argentina to Israel.

The Council discussed the matter on June 22 and 23. The Foreign Minister of Israel, who was invited to take part without vote, recognized that the persons who took Eichmann from Argentina to Israel had broken the laws of Argentina and said that the Government of

Israel apologized for this act. Nevertheless, Israel believed that the act should be seen in the light of the "exceptional and unique character of the crimes attributed to Eichmann."

The Council then adopted an Argentine resolution which stressed the essential need of safeguarding the sovereign rights of states, and requested "appropriate reparation" on the part of Israel. Before the vote, the Israel Foreign Minister declared that, in the Israel Government's view, its expression of regret constituted adequate reparation.

Question of Kuwait

On July 1, 1961, Kuwait asked the Security Council to consider its complaint "in respect of the situation arising from threats by Iraq to the territorial independence of Kuwait, which is likely to endanger the maintenance of international peace and security." On the same day, the United Kingdom informed the President of the Council that it supported the request of Kuwait.

The next day, Iraq requested that the Security Council consider its complaint "in respect of the situation arising out of the armed threat by the United Kingdom to the independence and security of Iraq, which is likely to endanger the maintenance of international peace and security."

The Council considered the two complaints at four meetings from July 2 to 7. Two draft resolutions submitted by the United Kingdom and the United Arab Republic, respectively, failed to be adopted. Subsequently, Kuwait stated, on October 19, 1961, that the withdrawal of the British forces from Kuwait had been completed and that the Arab League forces had replaced the British in safeguarding the independence and sovereignty of Kuwait.

[On May 7, 1963, on the recommendation of the Security Council, the General Assembly admitted Kuwait to the United Nations.]

Yemen

The question of Yemen first came before the United Nations in December 1962, when the Credentials Committee of the General Assembly considered a memorandum from the Secretary-General stating that credentials for the representatives of Yemen had been received from more than one delegation—from the President of the Yemen Arab Republic and from the Imam of Yemen. On the recommendation of the Credentials Committee, the Assembly accepted the credentials presented by the President of the Yemen Arab Republic.

In April 1963, the Secretary-General reported to the Security Council that, since late 1962, he had been in consultation with the

Governments of the United Arab Republic, Saudi Arabia and the Yemen Arab Republic regarding the situation in Yemen, where fighting had broken out between the republican forces and the forces of the revolutionary council which had taken over power from the Imam. As a result of a fact-finding mission on his behalf by Ralph J. Bunche, Under-Secretary for Special Political Affairs, and an independent but similar mission by Ellsworth Bunker, of the United States, the Secretary-General had received from Saudi Arabia and the United Arab Republic confirmation of their acceptance of identical terms of disengagement in Yemen.

Under these terms, Saudi Arabia would terminate all support and aid to the Royalists, and the United Arab Republic, which had supported the republican forces, would begin a phased withdrawal of its troops from Yemen. A demilitarized zone would be established on each side of the Saudi Arabia-Yemen border, and impartial observers would be stationed there to check on observance of the terms of disengagement.

The Secretary-General informed the Security Council that he had asked Major-General Carl von Horn, Chief-of-Staff of the United Nations Truce Supervision Organization (UNTSO) in Jerusalem, to visit the three countries concerned to consult on terms relating to the functions of United Nations observers. He later informed the Council that Saudi Arabia had agreed to pay a proportionate share of the costs of the observation operation and that the United Arab Republic had agreed to pay $200,000, approximately half the cost for a four-month period.

On June 11, 1963, the Council adopted, by 10 votes in favour to none against, with 1 abstention (Soviet Union), a resolution commending the parties concerned for arriving at the terms of disengagement and asking the Secretary-General to establish the observation operation, as defined by him, and to report to the Council on the implementation of the decision.

UNITED NATIONS OBSERVATION MISSION.   The United Nations Observation Mission in Yemen (UNYOM) began its operations on July 4, 1963, with the United Nations Emergency Force in the Middle East (UNEF) providing administrative and logistics support.

On September 4, the Secretary-General informed the Security Council that the functions of UNYOM were limited to observation, certification and reporting; that it could not effectively undertake any broader functions with the personnel, equipment and funds available to it; and that the agreement on disengagement concerned only Saudi Arabia and the United Arab Republic and, accordingly, UNYOM was not concerned with Yemen's internal affairs and did not have any authority to issue orders or directions in this respect.

The Secretary-General stated that, as the task of the mission would not be completed before the expiration, on September 4, of the original two-month period, he had sought and received assurances from both parties that they would defray the expenses of the operation for a further two-month period.

On October 31, the Secretary-General reported to the Security Council that Saudi Arabia had decided to participate in the financing of UNYOM for a further period of two months, from November 5 to January 4, 1964.

Considering that military observation should be complemented by a United Nations political presence to encourage the implementation of disengagement, the Secretary-General, on November 4, 1963, appointed Pier P. Spinelli, Under-Secretary and Director of the United Nations Office at Geneva, as his Special Representative for Yemen and Head of the Yemen Observation Mission.

Early in January 1964, the Secretary-General reported to the Council that while the fighting in Yemen was decreasing, the continued functioning of UNYOM was desirable and that, therefore, UNYOM would be extended for another two months ending March 4, 1964, with Saudi Arabia and the United Arab Republic agreeing to the extension and defraying the costs involved. Subsequently, UNYOM received three additional two-month extensions, the last one ending on September 4, 1964, when its activities were terminated by the Secretary-General in view of the expressed wishes of the parties concerned. The Secretary-General stated that, though UNYOM's terms of reference had been restricted to observation and report, it had exercised an important restraining influence on hostile activities in the area.

On August 25, 1965, the Secretary-General sent identical cables of congratulations to King Faisal of Saudi Arabia and President Gamal Abdel Nasser of the United Arab Republic on a peace agreement on Yemen which they had signed at Jidda on August 24.

QUESTIONS RELATING TO ASIA AND THE FAR EAST

India-Pakistan Question

On January 1, 1948, India reported to the Security Council that tribesmen and others had been invading the state of Jammu and Kashmir and that extensive fighting was taking place. India complained that Pakistan was assisting the tribesmen in the invasion and requested the Security Council to call on Pakistan to stop giving such assistance, since it was an act of aggression against India.

Jammu and Kashmir was an Indian princedom which, under the scheme of partition and the Indian Independence Act of 1947, became free to accede to India or Pakistan. It borders on both. After the fighting had begun, the Maharajah of the state requested accession to India, which India accepted on the understanding that, once normal conditions were restored, the question of accession "should be settled by a reference to the people."

Pakistan submitted countercharges against India on January 15, 1948, alleging that the accession to India of the state of Jammu and Kashmir was illegal, that Indian forces had unlawfully occupied Junagadh and other states, that mass destruction of Muslims was being carried out in a prearranged programme of genocide and that India had failed to implement agreements between the two countries. Pakistan and India agreed that the situation between them might lead to a breach of international peace.

UNITED NATIONS COMMISSION FOR INDIA AND PAKISTAN. On January 20, the Security Council established a three-member United Nations Commission for India and Pakistan (UNCIP) to investigate and mediate, first, on the Jammu and Kashmir situation and, when so directed by the Council, on other situations complained of by Pakistan.

India subsequently nominated Czechoslovakia to the Commission, and Pakistan nominated Argentina. When these two states failed to agree on the third member, the President of the Council, on May 7, designated the United States. Meanwhile, on April 21, the Council had decided to increase the membership to five and added Belgium and Colombia two days later. The Council also recommended various measures to stop the fighting and to create proper conditions for a free and impartial plebiscite. To assist in carrying out these measures, it instructed the Commission to proceed at once to the Indian subcontinent and there place its good offices and mediation at the disposal of the Governments of India and Pakistan.

The Commission arrived on the sub-continent on July 7, 1948, and, on August 13, proposed that both Governments issue cease-fire orders at the earliest possible date, to apply to all forces under their control in Jammu and Kashmir, and that they accept certain principles as the basis for a truce agreement. These included: (1) that Pakistan would withdraw its troops recently stationed in the state and do its best to secure the withdrawal of tribesmen and Pakistan nationals not normally resident there; (2) that, pending a final solution, the territory evacuated by the troops would be administered by the local authorities under the surveillance of the Commission; (3) that, when the Commission notified India that Pakistan was complying with these terms, India would begin to withdraw the bulk of its forces in stages to be agreed on with the Commission; and (4) that, pending the acceptance of conditions for final settlement, the Indian Government would maintain within the lines existing at the moment of cease-fire those forces considered necessary to assist local authorities in observing law and order.

Meanwhile, India, after a clarification of certain points, accepted the Council resolution of April 21. Pakistan, however, informed the Commission that it could not accept it without certain reservations, in particular the part concerning the organization of a plebiscite. The Commission reported in September that it had temporarily exhausted possibilities of further negotiations.

The Security Council considered the Commission's report in November. It informed the Commission of its full support and endorsed its appeal to India and Pakistan to refrain from any action which might aggravate the situation. Informal conversations with the parties then took place on the conditions and basic principles which should govern the plebiscite. As a result, the Commission proposed to the Governments that the accession of the state be decided by a free and impartial plebiscite and that the Secretary-General nominate, in agreement with the Commission, a plebiscite administrator.

Both Governments accepted the proposals, with clarifications and understandings, and ordered a cease-fire as from January 1, 1949. On January 5, the Commission adopted a formal resolution embodying the proposals. It then appointed observers from various nations to report on the observance of the cease-fire agreement. Agreement on a cease-fire line was reached on July 27, and a few days later was ratified by both India and Pakistan.

Meanwhile, in March, Fleet Admiral Chester W. Nimitz, of the United States Navy, was nominated as plebiscite administrator by the Secretary-General. He was to be formally appointed by the Government of Jammu and Kashmir when the details of the plebiscite were settled after the acceptance of a truce agreement.

On April 15, the Commission presented simultaneously to both Governments its proposals for implementation of the cease-fire agreement, emphasizing withdrawal on the entire cease-fire line. After considering the replies, the Commission, on April 28, presented its final terms and asked for unreserved acceptance. The replies, however, did not constitute acceptance. Resorting to another procedure, the Commission invited India and Pakistan to joint meetings at the ministerial level, but abandoned the idea in the face of disagreement on the agenda. As a final effort, the Commission asked the parties whether they would agree to submit the points at issue to arbitration, but this was not acceptable to India. In the circumstances, the Commission decided to report to the Council.

After considering the Commission's report, the Council requested its President, General A. G. L. McNaughton, of Canada, to hold informal discussions with the parties. On December 22, 1949, Mr. Mc-

Naughton submitted to them a set of proposals for demilitarization, to be implemented prior to a plebiscite. They provided for the withdrawal of the regular forces of Pakistan, the withdrawal of the regular forces of India not required to maintain security and law and order on the Indian side of the cease-fire line, and the reduction of local forces, including state armed forces and militia and the Azad Kashmir forces.

Mr. McNaughton reported to the Council in February that the two parties had submitted a series of amendments to his proposals which they said were mutually unacceptable. Mr. McNaughton considered that no useful purpose could be served by continued activity on his part.

In the discussions that followed in the Council, India proposed that not only the regular but also the irregular forces of Pakistan should be withdrawn and the Azad Kashmir forces disbanded, and that the provision regarding the disbandment and disarming of the Kashmir state forces and militia should be deleted. India further declared that Pakistan had created obstacles to the holding of a plebiscite by sending troops into Kashmir in disregard of the Council resolution of April 21, 1948. India stood by its offer of a plebiscite provided that Kashmir was restored to its normal condition prior to the vote, but the positions adopted by the two sides were irreconcilable, India stated.

Pakistan proposed that the functions of the plebiscite administrator should include the final disposal of all forces remaining in Kashmir after demilitarization. Later, during the Council's debate, Pakistan accepted the McNaughton proposals and agreed to submit to arbitration the differences which had arisen with regard to implementation of the United Nations Commission's resolution of August 13, 1948. Pakistan informed the Council that it had moved troops into Kashmir, in May 1949, to circumvent the imminent danger to its own security and economy resulting from the continued build-up of the Indian Army there, and that it had secured the evacuation of the tribesmen and of the Pakistan nationals who had entered the state to fight.

UNITED NATIONS REPRESENTATIVE FOR INDIA AND PAKISTAN. In March 1950, the Council decided to terminate the United Nations Commission and transfer its power and responsibilities to a United Nations Representative. The Council also, considering that steps should be taken forthwith to demilitarize Kashmir and determine its future in accordance with the freely expressed will of the inhabitants, called on India and Pakistan to prepare and execute within five months a programme of demilitarization based on the principles contained in the McNaughton proposals or a mutually agreed modification thereof. These arrangements would be without prejudice to the rights or claims of the parties and were to take due regard of the requirements of law and order. Both India and Pakistan accepted the Council's draft resolution before it was adopted.

In April, the Council appointed Sir Owen Dixon, of Australia, as United Nations Representative for India and Pakistan. Sir Owen reported to the Council in September that no agreement had been reached on demilitarization or other preparations for the holding of a plebiscite and that India had rejected his suggestions regarding demilitarization, administration of Kashmir prior to a plebiscite and conditions for the plebiscite. He said he had concluded that the only chance of settling the dispute by agreement lay in partition of the state and in some way of allocating the Valley of Kashmir, rather than in an over-all plebiscite, but he had not been able to secure agreement between the parties on a meeting to discuss his earlier suggestion for partition and a partial plebiscite in a limited area, including the Valley.

Sir Owen also reported that Pakistan had said it would consider the matter if the Valley of Kashmir was allocated to it, while India declined to consider an over-all partition in which the Valley would go to Pakistan.

Sir Owen declared that both the United Nations Commission and he, himself, had failed to secure an agreement on practical measures for a plebiscite, and he asked to be relieved of his position. The Security Council acceded to this request on September 26, without discussing the substance of his report.

On October 27, 1950, the General Council of the All Jammu and Kashmir National Conference adopted a resolution recommending the convening of a constituent assembly to determine the future shape and affiliations of the State of Jammu and Kashmir. On December 14, Pakistan asked the Security Council to call on India to refrain from proceeding with the proposal for a constituent assembly and from taking any other action which might prejudice the holding of a free and impartial plebiscite.

On March 30, 1951, the Council affirmed that the convening of a constituent assembly and any action that assembly might attempt to determine the future shape and affiliation of the entire state or any part of it would not constitute a disposition of Kashmir in accordance with the principle of a free and impartial plebiscite. The Council observed that the main points of difference preventing agreement were the procedure for and the extent of demilitarization of Kashmir preparatory to the holding of a plebiscite, and the degree of control over the exercise of the functions of government in the state necessary to ensure a free and fair plebiscite.

The Council decided to appoint a successor to Sir Owen Dixon, and on April 30 named Frank P. Graham as United Nations Representative for India and Pakistan. It instructed him, after consultations with the two Governments, to effect the demilitarization of Kashmir on the basis of the resolutions of the United Nations Commission and called on the parties to co-operate with him to the fullest degree. If the Representative had not effected demilitarization within three months, he was to report to the Council the points of difference preventing demilitarization. The Council called on the parties to accept arbitration of such points of difference, the arbitrator or arbitrators to be appointed by the President of the International Court of Justice after consultation with the parties.

The Council also decided that the United Nations Military Observer Group in India and Pakistan (UNMOGIP), which had been set up in 1949, would continue to supervise the cease-fire. It requested India and Pakistan to ensure the faithful observance of the cease-fire agreement, and called on them to take all possible measures to secure the creation and maintenance of an atmosphere favouring further negotiations and to refrain from any action likely to prejudice a just and peaceful settlement.

Pakistan accepted the resolution, but India said that it contained unacceptable provisions, particularly as regards arbitration, and that India could not leave to a third party, however chosen, the decision as to how Kashmir should be protected against a recurrence of the events of October 1947. Concerning the constituent assembly, India asserted that Kashmir was a unit of the Indian Federation, entitled to frame its own constitution and to convene an assembly for that purpose, and that the assembly was not intended to prejudice issues before the Council.

Early in May, Pakistan informed the Council of reports that steps were being taken by the Ruler of Kashmir to convene a constituent assembly. The Council approved a letter, to be sent by its President to India and Pakistan, stating that if the reports were correct, the action would be in conflict with the commitments of the parties to a fair and impartial plebiscite. The Council trusted that the parties would do everything in their power to ensure that the authorities in Kashmir did not disregard the Council or act so as to prejudice a determination of the future accession of the state in accordance with United Nations resolutions.

After conversations with the parties, Mr. Graham, the United Nations Representative, submitted to them, on September 7, a plan of demilitarization to be carried out over a period of ninety days. The plan provided for the withdrawal of Pakistan troops, as well as of the tribesmen and Pakistan nationals not normally resident in Kashmir who had entered the state to fight, and for the large-scale disbandment and disarming of the Azad Kashmir forces on the Pakistan side of the cease-fire line. On the Indian side, the plan called for withdrawal of the bulk of the Indian forces and then further withdrawals or reductions of the Indian and State armed forces remaining in Kashmir. An agreed number of civil armed forces would remain on the Pakistan side of the cease-fire line and an agreed number of troops would remain on the Indian side. The Plebiscite Administrator would be appointed to office by India by the end of this demilitarization period. On October 15, 1951, Mr. Graham reported to the Council that the parties had not agreed on this scheme. They had, however, accepted four points of his proposal, involving reaffirmation of their determination not to resort to force with respect to the Kashmir question, of their will to observe the cease-fire and of their acceptance of the principle of a free and impartial plebiscite and agreement to avoid warlike statements regarding Kashmir.

The Council instructed Mr. Graham to continue his efforts to obtain agreement of the parties on demilitarization and called on the parties to co-operate.

In his second report to the Council, presented on December 18, 1951, Mr. Graham said that agreement had been reached on certain of the points in his original proposal, but that fundamental differences remained with regard to the size of forces to be left on each side of the cease-fire line after demilitarization. His third report, on April 22, 1952, indicated no further progress on this point.

On July 16, 1952, Mr. Graham proposed to the parties that the number of troops on the Pakistan side after demilitarization be fixed at a figure between 3,000 and 6,000 and the number on the Indian side at between 12,000 and 18,000.

In his fourth report to the Council, on September 16, Mr. Graham said that there had been no agreement between the parties on the figures he had proposed. In order to reach agreement on demilitarization, he said, it was necessary either to establish the character and number of forces to be left on each side of the cease-fire line at the end of demilitarization, or to establish criteria to guide the parties in fixing the number of forces.

The Council, on December 22, adopted a resolution endorsing the general principles on which the United Nations Representative had sought to bring about agreement between India and Pakistan. It urged the two Governments to enter into immediate negotiations under the auspices of the Representative in order to reach agreement on the specific number of forces to remain on each side of the cease-fire line at the end of the period of demilitarization. That number, the Council added, should be between 3,000 and 6,000 on the Pakistan side of the cease-fire line and between 12,000 and 18,000 on the Indian side, as Mr. Graham had suggested.

During the discussion prior to adoption of the resolution, India told the Council that it was unable to accept the text, though it was prepared to join in talks in connection with the dispute. A force of 28,000 would be required on the Indian side of the line to maintain law and order and provide for the over-all security of the state. On the other side, a civil force of 4,000 would be sufficient, India contended.

India could not accept any parity, in either number or character of forces, between itself and Pakistan. It maintained that Kashmir's accession to India had been a legal act, while Pakistan had illegally occupied part of the state.

Pakistan said that it could go forward on the basis of the resolution, although it considered that the numbers suggested were not fair to its side of the line. It would agree to India's retaining 28,000 troops on the Indian side, with the question of disbandment and disarming of the Azad Kashmir forces to be taken up when the plebiscite administrator took over. Pakistan maintained that India's refusal to withdraw its troops was holding up the plebiscite.

In reply, India said that it was necessary to withdraw all armed formations from the Pakistan side, including Azad Kashmir troops.

Negotiations between the two Governments, at the ministerial level, began in Geneva on February 4, 1953, under the chairmanship of the United Nations Representative.

On March 27, Mr. Graham, in his fifth report to the Council, stated that the Geneva talks had not produced agreement. He had suggested revised figures on the number of forces to remain after demilitarization—21,000 on the Indian side and 6,000 on the Pakistan side. India, according to the report, did not agree to the retention of any military forces in the Azad Kashmir area, contending that a 4,000-man civil force would be sufficient there. Pakistan maintained that the arbitrary raising of the figures mentioned in the Council resolution would put the security of the Azad Kashmir area in serious jeopardy.

SECURITY COUNCIL CONSIDERATION IN 1957, 1962 AND 1964. On November 26, 1956, Pakistan informed the Security Council that a "so-called constituent assembly," meeting at Srinagar, had framed a constitution for Kashmir and that that part of the constitution integrating the state into India had come into force on November 17. Pakistan considered that this should be decided by a plebiscite.

At Pakistan's request, the Council began a series of meetings on Kashmir in January 1957. India told the Council that it stood by its commitments under resolutions of the United Nations Commission, but that Pakistan had committed aggression and must "vacate that aggression" and that, in view of the changed conditions, India could not forever regard past proposals as applicable or binding.

The Security Council declared that the convening of a constituent assembly, and any support by the parties of any such action, would not constitute a disposition of the state in accordance with the principles of a free and impartial plebiscite. The Council requested its President, Gunnar V. Jarring, of Sweden, to examine with the two Governments any proposals he considered likely to contribute towards settlement of the dispute, having regard to previous resolutions, and invited India and Pakistan to co-operate.

Mr. Jarring visited the two countries between March 14 and April 11, 1957. In his report, submitted on April 29, he said he was unable to report any concrete proposals likely to contribute towards a settlement. India's position, he indicated, was that discussions on preparations for a plebiscite could not begin until Pakistan had implemented those parts of the United Nations Commission's resolution of August 13, 1948, having to do with a military *status quo* and the creation of an atmosphere favourable to negotiations, and that the Council must express itself on what it considered Pakistan aggression, and Pakistan must "vacate that aggression." Pakistan, on the other hand, Mr. Jarring reported, considered that it had implemented the relevant parts of the Commission's resolution and that it was now time to implement those parts dealing with a plebiscite.

Mr. Jarring said that Pakistan had accepted his suggestion that the parties submit to arbitration the question of whether or not the first part of the Commission's resolution had been implemented, but that India maintained that such arbitration would not be appropriate, since it would be inconsistent with the sovereignty of Jammu and Kashmir and the rights and obligations of India in respect of the state.

On December 2, 1957, the Council requested the United Nations Representative, Mr. Graham, to make any recommendations to the parties for further appropriate action with a view to making progress towards implementing the Commission's resolutions and towards a peaceful settlement.

Mr. Graham submitted to the parties, on February 15, 1958, a five-point proposal calling for: (1) a renewed declaration by the two Governments appealing to their peoples to assist in creating an atmosphere favourable to negotiations and an undertaking to refrain from statements and actions which would aggravate the situation; (2) a reaffirmation by both Governments that they would respect the integrity of the existing cease-fire line; (3) a study of how the territory on the Pakistan side of the cease-fire line could be administered, with consideration to be given to the possibility of stationing a United Nations force there following withdrawal of the Pakistan army; (4) an early agreement between the two Governments on the holding of a plebiscite; and (5) a Prime Ministers conference between the two countries.

On March 28, Mr. Graham reported to the Council that Pakistan had agreed in principle to the five recommendations, but that India had been unable to accept them, considering that they had been made without regard to Pakistan's failure to implement past resolutions and that, moreover, India did not look with favour on the substance of the recommendations and regarded the Representative's approach as not feasible.

The Security Council met between February 1 and June 22, 1962 at the request of Pakistan, but took no decisions.

On May 18, 1964, after a series of meetings called at the request of Pakistan, the President of the Security Council set forth the points on which no differences of opinion appeared among Council members. The members had expressed their conviction that everything possible should be done to consolidate favourable elements and avoid jeopardizing advantages, which would require conciliation and moderation on the part of the parties and prudence and careful and vigilant attention on the part of the United Nations. The members had expressed the hope that the parties would abstain from any act that might aggravate the situation and that they would take measures to re-establish an atmosphere of moderation between the two countries and of peace and harmony among the communities. Finally, they had expressed the hope that the two countries would resume contacts as soon as possible to resolve their differences by negotiation.

The President reported that members had disagreed on the suggestion that the Secretary-General might be of assistance in facilitating resumption of negotiations. Some members considered that the negotiations might be complicated by the intervention of outside elements.

DEVELOPMENTS IN 1965.   The Security Council met on September 4, 1965, to consider a report by the Secretary-General, dated September 3, which stated that the 1949 cease-fire agreement had collapsed and that the Kashmir problem had again become acute.

In his report, the Secretary-General stated that, since the beginning of 1965, there had been a disturbing increase in the number of violations of the cease-fire line; as of mid-June, the investigations of the United Nations Military Observer Group in India and Pakistan (UNMOGIP) had confirmed that there had been 377 violations of the cease-fire line, 218 of which were committed by Pakistan and 159 by India.

The Secretary-General further reported that serious trouble had started on August 5, 1965, and consisted of a large number of violations by crossing of the line, by firing across it with artillery pieces and by the occupation of positions on the wrong side of the line.

The Chief Military Observer of UNMOGIP, General Robert H. Nimmo, had indicated to him, the Secretary-General stated, that the series of violations that had begun on August 5 were to a considerable extent in the form of armed men, generally not in uniform, crossing the cease-fire line from the Pakistan side for the purpose of armed action on the Indian side. There had also been heavy and prolonged artillery fire across the line from the Pakistan side on August 15-16, and similar incidents were reported from both sides with increasing frequency during the remainder of the month, followed by occupation of Pakistan positions by Indian army troops which crossed the line in several areas between August 15 and September 1.

The Secretary-General gave an account of the steps he had taken, including meetings with the permanent representatives of India and Pakistan, and the appeals which he had conveyed to the Prime Minister of India and the President of Pakistan on September 1.

The Secretary-General expressed the view that the restoration of the cease-fire and a return to normal conditions could be achieved only under the following conditions: (a) a willingness of both parties to respect the 1949 cease-fire agreement; (b) a readiness on the part of Pakistan to take effective steps to prevent crossings of the cease-fire line from the Pakistan side by armed men, whether or not in uniform; (c) evacuation by each party of positions of the other party now occupied and withdrawal of all armed personnel of each party to its own side of the line, which would include the withdrawal once more of Indian troops from Pakistan positions in the Kargil area; (d) a halt by both parties to the firing across the cease-fire line; and (e) allowing full freedom of movement and access to United Nations Observers by both parties on both sides of the line.

On September 4, the Council unanimously called upon both India and Pakistan to cease fire immediately and asked each of the two powers to withdraw to its own side of the cease-fire line.

At the Council's meeting on September 6, the Secretary-General circulated a report on new and serious developments. He said that no official response had been received from India or Pakistan to the Council's resolution of September 4. Reports from UNMOGIP indicated that the fighting had broadened and intensified. According to information received by UNMOGIP from the Pakistan army, Indian troops had attacked across the West Pakistan border and major attacks had been launched against Lahore, Sialkot and Kasur, all in Pakistan, by a large part of the Indian army.

At the Council meeting, India replied to Pakistan's charges of aggression against its territory by stating that its action was intended as self-defence and for the purpose of attacking bases from which Pakistan had launched aggression against Kashmir, which was a part of India.

In a resolution adopted the same day, the Council unanimously called on the parties to immediately cease hostilities in the entire area of conflict and to withdraw all armed personnel to the positions they held before August 5. The Council requested the Secretary-General to exert every possible effort to give effect to this resolution and to strengthen UNMOGIP.

Between September 7 and 15, the Secretary-General visited India and Pakistan for talks with the parties on implementation of the Council's resolutions. On September 14, he received a reply from India stating that it would agree to his appeal for a cease-fire, provided Pakistan also did so. A reply from Pakistan, received on the same day, said that Pakistan would welcome a cease-fire which provided for a self-executing arrangement for the final settlement of the India-Pakistan dispute.

On September 20, the Security Council adopted a resolution demanding that a cease-fire take effect on September 22 and calling on the two Governments to issue orders for a cease-fire and a subsequent withdrawal of all armed personnel to the positions held by them before August 5. The Council requested the Secretary-General to provide the necessary assistance to ensure supervision of the cease-fire and withdrawal of all armed personnel and called on all states to refrain from any action which might aggravate the situation. The Council also decided to consider, as soon as its call for a cease-fire and withdrawal of troops had been implemented, what steps could be taken to assist towards a settlement of the political problem underlying the conflict, and in the meantime it called on the two Governments to utilize all peaceful means to this end. Finally, the Council requested the Secretary-General to exert every possible effort to give effect to this resolution and to seek a peaceful solution.

Both India and Pakistan accepted the cease-fire demanded by the Council, and it entered into effect on September 22.

On September 23, the Secretary-General reported that he had decided to organize the observers who would supervise the cease-fire along the India-Pakistan border as the United Nations India-Pakistan Observation Mission (UNIPOM), an operation distinct from UNMOGIP in Kashmir. The next day, he announced the appointment of Major-General B. F. MacDonald, of Canada, as Chief Officer of UNIPOM. By September 27, he later reported, twenty-two UNIPOM observers had arrived in the area, and forty-nine were in transit or about to leave their home countries.

Meanwhile, forty-two additional observers had arrived in the area to strengthen UNMOGIP, with twenty-four others on the way.

On September 26, the Secretary-General reported to the Security Council that an artillery barrage and attack had occurred in the Lahore sector and that the cease-fire was not holding in that area. The following day, the Security Council unanimously demanded that the parties honour their commitments to the Council to observe the cease-fire and called on them to withdraw promptly all armed personnel as necessary steps in the full implementation of the September 20 resolution.

During the following month, the Secretary-General reported on numerous violations of the cease-fire investigated by United Nations observers. On October 18, he stated that although heavy fighting had decreased considerably, the existence of the cease-fire had to be considered precarious and that both sides had attempted to improve their positions by digging, wiring and mining in the forward areas or by edging forward for tactical purposes. Also on October 18, India and Pakistan accepted in principle a suggestion by the Secretary-General that their representatives meet with a suitable representative of his to formulate an agreed plan and schedule for withdrawals of armed personnel by both parties.

On November 5, the Security Council adopted a resolution requesting India and Pakistan to co-operate towards a full implementation of the cease-fire and withdrawal provisions of its resolution of September 20. It called on them to instruct their armed personnel to co-operate with the United Nations and cease all military activity, and insisted that there be an end to violations of the cease-fire.

The Council also demanded the prompt and unconditional carrying out of the proposal for a meeting on withdrawals of armed personnel, to be held by representatives of both parties and a representative of the Secretary-General. It urged that the meeting take place as soon as possible and that the withdrawal plan contain a time-limit on implementation.

During November and December, the Secretary-General continued to report on incidents occurring along the cease-fire line. At the end of December, a no-firing agreement at the military level was reached, followed by a general relaxation of tension along the front line and a marked decrease in the number of incidents.

On November 25, the Secretary-General announced the appointment of Brigadier-General Tulio Marambio, of Chile, as his Representative in talks between India and Pakistan on withdrawal of armed personnel. Talks beginning on January 3, 1966, led to an agreement on January 29 providing for disengagement and withdrawal, and implementation of the agreement began immediately.

Conclusion of this agreement followed a joint declaration at Tashkent, USSR, on January 10, by the Prime Minister of India and the President of Pakistan, stating that all armed personnel of their countries should be withdrawn not later than February 25 to the positions held by them before August 5, 1965.

On February 23, 1966, the Secretary-General reported to the Council that if the withdrawals were completed, as expected, by February 25, General Marambio's responsibilities would have come to an end, and his mission terminated, on February 28. The task of UNIPOM would also have been successfully completed, and that Mission would be disbanded no later than March 22. There would also be a gradual reduction of the fifty-nine new observers appointed in September 1965 to UNMOGIP.

On February 26, the Secretary-General reported that the troop withdrawals had been completed on schedule the day before, thus fulfilling the withdrawal provisions of the Council's resolutions.

Hyderabad Question

On August 21, 1948, the Government of Hyderabad drew the attention of the Security Council to a grave dispute which had arisen from

India's action in threatening Hyderabad with invasion and economic blockade, with the intent of coercing it into renunciation of its independence. India maintained that Hyderabad was not competent to bring this question to the Council, as it was not a state and was not independent.

The Council considered the subject during several meetings and received a number of communications pertaining to the question, some of them dealing with the right of Hyderabad to initiate the proceedings and some with the credentials of the Hyderabad delegation. The Council did not take any action on the matter, and after May 1949 no developments concerning the issue took place.

Indonesia

The question of Indonesia first came before the Security Council on January 21, 1946, when the Ukrainian SSR charged in a letter that military action against the local population in Indonesia by British and Japanese forces created a threat to international peace. The Japanese troops concerned were those which, after the surrender of Japan, had been empowered by the Allies to maintain law and order pending the arrival of British forces.

At a meeting held on February 7, 1946, the United Kingdom denied the charge that British troops had attacked the local population, and stated that the troops had defended themselves when attacked.

The Ukrainian SSR then proposed the setting up of a commission of inquiry, and Egypt proposed that British troops should not be used against the National Indonesian Movement and should be withdrawn from Indonesia as soon as the surrender of Japanese troops had been completed. Both proposals were rejected by the Council as they lacked the required number of votes, and the matter was considered closed.

On July 30, 1947, however, Australia and India drew the Council's attention to fighting between the Netherlands and the Republic of Indonesia. The Council, on August 1, called on both parties to cease hostilities. Shortly thereafter, the parties issued cease-fire orders, but some fighting continued, and on August 25 the Council requested members of the Council having consular representatives in Batavia to ask them to submit joint reports to the Council. The Council also offered its good offices in settling the political dispute through a committee to consist of two Council members, one selected by each of the parties, and a third chosen by those two. The members chosen were Australia (by the Republic of Indonesia), Belgium (by the Netherlands) and the United States (by Australia and Belgium).

As a result of negotiations conducted by the Good Offices Committee, the Netherlands and Indonesia signed a truce agreement on

January 17, 1948, and agreed on eighteen principles as the basis for a political settlement. However, in November 1948, the Committee notified the Council that there had been no progress towards a settlement and that, in fact, there had been an increase in political tension and a strain on the truce.

On December 18, the Netherlands denounced the truce agreement and commenced military operations against Indonesia. Meeting in emergency session, the Security Council, on December 24, called for a cessation of hostilities forthwith and the immediate release of the President of the Republic of Indonesia and other political prisoners taken since the renewal of hostilities. Four days later, it again called on the Netherlands to release the President and the other political prisoners.

On January 28, 1949, the Council further recommended the establishment of a federal, independent and sovereign United States of Indonesia, with transfer of sovereignty not later than July 1, 1950. The Good Offices Committee was named the United Nations Commission for Indonesia, with power to assist the parties in implementing the Council's resolution.

The Netherlands notified the Council on March 2 that it had lifted restrictions on the Republican leaders. It proposed a round-table conference at The Hague, at the earliest possible date, to arrange for hastening the transfer of sovereignty.

Three weeks later, the Council directed the Commission to assist the parties in implementing the Council's January 28 resolution and in arranging the conference. At the Commission's invitation, the Netherlands and Indonesian delegations met at Batavia, from April 14 to August 1, 1949, and agreed on the return of the Republican Government to its capital at Jogjakarta, on measures to halt guerrilla warfare, on discontinuance of military operations by the Netherlands Government, on the immediate and unconditional release of all political prisoners and on the holding of a round-table conference.

Republican leaders returned to the capital on July 6. Evacuation by Dutch troops and occupation by Indonesian forces were completed under the observation of United Nations military observers.

The Round-Table Conference met at The Hague from August 23 to November 2, 1949, with representatives of the Netherlands, the Republic of Indonesia, the Federal Consultative Assembly (representing areas of Indonesia other than the Republic) and the United Nations Commission for Indonesia participating.

The Conference drew up a Charter of Transfer of Sovereignty, which stated that the Netherlands unconditionally and irrevocably transferred complete sovereignty over Indonesia to the Republic of the United States of Indonesia and recognized the Republic as an independent and sovereign state. New Guinea, however, was to continue under the Netherlands, but within one year its political status was to be determined through negotiations between the Republic and the Netherlands.

The General Assembly, in December 1949, welcomed the results of the Round-Table Conference. The formal transfer of sovereignty to the Republic took place on December 27, 1949. In the months that followed, the United Nations Commission continued to observe the implementation of The Hague agreements.

On September 28, 1950, on the recommendation of the Security Council, the General Assembly admitted Indonesia to the United Nations.

Question of West Irian (West New Guinea)

On August 17, 1954, Indonesia requested the inclusion of "The Question of West Irian (West New Guinea)" in the agenda of the ninth session of the General Assembly. In view of the unsuccessful negotiations on this question between Indonesia and the Netherlands, Indonesia said it considered the problem—if left unsolved—a latent threat to the peace and security of that part of the world.

During the Assembly's debate, the Netherlands stressed that its administration of West New Guinea constituted a peaceful endeavour to create conditions for the self-determination of the population. A threat to the peace could occur only if Indonesia were to resort to aggressive action. Indonesia claimed that West Irian was an integral part of Indonesia and that "complete sovereignty over Indonesia" had been transferred by the Netherlands.

The Assembly took no action on the issue and the question was reintroduced at the tenth session, in 1955, when the Assembly adopted a resolution expressing the hope that negotiations between the Governments of Indonesia and the Netherlands would be fruitful.

In 1961, the Netherlands introduced in the Assembly a draft resolution which noted that the Netherlands was prepared to implement the 1960 Declaration on the Granting of Independence to Colonial Countries and Peoples (see page 396) and to transfer sovereignty to the people of the territory as soon as possible. But "recognizing the paramount importance of respect for the principle of self-determination," the draft proposed that a United Nations Commission for West New Guinea be set up to inquire into conditions in the territory, to ascertain the views of the inhabitants and to determine the possibility of a United Nations plebiscite "to register the wishes of the population" and of interim United Nations administration. A second draft resolution, originally sponsored by India, urged the two parties to negotiate but did not mention the principle of self-determination. A third draft, submitted by thirteen African powers, urged negotiations but stressed the importance of self-determination for the Papuans and, failing agreement by the Netherlands and Indonesia, envisaged a temporary "international system" of administration. The Assembly's debate covered all the issues once more, but neither the Indian nor the African-sponsored proposals received a two-thirds vote in plenary session; the Netherlands draft was not brought to a vote.

In December 1961, fighting broke out in the West New Guinea area between Dutch and Indonesian forces. On December 19, Secretary-General U Thant sent identical cables to the Prime Minister of the Netherlands and to the President of Indonesia expressing his deep concern over the possibility of a serious situation arising between Indonesia and the Netherlands and expressing his sincere hope that the two parties might come together to seek a peaceful solution to the problem. On January 15, 1962, U Thant sent another appeal, and on January 17, after a naval clash off West New Guinea, he asked that instructions be given to the permanent representatives of the two Governments to the United Nations to discuss with him the possibilities of a peaceful settlement of the whole question in conformity with the purposes and principles of the United Nations Charter. Both Governments then instructed their permanent representatives to consult with him.

After these consultations, the Secretary-General again appealed to the Netherlands, this time to agree to the release and repatriation of Indonesian prisoners "as a humanitarian gesture which might help in easing tensions all round"; the repatriation was completed on March 11.

Acting as mediator representing U Thant in those talks, Ambassador Ellsworth Bunker, of the United States, put forward proposals for negotiations between the two Governments.

In July, the Secretary-General announced that talks had resumed between the two countries in the presence of Ambassador Bunker "on the basis of the principles of the Bunker plan," and that a preliminary agreement had been reached by the Indonesian and Netherlands representatives regarding the transfer of authority over West New Guinea.

The agreement providing for the transfer of the administration of West New Guinea (West Irian) and for the eventual self-determination of the people was signed on August 15, at United Nations Headquarters, by the representatives of Indonesia and the Netherlands, and was ratified by the two Governments on September 20. It provided for a United Nations Temporary Executive Authority to take over administration of the former Netherlands dependency on October 1 for an interim period ending on May 1, 1963, after which full administrative responsibility for the territory would be transferred to Indonesia. Also under the agreement, Indonesia would make arrangements for the self-determination, by 1969, of the 700,000 Papuans of the territory by means of an act of self-determination, to be supervised by the United Nations, designed to give the people a choice of retaining or severing ties with Indonesia.

The General Assembly approved the agreement on September 21 and commended the Secretary-General for his part in bringing about the settlement.

The United Nations Temporary Executive Authority took over the administration of West New Guinea from the Netherlands on October 1, 1962, and carried on vital governmental functions until May 1, 1963, when the administration was transferred to Indonesia as scheduled. A security force of 1,500 was supplied by Pakistan. The cost of operations was borne by Indonesia and the Netherlands.

Korea

The independence of Korea was first stated formally as an Allied war aim at the Cairo Conference in 1943. In 1945, Korea was occupied by the USSR and the United States in order to accept the surrender of the Japanese troops north and south, respectively, of the 38th parallel. Under the Moscow Agreement of 1945, the occupying powers established a joint commission to set up a Provisional Korean Democratic Government. The Joint Commission's negotiations in 1946-1947 reached a deadlock, and the United States submitted the problem to the General Assembly in 1947. The Assembly, on November 14, created a nine-member temporary commission on Korea to facilitate the establishment of a National Government of Korea by means of duly elected Korean representatives and to provide for an early withdrawal of the occupation forces. Czechoslovakia, the Byelorussian SSR, Poland, the Ukrainian SSR, the USSR and Yugoslavia did not participate in the voting, and the Ukrainian SSR did not take its seat on the Commission.

The Commission was not allowed access to North Korea, but it observed elections in South Korea which led to the formation of a government there on August 15, 1948. In September, a separate government came into being in North Korea. In December, the General Assembly declared that the Government of the Republic of Korea had been established as a lawful government and the only such government in Korea. The Assembly recommended the withdrawal of the occupying forces and established a seven-member commission to bring about the unification of Korea and the integration of all Korean forces.

In July 1949, the United Nations Commission on Korea reported that it had not been able to make any progress towards unification. It had observed the withdrawal of United States forces but not the reported withdrawal of USSR forces from North Korea in December 1948. In October 1949, the Commission was assigned the additional task of observing and reporting developments which might lead to military conflict in Korea.

In 1948, as well as in 1949, the USSR had maintained that the

General Assembly did not have the right to act on Korea since the matter was covered by the Moscow Agreement and should be dealt with by the Allied Commission. The establishment of the United Nations Commission on Korea, it stated, was illegal; the unification of Korea must be left to the Korean people.

On June 25, 1950, the Secretary-General was informed, by the United States and by the United Nations Commission on Korea, that North Korean forces had invaded the Republic of Korea that morning and that, according to a statement by the Republic of Korea, they had attacked the Republic all along the 38th parallel.

On the same day, the Security Council, meeting at the request of the United States, determined, by 9 votes to none, with 1 abstention (Yugoslavia) and one member absent (USSR),* that the armed attack by North Korea was a breach of the peace and called for immediate cessation of hostilities, withdrawal of North Korean forces to the 38th parallel and the assistance of members of the United Nations in carrying out the resolution.

On June 27, the Council adopted a United States draft resolution noting that the authorities in North Korea had neither ceased hostilities nor withdrawn their armed forces and recommending that members furnish such assistance to the Republic of Korea as might be necessary to repel the armed attack and restore international peace and security in the area. The vote was 7 to 1 (Yugoslavia), with 1 member absent (USSR), and with Egypt and India not voting but later indicating their positions as abstention from and acceptance of the resolution, respectively.

On the same day, the United States announced that it had ordered its air and sea forces to give cover and support to the troops of the Korean Government and, three days later, it informed the Council that it had ordered a naval blockade of the Korean coast and authorized the use of ground forces as a further response to the June 27 resolution.

Fifty-one member states expressed support for the stand taken by the Council, while five, including the USSR, together with the People's Republic of China and the Democratic People's Republic of Korea, shared the view that the June 27 resolution was illegal because it had been adopted in the absence of two permanent members of the Council, the People's Republic of China and the USSR. The Soviet Union also declared that the events in Korea were the result of an unprovoked attack by South Korean troops and demanded the cessation of United States intervention.

On July 7, the Council, by 7 votes to none, with 3 abstentions (Egypt, India and Yugoslavia) and 1 member absent (USSR), re-

___

* The USSR had been absent from the Council since January 13, 1950, over the representation of China but resumed its seat in the Council beginning August 1 when the presidency of the Council again devolved upon it in accordance with the system of monthly rotation.

quested all member states providing military forces in pursuance of the Council's resolutions to make them available to a unified command under the United States. The next day, General Douglas MacArthur, of the United States, was designated Commanding General. Subsequently, combat units were provided by the following sixteen member states: Australia, Belgium, Canada, Colombia, Ethiopia, France, Greece, Luxembourg, the Netherlands, New Zealand, the Philippines, Thailand, Turkey, the Union of South Africa, the United Kingdom and the United States. In addition, five nations—Denmark, India, Italy, Norway and Sweden—supplied medical units. The Republic of Korea also placed all its military forces under the Unified Command.

Korea's capital, Seoul, fell on June 28, 1950, and in August the United Nations forces were confined within a small area in south-east Korea. By mid-October, however, following an amphibious landing at Inchon, they had regained almost all the territory of the Republic of Korea and were advancing far into North Korea.

Meanwhile, on October 7, the General Assembly adopted a resolution which recommended that "all appropriate steps be taken to ensure conditions of stability throughout Korea"; established the United Nations Commission for the Unification and Rehabilitation of Korea (UNCURK) of seven member states—Australia, Chile, the Netherlands, Pakistan, Philippines, Thailand and Turkey—to bring about the establishment of a unified, independent and democratic government of all Korea; and recommended that the United Nations forces should not remain in Korea otherwise than for the objectives stated and that all necessary measures be taken to accomplish the economic rehabilitation of Korea.

INTERVENTION OF THE PEOPLE'S REPUBLIC OF CHINA.   On November 6, 1950, a special report of the United Nations Command informed the Security Council that United Nations forces were in contact in North Korea with military units of the People's Republic of China. A representative of the People's Republic of China participated in the Council's subsequent combined discussion of complaints of aggression upon the Republic of Korea and of armed invasion of Taiwan (Formosa) (for the latter, see page 133).

On November 30, because of the negative vote of a permanent member (USSR), the Council did not adopt a resolution calling, among other things, on all states and authorities to refrain from assisting the North Korean authorities, and affirming that it was United Nations policy to hold inviolate the Chinese frontier with Korea. The Council rejected by a vote of 1 (USSR) to 9, with India not participating, a draft resolution condemning the United States for armed aggression against Chinese territory and armed intervention in Korea and demanding withdrawal of United States forces.

The Security Council, which had been unable to agree on a solution, decided unanimously, on January 31, 1951, to remove the item "Complaint of aggression upon the Republic of Korea" from its agenda. Meanwhile, in 1950, the General Assembly included the item "Intervention of the Central People's Government of the People's Republic of China in Korea" in its agenda and established a three-man Cease-Fire Group—the President of the Assembly, Canada and India —to recommend satisfactory cease-fire arrangements in Korea. The Group's programme, aimed at achieving a cease-fire by successive stages, was transmitted to the People's Republic of China on January 13, 1951.

After discussing the Chinese reply to the Cease-Fire Group's programme, the Assembly adopted a resolution, on February 1, 1951, which noted that the People's Republic of China had not accepted the United Nations proposals to end hostilities. The Assembly found that the People's Republic of China had engaged in aggression in Korea and called on it to withdraw its forces and nationals from Korea. The Assembly also requested a committee—the Additional Measures Committee—to consider measures for meeting the aggression, reaffirmed the policy of achieving United Nations objectives in Korea by peaceful means and created a Good Offices Committee, consisting of the President of the Assembly, Sweden and Mexico, to further those ends.

On May 18, the Assembly, in the absence of a satisfactory progress report from the Good Offices Committee, recommended that all states apply an embargo on the shipment, to areas under the control of the Chinese Central People's Government and of the North Korean authorities, of arms, ammunition and implements of war, items useful in their production, petroleum and transportation materials. The USSR and four other members did not participate in the voting on the ground that the matter was exclusively within the jurisdiction of the Security Council.

ARMISTICE NEGOTIATIONS. Armistice negotiations between the military commanders of the opposing sides began in Korea on July 10, 1951, but were recessed over the question of exchange and repatriation of prisoners until April 1953, when agreement was reached on the exchange of sick and wounded prisoners, followed by an agreement on June 8 on the question of all prisoners of war.

The prisoners-of-war agreement, which was later incorporated in the Armistice Agreement, provided for a United Nations Repatriation Commission, consisting of Czechoslovakia, India (Chairman), Poland, Sweden and Switzerland. No force or threat of force was to be used against the prisoners.

The Armistice Agreement was signed on July 27, 1953, by the Commanders of the United Nations Command, the Korean People's Army and the Chinese People's Volunteers, and hostilities ceased. The Agreement established a demarcation line and demilitarized zone; provided that no reinforcing personnel or combat equipment be introduced except on a replacement basis; set up a Military Armistice Commission of representatives from the two sides to supervise and settle any violations of the Agreement and a Neutral Nations Supervisory Commission of four—Sweden and Switzerland, appointed by the United Nations Command, and Czechoslovakia and Poland, by the other side—to observe and investigate troop withdrawals and weapons replacement; recommended to the Governments of the countries concerned a political conference within three months to settle, through negotiation, the question of the withdrawal of all foreign forces from Korea and the peaceful settlement of the Korean question; and declared that the Agreement would remain in effect until superseded by mutually acceptable changes or by provision in an agreement for a peaceful settlement at the political level between both sides.

Shortly thereafter, the sixteen powers contributing forces to United Nations action in Korea affirmed their determination to carry out the Armistice Agreement and to resist promptly in case of renewal of armed attack.

On August 28, 1953, the General Assembly reaffirmed United Nations objectives of the achievement by peaceful means of a unified, independent and democratic Korea under a representative form of government and the full restoration of peace in the area, and recommended that those member states contributing armed forces under the Unified Command should participate in the political conference envisaged in the Armistice Agreement. The participation of the USSR in the conference was also provided for.

In September, the People's Republic of China and North Korea rejected the Assembly's proposal. Subsequent negotiations on the conference between the two sides at Panmunjom broke down in December. On February 23, 1954, however, following a meeting in Berlin, the Foreign Ministers of France, the USSR, the United Kingdom and the United States announced that they would convene a conference at Geneva for the purpose of reaching a peaceful settlement of the Korean question. The conference would be composed of representatives of their Governments, the People's Republic of China, North and South Korea, and other countries whose armed forces had participated in the Korean hostilities.

The conference failed to find an agreed solution to the Korean question. On November 11, 1954, fifteen of the sixteen members of the United Nations which had participated in the Korean action and had been present at Geneva (the Union of South Africa was absent) reported that the failure of the conference did not prejudice the armistice, which remained in effect. The report included a declaration, to which the Republic of Korea was an additional signatory, of two principles: (1) the United Nations, under its Charter, was fully and rightfully empowered to take collective action to repel aggression, to restore peace and security and to extend its good offices in seeking a peaceful settlement in Korea; (2) in order to establish a unified, independent and democratic Korea, genuinely free elections, under United Nations supervision, should be held to constitute the Korean National Assembly, in which representation should be in direct proportion to the indigenous population in Korea.

The Soviet Union, among others, considered the Geneva Conference report biased and inappropriate to serve as a basis of a solution. It supported a programme for unification, to be based on an agreement between North and South Korea to be concluded at an all-Korean conference. Free elections, under international supervision and in the whole of Korea, were called for, as well as the withdrawal of all foreign troops before the elections.

The United Nations Commission for the Unification and Rehabilitation of Korea (UNCURK) continues to represent the United Nations in Korea and to observe and report annually to the General Assembly on political and economic developments in the Republic of Korea.

RELIEF AND REHABILITATION OF KOREA.   The Security Council, on July 31, 1950, inaugurated an emergency programme for civilian relief through the United Nations Command, with the Secretary-General and, later, the Agent General of UNKRA (*see below*), acting as clearing agents for requests and offers of assistance. With contributions valued at nearly $50 million from some thirty-two member states, seven non-member states, specialized agencies and non-governmental organizations and, in particular, assistance valued at more than $400 million from the United States, the United Nations Command carried out by September 1953, through a Civil Assistance Command, a large-scale civilian and refugee relief programme.

The United Nations Korean Reconstruction Agency (UNKRA) was established by the General Assembly on December 1, 1950, "to help the Republic of Korea and its people towards the restoration of their war-wrecked economy." By June 1958, when UNKRA's operational activities were concluded, thirty-four United Nations members and five non-member states had contributed over $141 million to UNKRA and over $7 million had been received in miscellaneous income.

OTHER MATTERS RELATED TO KOREA.   *Prisoners of War.* By September 23, 1953, the Neutral Nations Supervisory Commission appointed under the Armistice Agreement had assumed custody of 22,604 prisoners from the United Nations Command and 359 from the Korean People's Army and the Chinese People's Volunteers who had not exercised their right of repatriation. Because the political conference envisaged in the Armistice Agreement had not materialized at the end of the ninety-day period allotted for explanation of the right of repatriation, the Commission referred to the two commands the question of disposition of those prisoners who had not exercised their right of repatriation. Before the Commission dissolved itself on February 21, 1954, the custodial force, India, had restored to the United Nations Command some 21,805 prisoners, two-thirds of them Chinese and one-third Korean, without, however, declaring their civilian status. The United Nations Command released these former prisoners to civilian status. By 1961, all ex-prisoners had been resettled in the countries they had chosen, Argentina and Brazil providing resettlement facilities to many of them.

Geneva Protocol Against Use of Bacterial Weapons. In June 1952, at the request of the USSR, the Security Council considered the question of an appeal to states to accede to the 1925 Geneva Protocol for the Prohibition of the Use of Bacterial Weapons. Only six states among those which had acceded to the Protocol had not yet ratified it, the USSR pointed out. These were Brazil, El Salvador, Japan, Nicaragua, the United States and Uruguay.

The United States maintained that the Protocol had been withdrawn from the United States Senate in 1947, together with other treaties which had become obsolete. Citing the reservations made to the Protocol by the USSR, the United States said that, by charging the United Nations Command in Korea with the use of bacterial weapons, the USSR had set the stage for using the weapons itself should it declare that states resisting aggression in Korea were its enemies. The United States declared that it had never used germ warfare in the Second World War or at any other time; the United States further declared that it had not used and was not using germ warfare of any kind in Korea.

A USSR draft resolution, by which the Council would have appealed to states to accede to the Geneva Protocol, was rejected by 10 votes to 1 (USSR). A United States draft resolution proposed the complete elimination of weapons of mass destruction through the establishment of an effective system which would make their use impossible. The draft would further have referred the USSR draft to the Disarmament Commission. It was rejected by the Council because of the negative vote of the USSR.

Request for Investigation of Alleged Bacterial Warfare. The Security Council, in June 1952, also decided to include in its agenda the item "Question of a request for investigation of alleged bacterial warfare," which had been proposed by the United States. A USSR proposal to invite representatives of the People's Republic of China and the Democratic People's Republic of Korea was rejected by the Council.

The United States submitted a draft resolution which noted the concerted dissemination by certain governments and authorities of grave accusations alleging the use of bacterial warfare by United Nations forces in Korea and recalled that the United Nations Command had requested an impartial investigation by the International Committee of the Red Cross. The proposal then called upon all governments and authorities concerned to accord full co-operation to the Committee.

This draft resolution, as well as a second one also submitted by the United States, failed of adoption because of negative votes by the USSR.

At the request of the United States, the General Assembly, in 1952, considered the "Question of impartial investigation of charges of use by United Nations forces of bacteriological warfare." An explanatory memorandum stated that, since February 1952, such charges had been reiterated by Poland and the USSR, in spite of authoritative denials and offers of impartial investigation.

After the President of the Assembly had received an indication from all governments and authorities concerned of their acceptance of the proposed investigation, the Assembly, on April 23, 1953, decided to establish a commission which would carry out an investigation of the charges.

On July 28, the President of the Assembly notified members that the proposal to establish the commission of investigation had been accepted by Japan, the Republic of Korea and the United States and that no other replies had been received.

After the Assembly had decided to include the item in the agenda of its eighth session, the United States, on October 26, 1953, transmitted to the Secretary-General sworn statements by officers of the United States armed forces repudiating confessions regarding bacterial warfare which they had made while prisoners of war, charging that the confessions had been extorted. A USSR draft resolution calling upon all states which had not done so to accede to or ratify the Geneva Protocol of 1925 was referred by the Assembly to the Disarmament Commission.

Taiwan (Formosa) and Other Questions

Concurrently with the question of Korea, both the General Assembly and the Security Council considered, during 1950, a number of questions concerning Taiwan (Formosa) and complaints by the Chinese People's Republic and the USSR alleging United States attacks on the Chinese mainland.

The Security Council, on November 28, 1950, heard a representative of the People's Republic of China who recalled the June 27 announcement by President Harry S. Truman that the United States Navy had been ordered to prevent attacks on Formosa. The Chinese representative said that this constituted aggression against China because, according to the Cairo Declaration and the Potsdam communiqué of 1945, Formosa was Chinese territory.

The United States said that its action was designed to keep the peace and protect the security of United Nations troops in Korea and that while the United States Navy had orders to prevent attacks on Formosa, whose "liberation" had been threatened by the Chinese mainland forces, it had also been ordered to prevent attacks on the mainland by Marshal Chiang Kai-shek's forces based on Formosa.

After the Council had rejected proposals, sponsored by the USSR, condemning the United States for aggression, the USSR raised in the General Assembly the matter of United States aggression in Taiwan and United States air attacks on the Chinese mainland. At the same time, the United States proposed Assembly consideration of the status of Taiwan. In view of the priority then being attached to the question of the intervention by the Chinese People's Republic in Korea (*see page* 128), consideration of these items by the General Assembly was postponed.

In 1954, the USSR placed two items on the Assembly's agenda, one complaining of aggression against the Chinese mainland by forces "under the control" of the United States operating from Formosa and seeking a declaration by the Assembly that the United States take steps to end such aggression, and the other complaining of "piratical acts" by naval vessels based on Formosa and controlled by the United States Navy. The declaration sought by the USSR on the first complaint was not adopted. As regards the second, the General Assembly, on December 17, adopted a resolution by which it transmitted the records of the discussion to the International Law Commission, recalling that the Commission had been requested to complete its final reports on the law of the sea.

The question of Formosa was revived in another form in January 1955, when New Zealand requested the Security Council to consider armed hostilities between the forces of the People's Republic of China and the Republic of China in the area of Taiwan. New Zealand stated that since both Governments had the support of powerful forces, the hostilities constituted a danger to peace in the area.

At the same time, the USSR placed on the Council's agenda the question of United States aggression against the Chinese People's Republic in the area of Taiwan. Although the Council approved a proposal to invite a representative of the People's Republic of China, the invitation was not accepted because the latter considered that the liberation of Taiwan was its internal affair and because it could not participate in the deliberations of the Council until its representative attended in the name of China. The USSR request for a consideration of the item proposed by it was rejected by the Council and consideration of the New Zealand item was adjourned.

China's Complaint Against the USSR

In September 1949, China submitted to the General Assembly the question of "Threats to the political independence and territorial integrity of China and to the peace of the Far East, resulting from Soviet violations of the Sino-Soviet Treaty of Friendship and Alliance of August 14, 1945, and from Soviet violations of the Charter of the United Nations."

The USSR, the Byelorussian SSR, Czechoslovakia, Poland and the Ukrainian SSR announced that they would neither take part in the debate nor be bound by any decisions taken.

China called on the Assembly to pronounce judgment on the USSR for obstructing the efforts of the Chinese National Government in Manchuria and to recommend that all member states of the United Nations refrain from giving further military and economic aid to the Chinese communists.

The General Assembly, on December 8, 1949, called on all states to: (1) respect the political independence of China and be guided by the principles of the United Nations in their relations with China; (2) respect the right of the people of China to choose freely their political institutions and to maintain a government independent of foreign control; (3) respect existing treaties relating to China; and (4) refrain from seeking to acquire spheres of influence or to obtain special rights or privileges within the territory of China.

On February 1, 1952, the Assembly adopted another resolution which stated that the USSR, in its relations with China since the surrender of Japan, had failed to carry out the Treaty of Friendship and Alliance.

Representation of China in the United Nations

On November 18, 1949, the Foreign Minister of the Central People's Government of the People's Republic of China informed the President of the General Assembly and the Secretary-General that his Government repudiated the legal status of the delegation of the Chinese National Government, which, he said, had no right to speak for the people of China in the United Nations. On January 8, 1950, he informed the Security Council that his Government considered that the presence of the existing Chinese delegation in the Council was illegal and that it should be expelled. The USSR then proposed that the Council decide not to recognize the credentials of the representative of the "Kuomintang group" and to exclude him. When this proposal was rejected, on January 13, the representative of the USSR declared that his delegation would not participate in the Council's work until the "Kuomintang representative" had been removed, nor would the Soviet Government recognize as legal any decision adopted with his participation. The representative of the USSR then left the Council Chamber and did not return until August 1; during this period, the USSR and certain states supporting its position withdrew from other United Nations organs of which China was a member.

At a meeting of the Council on August 1, 1950, the representative of the USSR, who was President of the Council that month, ruled that the representative of the "Kuomintang group" did not represent China and therefore could not take part in the Council's meetings. The Council overruled the President, however, and two days later rejected a Soviet proposal to include in the agenda an item entitled "Recognition of the representative of the Central People's Government of the People's Republic of China as the representative of China."

Also in August 1950, the Minister for Foreign Affairs of the People's Republic of China requested that the necessary arrangements be made for the delegation of the People's Republic of China to attend the fifth session of the General Assembly. The Assembly established a special committee which failed to agree on any recommendations in the matter, and accordingly no decision was taken at the fifth session.

Since then, the question of the representation of China has been before the Assembly at each session and before other United Nations organs and specialized agencies. Between 1956 and 1959, India made repeated proposals for placing the question on the agenda, and in 1960 a similar proposal was made by the USSR, but in each instance the Assembly decided to reject the request. The question was also raised in the Credentials Committee.

In 1961, the Assembly decided that any proposal to change the representation of China was an "important question" under Article 18 of the Charter, thus requiring a two-thirds majority, and it rejected the proposal that China be represented by the Government of the People's Republic. Again in 1962, the Assembly rejected a Soviet proposal which would have had the Assembly "remove the Chiang Kai-shek representatives from all United Nations organs" and "invite representatives of the Government of the People's Republic of China to occupy China's place in the United Nations and all its organs." In 1963, the Assembly rejected a similar proposal made jointly by Albania and Cambodia.

At its twentieth session, in 1965, the Assembly reaffirmed its 1961 resolution that any proposal to change the representation of China in the United Nations was an important question and required a two-thirds majority. The Assembly then voted on a draft resolution, sponsored by Albania, Algeria, Burundi, Cambodia, Congo (Brazzaville), Cuba, Ghana, Guinea, Mali, Romania and Syria, which asked the Assembly to "restore all its rights to the People's Republic of China and recognize its representatives as the only lawful representatives of

China." The resolution received 47 votes in favour, 47 against, with 20 abstentions. It was therefore not adopted.

Complaint by Burma

The General Assembly, on March 31, 1953, included in its agenda the item entitled "Complaint by the Union of Burma regarding aggression against it by the Government of the Republic of China."

Burma stated that Kuomintang troops had crossed the border into Burma in 1950 and had refused to submit to disarmament and internment, that engagements had taken place between them and the Burmese army and that, by 1953, the number of Kuomintang troops had increased to about 12,000.

China replied that the idea of aggression against Burma had never entered the mind of the Chinese Government and that the army led by General Li Mi was no longer part of the regular forces of the Republic of China nor under the physical control of its Government.

On April 23, 1953, the General Assembly deplored the presence of foreign troops in Burma, condemned their hostile acts against that country and declared that they must be disarmed and either agree to internment or leave Burma forthwith.

On December 4, 1953, the Assembly again urged the evacuation of these forces. In 1954, it noted that nearly 7,000 persons had been evacuated and invited Burma to report on the situation as appropriate.

Request of Thailand

On May 29, 1954, Thailand brought to the attention of the Security Council the situation in Indo-China. Thailand stated that a very real danger existed that fighting in neighbouring territories might spread to Thailand and to other countries in the area. The Viet Minh forces which still remained in Laos and Cambodia were well organized; there was evidence that they had received support from outside Indo-China and that these forces intended to overthrow the legal governments of Cambodia and Laos. Thailand further stated that the propaganda of the Viet Minh and of the foreign government with which it was associated had spread serious and false charges against Thailand and that within Thailand itself, alien elements obedient to the political philosophy of the Viet Minh had been disquietingly active. A Thai draft resolution requesting the aid of the Peace Observation Commission failed of adoption because of the negative vote of the USSR.

In a letter of July 7 to the Secretary-General, the Thai Government proposed that an item entitled "Request of Thailand for observation under the Peace Observation Commission" be placed on the agenda of the eighth session of the General Assembly, which, technically, was still in session and could therefore be reconvened. On August 20, 1954, however, Thailand informed the Secretary-General that it would not press for a resumption of the eighth session of the Assembly.

Cambodia and Thailand

On November 29, 1958, Cambodia informed the Secretary-General that Thailand was threatening the peace by concentrating troops and military equipment on the frontier between the two countries and that Thailand had occupied the temple of Preah Vihear, which Cambodia considered part of its territory.

Thailand replied that while it had increased police enforcements along the border to prevent armed raids and infiltration by elements from Cambodia, it had not concentrated troops or military equipment. Thailand added that it was prepared to welcome a United Nations representative to observe the situation in the border area.

In response to an invitation by the two Governments, the Secretary-General, on December 22, designated Johan Bech-Friis, of Sweden, as his Special Representative, to help Cambodia and Thailand find a way out of their difficulties.

The Special Representative visited Cambodia and Thailand between January 20 and February 23, 1959. On February 6, it was announced that the two Governments had decided to re-establish normal diplomatic relations.

On October 6, Cambodia asked the International Court of Justice to adjudge that sovereignty over the Preah Vihear temple belonged to Cambodia and that Thailand should withdraw its forces from the area. On June 15, 1962, by 9 votes to 3, the Court found that the temple was situated in territory under Cambodia's sovereignty and that Thailand was obliged to withdraw any military or police forces stationed by it at the temple (*see also page* 441).

On October 19, the Secretary-General informed the Security Council that Cambodia and Thailand had exchanged accusations of aggression and had asked him to send a personal representative to inquire into the difficulties. In response, he appointed Nils G. Gussing, of Sweden, who arrived in the area on October 26.

On December 18, the Secretary-General reported that the parties had agreed that a Special Representative of the Secretary-General be appointed for a period of one year beginning on January 1, 1963. All costs of the mission were to be shared equally by the two Governments. Mr. Gussing then returned to the area as the Special Representative. The mission was withdrawn at the end of 1964 at the suggestion of Thailand and with the concurrence of Cambodia.

Question of Laos

In the introduction to his annual report to the General Assembly in 1959, the Secretary-General stated that during the course of the year "difficulties have developed at the north-eastern border of Laos," and he called attention to communications received on the matter.

On September 4, 1959, the Foreign Minister of Laos asked for assistance by the United Nations, and in particular the dispatch of an emergency force, to halt aggression along the north-eastern frontier of Laos by elements from North Viet-Nam. On September 5, the Secretary-General asked the President of the Security Council to convene the Council urgently to consider the Laotian request.

The Council considered the item and adopted a resolution, after having decided, over the objections of the USSR, that the subject matter of the resolution was of a procedural nature and that therefore its approval did not require the unanimity of the five permanent members. The resolution asked that a sub-committee, consisting of Argentina, Italy, Japan and Tunisia, examine the statements made concerning Laos, conduct inquiries into the matter and report to the Council. The USSR representative declared that the resolution had been adopted in violation of the Charter and the rules of procedure and that he therefore regarded it as illegal and not binding upon anyone.

The sub-committee visited Laos between September 15 and October 13, 1959, at the invitation of the Laotian Government. In its report, the sub-committee stated that the military action in Laos had been "of a guerrilla character" but that it appeared from statements of the Laotian authorities and of some witnesses that certain of the hostile operations "must have had a centralized co-ordination."

In the meantime, the Secretary-General, continuing his consultations with Laos, accepted on November 8 an invitation from the Laotian Government to visit the country in order to obtain independent and full knowledge of the problem.

After discussions with representatives of the Laotian Government, the Secretary-General instructed Sakari Tuomioja, Executive Secretary of the Economic Commission for Europe, to review the economic situation of Laos. In his report, Mr. Tuomioja made a series of proposals for the economic development of Laos within the general framework of that country's neutrality.

After a study of Mr. Tuomioja's report, the Secretary-General asked Roberto M. Heurtematte, United Nations Commissioner for Technical Assistance, to go to Laos and discuss the implementation of Mr. Tuomioja's recommendations.

The Laotian problem was later dealt with through direct negotiations between the interested parties.

Question of Tibet

The question of Tibet was discussed by the General Assembly in 1959 at the request of the Federation of Malaya and of Ireland, which said that there was *prima facie* evidence of an attempt by the People's Republic of China to destroy the traditional way of life of the Tibetan people.

The USSR and countries supporting it considered the accusation baseless. They held that since Tibet was an integral part of China, consideration of the case constituted a violation of Article 2, paragraph 7, of the Charter. Several members, although expressing concern at developments in Tibet, also believed that Article 2, paragraph 7, of the Charter prevented the Assembly from taking any action on the question.

Nevertheless, on October 21, 1959, the Assembly adopted a resolution affirming its belief that respect for the principles of the United Nations Charter and the Universal Declaration of Human Rights was essential for the evolution of a peaceful world order based on the rule of law. The resolution called for respect for the fundamental human rights of the Tibetan people and for their distinctive cultural and religious life.

At its sixteenth session the General Assembly, in a resolution adopted on December 20, 1961, reaffirmed its conviction regarding respect of the Charter and the Universal Declaration of Human Rights and renewed its call for the cessation of practices which deprived the Tibetan people of their fundamental human rights and freedoms, including their right to self-determination.

The item was considered again at the twentieth session, in 1965, when the General Assembly, on December 18, adopted a similar resolution.

Question Concerning Goa, Damao and Diu

In a series of letters addressed to the President of the Security Council between December 8 and 16, 1961, Portugal stated that India had started a military build-up on the frontiers of Goa, Damao and Diu and had violated the Portuguese frontier and air space in an attitude of clear provocation.

In letters of December 12 and 13 to the Council's President, India stated that in view of the recent attacks on Indian villages and citizens, it had been obliged to move units of its armed forces to the vicinity of Goa.

On December 14, the Secretary-General, U Thant, addressed identical cables to the Prime Ministers of India and Portugal, appealing to them and their Governments to ensure that the serious situation which had developed did not deteriorate to the extent that it might constitute a threat to peace and security. He also urged immediate negotiations.

Indian Prime Minister Jawaharlal Nehru, in a reply dated December 16, said that India had consistently abided by the provisions of the United Nations Charter and that the only solution to the problem was for Portugal to leave its colonies in India and allow the people to join their countrymen in freedom and democracy.

Prime Minister Antonio de Oliveira Salazar of Portugal said that, except in case of armed aggression, Portugal would do nothing which might constitute a threat to peace and security.

On December 18, Portugal declared in a letter to the Council's President that India had launched a full-scale armed attack on Goa, Damao and Diu, resulting in much damage and many casualties, and that Portugal was thus obliged to ask the Council to convene immediately in order to put a stop to the aggression of India and to order an immediate cease-fire and the withdrawal forthwith of all Indian troops from the Portuguese territories.

On the same day, the Security Council decided, over the opposition of Ceylon and the USSR, to place the question on its agenda. The following day, the Council voted on two draft resolutions. Under the first, submitted by Ceylon, Liberia and the United Arab Republic, the Council would have rejected the Portuguese complaint and called upon Portugal to terminate hostile action. Under the second, submitted by France, Turkey, the United Kingdom and the United States, the Council would have asked for a cessation of hostilities, called upon India to withdraw its forces and urged the parties to settle the question by peaceful means.

The three-Power draft resolution was rejected by the Security Council for lack of sufficient votes; the four-Power draft resolution received 7 votes in favour but was not adopted because of the negative vote of the Soviet Union.

Question of Malaysia

In May 1961, the Prime Minister of the Federation of Malaya proposed the formation of an enlarged Federation of Malaysia, to consist of the Federation of Malaya, North Borneo, Sarawak and Singapore. Following the report of a Commission of Inquiry which met in Sarawak and North Borneo, the United Kingdom (the administering Power for North Borneo, Sarawak and Singapore) and the Federation of Malaya issued, on August 1, 1962, a joint statement, on behalf of the Governments concerned, that, in principle, the Federation of Malaysia should be established by August 31, 1963.

On August 5, 1963, following a meeting of the heads of their governments in Manila, the Foreign Ministers of the Federation of Malaya, Indonesia and the Philippines jointly requested the Secretary-General to send a mission to Sabah (North Borneo) and Sarawak to ascertain whether or not the peoples of those territories wished to join the federation. The Federation of Malaya, Indonesia and the Philippines were to send observers to witness the investigations of the mission.

The Secretary-General informed the three Foreign Ministers on August 8 that he could undertake the task only with the consent of the United Kingdom. He proposed to set up two working teams, one for Sarawak and the other for Sabah, to work under the over-all supervision of his representative. They would be responsible directly and exclusively to him. On the basis of their report, the Secretary-General would communicate his final conclusions to the three Governments and to the United Kingdom. It was his understanding that neither the report nor his conclusions would be subject to ratification or confirmation by any of the Governments concerned.

The United Nations Malaysian Mission, appointed on August 12, consisted of eight members of the United Nations Secretariat and was headed by Laurence V. Michelmore as the representative of the Secretary-General. The Mission arrived in Sarawak on August 16 and remained there until September 5. Observers from the Federation of Malaya and the United Kingdom were present throughout all the Mission's hearings, but those from Indonesia and the Philippines arrived on September 1 and attended meetings on September 2, 3 and 4 only.

The Secretary-General's conclusions, based on the Mission's report, were made public on September 14, 1963. He stated that the majority of the people of Sabah and Sarawak had decided to realize their independence through freely chosen association with the people of the Federation of Malaya and Singapore, with whom they felt ties of ethnic association, heritage, language, religion, culture, economic relationship, ideals and objectives. The Secretary-General referred to the fundamental agreement of the three participating Governments and the statement by Indonesia and the Philippines that they would welcome the formation of the Federation of Malaysia provided that the support of the people of the territories had been ascertained by him. In the opinion of the Secretary-General, complete compliance with the principle of self-determination laid down by the General Assembly had been ensured.

The Secretary-General stated that, according to the findings of the Mission, there was no doubt about the wishes of a sizable majority of the people of the two territories to join in the Federation of Malaysia.

The Federation of Malaysia was proclaimed on September 16, 1963.

On the following day, at the opening of the eighteenth session of the General Assembly, the representative of Indonesia took exception to the seat of the Federation of Malaya being occupied in the Assembly Hall by a representative of the Federation of Malaysia. He referred to the fact that both Indonesia and the Philippines had withheld recognition of the Federation of Malaysia. Later, both countries expressed reservations about the findings of the United Nations Malaysian Mission.

Differences between Indonesia, the Philippines and the Federation of Malaysia continued, sometimes resulting in armed clashes on the borders of Sabah and Sarawak.

In September 1964, the Security Council met to consider Malaysia's charge that an Indonesian aircraft had dropped about thirty heavily armed paratroopers on South Malaya at about midnight on September 1-2. Malaysia, Indonesia and the Philippines were invited to participate without vote in the Council's deliberations. Malaysia said that Indonesia and the Philippines had refused to accept the Secretary-General's conclusions, had not recognized Malaysia and had broken off diplomatic relations with it. Indonesia had then, Malaysia said, announced its policy of a military and economic "confrontation" to "crush Malaysia"; armed Indonesian infiltrators had started flooding into the Borneo states from across the border and there had been evidence of a concentration of Indonesian troops all along the border. Malaysia had had talks with Indonesia, which had proved unsuccessful. Malaysia asked the Security Council to adjudge Indonesia guilty of aggression against a peaceful neighbour and enjoin it to desist from further acts of aggression.

Indonesia maintained that its neighbouring areas, at present called Malaysia, were being used by British colonialism as a base from which to subvert the Indonesian revolution. The idea of "Malaysia" had originated in London, but Indonesia had been anxious that the proposed enlarged Federation of Malaysia should come into being as a South-East Asian project, founded on the co-operative will for freedom of the peoples of the region—"Maphilindo" (a loose association between Malaya, the Philippines and Indonesia). The Philippines was interested in the question because of its claim to Sabah.

Indonesia further noted that under the Manila Agreement of August 1963, the establishment of the projected Federation was to have been postponed to await the outcome of the United Nations assessment of the wishes of the people of Sarawak and Sabah. But, Indonesia stated, the United Kingdom, which was opposed to "Maphilindo," had opposed this from the outset, and under its pressure, the Government in Kuala Lumpur had proclaimed the Federation of Malaysia on September 16, before the outcome of the United Nations assessment was known. Indonesia and the Philippines could not be bound by an assessment which Malaysia had itself not regarded as binding, and Indonesians had volunteered as guerrillas to fight together with the militant youth of Sarawak and Sabah for freedom and against neo-colonialism. There was a danger that the fighting and other actions from both sides would increase. The Indonesian policy of confrontation was a consequence, not a cause, of the conflict. This policy would end as soon as the political conflict was resolved.

The Philippines said that it regarded the Manila Agreement as a blueprint for peace. In Tokyo, President Macapagal had suggested the establishment of an African-Asian Conciliation Commission. Subject to concurrence by the other parties, the Philippines would be prepared to suggest a commission of four members.

The United Kingdom denied the charge that its Government had been trying to subvert the Government of Indonesia and said that Malaysia was a friend and ally of the United Kingdom.

On September 17, the Council considered a Norwegian-sponsored draft resolution by which the Council would have regretted all the incidents which had occurred in the whole region and deplored the incident of September 2, and would have called upon the parties to refrain from all threats or use of force and to respect each other's territorial integrity and political independence so as to create an atmosphere conducive to the continuation of their talks. The Council would have recommended further that the governments concerned resume their talks on the basis of the joint communiqué issued by the Heads of Government following the meeting at Tokyo on June 20, 1964. The vote on the draft was 9 in favour and 2 against (USSR and Czechoslovakia). The draft was not adopted because of the negative vote of a permanent member of the Council (USSR).

Withdrawal of Indonesia from Membership of the United Nations

In a letter dated January 20, 1965, Indonesia informed the Secretary-General that on January 7, after the seating of Malaysia as a member of the Security Council, the Indonesian Government had decided to withdraw from the United Nations, as of January 1, 1965.

The letter recalled that the formation of "Malaysia" had been rejected by two out of the three signatories to the Manila Agreement and that by means of "a successful manœuvre of neo-colonial powers in the United Nations," Malaysia had been forced into the United Nations. The letter further stated that "the pushing of this 'Malaysia' into the United Nations Security Council" was another "colonial manœuvre" and made a mockery of the Council, since, under the Charter, the election of a non-permanent member of the Security Council should be guided by the importance and contribution of the candidate-country in the maintenance of peace and security in the world. Malaysia's very birth, Indonesia charged, had caused trouble and insecurity in South-East Asia.

In a reply dated February 26, the Secretary-General noted Indonesia's decision to withdraw and also its assurance that Indonesia "still upholds the lofty principles of international co-operation as enshrined in the United Nations Charter." The Secretary-General expressed "the profound regret which is widely felt in the United Nations" over Indonesia's decision to withdraw from membership and "the earnest hope that in due time it will resume full co-operation with the United Nations."

[On September 19, 1966, Indonesia announced its decision "to resume full co-operation with the United Nations and to resume participation in its activities starting with the twenty-first session of the General Assembly."]

Violation of Human Rights in South Viet-Nam

The question of violation of human rights in South Viet-Nam was placed on the agenda of the eighteenth session of the General Assembly, in 1963, by fourteen countries—Afghanistan, Algeria, Cambodia, Ceylon, Guinea, India, Indonesia, Mongolia, Nigeria, Pakistan, Rwanda, Sierra Leone, Somalia, and Trinidad and Tobago, who were subsequently joined by Mali and Nepal. In a memorandum submitted on September 13, they said that the Government of South Viet-Nam had interfered with the manifestation of religious belief of the Buddhists, who formed 70 per cent of the population of South Viet-Nam.

In May 1963, the memorandum stated, the Government of President Ngo Dinh Diem had ruthlessly denied Buddhists the right to celebrate Buddha's birthday. Nine participants in the celebrations had been shot by government orders and hundreds of persons, including monks and nuns, had been injured and arrested; the total death toll was unknown. The intensity of feelings aroused was such that five monks and a nun had immolated themselves in protest. The memorandum also stated that, on August 25, hundreds of Saigon University student demonstrators had been arrested. The memorandum concluded by stating that the Government of South Viet-Nam was moving more and more towards the suppression of human rights, such as the right of assembly, freedom of speech and freedom of communication, and that the situation demanded urgent attention by the United Nations.

On September 23, the Secretary-General made public an exchange of correspondence between himself and President Ngo Dinh Diem, including a letter of August 31 from the Secretary-General expressing the "grave concern" of Asian and African member states at the situation in the Republic of Viet-Nam, and relaying to President Diem their request that the Viet-Namese Government take all necessary steps to normalize the situation by ensuring the freedom to exercise fundamental human rights for all sections of the population. In his reply of September 5, President Diem assured the Secretary-General that there had been no suppression of Buddhists in Viet-Nam and that his Government had acted only to free the Buddhist hierarchy from outside pressure and to shield the development of Buddhism from an external influence working against the interests of the Buddhist religion and against the higher interests of the State.

On October 8, the General Assembly agreed that its President, Carlos Sosa Rodriguez, of Venezuela, should act on the letter of October 4 from the Government of the Republic of Viet-Nam inviting a United Nations mission to visit that country to "see for themselves what the real situation is."

Three days later, a seven-member fact-finding mission was named by the Assembly President to investigate the situation regarding relations between the Government of South Viet-Nam and the Buddhist community. It reported on December 13 that it had visited that territory from October 24 to November 3 to ascertain the situation regarding alleged violations of human rights by the Government in its relations with the Buddhist community. The Assembly decided that in the light of recent events in Viet-Nam [on November 2, 1963, President Diem was assassinated and his régime overthrown], it would not be useful to discuss the matter at that time, and that no further action was required.

Complaints by Cambodia

The Security Council, in May 1964, considered complaints by Cambodia that armed forces of the United States and of the Republic of Viet-Nam (South Viet-Nam) had committed repeated acts of aggression against the territory and population of Cambodia which has common frontiers with the Republic of Viet-Nam; Cambodia listed some 261 such acts between 1963 and early 1964. It denied the charge that its territory was being used by Viet-Cong rebels and stated that to verify its statement it would accept a United Nations commission of inquiry. It also suggested that the International Control Commission established under the Geneva Agreements of 1954 might be reactivated and that the Geneva Conference on Indo-China should reconvene.

The United States and the Republic of Viet-Nam (the latter's representative participated without vote in the discussion) stated that while they had expressed regrets for the incidents, they felt that the fundamental reason for such border incidents was the absence of well-marked frontiers between the two countries. They urged that a United Nations commission of experts mark the borders and institute joint patrols from both countries. The International Control Commission (consisting of Canada, India and Poland), they felt, would be ineffective.

The Council, on June 4, adopted a resolution noting the apologies tendered to Cambodia, asked that compensation be paid to that Government and invited those responsible to take steps to prevent any further violations of Cambodian frontiers. The Council requested all states and authorities and in particular the participants of the Geneva Conference to respect Cambodia's neutrality and territorial integrity. The Council decided to send three of its members, the representatives of Brazil, Ivory Coast and Morocco, to the places where the most recent incidents had occurred in order to consider measures to prevent their recurrence.

On July 27, the three-member mission reported to the Council the results of its visit. It recommended that the Security Council establish and send to Cambodia a group of United Nations observers and entrust the Secretary-General with the implementation of this decision in consultation with members of the Council. The Council should, further, recommend that Cambodia and Viet-Nam adopt whatever measures might be necessary for the resumption of the political relations broken off in August 1963. The Council should appoint a person of high international standing, approved by both parties, to arrange for a preliminary meeting between the two Governments to re-establish relations and resume talks on matters in dispute, particularly the delimitation and marking of the common frontier. The Council should take note of the assurances given to the mission by the Republic of Viet-Nam that its armed forces had been issued definite instructions to take every precaution to avoid any risk of frontier violations, and of the statement by the Republic of Viet-Nam that it recognized and undertook to respect the neutrality and territorial integrity of Cambodia. No further action was taken by the Council on this question.

In later communications, Cambodia continued to complain to the Council of further incidents on its frontiers.

Gulf of Tonkin Incidents

On August 4, 1964, the United States requested an urgent meeting of the Security Council "to consider the serious situation created by deliberate attacks of the Hanoi régime on United States naval vessels in international waters."

The United States asserted that, on August 2 and 4, United States destroyers in international waters off the coast of North Viet-Nam had been fired upon by North Viet-Namese torpedo boats. After the first attack, hoping that the incident had been an uncalculated action, the United States, in accordance with the Geneva Agreement, called Hanoi's attention to its aggression and warned of the grave consequences which would result from any further unprovoked offensive military action against United States forces. When the second attack took place, however, there was no longer a shadow of doubt that a planned, deliberate military attack had occurred, the United States declared. Its Government had therefore determined to take positive but limited measures and, on the night of August 4, had carried out aerial strikes against North Viet-Namese torpedo boats and their support facilities. That action had been limited in scale and directed only against the weapons and facilities against which the United States had been forced to defend itself.

The United States stated that its vessels had been in international waters when attacked, that they had taken no belligerent action of any kind before they were subjected to armed attack and that their action in self-defence fell within the right of all nations and within the provisions of the United Nations Charter. The incident in question must be viewed, the United States said, in the context of developments in South-East Asia during the past fifteen years and was part of a pattern designed to subject the people of that area to an empire ruled by force and terror. The United States had sent additional forces to the area to make it unmistakably clear that military attack could not divert it from its obligations to help its friends establish and maintain their independence. Only when the political settlements freely negotiated at the conference tables in Geneva were enforced and made effective would the independence of South Viet-Nam and of South-East Asia be guaranteed and peace return to the area.

Following the meetings of the Council on August 5 and 7, communications were received from the Democratic Republic of Viet-Nam and the Republic of Viet-Nam in response to the Council's invitation that they submit information to it regarding the question.

In its response, the Democratic Republic of Viet-Nam charged that, since the end of July, the United States had repeatedly dispatched its aircraft and warships to violate the airspace and territorial waters of the Democratic Republic, bombing and strafing areas deep inside Viet-Namese territory and shelling coastal islands, and that on August 2 it had opened fire from a destroyer inside Viet-Namese territorial waters on patrol boats of the Democratic Republic, which had been obliged to defend themselves. During the night of August 3, American and South Viet-Namese warships had resumed their provocations, bombarding coastal regions.

The United States had then, the Democratic Republic of Viet-Nam charged, concocted the myth of a second attack by North Viet-Namese patrol boats on its destroyers and used that as a pretext to order aircraft of the Seventh Fleet to bomb and strafe several areas in the Democratic Republic on August 5, causing losses and damage among the local population. That act of war against the Democratic Republic was part of a United States plan to extend to North Viet-Nam the war of aggression in Indo-China which the United States had been carrying on for ten years, in systematic violation of the 1954 Geneva Agreements on Indo-China.

By submitting a complaint to the Security Council, the Democratic Republic of Viet-Nam charged, the United States was again revealing its opposition to a political settlement of the problems of Indo-China through the reconvening of the Geneva Conference and was seeking to misuse the name of the United Nations in order to disregard the 1954 Agreements. The consideration of the acts of war against the Democratic Republic and of the war of aggression in South Viet-Nam, carried on by the United States, lay within the competence of the 1954 Geneva Conference on Indo-China and not of the Security Council. Therefore, if the Council took an illegal decision on the basis of the United States "complaint," the Democratic Republic would be obliged to consider such a decision null and void. It continued to request the co-chairmen of the Geneva Conference and the participants therein to consult, in accordance with the final Declaration of that Conference, and "to study such measures as may prove necessary to ensure that the agreements on the cessation of hostilities . . . are respected."

In its response, the Republic of Viet-Nam offered its full co-operation to the Security Council and expressed its readiness to provide any information which the Council might need concerning the attacks by the Viet-Cong torpedo boats against United States ships in international waters in the Gulf of Tonkin; those attacks were additional evidence of the aggressive policy of the Hanoi régime, which had for many years directed its aggression not only against the Republic of Viet-Nam but also against Laos, and against peace and security in South-East Asia as a whole.

The refusal of the Hanoi régime to respond to the invitation of the Security Council, the Republic of Viet-Nam stated, indicated its awareness that its attacks on the high seas were indefensible, as well as its disregard for the role of the United Nations in the maintenance of international peace and security. Each time it committed aggression or created a serious situation, the Hanoi régime invariably advocated the convening of a new Geneva conference, but in the view of the Republic of Viet-Nam the usefulness of such conferences could be judged in the light of the repeated violations of the 1954 Geneva Agreements.

The Republic of Viet-Nam transmitted to the Council documents, covering the period July 1963 to June 1964, relating to its charges of terrorist acts by the Viet-Cong in South Viet-Nam, the illegal introduction of arms and war *matériel* and the infiltration of specialized cadres of the North Viet-Namese army into South Viet-Nam. It also cited a special report of June 2, 1962, by the International Control Commission in Viet-Nam describing such activities and terming them violations of the 1954 Geneva Agreements.

Question of Viet-Nam

On January 31, 1966, the United States requested an urgent meeting of the Security Council to consider the question of Viet-Nam. On the same day, the United States submitted a draft resolution whereby the Council would: call for immediate discussions, without pre-conditions, among the interested Governments to arrange a conference looking towards the application of the Geneva Agreements of 1954 and 1962 and the establishment of a durable peace in South-East Asia; recommend that the first order of business of such a conference should be arrangements for a cessation of hostilities under effective supervision; offer to assist in achieving the purposes of the resolution by all appropriate means, including the provision of arbitrators or mediators; call on all concerned to co-operate fully in the implementation of the resolution; and request the Secretary-General to assist as appropriate in the implementation of the resolution.

When the Council met on February 1 to consider the United States request for inclusion of the question in its agenda, the United States declared that despite all the efforts made by the United States and others to bring about negotiations, neither Hanoi nor Peking had shown any sign that they desired to move the problem to the conference table. Nevertheless, the United States had suspended the bombing of North Viet-Nam on December 24, 1965. The purpose of that suspension, which had lasted thirty-seven days, had been to ascertain whether the bombing was in fact a decisive barrier to negotiations and whether Hanoi also desired to reduce the range of armed conflict and to bring about a peaceful settlement.

During the suspension, the United States had consulted with more than 115 governments and had explained its objectives to Hanoi. Unfortunately, its restraint and patience had gone unrewarded. Infiltrations of men and material from the North to the South and acts of violence in South Viet-Nam had continued.

Finally, on January 29, Hanoi had made public a letter addressed by President Ho Chi Minh to certain Heads of State or Government, which laid down three pre-conditions for negotiations: (1) that the United States must accept the four-point stand of the Democratic Republic of Viet-Nam; (2) that the United States must end unconditionally and for good all bombing raids and other acts of war against the Democratic Republic of Viet-Nam; and (3) that the United States must recognize the National Front for the Liberation of South Viet-

Nam as the sole genuine representative of the people of South Viet-Nam.

In exchange for those demands, President Ho Chi Minh had offered nothing. He flatly rejected the two objectives which the United States had sought to achieve by the prolonged suspension of its bombings and in so doing assumed full responsibility for the United States decision that the suspension of bombing could not be continued beyond thirty-seven days. But the United States wanted to go on seeking a forum and a formula which would permit the beginning of negotiations. It had brought the Viet-Nam situation before the Council because that principal organ of the United Nations for the maintenance of international peace had not yet had the formal opportunity to ascertain whether it could find a new formula which would succeed where others had failed.

The United States would, of course, welcome the reconvening of the Geneva Conference, but it should be noted that a specific request made by the United Kingdom, one of the co-chairmen of the Conference, to the Soviet Union, the other co-chairman, had been turned down.

The USSR objected to the convening of the Security Council and to the inclusion of the question of Viet-Nam in the agenda, since the question should be settled only within the framework of the Geneva Agreements. By bringing the question to the Council simultaneously with the resumption of air raids on the Democratic Republic of Viet-Nam, the United States was not aiming at a genuine settlement of the question but had resorted to a diversionary tactic with a view to covering the expansion of its intervention and aggressive war in Viet-Nam and was using the Council to stage a propaganda show. In fact, the United States was unwilling to revert to a strict compliance with the Geneva Agreements of 1954, since it refused to recognize that the National Liberation Front was the sole genuine representative of the South Viet-Namese people, and the one with which it was necessary to negotiate. While the United States continued to act from a position of brute force, the Government of the Democratic Republic of Viet-Nam had again recently demonstrated its readiness to achieve a just settlement by sending messages to the Heads of State or Government of many countries stating that, if the United States was genuinely interested in peaceful settlement, it must recognize the four points of the position taken by the Democratic Republic of Viet-Nam and stop unconditionally and forever the bombing and all other military acts against the territory of the latter.

Bulgaria opposed the calling of a meeting of the Council for the same reasons which had determined the convening of the Geneva Conference in 1954, that is, the parties concerned could not come to the United Nations or were not yet members of the Organization.

The United Kingdom and New Zealand supported the United

States action in bringing the question to the Security Council, and Argentina, China, Japan and Uruguay favoured consideration of the problem by the Council.

The Netherlands observed that under Article 2, paragraph 6, of the Charter, the Organization was to ensure that states not members of the United Nations respected the principles of the Charter regarding the maintenance of international peace. It did not, therefore, matter that most of the countries involved were not members of the United Nations; this circumstance could not be regarded as a valid objection to Council consideration of the question. Also, all those concerned could and should be invited to particpiate in the discussion. The objection that the problem should be solved in the context, not of the United Nations, but of the Geneva Conference of 1954 was not justified since the purpose of the Council's discussion was only to arrange a pre-conference looking towards the application of the Geneva Agreements of 1954 and 1962.

France stated that the United Nations, where only one of the principal parties concerned, the United States, was represented, was not the proper forum for a peaceful solution. Even if the other parties were invited, the discussion could not be held on an equal footing. Moreover, United Nations intervention would only add to the existing confusion, as all parties to the conflict constantly referred to the need for respecting the principles of the Geneva Agreements of 1954 and 1962.

Mali thought that a discussion of the question of Viet-Nam in the Security Council did not seem appropriate in the absence of any of the conditions required for arriving at decisions acceptable to the parties concerned: most of these parties not only were not members of the Organization but had explicitly expressed their opposition to any discussion in the Council.

Nigeria felt that it was not an appropriate time to bring the question of Viet-Nam before the Council, since it coincided with the unfortunate resumption of bombing in North Viet-Nam. Both Mali and Nigeria, however, stated that they did not contest the right of any member state to call for a meeting of the Council if it felt that a situation threatened international peace and security.

Uganda asked whether any useful purpose would be served by pushing the inclusion of the question of Viet-Nam in the agenda to the vote and suggested that the President conclude the debate, summarizing it as best he could, and let the matter rest there.

On February 2, the Council voted on whether or not to include the question of Viet-Nam on its agenda; the result of the vote was 9 in favour to 2 against, with 4 abstentions. Following the vote, the President of the Council suggested that private consultations be held in order to decide on the most effective and appropriate way of continuing the debate. The Council adopted this suggestion.

On February 26, the President transmitted to the Secretary-General the text of a letter he had sent to the members of the Council. In his letter, the President reported that some members, in conformity with the position they had taken during the debate, had not participated in the consultations he had proposed. Serious differences remained unresolved, especially as to whether consideration of the problem of Viet-Nam in the Council would be useful in the circumstances. These differences had given rise to the feeling that a report in the form of a letter appeared better than a formal meeting of the Council. The President felt that he could detect a certain degree of common feeling among many members of the Council on the points that: (1) there was general concern and growing anxiety over the continuation of hostilities in Viet-Nam and a strong desire for the early cessation of hostilities and a peaceful solution of the Viet-Nam problem; and (2) there appeared also to be a feeling that the termination of the conflict in Viet-Nam should be sought through negotiations in an appropriate forum in order to work out the implementation of the Geneva accords.

The Security Council remained seized of the Viet-Nam problem.

VIEWS EXPRESSED BY THE SECRETARY-GENERAL ON VIET-NAM. In the introduction to his annual report to the General Assembly on the work of the Organization covering the period June 16, 1964 to June 15, 1965, the Secretary-General, U Thant, referred to the escalation of the conflict in Viet-Nam. He stated that the problem of Viet-Nam was one in regard to which the settlement reached at Geneva in 1954 prescribed no role for the United Nations. Neither North Viet-Nam nor South Viet-Nam was a member of the United Nations. Some of the parties to the conflict had openly voiced the view that the United Nations as such had no place in the search for a solution. However, in view of the profound effect that the Viet-Nam situation was having on problems of global as well as regional importance and the "shadow it cast" on every area of international co-operation, the Secretary-General had, he said, devoted considerable effort in a personal capacity and by way of "quiet diplomacy" to getting the parties concerned to stop the fighting and to begin discussions. He was fully convinced that total victory or total defeat for one side or the other was out of the question and that military action could not bring peace and restore stability to the area. In this connection, the Secretary-General, as early as July 1964, urging that diplomatic methods be tried, advocated a revival of the Geneva Conference of 1954. On February 12, 1965, noting the aggravation of the crisis that had just taken place, the Secretary-General issued a serious warning regarding the "dangerous possibilities of escalation" of the Viet-Nam conflict and appealed for a dialogue between the principal parties in order to prepare the ground for formal discussions.

In the introduction to his annual report for the period June 16, 1965 to June 15, 1966, the Secretary-General again noted that "the

chances of fruitful international co-operation on many crucial issues
. . . ranging from disarmament to development" had been "steadily
and seriously impaired" over the preceding two years by the deepening crisis in Viet-Nam, a situation over which the United Nations had
not been able to exercise any effective control. He had, he said, done
his best to help in the efforts that had been made to reduce the escalation of the conflict and to move to the conference table the quest for
a solution of the problem. But he had noted that discussions of the
matter had been largely dominated by consideration and analysis of
the power politics involved and that there had been much less concern for the tremendous human suffering which the conflict had entailed for the people of Viet-Nam, who had known no peace for twenty-
five years and whose present plight should be the first, and not the
last, consideration of all concerned.

Indeed, efforts by the Secretary-General were relentlessly pursued in 1965 and 1966. On July 7, 1965, the Secretary-General, asking again for a reconvening of the Geneva Conference, added that, in
order to achieve a really effective cessation of military activities, the
discussions must involve those who are actually fighting. On January
20, 1966, during a suspension of the bombings of North Viet-Nam, the
Secretary-General suggested to the parties to make concrete proposals
on "what type of government in South Viet-Nam, representative as far
as possible of all sections of the South Vietnamese people, could take
over the responsibility of organizing the exercise by the people of their
right to decide their own affairs." And, in February 1966, the Secretary-General suggested three preliminary steps which, in his view,
should be taken to facilitate the opening of negotiations: (i) cessation of bombing of North Viet-Nam, (ii) scaling down by all parties
of all military activities in South Viet-Nam and (iii) the willingness
by all sides to enter into discussions with those who are actually
fighting.

The real issue, U Thant stated in the introduction to his Annual
Report for the period June 16, 1965 to June 15, 1966, was the survival
of the people of Viet-Nam and that issue could not be resolved by
force. He believed that the moral influence of governments and peoples
outside the immediate conflict could help to bring about acceptance
of this approach on all sides and that "it should be possible to reach
a settlement which would end the suffering in Viet-Nam, satisfy the
conscience of the world at large and remove a formidable barrier to
international co-operation."

In a press conference on August 30, 1966, in Santiago, Chile, the
Secretary-General expressed the view that the Viet-Nam question was
basically "the continuous struggle of a people for independence." On
September 1, 1966, in a letter to all states members of the Organization concerning his own future, U Thant stated his concern for the
situation in South-east Asia. "The cruelty of this war," he said, "and

the sufferings it has caused the people of Viet-Nam are a constant reproach to the conscience of humanity." In speaking of the trend towards a larger war, he added that, in his view, "the tragic error is being repeated of relying on force and military means in a deceptive pursuit of peace." Finally, the Secretary-General repeated his conviction that peace in South-east Asia could only be obtained through respect for the principles formulated in Geneva in 1954 and indeed for those contained in the Charter of the United Nations. On November 11, 1966, in a letter to Lord Brockway, Chairman of the British Council for Peace in Viet-Nam, the Secretary-General reiterated the three "independent" steps towards negotiations which he had advanced in February 1966, and submitted that "if there are conflicting views among Vietnamese concerning the future of South Viet-Nam, these can only be reconciled by the people of South Viet-Nam and cannot be decided beforehand otherwise than through peaceful processes and without foreign intervention." On December 2, 1966, accepting a new term as Secretary-General of the United Nations, U Thant said to the General Assembly that the Vietnamese situation was for him a "continuing source of anxiety and even anguish." The Secretary-General pledged to "seize every occasion to recall that this war must be ended" and "to continue to regard it as his duty to make every effort on a personal basis to promote a solution which will bring peace and justice to the people of Viet-Nam."

QUESTIONS RELATING TO AFRICA

Apartheid in South Africa

The racial policies of the Government of South Africa have been before the United Nations, in one form or another, since the first session of the General Assembly in 1946. The matter was first raised by India in a complaint that the South African Government had enacted legislation discriminating against South Africans of Indian origin, in violation of treaty obligations and of the United Nations Charter.

In 1952, the wider question of racial conflict in South Africa arising from the Government's policies of *apartheid* (racial separation) was also placed upon the Assembly's agenda. The two related questions continued to be discussed as separate agenda items until they were combined under one title at the seventeenth session, in 1962, as "The policies of *apartheid* of the Government of the Republic of South Africa."

On both these questions, the South African Government consistently maintained that the matter was essentially within its domestic jurisdiction and that, under the Charter, the United Nations was barred from considering it.

COMPLAINT BY INDIA. When the Indian complaint first came before the General Assembly at the second part of its first session in 1946, South Africa proposed that the International Court of Justice be asked for an advisory opinion on whether the matter was not essentially within South Africa's domestic jurisdiction. Rejecting this proposal, the Assembly, on December 8, 1946, expressed the opinion that the treatment of Indians in South Africa should be in conformity with the international obligations under the agreements concluded between India and South Africa and the relevant provisions of the Charter. It asked the two Governments to report to the next session.

The reports by India and South Africa to the Assembly's second session showed that efforts to arrange discussions had failed. Two proposals were put before the Assembly, but neither received the necessary two-thirds majority.

After its admission to the United Nations in September 1947, Pakistan also began participating as a party in the discussion of the question.

In resolutions adopted on May 14, 1949, and December 2, 1950, the Assembly proposed that India, Pakistan and South Africa hold a round-table conference to explore ways and means of settling the question, taking into consideration the purposes and principles of the Charter and the Universal Declaration of Human Rights. Agreement on an agenda was reached at preliminary talks in Capetown in February 1950, but negotiations to convene the conference subsequently broke down.

When the conference failed to take place, the Assembly provided first, in 1951, for a special commission and later, in December 1952, when the commission was not set up, for a United Nations Good Offices Commission, composed of Cuba, Syria and Yugoslavia, to arrange and assist in negotiations between India, Pakistan and South Africa. The Assembly also called on South Africa to suspend implementation of the Group Areas Act of 1950 pending conclusion of the negotiations, but South Africa continued to enforce it.

The Good Offices Commission reported to the Assembly in 1953 that South Africa had refused to recognize it and, a year later, that it had been unable to discover any new procedure for negotiations between the parties, nor could it submit any proposal likely to lead to a peaceful settlement of the problem. The Assembly then suggested that if India, Pakistan and South Africa could not agree on direct negotiations within six months, the Secretary-General should designate a person to assist them.

As no agreement was reached, the Secretary-General, in June

1955, designated Ambassador Luis de Faro, Jr., of Brazil, to discharge the functions called for in the General Assembly resolution. India and Pakistan stated that they would extend full co-operation, but South Africa informed the Secretary-General that it was obliged, regretfully, to decline to collaborate with the Ambassador.

South Africa recalled its delegation from the tenth session of the General Assembly in 1955 and announced in 1956 that it would maintain only token representation at the United Nations. In 1958, South Africa returned to full participation in the United Nations, continuing, however, its refusal to discuss its racial policies and stating that it would ignore any resolutions adopted by the Assembly in this connection.

Between 1955 and 1961, the Assembly repeatedly appealed to South Africa to enter into negotiations with India and Pakistan. It also invited member states to use their good offices to bring about negotiations.

QUESTION OF RACIAL CONFLICT.   The over-all question of race conflict resulting from the policies of *apartheid* of the South African Government was dealt with by the Assembly for the first time in 1952.

The Assembly's decisions of December 5, 1952, on the issue were embodied in two resolutions. The first established a three-man commission to study the racial situation in South Africa and invited South Africa to extend its full co-operation. The second resolution called on all member states to bring their policies into conformity with their obligations under the Charter to promote the observance of human rights and fundamental freedoms.

South Africa maintained its position regarding domestic jurisdiction and refused to recognize the commission set up by the Assembly. The commission, nevertheless, submitted three reports to the Assembly, in 1953, 1954 and 1955.

Resolutions adopted by the Assembly between 1953 and 1959 repeatedly appealed to South Africa to revise its racial policies in the light of the Charter, and expressed concern and regret at South Africa's refusal to do so.

In 1960, following the Sharpeville incident of March 21, the Security Council met at the request of twenty-nine African and Asian members of the United Nations to consider "the situation arising out of the large-scale killings of unarmed and peaceful demonstrators against racial discrimination and segregation" in South Africa. Despite South Africa's protests, the Council discussed the matter and, on April 1, adopted a resolution stating that if the situation in South Africa continued, it might endanger international peace and security. The Council called on South Africa to abandon its policy of *apartheid* and racial discrimination, and asked the Secretary-General, in consultation with South Africa, to take adequate measures to uphold the purposes and principles of the Charter.

Subsequently, the Secretary-General visited South Africa between January 6 and 12, 1961, at the invitation of the Government. In his discussions with the South African Prime Minister, no mutually acceptable arrangement was found, but the Secretary-General informed the Council that, in his view, this lack of agreement was not conclusive and he looked forward to the continuation of consultations. The South African Government, having found the talks useful and constructive, decided to invite him again at an appropriate time, or times, in order to continue the contact.

The General Assembly continued to discuss the question at its following sessions, and on April 13, 1961, and again on November 28, 1961, it deplored South Africa's "continued and total disregard" of the repeated requests of the United Nations and world opinion to change its racial policies. The Assembly asked all states to consider taking separate and collective action to bring about the abandonment of these policies.

At its seventeenth session, in 1962, the Assembly considered for the first time the item "The policies of *apartheid* of the Government of the Republic of South Africa," which combined the two earlier items on South Africa's racial policies. In a resolution adopted on November 6, 1962, the Assembly requested member states to take the following specific measures: break off diplomatic relations with the Government of South Africa; close all ports to all vessels flying the South African flag; enact legislation prohibiting the ships of each state from entering South African ports; boycott all South African goods and refrain from exporting goods, including all arms and ammunition, to South Africa; and refuse landing and passage facilities to all aircraft belonging to the Government and companies registered under the laws of South Africa.

The Assembly also established an eleven-member Special Committee on the Policies of *Apartheid* of the Government of the Republic of South Africa to keep the situation under review between Assembly sessions, so that continuous attention might be given to the problem, and to report to the General Assembly and to the Security Council as necessary.

Finally, the Assembly requested the Security Council to take appropriate measures, including sanctions, to secure South Africa's compliance with the resolutions of the Assembly and of the Council and, if necessary, to consider action under Article 6 of the Charter, which provides that a member which has persistently violated the principles of the Charter may be expelled by the Assembly on the recommendation of the Council.

In fulfilment of its responsibilities, the Special Committee has heard petitioners and studied numerous communications and documents. In its reports to the General Assembly, the Committee has reviewed developments concerning the racial policies in South Africa and made recommendations for dealing with the problem. It has also submitted interim reports between sessions of the Assembly.

The Security Council considered the question twice in 1963—in August and December—and again in June 1964. On August 7, 1963, the Council solemnly called upon all states to cease the sale and shipment of arms, ammunition and military vehicles to South Africa; and on December 4, it urged extension of the arms embargo to include equipment and materials for manufacture and maintenance of arms and ammunition in South Africa. On each occasion, the Council called on the South African Government to liberate all persons imprisoned or subjected to other restrictions for having opposed *apartheid*. (A similar request was made by the General Assembly on October 11, 1963.)

Taking note of the Special Committee's reports, the Security Council expressed the conviction that the situation in South Africa was seriously disturbing international peace and security and called on South Africa to "cease forthwith" its discriminatory and repressive measures. The Council also asked the Secretary-General to establish a small expert group to examine methods of resolving the situation in South Africa "through full, peaceful and orderly application of human rights and fundamental freedoms to all inhabitants of the territory as a whole" and invited South Africa to avail itself of the assistance of this group to bring about peaceful and orderly transformation.

The expert group, with Mrs. Alva Myrdal, of Sweden, as chairman, recommended, in its report of April 20, 1964, the formation of a national convention fully representative of all the people of South Africa so that the people could be consulted and the future of their country decided at the national level. For the convention to succeed, the group stated, an amnesty must be granted to all opponents of *apartheid*, whether on trial, in prison, under restriction or in exile. A refusal by South Africa to discuss holding a national convention would leave the Security Council, in the group's view, with no effective peaceful means for helping to resolve the situation in South Africa except to apply economic sanctions. The group suggested that a technical study of the economic and strategic aspects of sanctions should be made by experts in those fields, pending a reply from South Africa.

The Security Council, on June 18, 1964, endorsed the group's main conclusion that all the people of South Africa should be brought into consultation, and invited South Africa to submit its views on national consultation by November 30, 1964. It decided to establish an expert committee of all members of the Council for the year 1964 to make a technical and practical study of the feasibility, effectiveness and implications of measures which could be taken by the Council under the Charter and to report to the Council by the end of February 1965.

Also, in line with the experts' proposals, the Council asked the

Secretary-General to establish, in consultation with appropriate specialized agencies, an education and training programme abroad for South Africans.

In another resolution, adopted on June 9, 1964, the Council urged South Africa to renounce the execution of persons sentenced to death for acts resulting from opposition to *apartheid*, and to end the Rivonia trial of the leaders of the anti-*apartheid* movement.

South Africa, on July 13, rejected this resolution as completely illegal and stated that the Council's intervention could be regarded as particularly blatant since the discussion in the Council had taken place before the Rivonia trial verdict had been announced. On November 16, South Africa also rejected the invitation in the Council's resolution of June 18, stating that what was sought was that a member state should abdicate its sovereignty in favour of the United Nations. Earlier, in May, South Africa had declined to comment on the experts' proposals for a national convention, since it considered that the subject matter of their report was essentially within South Africa's jurisdiction. South Africa also contended that the report contained a number of inaccuracies, distortions and erroneous conclusions based on false premises.

The Security Council's expert committee reported in February 1965 that it had been unable to reach full agreement on its conclusions, which were adopted by majority vote. The majority was of the view that while many economic measures against South Africa were feasible, their effectiveness would depend to a great extent on applying them universally, on the manner and duration of their enforcement and on the genuine desire of those imposing the measures, special attention being given to the states having close economic relations with South Africa. Emphasis was placed on the importance of a total trade embargo, an embargo on petroleum and petroleum products, on arms, ammunition of all types and military vehicles, and on equipment and materials for the manufacture and maintenance of arms and ammunition in South Africa; cessation of emigration of technicians and skilled manpower to South Africa; interdiction of communications with South Africa; and political and diplomatic measures already referred to by the Security Council and the General Assemby.

On December 15, 1965, the General Assembly declared that universally applied economic sanctions were the only means of achieving a peaceful solution of the problem. It drew the attention of the Security Council to the fact that the situation in South Africa was a threat to international peace and security and stated that in order to solve the problem, action was essential under Chapter VII of the Charter (which concerns action with respect to threats to the peace, breaches of the peace and acts of aggression). The Assembly urgently appealed to the major trading partners of South Africa to cease "their increasing economic collaboration" with South Africa "which encourages that

Government to defy world opinion and to accelerate the implementation of the policies of *apartheid*."

In addition, the Assembly: again asked all states to comply fully with all the resolutions of the Security Council on this question; called for the widest possible dissemination of information on *apartheid* and United Nations efforts to deal with the situation; invited the specialized agencies to deny assistance to the South African Government, except for assistance to the victims of *apartheid;* decided to enlarge the Special Committee on *Apartheid* from eleven to seventeen members; and established a United Nations trust fund, to be made up of voluntary contributions, to provide legal assistance to persons charged under discriminatory and repressive legislation in South Africa, relief for dependants of persons persecuted by the South African Government for their opposition to the policy of *apartheid,* education of prisoners and of their children and other dependants, and relief for refugees from South Africa.

The Former Italian Colonies

At the Paris Peace Conference in 1947, Italy renounced all claims to its former colonies—Libya, Eritrea and Italian Somaliland—and, under the Italian Peace Treaty, their final disposition was to be determined by France, the United Kingdom, the United States and the USSR within one year of the conclusion of the treaty, that is, by September 15, 1948.

When the four powers failed to reach agreement, the issue was referred to the General Assembly, which adopted a resolution, on November 21, 1949, dealing with all three territories.

Libya, comprising Cyrenaica, Tripolitania and the Fezzan, the Assembly decided, should become an independent and sovereign state not later than January 1, 1952, and should then be admitted to the United Nations. A United Nations Commissioner was appointed to assist the Libyans in drawing up a constitution and establishing an independent government.

The Assembly also decided that Somaliland should become a sovereign state ten years from the date of Assembly approval of a trusteeship agreement for the territory, with Italy as the administering authority in the interim period, assisted by an Advisory Council. (*See also page* 376.)

With regard to Eritrea, the Assembly stated that a commission of investigation should be dispatched to the territory to ascertain more fully the wishes of the people and the best means of promoting their welfare. It was instructed to report to the Assembly not later than June 15, 1950.

LIBYA. On November 17, 1950, the General Assembly adopted a resolution which called on the authorities concerned to ensure, among other things, the early realization of the unity of Libya and the transfer of power to an independent Libyan Government by January 1, 1952; recommended that a National Assembly, to be convened before January 1, 1951, establish a provisional government and that the United Nations Commissioner, aided by a Council of Ten, draw up a programme for the transfer of power in co-operation with the administering powers (the United Kingdom and France); and urged the Economic and Social Council, the specialized agencies and the Secretary-General to extend to Libya such technical and financial assistance as it might request.

Later, on December 15, the Assembly adopted resolutions relating to the economic and financial provisions to be applied under the Italian Peace Treaty, and established a United Nations Tribunal in Libya to give instructions and to decide all disputes between the authorities concerned regarding the application of these provisions. [The Tribunal was terminated on December 31, 1955, upon the establishment of an Italian-Libyan Mixed Arbitration Commission.]

In the meantime, on December 2, 1950, the Libyan National Assembly declared that Libya should be a federal state, with the Emir of Cyrenaica as King. On March 29, 1951, the National Assembly established a "provisional federal government" for Libya. The transfer of powers took place on October 2, 1951, and five days later the constitution establishing a United Kingdom of Libya was approved by the National Assembly.

On December 24, 1951, Libya was proclaimed an independent and sovereign state by King Idris I, and the administering powers transferred all authority to the Libyan Government. Libya immediately applied for membership in the United Nations; it was admitted on December 14, 1955.

In 1955, 1958 and 1960, the Assembly adopted resolutions on the question of assistance to Libya, all of which recognized the special responsibility assumed by the United Nations for the future of that country. In 1962, the Secretary-General received a communication from the Prime Minister of Libya stating that the economic prospects of Libya had been improved by the discovery of petroleum and that the question of assistance to Libya no longer required special consideration by the General Assembly. The Assembly therefore adopted, on December 18, 1962, a resolution requesting the United Nations and the aid agencies concerned to deal with the needs of Libya in the general framework of assistance to newly independent countries.

ERITREA. On December 2, 1950, the General Assembly adopted a resolution which included a plan, suggested by the United Nations Commission, whereby Eritrea was to constitute an autonomous unit federated with Ethiopia under the sovereignty of the Ethiopian Crown. An Eritrean Government was to be organized and a constitution prepared with the assistance of a United Nations Commissioner and experts.

In March 1952, a Representative Assembly was elected and on April 28 was officially opened. On May 14, the Eritrean Assembly unanimously adopted and ratified the Federal Act, and on July 10, 1952, the constitution was unanimously adopted. It entered into effect on September 11, 1952.

The establishment of the federation was formally welcomed by the General Assembly on December 17, 1952.

In accordance with a General Assembly resolution of January 29, 1952, a United Nations Tribunal in Eritrea was formally installed at Asmara on September 4, 1952, with executive jurisdiction on the disposal of the properties of the former Italian administration. Its functions formally ended on April 26, 1954.

Question of Morocco

The question of Morocco was first raised at the sixth session of the General Assembly, in 1951, when six Arab states complained of violation by France in Morocco of the principles of the Charter and the Universal Declaration of Human Rights and asked the Assembly to consider the matter. At that session, the Assembly postponed consideration of the question.

The question of Morocco was raised again at the next session by thirteen states which charged that stringent French rule had compromised the sovereignty of the country and its legitimate ruler and that the national movement in Morocco was being oppressed. On December 19, 1952, the Assembly adopted a resolution, sponsored by eleven Latin American states, expressing confidence that France would "endeavour to further fundamental liberties of the people of Morocco" and that the parties would "continue negotiations towards developing the free political institutions of the people of Morocco."

France maintained that the United Nations, under the Charter, had no right to intervene, since the question was one of domestic jurisdiction, and refused to take part in the discussion.

On August 21, 1953, fifteen Asian and African countries requested an urgent meeting of the Security Council to investigate the danger to international peace and security arising out of the intervention of France in Morocco and the overthrow of its legitimate sovereign. The Security Council, however, decided not to include the item in its agenda.

The issue was discussed at the eighth, ninth and tenth sessions of the General Assembly. On December 3, 1955, the Assembly noted that negotiations between France and Morocco were to be initiated regarding the question, and decided to postpone further consideration of the item.

On March 2, 1956, a joint declaration on the status of Morocco was signed by representatives of France and Morocco by which France recognized the independence of Morocco. Morocco applied for membership of the United Nations on July 4 and was admitted on November 12, 1956.

Questions Relating to Tunisia

The situation in Tunisia was first brought before the Security Council in April 1952 by eleven Asian and African states and, after the Council failed to place the matter on its agenda, the General Assembly was asked to discuss the question later the same year and again in 1953 and 1954. The sponsors of the item charged that France was depriving the people of Tunisia of their right to self-government and self-determination and that the deteriorating situation was endangering international peace and security.

France refused to take part in any discussion of the question and stated that interference by the United Nations in matters which it regarded as exclusively within France's national jurisdiction was wholly unacceptable.

On December 17, 1952, the Assembly expressed the hope that the parties would continue negotiations with a view to bringing about self-government for the Tunisians and appealed to the parties to settle their disputes in accordance with the spirit of the Charter.

On December 17, 1954, the General Assembly noted with satisfaction that the parties had entered into negotiations, expressed confidence that a satisfactory solution would result and decided to postpone further consideration of the question.

Negotiations between France and Tunisia resulted in a protocol agreement signed on March 20, 1956. Tunisia applied for membership in the United Nations on July 14, and was admitted on November 12, 1956.

Between 1958 and 1960, Tunisia complained to the Security Council on several occasions that French armed forces had violated Tunisian territory. On February 13, 1958, Tunisia told the Council that France had committed an act of aggression when French military aircraft subjected the border town of Sakiet-Sidi-Youssef to massive bombardment. In another incident, a year later, it stated that French military aircraft from Algeria had violated Tunisian air space and machine-gunned Tunisians.

France, for its part, maintained that the situation on the Algerian-Tunisian border was created by armed Algerian rebels operating from bases in Tunisia, and complained to the Council in February 1958 about the aid furnished by Tunisia to rebels whose operations, France stated, were directed against the integrity of French territory.

The Security Council discussed the respective complaints in February 1958, but decided to adjourn pending the results of conciliation efforts by the United States and the United Kingdom. Further meetings were held in June of that year at which new charges from France and Tunisia were considered.

On June 18, France and Tunisia informed the Council that it had been agreed that all French forces would be evacuated from Tunisia within four months, except those stationed at Bizerte.

DISPUTE OVER BIZERTE.   In July 1961, Tunisia asked the Security Council to put an immediate end to "acts of aggression" by French troops in Bizerte which, it reported, was under attack by the French navy and air force. Tunisia further asked the Council to help it repel the permanent danger constituted by the presence of French troops on its territory.

France maintained that it had abided scrupulously by the 1958 Franco-Tunisian agreement regarding Bizerte and that Tunisia bore full and sole responsibility for the events that had occurred there.

On July 22, the Council adopted an "interim" resolution calling for a cease-fire in Tunisia and the return of all armed forces to their original position. Tunisia complained a few days later that the French military forces had not complied with this resolution. None of the other resolutions subsequently submitted to the Council gained the required majority. Meanwhile, the Secretary-General made a brief visit to Tunisia in response to an appeal from the President of Tunisia for a direct and personal exchange of views between himself and the Secretary-General.

The failure of the Security Council to take action and the continuation of a grave situation in Tunisia led thirty-eight delegations to request a special session of the General Assembly to consider the matter.

On the last day of the session, the Assembly, which met from August 21 to 25, 1961, adopted a resolution sponsored by thirty-two nations, reaffirming the Security Council's "interim" resolution of July 22 and urging France to carry out fully its provisions regarding "an immediate cease-fire and return of all armed forces to their original positions." The Assembly also called upon the Governments of France and Tunisia "to enter into immediate negotiations to devise peaceful and agreed measures in accordance with the principles of the Charter for the withdrawal of all French armed forces from Tunisian territory."

After two years of negotiations, France and Tunisia reached an agreement for the withdrawal of French troops from Bizerte; the withdrawal was completed on October 15, 1963.

Question of the Sudan-Egyptian Border

At the request of the Sudan, the Security Council met on February 21, 1958, to discuss "the grave situation" on the Sudan-Egyptian border "resulting from the massed concentration of Egyptian troops moving towards the Sudanese frontiers."

Following conciliatory statements by Egypt and the Sudan, the Council did not deal with the item further.

Question of Algeria

The situation in Algeria was first brought to the attention of the Security Council and later the General Assembly in 1955 and subsequently was discussed by the Assembly from 1956 to 1961.

On January 5, 1955, Saudi Arabia informed the Council that the situation in Algeria was likely to endanger international peace and security. Saudi Arabia charged that the French Government was employing military operations in Algeria to liquidate the nationalist uprising against colonial rule.

Later that year, the question of Algeria was placed on the Assembly's agenda at the request of fourteen African-Asian states, but after some discussion, the item was not considered further.

France objected to any discussion of the question by the United Nations, arguing that Algeria was an integral part of Metropolitan France and had been so since 1834, that Algerian affairs were essentially within France's domestic jurisdiction and that, therefore, the United Nations was not competent to intervene.

On June 13, 1956, a meeting of the Security Council was requested by thirteen states on the ground that the situation in Algeria had become worse. Earlier, in April, seventeen states informed the Council that the situation had deteriorated to such an extent that the United Nations could not remain indifferent to the threat to peace and security, to the infringement of the basic rights of self-determination and to the flagrant violation of other fundamental human rights. The Council, however, did not include the question in its agenda. [The situation was again brought to the Security Council's attention by twenty-two member states in July 1959, but no meeting of the Council took place.]

In October 1956, at the request of France, an item entitled "Military assistance rendered by the Egyptian Government to the rebels in Algeria" was included in the Council's agenda but was not discussed.

The General Assembly, meanwhile, placed the matter on the agenda of its eleventh session and, on February 15, 1957, expressed the hope that, in a spirit of co-operation, a peaceful, democratic and just solution would be found, in conformity with the principles of the Charter.

Again, on December 10, 1957, the General Assembly expressed its concern over the situation in Algeria, took note of the offer of good offices made by the King of Morocco and the President of the Republic of Tunisia and expressed the wish that, in a spirit of effective co-operation, *pourparlers* would be entered into and other appropriate means utilized with a view to a solution in conformity with the purposes and principles of the Charter.

In 1960, the Assembly adopted a resolution stressing the right of the Algerian people to self-determination; and the following year, regretting the suspension of negotiations between France and the Provisional Government of the Algerian Republic, the Assembly called upon both parties to resume negotiations with a view to implementing the right of the Algerian people to self-determination and independence, respecting the unity and territorial integrity of Algeria.

Algeria became independent on July 1, 1962, and was admitted to the United Nations on October 8 of the same year.

Algerians Imprisoned in France

A resolution on the status of Algerians imprisoned in France was adopted by the General Assembly on November 15, 1961. The matter was raised by the representative of Pakistan, who pointed out that several thousand Algerian prisoners were on a hunger strike and that that matter, which was essentially a humanitarian question, should be dealt with urgently.

On the same day, the Assembly called upon France "in accordance with established international practice and humanitarian principles, to redress the legitimate grievances of the Algerian prisoners in recognizing their status as political prisoners with a view to making possible the immediate termination of the hunger strike."

Problem of Mauritania

In 1960, the problem of Mauritania was placed on the agenda of the fifteenth session of the General Assembly at the request of Morocco, which claimed that Mauritania, within the borders assigned to it by France, had always been an integral part of Moroccan national territory and that France, by intending to grant independence to Mauritania, was attempting to sanction the final separation of this region from the rest of Morocco.

France held that the Moroccan claim was not justified, whether on geographical or historical, ethnographic, juridical or political grounds; that Mauritania was not an issue between France and Morocco; and that if the Mauritanians wished to forge special bonds with any particular country, they were free to do so.

Without adopting a formal resolution on the subject, the Assembly, on December 18, 1960, took note of the report of the First Committee, where the question had been discussed. Mauritania attained independence on November 28, 1960 and on the same day it applied for membership in the United Nations. It was admitted on October 27, 1961.

The Congo

The Republic of the Congo (Leopoldville),* a former Belgian-administered territory in Central Africa, became independent on June 30, 1960. On July 5, a mutiny broke out in the *Force publique* (the national army) and grave acts of violence were committed against Belgian officers and civilians. The disorders led to a mass exodus of Belgian administrators and technicians, resulting in the breakdown of essential services and the stoppage of important economic activities in many parts of the country.

On July 10, metropolitan Belgian troops intervened, without the agreement of the Congolese Government, and occupied Elisabethville, Luluabourg and, later, other towns. In the wake of the entry of Belgian troops into Elisabethville (the present Lubumbashi), the independence of the province of Katanga was proclaimed by Moïse Tshombé, the President of the Provincial Government.

On July 12, Joseph Kasa-Vubu, the President of the Republic of the Congo, and Patrice Lumumba, the Prime Minister, jointly addressed a telegram to the Secretary-General of the United Nations, Dag Hammarskjöld, requesting urgent dispatch by the United Nations of military assistance to protect the national territory of the Congo against external aggression, which, they said, was a threat to international peace. The Congolese leaders also asked the United Nations to put an end to the secession of Katanga and accused Belgium of having fostered a colonialist conspiracy by carefully preparing that secession with a view to maintaining a hold on the Congo.

The Secretary-General brought the requests to the attention of the Security Council as a matter which, in his opinion, might threaten the maintenance of international peace and security. The Council, on July 14, 1960, adopted a resolution calling upon Belgium to withdraw its troops from the Congo and authorizing the Secretary-General to take the necessary steps, in consultation with the Congolese Government, to provide the latter with such military and technical assistance as might be necessary until the Congolese national security forces could fully meet their responsibilities. At the same time, the Council rejected three USSR amendments which would have condemned armed aggression

---

* Officially renamed the Democratic Republic of the Congo in July 1964. Leopoldville was renamed Kinshasa on July 1, 1966.

by Belgium, called for immediate withdrawal of Belgian troops and limited the military assistance to be provided to that of African member states of the United Nations.

In order to carry out the resolution, the Secretary-General set up the United Nations Operation in the Congo (*Opération des Nations Unies au Congo*), or ONUC. ONUC was composed, on the one hand, of civilian operations and, on the other, of an international armed peace force, the United Nations Force in the Congo. This force, made up of contingents from states other than the great powers but placed under the exclusive command of the United Nations, was under standing orders to use force only in self-defence and not to intervene in the internal affairs of the Congo. Later, however, when the internal conflict in the Congo worsened, the Security Council on February 21, 1961, authorized the use of force as a last resort to prevent civil war. In another resolution adopted on November 24, 1961, it authorized the use of force to eliminate mercenaries and other foreign personnel not under United Nations command.

The main problems faced by ONUC in carrying out its mandate were the withdrawal of Belgian troops, the maintenance of law and order, the constitutional crisis, the secession of Katanga and the provision of technical assistance.

WITHDRAWAL OF BELGIAN TROOPS.   Immediately after the adoption of the Security Council resolution of July 14, 1960, Dr. Ralph J. Bunche, the first Special Representative of the Secretary-General in the Congo, entered into negotiations with the Belgian representatives in Leopoldville for the speedy withdrawal of their troops. It was agreed that the Belgian troops would withdraw from the positions they occupied as soon as these positions were taken over by the United Nations Force.

On July 15, less than forty-eight hours after the Security Council resolution, the first United Nations contingent landed in Leopoldville. It was soon followed by others, until the strength of the United Nations Force reached a maximum of about 20,000. As soon as the United Nations soldiers arrived, they relieved the Belgian troops, first in Leopoldville, then in the other parts of the Congo except Katanga and the two military bases of Kamina and Kitona and, finally, in these three areas also. The entry into Katanga was achieved in August 1960. By the beginning of September, there were no Belgian troops left in the entire territory of the Congo.

The entry into Katanga gave rise to serious differences between the Secretary-General and Patrice Lumumba, the Prime Minister. Mr. Lumumba demanded that ONUC assist him in putting down by force the secession of Katanga. The Secretary-General refused to accede to this demand, maintaining that to do so would be contrary to ONUC's mandate. The Secretary-General's stand regarding ONUC's mandate was upheld by the Security Council in a resolution adopted on August 9, in which the Council stated, among other things, that ONUC "will not be a party to or in any way intervene in or be used to influence the outcome of any internal conflict, constitutional or otherwise."

The Secretary-General succeeded in his effort to secure the entry of United Nations troops into Katanga without using force, by means of negotiations through the Belgian authorities. On August 12, he personally led the first United Nations contingent into Katanga. The Secretary-General's stand regarding the use of United Nations troops in the Congo and the manner of the entry into Katanga were deeply resented by Mr. Lumumba, who henceforth refused to co-operate with the Secretary-General.

Mr. Lumumba's position was expressed in an exchange of correspondence between him and the Secretary-General, beginning August 14, in the course of which the Congolese Prime Minister described the Secretary-General's interpretation of the Security Council resolution as "unilateral and erroneous." He considered that under the Security Council resolution, United Nations troops could be used to subdue the rebel government of Katanga and that the Secretary-General had acted without authority in dealing directly with the provincial government. He declared that his Government had lost confidence in the Secretary-General.

MAINTENANCE OF LAW AND ORDER.   Deployed in various areas of the Congo, where their arrival brought about the prompt withdrawal of Belgian troops, the United Nations Force made every effort to assist the Congo Government in restoring law and order, protect the lives and property of the civilian population, Africans and Europeans alike, and ensure the continued operation of the essential services. In performing these functions, ONUC was enjoined by the Secretary-General to avoid any action that would put it in the role of a government and to limit its activities to giving advice and assistance to the Government of the Congo.

A constitutional crisis broke out on September 5, 1960, when the President of the Republic, Joseph Kasa-Vubu, dismissed Prime Minister Lumumba and asked the President of the Senate, Joseph Iléo, to form a new government. Mr. Lumumba, in turn, announced that President Kasa-Vubu was no longer Chief of State. On September 13, power in the Republic was seized by Col. Joseph Mobutu, Chief of Staff of the Army. The crisis thus engendered lasted for eleven months during which there was no legal government and, after a confused struggle for power, the country found itself divided into four opposing camps, each with its own armed forces. On the night of September 5, ONUC closed all major airports to traffic other than that of the United Nations on the ground that this step was required in the interest of maintaining peace and security. The next day, it temporarily closed the Leopoldville radio station. On September 12, ONUC reopened the airports and the radio station after the Congolese Parliament undertook surveillance of their use. Without a legal government with which it could deal, ONUC's policy was to continue to carry out its mandate in co-operation, on the local level, with the authorities actually in control of the area whenever necessary. During this period of deepening unrest, ONUC exerted its best efforts to protect the many political leaders threatened by their opponents. Measures had also to be taken to avert civil war between the rival factions and to prevent a resurgence of tribal violence.

During the constitutional crisis, ONUC's efforts were mainly directed at two objectives. ONUC endeavoured to prevent the leaders wielding power from subduing their opponents by force, while at the same time it encouraged all leaders to seek a solution of their differences through negotiation and conciliation.

This stand was endorsed by the General Assembly, which examined the problem at an emergency special session held from September 17 to 20, 1960, after the Security Council had failed to arrive at a decision. In its resolution of September 20, the Assembly appealed to all Congolese to seek a peaceful solution of their internal conflict and provided for the establishment of a Conciliation Commission to assist Congolese leaders for this purpose. The Assembly further appealed for urgent voluntary contributions to a United Nations fund for the Congo and called on all states to refrain from providing military assistance in the Congo, except upon request of the Secretary-General, and to refrain from any action which might undermine the unity, territorial integrity and political independence of the Congo.

ACTIONS REGARDING PATRICE LUMUMBA.   In December 1960, Ambassador Rajeshwar Dayal of India, who had succeeded Dr. Bunche as the Secretary-General's Special Representative in the Congo, reported that Mr. Lumumba, whose residence had been guarded by United Nations troops, had fled from his residence on November 27-28 but had been apprehended by Congolese troops on December 1. He had been brought to Leopoldville on December 2 and transferred to Thysville on December 3. Two members of Parliament, Mr. Mpolo and Mr. Okito, had also been arrested.

At the call of the USSR, the Security Council met from December 7 to 13 to consider the question but failed to adopt any of the draft resolutions submitted.

The transfer of Mr. Lumumba and his companions by the Congolese authorities from Thysville to Elisabethville in Katanga in January 1961 and their subsequent murder in February led to a fresh crisis both in the Congo and in the United Nations where the USSR called for the dismissal of Mr. Hammarskjöld and announced that it would not, henceforth, recognize him as Secretary-General of the United

Nations. A majority of member states, however, continued to support Mr. Hammarskjöld and the operations of the United Nations in the Congo.

A four-man Commission of Investigation was established on April 15, 1961, to investigate the death of Mr. Lumumba and his colleagues, and its report was circulated to members of the Security Council and the General Assembly on November 11, 1961. The Commission concluded that the weight of evidence was against the official version of the Katanga provincial Government that Mr. Lumumba and his colleagues had been killed by certain tribesmen on February 12, 1961; that the evidence indicating that the prisoners had been killed on January 17, 1961, in a villa near Elisabethville, probably by certain mercenaries, in the presence of Katanga provincial officials, seemed to be substantially true; and that President Kasa-Vubu and his aides and Mr. Tshombé and his aides should not escape responsibility. The Commission noted that it had been unable to visit the Congo, owing to objections by the Leopoldville authorities.

FORMATION OF A NATIONAL GOVERNMENT.   The Conciliation Commission established by the General Assembly on September 20, 1960, visited the Congo at the beginning of 1961. The Commission reported that its attempt to reconcile the opposing groups had not led to positive results because of the intransigent attitude of some of the leaders who held the reins of power. It considered that the crisis could be solved only if Parliament were reconvened and a national unity government were approved by it. It also found that one of the main obstacles to a speedy solution was foreign interference in the internal affairs of the Congo.

These views were similar to those expressed by the Secretary-General and were largely reflected in the decision taken by the Security Council, which met in February 1961 to examine once again the Congo problem. The Security Council urged that Parliament be convened and that the necessary measures be taken for this purpose.

In the first months of 1961, a number of meetings were held between various Congolese leaders in an attempt to solve the crisis, but none of them led to a positive result. During the Conference of Coquilhatville (the present Mbandaka), in May 1961, President Kasa-Vubu announced his intention to reconvene Parliament in the near future and requested United Nations assistance and protection for this purpose. ONUC acceded to this request and played a major role in bringing about an agreement between the main political groups on the reopening of Parliament. It also assumed the responsibility for making arrangements for the opening session of Parliament and for ensuring full protection to the parliamentarians.

Parliament was reopened on June 22, 1961, with more than 200 members attending out of a total of 221. Only Antoine Gizenga, head of the Stanleyville (the present Kisangani) group, and the whole of Moïse Tshombé's South Katanga group were absent. On August 2, Cyrille Adoula, at the request of President Kasa-Vubu, formed a national unity government, which was unanimously approved by Parliament. With the approval of the national unity government, the constitutional crisis was ended, but two leaders still stood in the way of full national unity: Mr. Gizenga in Orientale province and Mr. Tshombé in the south of Katanga province. Mr. Gizenga, although appointed Vice-Prime Minister in the new Government, subsequently opposed its authority. He was censured by Parliament, and his parliamentary immunity was lifted. He was later detained by the Congolese authorities pending trial.

SECESSION OF KATANGA. The secession of Katanga, which was made possible by foreign interference, was undoubtedly the most difficult problem facing ONUC. From the very outset, ONUC was wholly opposed to the secession but, despite the insistence of Prime Minister Lumumba, it refused to intervene directly and help him put down the secession. What ONUC sought to do was to eliminate the foreign interventions which brought about the secession and to encourage and facilitate negotiation and reconciliation between the Central Government and Katangese authorities.

The withdrawal of the Belgian troops from Katanga was completed at the beginning of September 1960, but after the departure of these troops, foreign interference took more subtle forms and the secessionist régime was further strengthened, particularly during the constitutional crisis, by the introduction of foreign political advisers, military and paramilitary personnel, and mercenaries. This aspect of the problem was stressed by the Security Council in its resolution of February 21, 1961, when it urged that measures be taken for the immediate withdrawal of such foreign personnel.

Measures were taken by the Secretary-General to carry out this decision, but they were hampered by the unco-operative attitude of Katangese authorities and the absence of a legal central government. Belgian advisers and officers were recalled by their Government; some foreign personnel were evacuated by ONUC. However, most of them remained. In June 1961, there were more than 500 foreign military personnel and mercenaries in the Katangese *gendarmerie*.

During the discussions and negotiations which had taken place prior to the reopening of Parliament, many overtures had been made in vain to Mr. Tshombé by the other leaders. After the formation of the national unity government in Leopoldville in August 1961, Prime Minister Adoula again attempted to win him over, and again his attempts were frustrated. In order to remove what it believed to be the main obstacle to a peaceful solution of the Katanga problem, the Gov-

ernment ordered, on August 24, the expulsion of mercenaries serving
in Katanga and requested onuc's assistance in carrying out this decision, a course to which onuc was already committed.

On August 28, onuc proceeded to round up mercenaries in
Elisabethville for deportation, after having taken certain security
precautions, including surveillance over the Elisabethville radio station,
the *gendarmerie* headquarters and other key points. The rounding up
operation, which lasted only a few hours, was successful and peaceful.
Mr. Tshombé, who had been informed of the goals of onuc's action,
expressed his readiness to co-operate. Some 273 military personnel
were rounded up, and the operation was suspended when the consular
corps assumed the responsibility and promised to bring about the
repatriation of the remaining foreign elements.

Unfortunately, this promise was not fully kept. Many mercenaries
were "missing" and went underground, while the Katangese authorities
launched a violent propaganda campaign against onuc. On September
13, onuc decided to repeat the August 28 operation under the same
conditions, but before the operation could get under way, United Nations troops were attacked by Katangese *gendarmerie*. Thus began the
hostilities of September 1961.

As soon as the hostilities began, onuc endeavoured to achieve a
cease-fire. The Secretary-General, who had earlier arrived in Leopoldville, decided to deal personally with the matter. It was on his flight
to Ndola, Northern Rhodesia, to meet Mr. Tshombé, on September 17,
that Mr. Hammarskjöld and seven other United Nations staff members
and the crew of the aircraft were killed in the crash of the aircraft
(*see page* 205). The peace-making task was immediately taken over
by other United Nations officials and three days later a cease-fire
agreement was concluded between Mr. Tshombé and onuc. The
agreement was endorsed by United Nations Headquarters on the understanding that it would in no way impede the implementation of
Security Council and General Assembly resolutions.

However, the Katangese authorities were soon flouting the provisions of the cease-fire agreement, and the situation continued to
worsen. In November, shortly after the appointment of U Thant as
Acting Secretary-General, the Security Council met once again to examine the situation in the Congo. In its resolution of November 24, the
Council opposed the secessionist activities in Katanga and authorized
the Secretary-General to use the requisite measure of force to complete
the removal of mercenaries.

Immediately after the adoption of the resolution, the Katangese
authorities launched a propaganda campaign against onuc, which soon
led to open violence. Onuc personnel were beaten, abducted and killed
by Katangese *gendarmerie*, and roadblocks were erected to impede the
movements of United Nations troops. After attempting in vain to settle
the crisis by peaceful negotiations, onuc decided on December 5 to

take action to remove the roadblocks and regain its freedom of movement. Fighting ensued once again between United Nations and Katanga forces.

During the fighting, ONUC troops and aircraft took all possible measures to ensure that their attacks were limited strictly to military objectives. Strict orders were given to ONUC troops to safeguard to every possible extent the lives and properties of the civilian population. These orders were generally observed, although it was often difficult to do so as time and again ONUC troops found themselves subjected to heavy fire from civilian installations by persons in civilian dress. As soon as it had occupied the positions necessary for its security and freedom of movement, ONUC ordered its troops, on December 19, to hold fire unless fired upon. Immediately thereafter, it turned its efforts to re-establishing normal conditions in Elisabethville, in co-operation with the Katangese police wherever possible.

Mr. Tshombé left Elisabethville on December 19 to confer with Prime Minister Adoula in Kitona. The meeting had been arranged with the assistance of ONUC and the United States Ambassador in the Congo, following a request made by Mr. Tshombé. As a result of the Kitona talks, Mr. Tshombé signed, on December 21, 1961, an eight-point declaration whereby he accepted the application of the *loi fondamentale*, recognized the authority of the Central Government and agreed to a number of steps aimed at ending the secession of Katanga.

On his return from Kitona, Mr. Tshombé sent several Katangese parliamentarians to Leopoldville to participate in the Central Parliament, but referred the Kitona Declaration to the provincial assembly, which, on February 15, 1962, accepted it only as a basis for discussion. From March to June 1962, Mr. Tshombé held two series of negotiations in Leopoldville with Prime Minister Adoula under United Nations auspices and safe conduct. These finally broke down as a result of the procrastination and intransigence of the Katangese leader.

In view of the failure of the negotiations, the Secretary-General himself, after consultations with various member states, proposed in August 1962 a "Plan of National Reconciliation," which was presented to both Mr. Adoula and Mr. Tshombé as a reasonable basis for settling the differences between the Central Government and the Province of Katanga. In the main, the Plan provided for a federal system of government; division of revenues and foreign exchange earnings between the central and provincial governments; unification of the currency; integration and unification of all military, paramilitary and *gendarmerie* units into the structure of a national army; proclamation of a general amnesty; reconstitution of the Central Government to provide representation for all political and provincial groups; withdrawal of all representatives abroad not serving under the authority of the Central Government; and freedom of movement for United Nations personnel throughout the Congo.

The Plan was immediately accepted by Prime Minister Adoula and, after a short delay, by Mr. Tshombé. A draft federal constitution was speedily prepared by experts provided by the United Nations. Moreover, on November 26, President Kasa-Vubu issued a Proclamation of Amnesty. On the Katanga side, however, no substantial steps were taken towards implementing its acceptance. Accordingly, and after further consultations with member governments, the Secretary-General, on December 13, requested various member states in a position to do so to bring economic pressure on the Katanga authorities, in particular by stopping the exports of copper and cobalt from Katanga. Before these measures could take effect, the security situation in South Katanga deteriorated once more. Onuc troops in Elisabethville were subjected to increased harassment culminating in a four-day period of unprovoked firing by the Katangese *gendarmerie* on United Nations positions, which onuc troops did not answer. After repeated unsuccessful discussions with Mr. Tshombé, United Nations troops on December 28, took action to remove *gendarmerie* road-blocks near Elisabethville and subsequently to secure for themselves freedom of movement throughout Katanga. During these operations, in which little resistance was met, every opportunity was given to Mr. Tshombé and his provincial ministers to give practical evidence of their readiness to put into effect the Plan of National Reconciliation, while at the same time they were warned against carrying out their threats of massive destruction of the mining and power installations in South Katanga.

On January 14, 1963, Mr. Tshombé and his ministers indicated that they were ready to proclaim the end of Katangese secession, to grant freedom of movement to United Nations troops and to co-operate with the United Nations in the implementation of the Plan. They asked, however, for confirmation that the Amnesty Proclamation remained valid, and this was immediately provided by both President Kasa-Vubu and Prime Minister Adoula. On January 17, the Provincial President returned to Elisabethville; the onuc representatives there reached agreement with him on arrangements for the peaceful entry of onuc troops into Kolwezi, the last important stronghold held by the Katangese *gendarmerie*. Onuc troops entered Kolwezi unopposed on January 21 and within a few days established their presence and freedom of movement throughout the province. On January 23, Mr. Iléo arrived in Elisabethville as Minister Resident of the Central Government for the reintegration of South Katanga.

On February 4, the Secretary-General reported to the Security Council that the secession of Katanga had ended and that the removal of foreign military and paramilitary personnel and mercenaries had, for all practical purposes, been fulfilled. However, efforts over the next few months to negotiate, with the Government, arrangements for retraining the Congolese army with onuc assistance were inconclusive.

WITHDRAWAL OF UNITED NATIONS FORCE. Acting upon a request of the Congolese Government, the General Assembly decided, on October 18, 1963, to extend the stay of the United Nations Force until June 30, 1964, to continue to assist the Congolese Army and police in the maintenance of law and order in the country. The Force, whose total strength had been brought down to 5,871 officers and other ranks by the end of 1963, was further gradually reduced during the first half of 1964 until its complete withdrawal by the target date.

In a report to the Security Council on June 29, the Secretary-General stated that most of the objectives of ONUC had, in large measure, been achieved. There remained the objective of rendering technical assistance, and this the United Nations would continue to do to the fullest extent of finances available.

Summing up the experience of the United Nations Force, the Secretary-General made the following observations: (a) the creation of the Force in July 1960 proved the ability of the United Nations to meet grave emergency situations and to set up the largest peace-keeping operation in its history within an incredibly short time; (b) despite its limited authority and resources, the United Nations offered the only possible hope of keeping the peace and of facilitating the finding of a solution; (c) four years were gained in which the Government and the people of the Congo had the opportunity to come to grips with their vast problems and in which Congolese public administrators, doctors, professional people and technicians could begin their training and acquire experience; (d) on the whole, the record of the United Nations Force in the Congo, in all respects, was distinguished; (e) the relations with the Congolese Government were generally good and weathered the relatively few major crises.

It was inevitable, the Secretary-General pointed out, that in a situation as complex and politically controversial as the Congo, certain impressions, assumptions and even myths developed, some of them having, no doubt, political overtones or motivations. But these were countered by the following well documented and firmly established facts: the United Nations operation had at all times scrupulously avoided intervention in the internal affairs of the Congo; it had not taken sides in political or constitutional differences; it had not sought to exercise any governmental authority; from beginning to end, the Force was under strict instructions to use its arms for defensive purposes only; it launched no offensive, nor did it take any military initiative involving the use of force other than its successful efforts to eliminate the mercenaries in South Katanga, in pursuance of a Security Council mandate; it never permitted itself to become an arm of the Government and remained at all times under United Nations command. The presence of the United Nations Force was the decisive factor in preserving the territorial integrity of the country and it was a major factor in preventing widespread civil war in the Congo.

For its part, the Democratic Republic of the Congo, in a note to the Secretary-General on September 19, expressed its sincere and profound gratitude for the efforts made by the United Nations forces to preserve the unity and integrity of the Congo.

THE STANLEYVILLE OPERATIONS.   Following the withdrawal of the United Nations Force, the situation in the Congo rapidly deteriorated. At the beginning of July 1964, a new Constitution came into force. On July 9, Mr. Adoula, who had resigned as Prime Minister, was succeeded by Mr. Tshombé. Shortly thereafter, a movement of rebellion gained increased momentum; insurgent forces extended their control over large areas in the eastern part of the country, including Stanleyville, where a dissident government was set up. Mr. Tshombé fought back to regain the lost ground and recruited foreign mercenaries to assist the Congolese National Army.

On November 21, Belgium and the United States drew the Security Council's attention to the danger threatening the foreign residents of Stanleyville, among whom more than 1,000 persons belonging to nineteen nationalities were being held as hostages by the rebel authorities. The two Governments subsequently informed the Council that following a refusal by the rebel authorities to guarantee the safety of the civilians in Stanleyville, Belgian paracommandos carried by United States aircraft had been parachuted into Stanleyville and rescued as many of the hostages as possible before departing from the Congo on November 29. The Democratic Republic of the Congo informed the Council that it had authorized the rescue operation; and the United Kingdom reported that it had granted the use of facilities on Ascension Island to the Governments of Belgium and the United States.

On December 1, twenty-two United Nations member states called for a Security Council meeting to consider the situation created by this military operation which they considered an intervention in African affairs and a threat to the peace and security of the African continent. A Council meeting was also requested by the Prime Minister of the Congo on December 9 to examine the intervention in Congolese domestic affairs by various states which were assisting the rebel movement in the Congo.

The Council held seventeen meetings on these two complaints between December 9 and 30. It called for an end to foreign intervention in the Congo, appealed for a cease-fire there and considered that the mercenaries should as a matter of urgency be withdrawn. The Council also gave its support to efforts by the Organization of African Unity (OAU) to help the Government of the Democratic Republic of the Congo to achieve national reconciliation and asked the OAU to keep the Council fully informed of any action it might take in this connection.

FINANCING. Total expenditures authorized for ONUC for the period July 14, 1960 to September 30, 1965 amounted to $392.8 million. The first financing arrangements were made by the General Assembly on December 20, 1960, when it decided to apportion $48.5 million in expenses for ONUC during 1960 among member states on the same scale of assessments as for the United Nations regular budget, subject to certain reductions. The Assembly opened a special account for the expenses of ONUC and in subsequent resolutions authorized the Secretary-General to spend up to $120 million in 1961, $120 million in 1962, $83.7 million in 1963 and $18.2 million in 1964. An additional $2.4 million was authorized to meet expenses involved in the closure of the operation through September 30, 1965.

For various political reasons, some member states refused to pay their assessed contributions for ONUC, and the Organization consequently began to accumulate a substantial deficit and faced a mounting problem in meeting the expenses of the operation.

The Assembly took the position that the expenses involved in ONUC for 1960 were "expenses of the Organization" within the meaning of Article 17, paragraph 2, of the Charter and that, therefore, member states had binding legal obligations to pay their assessed shares. This view was upheld by a majority opinion of the International Court of Justice which found, on July 20, 1962, that these expenditures were "expenses of the Organization" within the meaning of the Charter (see page 450).

The Assembly subsequently decided that the extraordinary expenses of ONUC were essentially different in nature from those of the Organization's regular budget and that, therefore, a different procedure for meeting them was required. The Assembly noted in this connection that the five permanent members of the Security Council had a special responsibility for contributing to the cost of peace-keeping operations. Accordingly, the Assembly worked out a special formula under which developing nations were given a substantial reduction on their assessments, with the difference to be made up by voluntary contributions from the developed countries. Twenty-six countries were subsequently designated as "developed" by the Assembly, but a number of these countries did not contribute towards the peace-keeping operations.

The Assembly later appealed to members in arrears to make their payments, without prejudice to their respective political positions, and set up machinery and guide-lines to evolve special methods for financing peace-keeping operations involving heavy expenditures, such as those for the Congo and the Middle East (see page 77, "Peace-keeping Operations").

A financial report issued by the Secretary-General in January 1966 showed that the actual cash expenses incurred by ONUC through September 30, 1965, totalled $337.4 million, with unliquidated obligations amounting to $30.8 million. The funds obtained to meet cash expenditures totalled $348.2 million. Of this sum, $159 million was the total amount collected from member states in assessed contributions for ONUC; voluntary contributions to the ONUC Account totalled $36 million; the amount met from the proceeds of the United Nations Bond Issue was $143.2 million; and miscellaneous income was $10 million.

CIVILIAN OPERATIONS. When the United Nations went into the Congo in July 1960, the country was in the throes of a dire emergency. The mass exodus of Belgian technicians and administrators was threatening to paralyse its entire economy, essential services were in imminent danger of breaking down, unemployment was rapidly rising in the cities, and hunger and disease loomed. To provide the Congo Government with the technical assistance it needed, the Secretary-General set up, in close co-operation with the specialized agencies, the civilian operations of ONUC.

In the beginning, at the same time as United Nations troops were striving to restore law and order, ONUC experts were helping to ensure the continued operation of essential services.

Relief operations were also undertaken by ONUC, both alone and in conjunction with the Red Cross. The most important of the relief operations undertaken by ONUC related to the famine in South Kasai in the autumn of 1960, where some 200 persons daily were reported dying from starvation. Over a period of six months, ONUC shipped and distributed food and medical supplies in the area; it was estimated that the operation saved the lives of about 250,000 persons.

After the emergency had been met, long-range programmes were drawn up in consultation with the Congo Government, to restore and reorganize the government services and to ensure the continued development of the national economy. Particular emphasis was placed on the training of qualified Congolese in various services.

The implementation of these programmes was begun without delay, but was soon slowed down, first by the refusal of Prime Minister Lumumba to co-operate with ONUC and later because of the constitutional crisis, which for eleven months deprived the country of a legal government. ONUC continued its efforts nevertheless, but it was only after the formation of the Adoula Government that its programmes could be carried out at full speed.

With ONUC's efforts, the government services were fully restored. Economic and financial specialists, working in close co-operation with the Government, helped towards an improvement of the Congo's monetary and budgetary position. Other experts constituted the backbone of many essential services, such as the judiciary and law enforcement, civil aviation and telecommunications, public works, meteorology, public health and education. Experts were provided in mining and natural resources, public administration, transport, social affairs, community development, labour administration, food and agriculture, and postal services. In-service training of Congolese was begun, under the supervision of United Nations experts, in practically all of the ministries receiving technical assistance.

At the same time, institutes were set up to train Congolese teachers, engineers and public works foremen; to provide vocational training; and to produce qualified personnel in mining, meteorology, civil aviation and telecommunications. A national school of law and administration was established to produce competent civil servants. Courses were arranged in the techniques of customs inspection, farm machinery, poultry breeding, clerical trades and other fields. A 400-man police contingent from Nigeria helped not only in the maintenance of law and order but also in the direct training of, and in joint patrols with, the Congolese police.

By the end of 1963, qualified Congolese were beginning to replace some international personnel. Towards the end of 1963, the first fifty-five out of a total of 130 medical assistants sent abroad in 1960 and 1961 for training as doctors at French and Swiss universities under the auspices of the World Health Organization returned to the Congo. As they returned, the Congolese doctors replaced internationally recruited doctors.

The technical assistance provided to the Congo has been the largest programme of the United Nations and its specialized agencies in any part of the world. Until the end of 1962, the programme was financed entirely from the United Nations Fund for the Congo, a trust fund made up of voluntary contributions from member states of the United Nations and the specialized agencies. Beginning in 1963, a part of the over-all programme began to be provided through the conventional programmes of technical assistance of the United Nations and the specialized agencies.

From July 1960 to the end of 1963, the United Nations spent approximately $29.9 million for civilian assistance from the United Nations Fund for the Congo. This sum included the equivalent of about $7.3 million in local currency contributed for 1962 and 1963 by the Government of the Congo. During this period, the United Nations also administered a trust fund, valued at $10.9 million, of donations in cash and kind from governments and non-governmental organizations for famine relief in the Congo. The United Nations also assisted the Government of the Congo in the programming and administration of foreign exchange and goods totalling the equivalent of approximately $165 million, which had been provided on a bilateral basis to the Republic of the Congo to maintain essential imports and to generate local currency for the support of the Congolese economy.

With the completion in June 1964 of the military phase of ONUC, the civilian operations programme was formally discontinued. The over-all programme of technical assistance which had been supplied by the United Nations family of organizations continued, but the responsibility for it was transferred by the Secretary-General to the normal inter-agency machinery for technical co-operation.

Since January 1964, the programme of technical assistance has been financed under United Nations conventional programmes of technical co-operation, as well as by funds-in-trust provided by the Government of the Congo and other interested governments and by the United Nations Fund for the Congo. The total cost of this programme was $16.9 million in 1964 and $14.7 million in 1965, of which the equivalent of some $8 million in local currency and $5.9 million in foreign exchange were contributed by the Government of the Congo for the two-year period.

During 1965, United Nations experts were continuing to advise, assist and train their Congolese counterparts in carrying out the many functions of the Government. A total of 500 United Nations experts, drawn from fifty-two countries, were working on twenty projects under the over-all programme of technical co-operation. In addition, 800 secondary-school teachers were recruited with the help of UNESCO.

Complaints by Senegal

The Security Council has twice considered charges by Senegal that Portuguese aircraft and troops had violated its airspace and territory on a number of occasions and attacked Senegalese villages. The first discussion took place in April 1963, after Senegal charged that four Portuguese aircraft had dropped grenades on the Senegalese village of Bougniack. Senegal recalled that in December 1961 its territory and airspace had also been violated by Portugal on three occasions. In May 1965, Senegal complained that Portuguese authorities had committed sixteen new violations of Senegalese airspace and territory since the incidents of April 1963.

Portugal denied that its aircraft had flown over or bombed Bougniack, rejected the charges made by Senegal in May 1965 as completely baseless and unwarranted and suggested that a small inquiry team should be set up to investigate the allegations. Portugal, for its part, charged that Senegal was aiding armed gangs in its territory to attack the population of Portuguese Guinea.

The Security Council, on April 24, 1963 and May 19, 1965, unanimously deplored any incursion by Portuguese forces into Senegalese territory and requested Portugal to take action in accordance with its declared intentions "to prevent any violation of Senegal's sovereignty and territorial integrity." The Secretary-General was also asked to keep the situation under review.

QUESTIONS RELATING TO EUROPE

Spanish Question

The relations of members of the United Nations with Spain were first discussed by the General Assembly in 1946 at the request of Panama. Earlier, at the Potsdam Conference, the United Kingdom, the United States and the USSR had stated that they would not support the Franco Government for admission to the United Nations. The San Francisco Conference had also resolved that Charter provisions for United Nations membership could not apply to states whose régimes had been installed with the help of the armed forces of ex-enemy countries so long as those régimes were in power.

On February 9, 1946, the General Assembly recommended that member states act in accordance with these decisions. On December 12 of the same year, the Assembly recommended that the Franco Government be barred from membership in specialized agencies having relations with the United Nations. It further suggested that if a democratic Spanish Government were not established within a reasonable time, the Security Council should consider adequate measures to remedy the situation. Finally, it recommended that members immediately recall their ambassadors and ministers plenipotentiary accredited to Madrid.

These recommendations of December 1946 were revoked by the Assembly on November 4, 1950. The Assembly declared that the establishment of diplomatic relations and the exchange of ambassadors and ministers with a government did not imply any judgment on the domestic policy of that government. Moreover, because the specialized agencies were technical and largely non-political in character and had been established to benefit the peoples of all nations, they should be free to decide for themselves whether the participation of Spain was desirable.

The question of Spain was also discussed by the Security Council, which, in April 1946, considered a request by Poland to declare the existence of the Franco régime a threat to international peace and security, and to call on all members of the United Nations to sever diplomatic relations with it. This proposal was not adopted.

The Council subsequently set up a sub-committee of five, and on June 6 the majority of the sub-committee reported that the Franco régime constituted not an existing threat but a "potential" menace to international peace. It suggested that its findings be transmitted to the Assembly with a recommendation that, unless the Franco régime were withdrawn and other conditions of political freedom satisfied, the Assembly recommend the severance of diplomatic relations. A resolution embodying these recommendations was not adopted, however, because of the negative vote of the USSR, which held that the findings had incorrectly labeled the Franco régime a "potential" rather than an "existing" threat to peace and that the Council, rather than the Assembly, was the appropriate organ to call for the severance of diplomatic relations.

[Spain applied for United Nations membership on September 22, 1955, and was admitted on December 14 of that year.]

Greek Question

A number of complaints alleging foreign interference in Greece were considered by the Security Council in 1946 and 1947 and by the General Assembly from 1947 to 1951.

The Security Council in 1946 received separate complaints from the USSR, the Ukrainian SSR and Greece. The USSR complained on January 21, 1946, that the continued presence of British troops in Greece constituted interference in Greek internal affairs and was likely to endanger peace and security. The United Kingdom stated that British troops were in Greece by agreement with the Greek Government, and Greece denied interference. After discussion, the Council accepted its President's suggestion to take note of the declarations and consider the matter closed.

The Ukrainian SSR, on August 24, 1946, complained that the policies of the Greek Government constituted a threat to peace. Greece denied the charges and referred to frontier incidents allegedly provoked by Albania. On September 11, Albania itself asked the Council to take up the situation on the Greek-Albanian frontier allegedly resulting from continued violations by Greek soldiers. Four draft resolutions were proposed, but all were rejected and the Council regarded the case as closed.

Greece asked the Council on December 3, 1946, to consider the situation in northern Greece resulting from aid provided to Greek guerrillas by the country's northern neighbours. These charges were denied by Albania, Bulgaria and Yugoslavia.

On December 19, the Council established a commission of investigation, composed of one representative of each member of the Council for 1947, to ascertain the causes and nature of the border violations and to make proposals for averting a repetition of those violations. The commission conducted investigations in northern Greece in 1947 and submitted a report with recommendations accepted by nine of its members.

Greece again asked the Council in August 1947 to consider the question, this time as a threat to the peace under Chapter VII of the Charter, but draft resolutions submitted by Australia and the United

States failed of adoption. As the Council was unable to adopt any resolution, it decided on September 15 that the question should be taken off the list of matters of which the Council was seized.

The General Assembly then took up the question. On October 21, 1947, and again on November 27, 1948, the Assembly called on Albania, Bulgaria and Yugoslavia to stop aiding the Greek guerrillas. It asked those three countries and Greece to co-operate in settling their disputes peacefully and, to this end, recommended the establishment of diplomatic relations between them; frontier conventions; and co-operation in solving refugee problems.

An eleven-member United Nations Special Committee on the Balkans (UNSCOB) was set up by the Assembly in its 1947 resolution to assist the four Governments in complying with its recommendations and to observe how far they did so. Poland and the USSR, two of UNSCOB's members, declared that they would not participate in the Committee's work because they considered that its functions violated the sovereignty of Albania, Bulgaria and Yugoslavia.

In its first report, UNSCOB stated that it had been unable to aid the four Governments substantially in implementing the Assembly's recommendations. UNSCOB further reported to the Assembly in 1949 that Albania and Bulgaria had assisted the Greek guerrilla movement and had also encouraged the Greek guerrillas in their attempts to overthrow the Greek Government; it added that Yugoslavia had aided the guerrillas, but that this aid had diminished and might even have ceased.

Following this report, the Assembly adopted a resolution on November 18, 1949, stating that active assistance given to the Greek guerrillas by Albania in particular and by Bulgaria and certain other states, including Romania, was contrary to the Charter and endangered peace in the Balkans. It declared that further foreign assistance to the guerrillas would justify a special session of the Assembly.

A year later, on December 1, 1950, the Assembly took note of UNSCOB's conclusion that there remained a threat to Greece's political independence and territorial integrity.

In its report to the sixth session of the Assembly, in 1951, UNSCOB stated that the threat to Greece continued, although changed in character since the retreat of the guerrilla forces in 1949. The guerrillas were receiving external aid from Albania, Bulgaria, Czechoslovakia, Hungary, Poland and Romania. The Committee recommended considering the advisability of maintaining United Nations vigilance over the Balkans in the light of the nature of the threat to peace in that area.

On December 7, 1951, the Assembly endorsed this report and discontinued the Committee. It then provided for the establishment of a Balkan Sub-Commission by the Peace Observation Commission. It gave the Sub-Commission authority to dispatch observers to any area of international tension in the Balkans on the request of any state or states concerned, but only to the territory of consenting states.

At the request of Greece, the Sub-Commission decided, on January 31, 1952, to conduct observations in the frontier areas of Greece. Quarterly reports were submitted on conditions and incidents along the Greek-Bulgarian and Greek-Albanian border, but the Sub-Commission did not find it necessary to report to the Peace Observation Commission. On August 1, 1954, the observer group was discontinued at the suggestion of Greece.

REPATRIATION OF GREEK CHILDREN. UNSCOB had reported that during 1948 some 25,000 Greek children had been removed from Greece and retained in the territories of Greece's northern neighbours and other countries. In November 1948, the Assembly recommended the return to Greece of Greek children abroad when the children or their close relatives requested it and asked the International Committee of the Red Cross and the League of Red Cross Societies to help in this connection.

A year later, the Assembly urged all states harbouring Greek children to arrange for their early return, and asked the international Red Cross organizations to continue their efforts.

Despite these efforts, the Assembly noted "with grave concern" on December 1, 1950, that not a single child had been returned to his native land and that, with the exception of Yugoslavia, no country harbouring those children had complied definitely with the previous resolutions. In a new effort to bring about repatriation, the Assembly set up a standing committee and asked the international Red Cross organizations to continue their efforts.

In February 1952, the Assembly recognized that efforts must be continued towards the repatriation of Greek children, noted "with satisfaction" that some children had been repatriated from Yugoslavia and expressed the hope that rapid progress would be possible with the repatriation of those in Czechoslovakia. In December, the Assembly decided that work for the repatriation of Greek children, except in Yugoslavia, should be suspended until conditions were established which would make such action practical and useful, and that the standing committee should be discontinued. The Assembly asked the Red Cross to continue its work in Yugoslavia until all children had been repatriated.

Free Territory of Trieste

The responsibility of ensuring the independence and integrity of the Free Territory of Trieste, including the appointment of a Governor, was accepted by the Security Council on January 10, 1947. However, the Council was unable to agree upon any candidate for appointment as Governor in 1947, 1948, or 1949, despite consultations in 1947 between its permanent members and later between Italy and Yugoslavia. On October 5, 1954, a Memorandum of Understanding concerning the Free Territory of Trieste was transmitted to the Security Council by Italy, the United Kingdom, the United States and Yugoslavia. The Memorandum provided for certain boundary adjustments between Yugoslavia and the Free Territory, on the completion of which the United Kingdom, the United States and Yugoslavia would withdraw their military forces from the area north of the new boundary and relinquish the administration of that area to Italy. Italy and Yugoslavia would then extend their civil administration over the areas allotted to them. On October 12 the representative of the USSR informed the President of the Security Council that his Government had taken cognizance of the agreement.

Czechoslovak Situation

At the request of Chile, the Security Council in March 1948 considered a request from Jan Papanek, permanent representative of Czechoslovakia, for an investigation of events preceding and succeeding the change of government in Czechoslovakia in February 1948. Mr. Papanek was replaced by Dr. Vladimir Houdek as permanent representative of Czechoslovakia on March 15.

Czechoslovakia subsequently declined an invitation to participate in the discussion on grounds of domestic jurisdiction and rejected as unfounded the complaint of Chile.

A proposal to appoint a sub-committee to receive evidence was not adopted because of the negative vote of the USSR.

Berlin Question

On September 29, 1948, France, the United Kingdom and the United States drew attention to the serious situation which had arisen "as the result of the unilateral imposition by the Government of the USSR of restrictions on transport and communications between the Western zones of occupation in Germany and Berlin."

The Security Council considered this question at several meetings beginning on October 4, 1948. The USSR questioned the Council's competence, and after the question was placed on the Council's agenda, the USSR and the Ukrainian SSR announced that they would not take part in the discussion.

Between October 1948 and May 1949, a number of Council members informally considered ways of solving the problem, but no agreement was reached. In addition, the Council President set up a Technical Committee on Currency Problems and Trade in Berlin, but the Committee was unable to work out an acceptable solution. Following informal conversations at the United Nations between the representatives of the four occupying powers, the Secretary-General was requested on May 4, 1949, by France, the United Kingdom and the United States to notify the Security Council that an agreement had been concluded between them and the USSR. This agreement removed, as of May 12, 1949, all restrictions imposed by both sides since March 1, 1948, on communications, transport and trade between Berlin and their respective zones of occupation in Germany, and between those zones themselves.

Complaints of United States Intervention in the Domestic Affairs of Other Countries

Three complaints of intervention by the United States in the domestic affairs of other states were placed on the General Assembly's agenda—two of them, in 1951 and 1956, at the request of the USSR and one, in 1952, at the request of Czechoslovakia.

In 1951, the Assembly considered an item entitled "Complaint of aggressive acts of the United States of America and its interference in the domestic affairs of other countries, as instanced by the appropriation of $100,000,000 to finance the recruitment of persons and the organization of armed groups in the Soviet Union, Poland, Czechoslovakia, Hungary, Romania, Bulgaria, Albania and a number of other democratic countries, as well as outside the territory of those countries."

A Soviet draft resolution condemning the United States Mutual Security Act of 1951 was rejected by the Assembly in January 1952. A similar complaint was submitted by Czechoslovakia in October 1952, but its draft resolution was also rejected.

During the discussion on the second Soviet complaint in the Assembly's Special Political Committee in February 1957, the USSR, Czechoslovakia, Bulgaria, Albania, the Ukrainian SSR, Romania, the Byelorussian SSR and Poland described various aspects of hostile activity by the United States in their countries.

The United States rejected the allegations and stated that the USSR was endeavouring to divert world attention from its own attempts to undermine the governments of free countries all over the world, and particularly from its intervention in the domestic affairs of Hungary.

A draft resolution submitted by the USSR on the subject was not adopted.

Investigation of Conditions for Free Elections in Germany

France, the United Kingdom and the United States, acting on a proposal by the German Federal Chancellor, brought to the General Assembly's sixth session, in 1951, a request for the appointment of an impartial international commission to carry out, under United Nations supervision, an investigation in the Federal Republic of Germany, in Berlin and in the Soviet Zone of Germany to determine whether existing conditions there made it possible to hold genuinely free elections throughout those areas, which would be a decisive step towards reunification.

The representatives of the German Democratic Republic and of the eastern sector of Berlin stated that the establishment of a commission of investigation would constitute intervention in the domestic affairs of the German people.

On December 20, 1951, the Assembly established a commission to ascertain and report whether "genuinely free and secret elections" throughout those areas were possible. Poland declined to accept membership on the commission on the grounds that its establishment was illegal and contrary to the Charter.

On April 30, 1952, the commission submitted a report stating that during a visit to Germany in March, it had concluded satisfactory agreements for carrying out its task with the Allied High Commission for Germany, the Government of the Federal Republic of Germany, the Inter-Allied Kommandatura in Berlin and the Government of the western sector of Berlin. It had not, however, been able to establish contact with the authorities in the Soviet Zone of Germany and in the eastern sector of Berlin and had thus been unable to make the necessary arrangements with them. The commission regretfully concluded that at that time there was little prospect of its being able to pursue its task, but it would remain at the disposal of the United Nations to implement its mandate whenever it seemed likely that new steps might lead to positive results.

Complaint of Hostile Activities Against Yugoslavia

Yugoslavia complained on November 9, 1951, that for more than three years the USSR had been organizing pressure against it in order to threaten its territorial integrity and national independence and that that pressure had been applied both directly and through the Governments of Albania, Bulgaria, Czechoslovakia, Hungary, Poland and Romania in actions which violated the generally accepted principles regarding relations among nations.

The General Assembly, on December 14, 1951, adopted a Yugoslav draft resolution recommending that Yugoslavia and the seven other states conduct their relations and settle their disputes in accordance with the spirit of the Charter, conform in their diplomatic intercourse with the rules and practices customary in international relations and settle frontier disputes by means of mixed frontier commissions or other peaceful means of their choice.

Austrian Peace Treaty

The question of an appeal to the signatories to the Moscow Declaration of November 1, 1943, for an early fulfilment of their pledges towards Austria was taken up by the General Assembly in 1952, at the request of Brazil.

In a resolution adopted on December 20, 1952, the Assembly earnestly appealed to France, the USSR, the United Kingdom and the United States—the Governments concerned—to make a renewed and urgent effort to reach agreement on the terms of an Austrian treaty so that the occupation might soon be terminated and Austria might fully exercise the powers inherent in its sovereignty.

The Byelorussian SSR, Czechoslovakia, Poland, the Ukrainian SSR and the USSR did not participate in Assembly consideration of the item because they contended that, according to Article 107 of the Charter, the Assembly was not legally entitled even to consider the subject. (Article 107 states: "Nothing in the present Charter shall invalidate or preclude action, in relation to any state which during the Second World War has been an enemy of any signatory to the present Charter, taken or authorized as a result of that war by the Governments having responsibility for such action.")

An Austrian State Treaty restoring Austria's independence was signed in Vienna on May 15, 1955, by representatives of Austria, France, the USSR, the United Kingdom and the United States.

Austria was admitted to membership in the United Nations on December 14, 1955.

Hungarian Question

On October 27, 1956, France, the United Kingdom and the United States requested the Security Council to consider the situation in Hungary in connection with events which had occurred in that country on October 22 and the ensuing days. The three countries stated that foreign military forces in Hungary were violently repressing the rights of the Hungarian people, which were secured by the treaty of peace to which Hungary and the Allied and Associated Powers were parties.

On October 28, the Hungarian People's Republic protested against consideration by the Security Council of the situation in Hungary on the grounds that the events there were exclusively within Hungary's domestic jurisdiction. The USSR maintained that discussion by the Council would amount to gross interference in the domestic affairs of Hungary and to contravention of the Charter and would encourage the armed rebellion being conducted by a reactionary underground movement against the legal government.

On November 1, Imre Nagy, President of the Council of Ministers of the Hungarian People's Republic, informed the Secretary-General that new Soviet troops were entering Hungary and that he was demanding their withdrawal. The following day, Mr. Nagy asked the Security Council to instruct the Soviet and Hungarian Governments to start negotiations for the withdrawal of Soviet troops from Hungary, the termination of the Warsaw Treaty and the recognition of Hungary's neutrality.

A United States draft resolution, submitted on November 3 and later revised, called upon the USSR not to introduce additional armed forces into Hungary and to withdraw without delay all its forces from that country. The draft resolution was not adopted because of the negative vote of the USSR. The United States then submitted another draft resolution, which the Council adopted by 10 votes to 1, calling an emergency special session of the General Assembly—as provided for by its "Uniting for Peace" resolution of 1950—to consider the situation in Hungary.

The emergency special session of the Assembly met from November 4 to 10, 1956. The USSR opposed the inclusion of the item in the agenda of the session on the grounds that discussion of it was barred by the Charter. The new Hungarian Government, headed by Janos Kadar, had informed the Secretary-General that all communications from Mr. Nagy were invalid and had reiterated the Hungarian Government's objections to discussion of the situation in the United Nations.

The Assembly, after discussion on November 4, adopted a resolution calling upon the USSR to withdraw all its forces from Hungary without delay. It further affirmed the right of the Hungarian people to a government responsive to its national aspirations and requested the Secretary-General to investigate the situation directly through representatives named by him, to report thereon to the Assembly and to suggest methods of bringing to an end foreign intervention in Hungary in accordance with the Charter. The Assembly then called upon Hungary and the USSR to permit United Nations observers to enter the territory of Hungary and requested the Secretary-General to inquire into the needs of the Hungarian people for food, medicine and similar supplies. In the meantime, the Office of the United Nations High Commissioner for Refugees was working with welfare agencies to provide these supplies.

On November 9, the Assembly adopted three further resolutions, calling again upon the USSR to withdraw its forces from Hungary without delay and dealing with the humanitarian aspects of the question and assistance to refugees from Hungary.

On November 10, the Secretary-General sent an *aide-mémoire* to the Government of Hungary proposing discussion of his earlier request for the admission of United Nations observers to Hungary and also requesting information concerning the needs of the people.

Two days later, the Acting Minister for Foreign Affairs in the Revolutionary Workers' and Peasants' Government of the People's Republic of Hungary informed the Secretary-General that law and order were being restored and that the Hungarian and Soviet Governments considered themselves to be exclusively competent to negotiate the withdrawal of Soviet troops. Any General Assembly resolution concerning the Hungarian situation was contrary to Article 2, paragraph 7, of the Charter, and the sending of representatives appointed by the Secretary-General was not warranted. As for relief assistance to its people, the Hungarian Government was thankful and would facilitate the receipt and distribution of any food and medicine sent.

At its eleventh session, the Assembly, on November 21, December 4 and 12, 1956, and January 10, 1957, adopted a number of resolutions on the Hungarian question in which it: condemned the violation of the Charter by the Soviet Government in depriving Hungary of its liberty and independence; reiterated its call upon the USSR to desist forthwith from any form of intervention in the internal affairs of Hungary; again called on the Soviet Government and the Hungarian authorities to admit United Nations observers to Hungary and to comply with the Assembly's other resolutions, including the withdrawal, under United Nations observation, of Soviet armed forces from Hungary; urged the Soviet Government and the Hungarian authorities to cease immediately the deportation of Hungarian citizens; urged governments and non-governmental organizations to make contributions for the care and resettlement of Hungarian refugees; asked the Secretary-General to take any initiative that he deemed helpful; and established, on January 10, 1957, a United Nations Special Committee on the Problem of Hungary, which was to maintain direct observation in Hungary and elsewhere, taking testimony, collecting evidence and receiving information, as appropriate, in order to report its findings to the General Assembly.

Among the conclusions in the report of the Special Committee, which was submitted in September, were the following: what had taken place in Hungary in October and November 1956 was a spontaneous national uprising; the uprising, far from having been fomented by reactionary circles in Hungary, had been led by students, workers, soldiers and intellectuals; the uprising had not been planned in advance but had started as a peaceful demonstration which was transformed into an armed uprising when the political police opened fire on the people; and in the light of the extent of foreign intervention, consideration of the Hungarian question by the United Nations had been legally proper and, moreover, had been requested by a legal Government of Hungary.

In a supplementary report, submitted on July 14, 1958, the Special Committee expressed the hope that the Hungarian Government would cease carrying out the death sentence for participants in the 1956 uprising and would effectively re-establish the inalienable principles of human rights.

The General Assembly endorsed the Special Committee's reports and, on December 12, 1958, denounced the executions in Hungary of Imre Nagy and three of his associates.

In a further attempt to achieve the objectives of the Assembly's resolutions on Hungary, Prince Wan Waithayakon, of Thailand, President of the eleventh session, was appointed the Assembly's Special Representative on the Hungarian Problem in September 1957. He was succeeded in this post, on December 12, 1958, by Sir Leslie Munro, of New Zealand, President of the Assembly's twelfth session. Both Special Representatives subsequently reported that their efforts to induce the USSR and Hungary to co-operate had been unsuccessful.

The question continued to be discussed at each session of the Assembly from 1959 to 1962, and resolutions adopted by the Assembly deplored the continued disregard by the USSR and Hungary of its decisions on Hungary. In his fourth and last report, submitted on September 25, 1962, the Special Representative stated that none of the Assembly's resolutions had been complied with on this question.

RELIEF TO THE HUNGARIAN PEOPLE. In its resolution on Hungary of November 4, 1956, the General Assembly requested all member states, and invited international and national humanitarian organizations, to co-operate in supplying relief to the Hungarian people.

Relief in the form of food, clothing, medicine and other supplies, valued at $20 million, was distributed by the International Committee of the Red Cross, which acted as the sole agency for the distribution of aid furnished through the United Nations. Relief needs were evaluated by requesting the information from Hungarian authorities and through a joint United Nations/FAO mission which visited Hungary early in January 1957. The relief programme was formally concluded on September 30, 1957.

In regard to the problem of refugees from Hungary, the General Assembly authorized the Secretary-General and the United Nations High Commissioner for Refugees to make joint appeals to governments and non-governmental organizations for assistance to Hungarian refugees. The total influx of Hungarian refugees into Austria and Yugoslavia was about 200,000.

USSR Complaints Regarding United States Military Flights

Complaints by the USSR regarding flights by United States military aircraft were submitted to the Security Council on April 18, 1958, and on May 18 and July 13, 1960. Each complaint was discussed, but none of the resolutions proposed to the Council was adopted.

In 1958, the USSR asked the Council to consider "urgent measures to put an end to flights by United States military aircraft armed with atomic and hydrogen bombs in the direction of the frontiers of the Soviet Union." The United States rejected the Soviet charges and stated that it was merely complying with the inescapable requirements of legitimate self-defence and guarding against the possibility of a surprise attack.

In 1960, the USSR asked the Council to consider "aggressive acts by the United States Air Force against the Soviet Union, creating a threat to universal peace." The USSR told the Council that on May 1, 1960, a United States Air Force military plane of the U-2 type had penetrated into USSR territory for purposes of espionage and sabotage to a depth of more than 2,000 kilometres until it was brought down by USSR rocket units. The United States denied that it had committed any aggressive acts against the USSR or any other country, either through its Air Force or through any agency of the Government.

Two months later, the USSR informed the Council that on July 1 it had shot down in Soviet airspace a six-engined armed bomber of the United States Air Force on a military reconnaissance mission which had penetrated into Soviet territory from the Barents Sea. The United States proposed a full investigation of the facts of the case after stating that the plane was on an electro-magnetic observation flight and that its route had been over international waters at all times.

The USSR also submitted its complaint to the General Assembly on August 20, 1960, but did not insist on discussing it after noting that the new United States President had issued an order prohibiting United States military aircraft from violating the airspace of the Soviet Union.

Status of the German-speaking Element
in the Province of Bolzano (Bozen)

Austria's dispute with Italy concerning the status of the German-speaking element in the Province of Bolzano (Bozen) was considered by the General Assembly in 1960 and 1961. Austria contended that Italy had implemented neither the letter nor the spirit of the Paris Agreement, which had been signed by the two countries on September 5, 1946 and which provided for legislative and executive autonomy for the South Tyrolean population. Austria charged that South Tyroleans were discriminated against and denied their democratic rights. Italy, on the other hand, asserted that the German-speaking inhabitants of the area had full civil and political liberties and that theirs was an active, autonomous region with wide legislative and executive powers and considerable financial resources.

On October 31, 1960, the Assembly recommended that Austria and Italy resume negotiations on the matter and that, failing an agreement within a reasonable period of time, both parties should consider a solution "by any of the means provided in the Charter, including recourse to the International Court of Justice, or any peaceful means of their own choice."

The following year, on November 28, the Assembly noted that the dispute remained unsolved, although negotiations were in progress, and called for further efforts by Austria and Italy to find a solution in accordance with its 1960 resolution.

QUESTIONS RELATING
TO THE WESTERN HEMISPHERE

Complaint of Guatemala

On June 19, 1954, Guatemala requested a meeting of the Security Council to consider measures necessary to prevent the disruption of peace and international security in Central America and also to put a stop to the aggression in progress against Guatemala. Guatemala charged that expeditionary forces had advanced about 15 kilometres inside Guatemalan territory and that, on June 19, aircraft flying from the direction of Honduras had dropped bombs on the port of San José and attacked Guatemala City. The attack, it was stated, was part of a vast international conspiracy to subjugate Guatemala.

When the Council met, Brazil and Colombia proposed that the Security Council refer the complaint of Guatemala to the Organization of American States (oas). France proposed that a final paragraph be added to the joint draft resolution whereby the Council, without prejudice to such measures as oas might take, would call for immediate termination of any action likely to cause further bloodshed. The amendment was accepted by the sponsors of the joint draft resolution. When the resolution, as modified by France, came to the vote, it was not adopted because of the negative vote of the USSR.

The representative of France then reintroduced his amendment as a separate draft resolution; this was adopted unanimously.

At the request of Guatemala and the USSR, the Council met again on June 25. The provisional agenda read: "Cablegram dated June 19, 1954, from the Minister for External Relations of Guatemala addressed to the President of the Security Council and letter dated June 22, 1954, from the representative of Guatemala addressed to the Secretary-General."

After a discussion on a question of procedure, the agenda was not adopted because of lack of a majority.

On July 9, in a cablegram to the President of the Security Council, Guatemala stated that "the occurrences that had prompted the previous Government to appeal to the Security Council in the communication of June 19 and subsequent correspondence" had ceased and that peace and order had been restored.

Complaints by Cuba

On July 18, 1960, the Security Council considered a complaint by Cuba accusing the United States of repeated threats, reprisals and aggressive acts against Cuba.

The United States denied aggressive designs against Cuba, accused Cuba of carrying out a violent propaganda campaign against the United States and said that the matter was already under consideration by the Organization of American States (OAS), which was the proper forum for its discussion.

On July 19, the Security Council noted that the situation was under consideration by OAS and adjourned consideration of the question pending a report from OAS. It invited the members of OAS to lend their assistance in achieving a peaceful solution.

Later, OAS transmitted to the Security Council a number of its documents by which it condemned intervention or the threat of intervention from an extra-continental power in the affairs of the American Republics. It singled out what it called the attempt of the Sino-Soviet powers to destroy hemispheric unity, and it reaffirmed the principle of non-intervention by any American state in the internal or external affairs of the other American states. In addition, it proclaimed that all members of OAS were "under obligation to submit to the discipline of the inter-American system."

It also informed the Security Council of the forthcoming meeting of its Committee of Good Offices which would seek to clarify the facts relating to the Cuba-United States controversy.

On December 31, 1960, Cuba, in a letter to the President of the Security Council, asked for an immediate meeting of the Council to consider United States intention to commit direct military aggression against Cuba. Cuba said that it had in its possession evidence of a plan for United States armed aggression against Cuba and that in its preparation the United States was exerting pressure to bring about the diplomatic isolation of Cuba from Latin America. Cuba later informed the Council that the United States had severed diplomatic relations with it.

On November 21, 1961, Cuba requested a meeting of the Council to consider its charges that the United States was carrying out a plan of armed intervention in the Dominican Republic in violation of the latter's sovereignty. After discussion, the President of the Council stated that the item would remain on the Council's agenda for further discussion, if required.

CONSIDERATION BY THE GENERAL ASSEMBLY. The Cuba-United States issue was included in the Assembly's agenda in 1960 as a result of the Cuban complaint that the United States had intensified its plans for aggression and intervention in the domestic affairs of Cuba.

When the Assembly started to consider the item on April 15, 1961, Cuba charged the United States with a number of acts of aggression, and on April 17 announced the invasion of Cuba by a mercenary force from Guatemala and Florida, organized, financed and armed by the United States.

The United States denied that any attack against Cuba had been launched from any part of the United States and stated that while the United States sympathized with those who opposed the Castro régime, it was opposed to the use of its territory for mounting an offensive against any foreign government.

On April 21, the Assembly adopted a resolution, sponsored by seven Latin American countries, which referred to the Security Council's resolution of July 19, 1960, and the procedures adopted at the seventh meeting of the Committee of Consultation of OAS, and exhorted all member states to take such peaceful action as was open to them to remove existing tension.

In September 1961, the item "Complaint by Cuba of threats to international peace and security arising from new plans of aggression and acts of intervention being executed by the Government of the United States of America against the Revolutionary Government of Cuba," was inscribed in the agenda of the sixteenth session of the Assembly.

Subsequent to the item's inscription, further communications from Cuba were received, containing additional charges of United States intervention in Cuba's internal affairs. Also, in a letter dated October 30 addressed to the President of the General Assembly, Guatemala protested against the allegations made by Cuba of Guatemalan participation in the invasion of Cuba in 1961. The Cuban complaint was considered by the General Assembly during February 1962, but no resolution was adopted.

The Critical Situation in the Caribbean

The Security Council met from October 23 to 25, 1962, to discuss the critical situation in the Caribbean in response to separate requests by the United States, Cuba and the USSR.

The United States requested that the Council deal with the dangerous threat to the peace and the security of the world resulting from the secret establishment in Cuba by the USSR of launching bases and the installation of long-range ballistic missiles capable of carrying nuclear warheads to most of North and South America.

Cuba asked the Council to consider "the act of war unilaterally committed" by the United States in ordering what it called a "naval blockade" and what the United States termed a "quarantine" of Cuba. Cuba charged that this was the culmination of a series of aggressive acts against it by the United States.

The USSR, contending that all weapons sent to Cuba were for defensive purposes, requested the Council to condemn the United States for "violating the Charter" and "increasing the threat of war" and to insist that it revoke its decision to inspect ships bound for Cuba. Both the United States and the USSR expressed readiness to confer on the situation.

On October 24, Secretary-General U Thant informed the Council that, at the request of a large number of delegations, he had sent identically worded appeals to President Kennedy and Chairman Khrushchev to suspend voluntarily the arms shipments and quarantine measures for a period of two to three weeks and to enter into immediate negotiations for a peaceful solution. He had also appealed to Prime Minister Castro to assist in finding a way out of the "impasse" by halting work on the installations under discussion, and had declared himself available to all parties for whatever services he might be able to perform. The Secretary-General had warned that what was at stake was not just the interests of the parties concerned, or even of all member states, but "the very fate of mankind."

During the course of the Security Council's debate, the Secretary-General received favourable replies from President Kennedy and Chairman Khrushchev, and the Council adjourned on the understanding that future work would be decided in the light of the results of the discussions that were to take place.

On October 30 and 31, U Thant held talks with Cuban authorities in Havana. He reported afterwards that he had been reliably informed that the missiles were being dismantled and that there had been agreement "that the United Nations should continue to participate in the peaceful settlement of the problem."

On January 7, 1963, the Secretary-General received a joint letter from the USSR and the United States expressing the appreciation of the two Governments for the Secretary-General's efforts in assisting them in averting the serious threat to the peace. While not all the related problems in the matter had been resolved, the two Governments believed that, in view of the degree of understanding reached between them on the settlement of the crisis and the extent of progress in the implementation of this understanding, it was not necessary for the item to occupy further the attention of the Security Council.

A letter from Cuba, also delivered to the Secretary-General on January 7, expressed the view that the negotiations carried out with the Secretary-General's assistance had "not led to an effective agreement capable of guaranteeing, in a permanent way, the peace of the Caribbean and in liquidating existing tensions." The Cuban Government felt that the negotiations had not produced agreements acceptable to Cuba mainly because the United States had not "renounced its aggressive and interventionist policy" and was maintaining the "position of force assumed in flagrant violation of international law."

U Thant, in his reply of January 9, took note of the position of the Cuban Government.

Question of Boundaries between Venezuela and British Guiana (the present Guyana)

On August 18, 1962, Venezuela requested the inclusion, in the agenda of the seventeenth session of the General Assembly, of the question of boundaries between Venezuela and the territory of British Guiana (the present Guyana). An explanatory memorandum stated that an award made in 1899 by an Arbitral Tribunal had not recognized Venezuela's rights even over territories which had not been held by the British for fifty years and that the boundary had been traced in an arbitrary way. Venezuela had reserved its rights at the Fourth Meeting of Consultation of Ministers of Foreign Affairs of the American Continent in 1951 and at the Tenth Inter-American Conference in 1954. Since then, Venezuela had approached the United Kingdom with a view to arriving at an amicable solution of the problem before the proclamation of independence of British Guiana in order to avoid future controversy with a newly independent state. Venezuela believed that the Assembly should be informed of the results of those negotiations.

The Special Political Committee considered the item at three meetings in November, at which statements were made by the Foreign Minister of Venezuela, the representative of the United Kingdom and others. On November 16, the Chairman of the Committee stated that "in view of the possibility of direct discussions among the parties concerned, we should not proceed further with our debate here." The Committee, therefore, had no recommendation to make to the General Assembly.

Complaint by Haiti

On May 8, 1963, the Security Council met to consider a complaint by Haiti that the Dominican Republic was trying to precipitate war in the Caribbean by threatening an invasion of Haiti. The Dominican Republic, Haiti stated, had issued a 24-hour ultimatum on the basis of false allegations of violations of the Dominican Embassy at Port-au-Prince by Haitian security forces. Haiti further charged that the Dominican Republic had aided Haitian exiles in activities hostile to the Haitian Government, that there was a massive concentration of Dominican troops on the Haitian border and that the aim of the Dominican Republic was to destroy the only Negro republic in the Americas.

The Dominican Republic rejected the charges and stated that the cause of the tension between the two countries lay in the systematic acts of provocation and the outrage to the dignity and sovereignty of the Dominican State committed by Haiti, which had culminated in the attack on the Dominican Embassy at Port-au-Prince, the arrest of those who had sought asylum there and the military occupation of the Embassy. The Dominican Republic also stated that its troops had been placed on the border to prevent Haitian forces from making incursions into Dominican territory and that the chaotic situation within Haiti was a source of danger for the peace in the Caribbean.

It further stated that the controversy between the two countries was under consideration by the oas, which had already taken steps with a view to finding a solution of the problem. The Dominican Republic asked the Council to suspend consideration of the question and leave the matter to the oas.

At the meeting on May 9, the President of the Council drew attention to the text of a resolution adopted by the Council of the oas the previous day providing for further study of the Dominican-Haitian situation by a committee of five which had been appointed in April to study the events denounced by the Dominican Republic and for an increase, if necessary, in the membership of the committee.

Haiti, while maintaining its right to resort to the Security Council, said that it would agree to a decision of the Council to await the results of the peace mission of the oas, provided the Security Council remained seized of the question.

The Council adjourned on the understanding that the question would remain on its agenda.

Complaint by Panama

At a meeting held on January 10-11, 1964, the Security Council considered a complaint by Panama that, on January 9-10, United States forces garrisoned in the Panama Canal Zone had committed an armed attack against Panama in which twenty persons had been killed and over 300 wounded. The incidents had arisen in connection with the implementation of an agreement between Panama and the United States whereby the flags of both countries should fly together at certain places and on certain buildings in the Canal Zone. United States residents of the zone, however, had done all they could to prevent the implementation of the agreement. As a concession to their views, the United States Governor of the Canal Zone had arbitrarily decided that in some places neither flag should be hoisted. Nevertheless, United States students at a school in the Canal Zone had decided, on their own initiative, to fly only the United States flag. This had greatly disturbed the Panamanian community, with the result that a number of Panamanian students and citizens had decided to hoist the Panamanian flag at those places where it should legally be hoisted. The United States military forces had, thereupon, opened fire with machine-guns on the peaceful demonstrators.

Under the Canal Treaty of 1903, Panama had granted the United States certain limited rights which were necessary for the construction, maintenance and protection of the Canal, but Panama had always maintained its sovereignty over the Canal Zone. The United States, however, Panama charged, had unilaterally arrogated to itself functions and prerogatives in the Canal Zone to the detriment of Panama's rights. Panama asked that the status of the Canal, which was a source of permanent discord, should be changed and that lasting solutions be found which would guarantee the well-being and economic development of Panama.

The United States rejected the charges, stating that violence had started after a group of Panamanian high school students had been permitted by United States Zone authorities to move peacefully to the Balboa High School within the Zone for the purpose of raising the Panamanian flag. On the way out of the Zone, some students had become unruly and had damaged property; the Zone police, however, had escorted them to the zone boundary and most of them had peacefully withdrawn. Subsequently, since the police had been unable to maintain order, the United States armed forces had assumed responsibility for the protection of the Zone. There was no evidence that either the police or the army had ever gone outside the Zone, and they had only taken minimum measures to insure the safety of the Zone and its residents. The OAS Inter-American Peace Committee, which had been jointly requested by Panama and the United States to investigate the situation, was on its way to Panama and the problem should continue to be dealt with in the regional forum.

On a proposal by Brazil, which was accepted by Panama and the United States, the Council authorized its President to appeal to the two Governments to put an immediate end to the exchange of fire and the bloodshed, and to request that they impose the utmost restraint over the military forces under their command and the civilian population under their control.

The Council retained the item on its agenda.

The Situation in the Dominican Republic

In a letter of April 29, 1965, the United States informed the Security Council that, armed hostilities having broken out in the Dominican Republic, the President of the United States had ordered American troops ashore to protect American citizens and escort them to safety. The letter stated that the President had acted after the Dominican military authorities had informed him that the safety of Americans in the country could no longer be guaranteed and that the assistance of United States military personnel was required. The letter further stated that the United States had requested the Council of the Organization of American States (OAS) to consider the situation in the Dominican Republic.

On May 1, the USSR requested an urgent meeting of the Security Council to consider the question of armed interference by the United States in the internal affairs of the Dominican Republic. On May 14, the Council called for a strict cease-fire and invited the Secretary-General to send a representative to the Dominican Republic to report on the situation. The Council called upon all concerned in the Dominican Republic to co-operate with the representative of the Secretary-General in his task.

The Secretary-General, on the same day, sent an advance party to the Dominican Republic, led by General Indar Jit Rikhye, his military adviser. He also appointed José A. Mayobre, Executive Secretary of the Economic Commission for Latin America, as his representative in the Dominican Republic. Mr. Mayobre arrived in Santo Domingo, the capital, on May 17, taking an urgent appeal from the Secretary-General to the contending factions—the Constitutional Government and the Government of National Reconstruction—to heed the Council's call for a cease-fire.

On May 19, at the suggestion of France, the Council appealed for a suspension of hostilities so that the International Red Cross could search for the wounded and the dead. Mr. Mayobre was asked to direct his efforts to securing a truce. On May 21, Mr. Mayobre reported that both factions had agreed to a truce.

The following day, the Council requested the parties in conflict to extend the truce into a permanent cease-fire and asked the Secretary-General to report to it on the implementation of the resolution. The draft resolution, submitted by France, was adopted by a vote of 10 in favour, none against, with 1 abstention (United States). Three days later, Mr. Mayobre reported that, except for minor incidents, the cease-fire was effective.

In the course of its meetings in May, the Council rejected a USSR proposal to condemn United States intervention in the Dominican Republic and to demand the immediate withdrawal of United States forces, and a draft resolution by Uruguay calling for immediate compliance with the cease-fire, as well as USSR amendments to it proposing that the Council call for the immediate withdrawal of United States troops and that it condemn the armed intervention.

On May 21, the United States submitted a draft resolution calling for the strict observance of a cease-fire, urging the OAS to intensify its efforts to attain democratic institutions in the Dominican Republic and to assure observance of the cease-fire, and requesting the Representative of the Secretary-General to co-ordinate his activities with those of the Secretary-General of the OAS. The United States, however, withdrew its draft on May 24 in view of the new mandate given the Secretary-General of the OAS, who had been appointed Special Representative of the OAS in the Dominican Republic, and in the light of the Security Council's appeal for a permanent cease-fire.

In a report covering the period June 19 to July 15, based on information received from his representative, the Secretary-General stated that, despite isolated incidents, the cease-fire had been maintained in Santo Domingo during that time. It referred to negotiations for a political settlement which the *Ad Hoc* Committee of the OAS had undertaken and to violations of human rights allegedly committed by the Government of National Reconstruction. The Secretary-General also drew the Council's attention to the serious social and economic situation.

On July 26, 1965, the President of the Security Council summed up the agreed views of the members of the Council. First, information received by the Council, as well as the Secretary-General's reports, showed that in spite of the Council's resolutions, the cease-fire had been repeatedly violated. Acts of repression against the civilian population and other violations of human rights, as well as data on the deterioration of the economic situation in the Dominican Republic, had been brought to the Council's attention. Secondly, members of the Council had condemned the gross violations of human rights in the Dominican Republic, expressed the desire that such violations should cease and indicated again the need for the strict observance of the cease-fire in accordance with the Council's resolutions. Thirdly, the Council members considered it necessary that the Council continue to watch the situation in the Dominican Republic closely and that the Secretary-General continue to report to it.

After July 26, there were no Security Council meetings on the Dominican question, but the Council was kept informed of developments there through the reports which the Secretary-General submitted to it at regular intervals and through the information submitted by the OAS pursuant to Article 54 of the United Nations Charter.

OTHER POLITICAL AND SECURITY QUESTIONS

United Nations Armed Forces

On February 16, 1946, the Security Council directed the Military Staff Committee to examine from the military point of view Article 43 of the Charter regarding agreements for making armed forces and assistance available to the Council. On April 30, 1947, the Committee presented a report on general principles to govern the organization of such armed forces. The Council accepted a large part of the report but an area of disagreement could not be overcome, and in July 1948 the Committee informed the Council that it was not able to make further progress until agreement had been reached in the Council on the general principles previously reported upon. The Council did not discuss the problem, and the Committee has continued to meet without being able to report any progress on the matter.

Interim Committee of the General Assembly

On November 13, 1947, the General Assembly established the Interim Committee as a subsidiary organ which would function between the Assembly's regular sessions.

The Interim Committee was prolonged for one year in December 1948, and on November 21, 1949, it was re-established for an indefinite period. The USSR and some other states have regarded the creation of the Interim Committee as contrary to the Charter and have never attended any of its meetings.

United Nations Field Service and Panel of Field Observers

Upon recommendation by the Secretary-General, the General Assembly adopted a resolution in November 1949 according to which the Secretary-General had authority to establish a United Nations Field Service to provide certain technical services to United Nations field missions, and a United Nations Panel of Field Observers, composed of a list of names of qualified persons, to assist United Nations missions in the functions of observation and supervision.

Since its establishment in 1949, the United Nations Field Service has rendered continuous services to United Nations missions around the world. Nominations made by member governments to the Panel of Field Observers have been duly listed and kept on file, but military observers lent by members for service with United Nations missions have not generally been selected from those named to serve on the Panel.

Recognition by the United Nations
of the Representation of a Member State

On December 14, 1950, the General Assembly approved a resolution under which it recommended that: (a) whenever more than one authority claims to be the government entitled to represent a member state in the United Nations and this question becomes the subject of controversy in the United Nations, it should be considered in the light of the purposes and principles of the Charter and the circumstances of each case; (b) when any such question arises, it should be considered by the General Assembly, or by the Interim Committee if the Assembly is not in session; and (c) the attitude adopted by the Assembly or the Interim Committee concerning any such question should be taken into account in other organs of the United Nations and in the specialized agencies.

Investigation into the Circumstances of the Death
of Dag Hammarskjöld and of Those Accompanying Him

Following the death of the Secretary-General, Dag Hammarskjöld, and of fifteen other persons in an airplane crash near Ndola, Northern Rhodesia, on September 17, 1961, the General Assembly decided to appoint a commission of five eminent persons to carry out an investigation into the conditions and circumstances of the tragedy. The Assembly asked that the commission investigate, in particular: (a) why the flight had to be undertaken at night without escort; (b) why its arrival at Ndola was unduly delayed, as reported; (c) whether the aircraft, after having established contact with the tower at Ndola, lost that contact, and why the fact of its having crashed did not become known until several hours afterwards; and (d) whether the aircraft, after the damage it was reported to have suffered earlier from firing by aircraft hostile to the United Nations, was in a proper condition for use.

The members of the United Nations Commission of Investigation were appointed by the Assembly on December 8, 1961. By a letter of the same date, the Assembly was informed by the United Kingdom that a Commission of Inquiry would be established by the Federation of Rhodesia and Nyasaland, which would conduct a public inquiry into the accident. On behalf of the Federation, the United Kingdom invited the United Nations to designate a member of this Commission. After careful consideration, the United Nations Commission decided that the United Nations would not appoint a member to the Federation Commission and that the two investigations could be best conducted through co-operation and exchange of information and should be kept separate.

The United Nations Commission met in the Congo (Leopoldville), in the Federation of Rhodesia and Nyasaland and in Geneva between January 24 and March 8, 1962. It took note of evidence submitted to the Federation Commission and to the Rhodesian Board of Investigation, visited the site of the crash, viewed the wreckage, which had been collected at Ndola, and heard ninety witnesses.

The Commission submitted its report to the President of the General Assembly on May 2, 1962. Its conclusions were that while it had examined all possible causes of the disaster, including sabotage, attack by hostile aircraft, mechanical trouble and human failure by the pilots, and while it had found no evidence to support any of the particular theories advanced, it was not able to exclude the possible causes considered.

Economic and Social Questions

UNITED NATIONS DEVELOPMENT DECADE

On September 25, 1961, the President of the United States, while addressing the General Assembly, proposed that the 1960's be officially designated as the United Nations Development Decade. He considered that within the framework of the Decade, the efforts of the United Nations in promoting economic growth could be expanded and co-ordinated. The matter was discussed during the sixteenth session of the Assembly, and a resolution was adopted unanimously on December 19, 1961.

The resolution stressed the importance of the economic and social development of the less advanced countries not only to those countries but also to the attainment of international peace and security and to an increase in world prosperity. It stressed the increasing gap in *per capita* incomes between the economically developed and the less developed countries. All member states and their peoples were to intensify their efforts during the 1960's to accelerate progress towards self-sustaining growth of the economy of individual nations and of their social advancement. The objective of these efforts would be the attainment, in each developing country, of a minimum annual growth rate of 5 per cent in aggregate national income by the end of the Decade.

The resolution called upon member states of the United Nations and of the specialized agencies to pursue certain policies in order to achieve the goal. It also called on the Secretary-General to develop proposals for the intensification of action in the fields of economic and social development by the United Nations system of organizations, after taking account of the views of governments and in consultation with the heads of international agencies, the Special Fund and Technical Assistance Board, and the regional economic commissions. The resolution invited the Economic and Social Council to transmit the Secretary-General's report, together with its views and its report on action taken thereon, to member states and to the General Assembly at its seventeenth session, in 1962.

In response to this request, the Secretary-General presented his proposals for action to the Council at its summer session in 1962. The proposals were grouped in seven chapters, entitled, respectively: setting and problems for the Development Decade; the approach to development planning; mobilization of human resources; sectoral development; international trade; development financing; and technical co-operation and other aids to development and planning.

Simultaneously with these proposals covering action by the whole United Nations family, the Secretary-General also submitted to the Council the individual reports from the specialized agencies describing their proposed programme for the Development Decade and the views submitted by governments concerning their action.

The Secretary-General's proposals were received with appreciation by the Council and subsequently by the General Assembly at its seventeenth session, in 1962. The Council requested the Secretary-General to prepare, in co-operation with the regional economic commissions and other United Nations bodies and agencies, a programme of detailed phased proposals for action in the more immediate future with respect to basic factors of economic growth.

The Council also urged the "prompt attainment" of the target of $150 million for the Expanded Programme of Technical Assistance and the United Nations Special Fund, as well as full support for the Freedom-from-Hunger Campaign and for the World Food Programme. The resolution also referred to the importance of the Conference on the Application of Science and Technology for the Benefit of Less Developed Areas and requested the Secretary-General to make appropriate recommendations for action resulting from the findings of the Conference.

In a related resolution, the Council decided to establish a Special Committee on Co-ordination, consisting of representatives of eleven states, with particular emphasis on the Development Decade. The Special Committee's task is to keep under review the activities of the United Nations and its related agencies in the Decade; to consider, in consultation with the agencies, priority areas or projects relating to the objectives of the Decade; and to submit recommendations on these matters to the Council.

The Council, in 1963, asked for a further progress report on the activities of the United Nations family of organizations, to be submitted in 1965. This report appeared together with an appraisal by the Secretary-General entitled *The United Nations Development Decade at Mid-Point.* In his appraisal, the Secretary-General pointed out that progress in the 1960's had been disappointing. Many indicators of economic advance showed that the rate of improvement between the 1950's and the 1960's had declined. The gap between the *per capita* incomes of the developing and the developed countries, which had caused concern at the beginning of the Decade, had widened by 1965.

The Secretary-General was able to point out, however, that the picture was not one of unrelieved gloom. Not only had progress been made in a significant number of important fields, but the means available to the international community for the betterment of the economic and social position of the disadvantaged countries had been improved. This was true both of the organizational and structural aspects of the United Nations system and of the techniques that had become available for promoting growth. Above all, the Secretary-General pointed out that the concept of the Decade had received wide acceptance and support and that it had become a focus for joint, international action.

Both the Economic and Social Council and the General Assembly adopted resolutions in 1965 calling for further action to translate the goals of the Development Decade into reality. The Council called on member states, and particularly the developed countries, to increase the flow of international capital to developing countries to the level recommended by the United Nations Conference on Trade and Development, namely, 1 per cent of the national income of the economically advanced countries, and to augment the resources available to the United Nations family for developmental activities. The Secretary-General and the heads of the specialized agencies were asked to review their work programmes and to explore the possibility of formulating further programmes of action with a view to intensifying areas in which their organizations could make a maximum contribution to the goals of the Development Decade.

The General Assembly endorsed the Council's resolution and reaffirmed the objectives it had laid down in 1961. It requested the Secretary-General, the specialized agencies and the regional economic commissions to report on the goals that had been established by the United Nations family of organizations in various fields and to try to establish goals in those fields where they had not yet been defined. The Assembly also requested that the possibility be explored of establishing a more comprehensive and coherent set of goals and objectives and that the plans and programmes of the United Nations family be reviewed in the light of these goals and objectives in order that appropriate international action might be taken to strengthen efforts being made at the national and regional levels.

In response to these requests, the Secretary-General, on behalf of all United Nations bodies and agencies, presented an interim report to the Council at its forty-first session, in July 1966. In this report, the Secretary-General described the evolution of the Decade into an organizing principle whose influence had pervaded the work of the entire United Nations family. The report also reviewed the action the various members of the United Nations family were planning to take both on some of the basic themes underlying economic and social development and in individual sectors and fields of activity.

The report concluded that the objectives of the Development Decade were not likely to be achieved by 1970 unless the governments of both developed and developing countries were willing to give a massive new impetus to development. Well-meaning declarations of intent had to be followed up by the actual implementation of specific programmes and policies, many of which would involve some sacrifice, but without which the aspirations embodied in the concept of the Development Decade would remain pious hopes.

ECONOMIC DEVELOPMENT: BROAD ISSUES AND TECHNIQUES

Development Planning and Projections

In its 1961 resolution designating the United Nations Development Decade, the General Assembly listed the approaches and measures which it considered necessary to be taken in order to further the objectives of the Decade. Among these, it listed measures for assisting the developing countries, at their request, to establish well-conceived and integrated national plans which would serve to mobilize internal resources and to utilize resources offered by foreign sources for progress towards self-sustained growth.

At the same session, the Assembly requested the Secretary-General to establish an Economic Projections and Programming Centre (now called the Centre for Development Planning, Projections and Policies) within the Department of Economic and Social Affairs to prepare, in co-operation with the international agencies concerned, long-term projections of world economic trends in order to facilitate the formulation of national economic plans and to provide studies of planning techniques under various economic and social systems which would be helpful to national and regional institutes of economic development and planning.

The Centre was established in June 1962, and a year later the Secretary-General submitted to the Economic and Social Council a progress report, including a work programme for the Centre which classified its activities into five major categories: studies on planning and programming; projections of world economic trends; technical assistance support activities; dissemination of information; and organization of meetings and seminars of experts.

The first volume of a two-volume study entitled *Planning for Economic Development* appeared in 1964. The report noted that the preparation of a plan for development was to be regarded as the first of a series of connected problems designed to solve deep-rooted social problems through rapid and sustained economic growth. The report contained a review of methods of plan formulation, implementation and organization, as well as an analysis of the interrelation between national plans and international policies. It emphasized the importance of the systematic and critical appraisal of programmes and of the reassessment of plan targets in the light of changing circumstances and possibilities.

Volume II of the report, which appeared in 1965, comprised two parts, one dealing with planning experience in private enterprise and mixed economies, and the other with planning experience in centrally planned economies.

At its summer session in 1965, the Economic and Social Council decided to appoint a Committee for Development Planning as a standing organ of the Council. The functions of the Committee are to consider and evaluate the programmes and activities of the organs of the United Nations and of the specialized agencies relating to economic planning and projections and to propose measures for their improvement, and also to consider and evaluate the progress made in the transfer of knowledge to developing countries and in the training of personnel of those countries in economic planning and projections.

The first of a series of seminars on economic planning was held in September 1965, at Ankara; the topic of the seminar was "Planning the external sector: techniques, problems and policies."

In October 1965, the Netherlands Government announced its decision to contribute $1,400,000 for establishing a United Nations Trust Fund. Of this contribution, $1,000,000 was to be allocated to the Centre for Development Planning, Projections and Policies and the associated centres of the secretariats of the regional economic commissions, and the remainder, $400,000, in equal amounts to the African Institute for Economic Development and Planning, the Asian Institute for Economic Development and Planning, the Latin American Institute for Economic and Social Planning and the International Institute for Educational Planning.

Financing of Economic Development

Financing the economic development of less developed countries has been the subject of many years' discussion and study in the General Assembly, the Economic and Social Council and other United Nations bodies dealing with economic questions. Deliberations have proceeded at two levels: at the general level of principle and policy and at the more detailed, practical and institutional level.

Discussions of policy and principle have been concerned, on the one hand, with ways and means of stimulating and mobilizing domestic savings in the developing countries and, on the other hand, with ensuring an adequate flow of external finance on appropriate terms and its most effective utilization for development purposes.

An important landmark in these discussions was the adoption in

1960 of a target for the amount of capital transferred by the economically advanced countries to the developing countries: this was set at 1 per cent of the combined national income of the former. This target was refined somewhat at the United Nations Conference on Trade and Development in 1964: the flows that were to be considered were enumerated and the 1 per cent ratio was made applicable to individual industrial countries. This recommendation was approved by 107 of the countries represented at the Conference.

The setting of a target threw into prominence the problem of measuring the resources that were being transferred to the developing countries. The forms in which resources are transferred have proliferated greatly in the post-war period. Private lending has played a much smaller part than it did in earlier years, and direct private investment has tended to vary erratically from year to year and to be concentrated very noticeably in areas in which there are mineral resources to exploit, particularly petroleum. Official transfers have not only increased markedly in over-all volume but have also extended in range to embrace both bilateral and multilateral cash loans, at various terms and with various degrees of constraint as to their use, and grants of cash and of many types of goods and services, most notably food and technical skills.

Efforts to measure the flow were first made separately for private transfers and for official transfers. The first studies were *International Capital Movements during the Inter-War Period*, published in 1947, and *The International Flow of Private Capital, 1946-1952*, published in 1954. Reports on the international flow of private capital were compiled periodically thereafter.

In 1957, the Economic and Social Council asked governments to submit information to the Secretary-General on international economic assistance, and this information was later published. In response to a resolution adopted by the Council in August 1960, the two types of flows were reported on together in *The International Flow of Long-Term Capital and Official Donations, 1951-1959*. A similar report has been published each year since then, the latest covering the period 1961-1965.

In the meantime, an effort has been made to solve some of the methodological problems associated with the measurement of capital flow in the sense in which the United Nations is interested in it. A group of experts submitted to the Economic and Social Council, in July 1966, an interim report on the measurement of the flow of resources from the developed market economies to the developing countries, and a final report was scheduled to be presented in 1967.

Parallel with its concern about the problem of financing development from domestic and external sources has been the United Nations interest in the machinery for assisting in the process of resource transfer. This machinery has also proliferated. It includes the United Nations Children's Fund, the Technical Assistance Programme, and the United Nations Development Programme, as well as various *ad hoc* arrangements, such as the United Nations Relief and Works Agency for Palestine Refugees, the United Nations Fund for the Congo and the United Nations Korean Reconstruction Agency, and also United Nations joint interest with FAO in the World Food Programme.

CAPITAL DEVELOPMENT FUND.   At its fifteenth session, in 1960, the General Assembly decided in principle that a United Nations Capital Development Fund should be established and resolved that a committee of twenty-five member states should consider concrete preparatory measures, including draft legislation, necessary for this purpose.

The Committee on a United Nations Capital Development Fund, meeting in May and June 1961, concentrated on the formulation of general principles applicable to any international financing institution. These principles dealt with the objectives of international assistance, the ways in which such assistance would be rendered and, finally, the question of co-ordinating the activities of the several institutions in this field.

At its summer session in 1962, the Economic and Social Council considered a draft statute which had been approved in June by a majority of the Committee. The statute stated that the purpose of the fund "shall be to assist under-developed countries in the development of their economies by supplementing existing resources of capital assistance by means of grants and loans, long-term loans made free of interest or at low interest rates." The financial resources of the fund would be derived from voluntary contributions by participating states, and participation in the fund would be open to any member of the United Nations, of the specialized agencies and of the International Atomic Energy Agency or "to any state which accepts the statute and which is admitted to participation by the General Conference of the fund." The statute also provided that the fund would be administered under the supervision of the Council and the authority of the Assembly and would have three organs: a general conference, an executive board, and a managing director and staff.

The Council transmitted the draft statute and the Committee's 1962 report to the Assembly at its seventeenth session, in 1962, together with a resolution which urged the economically advanced countries to reconsider, in consultation with the Secretary-General, possibilities of undertaking measures designed to ensure the establishment of a capital development fund.

The Assembly, in 1962, endorsed the Council's appeal to the economically advanced countries and instructed the Committee to continue to study the need for international financing in connection with the United Nations Development Decade.

The following year, the Assembly extended the Committee's mandate and requested the Secretary-General to prepare a study of the practical steps to transform the Special Fund into a Capital Development Fund in such a way as to include both pre-investment and investment activities. The study was presented in 1964 to the United Nations Conference on Trade and Development, which adopted two recommendations on the question, and to the Economic and Social Council.

At its twentieth session, in 1965, the General Assembly invited the Secretary-General to consult with member states regarding additional resources which might be obtained through voluntary contributions. It decided to extend the mandate of the Committee on a Capital Development Fund and instructed the Committee to make new efforts to achieve a larger measure of agreement on the draft legislation of the fund.

Reports on the World Economic Situation

The world economic situation is reviewed each year by the Economic and Social Council, in accordance with a General Assembly resolution of October 1947. Background information for the Council's discussion is provided by the Secretariat in the form of factual analyses of world economic conditions and trends.

These annual surveys of world economic conditions began with the *Economic Report: Salient Features of the World Economic Situation, 1945-1947*, which was published in 1948. Since 1955, the surveys have sought to analyse not only the current situation in the world economy but also various problems of longer-term significance. Thus, beginning with the *World Economic Survey, 1955*, the survey has consisted of two parts, one dealing with a topical economic problem and the other with current economic developments.

Between 1958 and 1962, the *World Economic Survey* was supplemented by a *Commodity Survey*, which was presented in the first instance to the Commission on International Commodity Trade as a background document for its discussion of the situation of world primary commodity markets with special reference to its implication for the export earnings of the developing countries. In 1963, a summary of the commodity survey was included as an annex in Part II of the *World Economic Survey*. Since then, the work has been carried on by the organization set up after the first United Nations Conference on Trade and Development.

In addition to the documentation produced by the Secretariat at Headquarters, the Economic and Social Council, as background for its discussion of the world economic situation, has before it economic surveys published annually by the regional economic commissions.

The subjects examined in successive surveys reflect both the course of the world economy and the United Nations efforts to implement the economic objectives of the Charter. The 1955 *Survey* contained a review of the first post-war decade. The course of production and trade was examined in the countries with market economies and those with centrally planned economies, and an assessment was made of the extent to which balanced growth had been achieved. In the 1956 *Survey*, attention was turned to the problem of keeping different types of economy in external balance; international payments experience in the post-war period was examined and its implications for growth discussed. The 1957 *Survey*, in response to a request by the Council in July 1956, analysed the problem of inflation in the 1950's, and the 1958 *Survey* took up the question of primary commodity trade and policies in the post-war period. In the 1959 *Survey* there was an appraisal of investment trends and policies; this was complemented in the 1960 *Survey* by an examination of sources and trends of saving.

The 1961 *Survey* studied the significance of industrialization policies for the process of economic development. The next two issues were devoted to the relationship between trade and development: the 1962 *Survey* was based on material prepared for the Preparatory Committee set up to arrange the first United Nations Conference on Trade and Development, and the 1963 *Survey* was based on papers prepared for the Conference proper. The 1964 *Survey* was devoted to an appraisal of targets and progress in development planning, and the 1965 *Survey* discussed the problems of financing economic development.

By covering economic trends on a continuing basis and dealing from time to time at greater depth with the major difficulties facing the world economy, the *Survey* is intended primarily to offer information and insight that might be useful to economic policy makers and advisers in national governments. Since it is couched in a broad analytical framework, however, it is also designed to stimulate interest among academic and other private economists in the practical problems facing the world economy.

Application of Science and Technology to Development

On the proposal of the Scientific Advisory Committee, the Economic and Social Council decided in 1962 that an international technical conference of governments should be convened under the auspices of the United Nations to explore the application of science and technology for the benefit of less developed areas.

The preparations and arrangements for the conference were carried out by the United Nations in consultation with the Scientific Advisory Committee and all the specialized and related agencies, and the conference—the United Nations Conference on the Application of

Science and Technology for the Benefit of Less Developed Areas (UNCSAT)—was held in Geneva from February 4 to 20, 1963. Compared to the other United Nations technical conferences which had preceded it, such as the United Nations Scientific Conference on the Conservation and Utilization of Resources, in 1948, and on New Sources of Energy, in 1961, and the three conferences on the Peaceful Uses of Atomic Energy in 1953, 1958 and 1963, UNCSAT was unique in that it touched on all the scientific disciplines and all aspects of modern life. Its agenda included: natural resources; human resources; agriculture; industrial development; transport; health and nutrition; social problems of development and urbanization; organization, planning and programming for economic development; international co-operation and problems of transfer and adaptation; training of scientific and technical personnel; and communications.

UNCSAT was mainly designed to focus world opinion on the practical possibilities of accelerating development through the application of science and technology. More particularly, it was intended to bring home the need for a reorientation of research towards the requirements of the developing countries and, at the same time, to emphasize the importance for those countries of utilizing scientific knowledge and techniques that were already available. As such, UNCSAT constituted a major event in the programme of the United Nations Development Decade.

More than 2,000 papers were presented to the Conference by governments, the United Nations and its regional economic commissions, the specialized and related agencies, and other participants, and there were more than 1,500 participants including representatives of almost all member states and of the United Nations family of organizations and observers of non-governmental bodies.

Unlike most United Nations conferences, UNCSAT was not empowered to make recommendations to governments or to take decisions regarding policy. However, any weight of opinion brought out in the discussions was reflected in the eight-volume report of the conference, which was issued in four languages. A summary of this report, presented by the Secretary-General to the Economic and Social Council in 1963, outlined his suggestions and recommendations with regard to follow-up action.

The Council was satisfied with the positive results achieved by UNCSAT and emphasized the important contribution which the more effective application of science and technology could make to the economic and social advancement of the developing countries and to the attainment of the objectives of the United Nations Development Decade. With a view to giving practical effect to the results of UNCSAT, the Council decided to establish an Advisory Committee on the Application of Science and Technology to Development.

The Committee, which was established in January 1964, is entrusted with a broad mandate, including that of keeping under review progress in the application of science and technology and proposing to the Council practical measures for the benefit of the less developed areas.

The Committee's eighteen members are appointed by the Council for a term of three years, on the nomination of the Secretary-General after consultations with governments and with the specialized and related agencies. The Committee members, who serve as individuals rather than as representatives of governments, include specialists in agriculture; atomic energy; biology; medicine; physics and space investigations; chemical, civil and electrical engineering; economics; scientific research; and administration.

In addition to its main functions, as outlined by the Council, the Committee was requested by the General Assembly in 1963 to examine the possibility of establishing a programme of international co-operation in science and technology for economic and social development. The Assembly also recommended that the Committee envisage the possibility of mobilizing the efforts of universities and scientific and technological institutions of the developed countries for active participation in such a programme.

In its first report to the Council, the Committee suggested a number of general measures aimed at establishing and strengthening the basic structures for the development of science and technology in the developing countries. The Committee began discussions looking towards the selection of a short list of especially important problems of research or application on which a concerted attack might be launched. It outlined a method of reporting whereby the organizations of the United Nations family could help it keep under review progress in the application of science and technology. The Committee also gave preliminary consideration to the possibility of establishing a programme on international co-operation in science and technology for economic and social development.

In its second report, the Committee emphasized that the most critical limitation on the capacity of a country to absorb and apply or adapt science and technology to development was its supply of trained manpower, and it reiterated its earlier findings that unless the cost of economic development could be financed, the existence of new or better methods might be of little use. It reviewed the current activities of the organizations of the United Nations family in the field of science and technology, and selected eight problem areas which it believed to be of special significance to a large number of developing countries and which lend themselves to a large-scale attack in which the developed countries might co-operate with the developing countries. These selected problem areas were: provision of adequate food supplies; improvement of health; more complete understanding of population problems; most effective exploration and utilization of natural resources;

industrialization; better housing and urban planning; improvement of transportation and communication; and raising levels of education, including new educational techniques.

At its summer session in 1965, the Council endorsed the views of the Committee that wider and more intensive application of existing knowledge, suitably adapted to local conditions, provided the best prospects of securing rapid advancement in the developing countries, and that those countries should be helped to build up as quickly as possible the policies, institutions and supply of skilled personnel on which their capacity and readiness to assimilate science and technology would inevitably depend. The Council requested the Committee, in close co-operation with the Administrative Committee on Co-ordination, to examine periodically the proposed as well as the existing programmes of the United Nations family of organizations, and invited it to submit recommendations aimed at stimulating, co-ordinating and reorienting the activities of those organizations in the application of science and technology to development. Governments of states members of the United Nations were requested to assist the Committee by every possible means; they were also requested to encourage bilateral relationships between their universities, research institutes and laboratories.

Commenting on the views expressed by the Committee in its second report regarding the proposed programme of international co-operation in the field of science and technology, the General Assembly, in 1965, agreed with the Committee that it would not only be possible but highly desirable to develop such a programme in order to strengthen existing programmes and to add appropriate new arrangements for rounding out total effort.

In its third report, the Committee expressed the view that the time had come for the United Nations and related organizations to take firm decisions leading to effective action and proposed to the Council the launching of an international co-operation programme as envisaged by the General Assembly. Hence, it recommended that the Council adopt a resolution launching a "World Plan of Action for the Application of Science and Technology to Development" for intensifying the impact of science and technology in the developing countries in the remaining years of the Development Decade.

The proposed World Plan of Action has four main objectives: to help developing countries build up the institutions and train personnel on which their capacity to apply science and technology to development problems will depend; to promote the more effective application of existing scientific knowledge and technology in developing countries; to focus increasing attention on problems whose solution would be of specific benefit to developing countries; and to promote greater knowledge of the needs of developing countries for science and technology. To help facilitate the implementation of the Plan, the United Nations

Development Programme and the International Bank for Reconstruction and Development were invited to make funds available for the financing of the projects directed towards the application of science and technology, and governments of member states of the United Nations were recommended to give full attention to the needs of the developing countries for assistance in the field of science and technology when conducting bilateral aid programmes.

Within the framework of the proposed Plan of Action, the Committee, in its report, presented specific recommendations in the following fields:

(a) Essential structure for science and technology in the developing countries: the Committee recommended goals for the next five to ten years, including the setting up or reinforcement of a suggested number of national training institutions at various levels, the establishment of centres for the scientific and teaching equipment of primary and secondary schools, the granting of fellowships to be used for the training of research workers and teaching staff and the development of faculties of science and research institutes in the developing countries;

(b) Access to scientific and technological information and transfer of technology: the Committee recommended that members of the United Nations be invited to set up a central body responsible for policy concerning documentation centres and technology transfer centres; that a programme be developed for the development of publishing enterprises to produce low-cost books and periodicals dealing with subjects relating to science and technology; that case studies be made of existing facilities for the transfer of technology in a limited number of developing countries; that a pilot programme be developed to promote visits to enterprises in other countries by technologists from developing countries, and that pilot case studies be undertaken in selected countries in the different regions, on the actual experience in the transfer of technology to developing countries through enterprise-to-enterprise (public and private) arrangements;

(c) Wider application of existing knowledge and the need for new knowledge: the Committee recommended early action in finding solutions to a limited number of problems, namely, increasing water for irrigation, expanding the supply of edible protein and controlling African tryponosiamiasis, the more complete understanding of population problems, exploration and utilization of non-agricultural natural resources, acceleration of industrialization, and development of new educational techniques.

THE ROLE OF PATENTS. In 1961, the General Assembly requested the Secretary-General to prepare a report on the role of patents in the transfer of technology to under-developed countries. In making this request, the Assembly affirmed that "it is in the best interest of all countries that the international patent system should be applied in such a way as to take fully into account the special needs and requirements of the economic development of under-developed countries, as well as the legitimate claims of patentees."

The Secretary-General's report, which was issued in 1964, reviewed the major characteristics of national patent laws and the international patent system and analysed the economic implications of the introduction of patents in developing countries. The report concluded, among other things, that the spread of the patent system to developing countries might, on balance, be beneficial to the introduction of new technology and the advancement of industry in those countries.

The report noted, however, that the monopoly position created by patents might operate to restrain ready access to new technology unless governments applied necessary legislative and administrative safeguards and made sure that the patented technology was put to work in the recipient countries in financial and operational terms which were favourable to their economic development.

The report also pointed out that patents covered only a part of the available technology and therefore any further consideration of the problems affecting the transfer of technology should extend to the entire field of patented and unpatented technology and know-how. The question of patents, in the final analysis, could best be seen, the report noted, in the broader context of facilitating the transfer of technology in general to the developing countries and enhancing the ability of those countries to adapt and use such foreign technology in the implementation of their development programmes.

The question in its broader context was considered in 1965 by the Advisory Committee on the Application of Science and Technology to Development (see above) and by the General Assembly. In a resolution adopted unanimously on December 20, 1965, the Assembly requested the Secretary-General to continue studies of (a) the adequacy of existing national and international practices for the transfer of patented and unpatented technology to developing countries and the possible development of improved practices, including model clauses; (b) national and international action and institutional arrangements, including the systematic collection and dissemination of scientific and technological data and materials, so as to promote the expeditious and effective transfer of technology, especially from private and public industrial enterprises in the developed countries to industrial enterprises in the developing countries; (c) the problems encountered, especially by developing countries, in obtaining technical know-how; and (d) other measures for specific technical and financial assistance to developing countries in their efforts to secure an increased flow of technological and managerial know-how and to adapt it to their individual needs.

Fiscal and Financial Questions

Fiscal and financial problems have for many years been a matter for consideration by the Economic and Social Council and other United Nations bodies. The work programme of the Secretariat has consisted mainly of providing technical assistance, information and advice, on request, to governments, as well as to organs of the United Nations and to the specialized agencies, and of preparing studies and reports on subjects considered by the Economic and Social Council.

In the field of government budgeting, two early studies of the Secretariat were *Budgetary Structure and Classification of Government Accounts* (1951), which included an analysis of the main features of various national budget systems, and *Government Accounting and Budget Execution* (1952), an analysis of representative government accounting systems and procedures.

In response to the interest expressed by member governments, regional workshops on problems of budget reclassification and management have been organized by the Secretariat in Asia and the Far East, Latin America and Africa, under the auspices of the United Nations technical assistance programme. In 1958, the Secretariat prepared *A Manual for Economic and Functional Classification of Government Transactions* to serve as a guide in the reclassification of government transactions with a view to providing required data for programming economic stability and development.

In recent years, economic planning in less developed countries has focussed attention on the problems of improving budget management so as to establish a close link between budgeting and planning. In this regard, the regional budget workshops have considered budgetary techniques which are primarily designed to facilitate budgeting in terms of programmes, projects or activities. These techniques, therefore, shift the emphasis from accountability in purely financial terms to results in real or physical terms and their cost. As a guide in this new field of budgeting, a *Manual for Programme and Performance Budgeting* prepared by the United Nations Secretariat was issued in 1966.

In the tax field, the publication by the Secretariat of *The Effects of Taxation on Foreign Trade and Investment* in 1950 was followed by research on the taxation of foreign private investments in a number of capital-exporting and capital-importing countries. Since 1960, a series of reports, submitted to the Economic and Social Council, on promotion of the international flow of private capital have included a survey of tax measures designed to encourage the flow of such capital to under-developed countries.

The various aspects of the transfer of technological and managerial know-how in the context of capital transfers were highlighted in a report on *The Role of Enterprise-to-Enterprise Arrangements in Supply-*

ing Financial, Managerial and Technological Needs of Industrial Enterprises in Developing Countries, which was submitted to the Council in 1965.

In accordance with Council resolutions, highest priority among the activities of the United Nations in the fiscal and financial field has been given to rendering technical assistance to governments at their request. Such aid has been provided through expert missions working in, and training courses in fiscal subjects established in, the recipient countries, and also training within the Fiscal and Financial Branch of the Secretariat.

As part of its fiscal information service, the United Nations Secretariat has published public finance information papers and surveys of several countries. The chapter on public finance statistics in the *Statistical Yearbook* gives information on public debt and on major components of government expenditures and receipts according to economic character and function.

In the tax field, the United Nations publishes, in the series *International Tax Agreements,* the texts of agreements for the avoidance of double taxation and the prevention of fiscal evasion, as well as information on the status of all known tax agreements. In response to an invitation of the Economic and Social Council to co-operate with the Secretary-General, the publication of a *World Tax Series,* consisting of comprehensive reports on national tax systems and administration, was initiated in 1957 by the Harvard Law School International Program in Taxation, with the co-operation of the Fiscal and Financial Branch of the Secretariat.

SOCIAL POLICY, PLANNING AND DEVELOPMENT

Reports on the World Social Situation

The General Assembly in 1949 invited the Economic and Social Council to consider drafting a general report on the world social and cultural situation. At the request of the Council, a preliminary report limited to the social situation was prepared by the Secretary-General in co-operation with the specialized agencies concerned—ILO, FAO, UNESCO and WHO—and submitted in 1952 to the Social Commission and the Council. A supplementary report on the main trends in social programmes over the ten-year period 1945-1955 was issued in 1955.

In 1957, a second *Report on the World Social Situation* gave special attention to the problem of urbanization. The 1959 *Report* reviewed international and national measures taken since 1953 to improve social conditions. A brief survey of major social trends and a study of balanced economic and social development was included in the 1961 *Report*. The Council then decided that an analytic report on the world social situation should be issued biennially, beginning in 1963 and covering, in alternate editions, social conditions and social programmes on the one hand and urgent comprehensive social problems on the other. The 1963 *Report* summarized trends in social conditions and programmes since 1950 and included regional chapters. The theme of the 1965 *Report* was "motivation for development"; it was concerned with the incentives, methods and techniques of inducing change at the local level, including citizen participation in development, and the results achieved.

Balanced and Integrated Economic and Social Development

In recent years, the General Assembly, the Economic and Social Council and the Social Commission (now called the Commission for Social Development) have adopted a number of resolutions reflecting their interest in questions of balanced and integrated social and economic development. They have also emphasized planning, research and training as means of achieving these goals. The Council, after considering the 1957 *Report on the World Social Situation*, agreed that special attention should be given to the important problem of "balance" in development. In 1959, the Council and the Assembly further examined the social aspects of economic planning and the different stages of development programming designed to meet more adequately the interrelated problems of population growth, urbanization and housing.

As noted above, the 1961 *Report on the World Social Situation* stressed the interrelations between economic and social development. The problem of the definition of "balanced" development was also considered, as were the actual patterns of development in different countries as revealed by different social and economic indicators. Several country case studies were prepared.

In 1962, the Social Commission, the Council and the Assembly approved the general acceptance of the principle of planning as essential to the rapid and balanced economic and social growth of developing countries. On the Council's recommendation, regional seminars have been held on specific aspects of planning. The Council also recommended the preparation of a report setting out, for the use of governments, methods of determining the appropriate allocation of resources to the various social sectors and summarizing various organizational arrangements for social planning in relation to development goals. The Commission, in 1963, approved the increasing attention being given to comprehensive development planning and noted that assistance was being provided to a number of countries for various sectors of their development plans. In 1965, two new posts were established for inter-regional advisers in social development planning and programming.

The United Nations Research Institute for Social Development, which was established through a gift by the Government of the Netherlands and which began operations in 1964, is engaged in a number of studies related to the subject of balanced and integrated economic and social development.

A General Assembly resolution arising out of its debate on the 1963 *Report on the World Social Situation* requested a series of actions which would include a draft programme of social development for the second half of the United Nations Development Decade and, in particular, a review of priorities in international social action. In this connection, a preliminary report was prepared on targets of social development based on data and development plans from a number of countries. The Council considered this report in 1965 and agreed to make further studies of the problem, and particularly to examine the question of the relationship of social targets to economic projections for the second half of the Development Decade. The Council also considered the report on social allocations and recommended that further studies of a more detailed nature, and drawing more far-reaching conclusions, be made, taking into account the experiences of countries with various social systems.

In a General Assembly resolution in 1965, stress was again given to the need to recognize the interrelationship of economic and social factors in formulating social policies and to take into account the experiences of countries with varying economic and social systems. The Secretary-General was requested to prepare, in consultation with the specialized agencies, a draft long-range social programme and to consider the possibility and advisability of preparing a declaration on social development.

In 1965, the Council and the Assembly adopted resolutions on the development and utilization of human resources, stressing the need for continued concerted action, by the competent organs of the United Nations and its interested specialized agencies, for promoting training and the utilization of human resources for the economic and social development of the developing countries.

The Council also adopted a resolution which recognized both the contribution and the needs of young people in relation to economic and social development. It urged governments to include, in their planning and policies, arrangements for enabling young people to participate in national development and measures to combat unemployment and under-employment among young people and to enable them to take part in service to their communities.

To implement this resolution at the international level, consultations were held between the United Nations and the specialized agencies. It was agreed to establish concerted inter-agency action in the field of youth under the general leadership of the United Nations and with the full participation of the specialized agencies, each acting within its own field of competence. An inter-regional adviser on youth policies and programmes was appointed and undertook missions in some ten African countries in the latter half of 1965 to collect information and, where requested, to advise governments. Subsequent missions are being undertaken in the other regions, and arrangements are being made to provide governments with technical assistance and advice on the problems and special needs of youth and the role of young people in national development.

Definition and International Comparability of Living Standards

The lack of generally accepted definitions of standards and levels of living, and of yardsticks by which these standards and levels can be internationally compared and changes in them measured has given rise to difficulties in the preparation of international surveys of social conditions, as well as to efforts to assess the effects of technical assistance programmes and to measure progress in development.

The United Nations and the specialized agencies collaborated on a report published in 1953 entitled "International Definition and Measurement of Standards and Levels of Living" which concluded that there was no single index of the levels of living as a whole that could be applied internationally. A series of components and indicators was suggested to measure and define levels of living. In 1961, the Social Commission, after considering a progress report on the subject, concluded that the work accomplished had reached a stage where the Secretary-General should be requested to distribute the first part of the progress report to member states for their interim guidance. A *Compendium of Social Statistics* dealing with basic statistical indicators showing changes and trends in levels of living over the decade 1950-1960 was issued in conjunction with the 1963 *Report on the World Social Situation*. The work programme adopted by the Social Commission in 1965 made provision for selected country case studies and for co-operation with the Division of Human Rights and the Statistical Office in giving attention to the non-material aspects of levels of living.

Income Distribution

The 1957 *Report on the World Social Situation* drew attention to the varying increases in national income, especially in the less developed countries, and to the unevenness in the distribution of income among the population. In the programme of work adopted by the Social Commission in 1961 and approved by the Council, it was agreed that studies should be undertaken of income distribution and social and economic development in selected countries.

In 1965, the Economic and Social Council, on the recommendation of the Social Commission, requested the Secretary-General to convene a small group of experts to review the relationship between distribution of income in the nation and social policy, including questions of definition and measurement. The aim of this new effort is to develop criteria for the formulation of social policy in a way that would best contribute to a more just and equitable distribution of income.

Social Aspects of Urbanization and Industrialization

In the 1957 *Report on the World Social Situation,* special attention was given to the problems of peoples undergoing rapid transition, especially through urbanization. A Social Commission resolution provides for assistance to be given to governments, on request, to establish national centres to deal with urbanization problems and, in particular, with studies of various kinds concerned with urban development. Since 1962, regional workshops and seminars have been held in different places, including Addis Ababa, Warsaw and Beirut.

The Commission has paid special attention to the social aspects of industrialization. An interregional seminar on this subject was held in Minsk in 1964, and the findings and conclusions of the seminar were discussed in the Committee for Industrial Development in 1965. Under the programme of work adopted by the Social Commission in 1965, case studies have been undertaken of the social aspects of cities and localities in the process of rapid industrialization.

In 1965, the Council adopted a proposal by the Social Commission to initiate a new United Nations programme in the area of regional development with major emphasis on research and training in the social field. A principal aim of this programme will be to assist countries with problems of excessive migration from rural to urban areas and concomitant unemployment and other social ills.

DEVELOPMENT AND UTILIZATION
OF HUMAN RESOURCES

Population Questions

Numerous censuses taken since 1960 have confirmed that a considerable acceleration of population growth now affects a majority of the world's peoples, and it is generally accepted that for some time many countries will continue to experience high rates of population growth. It is also recognized that changes in population characteristics have important implications for plans and programmes of economic and social development.

These and related questions have been the subject of debate in the Population Commission and the Economic and Social Council, where it has been emphasized that it is the responsibility of each government to determine its own policies and action programmes in dealing with problems likely to arise from population change. It has also been affirmed to be in the interest of the United Nations that national policy decisions be made and national programmes implemented in the light of as full a knowledge of the relevant demographic facts as is possible, and that the policies should be designed to ensure satisfactory economic and social progress. The role of the United Nations in the population field is to encourage and assist governments in obtaining relevant demographic information and to provide technical assistance on request in national, regional and interregional projects of research and action related to problems posed by population changes and trends.

The United Nations carries on a continuing programme of demographic research, and the results of this work have been published in many reports. Studies of the interrelationships between demographic, economic and social factors have occupied a prominent place in the Secretariat's work in the field of population. A comprehensive study entitled *The Determinants and Consequences of Population Trends* was issued in 1954, and a new, revised edition is being prepared. The Secretariat has also undertaken, in co-operation with interested governments, pilot studies of population growth and human resources in relation to national development needs, as well as a study of demographic, economic and social change in Mysore State, India. Other studies emphasizing interrelationships have included reports on the economic and social consequences of aging and on the demographic aspects of manpower. Reports relating to formal demography have included analysis of infant and early childhood mortality, methods of measuring infant and general mortality, and demographic aspects of fertility trends in industrialized countries. Recent reports have dealt with conditions and trends of mortality and fertility throughout the world. A revised report on *World Population Prospects* was issued in 1966.

As a part of its programme to enhance the utilization of demographic data, the United Nations has developed a series of technical manuals on methods of population analysis and population estimates and projections. These materials are being widely used by scholars and by regional and national institutions concerned with the development and implementation of economic and social plans and programmes.

The International Union for the Scientific Study of Population (IUSSP) has continued to promote the issuance in various languages of the *Multilingual Demographic Dictionary*, a publication prepared by the United Nations in co-operation with the IUSSP.

Population Growth and Economic Development

The interrelations between population growth and economic development were discussed in 1962 by the General Assembly, which requested the Secretary-General to conduct an inquiry among governments concerning the particular problems confronting them as a result of the reciprocal action between economic development and population change and to intensify the Secretariat's studies related to this subject. The results of the inquiry, conducted in 1963, were reported to the General Assembly in 1964, and in 1965 the subject continued as an item of the Assembly's deliberations. The Population Commission recommended, in 1965, that similar inquiries be undertaken in the future.

In 1964, an *ad hoc* committee of experts convened by the Secretary-General recommended an amplified long-range programme of United Nations work in population fields with respect to: (1) the improvement of demographic statistics; (2) the intensification of research and technical work on certain priority topics, such as fertility, mortality, internal migration and urbanization, and the demographic aspects of economic and social development; and (3) the programme of technical assistance and of conferences in the population field.

One of the steps taken to implement the new programme was the convening in 1966 of an expert group to recommend a practical framework for a programme of research, technical work and technical assistance in the field of fertility.

A large part of United Nations technical assistance in the population field has taken the form of training programmes in demographic analysis for personnel in developing countries, furnished at the three United Nations regional demographic training and research centres, located in Bombay, Cairo and Santiago, Chile. Advisory services in demographic analysis are rendered on the national and regional level at government request both by technical assistance experts financed under United Nations technical assistance programmes and by the regional economic commissions. The authority of the United Nations to provide advisory services and training in action programmes in the field of population at government request was confirmed by a 1965 resolution of the Economic and Social Council. At the request of the Government of India, a United Nations advisory mission has carried out an evaluation of the family planning programme in that country.

Population Conferences

The World Population Conference held in Rome in 1954 under the joint auspices of the United Nations and the IUSSP was the first international scientific conference on problems of population to be sponsored by the United Nations. A second World Population Conference was convened under the same auspices in Belgrade, Yugoslavia, in 1965, with a much larger attendance and a wider geographical coverage. Both conferences served as forums for the exchange of views and experience among experts in demography and related disciplines. The first volume of the proceedings of the conference was published in 1966; this and succeeding volumes will, like those covering the first World Population Conference, provide useful reference material on the present state of demographic knowledge.

A number of regional conferences and seminars on population have been held over the years, the most recent being the Asian Population Conference convened in New Delhi in 1963. Future plans include the convening of a series of regional and interregional seminars on various population questions, in compliance with recommendations contained in the long-range programme of work in the field of population.

Migration

The problem of migration has long been recognized as one which requires international action. While bilateral arrangements on migration, for the purpose of employment and land settlement, have played an important role, more and more frequently governments have called for the help of international organizations.

The United Nations deals with the social, economic and demographic aspects of migration; ILO with migratory movements in connection with its manpower programme; FAO with land settlement as an important aspect of migration; and WHO and UNESCO with those aspects falling within their respective competences. The United Nations High Commissioner for Refugees has an interest in the question, inasmuch as it is closely connected with his mandate of protection of refugees and the solution of their problems.

The Economic and Social Council very early recognized the need to avoid duplication in the work of the different organs of the United Nations and the specialized agencies. Thus, in March 1947, it invited the Population and Social Commissions, after appropriate consultations, to report to the Council on a practical plan for allocating functions among the various organs concerned in the field of migration. The recommendations of the Commissions were considered by the Council in 1948 and resulted in a resolution allocating responsibilities in the field, including a working arrangement between the Secretariat of the United Nations and ILO. It also provided the basis for achieving the co-ordination of these responsibilities through a Technical Working Group on Migration, established under the auspices of the Administrative Committee on Co-ordination (ACC). This group is now convened as appropriate and serviced by ILO, which assumes, under the ACC, the responsibility at the inter-secretariat level for promoting co-operation and co-ordination in this field.

In following up the pre-war endeavours of the League of Nations and of the International Institute for the Unification of Private Law towards the solution of this problem, and as a result of a study prepared for the Economic and Social Council, the texts of two international conventions have been drawn up with a view to ensuring that destitute families receive support—without delay, with a minimum of formalities and free of costs—from the head of the family when he is living in another country. One of these conventions—the Convention on Enforcement Abroad of Maintenance Orders—to be applied in countries whose laws permit the execution of foreign judgments, was approved by the Council in 1954 with the recommendation to governments that they use it as a guide for the preparation of bilateral treaties or uniform legislation to be enacted by individual orders. The other instrument—the Convention on the Recovery Abroad of Maintenance—the objective of which is to facilitate a support order in the country where the person responsible for the family's support lives, was adopted on June 20, 1956, at a United Nations Conference on Maintenance Obligations. It came into force on May 25, 1957.

A compilation of laws relating to the legal situation of immigrants in some principal countries of immigration was completed for the United Nations by the International Institute for the Unification of Private Law in 1953. Another compilation, completed in 1954, covered the international instruments related to the same question. A *Handbook of International Measures for the Protection of Migrants and General Conditions to be Observed in Their Settlement* was published in 1953.

In implementing its programme in the field of migration, the United Nations and the interested specialized agencies maintain close co-operation with non-governmental organizations which are active in this field. The United Nations, together with ILO, has sponsored the biennial sessions of the Conference of Non-Governmental Organizations Interested in Migration.

Social Welfare

The foundations of the United Nations social welfare programme were laid by the General Assembly at its first session in 1946 by the transfer from the League of Nations to the United Nations of certain responsibilities in the field of child welfare and the transfer to the Organization of the advisory services of the United Nations Relief and Rehabilitation Agency (UNRRA). From this relatively modest beginning the social welfare programme has gradually expanded to comprise the whole area of social welfare services. An extensive programme of advisory services, material aid and technical assistance has been developed in co-operation with UNICEF and the specialized agencies.

In the course of time, there have been changes of emphasis in the United Nations social welfare programmes, mostly in connection with important shifts of focus in the general economic and social policy of the Organization. In general, the development has been towards increasing recognition of the role of social welfare in over-all national development. In 1962, the Economic and Social Council, recognizing that the achievement of the goals of the United Nations Development Decade required increasing emphasis on the planning and development of social welfare services, called for a comprehensive reappraisal of the United Nations social welfare programme with a view to strengthening it. In 1965, the Council considered a report on this subject aimed at the development of an over-all policy for future United Nations action in the field of social welfare. The general goal of the reappraisal has been to increase the capacity of the Organization to assist governments in developing their social welfare services as an integral component of national social and economic development.

In recent years, the social welfare activities of the United Nations have mainly focused on three areas: planning, organization and administration of social welfare services; family, youth and child welfare; and training of social welfare personnel.

PLANNING, ORGANIZATION AND ADMINISTRATION OF SOCIAL WELFARE. In order to help governments establish and develop effective systems of social welfare administration, adapted to the local circumstances and manpower resources of each individual country, the United Nations has been giving increasing attention to problems of organization and administration of social welfare. Information has been continuously collected about the developments in this field. The subject has been discussed in expert groups, seminars and workshops, and advisory services have been made available to governments. A report on *The Organization and Administration of Social Services* was issued in 1961. In recent years, problems of social welfare planning within the context of over-all national planning have increasingly come into focus. Special attention has been given to methods of assessing social needs, establishing priorities, determining allocations and evaluating implementation of plans.

FAMILY, YOUTH AND CHILD WELFARE. The early efforts of the United Nations in the field of social welfare were directed towards meeting the pressing emergency needs of children and families in the areas devastated by war. In both operational activities and social welfare programmes, a remedial approach was taken to the needs and problems of certain particularly vulnerable groups.

With the shift in the United Nations policy in 1950 towards assisting developing countries in raising levels of living, the focus of the social welfare programme was changed from remedial assistance to more preventive measures in relation to mass social problems associated with vast and rapid changes in the social structure of industrializing and urbanizing societies. Accordingly, increasing attention has been given to the general economic and social prerequisites of a healthy and balanced family life. In 1952, a report on *Economic Measures in Favour of the Family* was issued, and in 1957 another report on a *Co-ordinated Policy Regarding Family Levels of Living* was published in co-operation with several specialized agencies. These were followed by a series of reports more directly aimed at assisting governments in the establishment and development of their social welfare services. In 1959, a report on *The Development of National Social Service Programmes* was issued, and in 1965 a report on *Family, Child and Youth Welfare Services* was published, containing guidelines to governments in the establishment and extension of family, youth and child welfare services. Both reports underlined the role of social welfare in the mobilization of human resources for national development.

The growth of the United Nations social welfare programme and operational activities in the field has taken place in close connection with the development of the activities of UNICEF. UNICEF, which was established in 1946 on a temporary basis, was placed on a continuing basis in 1952, and its terms of reference were broadened to include the provision of material aid, combined with the technical assistance of the United Nations and the specialized agencies, to assist governments in the development of long-term programmes for child health and welfare. In 1959, the UNICEF Executive Board decided to extend its aid to social service programmes for children. On this basis, a close co-operation between UNICEF and the technical assistance provided by the United Nations has been developed in the planning, implementation and evaluation of aid to country programmes. (*See also page 334*.)

The increasing co-operation with UNICEF in operational activities has enhanced the possibilities of the United Nations to assist governments in finding practical and indigenous solutions to their social welfare problems. Direct assistance to governments in strengthening family and child welfare programmes is normally provided through the services of social welfare advisers, the granting of fellowships and the organization of seminars and workshops. A great number of expert meetings, seminars and workshops have been arranged on family, youth and child welfare, as well as on training of personnel and organization and administration of social welfare, in Asia and the Far East, the Middle East, Europe, Latin America and Africa.

TRAINING OF SOCIAL WELFARE PERSONNEL. The United Nations has been giving increasing attention to the training of various categories of social welfare personnel. In 1950, a study entitled *Training for Social Work—An International Survey* was published, providing a detailed description and analysis of the methods of social welfare training in various countries. *The Second International Survey*, more particularly directed to the training of social workers in organized schools of social work, was published in 1955 and was supplemented by an *International Directory of Schools of Social Work*. *The Third International Survey*, analysing the essential elements in a curriculum for social welfare training, was issued in 1958, and *The Fourth International Survey*, identifying significant developments and trends in training for social welfare, in 1965.

The Economic and Social Council has recognized that social work, in principle, should be performed by persons who have received professional training in that field, and social work has been accepted as a distinctive discipline. The efforts of the United Nations have been mainly directed towards assisting governments in establishing and developing professional training in social work.

However, because of the particular needs of the developing countries as well as the insufficient number of trained social workers everywhere, increasing attention has been paid in recent years to the training of auxiliary workers and volunteers, as well as to the in-service training of both trained and untrained personnel. A special feature of recent developments has been the emphasis laid by the United Nations on the development of indigenous solutions and new approaches to the training problems of the developing countries.

Expert meetings, regional and interregional seminars, and workshops have been held to discuss problems relating to social work training, including training for policy-making, administration, supervision and teaching in the social welfare field. Experts have been available to governments to advise nationals of various countries in the training of social welfare personnel in their countries. Much attention has been given to the creation of indigenous teaching material and to the development of training facilities on a regional or subregional basis to promote the training of social welfare personnel in their own country or region.

REHABILITATION OF THE DISABLED. The General Assembly, by adopting in December 1946 a resolution concerning the establishment of the programme of advisory social welfare services, included rehabilitation of the handicapped as an area in which technical assistance should be made available to governments. The provision of assistance in the form of expert advice, fellowships and technical equipment began in 1947.

To strengthen international co-operation in this field, the Social Commission, in 1949, requested the Secretary-General to draft a comprehensive programme to be carried out by the United Nations and appropriate specialized agencies in co-operation with interested nongovernmental organizations. This programme was approved in its final form by the Economic and Social Council in 1950.

The purpose of the co-ordinated international programme is to assist governments, at their request, to develop adequate services for the prevention of disability and the rehabilitation of handicapped persons, including their education. Through the years, emphasis has been on technical assistance to under-developed countries in Asia, the Middle East, Africa and Latin America.

A close working relationship exists between the United Nations, the specialized agencies and several international non-governmental organizations. In 1953, these non-governmental organizations established the Conference of World Organizations Interested in the Handicapped, which acts as a co-ordinating body among twenty-six international non-governmental organizations and maintains liaison with the United Nations and the specialized agencies.

Rural and Community Development

In the operation of the technical assistance programmes of the United Nations and the specialized agencies, an increasing role has been assigned to approaches and techniques seeking to stimulate local initiative and leadership. Governmental agencies make special efforts to provide, locally, technical services in such fields as agriculture, health, education and public works in a co-ordinated and integrated manner, combining outside assistance with organized local self-determination and effort. Such methods and techniques are often identified under the broad term "community development."

One of the most important single factors which has influenced community development programmes is the growing emphasis given by governments to over-all planning and the attempt to make community development a part of the national development plan. In various countries of all regions, the community development plans with which the United Nations advisers have been associated are actually part of the over-all plan. An interesting variation of this is the experience of United Nations experts in certain Latin American countries where they have assisted in devising schemes designed to translate national and regional objectives and plans into programmes of local action.

The emphasis on the economic aspects of community development programmes is also evident in the technical assistance provided by the United Nations. Examples in this regard include the emphasis on agriculture and cottage-industry activities in the rural development programme in Afghanistan, opportunities for economic gain for the unemployed youth in Nigeria, market-gardening for rural families in Sudan and the promotion of co-operatives in Saudi Arabia.

Other trends in United Nations-assisted community development programmes have included the relating of these programmes to regional development, including resources development, institution building and local government, as well as to social reform, including land reform.

Both the Economic and Social Council and the General Assembly have, in recent years, called for concerted action in the field of community development and land reform. In 1963, the Assembly requested high priority for programmes which may facilitate the execution of land reform plans and assistance for community development programmes.

A World Land Reform Conference, convened in 1966, in Rome, pursuant to proposals by the Council and the Social Commission, was organized by the United Nations and the Food and Agriculture Organization (FAO), with the co-operation of the International Labour Organisation (ILO). The Conference provided an opportunity for a wide exchange of experience among the seventy-eight countries which took part in it. The subjects discussed included programmes of land tenure and structural reforms, the social and economic impact of such reforms, and related financial and administrative problems.

STUDIES AND SEMINARS.   The research being carried on by the United Nations is based in large measure on material supplied by members and non-governmental organizations, as well as on the findings of special survey missions. Among the studies which have been made are: "Community Development in Urban Areas" (1961), "The Social Training of Front-Line Rural Development Workers" (1962) and "Community Development and National Development" (1963). A paper entitled "The Participation of Women in Community Development" was prepared for the seminar on the participation of women in public life which took place in Mongolia in 1965. A joint study with FAO on land reform entitled "Progress in Land Reform—Fourth Report" has been issued as a sequel to three earlier reports, issued in 1954, 1956 and 1963, respectively.

Pilot projects, seminars and workshops have also been organized, among them the Asian seminar on urban community development, held in Singapore in 1961; a workshop in community development, held in Quito, Ecuador, in 1962; a seminar on the role of popular participation in the acceleration of social and economic development, held in Santiago, Chile, in 1964; and a seminar and round-table discussion on the relationship of community development to economic and social development, held in Pátzcuaro, Mexico, in 1965.

Social Defence

PREVENTION OF CRIME AND TREATMENT OF OFFENDERS. In 1946 the Economic and Social Council instructed the Social Commission to consider the development of effective international machinery to study the prevention of crime and the treatment of offenders on a broad international basis and to consult with the International Penal and Penitentiary Commission (IPPC) on the subject.

The Council, in August 1948, considered that the United Nations should assume leadership in the promotion of work in this field, making the fullest use of the knowledge and experience of competent international organizations; thus, after negotiations between the United Nations and IPPC, an agreement was reached providing for the dissolution of the latter body in 1951 and the assumption of its functions by the United Nations.

Whereas in previous efforts at international co-operation in dealing with social defence, the problem had been looked upon as primarily juridical or legal, the United Nations considers it largely a social problem which can be tackled most effectively only through the development of an integrated social defence policy as part of an over-all social welfare programme or, as it has been put more recently, within the scope of general social and economic development planning. The United Nations does not seek standardization, and leaves specific methods of carrying out preventive and treatment policies to the discretion of individual governments, but within the framework of its concept of social defence it nevertheless attempts to set up certain basic standards and objectives and to disseminate information about policies and practices that have proved their worth and which may be suited, with appropriate modifications, to national and local needs.

In 1954, at the request of the General Assembly, the Secretary-General presented to the Economic and Social Council a review of the work of the Secretariat in the economic and social field indicating that, in view of the overriding objective of the Organization's programme to promote the economic and social development of developing countries, priorities must be established. He proposed that primary attention be given to projects pertaining to the prevention and treatment of juvenile delinquency.

A resolution adopted by the General Assembly in 1959 noted the increasing concern in many countries with the problem of juvenile delinquency and expressed the hope that the Secretary-General would give urgent attention to this problem.

The question of juvenile delinquency and of the prevention of criminality resulting from social changes accompanying economic development has, in subsequent years, received the close attention of the Social Defence Section which is the technical administrative organ responsible for the implementation of the social defence policy established by the Social Commission, the Economic and Social Council, the General Assembly and the specialized technical bodies set up in this field. Among these are the Committee of Experts on the Prevention of Crime and the Treatment of Offenders, which advises the Secretary-General and the Social Commission; the Consultative Group on the Prevention of Crime and the Treatment of Offenders; and such special bodies as the Council, the Commission and the Secretary-General may wish to set up from time to time.

In recent years, there has been a shift of emphasis from treatment to prevention in the United Nations work in the social defence field, and also a growing emphasis on research as a prerequisite of adequate programmes for the prevention and control of criminality, particularly of the young. This emphasis was reflected in the European seminar on the evaluation of methods for the prevention of juvenile delinquency, held in Frascati, Italy, in October 1962. The meeting, as well as that of the *ad hoc* Advisory Committee of Experts on the Prevention of Crime and the Treatment of Offenders, held in January 1963, recommended that research activities receive increasing attention. In view of the acute shortage of qualified personnel in the social defence field, the urgent priority assigned to the training of such personnel was reaffirmed. The first regional institute set up in recognition of personnel training needs began operation in Fuchu, Japan, in 1962. Special courses for the training of specific categories of personnel have also been organized in other regions, for example in Africa.

The prevention of criminality, particularly of juvenile delinquency, with special attention to research and training needs, was the subject of a series of regional seminars convened in preparation for the Third United Nations Congress on the Prevention of Crime and the Treatment of Offenders, held in Stockholm in August 1965, and was the dominant theme of the Congress itself. Immediately prior to the Congress, moreover, a special inter-regional meeting on research in criminology was held in Krogerup, Denmark, followed by a study tour of criminological research facilities in Norway and Sweden.

The leadership role of the United Nations in social defence was reiterated by the Economic and Social Council in the summer of 1965 when it welcomed the Secretary-General's proposals "for strengthening the Organization's capacity to meet the demands for action appropriate to the role which the United Nations is expected to play in the field of social defence"; requested the establishment of a funds-in-trust account to be administered by the United Nations for the purposes of strengthening the capacity of the Organization to carry out its respon-

sibilities in the social defence field; and invited member states to contribute to this account. The Council also requested that technical
assistance in social defence, which had been strengthened in recent
years, be continued, particularly through regional training and research
projects and the use of regional advisers.

The social defence work programme has included the problem
of the traffic in persons and of the exploitation of the prostitution of
others. Efforts have been made to encourage government support for
the Convention for the Suppression of the Traffic in Persons and of the
Exploitation of the Prostitution of Others, which was approved by
the General Assembly in 1949, and to adopt measures designed to
eliminate the causes leading to the problem.

STUDIES AND REPORTS.   In collecting and disseminating information, the Social Defence Section relies heavily on its network of over
100 national correspondents who have the responsibility of keeping
the Secretariat informed of current developments relating to the prevention of crime and the treatment of offenders in their respective
countries, collecting information requested for studies and research
carried out by the United Nations, disseminating information on desirable policies and practices, and otherwise assisting the Secretary-
General in carrying out the Organization's programme in this field.

A large number of studies, often prepared by special consultants,
have been produced by the Social Defence Section on a wide variety
of subjects. In the past, such studies were primarily surveys, covering
such topics as probation and related measures, parole and after-care,
the indeterminate sentence, short-term imprisonment, and prostitution
and the traffic in persons. Some of the studies, such as the comparative
surveys of juvenile delinquency, dealt with the subject from a regional
point of view. Others, such as those on short-term imprisonment,
prison labour, criminality and social change, programmes for the prevention of juvenile and young adult delinquency, and capital punishment, were prepared for the United Nations social defence congresses,
which are held every five years, and for other meetings.

Recently, an effort has been made in the direction of studies involving a larger amount of original research; a number of case studies
have been prepared by a group of research specialists on "The real
extent of the increase of juvenile delinquency as well as the extent to
which such increases may be due to economic, social and/or psycho-
logical causes." Another study is being undertaken on the prevention
of delinquency in the context of national development.

The *International Review of Criminal Policy*, which has been issued by the United Nations Secretariat since 1952, is designed to
serve as an authoritative international channel for the dissemination
and exchange of technical information in the field of social defence.
Several issues of the *Review* have been devoted to particular themes,

for example, the evaluation of methods for the prevention of juvenile delinquency, the training of social defence personnel, and criminological research trends, needs, methodology, planning and co-ordination. Topical bibliographies of technical literature in the field have been issued as part of and, since 1965, as a supplement to the *Review*.

INTERNATIONAL CONFERENCES. The international congresses on the prevention of crime and treatment of offenders that are held by the United Nations every five years offer a forum for the presentation of policies and practices that have been found useful by the various countries and, through the exchange of opinion which they permit, provide a stimulus to progress in social defence. The First Congress, held in Geneva from August 22 to September 3, 1955, adopted a set of standard minimum rules for the treatment of prisoners and recommendations on the selection and training of personnel for penal and correctional institutes, open institutions, prison labour and the prevention of juvenile delinquency. The Second Congress, held in London from August 8 to 29, 1960, considered various measures for the prevention of juvenile delinquency and of crime resulting from social changes accompanying economic development in less developed countries; it also dealt with pre-release, parole and after-care, prison labour and short-term imprisonment. The Third Congress, held in Stockholm from August 9 to 18, 1965, and attended by over 1,200 participants from eighty-five countries, dealt with social change and criminality; social forces and the prevention of criminality; community preventive action, including the planning and execution of medical, police and social programmes; measures to combat recidivism, with particular reference to adverse conditions of detention pending trial and inequality in the administration of justice; probation and other non-institutional measures, and special preventive and treatment measures for young adults.

In addition to the world-wide congresses and meetings of consultative groups, the United Nations has convened expert groups and seminars on a regional basis and held meetings devoted to special subjects.

TECHNICAL ASSISTANCE ACTIVITIES. United Nations technical assistance activities in the social field include—in addition to seminars, expert groups and study tours, which are usually organized under the United Nations technical assistance programme—the provision of fellowships for advanced study to candidates nominated by their governments for observation and study elsewhere, the establishment of, or assistance in the establishment of, regional or national training and research facilities and the provision of expert advice.

One of the most fruitful ways of combining expert advice with the provision of fellowships has been through the establishment of re-

gional social defence institutes, the primary purpose of which is the
training of personnel. The United Nations Asia and Far East Institute,
established with the co-operation of the Government of Japan and
supported also by other countries, has held a number of international
training courses for correctional personnel, mostly senior, from the
region, offered expert assistance and issued a study on open correctional
institutions based on the experience of the region. The Institute is also
preparing basic training manuals and other teaching aids. A similar
institute for Latin America has been planned. In addition, special
courses have been organized, using the facilities of existing national
institutes—for example, the course for personnel of institutions for
juvenile delinquents held at the National Centre for Social and
Criminological Research, in Cairo, in 1964.

CO-ORDINATION OF ACTIVITIES OF INTERNATIONAL ORGANI-
ZATIONS. Increased co-operation and co-ordination of activities
with the specialized agencies, inter-governmental agencies and non-
governmental organizations having special interest in the social defence
field has been achieved in recent years. Inter-agency meetings on specific topics, such as juvenile delinquency, have also been held periodically to ensure integration of efforts, particularly for events such as
the quinquennial Congress on the Prevention of Crime and Treatment
of Offenders.

HOUSING, BUILDING AND PLANNING

The United Nations has given steadily growing attention to world-wide
problems in housing, building and environmental planning ever since
1946, when the first session of the General Assembly noted with concern the magnitude and gravity of these problems and called upon the
Economic and Social Council to initiate remedial action at the international level. More specifically, the Assembly recommended the creation by the United Nations of international arrangements for the promotion and co-ordination of research and exchange of information
among nations and for the definition of suitable housing standards to
raise levels of living.

In 1949, the Council requested the Secretary-General to formulate an integrated programme for housing and town and country planning. The programme was prepared in consultation with interested
specialized agencies, other inter-governmental bodies and competent
non-governmental organizations and was approved by the Council in
1950.

The continuing deterioration of the housing situation throughout the world and its serious social consequences, particularly in developing countries, led both the Assembly and the Council in 1952 to reiterate the urgent need for international action designed to alleviate low-cost-housing shortages. Among the measures recommended were application of practical methods to finance housing and environmental development programmes, strengthening of activities at the regional level and provision of technical assistance to requesting governments.

In subsequent years, the Social Commission repeatedly underlined the importance of finding practical solutions for the financing of housebuilding programmes. The Commission also urged the adoption of a regional approach to physical planning as a prerequisite for achieving a more balanced development of economic, social and technological resources within the national framework. The Council endorsed these proposals and recommended the organization of regional meetings of experts to discuss the relevant issues in depth.

As a next step, the Council approved in 1959 a long-range programme of concerted international action in the field of low-cost housing and related community facilities which the Secretary-General had prepared in response to a proposal of the Social Commission. Later that year, the General Assembly stressed the importance of governmental action, technical assistance and exchanges of technical information within that long-range programme.

In 1960, the Assembly requested the Secretary-General to investigate the possibility of obtaining technical services, equipment and funds for undertaking pilot projects to improve housing and community facilities. At the same time, the Assembly called upon the Council to investigate ways and means of financing such projects from domestic and external sources and invited member governments to indicate those areas in which international assistance was most urgently needed.

In 1961, the Council decided to convene an *ad hoc* group of experts on housing and urban development to advise the Social Commission on methods for accelerating and expanding programmes in these fields, including techniques for mobilizing the required national resources. That decision was closely linked to a concurrent one of the General Assembly designating the period 1960-1970 as the United Nations Development Decade during which priority was to be given, *inter alia*, to housing and to urban development because of their importance to the achievement of economic and social progress.

One of the major recommendations of the group of experts led the Council in 1962 to create a Committee on Housing, Building and Planning. The first session of the twenty-one member Committee was held in January-February 1963. Its recommendations covered: co-ordination of national and international efforts during the United Nations Development Decade as a means to improve housing, building and environmental conditions; finance of housing and community facilities from international and national resources; the formulation of a United Nations programme of pilot projects in these fields; the promotion of training and informational activities through regional and national institutes on the one hand and the possible creation of an international documentation institute on the other; and the need for reviewing existing arrangements to deal with housing, building and planning activities at the international level. When the Council approved these recommendations later in 1963, it requested the Secretary-General more specifically to obtain expert advice on the question of organizational arrangements.

A comprehensive consultant's report on those arrangements was reviewed by the Committee on Housing, Building and Planning at its second session in January-February 1964. Among the suggestions made by the Secretary-General's consultant was one which led the Committee to recommend the establishment of a centre for housing, building and planning within the United Nations Secretariat as a means to achieve a closer integration of environmental planning with planning in the industrial and economic sectors and as an important step forward in the development of a comprehensive United Nations programme for housing, building and physical planning. In addition, it was suggested that the proposed centre should have the services of a team of specialists provided within the United Nations Development Programme to assist developing nations, at their request, in the formulation of basic housing, building and planning programmes and the establishment of efficient construction and building materials industries. The Committee also recommended that the Secretary-General initiate a comprehensive study on the industrialization of building processes and that the General Assembly authorize the preparation of world-wide periodic reports on progress in the fields of housing, building and planning in the member states of the United Nations.

The Council endorsed the Committee's recommendations later in 1964 and, in June 1965, the Secretary-General established the Centre for Housing, Building and Planning within the Department of Economic and Social Affairs. In December 1965, the General Assembly approved the preparation of the suggested progress reports on a biennial basis.

At its third session in September 1965, the Committee on Housing, Building and Planning recommended early approval by the Council of establishing, under the auspices of the United Nations, an international institute for documentation on housing, building and planning which would co-operate closely with the Centre for Housing, Building and Planning; the preparation of a comprehensive study on the needs of developing countries in regard to training national cadres skilled in housing, building and planning, including the financing of such training from domestic and international sources; and the initiation of another study of countries having substantial experience in solving social problems of housing and urban development with particular reference to raising standards of living, housing for low-income families at reasonable rents, improvement of existing dwellings and slum clearance.

NON-AGRICULTURAL RESOURCES, TRANSPORT AND CARTOGRAPHY

Permanent Sovereignty over Natural Resources

One of the essentials of economic development is the encouragement of under-developed countries to exploit their natural resources. An Assembly resolution in 1952 pointed out that "the right of peoples freely to use and exploit their natural wealth and resources is inherent in their sovereignty and is in accordance with the United Nations Charter." The question of sovereignty over natural wealth and resources was frequently raised and discussed in the Commission on Human Rights, the Economic and Social Council and the General Assembly.

In 1958, the Assembly, on the recommendation of the Commission on Human Rights and the Economic and Social Council, established a Commission on Permanent Sovereignty over Natural Resources to conduct a full survey of the status of permanent sovereignty of peoples and nations over their natural wealth and resources.

The Commission, composed of nine members, met in 1959, 1960 and 1961 and discussed the subject, as well as a study entitled *The Status of Permanent Sovereignty over Natural Wealth and Resources*, prepared by the Secretariat at its request. This study, which incorporated information supplied by forty-one member governments and certain specialized agencies, consisted of five chapters: (1) national measures affecting the ownership or use of natural resources by foreign nationals or enterprises; (2) international agreements affecting the foreign exploitation of natural resources; (3) international adjudication and studies prepared under the auspices of inter-governmental bodies relating to responsibility of states in regard to the property and contracts of aliens; (4) status of permanent sovereignty over natural wealth and resources in newly independent states and in non-self-governing and trust territories; and (5) economic data pertaining to the status of sovereignty over natural wealth and resources in various countries.

The Commission's report, covering the work of its three sessions, together with all relevant documents and records of debates of the Economic and Social Council, was discussed by the General Assembly at its seventeenth session, in 1962, and on December 14, the Assembly adopted a resolution containing a declaration of eight principles:

(1) The right of peoples and nations to permanent sovereignty over their natural wealth and resources must be exercised in the interest of their national development and of the well-being of the people of the state concerned.

(2) The exploration, development and disposition of such resources, as well as the import of the foreign capital required for these purposes, should be in conformity with the rules and conditions which the peoples and nations freely consider to be necessary or desirable with regard to the authorization, restriction or prohibition of such activities.

(3) In cases where authorization is granted, the capital imported and the earnings on that capital shall be governed by the terms thereof, by the national legislation in force and by international law. The profits derived must be shared in the proportions freely agreed upon, in each case, between the investors and the recipient state, due care being taken to ensure that there is no impairment, for any reason, of that state's sovereignty over its natural wealth and resources.

(4) Nationalization, expropriation or requisitioning shall be based on grounds or reasons of public utility, security or the national interest which are recognized as overriding purely individual or private interests, both domestic and foreign. In such cases, the owner shall be paid appropriate compensation, in accordance with the rules in force in the state taking such measures in the exercise of its sovereignty and in accordance with international law. In any case where the question of compensation gives rise to a controversy, the national jurisdiction of the state taking such measures shall be exhausted. However, upon agreement by sovereign states and other parties concerned, settlement of the dispute should be made through arbitration or international adjudication.

(5) The free and beneficial exercise of the sovereignty of peoples and nations over their natural resources must be furthered by the mutual respect of states based on their sovereign equality.

(6) International co-operation for the economic development of developing countries, whether in the form of public or private capital investments, exchange of goods and services, technical assistance or exchange of scientific information, shall be such as to further their independent national development and shall be based upon respect for their sovereignty over their natural wealth and resources.

(7) Violation of the rights of peoples and nations to sovereignty over their natural wealth and resources is contrary to the spirit and principles of the Charter of the United Nations and hinders the development of international co-operation and the maintenance of peace.

(8) Foreign investment agreements freely entered into by or between sovereign states shall be observed in good faith; states and in-

ternational organizations shall strictly and conscientiously respect the sovereignty of peoples and nations over their natural wealth and resources in accordance with the Charter and the principles set forth in the present resolution.

In its resolution of December 14, 1962, the Assembly requested the Secretary-General to continue the study of the various aspects of permanent sovereignty over natural resources, taking into account the desire of member states to ensure the protection of their sovereign rights, while encouraging international co-operation in the fields of economic development, and to report to the Economic and Social Council and to the Assembly. The Secretary-General's report, prepared in accordance with this request and published in 1963, dealt largely with recent legislative developments and factual economic data germane to the topic, particular attention being given to the newly independent states.

Development and Use of Non-Agricultural Resources

The United Nations Scientific Conference on the Conservation and Utilization of Resources, which was held at Lake Success from August 17 to September 6, 1949, brought together 700 scientists and experts from over fifty countries for an exchange of views on techniques in conservation and utilization of resources, their economic costs and benefits, and their interrelations.

At the request of the Economic and Social Council, the Secretary-General studied the proceedings of the Conference and submitted a report and proposals for follow-up action. Upon considering the report, in March 1951, the Council noted that the Food and Agriculture Organization of the United Nations (FAO) was developing a programme for continuing co-operation with respect to soils, forests and other natural resources important to food and agriculture, but that no over-all facilities were provided for similar co-operation in the field of non-agricultural resources. The Council accordingly requested the Secretary-General to initiate a programme to promote the systematic survey and inventory of non-agricultural resources; to give consideration to requests from governments for technical assistance in the organizing and planning of national surveys and inventories of such resources; and to explore, at the request of member states concerned, the possibility of holding international conferences pertaining to particular types of resources or specific resource problems common to a group of countries.

The Council also considered for the first time the question of international co-operation on water control and utilization and asked the Secretary-General to prepare a report on the work of the specialized agencies and other international organizations engaged in this broad field.

Begun in this way, United Nations work in non-agricultural resources use and development, including mineral, energy and water resources, has evolved continuously under the Council's general guidance and on the basis of further specific directives issued from time to time. The activities take three forms: the rendering of assistance to developing countries under United Nations programmes of technical co-operation; the organization and convening of conferences or seminars to pool experience; and the carrying out and publication of studies compiling information and analysing needs in respect of particular resources or resource problems.

ASSISTANCE TO DEVELOPING COUNTRIES. Assistance to developing countries has been steadily increased and intensified, particularly since the creation in 1958 of the United Nations Special Fund. In 1965, the United Nations was executing fifty-nine Special Fund projects in the field of non-agricultural resources, at an aggregate estimated cost when completed of $105.4 million, consisting of $50.1 million in Special Fund allocations and $55.3 million in counterpart government contributions. These were pre-investment type projects of two- to five-year duration, such as large-scale mineral and/or groundwater investigations, major hydraulic development studies, integrated river development studies, power development surveys, surveys of geothermal energy, and projects to aid or establish technical institutions. In addition, some 140 internationally recruited experts—in fields ranging from photogeology and petroleum refining to hydroelectric engineering and dam design—served on field assignments under the regular and expanded programmes of technical assistance.

CONFERENCES AND SEMINARS. The United Nations Conference on New Sources of Energy, held in Rome in the summer of 1961, was the first world-wide meeting devoted to three new sources of energy—solar energy, wind power and geothermal energy. The Conference was attended by 447 persons representing a wide range of professional disciplines and organizational backgrounds from seventy-four countries and territories. The new sources of energy were discussed from the point of view of their potentialities and applications, particularly with reference to developing countries. The report of the Conference was published and widely disseminated.

The United Nations has also held a number of training seminars for from twenty-five to forty-five qualified participants in each instance—usually technicians, administrators or policy-makers in the field of the seminar—drawn from interested developing countries. The following inter-regional seminars have been held: on techniques of petroleum development, in 1962, at United Nations Headquarters; on energy policy in developing countries, in May 1965, at Bréau, France; on geo-chemical methods for mineral exploration, organized in collaboration with the Government of the USSR, in August 1965, at Moscow; on the economic application of water desalination, in September-October 1965, at United Nations Headquarters; on ore concentration in water-short areas, in February 1966, at United Nations Headquarters; and, in collaboration with the Government of the USSR, on integrated use of water resources in developing countries, in August 1966, at Fergana, in Uzbekistan, USSR.

STUDIES AND REPORTS.   In support of its operational activities, and in some instances as a by-product of this practical work, the United Nations has issued a number of global studies, notably the following: *Survey of World Iron Ore Resources: Occurrence, Appraisal and Use* (1954); *Non-Ferrous Metals in Underdeveloped Countries* (1955); *Economic Applications of Atomic Energy: Power Generation and Industrial and Agricultural Uses* (1957); *New Sources of Energy and Economic Development—Solar Energy, Wind Energy, Tidal Energy, Geothermic Energy and Thermal Energy of the Seas* (1957); *Integrated River-Basin Development* (1958); *Water for Industrial Use* (1958); *Large-Scale Groundwater Development* (1960); *Water Desalination in Developing Countries* (1964); and *Water Desalination: Proposals for a Costing Procedure and Related Technical and Economic Considerations* (1965).

In addition, the Secretary-General submits to the Economic and Social Council a biennial report on the work done in the field of non-agricultural resources, as well as a biennial report specifically on water resources development which includes coverage of the work in this field of the other organizations of the United Nations family.

Transport and Communications

TRANSPORT DEVELOPMENT.   United Nations work in transport development, which has evolved relatively recently as compared to United Nations activities in a number of other transport and communications matters, is of central importance, particularly for the world's developing countries.

In April 1963, the Economic and Social Council considered a report by the Secretary-General on work done and recommendations concerning transport development. The report reviewed in historic perspective some of the major efforts for international co-operation in the field of transport through the United Nations system of organizations and suggested a programme of future activities for the United Nations itself.

The Council drew the attention of governments to the facilities available at the United Nations for assistance in transport training and development and to the desirability of giving transport development priority commensurate with its importance as a prerequisite for overall economic and social development and in light of the objectives of the United Nations Development Decade. The Council also recommended that the Secretary-General organize regional and inter-regional seminars on the economic and financial, as well as administrative, aspects of transport development and requested him to inform it periodically on the progress of work in the transport field.

A brief progress report was submitted to the Council in June 1965, giving an account of the assistance provided to developing countries and of other activities in transport economics, planning and administration; regulatory questions; transport technology; highway transport; railways; inland navigation; and maritime transport. The report pointed out that the transport situation in the world was characterized by an extreme disparity between the developed and the developing countries and that one of the complex questions confronting the latter countries was that of determining the proportion of resources that should be allocated to transport. It concluded that increased research was needed to assist developing countries in formulating and implementing their transport policies.

The Council recommended that a programme of studies be undertaken, including studies on the adequacy and limitations of transport-related institutions and institutional arrangements in developing countries in relation to their needs and potential, and that regional and inter-regional seminars on transport development be organized, with particular emphasis on regional and international highways.

In 1965, 116 United Nations experts served on field assignments in developing countries in various branches of transport development under the United Nations technical assistance programmes, and four Special Fund projects—representing the beginning of Special Fund aid in the transport field—were put into operation, at an aggregate cost when completed of over $9 million: a Kabul-Herat direct road survey (Afghanistan); the establishment, at Taipei, Taiwan, of a National Maritime Development Institute; a railway survey in Madagascar; and a navigation study of the Paraguay River south of Asunción.

Ports and shipping training seminars, first organized in 1959, are held on an annual basis in co-operation with the Danish Government. The sixth seminar was held in Copenhagen, Denmark, from May 1 to 21, 1966, for the benefit of thirty participants from twenty-seven countries. The United Nations has also helped to establish a number of training centres—for example, a regional training centre at Auki, Solomon Islands, and at Noumea, New Caledonia, for boat building; one in Turkey for highway engineering; and another at Lahore, Pakistan, for railway signalling and operation.

Studies in preparation include a port administration manual and a study on containerization. Work has also begun on research into transport institutions, evaluation of transport capacities and facilities, applied research and transport technology, and methods of allocation of resources to transport projects.

DEVELOPMENT OF INTERNATIONAL TRAVEL AND TOURISM. In February 1955, the Transport and Communications Commission (a subsidiary body of the Economic and Social Council which the Council terminated in 1959) considered a report by the Secretary-General on developments in international travel, including relevant activities of the specialized agencies and other international organizations.

Shortly thereafter, in March 1955, the Council invited governments to examine the beneficial effects of increased tourism; survey their tourist facilities to determine existing deficiencies; simplify entry and exit procedures and formalities applicable to tourists; and take certain other measures designed to develop tourism. The Council also requested the United Nations organs and appropriate specialized agencies to give favourable consideration to constructive projects designed to increase tourist facilities and to promote travel, and asked the Secretary-General to study the available statistics on tourist travel and to report to the Statistical Commission regarding the establishment of uniform definitions, standards and methods in this sphere.

In 1959, the Council asked the Secretary-General to bring up to date and continue his technical studies in the field of international travel and tourism and to make recommendations on the question of calling an international conference on this subject.

After considering a note of the Secretary-General on the subject, in 1961, the Council requested him to call a conference on international travel and tourism as soon as possible and, in consultation if necessary with a group of experts, to prepare recommendations concerning the nature, scope, and location of the conference. The Secretary-General constituted a group of seven experts, who met in Geneva from January 29 to February 9, 1962, and whose report was transmitted to the Economic and Social Council in April.

The Council, on April 9, asked the Secretary-General to invite all states members of the United Nations and the specialized agencies to send representatives to the United Nations Conference on International Travel and Tourism, which was held in Rome in the autumn of 1963. The Conference adopted recommendations covering facilitation of governmental formalities for international travel and the development, organization and promotion of tourism. In December 1963, the Council called on governments and specialized agencies to consider and implement these recommendations. A progress report on the implementation of the Conference's recommendations was submitted to the Council in February 1966.

REGULATION OF ROAD AND MOTOR TRANSPORT. The United Nations Conference on Road and Motor Transport, which was convened in August-September 1949, adopted a new Convention on Road Traffic, which came into force on March 26, 1952, and prepared an optional Protocol on Road Signs and Signals, which came into force on December 20, 1953. As of December 31, 1965, there were seventy-seven parties to the former and thirty-four parties to the latter.

As a step towards eventual establishment of a common world-wide system, a group of experts on road signs and signals was appointed in 1950. They prepared what became known as the 1953 Draft Protocol on a Uniform System of Road Signs and Signals. The Economic and Social Council in 1955 recommended to governments that they consider, either unilaterally or bilaterally or in regional agreements, the provisions of the Draft Protocol when revising their systems of road signs and signals, in order to further the progressive achievement of uniformity in this field.

Minimum uniform regulations pertaining to the licensing of drivers were drafted by a group of experts convened in 1952 and were recommended to governments for their consideration. In addition, consideration has been given, with the assistance of the World Health Organization, to the question of mental and physical fitness of applicants for driving permits. Recommendations on this subject were prepared and circulated to governments for comment.

In July 1964, the Economic and Social Council requested the Secretary-General to prepare, on the basis of the 1949 Convention and the draft Supplementary European Convention, the draft of a revised traffic Convention to replace the 1949 instrument. The Secretary-General was also requested to prepare, taking into account the 1953 Draft Protocol and the various systems of signs and signals in existence, the draft of a new instrument on road signs and signals based on symbolic signs and road markings. These two drafts were scheduled to be examined at a conference to be held in 1967 or 1968.

PASSPORT AND FRONTIER FORMALITIES. A meeting of experts on passport and frontier formalities, held in Geneva in April 1947, made a number of recommendations for the easing and simplification of frontier formalities concerning passports, visas, police controls, customs inspection, currency control and other matters. On the advice of the Transport and Communications Commission, the Council recommended to governments the use by all means of transport of the International Civil Aviation Organization standard visa format for international travel.

CUSTOMS FORMALITIES. Pursuant to a 1951 resolution of the Economic and Social Council, the Secretary-General ascertained the views of governments on certain aspects of customs formalities and reported thereon to the Transport and Communications Commission in February 1953. As a result, the United Nations Conference on Customs Formalities for the Temporary Importation of Private Road Motor Vehicles and for Tourism was convened in New York in mid-1954. The Conference prepared and opened for signature the following three instruments: the Convention concerning Customs Facilities for Touring, which came into force on September 11, 1957, and to which there were fifty-three parties as of December 31, 1965; an Additional Protocol to the Convention Relative to the Importation of Tourist Publicity Documents and Material, which came into force on June 28, 1956, and to which there were forty-seven parties as of December 31, 1965; and the Customs Convention on the Temporary Importation of Private Road Vehicles, which came into force on December 15, 1957, and had been ratified by fifty-two states as of December 31, 1965.

TRANSPORT OF DANGEROUS GOODS.   Following a proposal of the Transport and Communications Commission in 1950 that work on the subject of transport of dangerous goods be started, the Secretary-General examined, together with competent international and national bodies, various aspects of the problem, to determine which were appropriate for uniform regulation. A report was published in 1953 embodying the results of this study.

In 1954, a committee of experts, appointed by the Secretary-General, was convened in Geneva. It prepared a report which was subsequently circulated to governments for comment, revised at a second meeting of the experts in the fall of 1956, and published under the title *Transport of Dangerous Goods—Recommendations Concerning the Classification, Listing and Labelling of Dangerous Goods and Shipping Papers for Such Goods.*

In 1957, the Economic and Social Council decided to set up a new committee to complete the list of dangerous goods, keep it up to date and generally pursue the tasks begun by the previous committee of experts. The Committee of Experts for Further Work on the Transport of Dangerous Goods held its first session in 1959.

Meanwhile, the International Atomic Energy Agency (IAEA) had been entrusted by the Council in 1959 with the task of drafting recommendations on the transport of radioactive substances consistent with the United Nations recommendations. In addition, a group of three experts on explosives was appointed and met in Geneva in August 1961, their task being to list and recommend methods of packing explosives. The Committee of Experts, at its second session in 1961, noted with approval the progress report of the experts on explosives and also recommended incorporating into the United Nations recommendations the regulations which had been worked out by IAEA.

In 1962, 1964 and 1965, reports, both of the Committee of Experts and the group of experts on explosives, were submitted to the

Council, which approved the principles established and recommendations made. The Secretary-General was requested, among other things, to amend the classification and list of principal dangerous goods set out in the United Nations 1956 Recommendations. Studies are in progress in respect of the packing of explosives and other dangerous goods.

[For the role of ICAO, ITU, UPU and IMCO in the field of transport and communications, see Part Three. Transport development is also considered by UNCTAD, by its Trade and Development Board and by the Board's Committee on Shipping (*see page 257*).]

International Co-operation in Cartography

The need for regional and world-wide co-ordination of cartographic services, as well as for further surveying and mapping of vast areas of the world, was already widely felt at the time of the establishment of the United Nations. In 1948, the Economic and Social Council asked the Secretary-General to further the stimulation of national programmes of surveying and mapping by promoting, among other things, the exchange of technical information, including the preparation of a study of modern cartographic methods; to co-ordinate the plans and programmes of the United Nations and the specialized agencies in the field of cartography; and to develop close co-operation with cartographic services of interested member governments.

To secure a plan of work for carrying out this task, the Secretary-General appointed a group of experts, whose report and a study prepared by the Pan American Institute of Geography were published in 1949 under the title *Modern Cartography—Base Maps for World Needs*.

In the light of the findings of the experts and a report by the Secretary-General, the Council laid down further instructions in July 1949. The Secretary-General was to: (1) consult with governments concerning the early calling of regional meetings on cartography; (2) set up a cartographic office capable of dealing with the existing and future needs of the United Nations and of providing, in co-operation with international scientific organizations, such assistance as might be requested by the specialized agencies; (3) continue co-ordinating the plans and programmes of the United Nations and the specialized agencies in the field of cartography; (4) publish periodical summaries on cartography that would constitute a report on activities, progress and plans in this field and would, it was hoped, facilitate the co-ordination of national programmes; and (5) examine the possibility of absorption by the United Nations of the Central Bureau of the International Map of the World on the Millionth Scale (IMW).

An office to deal with cartography was set up at United Nations Headquarters in 1950.

INTERNATIONAL MAP OF THE WORLD ON THE MILLIONTH SCALE (IMW). The Central Bureau of the International Map of the World on the Millionth Scale (IMW) was transferred to the United Nations in 1951. The functions carried out by the United Nations consist mainly in assisting the governments concerned in co-ordinating the publication of the sheets of the map and in exchanging related information.

Pursuant to an Economic and Social Council request of 1961, the Secretary-General convened in Bonn, Germany, in August 1962, an international technical conference, which reviewed and revised the specifications for uniform presentation of the map. In carrying out its functions, the United Nations maintains liaison with the national cartographic agencies in charge of the publication of the IMW, and publishes annually a report under the title *An International Map of the World on the Millionth Scale.*

INTERNATIONAL STANDARDIZATION IN THE WRITING OF GEO-GRAPHICAL NAMES ON MAPS. The need to establish as much uniformity as possible in the writing of geographical names became increasingly apparent with the growing variety of maps, the quantity produced and the uses to which they were put. A proposal concerning this matter was submitted to the United Nations in 1951 by Iran. Pursuant to Council instructions in 1953, 1956 and 1959, the following steps were taken: consultations were held with governments and the results were reported to the Council; a programme was drafted for bringing about maximum international uniformity in the writing of geographical names; and a group of experts was appointed and charged with examining the technical problems of domestic standardization, as well as the desirability of holding an international conference on this subject.

In April 1961, the Council, having received the report of the group of experts, invited governments to take steps, as appropriate, for the early implementation of the experts' recommendations and to transmit to the Secretary-General information on the progress being made in the standardization of geographical names and related information. In addition, the Secretary-General was asked to submit, within two years, a report to the Council on the progress being made by governments and on the desirability of convening an international conference on the standardization of geographical names.

Accordingly, the Secretary-General submitted a report in April 1963, in the light of which the Council asked him to explore the possible scope and arrangements for a conference. Further reports were submitted to the Council in August 1964 and July 1965 and on the basis of these the Council decided that the conference should be convened in Geneva in August 1967.

REGIONAL CARTOGRAPHIC CONFERENCES. The Council's instructions of July 1949 included one to the effect that the Secretary-General should consult with governments concerning the early calling of regional meetings on cartography. The first of what turned out to be a series of such conferences was convened in February 1955, in Mussoorie, India.

The second, third and fourth United Nations Regional Cartographic Conferences for Asia and the Far East were held in Tokyo in October 1958, in Bangkok in October 1961 and in Manila in November 1964, respectively. The conferences were attended by representatives from a number of countries in the region and several cartographically advanced countries from outside the region, as well as by observers from the specialized agencies and interested international organizations. The Manila Conference recommended that a fifth United Nations Regional Cartographic Conference for Asia and the Far East be convened in Canberra in March 1967.

At the request of the Council in 1961, the Secretary-General, in co-operation with the Executive Secretary of the Economic Commission for Africa, convened the first Regional Cartographic Conference for Africa in Nairobi, in July 1963. The second Regional Cartographic Conference for Africa was scheduled to be held in Tunis, in September 1966.

TECHNICAL ASSISTANCE IN CARTOGRAPHY. Governments have received, at their request, technical assistance in surveying and appraising existing and future needs in cartographic facilities; in establishing national cartographic centres and, in particular, photogrammetric departments, including installation of equipment and training of personnel; in introducing techniques of photo-interpretation and airborne geophysical surveys in connection with resource development projects; in carrying out topical mapping projects and other studies, such as geological maps, and in preparing economic atlases; in setting up cadastral services required for modern urban and rural development; and in training technical personnel, through provision of fellowships, and by organizing pilot courses and seminars. Among the latter have been the seminar on topographic mapping as a means for economic development, which was convened in co-operation with the Government of Iran and held in Teheran in 1957, and the seminar on aerial survey methods and equipment, which was held in Bangkok in early 1960.

An inter-regional seminar on the application of cartography for economic development, attended by cartographers from both Latin America and Africa, was held in Elsinore, Denmark, in October 1965.

TRADE AND DEVELOPMENT

Developments Prior to the United Nations Conference on Trade and Development

CONFERENCES ON COMMODITY PROBLEMS. The Economic and Social Council, in August 1950, authorized the Secretary-General to convene inter-governmental conferences on specific commodity problems.

A five-year International Tin Agreement was concluded after two sessions of a United Nations Tin Conference held in 1950 and 1953, and came into force on July 1, 1956. In 1960, another United Nations Tin Conference was held, at which the text of the second International Tin Agreement was approved. This Agreement, also for five years, entered into force provisionally on July 1, 1961, and definitively on March 7, 1962.

A United Nations Sugar Conference held in 1953 concluded an International Sugar Agreement, which came into effect on January 1, 1954. The five-year agreement was reviewed and revised during the third year of its operation at a second Conference, and a protocol modifying the agreement came into force on January 1, 1957. In the latter part of 1958, the Secretary-General convened a third United Nations Sugar Conference, which concluded a further five-year agreement. This agreement entered into force on January 1, 1959.

At the first and second sessions of a United Nations Wheat Conference, held in 1955 and 1956, a three-year International Wheat Agreement was concluded. The Agreement expired on July 31, 1959. A second Conference was held in October 1958 and in January-March 1959, and a new three-year International Wheat Agreement was concluded. It entered into force on August 1, 1959. Another United Nations Wheat Conference, held in January-March 1962, negotiated a new three-year Agreement, which entered into force on August 1, 1962.

An International Agreement on Olive Oil, adopted in October 1955 by a United Nations Conference on Olive Oil, did not come into force as scheduled in October 1956 because the required number of main producing and importing countries had not ratified the Agreement. The signatories to the Agreement met in 1956, 1957 and 1958 and drew up a protocol making certain procedural amendments to the proposed Agreement. The Agreement came into force on June 26, 1959, and expired on September 30, 1963.

United Nations exploratory meetings on copper and on lead and zinc were held in London in September 1958. At the exploratory meeting on lead and zinc, it was decided to seek the views of governments on methods of dealing with short-term problems and long-range actions and to establish a committee to examine these views. The Lead and Zinc Committee submitted its report to a United Nations Conference on Lead and Zinc, held in Geneva in November 1958, at which it was decided to continue and expand the Committee and to set up an inter-governmental study group, called the International Lead and Zinc Study Group.

During July and August 1962, representatives of seventy-one coffee-exporting and coffee-importing countries and interested organizations attended a United Nations Coffee Conference in New York, which approved a five-year International Coffee Agreement. The Agreement, which entered into force on December 27, 1963, is designed to increase the purchasing power of coffee-exporting countries by keeping prices at fair levels and increasing world consumption, and is also intended to achieve a reasonable balance between supply and demand by bringing about long-term equilibrium between production and consumption. Quotas have been assigned, dividing the annual global imports, estimated at more than 45 million bags, among thirty-six producing nations.

INTERIM CO-ORDINATING COMMITTEE FOR INTERNATIONAL COMMODITY ARRANGEMENTS.   In March 1947, the Economic and Social Council established an Interim Co-ordinating Committee for International Commodity Arrangements, the functions of which were to convene inter-governmental study groups, make recommendations to the Secretary-General on convening commodity conferences and coordinate the activities of individual commodity study groups and councils.

The Interim Co-ordinating Committee prepared, until the establishment of UNCTAD in December 1964 (see below), an annual Review of International Commodity Problems dealing with their relation to general economic conditions. From 1955 onwards, the Review was confined to a discussion of inter-governmental consultation and action, the task of reviewing the commodity situation having been assigned to the Commission on International Commodity Trade.

COMMISSION ON INTERNATIONAL COMMODITY TRADE.   In 1954, the Economic and Social Council established a subsidiary organ called the Commission on International Commodity Trade. Consisting of eighteen members, its terms of reference were to examine measures designed to avoid excessive fluctuations in the prices and volume of trade in primary commodities and to keep under review the situation in world markets for such commodities.

In 1958, the Council expanded the Commission's terms of reference to include the study of movements in the terms of trade and their effect on both the international and domestic economic position of countries participating in international commodity trade, with special attention given to the position of the less developed countries. The Commission was asked to continue to keep the movement of world primary markets under constant review.

In August 1962, the Economic and Social Council endorsed the Commission's work programme, as defined at its tenth session in May. The Commission had concluded that the average price of primary commodities moving in international trade had declined for the fourth successive year in 1961 and that the terms of trade of primary-producing countries had declined to their lowest level since 1950. The view was reaffirmed that the long-term problem should be approached by action on the part of both industrial and primary-producing countries. Thus, in addition to deciding to set up a technical working group to study in detail systems of compensatory financing to offset fluctuations in the export earnings of primary-producing countries, the Commission also decided to ask the group to consider measures needed to remedy the unsatisfactory long-term trend in commodity earnings of primary-exporting countries.

The Council also took note of the joint session of the Commission and the FAO Committee on Commodity Problems, held from May 7 to 14, 1962, where problems arising in connection with the study of long-term projections of supplies of and demand for agricultural and non-agricultural commodities had been considered and where attention had also been given to the role of national marketing boards and stabilization funds, particularly in less developed areas, and to the possibility of using international compensatory financing in connection with fluctuations in prices of individual primary commodities. The Council asked the Secretary-General and the Director-General of FAO to continue their work on projections of the prospective production of, and demand for, primary commodities.

In December 1962, the General Assembly approved the establishment of the technical working group on compensatory financing and asked that the report of the group be sent to the Economic and Social Council for transmission to the Preparatory Committee of the Conference on Trade and Development (*see below*). In addition, the Assembly urged the Commission and the Council to accelerate the study of the long-term trade problems of countries producing primary commodities, especially measures aimed at the long-term stabilization of prices, with a view to facilitating the work of the Preparatory Committee.

United Nations Conference on Trade and Development

When the Economic and Social Council, at its 1962 summer session, resolved to convene a United Nations Conference on Trade and Development relating particularly to commodity markets, it recalled earlier Assembly resolutions, particularly that on international trade as the primary instrument for economic development, and referred to the aims of the United Nations Development Decade. It noted the difficulties which hamper international trade, took into account the fact that the developing countries in recent years have suffered from the drop in prices of primary products and, finally, recognized that measures to impart stability in international commodity markets at remunerative levels are vital for these countries.

In December 1962, the General Assembly, at its seventeenth session, endorsed the Council's action and asked it to convene the first session of a Preparatory Committee for the Conference by January 1963 so that the Conference itself could be held in the latter part of 1963 or the early part of 1964.

The Conference was convened in Geneva on March 23, 1964, with representatives from 120 countries attending. During the course of the Conference, which lasted until June 16, 1964, a number of fundamental problems connected with the expansion of international trade and its impact on economic development were examined, and issues ranging from international commodity problems and the improvement of the invisible trade (for example, insurance) of developing countries, to the financing of trade expansion and the implications of regional economic groupings were discussed. In a Final Act, the Conference formulated a number of principles governing trade relations and trade policies and recommended that the Conference itself should be established as a permanent organ of the General Assembly, with a Trade and Development Board and subsidiary bodies, and a full-time secretariat.

ESTABLISHMENT OF UNCTAD AS A PERMANENT ORGAN.   In a resolution adopted on December 30, 1964, the Assembly decided to establish the United Nations Conference on Trade and Development (UNCTAD) as a permanent organ of the Assembly. The Assembly resolution provided that the main functions of UNCTAD should be:

to promote international trade, especially with a view to accelerating economic development, particularly trade between countries at different stages of development, between developing countries and between countries with different systems of economic and social organization;

to formulate principles and policies on international trade and related problems of economic development and to make proposals for putting those principles and policies into effect;

to review and facilitate the co-ordination of activities of other institutions within the United Nations system in the field of international trade and related problems of economic development;

to initiate action, where appropriate, in co-operation with the competent organs of the United Nations, for the negotiation and adoption of multilateral agreements in the field of trade; and to be available as a centre for harmonizing the trade and related development policies of governments and regional economic groupings.

The Conference comprises those states which are members of the United Nations, its specialized agencies or the International Atomic Energy Agency. It is to be convened at intervals of not more than three years.

The Conference's permanent organ, the Trade and Development Board, normally meets twice a year. Its functions are to keep under review, and take appropriate action for the implementation of, the recommendations and other decisions of the Conference, to ensure the continuity of its work and to make or initiate studies and reports in the field of trade and related problems of development. The Board consists of fifty-five members, elected by the Conference from among its membership with full regard for both equitable geographical distribution and the desirability of continuing representation for the principal trading states.

For the effective discharge of its functions, the Board has set up four main subsidiary organs: the Committee on Commodities, the Committee on Manufactures, the Committee on Invisibles and Financing related to Trade, and the Committee on Shipping. Each Committee is convened once a year, but may be called in special session to deal with urgent issues. An Advisory Committee assists the Board, the Committee on Commodities and the Secretary-General of UNCTAD, at their request, on matters concerning commodity arrangements and such other matters as are referred to it.

The secretariat is headed by a Secretary-General, who is appointed by the Secretary-General of the United Nations and confirmed by the General Assembly. The headquarters of the secretariat are in Geneva, with a liaison office at United Nations Headquarters.

The first session of the Trade and Development Board was held in April 1965, the second in August-September and the resumed second session in October of the same year. These two sessions were largely devoted to completing preparatory and organizational arrangements. The Board established its own programme of work and adopted the terms of reference for its four major technical committees.

The third session of the Board, held in January-February 1966, considered the scope and objectives of the second session of the Conference on Trade and Development, which was scheduled to be held in 1967. The consensus was that, the first session of the Conference, in 1964, having laid down what in essence constitutes the framework of a new international policy for trade and development, the second session should concentrate on ways and means of implementing the recommendations of the first session. It was widely agreed that the theme of the second session should be "action and achievement" and that it should concentrate on matters of fundamental importance.

The Committee on Commodities, which carries out the functions of the Commission on International Commodity Trade and the Interim Co-ordinating Committee for International Commodity Arrangements, held its first session in July-August 1965. The Committee reviewed the situation of international trade in primary commodities and examined the particular situation of individual commodities. It listed as commodities giving cause for immediate concern, cocoa, sugar and coffee and as requiring close attention, *inter alia*, copper, cotton, iron ore, lead and zinc, rice, rubber, tea, tobacco and vegetable oils. The Committee set up a permanent Sub-Committee on Commodities to carry out, in inter-sessional periods, functions assigned to it by the Committee, and a Permanent Group on Synthetics.

The Committee on Manufactures, which held its first session in August 1965, examined the report of a Special Committee on Preferences appointed by the Secretary-General of the United Nations in accordance with a recommendation of the first session of the Conference on Trade and Development, and decided to set up a Group on Preferences.

At the first session of the Committee on Shipping, in November 1965, it was agreed that consultative machinery between shipowners and users of sea transport should be expanded throughout the world and that such machinery should be established both on the national and regional level. It was decided that the UNCTAD secretariat should prepare models for establishing consultative machinery adaptable to the needs of varying conditions in different parts of the world.

The Committee on Invisibles and Financing related to Trade held its first session in December 1965. In the field of invisibles, the Committee mapped out a programme of future work covering statistics of international services transactions, insurance and reinsurance, and tourism. In the field of financing related to trade, the Committee discussed the question of the recent decline in the rates of growth of developing countries and began consideration of three major reports.

With regard to the report of the International Bank for Reconstruction and Development (IBRD) on the Horowitz Proposal, the Committee, after a preliminary exchange of views, requested the Secretary-General of UNCTAD to appoint a special group of experts to consider the economic and financial problems involved. The Proposal contemplates that funds would be raised by an international agency at commercial rates of interest and then re-lent at lower rates to developing countries, the difference being met by allocations from the developed countries.

The second report before the Committee was by a group of experts on international monetary issues. The report stated that there is need for a reform of the international monetary system that would make it more responsive to the need for economic development and that it is both feasible and desirable to establish a link between the creation of international liquidity and the provision of development finance.

The third major report before the Committee was by the IBRD on the question of supplementary financing. It dealt with a scheme aimed at providing financial assistance to developing countries pursuing agreed development policies when progress is threatened by unexpected export shortfalls which cannot be adequately neutralized by short-term balance-of-payments support.

Several meetings on individual commodities or on specific questions have been organized under the aegis of UNCTAD. The third International Tin Agreement, the first commodity agreement to be negotiated under the aegis of UNCTAD, was adopted in April 1965 and came into force on June 30, 1966.

In June-July 1965, a Conference on Transit Trade of Land-Locked Countries prepared and adopted a convention that was immediately opened for signature. The Convention, among other things, sets forth the principles that land-locked states should have free access to seas, that they should enjoy the freedom of the seas on equal terms with coastal states and that they should be afforded by all states free and unrestricted transit.

The United Nations Sugar Conference convened in September-October 1965 to consider the proposals for a new International Sugar Agreement submitted by the Executive Director of the International Sugar Council. The Conference recognized that further preparatory work was needed in order to negotiate a comprehensive international agreement. Before adjourning, the Conference, by a new Protocol, extended to December 31, 1966, the Protocol which was due to expire at the end of 1965.

The United Nations Cocoa Conference, which met in May-June 1966, agreed that a suitable international cocoa agreement should contain provisions relating to quotas, buffer stock mechanism, price range, regular income for the buffer stock and diversion of structural surpluses of cocoa to non-conventional uses. The Conference invited the Secretary-General of UNCTAD to arrange bilateral and multilateral consultations between interested governments, to establish technical working groups for the study of particular provisions of the contemplated agreement and to reconvene the Conference not later than the end of 1966.

INDUSTRIAL DEVELOPMENT

The need for a continuing, comprehensive and methodical study of economic development in achieving a better direction of effort and resources for the economic advancement of under-developed countries was recognized by the General Assembly in a resolution of January 12, 1952, which addressed two requests to the Economic and Social Council: first, that the Council should promote studies of a programme for the rapid industrialization of under-developed countries, including the economic, social, fiscal, technical and organizational problems involved, and the roles which both industrially advanced and under-developed countries have to play in such a programme; and second, that the Council should, as soon as practicable, submit concrete proposals to the Assembly for measures that might aid such countries in connection with these problems.

The Assembly also asked the Council to study the varying ways in which the productivity of peoples everywhere could be increased by the application of existing scientific and technological knowledge.

At its spring session in 1952, the Council stressed the need for co-ordinated and integrated policies of economic development, in particular for industrial diversification in harmony with the development of agricultural production. The Council drew the attention of governments to the technical assistance services available through the United Nations and specialized agencies for preparing and executing integrated development programmes.

Since then, questions concerning the industrialization of under-developed countries have been considered at nearly every session of the Council and the General Assembly. Among various recommendations made by the Council, one in 1957 asked that special attention be given to the needs of the Middle East and Africa, and another in 1959 asked the regional economic commissions and the specialized agencies to assign high priority to the assistance needed by countries seeking to diversify their exports. Later, in 1959, the General Assembly noted the need for speedier industrial development and called attention to the useful role which individual development banks and development corporations could play in promoting industrialization in the under-developed countries.

Committee for Industrial Development

In 1960, the Council, acting upon the recommendations of the Assembly, established a standing Committee for Industrial Development, composed of the eighteen Council members and six additional members and charged with the task of advising the Council. Acting on a later recommendation of the Assembly, the Council increased the membership of the Committee to thirty to ensure a more balanced representation of member states. The Committee was asked to examine the work programme on industrialization and recommendations related to this programme and to make arrangements for relevant studies and collection of data. The first session of the Committee was held in March 1961.

In its report to the Council in April 1961, the Committee presented a number of recommendations. In the field of industrial programming and policies, it recommended that measures be taken to collect and disseminate information on the institutional arrangements for, and the methods applied in, planning and programming industrial development in member states. Further, it suggested that the financing of industrial development be considered in the context of long-term development plans for the economic and industrial development of under-developed countries and recommended that international assistance be directed towards the achievement of this purpose.

As regards the organizational aspects of its work, the Committee recommended that a Centre for Industrial Development be established within the Secretariat to undertake the collection, analysis and dissemination of experience gained through technical assistance programmes in the field of industrialization and also to provide a mechanism for co-ordinating the activities of the various United Nations bodies and members of the United Nations family.

The Council endorsed the recommendations of the Committee and later in 1961 called upon the Secretary-General and the heads of the agencies concerned to give effect to suggestions by the Secretary-General and the Administrative Committee on Co-ordination (ACC) for concerted action in the field of industrialization.

Centre for Industrial Development

At its sixteenth session, the General Assembly, on December 19, 1961, endorsed the recommendations of the Council and the Committee and requested that the Centre for Industrial Development, which had been established in July 1961, begin its work without delay and that special attention be devoted to the question of financing industrial development, particularly the utilization of internal resources.

The Commissioner for Industrial Development was appointed by the Secretary-General on June 1, 1962. In a memorandum to the summer session of the Economic and Social Council, the Commissioner outlined the structure of the Centre, stressing the link that existed between United Nations activities in the field of industrial development and international trade, and noted that the programme of the Centre was essentially intended to mobilize, co-ordinate and strengthen the efforts of the United Nations family in the industrial field.

At its seventeenth session, in 1962, the General Assembly adopted two resolutions on the subject of industrial development. One resolution recommended that the ten-member Advisory Committee established earlier in the year by the Council consider the advisability of dealing with problems of industrial development, natural resources, energy and possibly other related fields, within the framework of one organizational structure, and the possibility of bringing about a closer co-ordination of all activities related to industrialization at the national, regional and international levels. The other resolution asked the Secretary-General to prepare a report, in conjunction with governments and other United Nations organs, which, among other things, would estimate the requirements of the developing countries for technical personnel of the intermediate and higher levels and assess the feasibility for training such personnel in those countries.

The work programme of the Centre for Industrial Development has included, among other things, the promotion of small-scale industry, the dissemination of information on industrial technology, the formulation of industrialization policies and programmes, the selection of high priority industrial projects and the preparation of bankable projects for submission to financing institutions. It has also included the preparation of studies and manuals on general and specific aspects of industrialization, such as *Management of Industrial Enterprises in Under-developed Countries, Establishment of Industrial Estates, Industrial Standardization in Developing Countries* and a report on the use of second-hand equipment in developing countries.

The Centre has also organized seminars and technical meetings on such subjects as industrial programming, industrial complexes, industrial research and development techniques, social aspects of industrialization, industrial standardization, evaluation of industrial projects and training of economic administrators in industrial development, as well as on particular industries, such as iron and steel, cement, textiles, petro-chemicals, food, chemicals and fertilizers.

An advisory committee of ten experts on the industrial development activities of the United Nations system, which had been requested to make recommendations concerning the organizational changes needed to intensify, concentrate and expedite the United Nations effort for the industrial development of the developing countries, submitted its report to the Secretary-General in 1963. The report stated that a review of the work being carried out in the field of industrial development disclosed a vast array of activities but that the total amount of resources devoted by the United Nations to the promotion of industrial development was inadequate.

In 1963, the Economic and Social Council, and later the General Assembly, endorsed this view and recommended that the Committee for Industrial Development be instructed to consider setting up an organization capable of dealing with the problems being encountered by the developing countries. The Assembly also called upon the Secretary-General to initiate consultations with members of the United Nations, the specialized agencies, the IAEA, the regional economic commissions and the Committee for Industrial Development on the advisability of holding an international symposium, preceded by regional and sub-regional symposia, relating to the problems of industrialization of the developing countries. The Secretary-General reported to the Economic and Social Council in 1964 that both the replies received from governments and the response of the regional economic commissions indicated a consensus in favour of holding the symposia, the regional and sub-regional symposia being viewed as phases of an extensive process of consultations which would culminate in a world-wide symposium. The Council endorsed the decisions to hold regional and sub-regional symposia in Africa, Asia and Latin America and welcomed the co-operation of the Economic Commission for Europe in this connection. The Council later decided that the international symposium should be postponed until early in 1967, the regional commissions having decided upon the following dates for holding their industrial development symposia: ECAFE, December 1965; ECA, January 1966; and ECLA, February 1966.

The question of training technical personnel has long been recognized as one of the major problems in accelerating the industrialization of the developing countries. In pursuance of a resolution adopted by the General Assembly in 1962, the Secretary-General, in close co-operation with organizations of the United Nations family, prepared a report covering the entire range of problems in the field of training for industrial development. The report contained a review of existing facilities in developing countries for the education and training of technical personnel; information and recommendations on objectives, systems and methods of technical education and vocational training for technical personnel, including in-plant training of graduate engineers, training of higher administrative personnel in government organizations, and education and training of higher administrative and managerial personnel for public and private industry. An attempt was also made to estimate the financial implications of the required technical education and vocational training. At the request of the Economic and Social Council in 1964, the report was transmitted to governments, the specialized agencies and the IAEA, the regional economic commissions and the Committee for Industrial Development for their comments and recommendations.

In 1965, the Council reaffirmed that one of the principal functions of the Centre for Industrial Development was to act as the focal point for co-ordination of the work of the United Nations system in the field of industrial development. The Council requested that the Centre, in fulfilling this function, should prepare a single, analytical annual report summarizing United Nations work in this field, including that of the regional economic commissions and of the other agencies of the United Nations system. At its twentieth session, the General Assembly reiterated the request to governments and the other organs concerned to submit to the Secretary-General their views on the recommendations contained in the Secretary-General's report.

United Nations Industrial Development Organization

When the Committee for Industrial Development, at the request of the Assembly and the Council, considered at its third session, in May 1963, the question of the organizational changes needed in the United Nations machinery for industrial development, it concluded that there was an urgent need to establish a specialized agency for industrial development within the framework of the United Nations family. A recommendation to this effect was also contained in the Final Act of the United Nations Conference on Trade and Development in June 1964.

When the question came before the Economic and Social Council in 1964, the Council requested the Secretary-General to make any necessary changes in organization and procedures which would enable the Centre for Industrial Development, acting as a catalytic agent, to carry out a dynamic programme of activities, among them: the provision of help to governments in formulating requests for technical assistance; assistance to developing countries in strengthening national institutions; effective co-ordination by the United Nations system of its activities in the field of industrial development, and the provision of research results which would be of practical use to the developing countries. The Council made recommendations on the budgetary requirements of that programme and requested the Secretary-General to draw the attention of governments to the possibility of making voluntary contributions for activities in that field.

In 1965, the Council reaffirmed the need for urgent action to be taken towards the establishment of a specialized agency for industrial development and, pending its establishment, requested the Secretary-General to provide a substantial increase in the budget of the Centre for Industrial Development with a view to carrying out its existing and expanding functions. When the question came before the General Assembly in 1965, a resolution was adopted whereby an autonomous organization for the promotion of industrial development was established within the United Nations, its administrative and research activities to be financed from the United Nations regular budget and its operational activities to be financed from voluntary contributions to it, as well as through participation in the United Nations Development Programme. The resolution called upon the Secretary-General to appoint an executive director to head the secretariat of the organization and set up a special *ad hoc* committee composed of thirty-two member states, the specialized agencies and the IAEA to prepare the necessary operating procedures and administrative arrangements.

DEVELOPMENT AND PROVISION OF BASIC STATISTICAL INFORMATION

The statistical activities of the United Nations are carried out under the guidance of the Statistical Commission, a functional commission of the Economic and Social Council which advises the Council and the Secretary-General. The Commission first met in 1947, thereafter holding annual sessions and, more recently, biennial sessions. The membership of the Commission increased from twelve to fifteen in 1951 and to eighteen in 1962.

The central unit for the collection, analysis, publication, standardization and improvement of statistics is the United Nations Statistical Office, which functions in co-operation with the secretariats of the regional economic commissions and the specialized agencies, each of the specialized agencies being responsible for the collection of statistics relating to its own field of activity.

An International Trade Statistics Centre, established in January 1963, was by the end of 1965 receiving and processing data from over ninety countries by electronic computer. After publication in *Commodity Trade Statistics* and the *World Trade Annual*, the data are stored on magnetic tape so that rearrangements and summaries can be made at cost for interested users; generalized computer programmes have been developed by the Statistical Office to make possible a large variety of arrays of data without special programming.

In November 1965, the United Nations International Computing Centre came into operation as part of the Statistical Office. The Centre is equipped with an IBM 7044 computer and an auxiliary IBM 1401. The Centre provides electronic data processing and computing services to all units of the United Nations and, on request and against payment of costs, to specialized agencies and other United Nations agencies, as well as to governments and private institutions.

Regional Activities

In 1949, the Economic and Social Council recommended that meetings of regional statisticians be convened in order to provide an exchange of experience and discussion of problems peculiar to each region. As a result, three regional conferences have been set up. By the end of 1965, thirteen plenary sessions of the Conference of European Statisticians had been held, six of the Conference of Asian Statisticians and four of the Conference of African Statisticians, the "youngest" of the regional meetings. In Latin America, the Inter-American Statistical

Institute co-operates with the United Nations with respect to activities similar to those carried out by the regional conferences.

In 1956, the Council, recognizing the need for more adequate arrangements covering advisory statistical services to governments, recommended measures to systematize and strengthen statistical assistance on a regional basis. Following this, regional statisticians were appointed and are now in posts in Europe, Asia and the Far East, Africa and Latin America, each attached to the corresponding United Nations regional economic commission. In addition, a network of regional statistical advisers is operating in various regions, providing short-term help in specialized fields to requesting countries. At the end of 1965, there were six such advisers in Africa, three each in Asia and the Far East and in Latin America and one in the Middle East.

Development and Application of International Standards

The Statistical Office has as one of its principal functions the development and improvement of national statistics, especially in the less developed areas of the world. Much of its work has, therefore, been devoted to the formulation of standards, guiding principles, uniform definitions and concepts.

One of the standards, promulgated by the Economic and Social Council in 1950, is the Standard International Trade Classification (SITC). In 1960, the Statistical Commission requested revision of the SITC in order to make it possible for countries to base both customs nomenclature and statistical classification on a single list of goods. By the end of 1965, an analysis of the data of approximately eighty countries could be made according to the revised SITC.

The International Standard Industrial Classification of All Economic Activities (ISIC), promulgated by the Council in 1948, was at the end of 1965 known to have been used by fifty-seven countries as a basis for formulating their industrial classifications; about thirty additional countries had national classifications convertible to the ISIC.

In addition to these two classification schemes, standards have been established in numerous other fields. The Statistical Office has also prepared a series of technical studies and handbooks on a variety of subjects, with special emphasis on the application of international standards and recommendations.

The 1960 World Population Census Programme, covering censuses carried out by countries during the decade 1955-1964, began in 1953. A total of 196 countries took population censuses and 125 took housing censuses as part of the Programme. The 1970 World Population and Housing Census Programmes, covering censuses to be taken during the period 1965-1974, started in 1965.

The 1963 World Programme of Basic Industrial Statistics, covering censuses carried out for the year 1963, or a year close to 1963, was launched in 1958. By the end of 1965, over ninety countries were participating in the Programme.

Revision and extension of the 1952 United Nations System of National Accounts was undertaken in 1964 to devise an integrated and comprehensive system of national accounts which would meet the needs of economic and social analysis and planning and serve as a basis for developing co-ordinated systems of basic statistics.

Technical Assistance in the Field of Statistics

Between 1948 and the end of 1965, over 425 consultants had been placed at the disposition of governments and over 700 fellowships had been awarded, not counting awards given to enable technicians to attend short-term training centres, seminars and group study tours sponsored by the United Nations.

To meet the needs of Africa for trained statisticians, five permanent training centres under United Nations auspices had opened by the end of 1965: in Rabat for university-level trainees and in Accra, Addis Ababa, Dar-es-Salaam and Yaoundé for middle-level trainees.

A Statistical Centre was established in June 1954 at the University of the Philippines with the assistance of the United Nations and is now in full operation without external help.

Between 1952 and 1955, the United Nations and the World Health Organization co-sponsored an Inter-American Centre of Biostatistics in Santiago, Chile. United Nations sponsorship ceased at the end of 1955, when the Centre was incorporated into the regular programme of the University of Chile's School of Public Health.

In addition to these long-term training activities, the Statistical Office participated, as organizer, co-sponsor or collaborator, in over forty-five short-term training centres, seminars and group study tours between 1948 and the end of 1965.

Data Collection and Publication Programme

One of the functions of the United Nations Statistical Office is the collection and publication of statistics to show the main economic and social characteristics of the world as a whole and the national components by means of periodic as well as *ad hoc* reports.

Six basic reference works are published every year: the *Statistical Yearbook*, the *Demographic Yearbook*, the *Yearbook of International Trade Statistics*, the *World Trade Annual* (published commercially), *World Energy Supplies* and the *Yearbook of National Accounts Statistics*. The need for current information is met by more frequent publications, among which is the *Monthly Bulletin of Statistics*. Periodically, a *Supplement* to the *Bulletin* is issued to provide more detailed definitions and explanatory notes about the scope, coverage, methods of compilation and other factors affecting the international comparability of statistics. Current figures are also given in the *Population and Vital Statistics Report*, a quarterly, and *Commodity Trade Statistics*, issued in fascicles, as quarterly data are reported by governments. Other recent data publications include the *Compendium of Social Statistics, 1963*, a joint publication of the United Nations, ILO, FAO, UNESCO and WHO, and *The Growth of World Industry, 1938-1961*, in two volumes: *National Tables* and *International Analyses and Tables*.

In addition to these publications which present data and to those which set forth standards, guiding principles and methodological studies, the Statistical Office has published reports of training centres, bibliographies, notes on current events in international statistics, information on current sample surveys and retail price comparisons for international salary determination.

TECHNICAL CO-OPERATION
AND OTHER PROGRAMMES

Programmes of technical assistance to the less developed countries through the United Nations and its family of related agencies have been described as a concrete manifestation of the will of the international community to honour a pledge—embodied in the United Nations Charter—to promote the economic and social advancement of all people.

Technical assistance is provided to governments, at their request, by the United Nations and its related agencies through two main types of programmes. One is the United Nations Development Programme, financed by voluntary contributions from governments which are members of the United Nations family of organizations, the funds being shared among the United Nations and eleven of the agencies related to it. The second type of assistance operations are commonly known as regular programmes because they are financed from the regular budgets of the organizations concerned.

United Nations Development Programme

At its twentieth session, in 1965, the General Assembly, acting on the recommendation of the Economic and Social Council, decided to combine the Expanded Programme of Technical Assistance (EPTA) and the Special Fund in a programme to be known as the United Nations Development Programme. In taking this action, the Assembly expressed its conviction that such a consolidation would go a long way towards streamlining the activities carried on separately and jointly by the two programmes, would simplify organizational arrangements and procedures and would facilitate over-all planning and needed co-ordination of the several types of technical co-operation programmes carried on within the United Nations system of organizations and increase their effectiveness.

As was the case with EPTA, which was established in 1950, and the Special Fund, established in 1959, the work of the Development Programme is financed by the voluntary annual contributions of members of the United Nations or of its related agencies. Pledges of financial support for 1966 exceeded $150 million, and the General Assembly recommended a $200-million target for subsequent contributions.

The resources of the Programme are divided among the twelve organizations which share the responsibility for carrying out UNDP projects: the United Nations, the International Labour Organisation (ILO), the Food and Agriculture Organization of the United Nations (FAO), the United Nations Educational, Scientific and Cultural Organization (UNESCO), the International Civil Aviation Organization (ICAO), the World Health Organization (WHO), the International Bank for Reconstruction and Development (IBRD), the International Telecommunication Union (ITU), the World Meteorological Organization (WMO), the International Atomic Energy Agency (IAEA), the Universal Postal Union (UPU) and the Inter-Governmental Maritime Consultative Organization (IMCO).

Direct policy control is provided by the thirty-seven members of the Governing Council of the UNDP, who are elected from among the developing and developed nations. The Governing Council has final responsibility for approving all projects, overseeing Programme operations and allocating funds.

The Economic and Social Council and the General Assembly also periodically review the work of the Programme.

Day-to-day operations of the Programme are managed by an Administrator and Co-Administrator and their staff at United Nations Headquarters. The Administrators are advised by an Inter-Agency Consultative Board composed of the heads of the twelve executing agencies and, where appropriate, by representatives of the United Nations Children's Fund and the World Food Programme.

In the field, UNDP is serviced, in addition to the facilities provided by the executing agencies, by eighty-two field offices. Headed by resident representatives of the UNDP, these offices work closely with governments and with the international organizations to identify needs for assistance, facilitate the obtaining of that assistance, smooth the path of project implementation and help assure effective follow-up.

The UNDP is currently engaged in helping the governments of 150 countries and territories carry out more than 3,000 projects in agriculture, industry, education, health, public utilities, development planning and social services, ranging from the provision of experts' services and fellowship grants to assistance in executing major pre-investment undertakings.

UNDP projects are divided into two general sectors: the large-scale pre-investment work which formerly fell within the competence of the Special Fund and which is now considered as the Special Fund sector; and the smaller technical assistance projects which were formerly carried out under the Expanded Programme of Technical Assistance.

SPECIAL FUND SECTOR.   Within the Special Fund sector, over 600 high priority pre-investment projects have been approved for operation, seventy of which had been completed before 1966. Aimed at helping the low-income countries create the conditions with which capital investment would be both feasible and effective, these projects encompass four main types of assistance: surveys and feasibility studies to identify and plan utilization of natural resources (254 projects); the establishment or strengthening of permanent educational institutions to produce the teachers and instructors for advanced technical and educational training programmes (213 projects); the setting up or expansion of applied research centres to improve efficiency and productivity in both agricultural and industrial enterprises (127 projects); and the provision of advisory and consultant services in development planning and in the execution of programmes (10 projects). A total of over $1,400 million has been committed for these undertakings, $823 million to be expended by the recipient countries for facilities, counterpart staff and follow-up costs, and $583 million being provided by the Development Programme. UNDP expenditures cover the provision of expert personnel on a direct or sub-contract basis, the provision of major items of equipment and the awarding of fellowships for study abroad. The regional distribution of these projects is as follows.

Region	Number of Projects	Total Cost	UNDP Share	Government Share
			(in millions of U.S. dollars)	
Africa	200	$467	$206	$261
The Americas	165	367	154	214
Asia and the Far East	157	363	152	212
Europe	37	108	34	74
Middle East	44	95	33	62
Inter-regional	1	3	4	—
	604	$1,403	$583	$823

TECHNICAL ASSISTANCE SECTOR. In the 1965-1966 biennium, the UNDP was carrying out some 2,500 smaller-scale technical assistance projects at a cost of approximately $101 million. These projects allow for consultant and advisory services by international experts in a wide range of economic and social subjects, such as the organization of a malaria-control campaign, the management of an airport or the planning of a statistical service; the training abroad of technicians and administrators through fellowship awards; and the planning and preparation on a limited basis of institutional facilities for education, training, management, research and administration, which may sometimes be expanded into a larger undertaking in the Special Fund sector.

For the 1965-1966 Programme, the following allocations were made to the UNDP executing agencies to carry out the technical assistance projects which fall within their respective field of competence:

Agencies	Amount	Per cent
United Nations	$19,988,850	19.80
International Labour Organisation	10,655,666	10.55
Food and Agriculture Organization of the United Nations	24,700,405	24.47
United Nations Educational, Scientific and Cultural Organization	16,556,972	16.40
International Civil Aviation Organization	4,636,807	4.59
World Health Organization	16,473,267	16.32
International Telecommunication Union	2,638,206	2.62
World Meteorological Organization	2,618,934	2.61
International Atomic Energy Agency	1,935,302	1.91
Universal Postal Union	737,080	0.73
	$100,941,489	100.00

RESULTS OF INTERNATIONAL DEVELOPMENT ACTIVITIES. Although the Development Programme as such was only created at the beginning of 1966, the operations that fall within its scope have, in the past fifteen years, been associated with a substantial record of accomplishment in the 150 developing countries and territories receiving such assistance. This record includes: over $1,000 million in capital investment attracted to develop agriculture, power, mining, manufacturing, transport, communications and forest industries; nearly 250,000 men and women equipped with vitally needed productive skills, among them thousands of administrators and planners; agricultural, industrial and public service technicians; engineers, plant managers and supervisors; educators and industrial instructors; and medical personnel; scores of permanent institutions, many regional in scope, established to plan, administer and stimulate economic and social progress, among them water authorities; medical, health, community and social services; forestry departments; transport and light industry boards; and other development agencies, both public and private; effective new methods developed for farming, fishing, forestry, manufacturing, construction and the use of local raw materials; new low-cost products made available for domestic consumption; and new high-earning markets opened abroad.

INTERNATIONALISM OF THE PROGRAMME. The United Nations Development Programme draws on the participation of all members of the United Nations family. Some two-thirds of the recipients of UNDP assistance are also contributors—in the sense that they pledge funds to the Programme's global activities, offer training facilities for UNDP fellows, or provide experts for missions abroad. Among the 5,633 United Nations and agency advisers and technicians who were in the field during 1965, about 100 nationalities were represented; at least as many countries were hosts to the 3,080 UNDP fellows or suppliers of the $19 million in equipment purchased for UNDP-supported projects.

Operational Activities of the United Nations

United Nations technical assistance activities take the form of expert advice and assistance, fellowships, training courses and seminars, pilot projects, and demonstration projects. More recently, however, operations and action have commanded increased attention, especially as regards assistance in the development of Special Fund and other long-range projects.

Another important development has been the steady strengthening of the technical assistance activities undertaken by the regional economic commissions. Besides decentralization of many of the regional technical assistance projects, a number of regional advisers and experts have been attached to the regional secretariats to render advisory services to member countries coming within the geographic jurisdiction of these commissions.

There has been a major increase in the work on natural resources development, statistics, industrial development and economic planning and programming activities and, finally, in social activities. Much headway has been made in developing integrated projects such as economic surveys and programming industrial development and productivity, and general economic and advisory services.

The financial value of the assistance provided under the United Nations programmes of technical co-operation in 1965 was $34 million, including funds expended under the regular and expanded programmes and Special Fund projects and activities financed under funds-in-trust arrangements but excluding special educational and training programmes for South West Africa and territories under Portuguese administration.

The rise in available resources was due mainly to the increasing role of the United Nations as an executing agency of Special Fund projects. By the end of 1965, it was the executing agency for 109 projects, distributed by region and by field of activity as follows:

Geographic Region		Field of Activity	
Asia and the Far East	34	Natural resources	72
Latin America	33	Industrial development	14
Africa	29	Economic surveys	7
Middle East	8	Housing and planning	6
Europe	5	Public administration	4
		Transport and communications	4
		Statistics	2

If 1960 were taken as a base of 100 in measuring the growth of technical assistance operations for which the United Nations was responsible for the period 1959 through 1965, excluding Special Fund projects and the World Food Programme obligations, expenditures in 1965 were at an index of 218.

The level of the regular programme was maintained at $6.4 million in 1965, as had been the case since 1962, when the General Assembly raised the level from $3.5 million in order to provide greater assistance to former trust territories and other newly independent states. The share of the regional and inter-regional projects under the regular programme rose to 43.3 per cent, as compared with 35.3 per cent in 1963. On an over-all basis, taking into account all programme resources, 30.3 per cent was spent on regional and inter-regional programmes, as compared with 26.2 per cent in 1963.

The increased allocations to regional and inter-regional projects were due in part to the demand for and use of regional and inter-regional advisers. The regional economic commissions, in the case of the former, and United Nations Headquarters, in the case of the latter, were able to respond promptly to requests for technical assistance in collaboration with the resident representatives. This also permitted the United Nations to respond to emergency needs, which would not otherwise have been met without the delay resulting from recruitment.

United Nations activities in economic and social development increased in 1965 as compared with 1964, taking into account all of the resources available to the Organization (regular and Expanded Programmes, Special Fund and extra-budgetary operations). Obligations for economic development activities totalled $25.9 million in 1965 as compared with $24.7 million in 1964, and social development activities totalled $5.1 million in 1965, as compared with $4.7 million in 1964.

The total number of experts under all programmes, but exclusive of those working under Special Fund projects, was 2,058 in 1965. There were an additional 306 experts working on Special Fund projects. More experts were used in economic surveys; programming and projections; industrial development; development of natural resources; statistics; social development; population; and housing, building and planning.

Fellowships under all programmes in 1965, exclusive of those under Special Fund projects, totalled 1,887, including 764 participants in regional and inter-regional training programmes.

Public Administration

ADVISORY SERVICES, TRAINING AND RESEARCH.   United Nations programmes in the field of public administration include the provision of advisory services, the fellowships programme in public administration and a programme of research which supports regional and country activities.

In the field of personnel and training, advisory experts assist in the establishment of in-service training courses, job evaluation, pay grades, retirement and pension plans, and in training personnel for public administration institutes.

In the field of organization and methods, experts have given advice in such specialized aspects of government operations as the establishment of organization and methods agencies, government purchasing and supply management, records management, public corporations, administration of development programmes, free-port zone administration, public works, passport and nationality affairs.

In the field of local government, experts have advised on municipal administration, training of local government personnel, local government financing, correspondence courses for local government personnel, administrative aspects of community development and municipal management.

A considerable amount of technical assistance in public administration is directed towards the establishment of national institutes of public administration and is subsequently channelled through them. The concept of the institute, to provide leadership in the improvement of administrative organization and practices through training, research and advisory services, is understood as the general role. Several institutes are receiving assistance from the United Nations technical assistance programmes in the form of lectures and support for their research and teaching activities. In addition, the Special Fund has taken an increasing interest in the institutes as potential nuclei of administrative reforms.

Seminars in public administration can be classified both as training and research activities since they pursue a twofold objective: on the one hand, country participants are expected to benefit from exposure to consultants of international calibre and to experienced colleagues from other countries while at the same time they add to the comparative knowledge in the various technical fields and contribute to new approaches that can be applied in a development context.

PROVISION OF OPERATIONAL, EXECUTIVE AND ADMINISTRATIVE PERSONNEL.   The programme for the provision of operational, executive and administrative personnel (OPEX) was initiated in 1959 to help meet the needs of many governments, particularly those in newly independent countries, for experts to fill executive and operational posts in their administrative machinery, as well as for advisers.

The OPEX programme thus supplements the main programmes of technical assistance—which provide experts whose role is advisory and who remain officials of either the United Nations or a specialized agency—by arranging for the temporary appointment of experts to fill government posts, as the servants of governments. Governments contribute to the programme by paying each OPEX officer the salary usually paid to a national for the same post. The United Nations supplements the local salary by a stipend and other allowances calculated to bring the total remuneration each officer receives up to the level of what he would have received as an international expert employed by the United Nations. Each OPEX officer is under an express obligation, with the co-operation of the government, to train a national to succeed him in his post as rapidly as possible. A feature of this programme is that experts are not confined to United Nations fields of activity, but cover the fields of the specialized agencies also. In 1965, fifty-one posts were filled for all or part of the year in twenty-nine countries. In addition, the United Nations made nineteen operational personnel available to governments.

World Food Programme

In 1961, the General Assembly adopted a resolution approving the establishment of a three-year experimental World Food Programme to be undertaken jointly by the United Nations and FAO in co-operation with other interested United Nations agencies and appropriate inter-governmental bodies. The Assembly, at the same time, approved the establishment of a United Nations/FAO Inter-Governmental Committee of twenty member states of the United Nations and FAO to provide guidance on policy, administration and operations of the Programme, and of a joint United Nations/FAO Administrative Unit to be responsible for Programme administration.

The Inter-Governmental Committee met in Rome in February 1962, and in its report recommended certain preparatory measures to the Economic and Social Council and FAO. The Council, in mid-1962, invited governments to prepare for pledging contributions to the Programme, bearing in mind the target of $100 million. At a pledging conference held in New York on September 5, 1962, and subsequently, governments pledged approximately $90 million in commodities, cash and services.

The World Food Programme started operations on January 1, 1963. Under the Programme, contributions of food, cash and services are used to relieve emergency needs, to assist in pre-school and school feeding and to implement economic and social development projects.

At the end of the three-year experimental period, on December 31, 1965, 101 countries had taken part in the Programme as donors, as recipients, or as both. The final figure for contributions as of December 31, 1965 was $94.7 million. By that date, virtually all the resources had been committed to thirty-two emergency operations in twenty-five countries and to 116 projects for economic and social development, covering a wide variety of economic and social activities.

As a result of formal actions taken by the General Assembly at its twentieth session and by the Conference of the Food and Agriculture Organization, the Programme was extended on a continuing basis for as long as multilateral food aid is found feasible and desirable.

The administration of the Programme has continued to be carried out, under the guidance of the United Nations/FAO Inter-Governmental Committee, by a joint United Nations/FAO Unit, headed by an Executive Director reporting to the Secretary-General of the United Nations and the Director-General of FAO. Efforts have been made to co-ordinate the Programme's projects with those of other aid programmes, such as the regular programme of technical assistance, the Expanded Programme, the Special Fund, UNICEF, the International Bank for Reconstruction and Development, regional financing institutions, and bilateral aid programmes. Procedures have been established for participation of the regional commissions in the work of the World Food Programme.

In recommending the extension of the Programme on a continuing basis, the FAO Council and the Economic and Social Council established a target of $275 million for the three-year period 1966-1968. A pledging conference was held on January 18, 1966, when forty-three countries contributed approximately $209 million in commodities and cash. (*See also page 497.*)

United Nations Institute for Training and Research

In 1962, the General Assembly expressed belief that the training of personnel of the highest calibre, particularly from the developing countries, for service in the United Nations or in their own countries was important for the fulfillment of the objectives of the United Nations Development Decade, and asked the Secretary-General to study the possibility of establishing an institute for this purpose.

In 1963, the Economic and Social Council endorsed the broad lines of the Secretary-General's plan for such an institute, and the Assembly asked the Secretary-General to take steps to set it up and to explore sources of financial assistance.

By the end of 1964, plans were under way for launching the United Nations Institute for Training and Research (UNITAR) in 1965, as an autonomous institution within the framework of the United Nations, financed through voluntary contributions from governmental and non-governmental sources. Contributions, either paid in or pledged for the Institute, came to nearly $2.5 million, and the Institute had acquired a building of its own, through a donation by the Rockefeller Foundation, on United Nations Plaza opposite United Nations Headquarters.

The twenty-one-member Board of Trustees of UNITAR met for the first time in March 1965, and the Statute of the Institute was promulgated by the Secretary-General in November. The Institute is headed by an Executive Director appointed by the Secretary-General.

The functions of UNITAR are (1) to train persons, especially from developing countries, for assignment with the United Nations family of organizations or with their own national services; and (2) to conduct research and study related to the functions and objectives of the United Nations. The Secretary-General reports annually to the Assembly and the Council on the work of UNITAR.

During its first year of operation, the Institute took over three training programmes previously conducted by the United Nations Secretariat—one for foreign service officers from newly independent countries; one in techniques and procedures of technical assistance; and one in development financing—and organized two new programmes—training for deputy resident representatives of the United Nations Development Programme and a seminar on major problems of United Nations technical assistance. The Institute will also administer the Adlai E. Stevenson Memorial fellowships, granted by the United States Government.

By mid-1966, about $3.5 million had been pledged to the Institute by sixty-eight governments and $552,000 by non-governmental donors.

Assistance in Cases of Natural Disaster

At its summer session in 1964, the Economic and Social Council recalled its earlier request that the Secretary-General should take the lead in establishing, in conjunction with the specialized agencies and the League of Red Cross Societies, appropriate arrangements for assistance in relief and reconstruction in cases of natural disaster, and requested him to study and report to the General Assembly on types of assistance which it might be appropriate for the United Nations to provide, the order of magnitude of the resources that might be required for this purpose and alternative methods of providing such resources.

The Secretary-General submitted a report to the General Assembly in accordance with this request, pointing out certain gaps in the arrangements within the United Nations system which it seemed important to fill and which, along certain lines suggested by the League of Red Cross Societies, could be filled by the United Nations with quite modest additional resources. He proposed that for this purpose he be authorized to draw from the Working Capital Fund up to a total of $100,000 for emergency aid in any year, with a normal ceiling of $20,-000 per country in the case of any one disaster.

At its twentieth session, in 1965, the General Assembly agreed with the Secretary-General's proposal, for an initial experimental period until 1968, and invited governments to consider the advisability of setting up the national planning and operating machinery most suited to their own conditions and designed to determine the degree and character of the relief required and to give unified direction to relief operations. Resident representatives of the United Nations Development Programme were to be associated with this work. Governments were also requested, when offering emergency assistance in cases of natural disaster, to make use of the standing machinery set up in the stricken countries and to inform the Secretary-General of the type of emergency assistance they are in a position to offer.

The Administrative Committee on Co-ordination has had under consideration for some time the question of the resources available to the United Nations family for responding to appeals for assistance in major disasters. As a result of its study, a manual has been prepared outlining the resources and procedures to be followed and covering the United Nations, ILO, FAO, UNESCO, WHO, IMF, ICAO, UNICEF, the World Food Programme and the League of Red Cross Societies. The manual is intended to serve as a guide for governments in securing and mobilizing assistance from the members of the United Nations family.

REGIONAL ECONOMIC COMMISSIONS

The basic aim of the four regional economic commissions—the Economic Commission for Europe (ECE) and the Economic Commission for Asia and the Far East (ECAFE), both established in 1947; the Economic Commission for Latin America (ECLA), established in 1948; and the Economic Commission for Africa (ECA), established in 1958—is to assist in raising the level of economic activity in their respective regions and to maintain and strengthen the economic relations of the countries in each region both among themselves and with other countries of the world.

As subsidiary organs of the Economic and Social Council, the commissions report to it annually on their activities. The commissions adopt their own rules of procedure, including the methods of selecting their chairman. The secretariats of the commissions are integral parts of the United Nations Secretariat as a whole. Each commission is headed by an Executive Secretary, who holds the rank of Under-Secretary of the United Nations.

All action taken by the commissions is intended to fit into the framework of the over-all economic and social policies of the United Nations. The commissions are empowered to make recommendations directly to member governments and to the specialized agencies concerned, but no action can be taken in respect of any country without the agreement of the government of that country.

Since 1960, the work of the four commissions has been expanded and intensified, following decisions in that year by both the Economic and Social Council and the General Assembly on decentralization of the economic and social activities of the United Nations and strengthening of the regional economic commissions.

Economic Commission for Europe (ECE)

The Economic Commission for Europe (ECE) was established by the Economic and Social Council in 1947 "to initiate and participate in measures for facilitating concerted action for the economic reconstruction of Europe, for raising the level of European economic activity, and for maintaining and strengthening the economic relations of the European countries both among themselves and with other countries of the world." To this major aim was added that of providing governments with economic, technological and statistical analyses and information.

Severe post-war shortages of some commodities and surpluses in others made international co-operation in Europe a necessity. Moreover, governments felt that the valuable work done by the organizations for economic co-operation set up during the Second World War by the Allies should be continued in the post-war period and that the instrument of a United Nations regional commission for Europe might be useful for achieving international economic co-operation in the interest of the world as a whole.

Begun as an experiment, the Economic Commission for Europe

has become a permanent instrument of the United Nations—a centre for the promotion of trade, for the exchange of technical information, for the negotiation of inter-governmental agreements and for research on and analysis of economic developments in the region. Through meetings of policy makers and experts, through publication of economic analyses and statistics and through study tours and exchanges of technological information, the Commission provides a link between governments having different social systems and belonging to different sub-regional associations.

MEMBERSHIP AND ORGANIZATION. The members of the Commission are: Albania, Austria, Belgium, Bulgaria, the Byelorussian SSR, Cyprus, Czechoslovakia, Denmark, the Federal Republic of Germany, Finland, France, Greece, Hungary, Iceland, Ireland, Italy, Luxembourg, Malta, the Netherlands, Norway, Poland, Portugal, Romania, Spain, Sweden, Turkey, the Ukrainian SSR, the Union of Soviet Socialist Republics, the United Kingdom, the United States and Yugoslavia. Switzerland, which is not a member of the United Nations, takes part in a consultative capacity in the work of the Commission and its subsidiary organs.

The Commission holds one public session each year, lasting two and a half weeks; closed meetings of its subsidiary organs are held throughout the year. The permanent committees of the Commission operate in the following sectors: agricultural problems; coal; electric power; gas; inland transport; steel; timber; development of trade; housing, building and planning; and statistics.

Each committee has subsidiary bodies to deal with questions requiring special attention. The committees and their subsidiary bodies provide regular opportunities to participating governments for confronting and harmonizing national policies on problems arising in major sectors of the economy of the region; for standardizing and unifying economic and commercial practices; and for promoting technological and scientific co-operation. The committees, sub-committees and working parties of the Commission meet in private sessions to deal with technical problems. No official records are kept, and only agreed reports of meetings and annual reports to the Commission are made public. This procedure, followed over a number of years, has aided unhampered and businesslike execution of their work.

The Commission maintains close relations with the other regional economic commissions of the United Nations, with specialized agencies, with the United Nations Conference on Trade and Development (UNCTAD), and with inter-governmental and non-governmental organizations concerned with its work.

The Technical Assistance Office of the Commission arranges for participation in training courses. Because of the richness and variety of facilities in Europe and the willingness of European countries to make them available to the developing countries, more than 60 per cent of all United Nations fellows, as the trainees are called, take their training in Europe. The Commission's in-service training programme offers its facilities to young economists and statisticians from developing countries outside the ECE region.

The secretariat of the Commission is part of the United Nations Department of Economic and Social Affairs and utilizes the facilities of the United Nations Office at Geneva. Besides servicing the meetings, it prepares documentation and publishes bulletins, surveys and other studies.

One of the important services which the Commission furnishes to policy makers and the public is the publication of facts and figures on the European economy and analyses of its developments and prospects in their world setting. Major responsibility for this periodic reporting rests with the Research and Planning Division of the secretariat. Its two most important periodic research publications are the *Economic Survey of Europe*, appearing early every year, and the *Economic Bulletin for Europe*, published at least twice in the interval between *Surveys*. The *Survey* includes a review of economic developments in Europe during the preceding year, as well as chapters devoted to special problems.

The Division is responsible for the agenda for the meetings of senior economic advisers to the governments participating in the work of the Commission. These meetings are based on the need for better understanding of economic questions of mutual interest to participating countries operating under different economic systems.

AGRICULTURE. In the period since the establishment of ECE in 1947, changes in European agriculture have been proceeding much faster and on a larger scale than in any earlier period. As a result of recent changes in national policies, plans and programmes and of an increase in the amount and variety of agricultural products in countries which have traditionally imported agricultural products, many new problems have arisen with respect to trade in such products. These problems are reviewed annually by the Committee on Agricultural Problems, one of the earliest of ECE's committees, serviced by a joint secretariat of the ECE and the Food and Agriculture Organization (FAO). Quality standards have been laid down under the Committee's auspices for virtually all the important fruits and vegetables being traded by ECE countries. The Codex Alimentarius Commission, a joint FAO/WHO body, is using the ECE's European standards as a basis for the elaboration of world-wide norms. Work has advanced on the standardization of fruit juices and deep-frozen foods.

A valuable part of the Committee's work consists of annual reviews of the market situation of major agricultural products: cereals, meat, milk products, poultry and eggs. Periodic reviews of the production and market situation of other products—vegetables, fruits, potatoes —are also made. These reviews are based on statistical material submitted by member countries and are prepared by the secretariat in the form of comprehensive analytical and statistical documents. They provide valuable information for experts on foreign trade in agricultural products.

Subsidiary bodies of the Committee are the working parties on standardization of perishable foodstuffs and on standardization of conditions of sale for cereals and mechanization of agriculture and the Joint FAO/ECE Study Group on Food and Agriculture Statistics.

HOUSING.   The first task of ECE's Housing Committee when it was established in 1946 was to deal with the acute housing needs arising from the destruction caused by the Second World War and the cessation of housing activity during the war.

In the next phase of activity, the Committee promoted systematic arrangements for international technical co-operation, recommending the establishment in each country of national organizations for building research and documentation. This culminated in the formation, in 1953, of the International Council for Building Research, Studies and Documentation (CIB), an international non-governmental organization. During this period, the Committee also sought a way towards intergovernmental co-operation in housing policy, particularly the economic and social aspects of housing.

In 1964, the Housing Committee, in recognition of its broadening scope of activity, became the Committee on Housing, Building and Planning. Among its aims are: facilitating action for improvement of the housing situation; raising the standards of related social and community facilities, and improving the efficiency of building materials and construction.

A comprehensive study authorized by the Committee attempts to link up the major long-term problems of housing policy to related problems of urbanization, physical planning and land use. Because of the urgent need to speed up the construction of dwellings, community facilities including hospitals and schools, and factories, a sub-committee on the building industry with a long-term programme of work has been established. Another sub-committee, on urban renewal and planning, studies techniques of appraising the quality of neighbourhoods, housing areas and individual dwellings and makes inquiries on regional physical planning. It also studies the use of electronic computers in construction programming and physical planning and examines major problems of government housing policy.

STEEL.   All European countries are represented, together with the United States, in ECE's Steel Committee, whose meetings are attended not only by government delegations but also by representatives of governmental and international non-governmental organizations. The national delegations normally include both government officials and senior industrialists. In its early days, the Committee was concerned primarily with raw materials problems, particularly with the availability and proper distribution of coke, scrap and, to a lesser extent, ore in the post-war years.

At present, the Steel Committee reviews the main features of Europe's steel market, examines, in an annual market review, major trends in steel and steel-making raw materials and, on the basis of this review, considers what action might be taken. It also studies the long-term trends of the European steel industry. A study on this subject, published in 1959, provides projections of the steel demand in Europe and in other regions until 1972-1975. The Committee is also concerned with developments in the principal steel-consuming sectors and with major technical changes in the iron and steel industries. One of its studies, entitled "Comparison of Steel-Making Processes," was published in 1962.

The Committee endeavours to promote European co-operation on technical problems relating to steel. Technical and scientific steel institutes in participating countries are invited to develop mutual contacts, and efforts are being made to increase reciprocal visits of a general character and follow-up visits by specialists. Under its current work programme, the Steel Committee is conducting inquiries on productivity in the iron and steel industry and on automation of rolling and finishing of steel, as well as studies on the use of steel in construction.

The Committee has undertaken two major studies, on the economic aspects of iron ore preparation and on long-term trends in the competitive uses of steel in comparison with other materials, and has also started an inquiry into the economic aspects of continuous casting. In co-operation with the former Centre for Industrial Development, now the United Nations Industrial Development Organization, it has undertaken an examination of the world market for iron ore, and a study of world trade in steel and steel demand. Other studies made by the Committee include those on productivity and automation in the iron and steel industry and short and long-term trends in the production and consumption of stainless steels.

ENERGY.   The ECE committees dealing with coal, gas and electric energy produce studies involving a comparative assessment of the effectiveness of various forms of energy for different purposes. The committees convene symposia on carefully defined subjects of major economic importance. These symposia make it possible to associate with ECE's work not only governmental experts but also specialists from research institutes and from private and public enterprises.

The Coal Committee reviews twice a year, through its Coal Trade

Sub-Committee, trade in coal, and prepares an annual review of the coal situation in Europe. Under the direction of the Committee, experts have studied production problems. The Coal Committee has also studied automation in mining techniques.

The Committee on Electric Power prepares, every three years, a detailed report on the situation and future prospects of Europe's electric power supply industry. In intervening years, it prepares brief reports, mentioning outstanding developments during the year. The secretariat, which prepares these basic reports for the Committee, also prepares for it, and for the Coal and Gas Committees, a survey of the general energy situation in Europe. Other fields of activity of the Committee include legal questions, hydroelectric resources in Europe and their utilization, rural electrification, covering of peak loads, thermal power stations, methods and criteria for selection of investments, and rationalization of electric power consumption.

The Gas Committee makes an annual review of the gas situation in Europe, where the demand for and consumption of gas has continued to rise with industrial production. In addition, special studies are made on the transport and storage of natural gas, natural gas markets in Europe, the status of international gas pipelines, the preferential uses of gas, the use of various petroleum products as raw material for gas production, methods of forecasting gas demand and productivity in the gas industry.

The three committees sponsor a survey primarily designed to give a general picture of the energy situation in the world as a whole, and in Europe in particular.

INLAND TRANSPORT. The Inland Transport Committee, set up by ECE in 1947, is the main inter-governmental instrument used to facilitate international transport and travel in Europe and to promote European co-operation through increased trade by reduction of customs and frontier formalities and standardization of equipment.

An important contribution to increased trade in Europe by road transport has been the convention, worked out in the ECE, called TIR— Transport International Routier. The Convention makes it possible for a shipment of goods listed on a manifest and enclosed in the body of a truck to pass from Sweden, for example, to Italy, crossing frontiers on the way without inspection by customs officials.

In recent years, the Sub-Committee on Road Transport has been drafting articles for a new convention on road traffic and road signs and signals to be used as the basis of discussion for a world convention to be held some time in late 1967 or early 1968. In other fields, the Committee seeks to simplify or abolish the special documents required of motorists travelling abroad; considers applications for authorization to operate regular road passenger transport lines passing through the territory of more than one country; studies fiscal discrimination in in-

ternational road transport; promotes entry into force of the European
agreement of January 19, 1962, concerning the work of crews of vehicles engaged in international road transport; and, with the Committee on the Development of Trade, works towards standardization of
export documents through the drawing up of a standard model con-
signment note for international transport of goods by road.

In addition to earlier agreements drawing up a comprehensive
code of signals on inland waterways, the Commission has been responsible for a convention and two protocols on the registration of
inland navigation vessels and a convention on the measurement of
vessels used in inland transport by water.

The Commission keeps under review economic and technical
studies on major technical problems and economic simplification of a
unified system of inland waterways in Europe, including the characteristics of navigable waterways and measures to be taken to prevent the
pollution of waterways.

In the field of rail transport, the Committee has worked on adoption of automatic couplings for railway rolling stock, economic studies
on allocation of track costs, combined transport and containers, speeding up of international goods transport by rail and widening the scope
of the customs convention on the international transport of goods under
cover of carnets, the TIR Convention now in force for goods trans-
ported by road.

The Committee has stressed the importance of the need for harmonization between various national and international regulations on
the transport of dangerous goods by all means of transport. It has requested governments to instruct their delegates to international bodies
to take due account of the work done by the Committee of Experts
set up by the United Nations Economic and Social Council; that work
has already been taken as a basis for the regulations applying to
maritime transport.

TRADE.   ECE's work in the field of trade is carried out both
through the various sectoral committees and through its Committee on
the Development of Trade.

The Committee holds annual sessions at which the improvement
of trade relations between countries with different economic systems
is a main objective. It reviews the progress made in expanding commercial exchanges inside the region and with countries in other regions;
examines policy issues and tries to remove obstacles to trade; and seeks
to provide facilities which would promote trade.

The Committee has adopted recommendations to governments, of
which two are of special policy importance. The first is designed to
encourage transferability and convertibility in payments relations and
the second to stimulate negotiations between members of sub-regional
trade groups in Europe and non-members. In addition, an *ad hoc*

group of experts to study problems of east-west trade has drawn up certain agreed conclusions which have been transmitted to ECE governments. In the field of insurance, studies made by an expert group have led to the adoption of recommendations, in particular as regards reinsurance operations.

Under the Committee's auspices, the Convention on International Commercial Arbitration was concluded in 1961 and has been signed by eighteen European governments; standard contracts for sale of engineering equipment, grains, citrus fruits, timber and other commodities have been formulated; governments have adopted procedures facilitating the operations of international fairs, and international measures have been introduced for the simplification and standardization of documents used in international trade.

Since 1957, the ECE secretariat has acted as agent for a multilateral clearing system whereby balances held by central banks' bilateral accounts may be rendered transferable. Transfers totalling over $100 million have been arranged for European governments and for governments in Latin America and Africa.

In conjunction with the Committee's annual sessions, trade consultations are held at which experts hold bilateral talks aimed at the expansion of commercial exchanges. As a result of these consultations, it has in some cases been possible to arrange for trade flows even between countries which have not had diplomatic relations.

In recent years, the Committee has been giving special attention to its role in the light of the establishment of the United Nations Conference on Trade and Development (UNCTAD). At its 1965 session, the Committee adopted a resolution recommending that ECE countries continue their efforts to apply the relevant UNCTAD recommendations, without prejudice to their attitude towards individual recommendations, and confirming its readiness to co-operate with UNCTAD. In order to assist the UNCTAD programme, the Committee has initiated certain studies, particularly on changes in demand in European countries and the implications for trade of those changes, with special reference to developing countries.

STATISTICS.   Under arrangements made by the Economic and Social Council, three regional meetings of European statisticians were held in 1949, 1951 and 1953. In response to the need for closer and more systematic co-operation among the national statisticians responsible for the practical execution of statistical work and for improved co-ordination among the international agencies active in European statistics, the participants agreed to meet as a continuing body, to be known as the Conference of European Statisticians.

The Conference is a permanent organization under the joint auspices of, and reporting to, the Statistical Commission (a functional commission of the Economic and Social Council) and ECE. The members are the directors of the central statistical offices, or equivalent officials, of countries participating in the work of ECE.

The methods of work of the Conference are flexible and vary with the subject under study and sometimes also with the stage of development of each project. A common procedure is to set up a working group for the study of a particular subject. Another method is to appoint an individual rapporteur from a national office to prepare a general report for the Conference on a given subject. He may work alone or obtain information and suggestions from a small number of other rapporteurs.

Of the many fields in which the Conference of European Statisticians works, particular mention may be made of its studies on national accounts and balances. The system of national accounts which reflects the economic structure of countries with market economies is being reviewed and extended to fit the modern needs and possibilities of the countries concerned. The system of balances of the national economy in use in countries with planned economies is also being reviewed. The Conference is forging the links between the two systems and identifying the maximum of common ground.

The Conference also devotes much time to population censuses. Most countries will take such censuses in or around 1970 and, because of the complexity of the problems involved, it is essential to get a good start on the work of standardizing the methods so as to render them of the utmost possible practical use.

Other subjects covered are industrial statistics, electronic data processing, statistics of the distributive trades, activity and commodity classifications and price statistics. In joint meetings with other bodies, the Conference examines statistics on agriculture, education, housing and building and health expenditure. The Conference's responsibilities also include the promotion of co-ordination of international statistical activities in Europe and the co-ordination of statistical activities of ECE committees.

Economic Commission for Asia and the Far East (ECAFE)

The Economic Commission for Asia and the Far East (ECAFE) was established by the Economic and Social Council in March 1947, and the first session of the Commission was held in June of that year.

The terms of reference approved by the Council for ECAFE defined the geographic scope of the Commission and listed its original membership. From time to time, the terms of reference have been amended in order to meet the extension of the Commission's work and role.

The geographic area covered by the Commission's activities includes: Afghanistan, Brunei, Burma, Cambodia, Ceylon, China, Continental Australia, Hong Kong, India, Indonesia, Iran, Japan, Korea, Laos, Malaysia, Mongolia, Nepal, New Zealand, Pakistan, the Philippines, Singapore, Thailand, Viet-Nam and Western Samoa.

The purposes and scope of action of the Commission are set out in its terms of reference. In summary, its tasks are:

to initiate and participate in measures for facilitating concerted action to raise the level of economic activity of Asia and the Far East and for maintaining and strengthening the economic relations of the countries of those areas both among themselves and with other countries of the world;

to make or sponsor investigations and studies of economic and technological problems; to undertake or sponsor the collection, evaluation and dissemination of economic, technological and statistical information; to perform such advisory services as the countries of the region may desire, provided the services do not overlap with those of the specialized agencies or those provided by the United Nations technical assistance programme;

to assist the Economic and Social Council in discharging its functions within the region in connection with any economic problems, including problems in the field of technical assistance; and

to deal with the social aspects of economic development and the relationship of economic and social factors.

In carrying out these tasks, the Commission acts within the policy directives laid down by its parent body, the Economic and Social Council, and by the General Assembly. It is precluded from taking any action in respect of any country without the agreement of the government of that country.

MEMBERSHIP AND ORGANIZATION. The Commission has twenty-seven members and two associate members. The twenty-seven members are: Afghanistan, Australia, Burma, Cambodia, Ceylon, China, France, India, Indonesia, Iran, Japan, Republic of Korea, Laos, Malaysia, Mongolia, Nepal, the Netherlands, New Zealand, Pakistan, Philippines, Singapore, Thailand, USSR, United Kingdom, United States, Republic of Viet-Nam and Western Samoa. The two associate members are: Brunei and Hong Kong.

The work of the Commission, whose headquarters are in Bangkok, is conducted through its annual sessions and through meetings of its main committees and subsidiary bodies. In the early stages of the Commission, sessions were held more than once a year, but since 1949, they have been held annually. At the sessions, the work of the Commission and the secretariat over the previous year is reviewed and the programme of work and priorities for the coming year are laid down. The Commission has adopted the practice of holding its sessions in different member countries. Each session decides the venue for the subsequent meeting.

ECAFE's continued efforts to strengthen economic co-operation among Asian countries led to the convening of the first ministerial conference on Asian economic co-operation, which was held in Manila in December 1963. A second ministerial conference was held, also in Manila, in November-December 1965. Unlike the Commission's annual sessions, the ministerial conferences are attended only by regional members and associate members.

The Commission has three standing committees: the Committee on Industry and Natural Resources, the Committee on Trade, and the Inland Transport and Communications Committee.

The Commission's subordinate bodies, which meet annually or every other year, are composed of representatives of all members and associate members. To handle specialized aspects of each Committee's work, a number of sub-committees have been established which meet regularly in advance of the full Committee. Working groups are also set up from time to time to consider particular questions. A number of the meetings of the working parties are convened jointly by ECAFE and other United Nations bodies, such as the Bureau of Technical Assistance Operations (BTAO) and interested specialized agencies.

Permanent regional bodies have evolved from working parties or similar subsidiary bodies. They are the Asian Conference on Industrialization, the Conference of Asian Economic Planners, the Conference of Asian Statisticians and the Regional Conference on Water Resources Development.

Working in close association with ECAFE, and particularly with its division of Water Resources Development, is the Committee for the Co-ordination of Investigations of the Lower Mekong Basin.

New institutions which have come into existence as a result of ECAFE's initiative are the Asian Development Bank, established in 1966 with headquarters in Manila; the Asian Institute for Economic Development and Planning, set up under the aegis of ECAFE in January 1964, with headquarters in Bangkok; and the Asian Highway Co-ordinating Committee, established with ECAFE in Bangkok.

The work of ECAFE is carried out in close working relationship and co-ordination with resident representatives of the United Nations Development Programme in the countries of Asia and the Far East and with regional and local representatives of all United Nations agencies. It also has the co-operation and support of many non-governmental organizations concerned with different fields of its activities.

A total staff of about 370 professional and general service personnel, working under the direction of an Executive Secretary, comprise the ECAFE secretariat.

ECAFE's activities have been increasingly focussed on regional economic co-operation and action-oriented projects. In recent years, the basis for ECAFE's regional economic co-operation efforts has been the six-point action programme, the "historic" Manila resolutions, adopted by the first ministerial conference in Manila in December 1963. Included in these resolutions were proposals for trade liberalization, stabilization of prices of commodity exports, joint ventures on a regional and sub-regional basis, establishment of an Asian Development Bank, rationalization of ocean freight rates and co-ordination of air transport facilities.

The second ministerial conference adopted a comprehensive resolution on "dynamic" Asian economic co-operation, in which particular attention was paid to specific programmes for regional harmonization of development plans, industrialization and natural resources, trade liberalization, shipping and ocean freight rates, the Asian Highway, telecommunications, typhoon damage control and demographic programmes.

ECAFE's main regional economic projects are the Asian Development Bank, with an authorized capital of $1,000 million; the Mekong Development Project; the Asian Highway; and the Asian Institute for Economic Development and Planning.

As a result of the decentralization policy adopted in 1962 for United Nations economic and social activities, ECAFE has assumed a greater role in technical assistance activities. It now has total responsibility in planning, programming, implementing and following up regional projects. ECAFE is also becoming more and more involved in country programming for technical assistance in the region and supervising the progress of country projects. The United Nations Bureau of Technical Assistance Operations (BTAO) allocates around $1 million annually for ECAFE's regional projects, and ECAFE in turn works out a programme within this allocation. About twelve regional advisers are stationed with ECAFE; they are available at short notice to provide advice and assistance to governments in the region.

ECAFE's activities have developed along three main lines: first, fact finding, fact recording, and analysis; second, recommendations for governmental and inter-governmental action; and third, the rendering of advisory services and operational functions. All of ECAFE's activities are directed towards helping governments to help themselves.

PLANNING FOR ECONOMIC DEVELOPMENT.   Main efforts are directed at helping governments to attain and, if possible, exceed the targets of economic growth indicated by the United Nations Development Decade. A standing forum for high-level policy discussions has been established in the form of the Conference of Asian Economic Planners. Particular attention has been given to studies of sectors of strategic importance and the identification of areas where co-operation among countries of the region could help achieve the most economic exploitation of natural resources. A series of working parties on economic development and planning has been held over the years.

ECAFE's efforts were strengthened by the setting up of a regional centre for economic projections and programming and by decisions facilitating co-operation among Asian countries for a regional harmonization of development plans.

The Asian Institute for Economic Development and Planning, at Bangkok, established jointly by the United Nations Development Programme and several countries which are members of ECAFE, was formally inaugurated in January 1964. Two main courses are conducted by the Institute each year: a general course, of six months' duration, for economists and administrative officials of different countries of the ECAFE region, and an advanced course of three months, which provides for specialization in key fields of development planning to officials occupying more senior positions. Short-term national courses are also organized by the Institute in particular countries, on request, covering a variety of subjects. During 1964 and 1965, seventy-three officials were trained in the Institute's regional courses and about 200 more in the short-term country courses. In addition, the Institute undertakes research into the problems, possibilities and techniques of economic and social development in Asia and the Far East.

RESEARCH AND STATISTICS. Since its inception, ECAFE has collected, assessed and disseminated statistics from the countries of the region and has sought to improve statistical methods through regional conferences of statisticians. The Conferences of Asian Statisticians, held regularly since 1957, together with subsidiary bodies meeting as seminars and expert groups, have assisted governments in building up their own statistical services and in working out national development programmes. Emphasis has recently been laid on foreign trade statistics. Seminars and working groups have been held on national accounts, sampling methods, and censuses of population and housing.

ECAFE's comprehensive investigations of economic conditions throughout the region are published in the annual *Economic Survey of Asia and the Far East*, which deals each year with a specific problem, in addition to containing a general description of Asia's economic situation.

INTERNATIONAL TRADE. Through its Committee on Trade and the work of its secretariat, ECAFE keeps under review the major trade problems of the region, its trade situation and national trade policies. ECAFE also played an important part in preparing the ground for the United Nations Conference on Trade and Development and has assisted regional economic co-operation and regional trading arrangements. It initiated and supported the first Asian International Trade Fair, which was held in Bangkok in late 1966.

To promote international and intra-regional trade, ECAFE has provided advisory services to member governments on shipping and ocean freight rates, international trade fairs, trade liberalization, commercial arbitration, trade promotion and customs administration.

Intra-regional trade promotion talks convened by ECAFE have produced practical results, and ECAFE working parties on customs administration have brought about an easing of frontier formalities and facilitated the flow of international trade. A Centre on Commercial Arbitration was established within the secretariat in 1962, and a conference on commercial arbitration was held in early 1966.

INDUSTRY AND NATURAL RESOURCES.   ECAFE's work in the field of industry and natural resources covers, broadly, the development of mineral resources, electric power, metal and engineering industries, chemical and allied industries, small-scale industries, and housing and building materials. This work is carried out by means of direct technical assistance to governments of the countries of the region; studies and the collection and dissemination of information; and conferences, seminars, expert working groups and study tours. In recent years, there has been increasing emphasis on the application of science and technology to industrial and natural resources development.

The Asian Conference on Industrialization, held at Manila in 1965, was a landmark in Asian joint efforts at industrialization. The Conference examined the present status, problems and prospects of industrialization in the region and laid down comprehensive guidelines for action at national, sub-regional or regional, and international levels for achieving harmonization of national industrial development plans, rapid growth of key industries, mobilization of financial resources, expansion of trade in manufactures and semi-manufactures, advancement of technological level, strengthening of institutional arrangements and the development of infrastructure.

By a decision of the Commission in early 1966, the Conference was made a permanent organ of the Commission, with an Asian Industrial Development Council as its executive counterpart. The Council's main function is to follow up the recommendations of the Conference and to assist the countries of the region in implementing them.

A regional Industries Promotion and Planning Centre was established in 1965 to assist the countries of the region in harmonizing their national industrial development plans and identifying projects suitable for development on a joint basis, and to render direct technical assistance to countries of the region at their request.

Mineral Resources Development. Emphasis has also been given by ECAFE to mineral resources development. A working party of senior geologists, which began work in 1954, has completed a geological map, an oil and natural gas map and a mineral map of the region. In some countries, geological survey departments have been established and in others the services and facilities of geological survey departments have been made available in the compilation of the maps.

The Sub-Committee on Mineral Resources Development reviews periodically the progress made in the development of mineral resources in the ECAFE countries and formulates a programme of work to be carried out by the secretariat in order to assist the countries in accelerating their development programmes in this field. The first symposium on the development of petroleum resources of Asia and the Far East was held in 1958 in New Delhi. As an outcome of the symposium, the Commission accepted an offer from the Government of Iran to establish, in Iran, the first regional petroleum institute. The second symposium was held in 1962 in Teheran, and the third in 1965 in Tokyo.

As geological mapping is closely related to topographical mapping, the secretariat has assisted in the organization of United Nations regional cartographic conferences for Asia and the Far East (*see page 254*).

Electric Power. Increased electric power for industry, agriculture and domestic use is one of the most urgent needs facing the region's development planners. One of the first tasks which ECAFE set itself, therefore, was the collection and compilation of data on the generation, transmission, distribution and utilization of electricity in countries of the region. It publishes annually the *Electric Power Bulletin* which gives such data.

The Sub-Committee on Electric Power holds sessions in which electric power experts discuss matters connected with the electric supply industry, such as utilization of wood poles for power line support and of low-grade coal for power production, standards and standardization of equipment and codes of practice, formulation of electricity tariff rates, safety regulations, training of personnel, and organization problems.

ECAFE has recognized the importance of extending electricity to rural areas and has carried out extensive studies covering technical, economic and administrative aspects of this problem. It has also set up a panel of experts on rural electrification to visit the countries of the region on request and advise on specific power problems.

Metals and Engineering. Through the ECAFE Sub-Committee on Metals and Engineering, Asian and non-Asian experts are regularly brought together to discuss the common problems of metals manufacture and the development of various engineering industries.

The Sub-Committee has suggested new techniques for iron and steel production, suitable ways of developing non-ferrous metals producing industries and engineering industries and, in general, the development of existing natural resources. ECAFE also facilitates tests and research on raw materials and gives advice on the planning of projects, the layout of plants, and cost and quality control methods. The Sub-Committee has examined the problems of the shipbuilding, boat-building and repairing industries, of the machine-tool industry and of various engineering industries in the ECAFE region, and has made recommendations for their development.

Chemical and Allied Industries. ECAFE has given special attention to the promotion of industries that utilize local raw materials. Thus, in collaboration with FAO, it organized in Tokyo, in 1960, the first Conference on Pulp and Paper Development in Asia and the Far East, which brought together leading research workers, industrial planners and industrialists both from within and outside the region to examine ways and means of developing the pulp and paper industry in ECAFE countries.

ECAFE also organized in Bangkok, in 1962, a seminar on the development of basic chemical and allied industries and in Bombay, in 1963, a Conference on the Development of Fertilizer Industry in Asia and the Far East, which devoted special attention to promoting the international flow of capital, technical "know-how," and knowledge of various kinds of equipment required for the development of these industries. It also considered the possibility of certain market-sharing arrangements, whereby each country would develop a complementary range of chemical products, thus enabling the countries of the region to pool their development efforts and ensuring better utilization of existing resources.

Small-Scale Industries. Through its Working Party on Small-Scale Industries, ECAFE's efforts have been directed towards modernization of small-scale industries, transformation of small industries into medium and large-scale industries, and development of small industries as ancillaries to medium and large-scale industries. The annual publication of *Small Industry Bulletin,* started in 1963, carries articles of topical interest to small industries in the countries of the region.

Housing and Building Materials. The ECAFE Working Party on Housing and Building Materials has tried to stimulate increased production of housing for low-income families. A comparative study of building costs in relation to the wages of workers in the countries of the region was made in order to help housing technicians and administrators reduce the over-all costs of building. Other ECAFE studies have dealt with the financing of housing, with building codes and with housing standards.

To promote the continued study of building materials and their better use, as well as of housing problems in the region, ECAFE, with the help of the United Nations and the host countries, has established regional housing centres in New Delhi and Bandung, the first for the hot and arid tropical zone and the other for the hot and humid tropical zone.

A study tour and workshop on the organization and functions of national housing agencies in Asia and the Far East was held in Oslo, Copenhagen and Stockholm in 1965 to give housing authorities from the ECAFE countries an opportunity to learn at first-hand the experience of Scandinavian countries in this field.

TRANSPORT AND COMMUNICATIONS. Since deficiencies in the region's transport facilities adversely affect economic development, ECAFE has made substantial efforts to tackle some of the outstanding transport problems through technical studies and research, study tours and exchange of information and, increasingly in recent years, by rendering advisory services to governments. The Inland Transport and Communications Committee has initiated studies on such subjects as co-ordination of different means of transport; transport development and planning; statistics and accounting procedures for transport undertakings; freight rate structures, and transport refrigeration. A number of country surveys of transport facilities and requirements have been undertaken as a basis for advising governments on the development of their inland transport systems.

Transport statistics are regularly compiled, analysed and disseminated by the secretariat, which also publishes twice a year the *Transport and Communications Bulletin for Asia and the Far East*.

Railways. ECAFE is giving special attention to railway accounting and budgeting procedures, dieselization of motor power, economic aspects of different types of motor power and increase in locomotive operating efficiency. Through the Railway Research Co-ordinating Committee, railway technical problems are referred to research institutes available both within and outside the region.

The Pakistan Regional Railway Training Centre, in Lahore, established by ECAFE in 1954, has continued to serve countries in the region by training railway officers. Under the auspices of ECAFE, the United Kingdom has prepared a handbook on single line railways.

Highways. ECAFE has prepared standard forms for a highway register, a highway bridge register and a register for recording data on concrete road pavements and for the preparation and presentation of highway project schemes to ensure uniformity, efficiency and economy in establishing useful inventories of highway assets and requirements.

Studies on traffic engineering and highway safety were carried out by a seminar held in Tokyo in May 1957 and in two study weeks, one in Bombay in 1959, organized by the Government of India under the auspices of ECAFE, and the other in Manila in 1961, organized by the Government of the Philippines.

The main aspects of road passenger transport for the region were discussed at a seminar on highway transport which met in Madras in

1961. The seminar's recommendations covered such subjects as the planning and consolidation of available transport facilities and ways and means of financing their expansion and improvement, and the regulation and control of passenger transport so as to ensure efficient operation and regular services.

The importance of developing adequate international highway communications in the region was formally recognized by ECAFE in 1958, when it proposed the development of an international network in Asia, based as far as possible on existing roads. Since then, considerable progress has been achieved in the implementation of the project. Agreement has been reached on the routes to be designated as international highways and priority routes; international standards have been evolved for highways and bridges; plans have been drawn up for the preparation of detailed maps, and information on transport and traffic aspects of the proposed network is being collected. ECAFE member countries have also agreed on a code providing a uniform system of road signs and signals, road markings, and signs for road works and two other codes relating to motor vehicles and trailers in international traffic, with special reference to rules of the road, equipment to be required of motor vehicles in international traffic, and conditions to be fulfilled by drivers of such vehicles.

When complete, the Asian Highway will be a 55,000-kilometre network of roads spread throughout the countries of Asia from Iran to Viet-Nam and Indonesia in the south-east. Westward from Iran, it will link up with the European highway system. The main through route, stretching 13,300 kilometres from Teheran to Singapore and Saigon, has been completed, except for 550 kilometres still not suitable for motor traffic. The missing links, measuring about 70 to 170 kilometres each, are in Burma, East Pakistan and southern Thailand.

Inland Waterways. To encourage development of inland waterway transport, ECAFE has published a collection of selected plans of vessels, prepared a comparative study of various types of marine engines which focussed attention on the economic advantages of diesel engines for marine propulsion as compared with conventional steam engines, and co-operated with the International Labour Organisation in setting up the regional Marine Diesel Training Centre at Rangoon. The Centre has been taken over by the Government of Burma but continues to be open to trainees from all countries of the region.

In view of the great economic significance of coastwise shipping for several countries of the region, ECAFE has defined the basic characteristics for two prototype coastal vessels that would be suitable to meet the more common requirements, and has sponsored the preparation of complete sets of contract drawings and specifications for such vessels.

ECAFE is giving special attention to the introduction of modern types of craft, improvement of dredging techniques, classification of inland waterways, and inland waterway transport statistics.

In order to improve port efficiency and the turn-round time of ships, a port survey team has been formed to make surveys of major ports of the countries of the region.

TOURISM AND INTERNATIONAL TRAVEL. The important role which tourism can play in the process of economic and social development has long been recognized by ECAFE, which has undertaken specific studies in the field of tourism and international travel and has also intensified and broadened its co-operation with the International Union of Official Travel Organizations (IUOTO) and other regional bodies in the promotion of tourism.

Training and study tours for tourist officials in the countries of the region have been organized by many countries under the auspices of ECAFE to examine specific aspects of tourist promotion problems. ECAFE also initiated a region-wide survey of tourism resources and potentials and set up a tourist potential and facilities advisory group to assist governments in formulating their promotional policies.

The ECAFE secretariat has continued to devote its efforts towards implementing the recommendations of the United Nations Conference on Tourism and International Travel, which was held in Rome in 1963.

FLOOD CONTROL AND WATER RESOURCES DEVELOPMENT. ECAFE began work on flood control and allied problems in 1949. In subsequent years, the scope of its work has been expanded to cover all important aspects of water resources development.

Various studies of specific importance to the region, such as those on integrated river basin planning, multiple use of water, river training and bank protection, and basic problems in surface and ground water were completed and published in the United Nations Water Resources Series. The Regional Conference on Water Resources Development is convened biennially to review progress made in countries in the region and to discuss problems affecting development policy. Symposia and seminars have been organized to deal with specific technical and economic subjects relating to development. In addition to technical subjects, ECAFE undertakes studies of the economic, social and legal aspects of water use and management.

In recent years, ECAFE has placed emphasis on action-oriented projects, such as the joint development of international river basins, that encourage regional co-operation. The most important project initiated by ECAFE has been the development of the water resources of the Lower Mekong Basin, involving Cambodia, Laos, Thailand and Viet-Nam.

Mekong River Project. The Mekong, one of the greatest rivers in the world, has its origin in the mountains of the Tibetan plateau in

China. It sweeps along the border of Burma and runs, in its lower basin, through Laos, Thailand, Cambodia and Viet-Nam into the South China Sea. Of the total drainage area of the river, some 77 per cent lies within these four countries of the Lower Basin, where 17 million people live. The purpose of the Mekong Development Project is the comprehensive development of the water resources of the Lower Basin, including mainstream and tributaries, for the generation of hydroelectric power, irrigation, flood control, drainage, improvements in navigation, water management and water supply. The over-all objective is the economic and social development of the area for the benefit of all its inhabitants, without distinction as to politics or nationality.

Ecafe took a special interest in the Mekong as early as 1951, when the Bureau of Flood Control, in co-operation with Cambodia, Laos, Thailand and Viet-Nam, initiated a series of field investigations of the Mekong River. These, in turn, led to the organization by ecafe in 1956 of a team of high-ranking international experts to conduct a comprehensive reconnaissance of the river's potential resources for irrigation, navigation, flood control and hydroelectric power. Their report stimulated the four Lower Basin riparian countries to realize the importance to their economies of developing the Mekong. In October 1957, they established, under the aegis of the United Nations, a Committee for the Co-ordination of Investigations of the Lower Mekong Basin, composed of representatives of each and serviced by the ecafe secretariat.

The Mekong Committee's first action was to request the United Nations to send a group of international experts to undertake further comprehensive studies and make detailed recommendations for joint action. The mission, organized under the Technical Asssistance Administration, carried out a three-month survey of the river, both by land and by air. Its report, submitted in February 1958, called for a multi-purpose programme of studies and data collection which could lead to a full development stage, and recommended a five-year programme of investigation, with an expenditure of about $9 million. The report further proposed that a "high-level international technical advisory board of engineers of world-wide reputation" be appointed by the Mekong Committee. Engineers from France, India, the United Kingdom and the United States were appointed to the Advisory Board when it was later set up.

The Mekong Development Project is being carried out by the four riparian countries with assistance from twenty-one governments, eleven United Nations agencies and other sources. Two power, irrigation and flood-control projects on Mekong tributaries in Thailand have been completed and four other tributary projects are under construction. Investigations for three larger, multi-purpose mainstream projects, as well as several tributary projects, are continuing, along with numerous ancillary projects, including mineral surveys in Cambodia, Thailand and Laos, a network of experimental and demonstration farms, power market projections, and industrial development analyses and recommendations. Financial resources available to the Mekong Committee have increased to over $100 million, of which almost one-third is made available by the four riparian countries.

AGRICULTURE.   ECAFE, in close co-operation with the Food and Agriculture Organization of the United Nations (FAO), has undertaken various projects to assist in food production and agriculture. The Joint ECAFE/FAO Agriculture Division within the ECAFE secretariat has been studying price policies since 1954. The Division convened a meeting on methods of agricultural development planning in 1957 and one on selected aspects of agricultural planning in 1960. In 1958, ECAFE joined FAO in sponsoring, in New Delhi, a regional seminar which reviewed price policies and other agricultural support measures and discussed the producer and consumer aspects of price policies.

The Division prepared a regional review of institutions for agricultural financing and credit, which was used as a background paper by a seminar on the subject held in September 1963.

The Division has also undertaken case studies relating to agricultural development and planning. Two reports—one on the impact on the agricultural economy of community development in Ghosi Block, Uttar Pradesh, India, and the other on farmers' associations in Taiwan—were published in 1960. Studies on the utilization of agricultural surpluses for economic development were undertaken for Japan in 1958, for Pakistan in 1961 and for the Republic of Korea in 1965. The Division also published, in 1963, a case study on the relationship between agricultural and industrial development for Taiwan, covering the period from 1953 to 1960, and, in 1964, a study of input-output relationships in Asian agriculture.

The Division undertakes periodic review of the food and agricultural situation in the region for inclusion in the annual *Economic Survey of Asia and the Far East*.

SOCIAL DEVELOPMENT.   Increasing awareness that rapid development depends heavily on social progress, as well as economic growth, led to the establishment of the ECAFE Division of Social Affairs in 1956. An important part of the Division's work is aimed at encouraging the close integration of social and economic planning that is required for rapid over-all development and for the effective use of human and financial resources. Special attention is given to questions of social policy and reform, and to the closely related problem of evolving practical policies and methods for mobilizing the widespread popular participation upon which substantial implementation of development plans largely depends.

An annual review of social development in the region is prepared to supplement the information provided in the *Economic Survey of Asia and the Far East*. In co-operation with the United Nations Bureau of Social Affairs, a number of case studies on key developmental problems of ECAFE countries have been undertaken on such subjects as balanced economic and social development, changes in income distribution in relation to economic growth, and social change in relation to economic growth.

The tasks of organizing and preparing people for joint developmental action with their governments are stressed in ECAFE's community development activities, which concentrate on the improvement of methods for stimulating community action, planning and implementation, leadership and institutional reorganization at the grass-roots level.

In 1961, a seminar on planning and administration of community development programmes was held in co-operation with the Government of Thailand; this was followed in 1962 by a seminar on urban community development and in 1963 by a regional workshop on the role of local leadership in community development. A regional programme, focussing upon professional education for community development, is in progress.

In the field of social welfare, ECAFE emphasizes aid to governments in the expansion and improvement of family, child and youth welfare programmes, especially through the provision of technical advice on training the required personnel. Technical assistance is also given in conjunction with the material and financial support provided by UNICEF for family and child welfare projects in countries of the region; joint projects of this nature have been established in Burma, Ceylon, China (Taiwan), Hong Kong, Iran, Korea, Pakistan, the Philippines, the Republic of Viet-Nam and Thailand.

A seminar on the organization and administration of family and child welfare services was held in 1960 in co-operation with the Government of the (then) Federation of Malaya; this was followed in 1962 by a seminar on training for family and child welfare, for which the Government of Thailand acted as host. Among its major proposals, the latter meeting recommended that high priority be given to the creation of a regional centre for training higher-level personnel and for related purposes. As a first step towards implementation, a working group on the development of indigenous teaching materials for social work was convened in 1964. As a result of the working group's discussions, a number of important initiatives have been taken, including the establishment, in several countries, of *ad hoc* committees for the development of local teaching materials, and the preparation of a newsletter on teaching materials.

ECAFE's work in the population field helps to meet member countries' needs for adequate demographic data, trained demographic personnel, more accurate knowledge of the relationships between population growth and socio-economic development, and the development and implementation of population policies.

The recommendations of the first Asian Population Conference, organized in co-operation with the Government of India in 1963, led to a strengthening of ECAFE's activities in the field of population and to an increasing emphasis on provision of assistance in fields of direct concern to governments. A regional advisory service was initiated in 1959 in connection with the collection and tabulation of data from national censuses held around 1960. Research activities are focussed on the preparation of population projections and studies of relationships between population characteristics and over-all development in ECAFE countries.

ECAFE has established a regional clearing-house of demographic information to facilitate exchange of information and dissemination of knowledge between government agencies and research and training institutions. The clearing-house will serve as a focal point of information and liaison and will build up comprehensive documentation on population questions. ECAFE continues to collaborate closely with the Bombay Demographic Training and Research Centre.

Economic Commission for Latin America (ECLA)

The Economic Commission for Latin America (ECLA) was established in February 1948 with the aim of helping Latin American governments promote the economic development of their countries and improve the standards of living of their peoples. In so doing, ECLA also endeavours to strengthen economic relations both among countries in the region and with other nations in the world. Its activities in this connection have been reinforced since 1962 by the creation, under its aegis, of the Latin American Institute for Economic and Social Planning.

In carrying out its work, ECLA maintains close co-ordination with the United Nations Secretariat and with other organs and regional commissions of the United Nations, as well as with the specialized agencies. In addition, every effort has been made to co-ordinate ECLA's activities with those of other international organizations operating in the region. A tripartite agreement was concluded in 1961 by the Executive Secretary of ECLA, the Secretary-General of the Organization of American States (OAS) and the President of the Inter-American Development Bank (IDB), whereby a number of joint programmes and activities were to be undertaken to ensure the best use of available resources. Agreements have also been reached with the IDB concerning joint activities in relation to integration, with particular reference to agriculture and industry. ECLA also works closely with the Latin American Free-Trade Association (ALALC) and with the organs of the General Treaty on Central American Economic Integration, and has consultative arrangements with numerous international non-governmental organizations accredited to its parent body, the Economic and Social Council.

The basic pattern of work and activities for ECLA and its secretariat was established by member governments during the initial meetings of the Commission. This programme has evolved and has been greatly expanded, but the central concepts motivating the work have remained essentially the same: first, that dynamic development policies and programmes are required in order to accelerate Latin America's growth from within; and secondly, that to be really effective, these policies, plans and programmes must be based on facts and systematic analyses of national economies and prospects of growth. Thus, the early fact-finding studies on individual countries and on the region as a whole and, similarly, the often pioneering and increasingly comprehensive studies on the different sectors of the economy have led to a programme geared more and more to the rendering of practical assistance to governments.

In the early period, particular stress was laid on the need to provide training for government officials concerned with the planning of economic development and, later, on the need to help governments develop machinery for planning purposes. In response to numerous requests by member governments, the ECLA secretariat began in 1959 to send advisory groups to those countries interested in introducing or improving their planning and policy-making machinery. Under the terms of the tripartite agreement concluded in 1961, the advisory group programme became a joint ECLA/OAS/IDB venture, with ECLA acting as the executing agency, but once the Latin American Institute for Economic and Social Plannning was founded in 1962, it assumed ECLA's responsibilities relating to training and advisory services.

Parallel with these operational activities, ECLA was undertaking research in problems of multilateral trade and economic integration. One aspect of this work has been to help the Latin American governments hammer out a unified policy with respect to their external trade problems and to emphasize the need for co-ordinated trade policies. Another aspect has been ECLA's role in developing a new philosophy designed to establish a more appropriate basis for the reorganization of world trade along lines that make due allowance for the particular situation and problems of the external trade of developing countries and of the relationship between trade and development. This philosophy has been embodied to a considerable extent in the principles and recommendations adopted by the United Nations Conference on Trade and Development (UNCTAD) and in the work being fostered by that organization.

Another important aspect of ECLA's work has been the development of both the Central American Economic Integration Programme, launched in 1952, and the Latin American Free-Trade Association, which came into force in June 1961. A further step forward was taken in 1965, when different proposals for accelerating progress towards a Latin American common market were examined at a special ECLA meeting of government experts from the countries in the region.

In line with this approach, special emphasis has been laid in ECLA's work on the effects of an integrated Latin American market on the development of industry, agriculture, transport, natural resources and so forth. Within the general programme, particular attention has been paid to the integration prospects for new or incipient industries which could take advantage of the economies of scale and other advantages of a Latin American common market, as well as the prospects for exports of manufactures to international markets.

MEMBERSHIP AND ORGANIZATION. The twenty-nine members of ECLA are: Argentina, Barbados, Bolivia, Brazil, Canada, Chile, Colombia, Costa Rica, Cuba, the Dominican Republic, Ecuador, El Salvador, France, Guatemala, Guyana, Haiti, Honduras, Jamaica, Mexico, the Netherlands, Nicaragua, Panama, Paraguay, Peru, Trinidad and Tobago, the United Kingdom, the United States, Uruguay and Venezuela. British Honduras, or Belize, is an associate member. As in the case of the other regional commissions, provision has been made for inviting any non-member of ECLA which is a member of the United Nations (and also the Federal Republic of Germany and Switzerland) to participate in a consultative capacity in discussions on any matter of particular concern to it.

Two permanent bodies have been established by the Commission: the Central American Economic Co-operation Committee and the Trade Committee.

The headquarters of the Commission are in Santiago, Chile. The secretariat, with about 350 staff members, is headed by an Executive Secretary.

The secretariat is organized into the following divisions: economic development and research; trade policy; social affairs; statistics; administration; and the joint ECLA/FAO agriculture division. There are also special programmes for natural resources and energy and for transport. In 1964, ECLA's industrial development division became part of a Joint Programme for the Integration of Industrial Development, established in conjunction with the Latin American Institute for Economic and Social Planning and the Inter-American Development Bank. There is also a Technical Assistance Co-ordinating Unit within ECLA's Executive Office and a Latin American Economic Projections Centre, which, until 1965, had functioned within the Economic Development and Research Division.

A branch office, servicing Mexico, Central America, Panama and the Caribbean countries, was established in Mexico City in 1952. The secretariat also maintains liaison offices in Washington and Monte-video. In conjunction with the Brazilian *Banco Nacional do Desen-volvimento Economico* (BNDE), a joint ECLA/BNDE Centre for Economic Development was founded at Rio de Janeiro in July 1960, to carry out training activities and research on economic problems in Brazil.

Between 1948 and 1951, the Commission held annual sessions; since 1953, it has met every two years. In alternate years, the Committee of the Whole—which has the same membership as the Commission—usually holds a brief two or three-day meeting at ECLA's headquarters to review the progress of work under way and to prepare the report which is submitted annually to the Economic and Social Council.

ECONOMIC DEVELOPMENT AND RELATED PROBLEMS.   Since little factual information was available to ECLA in its early years, its first tasks were to obtain adequate data on economic conditions in the region as a whole and in individual countries. This work has been concentrated principally around the annual *Economic Survey of Latin America*. Two other publications, which appear twice a year, are the *Economic Bulletin for Latin America* and the *Statistical Bulletin*.

An examination of theoretical and practical problems of economic growth was made in 1951 and was followed two years later by an introductory study of programming techniques. Developing out of these research activities, field work was undertaken in several countries with a view to analysing in greater depth the processes of economic and social development; as a result, a series of individual country studies was prepared and published. These studies led the Latin American governments, in 1957, to request ECLA's secretariat to provide assistance in the preparation of sectoral and over-all development programmes. In order to comply with this request, the advisory groups programme was established in 1959.

The advisory groups were originally designed as operational flying squads, but it soon became evident that the countries required assistance for much longer periods and of a more intensive nature than could be provided by ECLA's resources. As a first step towards ensuring co-ordination of all possible assistance to planning efforts, the OAS/ECLA/IDB tripartite agreement included provision for joint advisory groups, with ECLA as the executing agency, and in May 1961, the Commission took steps to expand and consolidate both training and advisory activities through the establishment of the Latin American Institute for Economic and Social Planning.

The Institute was established under the aegis of ECLA and with financial support from the United Nations Special Fund and the Inter-American Development Bank, which allotted $3 million and $1 million, respectively, for the first five years of operation of the Institute. Fellowship facilities for the Institute's training programme are furnished under the technical assistance programmes of the United Nations and of other international organizations. The participants at the annual courses at Santiago include economists, sociologists, statisticians, agronomists, engineers, other Latin American professionals and government officials, a total of 441 having attended up to the end of 1965. The annual course lasts ten months, the first six months being devoted to general economic development and techniques of planning, and the remaining four months dedicated to specialized training in sectoral aspects of programming, such as industry, agriculture, public investment and public works, transport, budget and finance. In collaboration with ILO, FAO, UNESCO, WHO and UNICEF, the Institute has taken steps to provide regular three-month courses in manpower, educational and public health programming. In addition to the regular annual courses, intensive training courses have taken place in different Latin American countries, giving national specialists an opportunity for on-the-spot training in the concepts and techniques of development planning.

In 1965, the Institute set up an Advisory Services Division, composed of a group of regional experts, with a view to strengthening the work of the advisory groups. These, in turn, have helped to create an awareness of the fundamental problems that the countries confront in relation to planning, and to bring about a change in their outlook in dealing with those problems. The experience obtained through the advisory groups and the training programme has led the Institute to strengthen its research activities. These are focussed mainly on economic integration, on social development and on an effort to interpret the Latin American economic development process.

With the establishment of the Latin American Institute for Economic and Social Planning, ECLA was able to assign some of the resources thus released to research on economic projections. There were a number of reasons for strengthening this aspect of the work, including the need for developing a systematic methodology; for preparing specific economic projections in order to help Latin American countries formulate their development plans and undertake research on factors limiting economic growth; for assessing the domestic and external resources needed to achieve given growth targets in the context of regional integration and of efforts to close the trade gap, as well as for purposes of estimating international financing requirements; and for ensuring proper co-ordination with the work on projections being undertaken by the United Nations Centre for Development Planning, Projections and Policies and of the UNCTAD secretariat.

This work was started on a permanent basis at the beginning of 1965, with emphasis on the preparation of an economic projections model suited to conditions in Latin American countries and of specific projections required in relation to UNCTAD's activities.

Parallel with this work, other research efforts were undertaken in relation to international co-operation and financing of development. A study prepared in 1954, and submitted to the Inter-American Conference of Ministers of Finance convened that year in Brazil by the OAS, contained a number of specific proposals, ranging from the creation of an Inter-American Development Bank (which was established five years later) to the need for combining well-planned structural reforms with ample technical and financial assistance from external sources, all within a long-range policy of international co-operation similar to that subsequently embodied in the Alliance for Progress programme adopted at Punta del Este in 1961.

An early study on foreign capital in Latin America (1954) was followed in 1961 by another on the role of external financing. That same year, ECLA brought up to date its analysis of the basic internal and external problems of Latin America by publishing a study on economic development, planning and international co-operation, followed in 1963 by proposals for action designed to achieve a dynamic development policy. In 1963 also, a comprehensive review of the economic and social development of Latin America since the end of the Second World War was completed.

Other ECLA activities of importance to economic development efforts have been related to fiscal policies. Four workshops, organized by ECLA in conjunction with the Bureau of Technical Assistance Operations (BTAO), the Division of Public Administration, and the Fiscal and Financial Branch of the United Nations Department of Economic and Social Affairs, and designed to improve knowledge of modern budget techniques and to promote an exchange of views among senior budget officials in the region, have been held. A special study group, set up in 1959 within ECLA's secretariat, analysed the problems of inflation in relation to economic development. In 1961, a regional conference on tax administration problems was held in Buenos Aires as part of the OAS/ECLA/IDB Joint Tax Programme, which subsequently organized a conference on fiscal policy, held at ECLA's headquarters in 1962. More recently, research has been undertaken on fiscal policies followed by different countries and their utility as instruments of economic development.

In 1963, ECLA made arrangements with the Government of Argentina for a joint study of income distribution in that country, with particular reference to the elaboration of the necessary statistical data. The results have been published in that country and are being used by ECLA as a model for similar work relating to other countries and for an over-all analysis of problems of income distribution in the region.

SOCIAL PROBLEMS.   As ECLA has progressed in the study of Latin America's economic development problems, it has gradually entered into research on the social aspects of these problems. As a first step, a general outline was drawn up in 1955, in a study on social conditions of economic development. This was followed by analyses of specific social problems and, as the research advanced, its results found expression in a number of specialized seminars or working groups. Operational activities were gradually developed to include support for advisory services to governments on community development, social services and, more recently, housing, as well as co-operation in establishing or maintaining research and training centres. At the same time, ECLA is the means for channelling to Latin America the recommendations and assistance of the Economic and Social Council and its subsidiary organs, such as the Commission for Social Development and the Population Commission. Hence, its activities are very closely co-ordinated with those of the United Nations Bureau of Social Affairs.

The subjects discussed at meetings and seminars on social problems organized or co-sponsored by ECLA have included financing of housing, urbanization problems, population census data, aspects of social development, development of information media, education and economic and social development, housing statistics and programmes, community development, and children and youth in national development.

Demographic studies have occupied an increasingly important place in ECLA's activities, particularly in view of the close working collaboration established with the Latin American Demographic Centre, which was set up in Santiago in 1957 under the auspices of the United Nations, the Government of Chile and the Population Council, Incorporated. Data and tables on population trends and structure are published regularly, and special studies have been prepared for meetings and seminars and, more recently, for the 1965 World Population Conference.

In 1964, research was started on over-all problems of housing policy in Latin America, with a view to co-ordinating that policy with general development planning and to providing support for the work being done by regional technical assistance advisers.

Studies have been completed on the post-war social development of Latin America, on rural settlement patterns and community organization, on the relationships of social services to development and, with financial assistance from UNICEF, on problems faced by young people in marginal urban settlements. Exploratory work has been done on the role of the industrial entrepreneur, and efforts have been made to co-ordinate activities relating to problems of skilled manpower through the Inter-Agency Working Party on Skilled Manpower in Latin America, set up in 1959.

INDUSTRIAL DEVELOPMENT.   An important part of ECLA's research has traditionally been directed towards industrial development problems. Early studies were focussed on the technical and economic aspects of production in key industrial sectors, and, in some cases, the findings were later examined by meetings of experts organized with the help of the United Nations technical assistance programme. The first studies on the iron and steel industry, for example, led to meetings of experts in 1952 and 1956 which, in turn, paved the way for the establishment, in 1959, of the Latin American Iron and Steel Institute. Studies on the pulp and paper industry were prepared in 1953 and 1954, and were examined at a meeting of experts in Buenos Aires in 1954 convened by ECLA and FAO. One result of that meeting was the setting up, in 1955, of the ECLA/FAO/BTAO Pulp and Paper Advisory Group, which has explored prospects for the industry in several Latin American countries. In 1962, studies were completed on timber trends and on the current situation and future prospects for pulp and paper on the basis of regional integration. A 1952 study on productivity in the cotton textile industry was followed from 1961 to 1965 by studies of the textile industries in eleven Latin American countries.

These initial studies indicated a need for more intensive research on the prospects that might be opened up by regional integration. This coincided with the movement towards a Latin American common market which gathered momentum in the 1960's, and studies undertaken since then have explored the possibilities of regional cooperation with the aim of promoting an improved utilization of resources.

Studies have been undertaken for railway equipment, followed by a meeting of government officials and railway executives in 1959, and for the chemical industry. In the latter case, the results of three years of research were reviewed at a seminar on the development of the chemical industry, held at Caracas in 1964. Another series of studies, carried out between 1961 and 1965, was aimed at obtaining a fuller comprehension of problems hindering industrial development; they dealt with the manufacture of basic equipment in selected countries (Argentina, Brazil and Chile); machine tools (Argentina and Brazil) and metal-transforming industries (Venezuela and Uruguay). These studies are now being extended to other countries and are used for regional assessments of the development prospects of given industries.

Parallel with this work, studies were undertaken on problems of productivity and economies of scale. The former were reviewed at a meeting convened by ECLA and ILO in 1962. The following year, ECLA, BTAO and the Centre for Industrial Development organized a seminar in São Paulo to review questions relating to industrial programming.

In June 1964, ECLA, the Latin American Institute for Economic and Social Planning and the Inter-American Development Bank launched a Joint Programme for the Integration of Industrial Development, designed to intensify efforts aimed at promoting regional integration of industrial development. Major attention has been devoted to the steel industry, as well as non-ferrous metals and chemicals, particularly fertilizers and petrochemicals, and to the regional prospects for textiles and metal-transforming industries.

Meanwhile, the ECLA secretariat undertook two major studies, one on the industrialization process in Latin America, and the other analysing the findings of the different sectoral studies and exploring the problems and issues involved in the region's industrial development.

NATURAL RESOURCES AND ENERGY. ECLA's early studies were focussed mainly on energy problems because of the need for strengthening this sector if Latin America's economic development is to proceed at an adequate pace. A pioneer study of current and estimated future production and consumption of energy, published in 1957, paved the way for the Latin American electric power seminar, which was held in Mexico in 1961 under the joint auspices of ECLA, BTAO, the Resources and Transport Division of the United Nations Secretariat, and the Government of Mexico. As a result of recommendations made at the seminar, ECLA has convened or provided technical advice for further, smaller meetings of experts, including two in 1962, on terminology and statistics for the electric power industry, and on electricity rates, and another in 1964, on rural electrification, organized by the Government of Argentina with ECLA's assistance.

A number of water resources survey missions have been undertaken with BTAO and with WMO and WHO. Those for Chile and Ecuador led the respective Governments to prepare projects for the improvement and expansion of the national networks of hydrometric and hydrometeorological stations subsequently carried out with the financial assistance of the United Nations Special Fund. Missions of the same sort have also been sent to Venezuela, Argentina, Bolivia, Colombia, Peru and Uruguay.

Recent studies on interrelated renewable natural resources and on geology and mineral generics were presented by ECLA at the UNESCO conference, held in Santiago in 1965, on the application of science and technology to the development of Latin America. In addition, field work and research has been carried out on petroleum and other mineral resources.

AGRICULTURE. ECLA conducts research into economic problems of agriculture in conjunction with FAO, the results being published in the annual *Economic Survey of Latin America* and in FAO's annual report on the state of food and agriculture. The early studies on economic development always included chapters on such agricultural activities as land utilization, production and commodity trade. Among the first agricultural studies prepared for the Commission was one, in 1957, relating to the selective expansion of agricultural production in Latin America. It was followed by specific studies on coffee economy, for Brazil, Colombia and El Salvador, and on livestock production, for Brazil, Colombia, Cuba, Mexico, Uruguay and Venezuela.

Considerable attention has also been devoted to the status and prospects of agricultural commodities in Latin American regional economic integration schemes. A first study on the subject, completed in 1961, analysed the role of agriculture in the Latin American agreements for the formation of common market and free-trade zones. Two years later, a special study on the agricultural development of Latin America during the period 1945-1960 was prepared. Then, in 1964, an experimental study covering one country was completed on the main physical inputs in agriculture and their relation to agricultural productivity within the context of regional integration. During 1965, this research was extended to other countries belonging to the Latin American Free-Trade Association. As an initial stage, the emphasis has been on fertilizers, and the IDB has collaborated in this aspect because of its interest in the development of specific projects which offered sound prospects for financing arrangements.

ECLA has also been concerned with problems of land reform. In 1961, the Commission reviewed a secretariat study stressing the need for well-conceived and properly executed programmes of land reform. More recently, ECLA, together with FAO, IDB, OAS and the Inter-American Committee for Agricultural Sciences, participated in the formation of the Inter-American Committee for Agricultural Development which has conducted research in Latin America on problems of land reform as well as on agricultural extension services.

STATISTICS.   Since the primary sources of data within each country are national statistical services, increasing attention has been given to advising governments about the scope of their statistical programmes and the technical requirements for adequate standards. Seminars have been organized, usually with assistance from BTAO, the United Nations Statistical Office, and the Inter-American Statistical Institute, on such subjects as national income estimates, industrial statistics, civil registration and national accounts. In addition, teams of statistical advisers, sometimes organized in conjunction with advisory groups, have assisted governments in bringing about necessary improvements.

Special attention is being devoted to statistics concerning social conditions. Sample household surveys, designed to collect information on a wide range of individual economic activities and conditions, have been given priority, as well as investigation into the complex factors involved in levels of living, such as housing, education, consumption patterns, family stability and migration. A comparative study on prices and purchasing power of currencies in Latin American countries was completed in 1963. This work is being extended by investigation into labour costs.

TRANSPORT. Questions relating to transport are of vital importance to economic development as well as to any regional integration scheme. The transport problems of the Central American countries were examined in 1951, and several solutions suggested. Other ECLA efforts have been concentrated on work required as part of the earlier country studies and on the transport aspects of the advisory groups programme.

Since 1962, research on transport has been conducted jointly with OAS, which provides two experts for the purpose. As a result of that co-operation, a comprehensive study on maritime, railway and air transport problems in Latin America was published in 1965. Considerable attention has been given, too, to the evaluation of the results of the United Nations Conference on Trade and Development in so far as trade in invisibles (maritime transport, insurance, the tourist trade, etc.) is concerned, and to the preparatory studies relating to transport and the economic integration of Latin America. As part of the latter project, a study was begun on the state of the international highways and railways between Argentina, Brazil and Uruguay.

Other studies include analyses of the incidence of maritime freights and insurance premiums in the price of the main import and export items between Chile, other ALALC countries and Venezuela, and of maritime freights in the price of steel products between Latin American ports, and between the latter and European and North American ports, prepared in connection with a study on Latin America's steel industry; and a study on methods and practices for facilitating international maritime and overland transport.

TRADE AND REGIONAL INTEGRATION. The expansion of trade with other parts of the world and within the Latin American region itself has been a major preoccupation of ECLA since its inception. Groundwork for action was laid in the relevant chapters of the annual *Economic Survey,* but soon specialized studies on this sector of the economy began to appear. They dealt first with trade between Latin America and Europe, but as early as 1952, ECLA was exploring the prospects for inter-American trade in the southern zone of the region, and the first steps towards Central American economic integration were being taken. The studies undertaken up to 1959 provided the necessary background for government action and underlined the need for Latin American countries to pool efforts in order to effect the gradual formation of a regional common market.

Central American Economic Co-operation Committee. In 1951, the Commission established the Central American Economic Co-operation Committee (CCE) as its first subsidiary body, in compliance with the wishes of the Governments of Costa Rica, El Salvador, Guatemala, Honduras and Nicaragua. The Government of Panama became a member in 1959. The secretariat of the Committee is provided by ECLA's Mexico Office, which prepares the necessary studies and research in co-operation with the governments concerned and with the help of technical assistance experts from the United Nations and the specialized agencies.

From the outset, the Committee has been concerned with setting up basic instruments for a Central American common market. In June 1958, a Multilateral Treaty on Central American Free Trade and Economic Integration was signed. This was followed in December 1960 by the signing of the General Treaty on Central American Economic Integration, at which time a Permanent Secretariat for the treaty was set up (SIECA).

Complementary agreements were signed at different times, relating to integration industries, road traffic and signals, and equalization of import duties, and to the establishment of the Central American Economic Integration Bank (BCIE), which was formed in 1961 with a capital of $16 million. Another important step was taken the following year with the signing of the Central American Agreement on Incentives for Industrial Development.

The groundwork was thus laid for achieving the main objectives of the Central American Economic Integration Programme, and by 1965—the final year of the transitional period before the full operation of the Common Market—regional trade amounted to $140 million, which was over four times the figure recorded for 1961 ($30 million) and stands out in sharp contrast to the 1950 figure of $8 million. The first two integration industries had been established (tires and inner tubes in Guatemala, caustic soda and chlorinated insecticides in Nicaragua) with financing from BCIE.

An evaluation study prepared by ECLA for the ninth session of the CCE showed that, following the period from 1958 to 1962, when basic instruments of integration were rapidly established, a second stage had commenced, marked by the consolidation and utilization of opportunities as part of the complex task of framing and executing a regional economic policy for the development of the Common Market in the main areas of activity.

In 1963, a Central American Joint Programming Mission was established under the terms of the OAS/ECLA/IDB tripartite agreement. It was directed by an Advisory Committee consisting of representatives of the three organizations mentioned, the Secretary-General of SIECA and the President of the BCIE. In 1965, the ECLA secretariat prepared a study on regional institutionalization of planning which paved the way for the incorporation into SIECA of the functions and staff of the Joint Programming Mission.

Trade Committee. ECLA's Trade Committee was set up in 1955 and held its first meeting in November 1956. Its objectives were to promote a common market encompassing all the Latin American countries and to foster trade within the region as well as with the rest of the world. Two working groups were established, one to study and suggest ways and means of introducing a Latin American multilateral payments system to facilitate trade, and a second to prepare detailed recommendations concerning the principles, purposes and structure for the proposed Latin American Common Market. Several meetings of government experts were convened to advise on specific problems.

These activities laid the groundwork for the Latin American Free-Trade Association (ALALC), which was established under the provisions of the Treaty of Montevideo, signed in February 1960 by Argentina, Brazil, Chile, Mexico, Paraguay, Peru and Uruguay. In 1961, Colombia and Ecuador also acceded to the Treaty, which entered into force in June of that year. In 1965, Venezuela announced its intention of acceding to the Treaty. ECLA has provided advisory services to the Standing Executive Committee and secretariat of ALALC, and has participated in the work of its specialized committees and of its five annual conferences on tariff negotiations.

In 1964, ECLA started an examination of economic activities in the region, in order to evaluate the results achieved and to evolve ways and means of hastening the transition to the stage of practical action. A series of alternatives was put forward, and these were reviewed by a meeting of government experts held in September 1965. On the basis of this exchange of opinion, the secretariat was able to fulfil its advisory functions to the members of ALALC, and prepared a list of suggestions for consideration by its Standing Executive Committee, prior to the meeting of ALALC Ministers of Foreign Affairs in November. Many of the resolutions adopted on that occasion reflected the guiding principles and ideas put forward at the meeting of government experts.

Research has been undertaken on ways of linking the Central American Common Market and the Latin American Free-Trade Association. In December 1965, representatives of the Government of Mexico and of the Central American integration organizations met for the first time, to explore ways and means of encouraging Central American exports to Mexico, with a view to balancing their trade and as a first step towards similar discussions with other ALALC countries.

Negotiations have also been under way between Central America and Panama concerning the possibility of concluding an agreement of economic association between Panama and the Common Market.

The emphasis and priorities placed on ECLA's efforts in relation to Latin America's economic integration have by no means lessened its interest in expanding and intensifying the region's trade with the rest of the world. Prior to the convening of the United Nations Conference on Trade and Development (UNCTAD) in Geneva in the spring of 1964, ECLA prepared studies which were considered at a meeting of government experts and served as a framework on which the Latin American governments developed a uniform approach for presenting their trade problems at the Conference. The results of the Conference were evaluated by ECLA's Trade Committee and recommendations were made concerning future courses of action at the regional and international levels. Some of these dealt with the placement of basic commodities and the potential markets for industrial products based on a system of preferences. This has led to joint research by ECLA and UNCTAD on the prospects for exports of manufactures, on problems of shipping and invisibles, and on trade projections.

In December 1965, the ECLA secretariat, together with a panel of senior consultants, examined a number of key questions arising out of the implementation of UNCTAD recommendations, with particular reference to basic commodities, manufactures and tariff preferences. Relationships between Latin America and the European Economic Community, the General Agreement on Tariffs and Trade and UNCTAD were also reviewed, together with measures for ensuring more effective trade policies for the Latin American countries. Problems of international liquidity were also explored, and different proposals for modifying the international monetary system were studied in relation to their effects on the external sector and on the economic development of Latin America.

Economic Commission for Africa (ECA)

A proposal, sponsored by twenty nations, to set up an Economic Commission for Africa (ECA) was introduced in the General Assembly in 1957 and was adopted by the Assembly on November 26. The Commission was established by a unanimous decision of the Economic and Social Council on April 29, 1958.

The tasks assigned to ECA are: to promote and facilitate concerted action for the economic and social development of Africa; to maintain and strengthen the economic relations of African countries and territories, both among themselves and with other countries of the world; to undertake or sponsor investigations, research and studies of economic and technological problems and developments; to collect, evaluate and disseminate economic, technological and statistical information; and to assist in the formulation and development of co-ordinated policies in promoting economic and technological development in the region.

ECA performs such advisory services as the countries and territories of the region may request. In carrying out its functions, the Commission is authorized to deal as appropriate with the social aspects of economic development and the interrelationship of economic and social factors.

It is also the duty of the Commission to assist the Economic and Social Council, at its request, by taking increasing responsibility within the region in connection with economic problems, specifically problems in the field of technical assistance. In its work, ECA takes measures to maintain necessary liaison and appropriate co-operation with other organs of the United Nations and with the specialized agencies, and gives particular attention to the avoidance of a duplication of effort.

MEMBERSHIP AND ORGANIZATION. ECA has thirty-nine members: Algeria, Botswana, Burundi, Cameroon, Central African Republic, Chad, Congo (Brazzaville), Congo (Democratic Republic of), Dahomey, Ethiopia, Gabon, Gambia, Ghana, Guinea, Ivory Coast, Kenya, Lesotho, Liberia, Libya, Madagascar, Malawi, Mali, Mauritania, Morocco, Niger, Nigeria, Rwanda, Senegal, Sierra Leone, Somalia, South Africa, Sudan, Togo, Tunisia, Uganda, United Arab Republic, United Republic of Tanzania, Upper Volta and Zambia. (By a 1963 resolution of the Economic and Social Council, the Republic of South Africa is excluded from participating in the work of ECA until "conditions for constructive co-operation have been restored by a change in its racial policy.")

Associate members of ECA are non-self-governing territories in Africa (including African islands) and countries other than Portugal responsible for the international relations of those territories (France, Spain and the United Kingdom).

ECA's terms of reference permit full membership to states members of the United Nations, and associate membership to non-self-governing territories in Africa, as well as to powers, other than Portugal, which are responsible for the international relations of those territories, "provided that states which shall cease to have any territorial responsibilities in Africa shall cease to be members of the Commission." Thus, Italy's membership of ECA ended with the independence of Somalia on July 1, 1960, and Belgium's membership ended with the independence of Rwanda and Burundi. Associate members have the right to attend meetings of the Commission and to take part in all discussions, as well as to participate and hold office in any committee or subordinate body of the Commission, but do not have the right to vote.

ECA's headquarters are in Addis Ababa. Sub-regional offices have been established in Tangier, Morocco, for the countries of North Africa; in Niamey, Niger, for the countries of West Africa; in Lusaka, Zambia, for the countries of East Africa; and in Kinshasa (formerly Leopoldville), Democratic Republic of the Congo, for the countries of Central Africa.

The ECA secretariat, consisting of a staff of about 340, is headed by an Executive Secretary. The work of the secretariat is determined, within the broad framework of ECA's terms of reference, by the decisions of plenary meetings of the Commission, which take place biennially. Emphasis is on assistance to African governments at critical points in their drive for economic and social development. In accordance with its terms of reference, ECA's major effort is in those fields where multi-national action is indicated, since, by reason of their smallness, many African countries cannot hope to achieve economic "take-off" single-handedly. The services of ECA specialists are also available to individual African countries for assistance in specific projects, a function performed largely by the regional advisers, supported by the United Nations programmes of technical assistance.

Since its sixth session, held in Addis Ababa in 1964, the work of ECA has followed two main lines. First, emphasis has shifted from research to execution. Previously, because of the relative paucity of detailed information on African economic problems, the secretariat was obliged to concentrate its main energies on research and basic studies. By 1964, however, it was felt that enough information had been accumulated to permit a start to be made on the task of identifying specific projects which could have a critical impact on the continent's economic development.

Secondly, with the completion of the chain of sub-regional offices, the secretariat has been able to help in creating mechanisms for systematic co-operation among countries belonging to a relatively limited geographical area and constituting economic units that would be suitable to rapid economic development.

The "sub-regional" approach has now been accepted by member countries of the Commission as being a realistic method of achieving economic development. It is appreciated that, with very few exceptions, African countries are too small to permit them to achieve any genuine economic advancement in isolation from each other. Co-operation with their neighbours offers several advantages: in particular, as in the case of iron and steel in West Africa, it enlarges the potential market for industrial products, thus permitting the introduction of reasonably large-scale industries, which offer, to consumer and producer alike, economies of scale.

Sub-regional machinery of this kind also constitutes an additional link in the chain of communication between the international agencies and individual countries in a given region, providing a realistic framework within which programmes of international co-operation can be devised and executed.

However, at its seventh session, held in Nairobi, in February 1965, the Commission recognized that there was some risk that sub-regional groupings might develop into watertight compartments. To counteract such a tendency, and to ensure the simultaneous development of regional initiatives, it decided to create seven working parties, composed of African specialists who would be chosen as representatives, not of individual countries, but of the sub-regions, and who would deal with the following subjects: intra-African trade; monetary management and inter-African payments; industry and natural resources; transport and telecommunications; agriculture; manpower and training; and economic integration. The role of the working parties would be, essentially, that of specialist intermediaries between the Commission and its constituent governments, empowered to follow up Commission decisions where these call for specific action by governments, such as provisions in national budgets and special legislation. The creation of the working parties also represents a further phase in the policy of co-operation between ECA and the Organization of African Unity (OAU), the secretariat of which is being closely associated with the activities of the working parties, as it is with all ECA meetings involving inter-governmental agreement.

TRAINING. The Commission has recognized from the very beginning that lack of skilled manpower is one of the major obstacles to African development. Thus, with the co-operation of United Nations technical assistance programmes, ECA has been responsible for the establishment and maintenance of three training centres for African statisticians in Africa, and has made arrangements to support two national institutions.

Concurrently, a major part of the schedule of meetings sponsored by the Commission consists of seminars and training courses covering the whole range of economic development questions—for example, population, national accounts, statistics, cartography, customs administration, local government, public administration, social work and, in co-operation with the General Agreement on Tariffs and Trade (GATT), commercial policy.

One of the most important achievements in the field of training was the establishment, with large-scale assistance from the United Nations Special Fund, of the African Institute for Economic Development and Planning, at Dakar, Senegal, in November 1963. The Institute gives a nine-month post-graduate course in economic development and planning to senior African civil servants, preferably officials with direct experience in government planning offices. Teaching at the Institute is linked to actual African experience and needs in planning, the aim being to develop eventually a specifically African philosophy of planning and a common African approach to development planning. In addition, the Institute offers short specialized courses for undergraduates from African universities and organizes other courses outside the university, as well as an annual seminar for teachers of economics from African universities and economic research institutes. Present facilities permit an enrolment of over thirty students a year for the main course; a diploma is awarded for successful completion of this course.

The secretariat also maintains, within its Division for Economic Co-operation, a training section, which is responsible for co-ordinating information on technical and academic training facilities available to Africans both within the continent and abroad, and which serves as a clearing-house for fellowships offered by the United Nations member countries.

TECHNICAL ASSISTANCE. ECA works in close co-operation with technical assistance programmes sponsored and operated by members of the United Nations family, particularly those under the aegis of the United Nations Development Programme. The secretariat has had some success in its efforts to persuade both potential donors of aid and African countries to re-examine their approach to aid. In particular, it has drawn the attention of both donors and recipient countries to certain inequalities which are necessarily produced by the bilateral approach. Thus, for example, the Executive Secretary pointed out to the seventh session of the Commission, held in Nairobi, Kenya, in 1965, that the greatest amount of aid tended to be channelled to those countries with the best administrative machinery, although other countries might have much greater need of external assistance. The idea of multi-national machinery for handling external aid has been accepted in principle.

ECONOMIC DEVELOPMENT PLANNING. Nearly all African countries now have some form of economic development planning. ECA has tried to ensure that, as far as possible, its member countries do not construct their plans in ignorance of those of their neighbours. Accordingly, ECA has carried out and published comparative studies of country plans and has sponsored the creation of the Conference of African Planners, which brings together the chief economic planners of member countries for a review of progress towards integrated planning. The Conference is also closely associated with the work of the African Institute for Economic Development and Planning, being responsible for choosing the institute's Governing Body and acting as the institutional link between ECA and the Institute.

TRADE AND PAYMENTS. A special characteristic of African countries is the virtual lack of intra-African trade. On a *per capita* basis, African countries trade with each other less than is the case in Latin America, Asia or other under-developed regions. A major part of the work of the ECA secretariat has been the promotion of intra-African trade.

In addition, the creation of the United Nations Conference on Trade and Development (UNCTAD) has had a considerable impact upon African trade policies and, consequently, on the secretariat's work programme. ECA assigned a team of specialists to the first session of the Conference in 1964 as advisers to the Co-ordinating Committee of the African countries, assisted individual African delegations and worked in close collaboration with the secretariat of the Conference. Since that time, ECA has kept under constant survey the impact of the Conference's decisions on African trade, and at the first session of the joint ECA/OAU Working Party on Trade and Payments, presented a study of the relations between African countries and UNCTAD. At this meeting, devoted primarily to studying ways and means of increasing trade among African nations, the secretariat was asked to draw up a list of commodities and products which could be exchanged among African countries.

Following a number of resolutions adopted by the Commission, ECA has undertaken a series of studies on payments arrangements for inter-African trade, and summoned, in September 1964, the first Conference of African Monetary Authorities, to consider proposals for creating an African Payments Union.

The secretariat has assisted a number of African governments with the transposition of their tariff nomenclatures to conform with the internationally accepted Brussels nomenclature.

FINANCING.   The Commission's experts have studied the flow of international aid to Africa, and their reports have served as a basis for ECA discussions on aid proposals and policies for Africa.

Following a decision of ECA's fourth session in 1962, the African Development Bank was established on September 10, 1964. The Board of Governors, comprising one representative from each member country, held its first meeting in Lagos, Nigeria, in November 1964. Membership is open to all independent African countries, which must subscribe to the nominal capital of $20 million according to a scale based upon national income, population and other economic factors. The Bank, with headquarters in Abidjan, Ivory Coast, is designed to promote the investment of public and private capital in Africa, to use its own resources to make or guarantee loans or equity investments and to provide technical assistance in the preparation, financing and implementation of development plans. The emphasis of its activities will be on multi-national projects concerned with the economic development of the region.

INDUSTRY.   The basis of the Commission's work in industry has been the document "Industrial Growth in Africa," which was published in 1962. Since that time, the secretariat has carried out surveys in all the sub-regions of the continent to determine, broadly, the points at which industrial development might be introduced or reinforced and, in particular, the scope for joint action by groups of countries to raise the level of industrial activity in Africa. In 1964, countries of West Africa met under ECA auspices to discuss a set of proposals concerning industrial development in the area. The major decision of this meeting was an agreement in principle to set up a large-scale iron and steel plant in Liberia, which would serve the whole West African sub-region. Later meetings of the countries concerned, sponsored by the Liberian government, have led to a further agreement to create a West African Iron and Steel Authority.

A similar meeting on industrial co-ordination was held in Lusaka, Zambia, in October 1965, for the countries of East Africa; and a meeting covering countries of Central Africa was held in Kinshasa, Democratic Republic of the Congo, in April 1966. In the north African sub-region, ECA has serviced a series of meetings convened by the Maghreb countries to establish institutional arrangements for harmonizing industrial growth, and has assisted in preparing a request to the United Nations Special Fund for assistance in the creation of an industrial centre for the Maghreb.

AGRICULTURE.   With more than three-quarters of the African population engaged in agriculture, this subject receives considerable emphasis in ECA's work programme. As in other regional commissions, agriculture is dealt with by a division jointly staffed by FAO and the Commission. At ECA, the main aim of the secretariat is to promote the transition from subsistence agriculture to market agriculture.

The activities of the Joint Division can be grouped under four headings: to improve African farmers' productivity; to promote new techniques of production and marketing; to improve and promote livestock and meat production; and to stimulate agricultural processing industries.

The Joint Division has carried out studies on land tenure, credit, co-operatives, extension services and rural animation. Its training programme has provided seminars and short-term courses in marketing and the economics of modern production techniques, an example being the seminar on the improvement of rural credit in French-speaking areas, which was held at Dakar, Senegal, in September 1965. ECA's specialists consider that the development of home and regional markets for industries processing agricultural raw materials will be an important factor both in the transition from subsistence to market cultivation and in the general move towards greater industrialization. In this connection, the first FAO African Regional Meeting on Animal Production and Health was held in Addis Ababa in March 1964. In addition, one of the basic secretariat papers presented to the West African Conference on Industrial Co-ordination, which was held in Bamako in October 1964, dealt in detail with the prospects for industrial processing of agricultural products. A team of ECA, FAO and Polish specialists has also surveyed the requirements for an integrated programme of livestock raising and meat processing and marketing in seven countries of West Africa.

TRANSPORT AND TELECOMMUNICATIONS. The state of intra-African communications reflects the continent's recent colonial history, the guiding principle of which was communication between colony and "metropolis," both in transport and in telecommunications. Independence has brought a desire for greater links within the continent, and member countries have requested ECA to undertake a series of studies on transport links throughout Africa. A survey of possible links in West Africa, as well as one of East and Central Africa, has been carried out, with assistance from bilateral aid sources. In addition, a preliminary survey on the possibility of establishing a trans-Sahara road has been completed and was discussed, in May 1964, by representatives of interested countries north and south of the Sahara who have now established a working committee comprising Algeria, Mali, Niger and Tunisia.

Studies on shipping in West and East Africa have also been completed. In air transport, member countries agreed, at an ECA-sponsored meeting in November 1964, on the need for a permanent African civil aviation organization and decided to work towards the creation of multi-national airlines, which would follow, as far as practicable, the lines of the Commission's pattern of sub-regions.

In the field of telecommunications, a joint ITU/ECA plan for the development of an African telecommunications network has been worked out in considerable detail. The plan includes two phases, one short-term and the other long-term. The short-term plan envisages telephone and telex links between African capitals. The long-term plan, which is tied to a training programme for African telecommunications engineers and administrators, would provide the continent with a highly sophisticated network operating with the most modern equipment and capable of carrying several kinds of traffic, including television transmissions.

STATISTICS AND DEMOGRAPHY. Because planning of any kind is impossible without adequate statistics, ECA's main task has been to help African countries meet their need for basic statistical information. The Conference of African Statisticians, established as a standing conference by the Commission in 1959, is ECA's main policy-making organ in the field of statistics. As a result of its recommendations, the main focus of the secretariat's activities has been on the training of statisticians, the compilation, processing and publication of data, the search for the best techniques of assembling statistical information, and technical assistance to African countries.

Up to the end of 1965, more than 100 professional statisticians and 400 executive-class personnel received training in United Nations aided national and international training centres in Africa, representing nearly a quarter of all trained staff in African statistical offices. ECA is closely associated with these training programmes, supplying lecturers from its regional funds and assisting with standardization of curricula.

In an effort to standardize techniques and to promote the exchange of information on problems and methods, ECA has also arranged meetings of African specialists in fields such as vital statistics, labour statistics and national accounts. In 1964, jointly with the International Labour Organisation (ILO), ECA convened the first African seminar on labour statistics. African experts on vital statistics have also met under ECA auspices, and the secretariat has drafted, with the advice of African experts, a handbook on national account statistics in Africa. ECA is also giving assistance to African countries with their preparations for the 1970 world censuses of population and housing.

ENERGY AND WATER RESOURCES.   In the field of water resources, the secretariat has carried out an inquiry, in collaboration with WMO, into the deficiencies of hydrological data in Africa. ECA has taken an active part in the evolution and work of two international organizations in West Africa—the Chad Basin Commission and a proposed inter-state organization for exploiting the Niger River Basin.

ECA specialists in mineral resources provided advisory services to twelve African countries in 1964. Plans are being made to establish training centres to serve several countries in photogrammetry, aerial geophysical surveying and the interpretation of aerial survey data. A preliminary survey on energy problems in North Africa was carried out with assistance from the secretariat of the Economic Commission for Europe.

SOCIAL PROBLEMS.   ECA's mandate calls on the Commission to pay special attention to the social aspects of economic development. The secretariat has been able to advise African governments on some of the social problems that affect economic development, including problems of juvenile delinquency, the imbalance between rural and urban development and the impact of industrialization on urban life. ECA has also organized training courses on social problems and has prepared and published a number of basic studies on some of the continent's major social questions.

In 1964, ECA carried out a survey of the social welfare activities of national governments, of United Nations specialized agencies and of international voluntary organizations in Africa, and compiled a directory of regional social welfare activities.

A monograph on social work training facilities in Africa has been published, as well as a study outlining the trends of social change and of juvenile delinquency in Africa. A training course on the institutional treatment of juvenile offenders, held in Cairo in 1964, brought together specialists in the treatment of young offenders from fourteen countries for an exchange of views and experiences.

United Nations Economic and Social Office in Beirut

There is no regional commission for the Middle East, but there is a United Nations Economic and Social Office in Beirut, which was established in 1963 to bring the United Nations staff closer to the countries in the Middle East for intensifying United Nations economic and social activities in the region. The Office comprises a Section for Economic Affairs and a Section for Social Affairs, and attached to it is a group of regional advisers serving upon request as consultants to governments in such fields as community development, demography, industrial development planning and statistics. The research and operational work of the Office is aimed at assisting governments in their efforts to formulate and implement comprehensive development plans.

SPECIAL PROGRAMMES

International Control of Narcotic Drugs

The basic aim of international, as well as national, narcotics control is the prevention of the misuse of narcotic drugs. In this sense, narcotics control is both a matter of public health and of social defence.

The first international conference on narcotics met in Shanghai in 1909, and three years later, at The Hague, the first international narcotics convention was concluded. The Hague Convention of 1912 established international co-operation in the control of narcotic drugs as a matter of international law, and its principles have remained the basis of international narcotics control. The Convention stipulated that the production and distribution of raw opium were to be controlled by law; that opium smoking was to be gradually suppressed; and that the manufacture, sale and use of manufactured narcotic drugs—that is, morphine, other opiates and cocaine—were to be limited by law exclusively to medical and other legitimate needs. Manufacturers of and traders in such drugs were also subjected to a system of permits and recording.

Before the Hague Convention had entered into force, the First World War broke out, in August 1914, and at the end of the war, at the Versailles Conference in 1919, it was recognized that the international control of narcotic drugs was to be a responsibility of the future League of Nations. It was not until 1925, however, that a new and more comprehensive treaty was drafted, under which a Permanent Central Opium Board was established and parties required to submit to that Board annual statistics concerning production of opium and coca leaves and the manufacture, consumption and stocks of narcotic drugs, as well as quarterly reports on the import and export of such drugs, including opium and coca leaves. The Permanent Central Opium Board also established a system of import certificates and export authorizations requiring governmental approval of each import and export.

The Hague Convention of 1912 and also the Geneva Convention of 1925 reflected the fact that opium and its two principal derivatives, morphine and heroin, and to a lesser extent the coca leaf and its derivative, cocaine, were practically the only dangerous substances capable of arousing international concern. Subsequent events showed, however, that many manufactured drugs, hitherto not subject to international control, were also potential sources of danger to public health. Another international convention was therefore signed at Geneva in 1931 with the object of limiting the manufacture and regulating the distribution of narcotic drugs; to ensure this limitation, it established a new international organ, the Drug Supervisory Body. Later, in 1936, a Convention for the Suppression of the Illicit Traffic in Narcotic Drugs was adopted.

NARCOTICS CONTROL UNDER THE UNITED NATIONS.   *Commission on Narcotic Drugs.* In 1946, the functions previously exercised by the League of Nations under the various narcotics treaties concluded before the Second World War were transferred to the United Nations, and in the same year the Economic and Social Council created the Commission on Narcotic Drugs.

Originally, the Commission was composed of fifteen governments, but in 1961 the Council increased the membership to twenty-one. The members of the Commission are elected by the Council with due regard to the adequate representation of countries which are important producers of opium or coca leaves, of countries which are important in the manufacture of narcotic drugs and of countries in which drug addiction or the illicit traffic in narcotic drugs constitutes an important problem. In 1965, the following countries were members of the Commission: Argentina, Canada, China, Federal Republic of Germany, France, Ghana, Hungary, India, Iran, Japan, Mexico, Morocco, Peru, Republic of Korea, Switzerland, Turkey, USSR, United Arab Republic, United Kingdom, United States and Yugoslavia.

The Commission on Narcotic Drugs:

(*a*) assists the Economic and Social Council in exercising such powers of supervision over the application of international conventions and agreements dealing with narcotic drugs as may be assumed by or conferred on the Council;

(b) carries out such functions entrusted to the League of Nations Advisory Committee on Traffic in Opium and Other Dangerous Drugs by the international conventions on narcotic drugs as the Council has found necessary to assume and continue;

(c) advises the Council on all matters pertaining to the control of narcotic drugs and prepares such draft international conventions as may be necessary;

(d) considers what changes may be required in the existing machinery for the international control of narcotic drugs and submits proposals to the Council;

(e) performs such other functions relating to narcotic drugs as the Council may direct.

Other Organs. The Permanent Central Opium Board (now called the Permanent Central Narcotics Board) and the Drug Supervisory Body were also transferred from the League of Nations to the United Nations.

The Permanent Central Narcotics Board and the Drug Supervisory Body meet twice a year. They are closely interrelated technical organs, the members of which serve in a personal capacity as experts and not as representatives of their governments. The eight members of the Board, appointed by the Economic and Social Council, review statistical returns of governments on the various phases of the licit trade in narcotics in the light of the advance estimates of drug requirements that governments furnish. The Board is empowered to take certain semi-judicial measures if it determines treaty violations in this connection.

The Drug Supervisory Body is composed of four experts: two appointed by the World Health Organization (WHO), one by the Commission on Narcotic Drugs and one by the Permanent Central Narcotics Board. The Supervisory Body reviews annually the estimates of drug requirements that governments furnish and can ask governments for explanations and amend the estimates with the consent of the government concerned. Governments must not manufacture or import drugs under control above the maximum amounts computed on the basis of the estimates.

The fourth international organ concerned with problems of narcotic drugs is the WHO Expert Committee on Dependence-Producing Drugs, which is mainly concerned with the pharmacological effects of dependence-producing substances and with the broader aspects of drug dependence of various types. Composed of technical experts, it evaluates the dangerous properties of new drugs to determine whether they should be placed under international control.

TREATY DEVELOPMENTS UNDER THE UNITED NATIONS.
Paris Protocol of 1948. The Commission on Narcotic Drugs, at its first
session in 1946, initiated a study of the procedures necessary for bringing under full international control the new synthetic drugs which
had been created and had turned out to be addiction-producing. Under the 1931 Convention for Limiting the Manufacture and Regulating the Distribution of Narcotic Drugs, the new synthetic narcotic
drugs could be placed only under partial control.

The Commission's study resulted in the preparation of an instrument known as the Paris Protocol of 1948, which was signed at
the Palais de Chaillot on November 19, 1948, and came into force
on December 1, 1949. It authorizes WHO to place under full international control any new drug (including synthetic drugs) which could
not be placed under such control by application of the relevant provisions of the 1931 Convention and which it finds either to be addiction-producing or convertible into an addiction-producing drug.

Opium Protocol of 1953. The Opium Protocol of 1953—the Protocol for Limiting and Regulating the Cultivation of the Poppy Plant,
the Production of, International and Wholesale Trade in, and Use of
Opium—was adopted by the United Nations Opium Conference,
which was held in New York in May-June 1953, and entered into
force in February 1963. Under the Protocol, the use of opium and the
international trade in it were limited to medical and scientific needs,
and legal overproduction of opium was eliminated through the indirect method of limiting the amounts that could legally be held in
stock by individual states. The Protocol provides for the licensing of
poppy farmers in opium-producing countries and for specifying the
areas which may be cultivated. Producing states are under obligation
to set up an agency to which all the opium thus produced has to be
delivered immediately after harvesting. Only seven countries—Bulgaria, Greece, India, Iran, Turkey, the USSR and Yugoslavia—are
authorized to produce opium for export. Of these, Iran banned all
poppy cultivation in 1955, Greece has ceased producing any opium
since 1952 and Bulgaria is a nominal producer.

Single Convention of 1961. In 1948, the Economic and Social
Council requested the United Nations Secretariat to begin work on
the draft of a new single convention on narcotic drugs.

The following year, the Council approved both the principles
suggested by the Narcotics Commission for the new convention and
the preparation of a draft treaty by the Secretariat. The work on the
single convention occupied the Commission during the ensuing nine
years.

On January 24, 1961, at United Nations Headquarters, a plenipotentiary conference was convened which brought together technical

experts and administrators from seventy-four countries. It adopted the Single Convention on Narcotic Drugs, 1961, which fulfilled the three main goals of the Council: (1) simplification of the international control machinery by fusing the Narcotics Board and the Supervisory Body into one body; (2) replacement of the international control instruments by one treaty; and (3) expansion of the control system to the cultivation of the plants (opium, cannabis and coca leaves) which are grown as raw materials of the natural drugs.

As a result of the new Convention, such practices as opium smoking, opium eating, coca-leaf chewing, hashish (cannabis) smoking, or the use of the cannabis plant for non-medical purposes are prohibited, after a transitional period to permit the countries concerned to overcome the difficulties arising from the abolition of these ancient customs. The Convention also puts parties under the obligation to take special measures of control in the case of particularly dangerous drugs (such as heroin and ketobemidone). Earlier treaty provisions, requiring (1) that exports and imports of narcotic drugs be made against express government authorization from both sides, (2) that governments make reports on the working of the treaty and (3) that they exchange through the Secretary-General laws and regulations passed to implement the treaty, have been retained. Provisos for controlling the manufacture of narcotic drugs and the trade and distribution of narcotic substances have also been continued, while measures for controlling new synthetic drugs laid down in the 1948 Protocol have been incorporated in the Single Convention.

In its penal provisions, the Single Convention requires each party —subject to its constitutional limits—to designate as punishable offences all intentional violations of its control provisions regarding cultivation, production, manufacture, trade, distribution, etc., of drugs as laid down in the treaty. Each such offence is similarly to be considered a distinct offence and foreign convictions are to be taken into account by courts for the purpose of establishing whether an offender has reverted to criminal activity. Extradition is recommended in the case of offences against the provisions of the Convention and if extradition is not practicable, a foreign offender is to be prosecuted in the country in which his offence was committed or in the country in which he was found.

Implementation of Treaties. In its annual review of the functioning of the control system, the Commission on Narcotic Drugs has the benefit of information furnished to the Secretary-General, the Permanent Central Narcotics Board and the Drug Supervisory Body by parties to the international treaties on narcotic drugs. These data include: (a) annual reports prepared in accordance with a form drafted by the Narcotics Commission and forwarded to the Secretary-General (the data on illicit traffic are published in full and the other data appear in an annual summary prepared by the Secretariat); (*b*) reports on important cases of illicit traffic having international significance; (*c*) texts of laws and regulations relating to the control of narcotic drugs; (*d*) lists of names and addresses of firms authorized to manufacture narcotic drugs; (*e*) information on national authorities empowered to issue certificates and authorizations for the import and export of narcotic drugs; (*f*) estimates of narcotics needed for medical and scientific purposes; and (*g*) statistics on production, manufacture, international trade in, stocks and consumption of narcotics.

PROBLEMS OF NARCOTICS CONTROL. *Illicit Traffic.* The Commission on Narcotic Drugs reviews annually the general problem of illicit trade in individual drugs as well as the situation of the traffic country by country. This review is based on information supplied by governments and by such other sources as the International Criminal Police Organization (INTERPOL). The Commission's review is assisted by the presence of observers from certain countries important within the international pattern of illicit trafficking.

Although the seizure reports furnished by governments may show here and there a decrease in the quantity of drugs seized in illicit trade, the recent surveys of the Commission indicate that, on the whole, the illicit traffic in drugs remains at a high level and is well organized.

The most important drugs in the illicit traffic, both international and national, are still opium and the opiates (principally morphine and heroin). The products of the opium poppy continue to present the greatest problem to international authorities. Opium, in the illicit traffic, originates mainly in the Middle East and in a well-defined area in south-east Asia along the borders of Burma, China, Thailand and Laos. In the Middle East, an important quantity of opium seems to escape local control where it is licitly cultivated, and some opium also comes from illicit cultivation. There is also illicit cultivation in other parts of the world, for example, Mexico.

The opium is used in clandestine factories for the manufacture of morphine, which is then often converted into heroin. Morphine and particularly heroin are much more potent than opium and much less bulky, thus much easier to smuggle to countries such as the United States, Canada, Iran and Thailand, where addiction, especially to heroin, has become a serious problem.

Cannabis, in its various forms, such as marijuana, hashish and maconha, continues to be, in quantitative terms, the biggest narcotic substance in illicit traffic. The plant grows in every part of the world and represents a particularly difficult problem to the enforcement agencies fighting the illicit traffic. In the Middle East, this drug crosses frontiers in bulk; in parts of Asia, Africa and Latin America, it is mainly a domestic problem. In recent years, the United Nations has urged that countries where cultivation is widespread take determined and effective action to put an end to it.

Research. Since opium and the narcotics derived from it are the principal drugs in the international illicit traffic, it is very important for governments and the Commission on Narcotic Drugs to know in which country the illicit opium has been produced. In this way it becomes possible to call the attention of the governments concerned to the need for improving their control and to assist them in doing so if such assistance is requested. The United Nations is therefore engaged in the development of scientific methods by which the origin of opium can be reliably determined.

The Division of Narcotic Drugs of the United Nations Secretariat carries out research on opium in its laboratory at Geneva, and national laboratories and individual scientists in various parts of the world also participate in the United Nations programme of opium research. The laboratory helps to co-ordinate the research being carried out by these scientists and arranges for the distribution of opium samples for this work.

The laboratory also publishes all of the findings in a special series of documents. The research is based on the analysis of hundreds of authenticated samples of opium, that is, opium authenticated by a government as having originated in that country. Several methods have been developed and extensively tested and are now being applied to determine the geographical origin of samples of opium seized in the illicit traffic.

TECHNICAL ASSISTANCE. With the aim of assisting developing countries to fulfil their obligations under the treaties and to help them meet special problems that they might face, the United Nations has been giving increasing attention to technical co-operation in this field.

In 1954, the Economic and Social Council recommended that the United Nations and the specialized agencies give due consideration to requests for technical assistance from countries concerned with combating the habit of coca-leaf chewing. In 1956, the Council invited governments to seek United Nations technical assistance for fighting their narcotics problems, including, in certain cases, the effort to introduce substitute crops in place of the cultivation of narcotics plants such as the opium poppy. After Iran banned the cultivation of the opium poppy, in 1955, the Council adopted a special resolution recommending that that Government make requests for such assistance as it considered necessary to help it to a successful and speedy achievement of the aims of its far-reaching reform.

On the basis of these resolutions of the Council, technical assistance began to be given in the narcotics field. Expert services and fellowships were provided, exploratory studies of special problems such as those in Iran and Thailand were made, and a special mission of experts (the Middle East Narcotics Survey Mission of 1959) was organized. In 1949 there had already been the Commission of Enquiry on the Coca Leaf to Peru and Bolivia, while the Andean Indian Programme, involving co-operation by several United Nations agencies and dealing in particular with certain aspects and consequences of the coca-leaf chewing habit, had also been initiated.

Impressed by the results of these early projects, the General Assembly in 1959 decided to establish a special programme of technical assistance in the narcotics field. It initially appropriated for this purpose $50,000, which was later increased to $75,000. The programme developed since then has given assistance to groups of countries in a region with similar problems or to specific countries. The assistance has taken various forms: the provision of experts; training for national officials concerned with narcotics problems; seminars and regional meetings to elucidate regional problems; visiting expert missions to selected groups of countries; and fellowships for the study of regional problems.

Several important regional projects have been completed in recent years. In 1963, the second of two expert missions to sixteen countries and territories in the Middle East and North African littoral up to Algeria completed its study of the regional problems and made recommendations to the governments concerned for action to deal with the situation. In 1963 also, a United Nations seminar on narcotics control problems in developing countries in Africa was held in Addis Ababa, with officials from sixteen African countries and one non-self-governing territory participating. The seminar reviewed the narcotics problems of the developing African countries and studied the obligations devolving upon the governments under the narcotics treaties.

Early in 1964, the Consultative Group on Narcotics Problems in Asia and the Far East met in Tokyo, with participants from fifteen Asian countries and two territories in the region. The group concentrated on the problem of the large-scale opium production which was known to exist in the region and which was one of the main sources of the increased morphine and heroin traffic in the region itself and in the world as a whole. A number of recommendations for dealing with the situation were made.

In December 1964, the Inter-American Consultative Group on Coca Leaf Problems met again at Lima, Peru, where its first meeting had taken place two years before. It reviewed the progress made in the control of coca bush cultivation, the eradication of the coca-leaf chewing habit and the illicit traffic in cocaine, and made a number of recommendations.

In 1965, two training seminars for enforcement officers were held, one in Manila, Philippines, and the other in Lagos, Nigeria. They were

attended by members of the police, customs and health services of the
countries in the region concerned, and reviewed the various problems
of enforcement in narcotics control.

In recent years, a number of fellowships have been awarded: for
training in the treatment and rehabilitation of addicts; to officials concerned with enforcement, for further training in the techniques of their
profession; for scientific research on opium and cannabis problems,
and for the control of the cannabis problem. For several years, Iran
has been given the services of an administrative expert to help the
government solve the manifold problems created by its total ban on
opium cultivation and on the use of opium by addicts. In 1964, a preliminary survey mission was sent at the request of the Government of
Burma to assist it to study the economic and social needs of an opium-
producing area in that country with a view to assisting the government
to replace opium cultivation by another means of livelihood for the
population affected. The same kind of aid has been requested by the
Government of Thailand, which has already had expert advice on the
problem of resettling hill tribes engaged in opium production.

This assistance by the United Nations is given as far as possible
in conjunction with WHO and FAO. The latter, for instance, was in the
field soon after the Iranian reform to advise the Government on replacing the large-scale legal opium cultivation in the country by other
crops.

DRUGS OUTSIDE INTERNATIONAL CONTROL.   Apart from the
narcotic drugs which fall under the régime of international control,
there are substances the use of which gives rise to some of the problems caused by narcotic drugs but which as yet are not thought to
constitute enough of a danger to justify their being placed under international control. The United Nations control bodies, in co-operation with WHO, are keeping a watchful eye on these substances in order
to determine the effects of their use upon the individual and society.

A study of khat and its properties has been completed by WHO at
the request of the Economic and Social Council, which has drawn the
attention of the governments concerned to the study for any action
they may consider necessary.

During the past several years, there has been increasing concern
over the possible harmful effects of such substances as barbiturates,
amphetamines and tranquillizers. WHO has found that barbiturates are
habit-forming, although, if consumed in doses not larger than the normal therapeutic amounts, not addiction-producing. The Commission
on Narcotic Drugs accordingly recommended that governments take
"appropriate legislative and administrative measures of control" to
prevent their abuse and recommended in particular that barbiturates
should be dispensed only on medical prescription.

The Commission also took note of the dangers arising from the abuse of stimulant drugs of the amphetamine group, and it was informed of cases of poisoning, accidents and even deaths resulting from abuse in many parts of the world. It accordingly recommended that governments provide adequate measures of control for the prevention of the abuse of these drugs.

The rapidly increased use of tranquillizers or ataraxic drugs in some countries induced WHO's Expert Committee on Addiction-Producing Drugs to classify these drugs as "potentially habit-forming," and the Commission has recommended that governments "keep a careful watch for any abuse of these substances."

In 1965, the Commission recommended to the Economic and Social Council that a Special Committee of the Commission meet to study the problems posed by the misuse of these substances, with a view to evolving the control and other measures required for them.

United Nations Children's Fund (UNICEF)

The United Nations Children's Fund (UNICEF) was created by unanimous vote of the General Assembly on December 11, 1946, to provide emergency relief for children who had been victimized by the Second World War. Originally called the United Nations International Children's Emergency Fund, from which its initials are derived, UNICEF took over about $30 million in unexpended assets of the United Nations Relief and Rehabilitation Administration (UNRRA), the mandate of which expired in the autumn of 1946. UNRRA had been the principal relief organization in liberated Europe at the end of the war, and many of the experienced personnel of UNRRA were transferred directly to UNICEF.

Following the establishment of UNICEF, the flow of emergency supplies into Europe, from the United States, the British Dominions and other countries, that had been going through UNRRA continued unabated, and $100 million in additional emergency contributions was obtained from governments and private citizens. Between 1946 and 1950, thousands of tons of skim-milk powder, lard, margarine, materials for clothing and shoes, and medical supplies were shipped into southern and eastern Europe.

It was UNICEF's responsibility to get these vital supplies where they were needed. It was the responsibility of the European governments to provide the facilities and personnel to distribute them. As the threat of widespread famine and epidemic receded, the beneficiary governments assumed the responsibility of re-establishing permanent services for children with the supplies furnished by UNICEF. The principle of shared responsibility, inherited from UNRRA, has remained the key ingredient in the "UNICEF formula." From the beginning, donor and beneficiary governments have had an equal voice in the deliberations of UNICEF's Executive Board, which decides policy and approves requests for assistance.

At the peak of its post-war emergency activities, UNICEF was providing direct assistance, in the form of food and supplies, to more than 6 million mothers and children and indirect assistance, through the re-establishment of vital services, to many more.

By 1950, the post-war emergency, *per se*, was over. In the normal course of events, UNICEF would have terminated operations or put them on a stand-by basis. UNICEF's supporters, however, saw the end of the emergency period as an opportunity to engage humanity's concern with the welfare of children on a broader front. In the developing countries, accounting for about two-thirds of the world's population, the great majority of children lived under what might be described as permanent emergency conditions. The General Assembly extended UNICEF's life for a three-year trial period, beginning in 1950, and directed it to turn its attention to long-range programmes for the benefit of those children. Three years later, the Assembly gave the agency a continuing mandate and changed its name to the United Nations Children's Fund.

In the face of the overwhelming needs of children in the developing countries and of UNICEF's limited resources, its strategy was to concentrate on fields of aid where relatively small expenditures of supplies and equipment could be most effect: /e; and it was in the fields of health and mass disease control that the most promising opportunities immediately presented themselves.

DISEASE CONTROL.   By 1950, it had been demonstrated that most of the mass diseases that killed or crippled millions of children in Africa, Asia and Latin America could be eradicated or controlled through modern medical and health techniques and often at a very low unit cost. It was a precarious period, for UNICEF's income fell to about $10 million a year in 1951 and 1952. But it was found that where governments were able to take care of the staffing and execution of a disease-control campaign, five cents would enable UNICEF to supply enough penicillin to cure two children of yaws; fifty cents would buy enough DDT to protect several children from malaria for a year; twenty-five cents would buy enough BCG vaccine to protect twenty children against tuberculosis. It was this matching of resources that became the hallmark of UNICEF's programme of assistance.

Working in close collaboration with the World Health Organization (WHO), UNICEF set out to fight these and other diseases with a high incidence among children, such as trachoma and leprosy. WHO provided the developing countries with technical advice and the assistance of international experts. UNICEF furnished the material support: insecticides, sprayers, laboratory equipment and jeeps for anti-malaria campaigns; drugs, vaccines, clinical supplies, transport, and health education materials for campaigns against other diseases. Some developing countries found manning these campaigns with qualified personnel a critical problem. As a result, UNICEF soon added a certain amount of aid to training as well.

Though UNICEF's income has gradually risen to $33 million a year, there have been increasing demands for assistance in new fields, and important as disease-control campaigns are to the welfare of children, UNICEF has never been able to devote more than an average of $10 million a year to their support; but in terms of the elimination of suffering and the restoration of youthful vitality, the results of these programmes have been incalculable. In Iran, where large-scale anti-malaria operations were launched in 1950, a peasant woman described the change that had come to her village with the disappearance of malaria in simple human terms: "Now we can see our children on their feet, playing and making noise. Before the malaria control operation they all died and our houses were mournfully quiet." It is a story that could be duplicated in thousands of villages in Asia, Africa and the Americas.

HEALTH SERVICES. Beginning in 1950, UNICEF embarked on a programme to help build up permanent health services for mothers and children. UNICEF has provided basic technical equipment, vehicles and supplies for networks of maternal and child health centres in 110 countries, and has provided stipends or fellowships for the training of more than 60,000 health workers, ranging from village birth attendants to pediatric specialists. About 135,000 UNICEF midwife kits have been shipped to all the continents of the world. By the beginning of 1966, more than 30,000 health centres—from simple village dispensaries to modern training wards—had been equipped by UNICEF, and funds had been committed to equip about 9,000 more. UNICEF-equipped health centres are currently serving more than 70 million persons, the great majority of them children and mothers. Many of these centres are located in areas where modern medicine had never before penetrated.

HUNGER AND MALNUTRITION. Conditions in the developing world have been changing rapidly in the past twenty years: new factories, highways and dams have appeared; widely publicized development plans, together with improved communications, have encouraged the rising expectations of the people. But the most basic of human problems, hunger, has still to be solved. It is the exceptional child, in the developing world, who gets the quota of proteins, vitamins and other "protective foods" he needs for optimum physical and mental development. Sickly and apathetic, the malnourished child seldom grows up to be an adult capable of helping his country prosper.

The shipment of surplus skim-milk powder had been a prominent feature of UNICEF's relief activities in Europe, and in the 1950's UNICEF shipped up to 100 million pounds a year of skim-milk powder to the developing countries for distribution through schools and health centres. Shipments have fallen off in recent years as dairy surpluses in the United States and other donor countries have dwindled. But in India, Pakistan, the Middle East and a number of countries in Africa and Latin America, modern UNICEF-equipped dairy plants are helping make up the difference. UNICEF has equipped—or is now equipping —over 200 dairy plants in thirty-eight countries, including Asia's largest dairy installation, the 400,000-litre-a-day Worli plant in Bombay.

Beginning in 1956, UNICEF embarked on a wider programme of aid to nutrition to develop other high quality protein foods where milk is not available. It has been working closely with FAO, WHO and a number of scientific and industrial groups on the development of new high protein foods such as cottonseed flour, peanut flour and fish flour. In recent years, UNICEF has concentrated on what are called applied nutrition projects to stimulate greater production and consumption of eggs, fish, garden vegetables and the like at the village level. Fish farming—the raising of rapidly growing varieties of fish in irrigation ponds and flooded rice paddies—is a prominent feature of many of these projects. In India, for example, it is by no means unusual to see a young man pedalling a UNICEF bicycle down a country road delivering a polyethylene sack full of carp fingerlings. The fingerlings, from a state hatchery, are bound for a village irrigation pond and when fully grown and "harvested," will provide nutritious meals for village children.

UNICEF-supported applied nutrition projects are now under way in over fifty countries. In thousands of villages, people have become aware, for the first time, of the importance of protective foods in their children's diet, and they have learned that it is not beyond their own capability to produce these foods. In Colombia, for example, a well co-ordinated assault is being made on the problem of malnutrition. With the help of UNICEF, FAO and others, training courses in nutrition have been established for teachers, nursing auxiliaries, midwives, extension agents and community leaders. More than eighty primary schools have started truck gardens, and both children and parents are being taught how to raise poultry and rabbits at home.

By 1966, UNICEF had equipped more than 5,400 nutrition centres, ranging from school gardens to training institutes, and had committed funds to equip over 2,000 more. More than 60,000 persons, from village workers to specialists, had been trained for applied nutrition work through UNICEF grants, and funds have been committed for the training of 40,000 more.

SOCIAL SERVICES.   UNICEF assistance to strengthen social services in the developing countries began in 1959. By this time, a number of developing countries were making definite progress towards industrialization, but with the breakdown of traditional ways of life in the villages and the migration of millions of persons to the cities in search of new opportunities, family life was suffering. More and more children were being threatened by neglect and even abandonment. UNICEF has been supporting the development of national programmes to strengthen family life and help young people acquire sound capacities and social habits. In many countries, the principal stress is on urban social services. Workers are being trained to help families newly arrived from the countryside bridge the enormous gap between old and new ways of life. UNICEF is equipping an increasing number of day-care centres and playgrounds, and it has made a number of grants to improve the care of children in welfare homes. Two projects have now been launched with UNICEF aid, one in Bangkok and one in Tunis, to clean up some of the worst shanty-town areas inhabited by large numbers of children and to provide these children with vital services.

UNICEF aid to community development and mothercraft-homecraft projects is designed to raise the standards of family life in rural areas. UNICEF is helping train community development leaders through nine country projects in Asia and the Americas and through a regional project embracing a number of African countries. Through its support to village women's clubs, UNICEF is helping twelve African and two Asian countries teach young women the essentials of better child care and homemaking. The women meet once every week or so at a crossroads schoolhouse or outside the home of the local chief—wherever it is most convenient. A visiting instructor or, perhaps, a member of the group who has herself attended a district level mothercraft-homecraft course leads the discussion. It is a pleasant social occasion, but also a useful one, for the women's real purpose in coming together is to improve their sewing, to learn how to cook meals for their families without losing any of the vital nutrients in the food and to learn how some of the commoner hazards of childhood can be avoided through cleanliness and sanitation.

EDUCATION.   The most recent developments in UNICEF assistance—aid to education, vocational training and national planning for children—grew out of a broad view of the needs of children conducted by the UNICEF Executive Board in 1961. Reports submitted by all the United Nations agencies directly concerned with the needs of children and background reports submitted by the governments of twenty-four developing countries pointed to an inescapable conclusion: that there is a limit to the improvement that can be made in the condition of children by attacking their needs piecemeal. Many Board members pointed out that, in an age of change and development, a child who is given medical attention and food still represents a life wasted if he has no opportunity to acquire an education and learn a useful trade. Again and again, the developing countries noted that in their list of children's priorities, preparation for life ranked as high as protection against disease and hunger.

UNICEF aid to education and vocational training, which was inaugurated in 1962, now accounts for about 10 per cent of its programme expenditures. Though a relatively small amount of money has been involved (currently about $2.5 million a year), the results are already appreciable. In 60 countries, UNICEF has helped equip 34 secondary schools, over 280 vocational training centres, 250 teacher training centres and more than 5,700 associated primary schools (for practice teaching). Here again, UNICEF aid is conceived as "yeast to make the bread rise." About half the school-age children in the developing countries still have no schools to go to, and much of the instruction offered has little practical value. A tremendous investment will be required to overcome these deficiencies. UNICEF, working in close cooperation with UNESCO and ILO, can only help to point the way. But UNICEF has already helped several countries to a good start in overcoming their most serious educational bottleneck: the shortage of qualified primary teachers.

In Algeria, for example, the government has carried out a remarkable emergency teacher-training programme over the past three years with aid from UNICEF and other sources. When Algeria attained independence, the sudden exodus of teachers threatened the entire primary education structure. About 5,000 primary school teachers were trained in the first two years following independence, and in the year ending in mid-1965, 5,000 more were trained. In addition, 1,572 school canteens had been established by mid-1965, serving a daily hot meal to more than 400,000 children.

In Thailand, UNICEF is helping the government strengthen its system of primary and secondary education with the object of giving children a better—and more realistic—preparation for life in a changing society. UNICEF is assisting 27 teacher training colleges in the country and, during 1965, completed the equipping of 180 village practice teaching schools. In 35 UNICEF-equipped vocational training schools for girls, enrollment has increased by 90 per cent since 1963. Thai educational officials consider this a remarkable achievement, in view of parents' past reluctance to let their children enrol in any but academic courses.

UNICEF's aid to education and vocational training ranges from the simplest classroom supplies for demonstration schools, to printing presses for the production of textbooks. Lathes, metal-working equipment and electric wiring kits have been supplied to vocational training centres. UNICEF recently supplied Burma with equipment to revitalize an ancient glass-blowing centre to produce science laboratory equipment for high schools. Thus an ancient skill was utilized to support a modern need. Globally, funds have been committed for stipends to train—or to improve the training of—more than 40,000 teachers and other educational personnel.

PROGRAMME INTEGRATION. In almost all the countries in which it is at work, UNICEF assists projects to meet a variety of children's needs. In India, for example, it is assisting seventeen different projects, ranging from vaccine production, peanut-flour production and the training of dairy personnel, to goitre control, pre-vocational education for elementary school "drop outs" and the strengthening of science teaching at the secondary level. UNICEF programme and field staff are now placing more and more emphasis on integrating projects for children in various fields so that they reinforce one another. Health and nutrition projects, for example, are being co-ordinated with health and nutrition education in the schools. Family and child welfare programmes are being planned as part of a comprehensive community development approach that includes the teacher, the public health nurse and the agricultural extension agent.

A broader objective of UNICEF is to encourage countries to integrate programmes for children and youth into their long-range economic and social development plans. An international round-table on "Planning for Children and Youth in National Development" was held in Bellagio, Italy, in the spring of 1964. In November 1965, key officials from twenty-five Latin American countries met in Santiago, Chile, to examine the situation confronting their children and to study how their needs could be met as part of a genuine "human resource development" programme. An Asian conference on children and youth in national development was held in Bangkok in March 1966, and a similar conference was held in Addis Ababa in May 1966.

STRUCTURE AND ADMINISTRATION. UNICEF is not a large agency. Its permanent staff, at headquarters and in the field, consists of about 700 persons, and its annual budget of about $33 million is hardly enough to keep the welfare services of a large city going for more than a month or two.

UNICEF is governed by a 30-nation Executive Board, which meets regularly to set policy and allocate aid to projects. The work is reviewed annually by the Economic and Social Council and the General Assembly. UNICEF personnel are members of the Secretariat of the United Nations, and its Executive Director is appointed by the Secretary-General, in consultation with the Executive Board.

Though a part of the United Nations, UNICEF is not financed through the regular United Nations budget, but by voluntary contributions. The number of governments contributing to UNICEF has steadily increased from thirty in 1950 to 117 in 1965. Contributions made by individuals and organizations or collected through the sale of greeting cards or through campaigns like the Hallowe'en Trick or Treat for UNICEF are increasingly important sources of revenue.

NOBEL PEACE PRIZE. In December 1965, UNICEF was awarded the Nobel Peace Prize. The Executive Board decided that the prize money, amounting to the equivalent of about $54,000, would be used for the establishment of a memorial fund honouring Maurice Pate, Director of UNICEF from its inception in 1946 until his death in January 1965. The memorial fund is to be used to train personnel in fields to improve conditions for children in developing countries or for some other special purpose closely related to the work of UNICEF.

Office of the United Nations High Commissioner for Refugees (UNHCR)

Assistance to refugees was first organized under international auspices in 1921 with the appointment of Dr. Fridtjof Nansen, of Norway, as League of Nations High Commissioner for Refugees.

After the beginning of the Second World War, the first major international agency concerned with refugees and displaced persons was the United Nations Relief and Rehabilitation Administration (UNRRA), which was established on November 9, 1943. Its broad objectives included the relief, maintenance, rehabilitation and, ultimately, repatriation of United Nations nationals who had been displaced as a result of the war. However, a large number of these displaced persons were reluctant or unwilling to be repatriated, either because they had lost all ties with their countries of origin or because of changed political conditions there. These people, together with non-settled pre-war and war-time refugee groups, represented the core of the refugee problem in Europe following the Second World War. At the beginning of 1946, it was estimated that there were some 1,675,000 persons who, to all intents and purposes, had to be considered as refugees for whom new homes had to be found.

In the wake of UNRRA came the International Refugee Organization (IRO), the Constitution of which was approved by the United Nations General Assembly on December 15, 1946. A Preparatory Commission for IRO was established and, on July 1, 1947, took over the functions and activities previously exercised by UNRRA on behalf of refugees and displaced persons. IRO succeeded the Preparatory Commission on August 20, 1948. By the time it had ceased its operations in February 1952, IRO had resettled more than a million displaced persons and refugees in new homes throughout the world, had repatriated approximately 73,000 to their former homelands and, altogether, had given some form of assistance to more than 1,600,000 persons.

On December 3, 1949, the General Assembly, recognizing the continuing responsibility of the United Nations for the international protection of refugees after the termination of IRO, decided to appoint a United Nations High Commissioner for Refugees.

OFFICE OF THE HIGH COMMISSIONER. On December 14, 1950, the Assembly adopted the Statute of the Office of the United Nations High Commissioner for Refugees (UNHCR). The Office came into existence on January 1, 1951, originally for a period of three years. Since then, its mandate has been renewed by the General Assembly for three five-year periods, most recently until December 31, 1968.

The United Nations High Commissioner for Refugees is elected by the General Assembly, on the nomination of the Secretary-General, and is responsible to the Assembly. The High Commissioner's programme is administered by a thirty-member Executive Committee, which generally meets twice a year at Geneva. It consists of representatives of members of the United Nations and of the specialized agencies, who are elected by the Economic and Social Council on the widest geographical basis from among those states with a demonstrated interest in and devotion to the solution of the refugee problem.

UNHCR headquarters are in Geneva. There are branch offices in Algeria, Australia (also covering New Zealand), Austria, Belgium, Burundi, the Democratic Republic of the Congo, France, the Federal Republic of Germany, Greece, Italy, Macao, Colombia (for Latin America), Lebanon, the United Arab Republic, Morocco, Nepal, the Netherlands, Senegal, Tanzania, Turkey, Uganda, the United Kingdom and the United States. In addition, UNHCR has an honorary representative in Tunisia, and correspondents in Argentina, Canada, Chile, Ecuador, Luxembourg, Portugal, the Republic of South Africa, Spain, Venezuela and Yugoslavia.

A joint representative of UNHCR and the Inter-Governmental Committee for European Migration (ICEM) in Hong Kong deals with the problem of refugees of European origin still on the mainland of China who seek resettlement opportunities in other countries.

TERMS OF REFERENCE. The work of UNHCR is humanitarian, social and non-political. Its basic tasks are to provide international protection for the refugees within the High Commissioner's mandate and to seek permanent solutions to their problems by facilitating their voluntary repatriation or their assimilation within new national communities. Mandate refugees, as defined in the UNHCR Statute, are persons who, owing to well-founded fear of persecution for reasons of race, religion, nationality or political opinion, are outside their country of origin and cannot or, owing to such fear, do not wish to avail themselves of the protection of that country.

UNHCR is not, of course, concerned with all refugees throughout the world. For example, refugees considered as nationals by the countries which have granted them asylum—by and large, refugees in "divided countries"—are not a UNHCR responsibility. Nor is UNHCR concerned with refugees for whom another United Nations body has assumed full responsibility, such as the Arab refugees from Palestine under the mandate of UNRWA (*see page* 95).

When the UNHCR Statute was drawn up, refugee problems of concern to UNHCR were essentially those of European refugees in Europe. Since 1957, however, UNHCR has been called upon more and more frequently to concern itself with refugee problems in other continents, particularly Africa and Asia. In meeting these "new" refugee situations, UNHCR acts under the directives of the General Assembly and on the basis of a series of resolutions generally referred to as the "Good Offices Resolutions." Originally used only for refugee groups outside the High Commissioner's mandate, the "Good Offices" procedure now covers the whole of the activities of UNHCR on behalf of new refugee groups. Provided they possess the essential characteristics of refugees coming within the UNHCR mandate, they are now entitled, without restriction, to the benefit of the High Commissioner's services —both aid and protection—without there being the need of first having to determine their elegibility in each individual case.

FINANCING OF ACTIVITIES.   UNHCR's administrative expenditure is financed under the United Nations budget, but its programmes of assistance to refugees are financed exclusively through voluntary contributions, primarily from governments. Contributions likely to be made by governments in support of UNHCR programmes are generally announced at pledging conferences held at United Nations Headquarters each year and, at times, are made in response to direct and specific appeals by UNHCR.

Occasionally, part of the proceeds of fund-raising campaigns in certain countries is earmarked to support the High Commissioner's programmes. A special venture, the objectives of which were to raise funds for refugees as well as to attract world-wide interest in their plight, was World Refugee Year, 1959-1960. It largely benefited refugees under the High Commissioner's mandate, both through the financing of UNHCR programmes, including that for the clearance of refugee camps in Europe, and through the application of increasingly liberal resettlement criteria, particularly in respect of handicapped refugees. Other special ventures have included the promotion of the world-wide sale of two long-playing records, "All-Star Festival" and "International Piano Festival."

However, it is to governments that the High Commissioner must look for most of the financial support needed to implement his programmes. By the end of 1965, nearly sixty governments were contributing financially to support UNHCR programmes, which for that year were based on a minimum budget of $3.5 million. The UNHCR programme as a whole is so conceived as to provide the basic starting point for wider action. It does not by itself cover all immediate needs, nor does it meet all aspects of the re-establishment of refugees. It is intended to stimulate other forms of international action, such as bilateral aid, zonal development projects and activities on behalf of refugees by inter-governmental organizations and voluntary agencies.

PROGRAMMES.   When UNHCR began its activities in 1951, it was estimated that there were at that time, throughout the world, some 1,250,000 refugees coming within the High Commissioner's mandate. Some 300,000 to 400,000 of these were non-settled and in need of some form of assistance. Most of these 300,000 to 400,000 refugees were in Europe, and some 120,000 of them were living in camps.

In spite of a never-ceasing influx of refugees into Europe over the years, including some 200,000 Hungarians who came to Austria and, subsequently, Yugoslavia in 1956-1957, the number of refugees still of concern to UNHCR had dropped to some 1,070,000 by the end of 1965. Most of these refugees—some 650,000—were located in Europe; some 260,000 were in North America, 100,000 in Latin America, 50,000 in Australia and New Zealand, 7,000 in various countries of Africa and Asia, and about 1,200 were still on the mainland of China, seeking resettlement opportunities elsewhere. Of the 650,000 refugees in Europe, only about 12,000, including 500 in camps, were still non-settled and required UNHCR assistance towards their final re-establishment. These remaining "old" refugees were located in Austria, Germany, France, Greece and Italy.

As the problem of the "old" refugees and certain other refugee situations were reduced or, sometimes, eliminated through the efforts of the international community and UNHCR, new refugee problems arose in practically every part of the world, particularly in Africa.

The first of these major "new" refugee problems which UNHCR had to face was in North Africa, where UNHCR was called upon to assist in the situation created by the arrival of over 200,000 Algerian refugees in Morocco and Tunisia. With the League of Red Cross Societies as its operational partner, the High Commissioner provided food, clothing and shelter to these refugees. UNHCR's main responsibilities were to act in a diplomatic and organizational capacity, as well as to raise the necessary cash contributions, which amounted to about $2 million a year between 1957 and 1962. The League of Red Cross Societies concentrated primarily on obtaining contributions in kind, amounting to some $5 million a year, and provided qualified personnel to man the operation.

Since then, UNHCR has provided assistance to nearly 500,000 refugees in Central, East and West Africa upon the request of the governments concerned and, generally, at the earliest possible stage of a newly arising refugee situation. This aid may range in scope from relatively modest financial contributions to help a government meet the cost of providing food and shelter to newly arrived refugees, to the setting up of a large-scale operation. Such an operation might include the provision of food, medical services and relief supplies by the League of Red Cross Societies upon the UNHCR's request; supplies from the World Food Programme; and other logistical support needed to safeguard life and health.

Since UNHCR is, in essence, non-operational and acts as the planner and diplomatic go-between to enlist the help of all those governments, organizations and individuals likely to be in a position to assist in any given refugee situation, it is concerned with the elaboration of plans and projects aimed at making refugees self-supporting as speedily as possible.

In Africa, where large areas of virgin land still exist, governments are frequently requested by UNHCR to provide land where the refugees can settle and, invariably, governments respond generously. But the actual settlement of refugees calls not only for a vast effort on the part of refugees themselves, but also for close partnership between host governments, UNHCR and those organizations which have the technical knowledge and strength to carry out projects whereby refugees, through their own work and efforts, will ultimately become fully self-supporting members of a new community in regions which, subsequently, may well receive development aid to benefit the population as a whole.

Altogether, over 260,000 refugees have entered the Democratic Republic of the Congo, including Angolans, Rwandese and Sudanese. About 50,000 Rwandese refugees are in Burundi. Uganda granted asylum to over 100,000 Rwandese and Sudanese refugees, and the United Republic of Tanzania accepted nearly 30,000 refugees, mostly from Rwanda and Mozambique.

Other refugee groups in Africa include 50,000 in Senegal, coming from Portuguese Guinea; about 18,000, mostly Sudanese, to whom asylum was granted in the Central African Republic; and about 5,000 in Zambia, coming from Mozambique. In addition, about 50,000 persons, displaced as a result of civil strife and upheavals in the Democratic Republic of the Congo, entered Burundi, the Central African Republic, the United Republic of Tanzania and Uganda.

In Asia, various types of projects are being implemented for the 80,000 Chinese refugees in Macao. The main effort in Macao is directed at seeking gainful employment for them. For the 1,100,000 Chinese in Hong Kong, UNHCR has channelled funds in support of the substantial efforts undertaken over the years by the Hong Kong authorities.

There are 7,000 Tibetan refugees in Nepal and 44,000 in India. The UNHCR programme in Nepal, carried out by the Nepalese Red Cross, is primarily directed towards the resettlement of the refugees

on the land. UNHCR assistance to the Tibetan refugees in India takes
the form of supporting a number of land-settlement projects undertaken on their behalf by the Indian Government and a number of international organizations and agencies.

INTERNATIONAL PROTECTION. International protection is
basic to the High Commissioner's work in favour of refugees. It is
designed to overcome the disabilities experienced by refugees because
they lack national protection, and to safeguard their basic rights and
legitimate interests. A refugee remains the High Commissioner's concern until he is finally integrated in his country of residence by acquiring the nationality of that country or until he has returned voluntarily
to his country of origin.

International protection, a day-to-day as well as a long-term task,
is effected through the conclusion and ratification of international conventions relating to the status of refugees, the supervision of their
application and the promotion, in agreement with governments, of
measures aimed at improving the situation of refugees. Over the years,
there has been considerable strengthening of various national, regional
and international arrangements aimed at safeguarding the basic rights
of refugees, and governments have pursued an increasingly generous
and liberal policy of asylum.

The most important international instrument drawn up in this
connection is the 1951 Convention Relating to the Status of Refugees,
which was drafted at a United Nations conference of plenipotentiaries,
held in Geneva from July 2 to 25, 1951. By the end of 1965, the Convention had been ratified or acceded to by forty-nine states, eighteen
of them in Africa.

The Convention sets out and codifies the minimum rights of refugees, such as the right to work, to education and to social security;
freedom of religion; and access to courts. It ensures that contracting
states shall not expel a refugee lawfully on their territory save on
grounds of national security or public order, and that no such refugee
shall be expelled or returned in any manner whatsoever to the frontiers
of territories where his life or freedom would be threatened on account
of his race, religion, nationality, membership of a particular social
group, or political opinion.

The Convention also provides for the issuance of travel documents
to refugees and makes special reference to the problem of refugee
seamen, who, serving as crew members on board merchant ships, have
been unable to set foot on shore owing to a lack of documents permitting them to return to any country.

At a colloquium held in Bellagio, Italy, in April 1965, various
eminent jurists, in their personal capacity, considered ways and means
of finding a simple, rapid procedure for updating the 1951 Convention
so as to take account of developments that have taken place since it

was drafted. UNHCR has started consultations with governments on the basis of a number of recommendations made.

Within the framework of its function of international protection, UNHCR has developed increasingly close relations with regional organizations such as the Council of Europe, the European Economic Community (EEC), the Organization of American States (OAS), the Asian/African Legal Consultative Committee and the Organization of African Unity (OAU). An important recent development is the link established with the OAU which, in a 1965 resolution, called upon those of its member states not yet party to the 1951 Convention to adhere to that instrument.

A special agreement was concluded on October 5, 1960, between the Government of the Federal Republic of Germany and the High Commissioner whereby a fund of approximately $10 million was established to enable the High Commissioner to undertake measures of assistance for those refugees who had been persecuted at the time of the National-Socialist régime by reason of their nationality, but who were not entitled to indemnification under existing German indemnification legislation. The agreement provided that those refugees who had suffered permanent injury to body or health should receive payments in the same amounts as those accorded to other categories of victims of persecution. The $10 million made available by the Federal Republic of Germany have since been distributed, and the fund closed.

UNHCR also operates projects within the framework of its programmes to provide refugees with legal assistance, advice, representation in court, or assistance in approaching administrative authorities to solve problems resulting from the very fact that they are refugees.

CO-OPERATION WITH OTHER AGENCIES. Because UNHCR is a co-ordinating rather than an operational body, it generally implements its programmes in close co-operation with the most suitable and effective operational partner or partners whenever called upon by governments to assist in refugee situations with which they can no longer cope on their own.

By acting as the co-ordinator and catalyzing agent to mobilize existing and potential sources of goodwill, UNHCR tries to bring about effective solutions to refugee problems through multilateral or bilateral action. The fact that UNHCR operates beyond all considerations of race, religion or political motive has been generally recognized as a strong element in the channelling of international assistance.

Organizations such as the United Nations Development Programme, the ILO, FAO, WHO, UNICEF and UNESCO have all at one time been associated with UNHCR programmes, or still are, as are also the World Food Programme; the International Committee of the Red Cross; the League of Red Cross Societies, often the UNHCR's operational partner in Europe and Africa; the United States Escapee Programme; and the Inter-Governmental Committee for European Migration (ICEM), whose mandate provides for the transportation of migrants and refugees from Europe to overseas countries. Seventy or more of the member agencies of the International Council of Voluntary Agencies have been actively associated in the implementation of UNHCR programmes.

NANSEN MEDAL AWARD.   The Nansen Medal Award was instituted by UNHCR in 1954. Named after Fridtjof Nansen (Norway), the League of Nations' first High Commissioner for Refugees, it is awarded each year for outstandingly meritorious work on behalf of refugees.

NOBEL PEACE PRIZE.   The Nobel Peace Prize for 1954 was awarded to the Office of the United Nations High Commissioner for Refugees. The prize money—approximately $35,000—was used for the closure of Camp Tinos in Greece.

Questions Concerning Human Rights

HUMAN RIGHTS

One of the purposes of the United Nations, according to Article 1 of the Charter, is to achieve international co-operation in promoting and encouraging respect for human rights and fundamental freedoms for all, without distinction as to race, sex, language or religion.

From its beginning, the United Nations has concerned itself with the promotion and protection of human rights. During its first ten years, activities in this field were directed primarily, although not exclusively, towards defining "human rights and fundamental freedoms" and establishing broad principles and general standards, chiefly through the adoption of international instruments. While such activities are continuing, a new programme has been developed since 1956 which lays emphasis on the value of the exchange of knowledge and experience in promoting human rights. The three main features of the new programme are: (1) a system of periodic reporting on human rights by governments; (2) a series of studies of specific rights or groups of rights; and (3) a programme of advisory services in the field of human rights. More recently, the General Assembly has initiated a positive drive towards the elimination of all forms of racial discrimination and religious intolerance.

Universal Declaration of Human Rights

The Commission on Human Rights, which came into existence in 1946, began its work in January 1947 under the chairmanship of Mrs. Franklin D. Roosevelt. The Commission devoted itself first to the preparation of a declaration of human rights and next to the drafting of a covenant on civil and political rights and a covenant on economic, social and cultural rights.

The Universal Declaration of Human Rights was prepared by the Commission in 1947 and 1948 and was adopted by the General Assembly on December 10, 1948. Of the fifty-eight nations represented at the Assembly session, forty-eight voted in favour of the Declaration, none voted against, eight abstained and two were absent.

In thirty articles, the Declaration sets forth basic rights and fundamental freedoms to which all men and women everywhere in the world are entitled, without any discrimination. These rights and freedoms include the right to life, liberty and security of person; freedom from slavery and servitude; freedom from arbitrary arrest and detention; the right to a fair trial by an independent and impartial tribunal; the right to be presumed innocent until proved guilty; inviolability of the home and secrecy of correspondence; freedom of movement and residence; the right to a nationality; the right to marry and to found a family; the right to own property; freedom of thought, conscience and religion; freedom of opinion and expression; freedom of peaceful assembly and association; the right to vote and to participate in government; the right to social security; the right to work; the right to an adequate standard of living; the right to education; and the right to participate in the cultural life of the community. [The full text of the Declaration is given on page 585.]

The Assembly proclaimed the Universal Declaration as "a common standard of achievement for all peoples and all nations" and called upon all member states and all peoples to promote and secure the effective recognition and observance of the rights and freedoms set forth therein.

In 1950, the General Assembly invited all states and interested organizations to observe December 10 of each year as Human Rights Day, a practice since adopted in many parts of the world.

In 1958 and 1963, special observances were held to mark, respectively, the tenth and the fifteenth anniversary of the adoption of the Declaration. A committee has proposed a series of special activities for 1968, the twentieth anniversary, which the General Assembly has designated as International Year for Human Rights.

In the years since its adoption, the Declaration has exercised a profound influence upon the minds of men. It has been translated into all the main languages of the world. The Declaration, or individual articles from it, are frequently quoted in United Nations resolutions as setting standards. The constitutions of many countries, including most countries which have recently gained their independence, reflect its influence. It has also influenced national legislations and jurisdictions.

A number of international conventions concluded under the auspices of the United Nations and the specialized agencies have been inspired by the Declaration—for example, the Convention Relating to the Status of Refugees; the Convention Relating to the Status of Stateless Persons; the Convention on the Political Rights of Women; the Convention on the Nationality of Married Women; the Supplementary Convention on Slavery, the Slave Trade, and Institutions and Practices Similar to Slavery; the Convention concerning the Abolition of Forced Labour; the Convention concerning Discrimination in Respect of Employment and Occupation; the Convention against Discrimination in Education; the Convention on Consent to Marriage,

Minimum Age for Marriage and Registration of Marriages; and the International Convention on the Elimination of All Forms of Racial Discrimination.

The human rights programme that has developed and is developing in the United Nations is, to a large extent, conceived within the framework of the Universal Declaration. In fact, it may be said that the purpose of the programme as a whole is to promote the observance and implementation of the rights and freedoms set forth in the Declaration.

International Covenants on Human Rights

Once the Universal Declaration was completed in 1948, the Commission on Human Rights concentrated on the draft international covenants. In 1954 it finished the preliminary texts of a draft covenant on civil and political rights and a draft covenant on economic, social and cultural rights. These were sent, through the Economic and Social Council, to the General Assembly and have been considered, article by article, at all the sessions of the General Assembly since 1955.

In the preliminary drafts completed in 1954 by the Commission on Human Rights, both covenants contained a preamble; an article on the right of peoples to self-determination; general provisions; substantive articles; measures of implementation; and final clauses.

Between 1955, when the two draft covenants came before the General Assembly, and 1965, the Third Committee (Social, Humanitarian and Cultural) adopted the preamble and the article on the right of peoples to self-determination, for inclusion in both draft covenants. It also completed consideration of, and adopted, all the general and substantive articles of the draft covenants.

The article, in both draft covenants, on the right of peoples to self-determination states that all peoples have the right freely to determine their political status and freely to pursue their economic, social and cultural development, and may, for their own ends, freely dispose of their natural wealth and resources without prejudice to any obligations arising out of international economic co-operation, based upon the principle of mutual benefit and international law. The article further states that in no case may a people be deprived of its own means of subsistence and that all states shall promote the realization of the right of self-determination and shall respect that right.

The substantive articles of the draft covenant on economic, social and cultural rights deal with the right to work; the right to just and favourable conditions of work; trade union rights; social security; rights relating to motherhood and childhood, marriage and the family; the right to adequate food, clothing, housing and standards of living and to freedom from hunger; the right to health; the right to education, including a plan for implementing compulsory primary education; and rights relating to science and culture.

The substantive articles of the draft covenant on civil and political rights cover the right to life; freedom from inhuman or degrading treatment; freedom from slavery, servitude and forced labour; the right to liberty and security of person and to be free from arbitrary arrest or detention; the treatment of persons deprived of their liberty; freedom of movement; the right to a fair trial; non-retroactive application of criminal law; privacy; protection against interference with privacy, family, home or correspondence and against attacks on honour and reputation; freedom of thought, conscience and religion; freedom of opinion and expression; the right of peaceful assembly and freedom of association; rights relating to marriage and family protection; the rights of the child; and the right to take part in the conduct of public affairs, to vote and to be elected.

At the end of 1965, there still remained to be considered the provisions relating to measures of implementation and the final clauses.

Prevention and Punishment of the Crime of Genocide

The General Assembly, on December 11, 1946, unanimously affirmed that genocide—the killing of a group of human beings—is a crime under international law which the civilized world condemns. Two years later, on December 9, 1948, the Assembly unanimously adopted the Convention on the Prevention and Punishment of the Crime of Genocide. The Convention came into force on January 12, 1951. As of December 31, 1965, it had been ratified or acceded to by sixty-eight states.

The purpose of the Convention is to prevent and punish genocide, whether committed in time of war or in time of peace. The Convention defines genocide as the commitment of certain acts with intent to destroy, in whole or in part, a national, ethnic, racial or religious group as such. The acts constituting genocide are killing, causing serious bodily or mental harm, deliberately inflicting conditions of life calculated to bring about physical destruction in whole or in part, imposing measures intended to prevent birth, and the forcible transfer of children. Not only genocide itself but also conspiracy or incitement to commit it, as well as attempts to commit genocide and complicity in the crime, are punishable under the Convention. Persons committing genocide must be punished "whether they are constitutionally responsible rulers, public officers or private individuals."

States adhering to the Convention are required to pass the necessary laws to give effect to it and to grant extradition in cases of genocide. Those persons charged with genocide are to be tried in the country where the crime was committed or by such international tribunals as may have jurisdiction.

In January 1965, the Sub-Commission on Prevention of Discrimination and Protection of Minorities noted that allegations of genocide occurring in various parts of the world had been made in recent years, and it expressed the belief that there still existed a need for further measures to prevent and punish the crime of genocide. It requested the Commission on Human Rights to give consideration to further measures that might be required to strengthen the prevention and punishment of the crime of genocide and to give wider effect to the Convention.

Slavery and Servitude

In 1949, the Economic and Social Council asked the Secretary-General to appoint a committee of experts to survey the field of slavery and other institutions and customs resembling slavery, to assess the nature and extent of these problems and to suggest methods of attacking them.

The four-member Committee, which completed its study in 1951, reported that, apart from slavery in its crudest form, a number of institutions or practices analogous to slavery or resembling slavery in some of its effects still existed in various parts of the world. Since many of these institutions or practices were not covered by the League of Nations Slavery Convention of 1926, the Committee proposed that a supplementary convention be drafted by the United Nations.

In 1953, the General Assembly adopted a protocol under which the functions exercised by the League of Nations under the Slavery Convention of 1926 were transferred to the United Nations.

In September 1956, a Supplementary Convention on Slavery, the Slave Trade, and Institutions and Practices Similar to Slavery was adopted and opened for signature at a conference of plenipotentiaries convened by the Economic and Social Council at Geneva. The Convention has been in force since April 30, 1957. As of December 31, 1965, it had been ratified or acceded to by sixty-one states.

Forced Labour

In 1951, the United Nations and the International Labour Organisation (ILO) jointly established a Committee on Forced Labour. In an inquiry it made on this subject, the Committee received, from governments, non-governmental organizations and individuals, allegations that forced labour existed in certain countries or territories. The Committee's study covered some twenty-four countries or territories.

The Committee completed its work in 1953. Its final report concluded that there were two systems of forced labour in the world: the first was employed as a means of coercion or punishment for holding or expressing political views; the second was employed for important economic purposes. The Committee considered that its inquiry had revealed that fundamental human rights were threatened and the freedom and status of workers were jeopardized in contravention of the obligations and provisions of the United Nations Charter. It urged that such systems of forced labour be abolished.

In 1954, both the Economic and Social Council and the General Assembly condemned those systems of forced labour, appealed to all governments to re-examine their laws and administrative practices and asked the Secretary-General and the Director-General of ILO to prepare a further report, including any new information on forced labour. The report was completed in December 1955.

Early in 1956, the Council again condemned all forms of forced labour which are contrary to the principles of the United Nations Charter and the Universal Declaration of Human Rights and, in particular, forced labour employed as a means of coercion or punishment for holding or expressing political views, and urged that action be taken to eliminate forced labour.

In June 1957, the International Labour Conference adopted a Convention on the Abolition of Forced Labour. Under this Convention, states parties undertake to suppress and not to make use of any form of forced or compulsory labour (a) as a means of political coercion or education or as a punishment for holding or expressing political views or views ideologically opposed to the established political, social or economic system; (b) as a method of mobilizing and using labour for purposes of economic development; (c) as a means of labour discipline; (d) as a punishment for having participated in strikes; or (e) as a means of racial, social, national or religious discrimination.

The Convention on the Abolition of Forced Labour entered into force on January 17, 1959. As of December 31, 1965, ninety-three countries had ratified it.

Refugees and Stateless Persons

In July 1951, a Convention relating to the Status of Refugees was adopted by a conference of plenipotentiaries convened in Geneva by the General Assembly. It entered into force on April 22, 1954, and as of December 31, 1965, it had been ratified or acceded to by forty-eight states.

The parties to the Convention undertake to apply three standards of treatment to refugees: (1) the same treatment that nationals receive with regard to religion, artistic rights, industrial property, access to courts, rationing, elementary education, public relief, labour legislation and social security, and fiscal charges; (2) the most favourable treatment accorded nationals of a foreign country with regard to the right of association and wage-earning employment; and (3) the most favourable treatment possible and, in any event, not less favourable than that accorded aliens generally, with regard to movable and immovable property, self-employment, the liberal professions, housing, education other than elementary education, and freedom of movement. Provision is also made in the Convention for issuing passports to refugees and for protecting them from expulsion from the country of refuge.

A Convention relating to the Status of Stateless Persons was adopted in September 1954 by a conference of plenipotentiaries convened in New York by the Economic and Social Council. It came into force on June 6, 1960, and as of December 31, 1965, had been ratified by eighteen states.

The Convention is based on the Refugees Convention, and many articles contain identical language. States parties undertake to grant to stateless persons almost the same standards of treatment as to refugees, except that in the case of the right of association and wage-earning employment, the treatment will be that accorded aliens generally. A stateless person is defined in the Convention as "a person who is not considered as a national by any state under the operation of its law." Included in the final act of the conference was a recommendation to governments concerning a person who has renounced the protection of the state of which he is a national, by which they consider sympathetically, in certain cases, the possibility of according to that person the treatment which the Convention affords to stateless persons. Contracting states to the Convention also agree to facilitate the assimilation and naturalization of stateless persons.

Plight of Survivors of Nazi Concentration Camps

The Commission on the Status of Women, in May 1950, called attention to the plight of women survivors of concentration camps who were subjected, during the Nazi régime, to so-called medical experiments. After considering the report of the Commission, the Economic and Social Council, in July 1950, requested the Secretary-General to consider as soon as possible, with the competent authorities, means for alleviating the plight of such victims, both male and female.

As the result of efforts made by the United Nations, the Government of the Federal Republic of Germany has accepted responsibility for compensating survivors of experimentation by Nazi doctors in concentration camps. Some 600 claims, as well as a substantial volume of follow-up correspondence, have been transmitted to the Government of the Federal Republic of Germany by the United Nations.

Prisoners of War

In 1950, the General Assembly asked the Secretary-General to appoint three "qualified and impartial persons" to settle the problem of prisoners of the Second World War who had not been repatriated or otherwise accounted for.

The three-member *Ad Hoc* Commission on Prisoners of War submitted to the Secretary-General in 1957 a full report on the progress in the repatriation of, and the accounting for, prisoners of war since 1950, stating that a total of 28,535 German prisoners (and 3,088 civilians) and 69 Italian and 33,778 Japanese nationals had been repatriated.

The Governments of Italy, Japan and the Federal Republic of Germany informed the Commission that there were still several thousand prisoners of war and civilians who had not been repatriated or otherwise accounted for. The Commission appealed to the Governments concerned to settle the problem in a purely humanitarian spirit, either directly or through the good offices of the Red Cross Societies.

Draft Declaration on the Right of Asylum

The text of a draft declaration on the right of asylum was prepared by the Commission on Human Rights in 1960.

The draft declaration has been described as an attempt to set forth general principles by which states and the international community should be guided in the matter of asylum. Among other things, it states that asylum granted by a state shall be respected by all other states; that the situation of persons forced to leave a country because of persecution or well-founded fear of persecution is a matter of concern to the international community; and that no one seeking or enjoying asylum should, "except for overriding reasons of national security or safeguard of the population," be subjected to measures such as rejection at the frontier, return and expulsion which would result in compelling him to return to or remain in a country where his life might be threatened.

The General Assembly began its consideration of the draft declaration in 1962. It adopted the preamble and a first article to the effect that territorial asylum granted by a state in the exercise of its sovereignty shall be respected by all other states, subject to the proviso that the right of asylum may not be invoked by any person guilty of a crime against peace, a war crime or a crime against humanity. Four further articles remain to be considered.

Protection of Trade Union Rights
(Freedom of Association)

The Economic and Social Council has worked in close co-operation with the International Labour Organisation (ILO) for the promotion of trade union rights since 1947, when the matter was brought to its attention by certain non-governmental organizations. As a result of this co-operation, the International Labour Conference adopted in 1948 the Freedom of Association and Protection of the Right to Organize Convention, and in 1949 the Right to Organize and Collective Bargaining Convention. ILO has also established, on its own behalf and on behalf of the United Nations, international machinery for the examination of allegations of infringements of trade union rights. All such allegations received by the United Nations which relate to states members of ILO are forwarded to the Governing Body of that organization; the Economic and Social Council considers only cases which are related to non-member states of ILO.

Freedom of Information

The General Assembly declared in 1946 that "freedom of information is a fundamental human right and is the touchstone of all the freedoms to which the United Nations is consecrated." In this spirit, the United Nations has engaged in a wide programme of activities aimed at promoting freedom of information.

In 1948 a Conference on Freedom of Information was held in Geneva to examine "the rights, obligations and practices which should be included in the concept of freedom of information." The Conference drew up three draft conventions: on the gathering and international transmission of news, on the institution of an international right of correction, and on freedom of information.

Of the conventions proposed by the Conference, only one, on the international right of correction, has been approved by the General Assembly and opened for signature. It entered into force on August 24, 1962. The Assembly approved the convention dealing with the international transmission of news, but has not opened it for signature. The draft convention on freedom of information has given rise to much controversy. It is still before the Assembly, which is engaged in an article-by-article revision of it.

In 1952, the Economic and Social Council appointed a rapporteur on freedom of information to prepare a substantive report covering "major contemporary problems and developments in the field of information together with recommendations for practical action." The Council considered the rapporteur's report in 1954 and asked the Secretary-General to study in greater detail certain of the problems raised. In 1955, the Council considered the studies prepared by the Secretary-General and adopted resolutions appealing to governments to cease censoring peace-time news dispatches and to facilitate the unrestricted transmission of news by telecommunications services.

Further work was carried out by a five-member committee which the Commission on Human Rights appointed in 1957 to review the work of the United Nations and the specialized agencies in the field of freedom of information. The Committee's report dealt, among other things, with the development of information media in under-developed countries, the free circulation of information, and the rights and responsibilities of information media.

Prevention of Discrimination and Protection of Minorities

In 1946, the Commission on Human Rights established a Sub-Commission on Prevention of Discrimination and Protection of Minorities to make studies and recommendations. The Sub-Commission is composed of eighteen persons selected by the Commission, subject to the consent of their governments. Members serve in their capacity as individuals and not as representatives of their governments.

Since 1952, the Sub-Commission has been studying concrete aspects of discrimination in various walks of life: discrimination in education; discrimination in employment and occupation; discrimination in the matter of religious rights and practices and in the matter of political rights; discrimination in respect of the right of everyone to leave any country, including his own, and to return to his country; discrimination against persons born out of wedlock; equality in the administration of justice; and racial discrimination in the political, economic, social and cultural spheres.

The study of discrimination in education was initiated by the Sub-Commission in 1952. Following upon this study, which was completed in 1956, the General Conference of UNESCO adopted, on December 14, 1960, a Convention and a Recommendation against discrimination in education.

On the initiative of the Sub-Commission, the United Nations in 1953 requested the International Labour Organisation to undertake a study of discrimination in employment and occupation. As a result of the study, the ILO adopted, on June 25, 1958, a Convention and a Recommendation concerning discrimination in respect of employment and occupation, which entered into force on June 15, 1960. Each member state ratifying this Convention undertakes "to declare and pursue a national policy designed to promote, by methods appropriate to national conditions and practice, equality of opportunity and treatment in respect of employment and occupation, with a view to eliminating any discrimination in respect thereof."

The Sub-Commission has also completed its studies of discrimination in the matter of religious rights and practices and in the matter of political rights, discrimination in respect of the right of everyone to leave any country, including his own, and to return to his country, discrimination against persons born out of wedlock, and equality in the administration of justice. In 1965, the Sub-Commission decided to undertake, in the light of the United Nations Declaration on the Elimination of All Forms of Racial Discrimination, a special study of racial discrimination in the political, economic, social and cultural spheres.

In January 1960, the Sub-Commission expressed its deep concern over the manifestations of anti-Semitism and other forms of racial prejudice and religious intolerance which had occurred in various countries late in 1959 and early in 1960.

In a resolution based on recommendations of the Sub-Commission and of the Commission on Human Rights, the General Assembly in 1960 condemned these manifestations as violations of the United Nations Charter and the Universal Declaration of Human Rights and called upon states to take all necessary measures to prevent such acts.

The following year, the Sub-Commission, and later the Commission, studied the question further on the basis of information obtained from governments, from UNESCO and from non-governmental organizations in consultative status.

At its seventeenth session, in 1962, the General Assembly, reiterating its condemnation of all manifestations of racial prejudice and of national and religious intolerance, called upon the governments of all states to take all necessary steps to rescind discriminatory laws and to adopt legislation, if necessary, to combat such prejudice and intolerance. The Assembly also requested the Economic and Social Council to ask the Commission on Human Rights to prepare, for the Assembly's consideration, a draft declaration and a draft convention on the elimination of all forms of racial discrimination and a draft declaration and a draft convention on the elimination of all forms of religious intolerance.

The United Nations Declaration on the Elimination of All Forms of Racial Discrimination was unanimously adopted by the General Assembly in 1963. Two years later, the International Convention on the Elimination of All Forms of Racial Discrimination was adopted by the Assembly and was opened for signature on March 7, 1966.

The draft declaration and the draft convention on the elimination of all forms of religious intolerance are still under consideration.

Declaration of the Rights of the Child

The General Assembly, on November 20, 1959, unanimously adopted a Declaration of the Rights of the Child. While many of the rights and freedoms were already included in the Universal Declaration of Human Rights, it was thought that the special needs of the child justified a separate declaration. The preamble to the Declaration states that the child, by reason of his physical and mental immaturity, needs special safeguards and care before as well as after birth. It also affirms that mankind owes to the child the best it has to give. Parents, individuals, voluntary organizations, local authorities, and governments are all called upon to recognize the rights and freedoms set forth in the Declaration and to strive for their observance by legislative and other measures.

In ten principles, the Declaration affirms the right of all children, without any exception whatsoever, to enjoy special protection and to be given opportunities and facilities to enable them to develop in a normal and healthy manner and in conditions of freedom and dignity; to have a name and a nationality from birth; to enjoy the benefits of social security, including adequate nutrition, housing, recreation and medical services; to receive special treatment, education and care, if handicapped physically and mentally; to grow up in an atmosphere of affection and security and, wherever possible, in the care and under the responsibility of their parents; to receive education; to be protected against all forms of neglect, cruelty and exploitation; and to be protected from practices which may foster racial, religious or any other form of discrimination. Finally, the Declaration emphasizes that the child shall be brought up "in a spirit of understanding, tolerance, friendship among peoples, peace and universal brotherhood and in full consciousness that his energy and talents should be devoted to the service of his fellow men."

Promotion Among Youth of the Ideals of Peace, Mutual Respect and Understanding Between Peoples

By a resolution of December 7, 1965, the General Assembly adopted a Declaration on the Promotion among Youth of the Ideals of Peace, Mutual Respect and Understanding between Peoples. The Declaration proclaims six principles which state, in particular: that the purpose of promoting these ideals is to secure equal rights for all human beings and nations, economic and social progress, disarmament and international peace; that education should be designed to bring peoples closer together and acquaint the young with the purposes and principles of the United Nations; that young people should be brought up in the knowledge of the equality of man, without distinction of any kind, and in respect for human rights and the right of peoples to self-determination; that international exchanges, travel, the study of foreign languages and the like among young people should be encouraged in order to bring them together in educational, cultural and sporting activities; that national and international associations of young people should be encouraged to promote the purposes of the United Nations, and that youth organizations should facilitate the free exchange of ideas; and finally, that a major aim in educating young people, both within and outside the family, should be the development of higher moral qualities, based on respect and love for humanity and its creative achievements, coupled with an awareness of their responsibilities in the world they will be called upon to manage.

Periodic Reports on Human Rights

In 1956, the Economic and Social Council, acting on a recommendation of the Commission on Human Rights, initiated a system of periodic reports on human rights. Members of the United Nations and of the specialized agencies were asked to submit, every three years, reports describing developments and progress achieved and measures taken by them in the field of human rights. The reports were to deal with "the rights enumerated in the Universal Declaration of Human Rights and the right to self-determination and independence." Since 1962, the non-governmental organizations in consultative status with the Economic and Social Council have been invited to submit comments and observations on the situation in the field of human rights.

Three series of reports have so far been completed, covering the periods 1954-1956, 1957-1959 and 1960-1962, respectively.

In 1965, the Council, acting on recommendations submitted by the Commission following its consideration of the third series of periodic reports, noted that, while the situation throughout the world with regard to human rights and fundamental freedoms continued to be unsatisfactory, particularly in connection with the policy of *apartheid* and the widespread racial, ethnic and religious discrimination throughout the world, the reports contained useful information indicating that some progress had been achieved in the protection of human rights. The Council noted that measures, including the conclusion of multilateral and regional agreements among member states, had been taken by various countries to eliminate or prohibit discrimination, particularly discrimination based on race or sex; to protect the rights of suspects and defendants in criminal procedures; to repeal provisions concerning various kinds of compulsory labour; to extend, increasingly, social insurance coverage to the agricultural population; to apply social insurance protection to workers and employees who are citizens of a foreign state; to improve conditions of work by widening the scope of minimum wage laws, shortening working hours and lengthening statutory vacations at full pay; and to make education more widely available by the extension of tuition-free instruction or by assistance to cover students' expenses by grants or loans repayable after graduation.

The Council expressed its concern that, despite its decision which called upon member states to submit reports on developments in the field of human rights relating, *inter alia*, to the right to self-determination and the right to independence, no information regarding the implementation of these rights had yet been received from states administering dependent territories.

Under the revised system of periodic reporting on human rights adopted by the Council in 1965, members of the United Nations or of the specialized agencies are invited annually, rather than triennially, to supply information on human rights and fundamental freedoms in the territories subject to their jurisdiction. The reports are to be submitted within a continuing three-year cycle, scheduled as follows: (*a*) in the first year, on civil and political rights, (*b*) in the second year, on economic, social and cultural rights, and (*c*) in the third year, on freedom of information.

The Secretary-General is requested, in accordance with the usual practice in regard to human rights communications, to forward any material received from non-governmental organizations which mentions states members of the United Nations or members of the specialized agencies, to those states for any comments they may wish to make.

An *ad hoc* Committee was established, composed of eight members of the Commission on Human Rights, to study and evaluate the periodic reports and other information received under the terms of the Council's resolution, and, in the light of the comments, observations and recommendation of the Commission on the Status of Women and of the Sub-Commission on Prevention of Discrimination and Protection of Minorities, to submit to the Commission on Human Rights comments, conclusions and recommendations.

Studies of Specific Rights or Groups of Rights

In 1956 the Council authorized the Commission on Human Rights to make studies of specific rights or groups of rights. The studies were to stress "general developments, progress achieved, and measures taken to safeguard human liberty," and they were to contain conclusions or recommendations of a general and objective character.

The first subject chosen for study was the right of everyone to be free from arbitrary arrest, detention and exile (article 9 of the Universal Declaration).

A study committee appointed by the Commission submitted its report to the Commission in 1961. The report contains comparative analyses of constitutional provisions concerning arrest, detention and exile; the grounds on which, and the procedures in accordance with which, a person suspected or accused of a criminal offence may be arrested; rights and privileges of a person under arrest or detention; remedies and sanctions against arbitrary arrest and detention; provisions relating to arrest and detention under civil and administrative laws; arrest and detention in emergency or exceptional situations; and laws relating to exile.

In 1961 also, the Commission decided to make a study of the right of arrested persons to communicate with those with whom it is necessary for them to consult in order to ensure their defence or to protect their essential interests, and charged the Committee with the making of this study also.

Advisory Services in the Field of Human Rights

In 1953 and 1954, the General Assembly, in three separate resolutions, authorized the Secretary-General to assist governments, at their request, in promoting and safeguarding the rights of women; in eradicating discrimination; in protecting minorities; and in promoting freedom of information. In 1955, the Assembly incorporated these provisions in a comprehensive resolution on advisory services in the field of human rights.

Three forms of assistance are now authorized: advisory services of experts; fellowships and scholarships; and seminars. Services are rendered at the request of governments on any human rights subject, provided it is not one for which adequate assistance is already available through the existing technical assistance programmes or from one of the specialized agencies.

The programme is designed to give governments an opportunity to share their experiences and to exchange knowledge on the promotion of human rights.

As the programme has developed, emphasis has been laid on the organization of seminars on various human rights problems. The seminars, whose participants are persons of high standing in various professions and services, make possible an exchange of experience in the protection of human rights to the end that each country may benefit from the experience of the others.

Human rights fellowships awarded under the programme are designed to meet the need for comparison of experience at a somewhat different level than through seminar discussions. These awards give recipients opportunities to observe institutions, practices and policies concerning human rights at the working level and on a day-to-day basis, so that the knowledge gained can be related to comparable practices in the fellows' own countries.

From very small beginnings—the first award was made in 1956 and the second in 1961—the programme has been increased by recommendations of the Commission on Human Rights, the Economic and Social Council and the General Assembly, so that about forty fellowships are now awarded every year to candidates nominated by the governments of member states.

Communications Concerning Human Rights

The United Nations receives each year several thousand communications concerning human rights from individuals and groups in all parts of the world. In conformity with a decision of the Economic and Social Council, the Secretariat forwards copies of these communications to the governments concerned, without, however, disclosing the identities of the authors except with their consent. Whether a government takes action on a communication thus forwarded is entirely at its own discretion.

The Secretariat also prepares confidential lists of the communications for the information of the Commission on Human Rights and the Commission on the Status of Women.

Yearbook on Human Rights

The United Nations publishes a *Yearbook on Human Rights,* containing constitutional provisions, legislative acts, executive orders and judicial decisions having a bearing on human rights in states, both members and non-members of the United Nations, and in trust and non-self-governing territories. It also includes international agreements concerning human rights.

STATUS OF WOMEN

The Commission on the Status of Women, established in 1946, is composed of member states of the United Nations and, like the Commission on Human Rights, is a functional commission of the Economic and Social Council. The membership of the Commission on the Status of Women was originally fifteen, but was later enlarged to eighteen and expanded to twenty-one in 1961. Its mandate is primarily to prepare recommendations and reports to the Economic and Social Council on promoting women's rights in political, economic, civil, social and educational fields.

Political Rights

Political rights are particularly important for women because only through participation in the legislative, executive and judicial organs of government can women obtain equality in other fields. At the time of the signing of the Charter, women had political rights in only half of the sovereign countries in the world. By 1966, over 100 countries had granted women full political rights, and those sovereign states of the world where women did not have the right to vote and were not eligible for election numbered only nine; in five countries, women's rights to vote and/or their eligibility to hold public office were subject to certain limitations not imposed on men. The overwhelming majority of new nations which have emerged in recent years have embodied in their constitutions or legislation provisions according political rights to men and women on equal terms.

The Commission on the Status of Women has taken several measures to ensure and to promote equal political rights for men and women. Of these, the most important is the Convention on the Political Rights of Women, which was adopted by the General Assembly in December 1952. This Convention is the first instrument of international law aimed at the granting and the protection of women's rights on a world-wide basis. It ensures that in those countries which are parties to the Convention, women shall have the right to vote, to be eligible for election, to hold public office and to exercise all public functions, on equal terms with men. The Convention was opened for signature in March 1953, and entered into force on July 7, 1954. By the end of 1965, forty-six countries had ratified or acceded to the Convention.

Education

The Commission on the Status of Women has also been deeply concerned with the question of the access of women to education. In cooperation with UNESCO and ILO, it has promoted the access of girls and women to education at all levels, to the teaching profession, and to vocational guidance and technical and professional training. It has advocated free and compulsory primary education for all, special measures to eliminate illiteracy among women and the development of programmes of adult education for women. The Commission has always expressed interest in those programmes of UNESCO which are of special importance to women, such as the various projects aimed at increasing the access of girls and women to education, particularly in the developing countries.

Economic Rights

The question of equal pay for equal work has figured prominently in the work of the Commission on the Status of Women. Collaboration between the ILO and the United Nations resulted in an ILO Convention and a Recommendation, adopted in 1951, on equal remuneration for work of equal value for men and women workers. The Commission, through the Economic and Social Council, has repeatedly urged the acceptance by governments of the principle of equal pay and has encouraged non-governmental organizations to influence public opinion on the subject.

The Commission and the Council have also concerned themselves with vocational and technical training opportunities, vocational guidance, age of retirement and conditions of employment for women, and have urged governments to avail themselves of services provided by technical assistance programmes in these fields.

Another question considered by the Commission has been the access of women to training and employment in the principal professional and technical fields. A report by the Secretary-General on the availability of opportunities for women jurists, architects and engineers was considered by the Commission in 1959, and another report on selected occupations in the principal professional and technical fields was discussed by the Commission in 1961.

In a resolution adopted in 1961, the Council called upon member states to pay special attention to the problems concerning the employment of women, to take all possible steps to promote, for women who desire to work, opportunities to obtain employment in accordance with their qualifications and abilities, and to take the necessary measures to eliminate restrictions on the right of women to work, including married women and women about to marry. Special aspects of the employment of women—including handicrafts and cottage industries, part-time work, work for older women, and the situation of working women with family responsibilities—have been considered by the Commission and the Council on the basis of reports prepared by the ILO and by the Secretary-General.

In the field of tax legislation applicable to women, the Economic and Social Council has supported the position taken by the Commission on the Status of Women that legislation should provide for equal treatment of men and women in regard to taxation of earned income, and that governments should ensure that married persons do not pay tax on earned income at a higher rate than that applied to single persons.

Private Law

The status of women under laws dealing with the family and with property rights of women has been extensively studied by the Commission on the Status of Women, which recommended that governments ensure the equality of rights and duties of spouses in conformity with the principle enunciated in Article 16 of the Universal Declaration of Human Rights. This recommendation has been adopted by the Council, as have specific recommendations made by the Commission for equality between parents in the exercise of rights and duties with respect to their children; for the right of a married woman to have a domicile independent of that of her husband; for the right of a married woman to engage in work without her husband's authorization; for statutory matrimonial régimes affording women equal rights with respect to separate or common property during marriage and equitable sharing of property at dissolution of marriage; for the application of the principle of equality to inheritance laws; and for equality of rights between men and women in the event of dissolution of marriage, annulment of marriage or judicial separation.

Certain ancient laws and customs relating to marriage and the family have been viewed by the Commission as impediments to the attainment of women's basic rights as contemplated in the United Nations Charter and in the Universal Declaration of Human Rights. Thus, the General Assembly in 1954 urged all states, including those administering trust and non-self-governing territories, to take measures to abolish such customs, ancient laws, and practices as child marriage and brideprice; to guarantee widows custody of their children and freedom to remarry; to ensure the right freely to choose a spouse; and to establish civil registers for marriages and divorces.

The Commission studied the question of marriage, especially from the point of view of the requirement of free consent of both parties, the minimum age of marriage, and the registration of marriages, and prepared texts of a draft convention and a draft recommendation on these subjects. On November 7, 1962, the Convention on Consent to Marriage, Minimum Age for Marriage and Registration of Marriages was adopted by the General Assembly, and on December 10, 1962, was opened for signature. It provides that no marriage shall be entered into without the full and free consent of both parties; that states parties shall undertake to prescribe a minimum age for marriage; and that all marriages shall be registered by a duly constituted authority. The Convention came into force on December 9, 1964. By March 1966, it had been ratified by seventeen states.

The Recommendation on Consent to Marriage, Minimum Age for Marriage and Registration of Marriages was adopted by the General Assembly in November 1965. Its substantive provisions are essentially similar to those of the Convention. One important difference is that a specific minimum age of fifteen years is mentioned in the Recommendation below which no person may legally enter into marriage. The Recommendation also introduces a reporting system whereby member states are requested to report, initially at the end of three years and thereafter at intervals of five years, on their law and practice with regard to the matters dealt with in the Recommendation. The reports of member states will be examined by the Commission on the Status of Women, which is invited to make recommendations on them to the Economic and Social Council.

Nationality of Married Women

Since its inception in 1946, the Commission on the Status of Women has been concerned with the problem of the nationality of married women. Its efforts in this field resulted in the preparation of the Convention on the Nationality of Married Women, which was adopted by the General Assembly in January 1957. The Convention was opened for signature in February 1957 and came into force on August 11, 1958. Under it, marriage to an alien shall not automatically affect the nationality of the wife; special privileged naturalization procedures are provided, however, for a wife who wishes to take the nationality of her husband. By March 1966, thirty-one states had become parties to the Convention.

Draft Declaration on the Elimination of Discrimination Against Women

Recognizing both the considerable achievement made in recent years and the distance which remains to be covered before women can contribute fully to the life of their country, the General Assembly, in 1963, unanimously adopted a resolution requesting the Economic and Social Council to invite the Commission on the Status of Women to prepare a draft declaration on the elimination of discrimination against women. The Commission has worked on the preparation of the draft declaration at two sessions, in Teheran in 1965 and in Geneva in 1966. At the latter session, the Commission unanimously adopted the text of a draft declaration for consideration by the Economic and Social Council and the General Assembly. The draft declaration contains substantive provisions dealing with political rights of women, nationality, civil law, penal law, education, and economic rights and opportunities.

United Nations Assistance for the Advancement of Women

An important development for the advancement of women in recent years was the adoption of a resolution by the General Assembly in 1962 calling for the study of the possibility of providing new resources for the establishment of a long-term programme for the advancement of women, with particular emphasis on women in developing countries. This study has been undertaken by the Secretariat in co-operation with the Commission on the Status of Women and with governments, specialized agencies, UNICEF and non-governmental organizations. After consulting governments, specialized agencies, UNICEF and non-governmental organizations, a first step in the study was to review existing resources for the advancement of women under United Nations programmes of technical co-operation and under programmes of non-governmental organizations.

Another report prepared by the Secretariat contains a number of suggestions concerning a unified long-term programme for the advancement of women, relating specifically to the establishment of goals to be achieved through such a programme, the determination of the special needs and problems of women in relation to these goals and in relation to economic and social development, and the intensification of action to meet these needs and overcome these problems.

Advisory Services

Under the advisory services programme (*described on page* 363), in addition to the award of fellowships to women, eight regional seminars have been organized on topics of interest to women. Four of these seminars, held in Bangkok (1957), Bogotá (1959), Addis Ababa (1960) and Ulan Bator (1965), dealt with the participation of women in public life. The other four, held in Bucharest (1961), Tokyo (1962), Bogotá (1963) and Lomé (1964), have dealt with the subject of the status of women in family law.

Questions Concerning Trust and Non-Self-Governing Territories

At the end of the Second World War, almost one quarter of the world's population lived in dependent territories. International interest in the welfare of dependent peoples led to the inclusion in the United Nations Charter of special provisions recognizing that their political, economic, social and educational advancement were the concern of the world community.

In Chapter XI, entitled "Declaration regarding Non-Self-Governing Territories," the Charter lays down the basic principles which are to be observed in the administration of all dependent territories. Specifically, states members of the United Nations responsible for the administration of territories whose peoples have not yet attained a full measure of self-government recognize the principle that the interests of the inhabitants are paramount and accept as a sacred trust the obligation to promote their well-being to the utmost. To this end, they accept the obligation, among others, to develop self-government, to take due account of the political aspirations of the peoples and to assist them in the progressive development of their free political institutions. In order to keep the international community informed of progress in the territories, the administering members also accept the obligation to transmit regularly to the Secretary-General "for information purposes, statistical and other information of a technical nature relating to economic, social and educational conditions in the territories for which they are respectively responsible."

Apart from the general principles and obligations which were intended to apply to all dependent territories, the Charter also established an International Trusteeship System for the administration and supervision of such territories as may by agreement with the United Nations be placed under it.

Trusteeship agreements subsequently signed for eleven territories which had either been former mandates or ex-enemy territories accounted for about 20 million people living in dependent territories. This left more than 200 million people who were, in principle, subject to the provisions contained in the Declaration regarding Non-Self-Governing Territories. Although the Charter envisages that non-self-governing territories may be voluntarily placed under international trusteeship, no such action has ever been taken. The Trusteeship Council has been concerned only with the trust territories, while the General Assembly itself took steps to establish procedures for the consideration of questions relating to non-self-governing territories. Although there still remained, ten years after the establishment of the United Nations, 100 million people in dependent territories, in the 1950's the movement towards the attainment of independence began to accelerate. Thus, from 1952 onwards, the General Assembly repeatedly requested the administering authority of each trust territory except Somaliland to include in its annual reports information on the measures taken or contemplated to lead the territory to self-government or independence within the shortest possible time and to establish intermediate target dates as well as a final time limit for the attainment of that objective. Increasingly also, decisions by the General Assembly on questions relating to trust and non-self-governing territories influenced and in turn were influenced by the changing world attitude towards colonialism.

In 1960, with the admission to the United Nations of seventeen new members, all of which had been former dependent territories, the General Assembly gave further impetus to this movement by the adoption of a Declaration on the Granting of Independence to Colonial Countries and Peoples. In this Declaration, the Assembly proclaimed the necessity of bringing a speedy and unconditional end to all forms of colonialism. The Declaration states that inadequacy of political, economic, social and educational preparedness should never serve as a pretext for delaying independence, and that immediate steps should be taken in trust and non-self-governing territories and all other territories which have not yet attained independence to transfer all powers to the peoples of those territories, without any distinction as to race, creed or colour, in order to enable them to enjoy complete independence and freedom.

This Declaration, together with the principles of the Charter, including those in Chapters XI, XII and XIII, provide the framework within which the United Nations seeks to encourage the accelerated advance of dependent peoples towards the goal of freedom and self-government or independence.

THE INTERNATIONAL TRUSTEESHIP SYSTEM

The objectives of the International Trusteeship System are: to further international peace and security; to promote the political, economic, social and educational advancement of the inhabitants of the trust territories, and their progressive development towards self-government or independence, in accordance with the circumstances of each territory and the wishes of its people; to encourage respect for human rights and fundamental freedoms for all, and to encourage recognition of the interdependence of the peoples of the world; and to ensure equal treatment in social, economic and commercial matters for all members of the United Nations and their nationals, and equal treatment for the latter in the administration of justice, provided this does not conflict with the attainment of the other objectives of the Trusteeship System.

The Trusteeship System can apply to territories formerly held under League of Nations mandates; territories taken from enemy states as an outcome of the Second World War; and others voluntarily placed under the Trusteeship System.

Trusteeship agreements must state the terms under which the trust territories are to be administered and must state what authority is to administer them. The administering authority can be a single state, a group of states or the United Nations itself.

The functions of the United Nations with regard to the trust territories are carried out by the General Assembly and, under its authority, by the Trusteeship Council, except in areas designated as strategic. The functions of the United Nations with regard to strategic areas are carried out by the Security Council, with the assistance of the Trusteeship Council.

By the end of 1949, eleven trusteeship agreements had been approved by the General Assembly. Ten of the trusteeship agreements concerned the following territories: Nauru, administered by Australia, on behalf of Australia, New Zealand and the United Kingdom; New Guinea, administered by Australia; Ruanda-Urundi, administered by Belgium; Cameroons and Togoland, administered by France; Somaliland, administered by Italy; Western Samoa, administered by New Zealand; and Cameroons, Tanganyika and Togoland, administered by the United Kingdom. The eleventh, the Trust Territory of the Pacific Islands, composed of the former Japanese-mandated islands of the Marshalls, Marianas (with the exception of Guam) and Carolines, is a strategic trust territory administered by the United States under an agreement approved by the Security Council in April 1947.

By the end of 1962, only three trust territories remained—New Guinea, Nauru and the Pacific Islands—the others having reached the Charter's goal of self-government or independence.

The regular supervision by the Trusteeship Council of the administration of the trust territories takes the form of an annual review of conditions in each territory based, in the first instance, on the annual report submitted by the administering authority in reply to a questionnaire adopted by the Trusteeship Council and containing detailed information on political, economic, social and educational conditions in the territories concerned. The procedure for the examination of these reports covers a number of distinct stages: (1) an opening statement by the special representative of the administering authority; (2) questions by Council members to the special representative for further explanation of points in the reports; (3) replies of the special representative; (4) general debate on the report, with expression of views and conclusions on conditions in the territory; (5) formulation, on the basis of these views, of conclusions and recommendations by a drafting committee of the Council; and (6) consideration and approval by the Council of the drafting committee's report. The recommendations thus adopted by the Council are included in its annual report to the General Assembly (or to the Security Council); the report also contains an outline of conditions in each territory and the observations of individual members of the Council.

Whenever a particular territory has recently been visited by a United Nations mission, the report of the mission is examined by the Trusteeship Council at the same time as the report of the administering authority. Since 1948, a periodic visit has been arranged to each trust territory every three years.

The visiting missions, which are composed of two persons nominated by member states administering trust territories and two persons nominated by member states which do not do so, submit reports on all main and some detailed aspects of conditions in the territory visited, with special attention to subjects in which the Council or the General Assembly has shown particular interest. In addition to regular missions, special missions dealing with important constitutional matters have been dispatched, for example, to Western Samoa in 1947 and to Togoland under French administration in 1957.

The Council also takes into consideration, during its annual review of conditions in trust territories, petitions concerning those territories. Some of these have been presented orally by petitioners who have requested hearings.

The General Assembly, for its part, regularly reviews progress in the territories through its examination of the annual report submitted to it by the Trusteeship Council. In recent years, the Assembly has also had before it the reports of the Special Committee on the Situation with regard to the Implementation of the Declaration on the Granting of Independence to Colonial Countries and Peoples (Special Committee of Twenty-Four), which have included chapters on the trust territories. As a result of its examination, the Assembly has adopted a number of resolutions on the trust territories as a whole and on individual trust territories.

In addition to its principal function of examining conditions in the trust territories, the Trusteeship Council has undertaken the study of a number of other questions relating to the operation of the international trusteeship system, such as rural economic development in trust territories; the abolition of discriminatory laws and practices and of corporal punishment in trust territories; the participation of indigenous inhabitants of trust territories in the work of the Trusteeship Council; and the preparation and training of indigenous civil cadres in the trust territories.

In accordance with procedures set out in Council resolutions, the Secretary-General annually submits reports on the dissemination, in trust territories, of information on the United Nations and the international trusteeship system, as well as on offers by United Nations member states of study and training facilities for inhabitants of trust territories.

The attainment by the trust territories of the objectives of the international trusteeship system, namely, self-government or independence, has been of primary importance to the Trusteeship Council and the General Assembly. Before 1960, when the Assembly adopted the Declaration on the Granting of Independence to Colonial Countries and Peoples, the Assembly and the Council had pressed for the establishment of intermediate target dates and final time limits for the attainment of the objectives of the trusteeship system in the trust territories. The adoption of the Declaration, which also applied to the trust territories, has caused particular attention to be directed to political advancement in the territories. This interest is shared by the Assembly's Special Committee of Twenty-Four, which also examines the situation in the trust territories. Co-operation is maintained between the two organs.

Former Trust Territories

TOGOLAND UNDER BRITISH ADMINISTRATION.					In 1955, the Trusteeship Council sent a special mission to Togoland under British administration to investigate the question of that territory's future. The mission submitted proposals to the General Assembly, which, in December 1955, resolved that a plebiscite—the first ever to be held in a trust territory—should be conducted in British Togoland to determine whether the people desired a union with the neighbouring Gold Coast (then about to attain independence) or wished to continue under trusteeship, pending an ultimate settlement of the territory's future.

The plebiscite, under United Nations supervision, took place on May 9, 1955. The resulting poll showed a vote of 93,365 favouring union with an independent Gold Coast and 67,422 supporting the alternative choice. The General Assembly approved the union and resolved that the trusteeship agreement should cease to have effect when the administering authority had taken the necessary steps to bring it about. The territory was united with the Gold Coast to form the new independent state of Ghana on March 6, 1957. Ghana became a member of the United Nations two days later.

TOGOLAND UNDER FRENCH ADMINISTRATION. Following the grant in 1956 of a new constitution to Togoland under French administration, a plebiscite was organized by the administering authority to ascertain the wishes of the people regarding their future. The result showed that a majority was in favour of autonomy within the French Union, as opposed to continued trusteeship. However, following discussions in the United Nations, it was decided that general elections should be held in the territory under United Nations supervision. Accordingly, a Commissioner for the elections, with United Nations observers, supervised the elections, which were held on April 27, 1958. A government in favour of independence was returned and the way thus opened for the termination of trusteeship.

In a resolution adopted on November 14, 1958, the General Assembly noted that the Governments of France and of the Republic of Togoland had mutually agreed that Togoland should attain independence on April 27, 1960. The Assembly resolved that the trusteeship agreement for the territory would be terminated on that date, and recommended that, upon attainment of independence, French Togoland should be admitted to the United Nations. Togo became a member of the United Nations on September 20, 1960.

CAMEROONS UNDER FRENCH ADMINISTRATION. In March 1959, the General Assembly voted to end the trusteeship agreement for the Cameroons under French administration. The Assembly, at the same time, expressed confidence that elections for a new Legislative Assembly in the country would be held as soon after the termination of the trusteeship agreement as possible and recommended that the Cameroons under French administration be admitted to the United Nations when it became independent. This was achieved on January 1, 1960, and the former trust territory, now the Republic of Cameroon, was admitted to United Nations membership on September 20, 1960.

CAMEROONS UNDER BRITISH ADMINISTRATION. Plebiscites to determine the future of the Cameroons under British administration were recommended by the General Assembly at its resumed thirteenth session, in March 1959. The Assembly took this step in order to give the inhabitants of the former German territory of Kamerun, estimated in mid-1959 at 1,632,000, an opportunity to express their wishes as to their future when Nigeria, with which the trust territory had been administered as an integral part, achieved independence on October 1, 1960. To this end, the Assembly decided that separate plebiscites should be held in the northern and southern sections of the trust territory. The plebiscites were to be conducted by the United Kingdom, as the administering authority, and supervised by the United Nations.

The first of the plebiscites took place in the Northern Cameroons in November 1959. The voters were asked if they wished the Northern Cameroons to be part of the Northern Region of Nigeria when the Federation of Nigeria became independent, or whether they favoured deciding the future of their country at a later date. Of the total votes cast, 70,546 were in favour of the second alternative and 42,788 were in favour of the first.

Since political leaders in the Southern Cameroons could not agree on such matters as the questions to be asked at the plebiscite, or the qualifications for voting, the General Assembly at its fourteenth session, in 1959, decided to defer consultation with the people to a time not later than March 1961. The Assembly also recommended that the administering authority, in pursuance of Article 76 b of the Charter and in consultation with the United Nations Plebiscite Commissioner, organize under United Nations supervision a further plebiscite in the Northern Cameroons during the same period as that for the Southern Cameroons. In both plebiscites, which took place on February 11 and 12, 1961, the voters were asked whether they wished to achieve independence by joining the independent Federation of Nigeria or whether they wished to achieve independence by joining the independent Republic of Cameroon.

The results of the two plebiscites showed that a majority of the voters in the Northern Cameroons wished to join the independent Federation of Nigeria, while in the Southern Cameroons a majority was in favour of joining the independent Republic of the Cameroon.

At its resumed fifteenth session, the General Assembly, on April 21, 1961, decided that the trusteeship agreement concerning the Cameroons under British administration should be terminated with respect to the Northern Cameroons on June 1, 1961, upon its joining the Federation of Nigeria; and with respect to the Southern Cameroons, on October 1, 1961, upon its joining the Republic of Cameroon.

SOMALILAND UNDER ITALIAN ADMINISTRATION.   In accordance with the Trusteeship Agreement of 1950, Somaliland was to become a sovereign independent state on December 2, 1960. By 1956, an elected Legislative Assembly, possessing wide legislative powers, and a cabinet system of government had been established. Elections were held early in 1959 for a new assembly, which was empowered to draw up a constitution for independent Somalia. The constitution was approved at the end of May 1960 and, in accordance with a resolution of the General Assembly at its fourteenth session, the country became independent on July 1, 1960, five months in advance of the date set by the trusteeship agreement. The Republic of Somalia— which includes not only the former trust territory of Somaliland but also the former British Protectorate of Somaliland—became a member of the United Nations on September 20, 1960.

TANGANYIKA. When elections were held in Tanganyika for the first time in 1958 and 1959, they were based on a system whereby the three main racial communities in Tanganyika were granted equal representation among the unofficial members of the Legislative Council. In 1960, reforms introduced in the electoral system and in the composition of the Legislative Council abolished the system of racial representation and created a legislature composed almost exclusively of elected representatives.

At its resumed fifteenth session, in April 1961, the General Assembly was informed that full internal self-government had been introduced in Tanganyika on May 1, 1960, and that Tanganyika would become a fully independent state in December 1961. During its sixteenth session, in 1961, the Assembly resolved, in agreement with the administering authority, that the trusteeship agreement should cease to be in force when Tanganyika became an independent state on December 9, 1961. It was admitted to membership in the United Nations on December 14, 1961.

WESTERN SAMOA. In 1959, a cabinet system of government was introduced into Western Samoa and the first prime minister was elected. During the same year, a working committee on self-government was established to consider the constitutional problems involved in the transition to independence, and in October 1960, a Constitutional Convention agreed upon a constitution submitted by the working committee.

A resolution adopted by the General Assembly in 1960 set forth the basis for a plebiscite to be held in Western Samoa under United Nations supervision; the questions to be put to the voters were:

"(1) Do you agree with the constitution adopted by the Constitutional Convention of October 28, 1960?

"(2) Do you agree that on January 1, 1962, Western Samoa should become an independent state on the basis of that constitution?"

The plebiscite, under United Nations supervision, took place on May 9, 1961. The final results of the plebiscite showed that 83 per cent of the people who voted were in favour of the constitution and 79 per cent were in favour of the independence of Western Samoa.

On October 18, 1961, the Assembly endorsed the results of the plebiscite and resolved that the trusteeship agreement for Western Samoa should cease to be in force on January 1, 1962, when Western Samoa became an independent sovereign state.

RUANDA-URUNDI. By 1960, communal elections on the basis of adult male suffrage had been held in Ruanda-Urundi. A provisional government was established in Ruanda, and six departments headed by indigenous commissioners were established in Urundi. The administering authority (Belgium) announced its intention of holding national elections in January 1961 on the basis of universal adult suffrage for the purpose of constituting national assemblies for Ruanda and Urundi, and invited the General Assembly to send a mission to observe the elections. The Assembly recommended, in December 1960, that a conference fully representative of political parties be held early in 1961 before the elections. It set up a three-man Commission for Ruanda-Urundi to attend the political conference and to supervise the elections, as well as the preparatory measures preceding them.

The Commission attended a conference in Ostend, Belgium, early in January 1961, on the future of Ruanda-Urundi, but a *coup d'état* in Ruanda at the end of that month made the implementation of the recommendations of the General Assembly infinitely more difficult. The Assembly re-examined the situation in April 1961, reaffirmed its previous resolutions on Ruanda-Urundi and decided that the elections, as well as the referendum on the question of the Mwami of Ruanda, should be held in August 1961, under United Nations supervision.

Elections were held in Burundi (vernacular for Urundi) on September 18, 1961, under United Nations supervision, and a government was formed on September 28. On October 13, the Prime Minister was assassinated, and the United Nations Commission was requested by the General Assembly to carry out an investigation.

In Ruanda, the elections, as well as the referendum on the Mwami, were held under United Nations supervision on September 25, 1961. The results of the referendum gave a four-to-one vote against the retention of the institution of the Mwami. As a result, the new legislature established a republican régime in Ruanda. Following its consideration of these events, the General Assembly, in February 1962, set up a five-member Commission to ensure the achievement, with the full co-operation of the administering authority and national authorities, of certain essential objectives before independence.

The General Assembly reconvened in June 1962 to consider the report of the Commission and, as a result, decided, in agreement with the administering authority, to terminate the trusteeship agreement for Ruanda-Urundi on July 1, 1962, on which date Rwanda and Burundi emerged as two independent and sovereign states. The two states were admitted to membership in the United Nations on September 18, 1962.

Remaining Trust Territories

NAURU.   Nauru, an island in the central Pacific, is administered by Australia on behalf of the joint administering authority of Australia, New Zealand and the United Kingdom. It has an area of 5,263 acres, two thirds of which contain extensive phosphate deposits, and in 1965 it had an estimated population of 5,561, consisting of 2,734 Nauruans, 1,481 other Pacific Islanders, 900 Chinese and 446 Europeans. The other Pacific Islanders (mostly Gilbertese), the Chinese and the majority of the Europeans are employed by the British Phosphate Commissioners.

The Trusteeship Council has been concerned with the future of the Nauruans ever since 1949. Both the Council and the administering authority are aware of the necessity of ensuring the continued well-being of the Nauruans when the phosphate deposits become exhausted in some thirty years' time. The Trusteeship Council has endorsed the efforts the Australian Government has been making, in consultation with the Nauruan leaders, to find another island on which the Nauruans could settle on terms suitable to them. It has also stressed the need for a larger degree of self-government for Nauruans through the granting of greater responsibilities to the Nauru Local Government Council.

Early in 1965, the Nauruan leaders rejected an offer of resettlement on an island off the Australian coast principally because the offer did not include provision for Nauruan sovereignty, which the Nauruans believe is necessary to preserve their national identity. The Nauruan leaders announced that, since no acceptable alternative was available, they had decided to stay on Nauru. However, at a conference held in Canberra in June 1965, it was agreed that the administering authority, in co-operation with Nauruan representatives, would actively pursue any proposals that might give promise of enabling the Nauruan people to resettle on a basis acceptable to them.

Most of the other major issues were also considered at the Canberra conference. The administering authority agreed to a Nauruan proposal that Legislative and Executive Councils be established by January 31, 1966, but could not agree to the granting of independence two years later, on January 31, 1968. It proposed instead that further political progress should be discussed after two or three years' experience of the new constitutional system. The administering authority also agreed to increase the royalty rates paid on phosphate and to set up an expert committee to investigate the feasibility of rehabilitating the worked-out phosphate land.

At its twentieth session, in 1965, the General Assembly reaffirmed the inalienable right of the people of Nauru to self-government and independence, called upon the administering authority to take immediate steps to implement the proposal of the representatives of the Nauruan people regarding the establishment of a Legislative Council by January 31, 1966, and requested the administering authority to fix the earliest possible date, but not later than January 31, 1968, for the independence of the Nauruan people in accordance with their wishes and to take immediate steps towards restoring the island of Nauru for habitation by the Nauruan people as a sovereign nation.

NEW GUINEA. The Trust Territory of New Guinea, administered by Australia, consists of the north-eastern part of the island of New Guinea, north of the Papuan and east of the West Irian border, the islands of the Bismarck Archipelago and the two northernmost islands of the Solomon Group, namely Buka and Bougainville. It has a land area of approximately 92,160 square miles. In 1965, its indigenous population was estimated at more than 1,550,000 and the non-indigenous, mostly Australians and Chinese, at 16,500.

The Trust Territory and the Territory of Papua are administered jointly under the Papua and New Guinea Act, 1949-1964. Recent legislation has provided for the reconstruction of the Administrator's Council and for the establishment of the House of Assembly.

The Administrator, appointed by the Governor-General, administers the Government of the Territory on behalf of the Australian Government. He is assisted by an Administrator's Council consisting of the Administrator himself, three official members and seven elected members of the House of Assembly. The House of Assembly, which has begun to play an important role in the life of the Territory, consists of sixty-four members, fifty-four of whom are elected on a common roll by adult suffrage; the remaining ten are official members. Of the elective seats, forty-four are open to candidates of all races and ten are special seats reserved to non-indigenous inhabitants. Following elections held in February and March 1964, the House of Assembly met for the first time in June 1964. A Select Committee of ten has been established to draft constitutional proposals to serve as a guide for future constitutional development in the Territory.

Elected local government councils have continued to grow in numbers and in total membership. At the end of June 1965, there were seventy-two, covering a population of approximately 880,000. This represents an increase of thirty-four over the previous four-year period. In addition, there is an advisory council in each district, as well as advisory councils in nine of the principal towns.

The Trusteeship Council in 1965 noted a tendency for more rapid advancement in the representative institutions than in executive organs and considered that a greater effort should be made to promote indigenous persons already in the public service to positions of authority. The Council believed that preparation for fully responsible government should be one of the principal tasks of the Select Committee on a constitution. It also recommended that the functions and responsibilities of the local government councils be extended as they grow in experience, so as to give the people further opportunity to exercise self-government in local matters.

In 1963, a mission from the International Bank for Reconstruction and Development (IBRD) conducted a comprehensive economic survey of the territory, the economy of which is based primarily upon subsistence agriculture, with production of copra, cocoa, coffee and rubber. Its report, which was presented to the administering authority in 1964, included detailed recommendations for economic growth in the next five years, the main ones of which the administering authority has accepted. The IBRD mission believed that acceleration of the process of development towards the goal of economic viability would require greater participation and involvement of the inhabitants and greater financial support from the administering authority, which has been subsidizing two thirds of the territorial budget.

The Trusteeship Council suggested, in 1965, that the administering authority draw a complete and balanced plan for economic development in New Guinea, which would provide for direct participation by the indigenous inhabitants of the territory. To this end, the Council suggested that technical training and the system of apprenticeship should be further advanced and every effort made to establish secondary industries. The Australian Government has appointed an economic adviser to give particular attention to economic planning for the territory and has accepted programmes, recommended by the Bank's mission, in agriculture, livestock and forestry as a working basis for planning over the next five years.

With regard to education, administration and mission primary schools have been registering notable increases in indigenous enrolments, and secondary education is being further developed with the setting up of more technical, teacher-training and other specialist schools. Following a recommendation by a Higher Education Commission which was appointed to study the potentialities for the development of higher education in the territory, a university and an institute of higher technical education were scheduled to begin operation in the Territory by 1967. Meanwhile, the status of the Papuan Medical College is being raised and there are plans for the further development of other institutions of higher education, including the agricultural college at Vudal and the administrative college and co-operative college in Port Moresby.

The General Assembly, in 1965, reaffirmed the inalienable right of the people of New Guinea and Papua to freedom and independence, noted that the administering authority had not yet taken sufficient steps towards the full implementation of the Trusteeship Agreement for New Guinea and of the Declaration on the Granting of Independence to Colonial Countries and Peoples and, to this end, called upon the administering authority to fix an early date for independence in accordance with the freely expressed wishes of the people.

TRUST TERRITORY OF THE PACIFIC ISLANDS.   The United States-administered Trust Territory of the Pacific Islands, comprising some 2,100 islands of varying sizes scattered throughout a vast area of some three million square miles in the Western Pacific north of the equator, has a total land area of only 700 square miles. Only ninety-five of the islands are inhabited; they are classified into three groups, the Marianas, excluding Guam, in the north, the Carolines in the south and the Marshalls in the east. In 1964, the territory had a population of 88,215, classed as Micronesians.

The Trusteeship Council has welcomed the action taken by the administering authority to promote political advancement at the district or local level but has expressed concern at the lack of territorial consciousness. To this end, it has urged the administering authority to transfer the centre of administration from Guam to a place within the Trust Territory and to establish a territorial legislature. In 1962, the administrative headquarters was established at Saipan and a twelve-member advisory body, the Council of Micronesia, was established. In 1965, on the recommendation of this body, a territory-wide Congress of Micronesia was inaugurated. The Congress is bicameral, consisting of two houses—a General Assembly of twenty-one members, elected on a population basis, and a House of Delegates of twelve, elected on a district basis.

In 1965, the Trusteeship Council referred to this development as the greatest single step forward in political development in the history of the territory. At the same time, it urged the administering authority to intensify its efforts to expand Micronesian control over and participation in the executive, now that a territorial legislature had come into existence. It also called for an extension of the powers of the legislature and expressed the hope that steps would be taken to enlarge the financial responsibility of the Congress of Micronesia by progressively relaxing restrictions on its power to appropriate the United States subsidies.

In recent years, the Trusteeship Council has recommended the formulation of an over-all and long-term economic development plan, the setting up of adequate machinery to execute such a plan and the association of Micronesians with the planning process at every stage.

The economy of the territory is based primarily upon subsistence agriculture, fishing and the making of copra. Government employment and the manufacture of handicrafts provide some supplementary cash income. Since 1963, funds made available annually to the territory by the administering authority have more than doubled, amounting to more than $18 million in 1965. In the same year, the administering authority engaged a private consulting firm to undertake a two-year economic development programme for the territory. A Resources and Development Department has recently been established to co-ordinate activities in such fields as economic development, co-operatives, credit unions, agriculture, fisheries, forestry, land management and transportation.

Considerable progress has been achieved through the education system, which provides free public schooling from the elementary stage through high school, with advanced training in agriculture, commerce and industry. However, the Council, noting the steady increase in both secondary school enrolment and in the numbers of Micronesian students attending institutions of higher learning abroad, asked that renewed consideration be given to the establishment of a junior college of Micronesia.

On the future of the territory in general, the Council, in 1965, reaffirmed the inalienable right of the people of the trust territory to self-determination (including the right to independence) in accordance with the Charter and with the Declaration on the Granting of Independence to Colonial Countries and Peoples. It urged the administering authority, in consultation with the Congress of Micronesia and in the light of the Charter and the Declaration on the Granting of Independence, to draw up realistic plans and programmes reflecting a proper sense of urgency for the rapid and planned advance of the territory in all aspects of its political life.

QUESTIONS RELATING TO
NON-SELF-GOVERNING TERRITORIES

Because Chapter XI of the Charter carries the title "Declaration regarding Non-Self-Governing Territories," the first questions which arose were how its provisions should be implemented and what responsibilities the United Nations had in relation to the inhabitants of such territories. Under Article 73 e, administering members accept the obligation to transmit regularly to the Secretary-General statistical and other information relating to economic, social and educational conditions in the territories. The application and interpretation of Chapter XI and the obligations involved have been determined mainly by decisions taken by the General Assembly relating to this obligation.

Although, in the early years, the discussions on non-self-governing territories were mainly concerned with establishing procedures for the transmission and examination of information, the underlying issue was the question of the competence of the General Assembly regarding non-self-governing territories.

Broadly speaking, discussions in the period before 1960 can be divided into three phases. In the first phase, covering the period approximately from 1946 to 1949, the General Assembly adopted decisions defining the scope, nature and procedures relating to the transmission of information under Article 73 e. In the second phase, covering approximately the period from 1949 to 1955, the Assembly established its competence to examine the information transmitted by the administering members and to make recommendations on conditions in the territories. In the third phase, the Assembly asserted its competence to determine when the obligation to transmit information could cease, and also to determine whether an obligation exists to transmit information.

Transmission of Information under Article 73 e

Early in 1946, at the first session, the General Assembly, declaring itself "keenly aware of the problems and political aspirations of the peoples who have not yet attained a full measure of self-government and who are not directly represented here," drew attention to the fact that the obligations under Chapter XI of the Charter were in force. In response, Australia, Belgium, Denmark, France, the Netherlands, New Zealand, the United Kingdom and the United States enumerated seventy-four territories on which they would transmit information. These territories varied in size and political status: the territories enumerated by the United Kingdom included colonies and protectorates; those enumerated by France included overseas territories, overseas departments and associated states; and the Cook Islands were enumerated without prejudice to the fact that they were "an integral part" of New Zealand.

Subject to reservations made by some of the members regarding the status of some of their territories and by other members regarding questions of sovereignty, the 1946 list had the effect of establishing the practical scope of Chapter XI: only the territories enumerated were, in effect, non-self-governing territories within the meaning of the Charter. As Portugal and Spain were not members of the United Nations, the question of their colonies did not arise at that time. Up to the end of 1959, no new territories were added to those enumerated in 1946, for although Portugal and Spain became United Nations members at the end of 1955, it was not until 1960 that the territories under their administration came to be included as non-self-governing territories. That year, the Assembly, having completed a special study on the obligations under Chapter XI, took note of Spain's declaration that it would send information to the Secretary-General; at the same time, the Assembly decided that the Portuguese overseas territories were non-self-governing within the meaning of the Charter and asked Portugal to transmit information accordingly. Portugal, however, maintained, and has continued to maintain, that as the territories named are overseas provinces and are an integral part of the Portuguese nation, it has no obligations under Chapter XI.

The territories enumerated by the General Assembly in 1946, the territories listed by the Assembly on December 15, 1960, and the territories declared to be non-self-governing by the Assembly after 1960, are shown on the following pages.

A. TERRITORIES ENUMERATED
BY THE GENERAL ASSEMBLY IN 1946

Australia

Cocos (Keeling) Islands[a]
Papua

Belgium

Belgian Congo (Republic of the Congo—1960) *

Denmark

Greenland (1954)

France

French Equatorial Africa:
Chad (1960) *
Gabon (1960) *
Middle Congo (Congo, Brazzaville—1960) *
Ubangi Shari (Central African Republic—1960) *
French establishments in India (1947)
French establishments in Oceania (1947)
French Guiana (1947)
French Somaliland (1957)
French West Africa:
Dahomey (1960) *
French Guinea (Guinea—1958)*
French Sudan (Mali—1960) *
Ivory Coast (1960) *
Mauritania (1960) *
Niger Colony (1960) *
Senegal (1960) *
Upper Volta (1960) *
Guadaloupe and dependencies (1947)
Indo-China (1947) [b]
Madagascar and dependencies (including Comoro Archipelago) (Malagasy Republic—1960) *
Martinique (1947)
Morocco (1956) *

New Caledonia and dependencies (1947)
New Hebrides under Anglo-French Condominium
Réunion (1947)
St. Pierre and Miquelon (1947)
Tunisia (1956) *

Netherlands

Netherlands Indies (Indonesia—1949) *
Netherlands New Guinea (West Irian) (1962)
Netherlands Antilles (Curaçao) (1951) *
Surinam (1951) [c]

New Zealand

Cook Islands (1965)
Niue Island
Tokelau Islands

United Kingdom

Aden Colony and Protectorate
Bahamas
Barbados (1966) *
Basutoland (Lesotho—1966) *
Bechuanaland Protectorate (Republic of Botswana—1966) *
Bermuda
British Guiana (Guyana—1966) *
British Honduras
British Somaliland (Somalia—1960) * [d]
Brunei
Cayman Islands[e]
Cyprus (1960) *
Falkland Islands
Fiji
Gambia (1965) *
Gibraltar
Gilbert and Ellice Islands Colony

Note: The dates in parentheses show the year of accession to independence ( ) * or other change in status as a result of which information was no longer sent to the Secretary-General.

Gold Coast Colony and Protector-
ate (Ghana—1957) *
Hong Kong
Jamaica (1962) *
Kenya (1963) *
Leeward Islands: [f]
 Antigua
 St. Kitts-Nevis-Anguilla
 Montserrat
 British Virgin Islands
Malayan Union (Federation of
 Malaya—1957) * [g]
Malta (1964) * [h]
Mauritius
Nigeria (1960) *
North Borneo (1963) [i]
Northern Rhodesia (Zambia—
 1964) *
Nyasaland (Malawi—1964) *
Pitcairn Islands
St. Helena and dependencies
Sarawak (1963) [j]
Seychelles
Sierra Leone (1961) *

Singapore (1963) [k]
Solomon Islands Protectorate
Swaziland
Trinidad and Tobago (1962) *
Turks and Caicos Islands[1]
Uganda (1962) *
Windward Islands:
 Dominica
 Grenada
 St. Lucia
 St. Vincent
Zanzibar (1963) *

United States of America

Alaska (1959)
American Samoa
Guam
Hawaii (1959)
Panama Canal Zone (1947)
Puerto Rico (1952)
Virgin Islands
 of the United States

[a] Originally administered as part of Singapore.
[b] Comprising Cambodia, Laos and Viet-Nam.
[c] The Assembly approved the change in status in 1955.
[d] British Somaliland with the Trust Territory of Italian Somaliland became independent as Somalia.
[e] Originally administered as part of Jamaica.
[f] The group of islands was enumerated in 1946 as one territory.
[g] In 1963, joined North Borneo, Sarawak and Singapore to form Malaysia.
[h] Information on this territory was not transmitted in the period from 1947 to
1959.

The enumeration of territories on which the administering members would transmit information led to a discussion on what should be
done with the information. Some administering members suggested
that it was clear from the Charter that the information was "for information purposes" and that no further action by the General Assembly
was necessary. Other members recalled that the intention at San Francisco was to keep the international community informed of conditions
in the territories; they suggested that the reports sent by the administering members should be made available to all members. Following
this suggestion, the Assembly, in the latter part of 1946, asked the
Secretary-General to summarize and analyse the information and established an *ad hoc* Committee, composed of an equal number of administering members and non-administering members, to recommend
procedures to be followed.

The *ad hoc* Committee, which met in 1947, reviewed the infor-

B. TERRITORIES LISTED BY THE GENERAL ASSEMBLY
ON DECEMBER 15, 1960

Spain

Fernando Póo[m]   Río Muni[m]
Ifni   Spanish Sahara

C. TERRITORIES DECLARED TO BE NON-SELF-GOVERNING
BY THE GENERAL ASSEMBLY SINCE 1960

1. *Territories under Portuguese administration as declared by the General Assembly on December 15, 1960:*

Angola, including the enclave of   Macau and dependencies
Cabinda   Mozambique
Cape Verde Archipelago   São João Batista de Ajuda[o]
Goa and dependencies[n]   São Tomé and Príncipe
Guinea (called Portuguese Guinea)   Timor and dependencies

2. *Territory under United Kingdom administration declared by the General Assembly on June 28, 1962 to be a non-self-governing territory:*

Southern Rhodesia

[i] In 1963, North Borneo (Sabah) joined the Federation of Malaya, Sarawak and Singapore to form Malaysia.
[j] In 1963, joined the Federation of Malaya, North Borneo and Singapore to form Malaysia.
[k] In 1963, joined the Federation of Malaya, North Borneo and Sarawak to form Malaysia. Singapore became a separate independent state in 1965.
[l] Originally administered as part of Jamaica.
[m] In 1963, Fernando Póo and Río Muni merged and were named Equatorial Guinea.
[n] Nationally united with India in December 1961.
[o] Nationally united with Dahomey in August 1961.

mation which had been transmitted by the administering members. As the information received from different members varied both in scope and in form, the Committee drew up a list of major headings and sub-headings relating to economic, social and educational conditions on which it considered it would be desirable to have detailed and comparable information from all administering members. In addition, it recommended that information should also be included on geography, history, people, government and human rights, which had been transmitted by some members. Although Article 73 e describes the information to be transmitted as "statistical and other information relating to economic, social and educational conditions," it was suggested that as the goal of advancement of the dependent territories is "full self-government," it was necessary for the United Nations also to receive information on constitutional and political developments. This view did not, however, prevail.

In 1947, the Assembly adopted the list of headings of a Standard Form for the guidance of members in preparing information transmitted under Article 73 e, with the additional information as optional. In 1948, although information on government was retained as an optional category in the Standard Form, the Assembly invited all administering members voluntarily to include political information in their annual reports.

The administering members have continued to follow procedures relating to the transmission of information under Article 73 e as approved by the General Assembly. Each year administering members transmit to the Secretary-General the most recent information at their disposal on all the non-self-governing territories for which they are responsible. They are asked to provide full information on all headings in the Standard Form every three years and, in the two intervening years, statistical information showing the changes that have taken place. In addition, the administering members make available to the Secretary-General other official publications for use in preparing the summaries and analyses required by the Assembly.

Among the original eight administering members, Australia, Denmark, the Netherlands, New Zealand and the United States have always included information on government institutions in their territories, and France transmitted information concerning changes in the constitutional status of its territories. Belgium, on the other hand, provided information only on economic, social and educational conditions. In 1961 and 1962 the United Kingdom voluntarily transmitted to the Secretary-General special information on political and constitutional developments.

Examination of Information Transmitted under Article 73 e

In addition to its recommendations on the form and content of the information to be transmitted under Article 73 e, the ad hoc Committee, in 1947, also proposed that the General Assembly establish a special committee to examine the information. Some administering members expressed reservations as to the right of the Assembly to do so as there were no Charter provisions to this effect. The Assembly, however, accepted the suggestion of the ad hoc Committee and set up a Special Committee with an equal number of administering and non-administering members to meet in 1948 to examine and to report on the economic, social and educational conditions in the non-self-governing territories.

In 1948, in spite of reservations of a legal nature of some of the administering members as to the competence of the Assembly, the Special Committee recommended to the Assembly that a similar Committee meet again the next year. In 1949, the Assembly established, on a three-year basis, the Special Committee on Information transmitted under Article 73 e of the Charter; the Special Committee was renewed in 1952, in 1955, when it was renamed the Committee on Information from Non-Self-Governing Territories, and in 1958.

Following the practice adopted in 1947, the Committee on Information from Non-Self-Governing Territories was always composed of the administering members transmitting information and an equal number of non-administering members, elected by the Fourth Committee on behalf of the Assembly, on as wide a geographical basis as possible. Representatives of the ILO, FAO, WHO and UNESCO also participated in its work. Its terms of reference were "to examine the summaries and analyses of information transmitted under Article 73 e of the Charter on the economic, social and educational conditions." It was also instructed to submit reports to the Assembly containing such procedural recommendations as it deemed fit and such substantive recommendations as it deemed desirable relating to the functional fields generally but not with respect to individual territories.

The Committee adopted the practice of reviewing the conditions in the territories once every three years on the basis of full summaries and in the two intervening years only the changes as shown by relevant statistical data. In addition, after 1950, the Committee adopted the practice of making a special study, in turn, of economic, social and educational problems once every three years. These reports generally covered a wide range of problems in the specific field, and included a consensus of observations and recommendations from the members of the Committee. After approval by the General Assembly, these special reports were sent to the administering members, to the Economic and Social Council, the regional economic commissioners, the Trusteeship Council and the specialized agencies for their consideration. Some of the administering members also sent these special reports to the governments of the territories under their administration.

In 1961, the General Assembly extended the Committee on Information for an indefinite period and also widened its terms of reference to include the examination of political and constitutional information transmitted by administering members, and to submit its observations and recommendations. Whereas previously the Committee had been precluded from making recommendations on individual territories, under its new terms of reference it was instructed to "undertake intensive studies of political, educational, economic and social conditions and problems of territories located in the same area or region, except where circumstances required individual consideration."

Because of its terms of reference, most of the Committee's work was concerned with economic, social and educational conditions in the territories, with a view to bringing about improvements which would enable the people to participate more fully in their own self-government. To this end, the Committee over a period of years, with the consensus of the administering members, drew up objectives of policy in each of these three fields which were approved by the General Assembly. On behalf of the Assembly, the Committee also considered and recommended action on problems of special importance in the territories because of their dependent status.

In 1953, the Assembly endorsed the following objectives drawn up by the Committee: to develop moral and civic consciousness and responsibility among the peoples and to enable them to take an increasing share of responsibility in the conduct of their own affairs; to raise the standards of living of the peoples by helping them to improve their economic productivity and standards of health; to promote the social progress of the territories, taking into account the basic cultural values and the aspirations of the peoples concerned; and to secure the extension of the intellectual development of the peoples so as to provide for them access to all levels of culture.

In 1956 and thereafter, the Committee was particularly concerned with the necessity for the expansion of educational facilities to meet the growing needs and aspirations of the inhabitants of the territories. This led the Assembly to recommend to the administering members that they intensify their efforts in all territories and formulate plans, with targets and dates, for providing various facilities and the attainment of established goals, including universal, free and compulsory education and general literacy.

In considering social conditions, the Committee was concerned especially with the problem of racial discrimination and, on the basis of its reports, the Assembly recommended action by governments designed to improve race relations in the territories, particularly, the abolition of all discriminatory laws and statutes and ordinances in force in the territories under their administration. The administering members were invited to include in their annual reports information on the measures taken by them to implement the Assembly's recommendations.

The Assembly also recommended that the administering members immediately rescind or revoke all laws and regulations which tend to encourage, directly or indirectly, discriminatory policies or practices based on racial considerations and that they give immediate effect to the recommendation of the Committee on Information that full political rights, including the right to vote, should be extended to all inhabitants in the territories.

On the basis of the special information requested from administering members, the Assembly, in 1961 and 1962, discussed racial discrimination in non-self-governing territories as a special item on its agenda. In both years, the Assembly reaffirmed its previous recommendations to the administering members and urged them to bring to an end all forms of racial discrimination as a means of contributing towards the implementation of the Declaration on the Granting of Independence to Colonial Countries and Peoples, which it had adopted in 1960 (*see page* 396).

With regard to economic development, the Committee on Information, from the outset, urged the formulation of long-term development plans and programmes for the territories and stressed the importance of government action to set in motion a process of sustained and balanced development supported by material, financial and technical assistance, especially as, in most territories, assistance provided by the administering members was insufficient to launch sustained economic growth. The Committee also stressed that many urgent social reforms were essential parts of economic programmes: populations deficient in health, education and welfare, the Committee noted, might be unable to increase productivity unless a vigorous policy were pursued for the expansion of social and educational services.

In 1955, the Assembly asked the Committee to make an over-all review of the progress made, since the establishment of the United Nations, by the territories towards the goals established by the Charter in Chapter XI. On the basis of this survey, the Assembly, in 1960, noted that in spite of the increased tempo of change, a substantial number of territories were still non-self-governing and that in the great majority of these, the achievements of the period reviewed fell short of the needs of the inhabitants. The Assembly considered that the inadequate level of economic, social and educational development in the territories should never serve as a pretext for deferring their accession to independence, and urged administering members to strengthen their efforts in all fields with the full participation of the indigenous inhabitants by transferring to them effective powers so that during the period of transition to independence the territories would be able to establish sound foundations for their future.

The Obligations under Chapter XI of the Charter

The obligation of administering members to transmit information under Article 73 e has been central to the whole question of the implementation of Chapter XI of the Charter and the political advancement of the territories. The Charter does not, however, specify which are the territories to which Chapter XI applies and who should determine whether or not such an obligation exists; nor does it indicate when the transmission of information may cease once it has been undertaken. For many years, these issues engaged the concern of the General Assembly.

In 1946, the Secretary-General, in drawing the attention of members to the obligations under Chapter XI, invited them, among other things (*a*) to give their opinion on the factors to be taken into account in determining which are the non-self-governing territories referred to in Chapter XI and (b) to provide an enumeration of such territories under their administration. As a wide range of opinion was expressed as to the criteria determining the status of a non-self-governing territory, the Assembly did not pursue the matter at that time but accepted the list of seventy-four territories enumerated by the eight administering members (see page 385).

In 1947, however, information was not transmitted on twelve of the enumerated territories. This led to discussions as to whether the administering members could unilaterally decide to cease transmitting information and when such transmission could cease. Since it was accepted that an obligation to transmit information existed so long as a territory was "non-self-governing," the discussion centred on whether, and in what form, apart from independence, a territory could be said to have attained "a full measure of self-government" and on the competence of the General Assembly to so decide.

In 1953, the Assembly approved a list of factors for use both by itself and by the administering members as a guide in determining whether a territory is or is not within the scope of Chapter XI of the Charter. The Assembly considered that for a territory to be deemed self-governing in economic, social or educational affairs, it is essential that its people shall have attained a full measure of self-government; that "each concrete case should be considered and decided upon in the light of the particular circumstances of that case, and taking into account the right of self-determination of peoples"; that the manner in which a territory can become fully self-governing is primarily through the attainment of independence, although this can also be achieved by union with or association of the territory on an equal footing with other component parts of the metropolitan country, or other countries; and that the validity of any form of association between a non-self-governing territory and a metropolitan, or any other, country depended upon the freely expressed will of the people at the time of the decision.

When, in 1955-1956, twenty states were added to the membership of the United Nations, the Secretary-General, following the procedure adopted in 1946, asked each of the new members to inform him whether they administered any territories whose people had not yet attained a full measure of self-government.

At the Assembly's session in 1956, the Fourth Committee examined the replies received. Albania, Austria, Bulgaria, Cambodia, Ceylon, Finland, Ghana, Hungary, Ireland, Italy, Japan, Jordan, Laos, Libya, Morocco, Nepal, Portugal, Romania, the Sudan and Tunisia replied that they did not have any non-self-governing territories within the meaning of Chapter XI.

The discussions in the Fourth Committee led to a debate on the competence of the Assembly to decide on the application of Chapter XI. Underlying this issue, however, was the question whether Portugal had an international obligation to transmit information on the overseas territories, especially those in Africa. The discussions omitted reference to Spain because no reply had yet been received from that Government.

In 1958, Spain informed the Secretary-General that it possessed no non-self-governing territories, since the territories subject to its sovereignty in Africa were, in accordance with Spanish legislation, considered to be classified as provinces of Spain, but that it would nevertheless, although there was no legal obligation to do so, place the publications on the African provinces of Spain at the disposal of the Secretary-General "for his enlightenment."

By 1959 it had become evident that the movement of colonial peoples towards self-government and independence was gaining pace. Many of the former French territories had by then become autonomous and many other territories were rapidly approaching the goal of self-government or independence. Against this background of events, the Assembly, in 1959, accepted a proposal by the Fourth Committee to set up a committee to study the principles which should guide members in deciding whether or not an obligation exists to transmit information under Article 73 e.

On the basis of that Committee's report, the Assembly, in 1960, adopted a list of twelve principles which should guide members in determining their responsibilities under Chapter XI. It concluded that, *prima facie,* there is an obligation to transmit information in respect of a territory which is geographically separate and is distinct ethnically and/or culturally from the country administering it, and decided that Cape Verde Archipelago; Guinea, called Portuguese Guinea; São Tomé and Príncipe, and their dependencies; São João Batista de Ajuda; Angola, including the enclave of Cabinda; Mozambique; Goa and dependencies, called the State of India; Macau and dependencies; and Timor and dependencies, were non-self-governing territories. It therefore declared that Portugal had an obligation to transmit information on these territories.

Noting also that, in the course of the discussions, Spain had undertaken to transmit information under Article 73 e, the Assembly in 1960 invited the Governments of Spain and Portugal to participate in the work of the Committee on Information from Non-Self-Governing Territories. Portugal, however, has reserved its position as regards this decision of the General Assembly, maintaining that the overseas provinces are an integral part of the Portuguese nation and that the General Assembly has no competence on matters relating to these provinces, which are essentially within its own domestic jurisdiction.

Other Action by the General Assembly

Under Article 73 e of the Charter, United Nations members responsible for the administration of non-self-governing territories accept the obligation "to promote constructive measures of development, to encourage research, and to co-operate with one another and, when and where appropriate, with specialized international bodies with a view to the practical achievement of the social, economic, and scientific purposes set forth." The principle that conditions in the non-self-governing territories are included within the purview of international economic and social co-operation is also indicated in Article 55 of the Charter, which provides that the United Nations shall promote measures of economic and social advancement "with a view to the creation of conditions of stability and well-being which are necessary for peaceful and free relations among nations."

Co-operation as set out in the Charter has developed within the general programmes of the Economic and Social Council and of the specialized agencies, as well as through the regional economic commissions. This co-operation involves, on the one hand, the consideration of conditions in the territories in any relevant study of economic and social problems and, on the other hand, the extension to the territories of international operational programmes of technical co-operation. Since 1950, many of the recommendations of the Economic and Social Council and those of the Assembly on economic and social matters, and particularly those relating to human rights, have included within their scope non-self-governing territories.

The participation of the non-self-governing territories as beneficiaries of the technical assistance programmes of the United Nations received the attention of the Assembly in 1948, and later, in 1950, following the establishment of the Expanded Programme of Technical Assistance, the Assembly invited the administering members which needed technical assistance for the economic, social and educational advancement of their territories to submit their requests under the Programme.

From 1950 onwards, there was a steady increase in the participation of non-self-governing territories in the technical assistance and development programmes of the United Nations and the specialized agencies, the IBRD and the Special Fund.

In recent years, to assist them in their transition, territories approaching independence have received greater attention under the United Nations programmes of technical assistance. Among specialized agencies and other bodies which provide technical services to the territories under their regular programmes are the ILO, FAO, UNESCO, WHO and UNICEF.

The General Assembly has also established programmes of scholarships for providing training for inhabitants of non-self-governing territories. The first of these programmes was established in 1954, when the Assembly invited member states to offer scholarships to students from non-self-governing territories for study and training not only at the university level but also, and in the first place, at the post-primary, technical and vocational levels. There are two other special training programmes, one for South West Africans and one for indigenous peoples of territories under Portuguese administration, both of which also provide scholarships financed by special United Nations allocations.

The General Assembly has on many occasions emphasized the importance of training indigenous inhabitants in the economic, social and educational fields as an integral part of their preparation for self-government. In 1960 and 1961, the Assembly noted that the information submitted showed evidence of a serious shortage of training facilities for personnel of all kinds in the territories, and that existence of adequate personnel was not only indispensable in the effective implementation of plans and programmes of development but also necessary in the transfer of full control of powers in conditions of stability. As the absence of trained personnel had in the past resulted in serious dislocations in certain territories upon their attainment of independence, the Assembly urged the administering members to take immediate steps aimed at the rapid development of training indigenous civil and technical cadres and at replacing expatriate personnel by indigenous officers. The Assembly also urged administering members to take immediately all steps necessary to increase the strength of the indigenous civil and technical cadres at all levels and to accelerate their training.

In the territories nearing independence, there has been a trend towards reorganization of the civil services to provide for the wider participation of the inhabitants, and greater efforts are being made for the provision of the necessary training. In many cases, international assistance has been requested for this purpose.

The General Assembly has also recommended measures aimed at associating the dependent peoples more closely with the work of the United Nations. The two principal recommendations have dealt with the participation of the territories in the work of the United Nations and specialized agencies and the availability to the territories of information on the work of the United Nations concerning non-self-governing territories.

On the recommendation of the Assembly, the participation of non-self-governing territories as associate members in the United Nations regional economic commissions and the specialized agencies had, by 1959, been accepted by most administering members. Associate members participate fully in the work of the subsidiary bodies of the regional commissions and in the discussions in plenary sessions, but normally without a vote.

In 1959, the Assembly requested the administering members to adopt necessary measures for the dissemination of information concerning the United Nations among the inhabitants of the non-self-governing territories and for this purpose to seek the active support and participation of the organizations that were representative of these inhabitants.

The Assembly has been especially concerned that peoples of the non-self-governing territories should have a wider knowledge of the principles and purposes of the United Nations, the Declaration of Human Rights and the Assembly's 1961 resolution calling for the removal of all forms of racial discrimination. It has asked the Secretary-General to ensure the circulation and dissemination of this information and it has also asked the administering members to include such information in the curricula of educational institutions in all the non-self-governing territories. Both the resolution on racial discrimination and the Declaration have been translated into some twenty principal local languages of the administering members, and texts have been printed in the form of leaflets and wallsheets. Special radio talks have also been prepared in as many of the languages as possible and, with the assistance of the administering members, the material has been used in various non-self-governing territories.

DECLARATION ON THE GRANTING OF INDEPENDENCE TO COLONIAL COUNTRIES AND PEOPLES

Adoption of the Declaration

Although some thirty trust and non-self-governing territories had attained self-government or independence in the period up to 1960, there was growing concern among members of the United Nations that the progress towards complete emancipation of many countries and peoples under colonial status was too slow and should be accelerated. This concern was reflected in the statements made by members during debates in the General Assembly, in its Committees and in the Trusteeship Council. It also found expression in decisions of the Assembly since 1952 inviting administering authorities of trust territories to furnish information on measures taken or contemplated to lead the territories to the objective of self-government or independence within the shortest possible time and to establish intermediate target dates as well as a final time-limit for the attainment of that objective.

The concept was expressed in a decision concerning non-self-governing territories for the first time in 1959. By that decision, the Assembly, in reiterating its request to administering members voluntarily to transmit information on political and constitutional developments in the non-self-governing territories under their administration, also requested them to include information on the establishment of intermediate timetables leading to the attainment of self-government.

The concern to accelerate the ending of colonialism culminated, in 1960, in the adoption by the Assembly of the Declaration on the Granting of Independence to Colonial Countries and Peoples.

The proposal to adopt a Declaration was made by N. Khrushchev, Chairman of the Council of Ministers of the USSR, in a statement to the General Assembly in September 1960. He proposed that, in keeping with the principles of its Charter, the United Nations must declare itself in favour of the "immediate and complete elimination of the colonial system in all its forms and manifestations."

The Assembly discussed two draft declarations, one proposed by the USSR, the other by forty-three African and Asian countries. The latter was eventually adopted, in the form in which it was proposed, by 89 votes to 0, with 9 abstentions, as resolution 1514 (XV), on December 14, 1960.

The Declaration solemnly proclaims the necessity of bringing colonialism to a speedy and unconditional end, in all its forms and manifestations, and declares that:

(1) the subjection of peoples to alien subjugation, domination and exploitation constitutes a denial of fundamental human rights, is contrary to the Charter of the United Nations and is an impediment to the promotion of world peace and co-operation;

(2) all peoples have the right to self-determination; by virtue of that right they freely determine their political status and freely pursue their economic, social and cultural development;

(3) inadequacy of political, economic, social or educational preparedness should never serve as a pretext for delaying independence;

(4) all armed action or repressive measures of all kinds directed against dependent peoples shall cease in order to enable them to exercise peacefully and freely their right to complete independence, and the integrity of their national territory shall be respected;

(5) immediate steps shall be taken, in trust and non-self-governing territories or all other territories which have not yet attained independence, to transfer all powers to the peoples of those territories, without any conditions or reservations, in accordance with their freely expressed will and desire, without any distinction as to race, creed or colour, in order to enable them to enjoy complete independence and freedom;

(6) any attempt aimed at the partial or total disruption of the national unity and the territorial integrity of a country is incompatible with the purposes and principles of the Charter of the United Nations;

(7) all states shall observe faithfully and strictly the provisions of the Charter of the United Nations, the Universal Declaration of Human Rights and the present Declaration on the basis of equality,

non-interference in the internal affairs of all states and respect for the sovereign rights of all peoples and their territorial integrity.

The Special Committee

In 1961, one year after the adoption of the Declaration, the Assembly considered the extent to which it had been implemented. In a resolution adopted in November 1961, it noted with regret that, with few exceptions, the provisions of the Declaration had not been carried out and that armed action and repressive measures continued to be taken against dependent peoples. The Assembly called on all states concerned to take action without further delay with a view to the faithful application and implementation of the Declaration. In a major provision of the resolution, the Assembly decided to establish a Special Committee of seventeen members, appointed by the President, to examine the application of the 1960 Declaration and to make recommendations on the progress and extent of its application.

The Committee, known as the Special Committee on the situation with regard to the implementation of the Declaration on the Granting of Independence to Colonial Countries and Peoples, began work in 1962. Enlarged to twenty-four members by the Assembly at the end of 1962, the Special Committee of Twenty-Four, as it is called, has played an important role in the work of the United Nations to acccelerate the process of decolonization.

The seventeen original members of the Special Committee appointed in 1961 were: Australia, Cambodia, Ethiopia, India, Italy, Madagascar, Mali, Poland, Syria, Tanganyika (now part of the United Republic of Tanzania), Tunisia, the USSR, the United Kingdom, the United States, Uruguay, Venezuela and Yugoslavia. The additional members appointed in 1962 were: Bulgaria, Chile, Denmark, Iran, Iraq, Ivory Coast and Sierra Leone. In 1965, Afghanistan was appointed to fill the vacancy caused by the resignation of Cambodia.

According to the terms of the Assembly resolution by which it was established, the Special Committee was requested to examine the application of the Declaration, to make suggestions and recommendations on the progress and extent of the implementation of the Declaration and to report back to the Assembly. It was empowered to establish its own procedures and authorized to meet elsewhere than at Headquarters whenever such meetings were required for the effective discharge of its functions.

In 1962, the Special Committee's mandate was set out in greater detail. In that year, the Assembly invited the Committee to continue to seek the most suitable ways and means for the speedy and total application of the Declaration; to propose specific measures for the complete application of the Declaration; to submit a full report containing recommendations on all the territories mentioned in paragraph 5 of the Declaration; and to apprise the Security Council of any developments in these territories which might threaten international peace and security.

In 1962 also, the General Assembly dissolved the Special Committee on South West Africa and the Special Committee on Portuguese Territories, and transferred their functions to the Special Committee of Twenty-Four, and, at its 1963 session, the Assembly dissolved the Committee on Information from Non-Self-Governing Territories and transferred its functions to the Special Committee. The Special Committee thus became the only United Nations body under the General Assembly concerned with matters relating to dependent territories with the exception of the Trusteeship Council, which is concerned with the three remaining trust territories.

In 1965, the Assembly reiterated the Committee's previous mandate and in addition requested it: (a) to pay particular attention to the small territories and to recommend the most appropriate ways, as well as the steps to be taken, to enable the populations of these territories to exercise fully their rights to self-determination and independence; (b) to recommend a deadline for independence in each territory whenever it considered it appropriate; (c) to apprise the Security Council of any developments in these territories which might threaten international peace and security and to make suggestions which might assist the Council in considering appropriate measures under the Charter.

The Committee examines the implementation of the Declaration in individual territories, the order of priority being decided on the basis of recommendations made by its Working Group, which is composed of the officers of the Committee and four other members.

To assist in its examination of each territory, the Special Committee normally has before it an information paper prepared by the Secretariat describing recent political and constitutional developments as well as current economic, social and educational conditions. This information is derived from published sources and, in relevant cases, from the information transmitted by administering powers under Article 73 e of the Charter. After the Committee has approved them, these information papers are included in its report to the General Assembly as part of the chapters on individual territories.

In addition, the Special Committee requests administering powers to submit information on political and constitutional developments. The Committee hears statements from administering powers, inviting those which are not members of the Committee to participate in its examination of the territories they administer. Petitions are circulated and the Committee may decide to hear petitioners at its meetings. Reservations concerning these proceedings have been expressed by Australia, the United Kingdom and the United States.

At the conclusion of its examination of a territory, the Committee adopts its recommendations in the form of a consensus formulated by the Chairman or by means of a resolution which is adopted by vote. The Committee is empowered by the General Assembly to send out visiting groups to territories in co-operation with administering powers, a procedure which has also been the subject of reservations expressed in the Committee by Australia, the United Kingdom and the United States.

The Committee maintains liaison with other United Nations bodies, such as the Trusteeship Council and the Special Committee on the Policies of *Apartheid* of the Government of the Republic of South Africa. Collaboration with the specialized agencies is maintained through the presence of representatives of ILO, FAO, UNESCO and WHO at the Committee's meetings.

The Committee reports to the General Assembly each year. The general aspects of the Committee's report are considered in the plenary meetings; the chapters on individual territories are referred to the Assembly's Fourth Committee for consideration and report.

The Committee has established a preliminary list of territories to which the Declaration applies. This includes the Trust Territories; the Mandated Territory of South West Africa; all non-self-governing territories on which information is transmitted; territories which the Assembly has declared to be non-self-governing, i.e. the Territories under Portuguese Administration and Southern Rhodesia; and French Somaliland, which the Committee added to its list in 1965.

The Committee normally meets at Headquarters, beginning its work for the year in February and ending at the opening of the Assembly session. As provided for in its mandate, it has held meetings away from Headquarters: in 1962, it met in Dar-es-Salaam, Addis Ababa and Tangier; in 1965, in Lusaka, Dar-es-Salaam and Addis Ababa; and in 1966 in Dar-es-Salaam, Mogadiscio, Addis Ababa, Cairo and Algiers.

Sub-committees have been established by the Special Committee to assist it in its consideration of individual territories, specifically Southern Rhodesia, Aden, British Guiana, Basutoland, Bechuanaland and Swaziland, South West Africa, and the smaller territories. There is also a Sub-Committee on Petitions.

The Special Committee has carried out the functions of the former Committee on Information from Non-Self-Governing Territories in relation to information transmitted under Article 73 e of the Charter in the following ways: at the Committee's request, the Secretariat uses the information transmitted by administering powers in the preparation of information papers on relevant territories, and the Committee takes this information into account when it considers these territories. It also considers questions relating to the transmission of information as a separate item, on the basis of a report by the Secretary-General setting out all the pertinent data, and makes recommendations to the Assembly.

IMPLEMENTATION OF THE DECLARATION

In the two years following the adoption of the Declaration by the Assembly, the following trust and non-self-governing territories attained their independence: Sierra Leone (1961), Tanganyika (1961), Western Samoa (1962), Ruanda-Urundi (as the two states of Rwanda and Burundi, in 1962), Jamaica (1962), Trinidad and Tobago (1962) and Uganda (1962). In addition, in 1961, the northern part of the British Cameroons joined the Federation of Nigeria while the southern part joined the Republic of Cameroon.

Between 1963, when the Special Committee drew up a preliminary list of sixty-four territories to which the Declaration applies, and 1965, six territories attained their independence, three became part of another independent state and one, the Cook Islands, became self-governing in free association with New Zealand. Those which attained independence are: Singapore, which became part of the Federation of Malaysia in 1963 and seceded from it as an independent state in 1965; Kenya in 1963; Nyasaland, which attained independence as Malawi in 1964; Malta in 1964; Northern Rhodesia, which attained independence as Zambia in 1964; and Gambia in 1965. The three joining other independent states were: North Borneo and Sarawak, which became part of the Federation of Malaysia in 1963; and Zanzibar, which joined independent Tanganyika in 1964 and became part of the United Republic of Tanzania. Four more territories, British Guiana, Basutoland, Bechuanaland and Barbados, became independent in 1966.

In its endeavours to ensure the speedy implementation of the Declaration, the Assembly relies to a great extent on the information and recommendations which are included in the reports of the Special Committee. In addition to the action the Assembly itself takes on the question in general and on individual territories, it has given the Special Committee broad terms of reference which have enabled it to take action of its own accord.

The measures taken by the Assembly and the Special Committee have normally been in the form of requests, appeals or recommendations. Most of these have naturally been directed to the administering power itself, but assistance has been sought from the Security Council, the Secretary-General, other member states, the specialized agencies and other international organizations.

The basic appeal to administering powers has been to take immediate steps to implement the Declaration, although in some instances, as in the case of the Portuguese territories, it has been necessary to call upon the administering power to accept the application of the Declaration to its territories. Administering powers have also been requested to co-operate with the Special Committee in other ways, such as by supplying it with information and agreeing to implement specific requests. Apart from these general appeals, specific measures have been called for, according to the situation in each territory. Thus the Special Committee and the Assembly, in relevant territories, have urged or called upon the administering powers to abrogate constitutions which are not representative, to convene fully representative constitutional conferences to devise suitable constitutions, to create representative legislatures, to establish universal suffrage, to apply the principle of "one man, one vote," to hold fresh elections, to repeal repressive and discriminatory legislation, to release political prisoners, to end states of emergency, to cease armed action against the people of the territories, to cease the systematic influx of foreign immigrants and the dislocation and transfer of indigenous inhabitants, and to fix dates for independence.

Emphasis has been placed on United Nations supervision of pre-independence elections and other procedures, such as plebiscites, for consulting the wishes of the people as to their future. The Assembly and the Special Committee have also stressed the importance of visiting groups from the Committee being permitted to visit the territories to collect information and learn at first-hand the wishes of the people.

The response of the administering powers to these requests has been varied. With the exception of Portugal and South Africa, all keep the Committee informed of developments and those who are not members are invited to participate in the Committee's discussions of the territories they administer. Many of the specific requests have not been acceded to, and this has led the Assembly and the Committee in some cases to condemn and deplore the administering power's failure to do so.

New Zealand responded favourably to a recommendation made by the Special Committee in 1964 by inviting the Secretary-General to nominate a person to be present in the Cook Islands on behalf of the United Nations for the elections scheduled for April 1965 and for the debate, in the newly constituted Legislative Assembly, on the constitution which provided for full internal self-government in free association with New Zealand. When the Assembly had approved this arrangement, the Secretary-General appointed a United Nations Representative for the Supervision of the Elections in the Cook Islands. After considering the Representative's report, the Assembly decided that since the Cook Islands had attained full internal self-government, the transmission of information under Article 73 e of the Charter was no longer necessary. It also reaffirmed the responsibility of the United Nations under the Declaration to assist the people of the Cook Islands in the eventual achievement of full independence, if they so wished, at a future date.

The Assembly has expressed concern over the military bases maintained by administering powers in their territories and, in 1965, requested the colonial powers to dismantle military bases installed in colonial territories and to refrain from establishing new ones. Specifically, it called upon South Africa and the United Kingdom to remove their bases from South West Africa and Aden, respectively.

The role of foreign economic interests in the implementation of the Declaration in colonial territories has also been examined by the Assembly. In 1963, the Assembly requested the Special Committee to report on the implications of the mining industry and other international companies having interests in South West Africa. This report was submitted in 1964. Since then, the Special Committee has submitted an interim report on the implications of the activities of foreign economic and other interests impeding the implementation of the Declaration in the territories under Portuguese administration and has begun a similar study on Southern Rhodesia. The conclusions resulting from these studies have led the Assembly to condemn the activities of the foreign companies and to request all states to prevent such activities by their nationals.

The Assembly has also made requests to all states. These include requests to support measures recommended against the illegal government of Southern Rhodesia and the Governments of South Africa and Portugal and to refrain from supplying them with arms and ammunition. The Assembly has also requested all states to assist the people of such territories as Aden, Southern Rhodesia, South West Africa and the Portuguese territories in their efforts to attain freedom and independence.

The plight of refugees from these territories has also been of concern to the Assembly, which has requested international relief organizations and the specialized agencies to render assistance to them. The specialized agencies have also been requested, along with all states, to withhold assistance of any kind to the illegal government of Southern Rhodesia and the Governments of South Africa and Portugal until they renounce their present policies.

The Assembly has also sought the assistance of the Secretary-General in an attempt to find solutions to some of the more difficult colonial problems, such as those of Southern Rhodesia, the territories under Portuguese administration, South West Africa and Aden.

In cases where the Assembly and the Special Committee have felt that the situation resulting from the delay to grant independence in accordance with the Declaration has become explosive and either threatens or is likely to threaten international peace and security, they have drawn it to the attention of the Security Council. Thus, the situations in the Portuguese territories, Southern Rhodesia, South West Africa and Aden have all been brought to the attention of the Security Council. As a result, the Security Council has taken action with respect to the Portuguese territories and Southern Rhodesia. In both cases, however, the action taken has fallen short of what the majority of the Assembly has sought.

Some of the territories with which the Assembly has been concerned have been the subject of conflicting territorial claims. These claims, however, as in the case of the former British Guiana, have not been allowed to stand in the way of the attainment of independence. In other instances, such as Gibraltar, the Falkland Islands (Malvinas), Ifni and Spanish Sahara, the Assembly has requested the parties concerned to negotiate a solution, bearing in mind the wishes or interests of the populations.

Although the Assembly has concentrated its attention on speeding up political development, it has also sought to promote economic, social and educational development in the territories. It has recommended that the administering powers increase assistance to the territorial economies and has requested the specialized agencies to consider increasing financial, economic and technical assistance to many of the territories. The importance of this question with regard to Basutoland, Bechuanaland and Swaziland led the Assembly to establish a fund for their development.

Most of the remaining territories are small in area and population and have limited economic resources. The Special Committee has stated that the Declaration applies to all dependent territories, regardless of their size, population or other factors, and that it is for the people of the territories and for them alone to express themselves freely on the form they wish to adopt to achieve the object of the Declaration. The Assembly has endorsed these views and has decided that the United Nations should render all help to the people of these territories in their efforts freely to decide their future status. The Assembly has also requested the Special Committee to pay particular attention to the small territories and to recommend the most appropriate ways, as well as the steps to be taken, to enable their populations to exercise fully their right to self-determination and independence.

Individual Territories

SOUTH WEST AFRICA.   South West Africa, administered by the Republic of South Africa, is the only remaining League of Nations mandate, all other mandated territories having either become independent or been placed under the international trusteeship system.

The territory covers about 318,000 square miles on the Atlantic coast of southern Africa. Its population of 526,004 (1960) consists of 428,-575 Africans, 73,464 Europeans and 23,965 Basters and other Coloureds. The economy of South West Africa is based chiefly on gem diamonds, copper, lead, zinc concentrates, fisheries, Persian lamb, and cattle.

At its first session, in 1946, the General Assembly was unable to accede to a proposal by South Africa that the mandated territory be incorporated into South Africa and recommended that South West Africa be placed under the trusteeship system. The following year, South Africa informed the United Nations that, in view of the Assembly's position, it had decided not to proceed with the incorporation. It further stated that while it would not place the territory under trusteeship, it would maintain the *status quo* and continue to administer the territory "in the spirit of the existing mandate," and would submit reports on its administration of the territory for the information of the United Nations. South Africa accordingly submitted, in 1947, a report covering its administration of the territory during 1946. Following the examination of that report by the Trusteeship Council, South Africa objected to the method of dealing with the report and claimed that the mandate had lapsed with the dissolution of the League of Nations and that the United Nations had no supervisory authority over the territory. It informed the United Nations, in 1949, that it would submit no further reports.

Consequently, in 1949, the General Assembly asked the International Court of Justice for an advisory opinion on the status of the territory and the obligations of South Africa. On July 11, 1950, the Court gave its opinion that South West Africa remained under mandate and that South Africa was not competent to modify that status except with the consent of the United Nations; that it continued to have international obligations under the mandate, including the obligation to submit annual reports and transmit petitions from within the territory to the United Nations; and that it was not legally obliged to place the territory under the international trusteeship system. Two supplementary advisory opinions, given in 1955 and 1956, dealt with the method of voting in the Assembly and the hearing of petitioners. (*See also page 447.*)

From 1950 to 1957, through various committees, the General Assembly sought by negotiation to reach agreement with South Africa on the implementation of the Court's 1950 advisory opinion. No agreement was reached, however, as the South African Government did not accept the advisory opinion and was unwilling to accept any form of United Nations supervision over the territory's administration. Further efforts at negotiations, from 1957 to 1959, to reach a basis for an agreement which would continue to accord an international status to the territory or to have the territory placed under the trusteeship system also failed to produce a solution acceptable both to the General Assembly and to South Africa.

In the absence of reports from South Africa, the General Assembly, in 1954, began examining conditions in the territory on the basis of annual reports submitted to it by successive committees, which have also examined and reported to the Assembly on petitions relating to South West Africa.

The Committee on South West Africa (1954-1961) observed that the South African Government administered the territory on the basis of a policy of *apartheid*, which was contrary to the mandate, the Charter, the Universal Declaration of Human Rights, the advisory opinions of the International Court of Justice and resolutions of the General Assembly. In 1956, it reported that the situation in the territory required close re-examination by the Assembly, particularly in regard to the failure of the South African Government to co-operate in the implementation of the advisory opinion of the Court concerning the status of the territory. That year, the General Assembly asked the Committee to study the question of legal action open to organs of the United Nations or to states members of the United Nations or of the former League of Nations to ensure that the South African Government fulfilled its obligations under the mandate.

In 1960, after the Assembly had drawn the attention of member states to the conclusions of the Committee on South West Africa covering the legal action open to them to refer any dispute with South Africa concerning the interpretation or application of the mandate to the International Court of Justice for adjudication, the Governments of Ethiopia and Liberia, both former members of the League of Nations, initiated contentious proceedings against South Africa before the International Court, charging that South Africa had violated its obligations under the mandate. In its judgment, delivered on July 18, 1966, the Court found that Ethiopia and Liberia could not be considered to have established any legal right or interest appertaining to them in the subject matter of their claims and that it had accordingly decided to reject them. (*See also page 442*.)

In 1961, the General Assembly proclaimed, and has since reaffirmed, the inalienable right of the people of South West Africa to independence and national sovereignty, and called for the achievement of the following objectives in the territory: the repeal of *apartheid* laws and regulations; preparations for general elections to the territorial Legislative Assembly based on universal suffrage, to be held as soon as possible under United Nations supervision; advice and assistance to the resulting government with a view to preparing the territory for full independence; and the co-ordination of economic and social assistance by specialized agencies to promote the moral and material welfare of the people.

These objectives, among others, were to be achieved in consultation with South Africa by the Special Committee for South West Africa, whose Chairman and Vice-Chairman visited South Africa and South West Africa during 1962 at the invitation of the South African Government. This Committee, which had replaced the Committee on South West Africa, was in turn dissolved at the end of 1962, and its functions were assigned, *mutatis mutandis,* to the Special Committee of Twenty-Four.

The Assembly also recognized the need to ensure the educational advancement of South West Africans and to prepare them for service in the administration of their country. Accordingly, at the Assembly's request, the Secretary-General in 1962 established a special educational and training programme for South West Africans, providing for the granting of fellowships by the United Nations and by individual member states.

In December 1962, the Assembly further requested the Secretary-General to appoint a United Nations Technical Assistance Resident Representative for South West Africa and to take all necessary steps to establish an effective United Nations presence in the territory. However, in 1964, South Africa informed the Secretary-General that it had come to the conclusion that it would be neither necessary nor desirable to make use of any outside expert advice which might be offered by the United Nations. As to the establishment of a United Nations presence in the territory, South Africa recalled that the whole issue of United Nations jurisdiction in South West Africa had long been a subject of unresolved controversy and was in dispute at the International Court of Justice.

Since 1961, both the Assembly and the Special Committee have repeatedly drawn the attention of the Security Council to the situation in the territory as a threat, or potential threat, to international peace and security, a charge disputed and denied by South Africa.

Since 1963, the Assembly and the Special Committee have urged all states which had not yet done so to refrain from supplying arms or military equipment, petroleum or petroleum products to South Africa and to refrain from any action which might hamper the implementation of Assembly resolutions on South West Africa. Both the Assembly and the Committee have also called upon South Africa to remove all bases and other military installations located in the territory and to refrain from utilizing the territory in any way whatsoever as a military base for internal or external purposes.

During 1964, the South African Government endorsed in principle recommendations made by its commission of inquiry into South West African affairs for the establishment of separate "homelands" in South West Africa for ten non-European groups, on a tribal or ethnic basis, and a separate "White area," in which non-Whites would constitute the majority. While deferring its decision on the establishment of such "homelands" pending the outcome of the dispute before the International Court of Justice, the Government decided to proceed with steps preparatory to their establishment and with the implementation of development plans proposed by its commission of inquiry.

In the same year, the Special Committee, viewing the situation with concern, called upon South Africa to desist from implementing the commission's recommendations, which it noted would result in the partition and disintegration of South West Africa and its absorption into South Africa.

When it took up the question in 1965, the Assembly considered that any attempt to partition the territory or to take any unilateral action, directly or indirectly, preparatory thereto constituted a violation of the mandate for South West Africa and of the Declaration on the Granting of Independence; it further considered that any attempt to annex a part or the whole of the territory would constitute an act of aggression. The Assembly condemned the policies of *apartheid* and racial discrimination practised in South West Africa, as it had on a number of earlier occasions, and also condemned the Government's policy of circumventing the political and economic rights of the indigenous people through large-scale settlement of foreign immigrants in the territory and its refusal to co-operate with the United Nations in implementing the Declaration. The Assembly appealed to all states to give the indigenous people of South West Africa all necessary moral and material support in their legitimate struggle for freedom and independence. The Assembly also requested the Security Council to keep watch over the critical situation in the light of the serious threat to international peace and security in that part of Africa.

In 1965, the Assembly also considered a special report submitted to it in 1964 by the Special Committee, concerning the implications of the activities of the mining industry and other international companies having interests in South West Africa. The Committee had found that foreign capital held a dominant position in the economy of the territory and that the main sectors of production were controlled by foreign enterprises or by settlers of European descent. It concluded that the foreign companies operating in South West Africa had no interest in developing a balanced economy there and that the desire of the South African Government to annex the territory was directly connected with the activities of international companies which were interested in keeping the territory as a field for the investment of their capital and a source of raw material and cheap labour.

The Committee recommended, among other measures, that the Assembly call upon the South African Government to take appropriate and urgent steps to put an end to the activities of international companies in South West Africa which were detrimental to the interests of the African population and that the Assembly appeal to all states whose nationals had public or private interests in the international companies in South West Africa to cease giving any support to the South African Government and to exert their influence to put an end to those activities of the international companies.

The Assembly, endorsing the Committee's conclusions and recommendations, condemned the policies of financial interests which exploited human and material resources and impeded the progress of the territory and the right of the people to freedom and independence.

TERRITORIES UNDER PORTUGUESE ADMINISTRATION. The territories under Portuguese administration together cover an area of some 3 million square kilometres with a population, in 1960, of more than 12 million. The largest of these territories are located in Africa and comprise: Angola, on the Atlantic coast, with an area of 1,241,700 square kilometres; Mozambique, on the east coast, with an area of 771,-125 square kilometres; and Guinea, called Portuguese Guinea, on the west coast, between Senegal and Guinea, with an area of 33,667 square kilometres. The other territories are the Cape Verde Archipelago, comprising ten islands off the west coast of Africa; the islands of São Tomé and Príncipe, on the Bay of Bafra; Macão, on the Asian continent; and Timor, consisting of the eastern half of the island of the same name located at the tip of the chain of islands forming the Republic of Indonesia. São João Batista de Ajuda and Goa and dependencies were nationally united in 1961 with Dahomey and India, respectively.

Since 1960, when the Assembly decided that the territories under Portuguese administration are non-self-governing territories, the basic issue before the Assembly has been the question of the compliance of Portugal with its obligations under Chapter XI of the Charter, including the obligation to transmit information called for under Article 73 e and also to recognize the right of the inhabitants of the territories to self-determination and to self-government or independence.

In 1961 and 1962, detailed reports and recommendations were drawn up by the Sub-Committee on Angola, which was set up by the Assembly in April 1961 following consideration by both the Assembly and the Security Council of the situation there, and by the Special Committee on the Territories under Portuguese Administration. Since 1962, through the Special Committee of Twenty-Four, the Assembly has kept the question of the Portuguese territories under continuous review, and since 1963, the Security Council has also been seized of the question.

The seven-member Special Committee on the Territories under Portuguese Administration was established by the Assembly in 1961 to examine, as a matter of urgency, within the context of Chapter XI and relevant Assembly resolutions, available information concerning all the territories under Portuguese administration, and to formulate its observations, conclusions and recommendations for the consideration of the General Assembly and any other body appointed to assist the Assembly in the implementation of the Declaration on the Granting of Independence to Colonial Countries and Peoples.

In the report which it submitted to the Assembly, the Special Committee on the Territories under Portuguese Administration concluded that the basic dissatisfaction of the people in the territories arose from the essentially colonial relationship of the territories with Portugal, which aimed at imposing, on the indigenous population, Portuguese culture and citizenship and which denied them opportunities for the development of their own personalities and the fulfilment of their own aspirations. While Portugal maintained that the territories were "overseas provinces," the majority of the indigenous inhabitants, the Committee found, did not have the same civil and political rights as the inhabitants of Portugal, and in many territories they had been subjected to forced labour practices. The Committee also found that the reforms which Portugal claimed to have introduced since 1961 not only did not meet the basic aspirations of the peoples but had not yet brought about any significant changes in the political, economic, social and educational conditions. Although the special status of the indigenous inhabitants had been abolished, no significant advance had been made in extending political rights to all the peoples.

At its seventeenth session, in 1962, the Assembly had before it the reports of the Special Committee on Territories under Portuguese Administration, the Special Committee of Twenty-Four and the Sub-Committee on Angola. After considering these reports, the Assembly reaffirmed the inalienable right of the peoples of the territories to self-determination and independence and upheld, without any reservations, the claims of those peoples for their immediate accession to independence.

It urged the Portuguese Government to take the following measures: (a) immediate recognition of the right of the peoples of the territories to self-determination and independence; (b) immediate cessation of all acts of repression and the withdrawal of all military and other forces employed for that purpose; (c) promulgation of an unconditional political amnesty and the establishment of conditions that would allow the free functioning of political parties; (d) negotiations, on the basis of the recognition of the right to self-determination, with the authorized representatives of the political parties within and outside the territories with a view to the transfer of power to political institutions freely elected and representative of the peoples; and (e) the granting of independence immediately thereafter to all the territories under its administration in accordance with the aspirations of the peoples.

In a separate resolution on Angola, the Assembly condemned what it described as the "colonial war" carried on by Portugal against the people of Angola and requested the Security Council to take appropriate measures, including sanctions, to secure Portugal's compliance with resolutions of the Assembly and the Security Council.

The Security Council, in July 1963, after having examined the situation in the territories at the request of thirty-two African states, determined that the situation there was seriously endangering peace and security in Africa, endorsed the measures for a peaceful solution recommended in 1962 by the Assembly and called on Portugal to implement them. In November 1965, the Council again affirmed that the situation resulting from the policies of Portugal, both as regards the African population of its colonies and the neighbouring states, was seriously disturbing international peace and security, and it urgently demanded that Portugal carry out the measures that had been recommended.

The Assembly, in a resolution adopted in December 1965, condemned the colonial policy of Portugal and its persistent refusal to carry out these measures.

Position of the Portuguese Government. The position of the Portuguese Government has remained unchanged since the question of the territories under its administration was first raised in 1956. Maintaining that it is a historical fact that Portugal is a unitary state and that constitutionally the overseas provinces together with the European territory form a single nation, Portugal rejects the Assembly's decision that it has responsibilities under Chapter XI for those territories. It considers the Assembly's decision illegal, holding that Chapter XI, as its title indicates, is intended as a unilateral declaration by the member states concerned, a view which it considers is substantiated by the fact that, unlike Chapters IX and X of the Charter, which provide for international economic and social co-operation, and Chapters XII and XIII, which establish the International Trusteeship System, Chapter XI does not establish an international responsibility for the non-self-governing territories. In Portugal's view, the fact that, in 1946, the Assembly invited member states to inform the Secretary-General of the territories on which they would transmit information, and later accepted their enumeration, showed that the Assembly did not consider that it had any competence to decide which are the non-self-governing territories.

Portugal has also denied the charge of colonialism in its overseas territories. It considers that the important factors to be taken into account in determining whether colonialism exists are those deriving from the nature of the juridical, political and economic relations and that if these relations are in keeping with fundamental human rights, the geographical, ethnical and cultural factors have no relevance. According to the Portuguese view, the Assembly's decisions did not take into account the true situation, namely the existence of a multi-racial civilization, in the Portuguese overseas territories. The Portuguese position is that there is no racial discrimination in these provinces and that the Portuguese electoral law is exactly the same for all citizens and all have the same opportunity to vote. Portugal has also stated that, in keeping with its traditional policy, it has continued to introduce measures for economic, social and political progress and that the disturbances which had been brought to the attention of the United Nations had never affected more than a small part of the territories concerned and, because they had been stimulated from the outside, did not represent the genuine desire of the people.

For all of these reasons, Portugal considers that the Assembly resolutions go beyond the provisions of the Charter and are therefore illegal, and it has refused to participate in the special committees appointed by the Assembly to examine conditions in the territories.

Requests to Member States and International Institutions. Both the Assembly and the Security Council have requested member states to use their influence with a view to securing the compliance of Portugal with its obligations under the Charter. In 1963, the Security Council requested all states to refrain from offering the Portuguese Government any assistance which would enable it to continue its repression of the peoples of the territories under Portuguese administration, and to take all measures to prevent the sale and supply of arms and military equipment for this purpose to the Portuguese Government. In 1965, the Council widened this request to member states by asking them also to stop the sale or shipment of equipment and materials for the manufacture or maintenance of arms and ammunition.

The Assembly later reaffirmed this request to member states and in particular to the military allies of Portugal within the framework of the North Atlantic Treaty Organization. On the basis of the conclusions of a study, by the Special Committee, of foreign economic and other interests in the territories under Portuguese administration, the Assembly in 1965 also requested all states to prevent activities on the part of their nationals in the foreign financial interests which are an impediment to the attainment by the people of their legitimate rights of freedom and independence. It further urged member states to break off trade, transport and diplomatic relations with Portugal.

In addition to these measures, the Assembly has requested all states and international institutions, including the specialized agencies of the United Nations, to withhold assistance of any kind from the Government of Portugal until it renounces its policy of colonial domination and racial discrimination.

SOUTHERN RHODESIA. Southern Rhodesia is a land-locked area of 150,333 square miles, situated in south central Africa. Its estimated population of nearly 4,330,000 includes 4,080,000 Africans, 224,000 Europeans, 13,000 Coloured and 8,100 Asians. The economy of the territory consists of a relatively developed and diversified European market economy and a rural African subsistence economy. Under the territory's land laws, certain lands are open only to particular races. Southern Rhodesia was first administered by the British South African Company under a Royal Charter granted in 1899. Company administration ended in 1923, when the United Kingdom Government annexed Southern Rhodesia to the Crown and granted the settlers internal self-government, retaining only certain reserved powers affecting, in particular, African interests and constitutional amendment. In 1953, Southern Rhodesia, with Northern Rhodesia and Nyasaland, became part of the Central African Federation; the Federation was dissolved in 1963.

In a referendum held in July 1961, the Southern Rhodesian electorate, consisting almost entirely of Europeans, approved proposals for a new Constitution which had been agreed upon with the United Kingdom Government. The new Constitution, which was promulgated in December 1961, abolished most of the reserved powers held by the United Kingdom Government, provided a new franchise system and granted to the legislature a general power to amend the Constitution. Under the new franchise system, fifty of the sixty-five members of the Legislative Assembly were to be elected from 'A' roll constituencies and fifteen from 'B' roll electoral districts. The franchise was limited to adults with certain property, income or educational qualifications, those for the 'A' roll being higher than those for the 'B' roll. Under this system, there was a preponderance of Europeans on the 'A' roll, and of Africans on the 'B' roll; most Africans were entirely excluded.

The question of Southern Rhodesia was first raised in the United Nations shortly after the promulgation of the new Constitution when the Assembly, early in 1962, requested the newly established Special Committee on the Situation with Regard to the Implementation of the Declaration on the Granting of Independence to Colonial Countries and Peoples to consider whether Southern Rhodesia had attained a full measure of self-government. In June 1962, after the Special Committee had considered the question and on its recommendation, the Assembly affirmed that Southern Rhodesia was a non-self-governing territory within the meaning of Article 73 e of the Charter.

In so doing, the Assembly also affirmed that the United Kingdom, as administering power, was responsible to the United Nations under the terms of the Charter and the Declaration on the Granting of Independence for ensuring that the people of Southern Rhodesia were enabled to exercise their right of self-determination and to achieve independence in accordance with their freely expressed wishes. The Assembly, and the Special Committee, have therefore directed requests to the United Kingdom Government to take action to achieve these objectives as soon as possible. It has also sought assistance from other states and from the Security Council.

Requests to the United Kingdom. The basic request, which was formulated in 1962 and has been reiterated many times since then, is that the United Kingdom should suspend the 1961 Constitution and call a fully representative constitutional conference for the purpose of formulating a constitution which would ensure the rights of the majority of the people, on the basis of "one man, one vote," and would lead to the granting of independence in accordance with the Declaration. Other requests made at the same time and also reiterated since are that the United Kingdom should repeal all discriminatory legislation, including the discriminatory land laws and all repressive legislation directed against the activities of the nationalist organizations, and should release all political prisoners and persons detained for political reasons.

The position taken by the United Kingdom was that any discussion of Southern Rhodesia would exceed the terms of the Charter and that the United Nations therefore had no authority to intervene. The United Kingdom maintained that Southern Rhodesia had been a self-governing colony since 1923 and that its special autonomous status had been repeatedly recognized over the intervening years. The United Kingdom could not now intervene in the internal affairs of Southern Rhodesia without the consent of the Government of Southern Rhodesia; in particular, it could not transmit information to the United Nations since it did not have the constitutional power or right to require the Government of Southern Rhodesia to provide the United Kingdom with information. Nor could it alter the constitutional arrangements for Southern Rhodesia without the consent of the Southern Rhodesian Government. Its position with regard to the Assembly's other requests was that they related to internal matters entirely within the competence of Southern Rhodesia.

The United Kingdom has maintained its position concerning the competence of the United Nations on the question and, although it has taken part in the debates on Southern Rhodesia in the Special Committee and the Assembly, it has not participated in the voting on the resolutions.

The first of a series of additional requests directed to the United Kingdom was made in 1962, when the Assembly requested the United Kingdom to cancel the elections scheduled to be held in Southern Rhodesia that year under the new Constitution. Following the elections, which brought into power a settler government opposed to any further extension of the franchise, and which formally requested independence, the Assembly asked the United Kingdom to declare that it would not transfer power until a fully representative government had been established. It also asked the United Kingdom not to transfer armed forces and aircraft to the territory, as envisaged by a conference held in June 1963 on the dissolution of the Central African Federation.

The position taken by the United Kingdom was that the question of independence for Southern Rhodesia, which in any case was beyond the competence of the United Nations, was the subject of difficult and delicate negotiations between the Government of the United Kingdom and Southern Rhodesia. The United Kingdom stated that its aims were similar to those of other members of the United Nations but those aims could not be achieved by precipitate action. The United Kingdom further stated that it had informed the Government of Southern Rhodesia that, before granting independence, the United Kingdom looked to the Southern Rhodesian Government to propose appropriate changes in the political structure, particularly a widening of the franchise so as to give greater representation to the Africans.

The Assembly has not accepted the United Kingdom's position. It has expressed its regret that the United Kingdom has not implemented the Assembly's resolutions and has urged it to do so without delay.

In 1964, the United Kingdom informed the Special Committee of an announcement made by the British Prime Minister on October 27 in which he had stated that a mere declaration of independence by the Southern Rhodesian Government would have no constitutional effect and that such a declaration would be "an open act of defiance and rebellion, and it would be treasonable to take steps to give effect to it." The Special Committee, while noting the steps taken by the United Kingdom to discourage a unilateral declaration of independence, considered that whatever the effect of these steps, energetic measures should be taken urgently by the United Kingdom to implement the United Nations resolutions on the territory.

Shortly before Southern Rhodesia's unilateral declaration of independence of November 11, 1965, the Assembly reiterated its position on such a declaration as well as its previous requests to the United Kingdom. In addition, it called upon the United Kingdom to employ all necessary measures, including military force, to implement the requests it had made.

Requests to Other States. In November 1963, the Assembly urged all states, particularly those having the closest relations with the United Kingdom, to use their influence to the utmost with a view to ensuring the realization of the legitimate aspirations of the peoples of Southern Rhodesia. This was followed in March 1964 by a request from the Special Committee to all states to refrain from supplying arms or ammunition in any form to the Government of Southern Rhodesia. In 1965, in the face of the threat of a unilateral declaration of independence, the Assembly requested all states to use all their powers against a unilateral declaration and in any case not to recognize any Government of Southern Rhodesia not representative of the majority of the people. It also called upon all states to refrain from rendering any assistance whatsoever to the "minority régime" in the territory.

Requests to the Security Council. As early as June 1962, the Assembly had referred to the situation in Southern Rhodesia as "explosive" and one which "endangers peace and security in Africa and in the world at large," and in October of the same year the Assembly considered that to hold elections under the 1961 Constitution would "aggravate the existing explosive situation in the Territory." In June 1963, following a request by the minority settler government for independence, the Special Committee drew the attention of the Security Council to "the deterioration of the explosive situation" in the territory.

When the Security Council took up the question in September 1963, a draft resolution was proposed inviting the United Kingdom not to transfer power until a fully representative government had been established and not to transfer armed forces and aircraft to the territory as envisaged by the conference on the dissolution of the Central African Federation. However, the draft was not adopted because of the negative vote cast by the United Kingdom.

In March 1964, the threat of a unilateral declaration of independence led the Special Committee again to draw the immediate attention of the Security Council to the explosive situation in the territory, which it described as a "serious threat to international peace and security." The Special Committee took similar action in June and October 1964, and again in April 1965.

When the Security Council met in May 1965, it requested the United Kingdom and all member states not to accept a unilateral declaration of independence, and also requested the United Kingdom to take all necessary action to prevent such a declaration and to implement the measures previously requested by the Assembly so that the earliest possible date might be set for independence under a democratic system of government in accordance with the aspirations of the majority of the population.

Action Following the Unilateral Declaration of Independence. On November 11, 1965, the day that the minority settler government of Southern Rhodesia unilaterally declared its independence, the Assembly adopted a resolution condemning this action and inviting the United Kingdom to implement the resolutions of the Assembly and the Security Council to put an end to the rebellion. It also recommended to the Security Council that it consider the situation as a matter of urgency. Having also received similar requests from the United Kingdom and the African states, the Security Council took up the question on November 12 and, after condemning the unilateral declaration of independence, called upon all states not to recognize the illegal racist régime and to refrain from rendering any assistance to it.

The United Kingdom informed the Security Council that the only legal government of Southern Rhodesia was now the United Kingdom Government, which had taken steps to restore constitutional government in Southern Rhodesia, including the prohibition of all export of arms to Southern Rhodesia, the imposition of a ban on all exports of United Kingdom capital, the denial of all Commonwealth trade preference and export credits, and the banning of the import into the United Kingdom of Southern Rhodesian tobacco and sugar.

On November 20, the Security Council called upon all member states to desist from providing Southern Rhodesia with arms, equipment and military material and to do their utmost to break off all economic relations, including an embargo on oil and petroleum products. The Council also called upon the United Kingdom to quell the rebellion of the racist minority and to take all other measures which would prove effective in eliminating the authority of the usurpers. The United Kingdom was further asked to take immediate measures, as the working of the 1961 Constitution had broken down, to allow the people of Southern Rhodesia to determine their own future consistent with the objectives of the Declaration on the Granting of Independence and to enforce urgently and vigorously all the measures it had announced, as well as those called for by the Council.

In addition, the Organization of African Unity was requested to do all in its power to assist in the implementation of the resolution in accordance with Chapter VIII of the Charter, which concerns appropriate regional action in dealing with matters relating to the maintenance of international peace and security.

In response to the call made to them by the Security Council, most states have not recognized the régime and have barred the export of arms, equipment and military material to Southern Rhodesia. The embargo on oil and petroleum products has been supported and many states have severed economic relations with Southern Rhodesia.

ADEN. Aden consists of the colony of Aden and twenty protected sultanates and sheikhdoms known as the Protectorate of South Arabia. It lies along the southern shore of the Arabian Peninsula and includes the Kuria Muria Islands, in the Indian Ocean, and the islands of Perim and Kamaran, in the Red Sea. Aden itself has an area of approximately 75 square miles; the Protectorate has a total area of about 112,000 square miles. The inhabitants are chiefly Moslem Arabs. The estimated population of Aden is 220,000 and that of the Protectorate approximately one million. Aden is the centre of an important entrepôt trade, which, together with the military base which the United Kingdom maintains there, constitutes the mainstay of its economy.

Until 1963, Aden was administered separately from the protectorates by a British Governor. In 1955, several sheikhdoms and sultanates joined to form the Federation of South Arabia and, in 1962, were joined by others. Aden was included in the Federation in January 1963 and there are now seventeen members. Four states remain outside the Federation.

By the terms of the treaty between the United Kingdom and the Federation of South Arabia, the Federal Government is obliged to accept the advice of the United Kingdom High Commissioner in matters concerning external affairs, defence and the public service. Each state has handed over certain powers to the Federation, the other powers remaining with the individual states.

The Federation has a Supreme Council (the executive body) and a Federal Council (the legislature). Each state is entitled to six seats in the legislature, except Aden, which has twenty-four seats, and four smaller sheikhdoms, which have from one to three seats each. All members of the legislature are appointed by the state governments or rulers.

Since December 1963, a state of emergency has existed in Aden and the Federation. Many incidents, involving bomb attacks, shooting and other acts of violence, have taken place in Aden, mainly directed against members of the British forces and of the administration, and in some areas of the Federation military operations have been carried out by British and Federal forces.

Elections were held in the state of Aden in October 1964 for the election of sixteen members of the Legislative Council. The People's Socialist Party and other groups boycotted the elections, and, of the 8,300 persons registered as voters, 6,000 cast their votes. Since September 1965, when the Aden constitution was suspended and the Ministers were dismissed, Aden state has been administered by the High Commissioner.

The question of Aden first came before the United Nations in 1963 when the Special Committee of Twenty-Four considered the situation there.

Acting on the recommendations of its Sub-Committee on Aden, which, although not permitted to visit the territory, had interviewed persons from it in neighbouring countries, the Special Committee in turn made recommendations to the General Assembly, which adopted them in December 1963. In its decision on the territory, the Assembly recommended that the United Kingdom should make the necessary constitutional changes with a view to establishing a representative government for the whole of the territory and that general elections should be held on the basis of universal adult suffrage before the attainment of independence. It requested the Secretary-General, in consultation with the administering power and the Special Committee, to arrange for an effective United Nations presence before and during these elections. The Assembly considered that the maintenance of a British military base in Aden was prejudicial to the security of the region and that its early removal was therefore desirable. It also called upon the United Kingdom to repeal the laws which restricted public freedom, to release political prisoners and detainees, to allow the return of political exiles and to cease all repressive actions forthwith.

The United Kingdom's position was that its aim was independence as soon as possible and that the best and quickest way to achieve that goal was through the union of the states of South Arabia in a federation. It blamed the difficulties and delays in achieving political progress on external intervention and claimed that a campaign of intimidation and violence had been launched to overthrow the Federal Government and incorporate South Arabia within Yemen. As to the presence of British military forces, these were there with the agreement of the Federal Government; they had helped to ensure the security of the Federation and thus to assist in its political development towards independence.

During 1964 and 1965, the Special Committee and its Sub-Committee continued to follow developments in the territory and to urge the United Kingdom to accept and implement the Assembly resolution on the territory. In 1964, the United Kingdom announced that the territory would be granted independence not later than 1968 and that the Governments of Aden and the Federation had agreed on the creation of a unitary state in South Arabia. In August 1965, a widely representative working party met in London to fix an agenda for a constitutional conference; however, after some delegates had insisted on unqualified acceptance of the United Nations 1963 resolution, agreement could not be reached and the working party broke up.

At the end of 1965, the Assembly reiterated its previous recommendations to the United Kingdom and urged it to implement them immediately. It deplored the attempts of the administering power to set up an unrepresentative régime in the Territory with a view to granting it independence, contrary to the resolutions of the General Assembly, and appealed to all states not to recognize any independence which was not based on the wishes of the people freely expressed through elections held under universal adult suffrage. The Assembly considered that the maintenance of military bases in the territory was a major obstacle to the liberation of the people from colonial domination and was prejudicial to peace and security in the region, and that the immediate and complete removal of these bases was essential. The Assembly also drew the attention of the Security Council to the dangerous situation prevailing in the area as a result of British military action against the people, and requested the Secretary-General to take whatever action he deemed expedient to ensure the implementation of the Assembly's decisions.

BASUTOLAND, BECHUANALAND AND SWAZILAND.   The question of Basutoland, Bechuanaland and Swaziland first came before the United Nations in 1962 when the Special Committee considered the situation in the territories. Subsequently, the Assembly and Special Committee made recommendations to the United Kingdom designed to speed up constitutional developments in the territories to enable them to achieve independence on the basis of constitutions reflecting the freely expressed wishes of the people. They also made repeated requests to the United Kingdom to take steps to return to the indigenous inhabitants the land taken from them. Other matters which were of continuing concern to the United Nations included the economic and social situation in the territories, their economic dependence on South Africa and the possibility of their becoming part of South Africa, and the need to guarantee their territorial integrity. The Assembly requested that increased efforts be made to provide economic, financial and technical assistance through the United Nations programmes of technical co-operation. In 1965, on the recommendation of a report by the Secretary-General, the Assembly established a fund for their economic development, to be made up of voluntary contributions.

Elections took place in Basutoland under universal adult suffrage on April 29, 1965. Basutoland achieved independence on October 4, 1966, as Lesotho.

Under the Bechuanaland Constitution which came into effect in January 1965, provision is made for a ministerial form of government drawn from and responsible to a Legislative Assembly consisting chiefly of members directly elected on the basis of a common voting roll. Elections for the new Assembly were held on March 1, 1965. Bechuanaland became the independent Republic of Botswana on September 30, 1966.

The 1964 Constitution for Swaziland provides for a purely advisory Executive Council and for separate racial representation in a partially elected Legislative Council. In August 1965, a local Committee, composed of Her Majesty's Commissioner and fourteen other members chosen by the Legislative Council, was appointed to make proposals for a new constitution.

According to the Committee's proposals, published in March 1966, Swaziland was to assume internal self-government later in the year on the British monarchical pattern under British protection, with the Paramount Chief recognized as King and Head of State and a Parliament consisting of a Lower House, with a majority of members elected by universal adult suffrage, and an Upper House, half of whose members are to be chosen by the Assembly and the other half appointed by the King.

FIJI.   Fiji, a group of islands in the central South Pacific, has a land area of 7,055 square miles and a population estimated in 1964 at 456,390, consisting of 189,169 Fijians, 228,176 persons of Indian origin and 39,045 Europeans and others.

Fiji has been administered by the United Kingdom since 1874. On the recommendation of a constitutional conference, held in London in July 1965, a new constitution was agreed on, providing for an elected majority in the Legislative Council and for an Executive Council, drawn principally from the elected members, which the Governor would be required to consult on all internal matters. Most members would continue to be elected on the basis of the three communal rolls, but some would be elected under a new cross-voting system.

The situation in Fiji was first considered by the United Nations in 1963. In seeking the implementation of the Declaration in Fiji, the Assembly and the Special Committee invited the United Kingdom to work out, together with the representatives of the people of Fiji, a new constitution providing for elections on the basis of "one man, one vote," and the creation of representative institutions. They also invited the United Kingdom, in co-operation with the people of Fiji, to seek the political, economic and social integration of the various communities. Commenting on the proposed constitutional changes, the Assembly, in 1965, considered that they would foment separatist tendencies and stand in the way of the integration of the people. It invited the United Kingdom to implement the Assembly resolutions immediately and requested it urgently to take measures to repeal all discriminatory laws and to establish an unqualified system of democratic representation based on the principle of "one man, one vote."

GIBRALTAR. Gibraltar, administered by the United Kingdom, has an area of 2¼ square miles and a population of about 24,500.

Spain has claimed that Gibraltar was ceded to the British by the Treaty of Utrecht in 1713 for use as a military base but that the United Kingdom expelled the original inhabitants and converted it into a colony of British subjects. This action, Spain has claimed, was in violation of paragraph 6 of the Declaration on the Granting of Independence to Colonial Countries and Peoples, which concerns attempts to disrupt the national unity and territorial integrity of a country. The United Kingdom has denied this claim and has stated that it has no doubts as to its rights in Gibraltar.

A new constitution came into effect in 1964 by which the people of Gibraltar were given greater control over internal affairs.

The question of Gibraltar has been considered by the Special Committee and the Assembly since 1963. In 1965, the Assembly endorsed the Special Committee's consensus on the territory which noted that there was a disagreement, or even a dispute, between the United Kingdom and Spain and invited the two Governments to begin talks without delay in order to reach a negotiated solution in conformity with the Declaration and bearing in mind the interests of the people.

In March 1966, the two Governments informed the Secretary-General that they had agreed to hold talks.

MAURITIUS. Mauritius, in the Indian Ocean, about 500 miles east of Madagascar, is administered by the United Kingdom. It has a population of approximately 680,000, mostly Indo-Mauritians, and, with its four island dependencies, an area of 809 square miles.

Under the 1964 constitution, there is a Council of Ministers and a Legislative Assembly consisting of a majority of elected members chosen by universal adult suffrage. External affairs, defence and internal security remain the responsibility of the Governor, in consultation with the Premier.

Following a constitutional conference held in London in September 1965 and attended by representatives of all the parties in the legislature, the United Kingdom Government announced that it considered that Mauritius should be independent, rejecting a proposal for continuing association with the United Kingdom and for a referendum on the question.

As the conference had been unable to agree on a new electoral system, the United Kingdom appointed a commission to recommend a new system that would safeguard the interests of all communities. It proposed that, after the commission had reported, a general election could be held and a new government formed; independence would follow after a period of six months of full internal self-government if the new Legislative Assembly passed, by a simple majority, a resolution asking for independence.

The situation in Mauritius was first examined by the Special Committee in 1964. On the basis of the Special Committee's recommendations, the Assembly, in 1965, invited the United Kingdom to take effective measures for the immediate and full implementation of the Declaration in the territory. With regard to an announcement by the United Kingdom that, as of November 1965, a dependency of Mauritius, along with three islands of Seychelles, would form a new colony to be used as a military base, the Committee noted that any step by the United Kingdom to detach certain islands from the territory would be in contravention of the Declaration, and invited the United Kingdom to take no action that would dismember Mauritius and violate its territorial integrity.

FALKLAND ISLANDS (MALVINAS). The Falkland Islands (Malvinas), in the South Atlantic, some 480 miles off Cape Horn, are administered by the United Kingdom. The population, mainly of British origin, numbered 2,172 in 1962.

Argentina has, at successive sessions of the General Assembly, expressed its reservations regarding sovereignty over the territory, claiming that the islands are an integral part of Argentine national territory. The United Kingdom has consistently maintained that it has no doubts concerning its sovereignty over the islands.

The territory has been considered by the Special Committee and the Assembly since 1964. In 1965, the Assembly, after noting the existence of a dispute between Argentina and the United Kingdom over the sovereignty of the islands, invited the two Governments to proceed without delay with negotiations, as previously recommended by the Special Committee, with a view to finding a peaceful solution, bearing in mind the provisions of the Charter, the Declaration and the interests of the people of the islands.

In February 1966, the two Governments informed the United Nations that they had agreed to begin these discussions.

EQUATORIAL GUINEA (FERNANDO PÓO AND RÍO MUNI). Equatorial Guinea, comprising Río Muni, on the west coast of Africa, and the islands of Fernando Póo and Annobón, in the Gulf of Guinea, is administered by Spain. It has a population of 246,000.

Following a referendum held in December 1963, the two territories were joined to form Equatorial Guinea under a new constitution by which they ceased to be Spanish provinces and were granted their own legislative and executive institutions. Spain is represented in the territory by a High Commissioner, who is responsible for external relations and defence.

The Special Committee and the Assembly, which have considered the territory since 1963, have requested Spain to set the earliest possible date for independence after consulting the people on the basis of universal suffrage, under the supervision of the United Nations. In 1966, the Special Committee, acting on an open invitation by Spain, decided to send a sub-committee to study conditions in the territory.

IFNI AND SPANISH SAHARA. Ifni, administered by Spain, is a small territory with some 50,000 inhabitants, on the north-west coast of Africa, bordered by Morocco. Spanish Sahara, with a population of about 24,000, is south of Ifni and is bordered by Morocco and Mauritania. Ifni is the subject of territorial claims by Morocco, and Spanish Sahara by Morocco and Mauritania.

The Special Committee and the Assembly have considered these territories since 1963. In a decision taken in 1965, the Assembly urgently requested Spain to take all necessary measures for the liberation of the territories from colonial domination and, to this end, to enter into negotiations on the problems relating to sovereignty presented by these two territories.

TRUST TERRITORIES. The situation with regard to the implementation of the Declaration in the three remaining Trust Territories has been examined by the Special Committee since 1964. The Committee usually takes up consideration of these territories after the Trusteeship Council has completed its report on them. When the Assembly considers the report of the Trusteeship Council, it also has before it the report of the Special Committee. The Assembly's decisions on the Trust Territory of Nauru and New Guinea, which are based on both reports, are described in the sections relating to those territories (*see pages* 378-381).

OTHER TERRITORIES. The remaining territories on the Special Committee's preliminary list of territories to which the Declaration applies, with the exception of British Honduras, Brunei, French Somaliland and Hong Kong, were examined by the Special Committee in 1964, and in 1965 were the subject of a decision by the Assembly. The territories, most of which are small in size and population, are the following: American Samoa, Antigua, Bahamas, Barbados,* Bermuda, British Virgin Islands, Cayman Islands, Cocos (Keeling) Islands, Dominica, Gilbert and Ellice Islands, Grenada, Guam, Montserrat, New Hebrides, Niue, Papua, Pitcairn, St. Helena, St. Kitts-Nevis-Anguilla, St. Lucia, St. Vincent, Seychelles, Solomon Islands, Tokelau Islands, Turks and Caicos Islands, and United States Virgin Islands.

In its decision on these territories in 1965, the Assembly endorsed the conclusions and recommendations of the Special Committee and called upon the administering Powers to implement the relevant resolutions of the Assembly without delay. It reaffirmed the inalienable right of the people of these territories to decide their constitutional status in accordance with the Charter, the Declaration and "other relevant General Assembly resolutions," and decided that the United Nations should render all help to the people of these territories in their efforts freely to decide their future status. The Assembly also requested the administering Powers to allow visiting missions to go to the territories and to extend to them their full co-operation and assistance.

OMAN. The question of Oman, which has been before the United Nations since 1957, was referred to the Special Committee in 1965, when the Assembly invited the Committee to examine the situation in the territory.

Oman, situated in the north-west of the Arabian peninsula, has been the subject of dispute between the Imam of Oman, supported by the Arab States on the one hand, and the Sultan of Muscat and Oman and the United Kingdom on the other.

The Imam claims that he is the rightful ruler of the Imamate of Oman, which includes the territory covered by the Sultanate of Muscat and Oman and the Trucial Sheikhdoms. The Imamate, he asserts, was dismembered in the nineteenth century, when the British established the Sultanate and the Sheikhdoms on the coast. Since that time, the Sultanate has been maintained through British support and, in 1955 and 1957, British forces annexed the remaining interior portion of the Imamate to the Sultanate. Because of British presence in the Sultanate and of its relationship with the United Kingdom, the Imam and the

* Barbados became independent on November 30, 1966, and was admitted to membership in the United Nations on December 9, 1966.

Arab States have claimed that the Sultanate is a territory of the colonial type.

The Sultan has denied the existence of the Imamate, stating that it went out of existence at the beginning of the nineteenth century, when it was succeeded by the Sultanate; the Imam and his followers were therefore rebels. The Sultan and the United Kingdom have asserted that the Sultanate is an independent sovereign state and have denied that a colonial relationship exists between it and the United Kingdom.

The question of Oman was first introduced in the United Nations in August 1957, when the representatives of eleven Arab States requested the Security Council to consider "the armed aggression by the United Kingdom of Great Britain and Northern Ireland against the independence, sovereignty and territorial integrity of the Imamate of Oman." The United Kingdom opposed the inscription of the item on the Security Council's agenda on the grounds that there was no "independent sovereign state" of Oman and that the "district" of Oman was part of the dominion of the Sultan of Muscat and Oman. The Security Council decided not to place the question on its agenda.

From 1960 to 1962, the question of Oman was included in the agenda of the Assembly and allocated to the Special Political Committee. However, draft resolutions approved by the Special Political Committee were not adopted since they failed to receive the required two-thirds majority.

In 1962, the representative of the United Kingdom, on behalf of the Sultan of Muscat and Oman, extended an invitation to a representative of the Secretary-General of the United Nations to visit the Sultanate on a personal basis to obtain first-hand information on the situation there. Mr. Herbert de Ribbing, who was appointed to undertake this task, visited Oman in June 1963. In his report, which was made available to the Assembly at the end of the year, he stated that many of the people interviewed had stated that they would not like to see the Imam return; others had commented that they would not object to his return provided he had made his peace with the Sultan. With regard to the status of the Imamate, the Special Representative stated that his mission did not have the time nor did it consider itself competent to evaluate the territorial, historical and political issues involved.

In 1963, the question of Oman was referred to the Assembly's Fourth Committee for consideration on grounds put forward by the Arab States that the question was essentially a colonial one. After taking note of the report of the Secretary-General's Special Representative, the Assembly decided to establish an *ad hoc* Committee—composed of Afghanistan, Costa Rica, Nepal, Nigeria and Senegal—to examine the question of Oman and to report to it at its next session.

After talks with the Sultan, the Imam, and others, the Committee stated that the Sultanate might not be considered a colony or a protectorate in a formal sense, but that the relationship of the United Kingdom with the Sultan, which enabled it to exercise great influence on the policies of the Sultanate, might be considered a very special and rather exclusive relationship. With regard to the status of the Imamate before 1955, the Committee believed that developments in the interior indicated very clearly the existence of an autonomous political entity that took steps to assert its competence in such important matters as the control of its foreign relations and of its natural resources. The Committee felt the action taken by the United Kingdom in 1957 to be extreme and difficult to justify. It also noted that it was the unanimous view of all persons interviewed from Muscat and Oman that, as a prerequisite of any solution, the British presence, in any form, must come to an end. The *ad hoc* Committee concluded that the question of Oman was a serious international problem requiring the special attention of the Assembly and that the problem derived from imperialistic policies and foreign intervention in Muscat and Oman.

The Assembly considered the Committee's report in 1965. In its decision on the question, the Assembly recognized the right of the people of the territory as a whole to self-determination and independence in accordance with their freely expressed wishes, and considered that the colonial presence of the United Kingdom in its various forms prevented the people of the territory from exercising this right. It also called upon the United Kingdom to cease its repressive actions against the people of the territory, to withdraw its troops, to release political prisoners and allow exiles to return, and to eliminate British domination in any form.

The Assembly also invited the Special Committee of Twenty-Four to examine the situation in the territory. It was explained by one of the co-sponsors of the resolution that the term "the territory as a whole" included Muscat and Oman and the Trucial Sheikhdoms. The rulers of the Trucial Sheikhdoms protested to the Secretary-General at the inclusion of the Trucial States on the agenda of the Special Committee, on the grounds that they are not of colonial status, and two members of the Special Committee, the United Kingdom and the United States, informed the Committee that they would not participate in any discussion on Oman in the Committee.

Legal Questions

INTERNATIONAL COURT OF JUSTICE

Contentious Cases Dealt with by the Court

CORFU CHANNEL. This dispute, which gave rise to three judgments by the Court, arose out of the explosions of mines by which some British warships suffered damage while passing through the Corfu Channel in 1946, in a part of the Albanian waters which had been previously swept. The ships were severely damaged and members of the crews were killed. The United Kingdom accused Albania of having laid, or allowed a third party to lay, the mines after mine-clearance operations had been carried out by the Allied naval authorities. Owing to the political situation at the time, the incident caused grave tension between the two states. The case was brought before the United Nations, and, in consequence of a recommendation by the Security Council, it was referred to the Court. The first of three judgments (March 25, 1948) dealt with the question of the Court's jurisdiction, which Albania had challenged.

The second and most important judgment (April 9, 1949) related to the merits of the problem. The Court found that Albania was responsible under international law for the explosions that had taken place in Albanian waters and for the damage and loss of life which had ensued. It did not accept the view that Albania had itself laid the mines. On the other hand, it held that the mines could not have been laid without the knowledge of the Albanian Government. In this connection, the Court took into account certain circumstantial evidence which established the responsibility of the territorial government. Albania, for its part, had submitted a counterclaim against the United Kingdom. It accused the latter of having violated Albanian sovereignty by sending warships into Albanian territorial waters and of carrying out mine-sweeping operations in Albanian waters after the explosions. The Court did not accept the first of these complaints. It upheld the generally admitted principle that states are entitled, in time of peace, to send their warships through international straits without first obtaining the leave of the coastal state. The Court found that this was a case of innocent passage. On the other hand, the mine clearance operation of November 12 and 13, 1946, having been effected against the will of the Albanian Government, the Court found that it constituted an inadmissible intervention in the affairs of Albania. In spite of the default of the Albanian Government and its dilatory attitude, the Court held that the action of the British Navy was a violation of Albanian sovereignty.

In a third and final judgment (December 15, 1949), the Court assessed the amount of reparation due by Albania to the United Kingdom. This amount had been determined as a result of an expert inquiry, and Albania was ordered to pay the United Kingdom a total sum of £ 844,000 for the damage caused to the ships and as compensation for the deaths of members of the crews and for personal injuries suffered by them.

FISHERIES. The judgment delivered by the Court in the Fisheries case set a term to a controversy which had been pending between the United Kingdom and Norway for a very long period. In 1935, Norway enacted a decree by which it reserved certain fishing grounds situated off the northern coast of Norway for the exclusive use of its own fishermen. The question at issue was whether this decree, which laid down a particular method for drawing the baselines from which the width of the Norwegian territorial waters had to be calculated, was valid in international law. This case, which aroused considerable interest, especially in maritime states, gave rise to prolonged and voluminous proceedings. In its judgment of December 18, 1951, the Court found that, contrary to the submissions of the United Kingdom, neither the method employed for the delimitation by the 1935 decree nor the lines themselves fixed by that decree were contrary to international law.

PROTECTION OF FRENCH NATIONALS AND PROTECTED PERSONS IN EGYPT. As a consequence of certain measures adopted by the Egyptian Government against the property and persons of various French nationals and protected persons in Egypt, France instituted proceedings in which it invoked the Montreux Convention of 1935, concerning the abrogation of the capitulations in Egypt. However, the case was not proceeded with, as the Egyptian Government desisted from the measures in question. By agreement between the parties, the case was struck off the Court's List (order of March 29, 1950).

ASYLUM. The granting of asylum in the Colombian Embassy at Lima on January 3, 1949, to a Peruvian national, Haya de la Torre, a political leader accused of having instigated a military rebellion, was the subject of a dispute between Peru and Colombia which the parties agreed to submit to the Court. The Pan-American Havana Convention on Asylum (1928) laid down that, subject to certain conditions, asylum could be granted in a foreign embassy to a political offender who was a national of the territorial state. The question in dispute was whether Colombia, as the state granting asylum, was entitled unilaterally to "qualify" the offence committed by the refugee in a manner binding on the territorial state, that is, to decide whether it was a political offence or a common crime. Furthermore, the Court was asked to decide whether the territorial state was bound to afford the necessary guarantees to enable the refugee to leave the country in safety.

In its judgment of November 20, 1950, the Court answered both these questions in the negative, but at the same time it specified that Peru had not proved that Haya de la Torre was a common criminal. Lastly, it found in favour of a counterclaim submitted by Peru that Haya de la Torre had been granted asylum in violation of the Havana Convention, as it considered that the asylum had been irregularly granted because Haya de la Torre had sought refuge in the Embassy some three months after the suppression of the military rebellion, which showed that the "urgency" prescribed by the Havana Convention as a condition for the regularity of asylum no longer existed.

On the very day on which the Court delivered this judgment, Colombia filed a request for an interpretation. By this request, Colombia sought to obtain from the Court a reply to the question whether the judgment implied an obligation binding the Colombian authorities to surrender the refugee, Haya de la Torre, to the Peruvian authorities. In a judgment delivered on November 27, 1950, the Court declared that the questions raised by Colombia were new questions, that they had not been presented in the preceding case and that, therefore, the Court could not decide upon them by way of interpretation. The Court further pointed out that a request for interpretation could only be founded on a dispute between the parties concerning the meaning of the judgment, which dispute could not have arisen because the request for interpretation had been submitted on the same day as the delivery of the judgment. The Colombian request was therefore dismissed.

HAYA DE LA TORRE.   This case, a sequel to the earlier proceedings, was instituted by Colombia by means of a fresh application. Immediately after the judgment of November 20, 1950 (*described under "Asylum" above*), Peru had called upon Colombia to surrender Haya de la Torre. Colombia refused to do so, maintaining that neither the applicable legal provisions nor the Court's judgment placed it under an obligation to surrender the refugee to the Peruvian authorities. The Court confirmed this view in its judgment of June 13, 1951. It declared that the question was a new one, and that although the Havana Convention expressly prescribed the surrender of common criminals to the local authorities, no obligation of the kind existed in regard to political offenders. While confirming that asylum had been irregularly granted and that on this ground Peru was entitled to demand its termination, the Court declared that Colombia was not bound to surrender the refugee; these two conclusions, it stated, were not contradictory because there were other ways in which the asylum could be terminated besides the surrender of the refugee.

RIGHTS OF UNITED STATES NATIONALS IN MOROCCO. By a decree of December 30, 1948, the French authorities in the Moroccan Protectorate imposed a system of licence control in respect of imports not involving an official allocation of currency, and limited these imports to a number of products indispensable to the Moroccan economy. The United States maintained that this measure affected its rights under treaties with Morocco and contended that, in accordance with these treaties and with the General Act of Algeciras of 1906, no Moroccan law or regulation could be applied to its nationals in Morocco without its previous consent.

In its judgment of August 27, 1952, the Court held that the import controls were contrary to the treaty between the United States and Morocco of 1836 and the General Act of Algeciras, since they involved discrimination in favour of France against the United States. The Court considered the extent of the consular jurisdiction of the United States in Morocco and held that the United States was entitled to exercise such jurisdiction in the French zone in all disputes, civil or criminal, between United States citizens or persons protected by the United States. It was also entitled to exercise such jurisdiction to the extent required by the relevant provisions of the General Act of Algeciras. The Court rejected the contention of the United States that its consular jurisdiction included cases in which only the defendant was a citizen or protégé of the United States. It also rejected the claim by the United States that the application to citizens of the United States of laws and regulations in the French zone of Morocco required the assent of the United States Government. Such assent was required only in so far as the intervention of the consular courts of the United States was necessary for the effective enforcement of such laws or regulations as against United States citizens. The Court rejected a counterclaim by the United States that its nationals in Morocco were entitled to immunity from taxation. It also dealt with the question of the valuation of imports by the Moroccan customs authorities.

AMBATIELOS.   In 1919, Ambatielos, a Greek shipowner, entered into a contract with the Government of the United Kingdom for the purchase of ships. Ambatielos claimed he had suffered damage through the failure of the United Kingdom Government to carry out the terms of the contract and as a result of certain judgments given against him by the English courts in circumstances which were alleged to be contrary to international law. The Greek Government took up the case of its national and claimed that the United Kingdom was under a duty to submit the dispute to arbitration in accordance with the treaties of 1886 and 1926 between the United Kingdom and Greece. The United Kingdom objected to the Court's jurisdiction. In a judgment of July 1, 1952, the Court held that it had jurisdiction to decide whether the United Kingdom was under a duty to submit the dispute to arbitration but, on the other hand, that it had no jurisdiction to deal with the merits of the Ambatielos claim. In a further judgment of May 19, 1953, the Court decided that the dispute was one which the United Kingdom was under a duty to submit to arbitration in accordance with the treaties of 1886 and 1926.

ANGLO-IRANIAN OIL COMPANY. In 1933, an agreement was concluded between the Government of Iran and the Anglo-Iranian Oil Company. In 1951, laws were passed in Iran for the nationalization of the oil industry. These laws resulted in a dispute between Iran and the Company. The United Kingdom took up the case of the latter and instituted proceedings before the Court. Iran disputed the Court's jurisdiction. In its judgment of July 22, 1952, the Court decided that it had no jurisdiction to deal with the dispute. Its jurisdiction depended on the declarations by Iran and the United Kingdom accepting the Court's compulsory jurisdiction. The Court held that the declaration by Iran, which was ratified in 1932, covered only disputes based on treaties concluded by Iran after that date, whereas the claim of the United Kingdom was directly or indirectly based on treaties concluded prior to 1932. The Court also rejected the view that the agreement of 1933 was both a concessionary contract between Iran and the Company and an international treaty between Iran and the United Kingdom, since the United Kingdom was not a party to the contract. The position was not altered by the fact that the concessionary contract was negotiated through the good offices of the Council of the League of Nations. By an order of July 5, 1951, the Court had indicated interim measures of protection, that is, provisional measures for protecting the rights alleged by either party, in proceedings already instituted, until a final judgment is given. In its judgment, the Court declared that the order of July 5, 1951, had ceased to be operative and that the provisional measures therefore lapsed.

MINQUIERS AND ECREHOS. The Minquiers and Ecrehos are two groups of islets situated between the British Channel Island of Jersey and the coast of France. Under a special agreement between France and the United Kingdom, the Court was asked to determine which of the parties had produced a more convincing proof of title to these groups of islets.

After the conquest of England by William, Duke of Normandy, in 1066, the islands formed part of the Union between England and

Normandy which lasted until 1204, when Philip Augustus of France conquered Normandy but failed to occupy the islands. The United Kingdom submitted that the islands then remained united with England and that this situation was placed on a legal basis by subsequent treaties between the two countries. France contended that the Minquiers and Ecrehos were held by France after 1204, and referred to the same medieval treaties as those relied on by the United Kingdom.

In its judgment of November 17, 1953, the Court considered that none of these treaties stated specifically which islands were held by the King of England or by the King of France. Moreover, what was of decisive importance was not indirect presumptions based on matters in the Middle Ages, but direct evidence of possession and the actual exercise of sovereignty. After considering this evidence, the Court arrived at the conclusion that the sovereignty over the Minquiers and Ecrehos belonged to the United Kingdom.

NOTTEBOHM.   In this case, Liechtenstein claimed restitution and compensation from the Government of Guatemala on the ground that the latter had acted towards Mr. Nottebohm, a citizen of Liechtenstein, in a manner contrary to international law. Guatemala objected to the Court's jurisdiction but the Court overruled this objection in a judgment of November 18, 1953. In a second judgment of April 6, 1955, the Court held that Liechtenstein's claim was inadmissible on grounds relating to Mr. Nottebohm's nationality. It was the bond of nationality between a state and an individual which alone conferred upon the state the right to put forward an international claim on his behalf. Mr. Nottebohm, who was then a German national, had settled in Guatemala in 1905 and continued to reside there. In October 1939, after the beginning of the Second World War, while on a visit to Europe, he obtained Liechtenstein nationality and returned to Guatemala in 1940, where he resumed his former business activities until his removal as a result of war measures in 1943. On the international plane, the grant of nationality was entitled to recognition by other states only if it represented a genuine connection between the individual and the state granting its nationality. Mr. Nottebohm's nationality, however, was not based on any real prior connection with Liechtenstein, since he always retained his family and business connections with Germany and had been settled in Guatemala for thirty-four years. Moreover, the object of his naturalization was to enable him to acquire the status of a neutral national in time of war. For these reasons, Liechtenstein was not entitled to take up his case and put forward an international claim on his behalf against Guatemala.

MONETARY GOLD REMOVED FROM ROME IN 1943.   A certain quantity of monetary gold, removed by the Germans from Rome in

1943, was later recovered in Germany and found to belong to Albania. The 1946 agreement on reparations from Germany provided that monetary gold found in Germany should be pooled for distribution among the countries entitled to receive a share of it. The United Kingdom claimed that the gold should be delivered to it in partial satisfaction of the Court's judgment in the Corfu Channel case (*see page 427*). Italy claimed that the gold should be delivered to it in partial satisfaction for the damage which it alleged it had suffered as a result of an Albanian law of January 13, 1945. In the Washington statement of April 25, 1951, the Governments of France, the United Kingdom and the United States, to whom the implementation of the reparations agreement had been entrusted, decided that the gold should be delivered to the United Kingdom unless, within a certain time limit, Italy or Albania applied to the Court requesting it to adjudicate on their respective rights. Albania took no action in the matter, but within the prescribed time limit, Italy made an application to the Court. Later, however, Italy raised the preliminary question as to whether the Court had jurisdiction to adjudicate upon the validity of the Italian claim against Albania.

In its judgment of June 15, 1954, the Court decided that, in order to determine whether Italy was entitled to receive the gold, it was necessary to determine whether Albania had committed an international wrong against Italy and whether it was under an obligation to pay compensation to Italy. To go into the merits of such questions would be to decide a dispute between Italy and Albania which the Court had no jurisdiction to do without Albania's consent. For this reason, the Court also could not decide the question of priority as between the claims of Italy and the United Kingdom, for this question could arise only if it was decided that, as between Italy and Albania, the gold should go to Italy.

ÉLECTRICITÉ DE BEYROUTH COMPANY. This case between France and Lebanon arose out of certain measures adopted by the Lebanese Government which the Electricité de Beyrouth Company, a French limited company, regarded as contrary to undertakings entered into by that Government. These undertakings, which related to concessions of French companies and companies with French capital in Lebanon, formed part of an agreement of 1948 between France and Lebanon. After the case had been brought before the Court by France on August 11, 1953, the Lebanese Government and the Electricité de Beyrouth Company entered into an agreement on March 26, 1954, for the settlement of the dispute by a repurchase of the concession. This agreement was ratified by the Lebanese Parliament on June 30, 1954. Moreover, it was agreed between the French and Lebanese Governments that as soon as a settlement was reached, France would discontinue the proceedings. On July 23, 1954, therefore, the French Government informed the Court that it was not going on with the proceedings, and on July 29, 1954, the Court made an order for the removal of the case from the List.

TREATMENT IN HUNGARY OF UNITED. STATES AIRCRAFT AND CREW. On March 3, 1954, the United States of America instituted proceedings against the Hungarian People's Republic and the Union of Soviet Socialist Republics "on account of certain actions of the Hungarian Government in concert with the Government of the Union of Soviet Socialist Republics" regarding an aircraft and crew of the United States which had been forced to land on Hungarian territory. The United States relied on Article 36, paragraph 1, of the Court's Statute, which provides that the jurisdiction of the Court comprises all cases which the parties refer to it, and it stated that it submitted to the Court's jurisdiction for the purpose of the two cases and indicated that it was open to the other two governments to do likewise. In a letter to the Court dated April 30, 1954, the Government of the Union of Soviet Socialist Republics attributed responsibility for the incident to the United States and said that it regarded as unacceptable the proposal of the United States Government that the Court should examine the case. In a letter to the Court dated June 14, 1954, the Hungarian Government stated that it was unable to submit to its jurisdiction in the matter. The Court found that in the circumstances it did not have jurisdiction to deal with these cases, and on July 12, 1954, it made two orders removing them from the List.

AERIAL INCIDENT OF MARCH 10, 1953. On March 29, 1955, the United States instituted proceedings against Czechoslovakia on account of "certain wrongful acts committed by MIG-type aircraft from Czechoslovakia within the United States zone of occupation in Germany on March 10, 1953." In its application to the Court, the United States Government stated that it submitted to the Court's jurisdiction for the purposes of the case and that it was open to the Czechoslovak Government to do likewise. The United States Government relied on Article 36, paragraph 1, of the Court's Statute, which provides that the Court's jurisdiction comprises all cases which the parties refer to it. In a letter to the Court, Czechoslovakia attributed responsibility for the incident to the United States and considered that there was no reason for the case to be dealt with by the Court. The Court found that Czechoslovakia had not accepted its jurisdiction to deal with the dispute, and on March 14, 1956, it made an order removing the case from the List.

ANTARCTICA. On May 4, 1955, the United Kingdom instituted proceedings before the Court against Argentina and Chile concerning disputes as to the sovereignty over certain lands and islands in the

Antarctic. In its applications to the Court, the United Kingdom stated that it submitted to the Court's jurisdiction for the purposes of the case, and although as far as it was aware, Argentina and Chile had not yet accepted the Court's jurisdiction, they were legally qualified to do so. Moreover, the United Kingdom relied on Article 36, paragraph 1, of the Court's Statute, which provides that the jurisdiction of the Court comprises all cases which the parties refer to it. In a letter of July 15, 1955, the Government of Chile informed the Court that, in its view, the application of the United Kingdom Government was unfounded and that it was not open to the Court to exercise jurisdiction. In a note of August 1, 1955, the Government of Argentina informed the Court of its refusal to accept its jurisdiction to deal with the case. In these circumstances, the Court found that neither Chile nor Argentina had accepted its jurisdiction to deal with the cases, and on March 16, 1956, it made orders removing them from the List.

AERIAL INCIDENT OF OCTOBER 7, 1952.   On June 2, 1955, the United States instituted proceedings against the Union of Soviet Socialist Republics on account of "certain wilful acts committed by fighter aircraft of the Soviet Government against a United States Air Force B-29 aircraft and its crew off Hokkaido, Japan, on October 7, 1952." In its application to the Court, the United States Government stated that it submitted to the Court's jurisdiction for the purposes of the case and that it was open to the Soviet Government to do likewise. The United States relied on Article 36, paragraph 1, of the Court's Statute, which provides that the jurisdiction of the Court comprises all cases which the parties refer to it. In a letter to the Court, the Soviet Union attributed responsibility for the incident to the United States and considered that there was no reason for the question to be dealt with by the Court. The Court found that the Soviet Union had not accepted its jurisdiction to deal with the dispute, and on March 14, 1956, it made an order removing the case from the List.

CERTAIN NORWEGIAN LOANS.   Certain Norwegian loans had been floated in France between the years 1885 and 1909. The bonds of these loans stated the amount of the obligation in gold or in currency convertible into gold, as well as in various national currencies. From the time when Norway suspended the convertibility of its currency into gold, the loans had been serviced in Norwegian kröner. The French Government, espousing the cause of the French bondholders, filed an application requesting the Court to declare that the debt should be discharged by payment of the gold value of the coupons of the bonds on the date of payment and of the gold value of the redeemed bonds on the date of repayment. The Norwegian Government raised a number of preliminary objections to the jurisdiction of the Court, and, in the judgment it delivered on July 6, 1957, the Court found that it was without jurisdiction to adjudicate in the dispute.

Indeed, the Court held that, since its jurisdiction depended upon the two unilateral declarations made by the parties, jurisdiction was conferred upon the Court only to the extent to which those declarations coincided in conferring it. The Norwegian Government was therefore entitled, by virtue of the condition of reciprocity, to invoke in its own favour the reservation contained in the French declaration which excluded from the jurisdiction of the Court differences relating to matters which were essentially within the national jurisdiction as understood by the Government of the French Republic.

RIGHT OF PASSAGE OVER INDIAN TERRITORY.   This dispute, which gave rise to two judgments by the Court, arose out of the following set of facts. The Portuguese possessions in India included, at some distance inland from the port of Daman, the two enclaves of Dadra and Nagar-Aveli which, in mid-1954, passed under an autonomous local administration. Portugal claimed that it had a right of passage to those enclaves and between one enclave and the other to the extent necessary for the exercise of its sovereignty and subject to the regulation and control of India; that that right derived from agreements concluded in the eighteenth century between Portugal and the Marathas, from local customs established between Portugal and the successive sovereigns of the Indian peninsula, from general international custom in regard to enclaves and from the general principles of law recognized by civilized nations; that, in July 1954, contrary to the practice previously followed, the Indian Government had prevented Portugal from exercising the right of passage claimed by it and that that situation should be redressed.

The first judgment (November 26, 1957) related to the jurisdiction of the Court, which was challenged by India. The Court rejected four of the preliminary objections raised by India and joined the other two to the merits. In the second judgment (April 12, 1960), after rejecting the two remaining preliminary objections, the Court gave its decision on the claims of Portugal, which India maintained to be unfounded.

After having examined the situation of Dadra and Nagar-Aveli during the Maratha period and the practice subsequently developed in regard to those enclaves, the Court found that Portugal had in 1954 the right of passage claimed by it but that such right was limited to the passage of private persons, civil officials and goods in general and did not extend to armed forces, armed police, arms and ammunition. The Court found finally that India had not acted contrary to the obligations imposed on it by the existence of the right of passage thus found to belong to Portugal.

APPLICATION OF THE 1902 CONVENTION GOVERNING THE GUARDIANSHIP OF INFANTS. The Swedish authorities had placed an infant of Netherlands nationality residing in Sweden under the régime of protective upbringing instituted by Swedish law for the protection of children and young persons. The father of the child, jointly with the deputy-guardian appointed by a Netherlands court, appealed against the action of the Swedish authorities, but the measure of protective upbringing was maintained. The Netherlands Government claimed that the decisions which instituted and maintained the protective upbringing were not in conformity with Sweden's obligations under The Hague Convention of 1902 governing the guardianship of infants, the provisions of which were based on the principle that the national law of the infant is applicable.

In its judgment of November 28, 1958, the Court held that the 1902 Convention on guardianship did not include within its scope the matter of the protection of children as understood by the Swedish law on the protection of children and young persons and that the 1902 Convention could not have given rise to obligations in a field outside the matter with which it was concerned. Accordingly, the Court did not, in this case, find any failure to observe the Convention on the part of Sweden.

INTERHANDEL. In 1942, the Government of the United States of America vested almost all of the shares of the General Aniline and Film Corporation (GAF), a company incorporated in the United States, on the ground that those shares, which were owned by Interhandel, a company registered in Bâle, belonged in reality to the I. G. Farbenindustrie of Frankfurt, or that the GAF was in one way or another controlled by that company. In an application dated October 1, 1957, the Swiss Government asked the Court to declare that the United States Government was under an obligation to restore to Interhandel the assets of that company which had been vested or, alternatively, that the dispute on the matter between Switzerland and the United States was one that was fit for submission for judicial settlement, arbitration or conciliation. Two days later, the Swiss Government asked the Court to indicate, as an interim measure of protection, that the United States should not part with these assets so long as proceedings in this dispute were pending and, in particular, should not sell the shares of the GAF which were claimed by the Swiss Federal Government as the property of its nationals.

On October 24, 1957, the Court made an order in which it noted that, in the light of the information furnished to the Court, it appeared that the sale of the shares in question could only be effected after the termination of judicial proceedings pending in the United States, in respect of which there was no indication of a speedy conclusion; that it was the stated intention of the United States Government not to take action at that time to fix a time schedule for the sale of the shares, and that, accordingly, there was no need to indicate interim measures of protection. The United States raised preliminary objections to the jurisdiction of the Court and, in its judgment of March 21, 1959, the Court found that the application of the Government of the Swiss Confederation was inadmissible in regard both to the principal claim and to the alternative claim for the reason that Interhandel had not exhausted the local remedies available to it in the United States courts.

AERIAL INCIDENT OF JULY 27, 1955. These three separate cases arose out of the destruction by Bulgarian anti-aircraft of an aircraft belonging to an Israel airline. Israel instituted proceedings before the Court by means of an application in October 1957. Bulgaria challenged the Court's jurisdiction to deal with the claim. Israel contended, however, that since Bulgaria had in 1921 accepted the compulsory jurisdiction of the Permanent Court of International Justice for an unlimited period, and since Bulgaria had been admitted to the United Nations in 1955, the jurisdiction of the present Court became applicable by virtue of Article 36, paragraph 5, of its Statute.

In its judgment on the preliminary objections, delivered on May 26, 1959, the Court found that it was without jurisdiction on the ground that Article 36, paragraph 5, was intended only to preserve declarations in force as between states signatories of the Charter, and not to revive undertakings which had lapsed on the dissolution of the Permanent Court.

On October 28 and November 22, 1957, respectively, the Governments of the United States and of the United Kingdom had filed separate applications with the Court in respect of the same aerial incident. Both Governments claimed damages for the death of their nationals who had been travelling in the aircraft and for the destruction of their property, and founded the jurisdiction of the Court on the acceptance of the compulsory jurisdiction of the Court by the states concerned.

Before the date fixed for the hearings of preliminary objections filed by Bulgaria on October 8, 1958, the United States Government informed the Court that, as a result of further considerations of questions of jurisdiction raised by Bulgaria in these objections, and the United States observations thereon, it had decided to request the discontinuance of the proceedings. The Bulgarian Government did not oppose such discontinuance and, on May 30, 1960, the Court directed that the case should be removed from the List.

The United Kingdom filed its memorial within the time-limit fixed but, before the date set for the filing of the Bulgarian counter-memorial, the Government of the United Kingdom informed the Court of its decision to discontinue the proceedings, having regard to the decision of the Court of May 26, 1959, that it had no jurisdiction in respect of the case. The Bulgarian Government did not oppose discontinuance of the proceedings and, on August 3, 1959, the Court made an order removing the case from the List.

SOVEREIGNTY OVER CERTAIN FRONTIER LAND. By a special agreement signed in March 1957 between the Netherlands and Belgium, the Court was asked to settle a dispute as to the sovereignty over two plots of land situated in an area north of the Belgian town of Turnhout where the frontier between the two countries presents certain unusual features, there being a number of enclaves formed by the Belgian commune of Baerle-Duc and the Netherlands commune of Baarle-Nassau. The Court was informed that this situation was of very ancient origin. From the documents produced by the parties, it appeared that a Communal Minute drawn up by the authorities of these two communes between 1836 and 1841 (on which the Netherlands relied) attributed the two plots in question to Baarle-Nassau, whereas the Descriptive Minute of the frontier annexed to the Boundary Convention of 1843 which was concluded after the separation of Belgium from the Netherlands (and on which Belgium relied) attributed them to Baerle-Duc, as did also the special map annexed to the Boundary Convention. The Netherlands Government maintained that the Boundary Convention recognized the existence of the *status quo* as determined by the Communal Minute, under which sovereignty over the disputed plots was recognized as vested in the Netherlands, and that the provision by which the two plots were attributed to Belgium was vitiated by a mistake, as was evident from a mere comparison of the terms of the Communal Minute with those of the Descriptive Minute. The Netherlands claimed further that its sovereignty over the disputed plots had been established by the exercise of various acts of sovereignty since 1843.

After considering all the evidence produced, the Court concluded that the Boundary Convention did determine to which state the various plots in each commune belonged and that no case of mistake had been made out and, finally, that the acts relied upon by the Netherlands as establishing its sovereignty were largely of a routine and administrative character and were insufficient to displace Belgian sovereignty established by the Boundary Convention. In its judgment delivered on June 20, 1959, the Court accordingly found that sovereignty over the two disputed plots belonged to Belgium.

ARBITRAL AWARD MADE BY THE KING OF SPAIN ON DECEMBER 23, 1906. On October 7, 1894, Honduras and Nicaragua signed a convention for the demarcation of the limits between the two countries, one of the articles of which provided that, in certain circumstances, any points of the boundary line which were left unsettled should be submitted to the decision of the Government of Spain. In

October 1904, the King of Spain was asked to determine that part of the frontier line on which the Mixed Boundary Commission appointed by the two countries had been unable to reach agreement. The King gave his arbitral award on December 23, 1906. Nicaragua contested the validity of the award and, in accordance with a resolution of the Organization of American States, the two countries agreed, in July 1957, on the procedure to be followed for submitting the dispute on this matter to the International Court of Justice.

In the application by which the case was brought before the Court on July 1, 1958, the Government of Honduras claimed that failure by the Government of Nicaragua to give effect to the arbitral award constituted a breach of an international obligation and asked the Court to declare that Nicaragua was under an obligation to give effect to the award. After considering all the evidence produced, the Court found that Nicaragua had in fact freely accepted the designation of the King of Spain as arbitrator, had fully participated in the arbitral proceeding and had thereafter accepted the award. Consequently, the Court found, in its judgment delivered on November 18, 1960, that the award was binding and that Nicaragua was under an obligation to give effect to it.

AERIAL INCIDENT OF SEPTEMBER 4, 1954.   On August 22, 1958, the United States of America instituted proceedings against the Union of Soviet Socialist Republics on account of "certain willful acts committed by military aircraft of the Soviet Government on September 4, 1954, in the international air space over the Sea of Japan against a United States Navy P2-V-type aircraft, commonly known as a Neptune type, and against its crew." In its application to the Court, the United States Government stated that it submitted to the Court's jurisdiction for the purposes of the case and that the Soviet Government was qualified to do likewise. The United States relied on Article 36, paragraph 1, of the Court's Statute, which provides that the jurisdiction of the Court comprises all cases which the parties refer to it. In a letter to the Court, the Soviet Union attributed responsibility for the incident to the United States and said it considered that in this case there were no questions which needed to be considered by the Court and that it saw no basis for turning this question over for examination by the Court. In the circumstances, the Court found that it had not before it any acceptance by the Soviet Government of the jurisdiction of the Court to deal with the dispute and that therefore it could take no further steps upon the application. The Court accordingly, in an order of December 9, 1958, removed the case from the List.

COMPAGNIE DU PORT, DES QUAIS ET DES ENTREPÔTS DE BEYROUTH AND SOCIÉTÉ RADIO-ORIENT.   This case between France and Lebanon arose out of certain measures adopted by the Lebanese Government with regard to two French limited companies, the Compagnie du Port, des Quais et des Entrepôts de Beyrouth and the Société Radio-Orient. The French Government considered these measures to be contrary to certain undertakings embodied in an agreement concluded between France and Lebanon in 1948 relating to concessions of French companies and companies with French capital in Lebanon. France instituted proceedings against Lebanon by means of an application on February 13, 1959. Lebanon raised preliminary objections to the jurisdiction of the Court but, before a date had been fixed for the hearings on the preliminary objections, the Court was informed by the parties that satisfactory arrangements had been concluded: the situation of the Compagnie du Port, des Quais et des Entrepôts de Beyrouth had been settled for the future by a convention of April 13, 1960, between the state of Lebanon and the company, together with an exchange of letters between the President of the Lebanese Council of Ministers and the French Ambassador at Beirut; and the Société Radio-Orient had been fully satisfied by a decision of the Lebanese Council of Ministers dated May 11, 1960. The President of the Court accordingly made an order on August 31, 1960, removing the case from the List.

AERIAL INCIDENT OF NOVEMBER 7, 1954.   On July 7, 1959, the United States of America instituted proceedings against the Union of Soviet Socialist Republics on account of the destruction, on November 7, 1954, of a United States Air Force B-29 aircraft in the Japanese territorial air space over Hokkaido, Japan. In its application to the Court, the United States Government stated that it submitted to the Court's jurisdiction for the purposes of the case and that the Soviet Government was qualified to do likewise. The United States relied on Article 36, paragraph 1, of the Court's Statute, which provides that the jurisdiction of the Court comprises all cases which the parties refer to it. In a letter to the Court, the Soviet Union attributed responsibility for the incident to the United States and said it considered that in this case there were no questions which needed to be solved by the Court and that it did not see any basis for the filing of this case with the Court. In these circumstances, the Court found that it had not before it any acceptance by the Soviet Government of the jurisdiction of the Court to deal with the dispute and therefore it could take no further steps upon the application. The Court accordingly made an order on October 7, 1959, removing the case from the List.

TEMPLE OF PREAH VIHEAR.   In an application instituting proceedings against Thailand, filed on October 6, 1959, Cambodia complained that since 1949 Thailand had persisted in the occupation of a portion of Cambodian territory where there are the ruins of a holy monastery, the Temple of Preah Vihear, a sacred place of pilgrimage and worship for the people of Cambodia. Cambodia asked the Court to declare that territorial sovereignty over the Temple belonged to the Kingdom of Cambodia and that Thailand was under an obligation to withdraw the detachments of armed forces it had stationed since 1954 in the ruins of the Temple. The Government of Thailand filed preliminary objections, on May 23, 1960, to the jurisdiction of the Court, and the proceedings on the merits were suspended.

On May 26, 1961, the Court delivered a judgment in which it rejected the two preliminary objections raised by Thailand, and upheld its jurisdiction. In its judgment on the merits, rendered on June 15, 1962, the Court found that the Temple of Preah Vihear was situated on Cambodian territory. It also held that Thailand was under an obligation to withdraw any military or police force, or other guards or keepers, stationed in the Temple or in its vicinity on Cambodian territory. Finally, it ruled that Thailand was under an obligation to restore any sculptures or similar objects removed by it since it occupied the Temple in 1954.

NORTHERN CAMEROONS.   On May 30, 1961, the Republic of Cameroon instituted proceedings against the United Kingdom. It complained that the United Kingdom, by administering the Northern Cameroons as an integral part of Nigeria, had been in breach of the Trusteeship Agreement for the Territory of the Cameroons under British Administration. It also complained that in its administration of the territory, the United Kingdom had created such conditions that the Trusteeship led to its attachment to Nigeria instead of to the Republic of Cameroon. The United Kingdom objected to the jurisdiction of the Court.

The Court dismissed objections relating to the non-existence of a dispute between the parties and non-compliance with its Rules, but found that it could not adjudicate upon the merits of Cameroon's claim. No decision on the merits could have any practical effect since, as had been recognized by Cameroon, no judgment of the Court could affect the decisions of the General Assembly terminating the Trusteeship Agreement and providing for the attachment of the territory to Nigeria, in accordance with the results of a United Nations supervised plebiscite, nor could it give the United Kingdom any possibility of satisfying the Republic of Cameroon.

SOUTH WEST AFRICA.   On November 4, 1960, Ethiopia and Liberia instituted proceedings against South Africa in a case concerning the continued existence of the mandate for South West Africa and the duties and performance of South Africa as mandatory power. The Court was requested to judge that South West Africa is a territory under mandate to South Africa and that South Africa continues to have obligations thereunder, including those relating to the supervisory functions of the United Nations, and is obliged to render annual reports regarding the territory and to transmit petitions from the territory's inhabitants to the General Assembly.

Regarding the administration of South West Africa, the Court was asked to judge that South Africa has practised *apartheid;* has failed to promote to the utmost the material and moral well-being and social progress of the inhabitants of the territory; has treated the territory in a manner inconsistent with its international status, thereby impeding opportunities for self-determination by the inhabitants of the territory; has established military bases within the territory; and has attempted to modify substantially the terms of the mandate without the consent of the United Nations.

The Court was asked to judge that these actions are in violation of South Africa's obligations under the mandate and that South Africa has the duty to cease such actions and to fulfil its obligations.

South Africa raised preliminary objections to the jurisdiction of the Court, which dismissed them in a judgment of December 21, 1962.

After further written proceedings on the merits, oral proceedings were held from March 15 to November 15, 1965. South Africa contended that the whole mandate for South West Africa had lapsed on the dissolution of the League of Nations and that South Africa was consequently no longer subject to any legal obligations thereunder; alternatively, in the event of it being held that the mandate as such continued in existence despite the dissolution of the League of Nations: (a) that South Africa's former obligations under the mandate to account to the Council of the League of Nations had lapsed upon the dissolution of the League and had not been replaced by any similar obligations relative to supervision by any organ of the United Nations and (b) that South Africa had not, as alleged, violated its obligations as stated in the mandate or in Article 22 of the League Covenant. In support of its arguments, South Africa called a number of witnesses and experts, including administrators and educators from South West Africa and South Africa, professors of sociology, anthropology, international relations, political studies and geography from universities in the United Kingdom, the United States and South Africa; newspaper editors from South West Africa and South Africa; and a military historian.

During the oral proceedings, the Court heard *in camera* the contentions of the parties with regard to an application by South Africa concerning the composition of the Court and, in an order of March 18, 1965, decided, by eight votes to six, not to accede to it. South Africa also applied for the Court to make an inspection in South West Africa and to visit other parts of Africa, including Ethiopia and Liberia. This application was opposed by Ethiopia and Liberia, and on November 29, 1965, the Court announced its decision not to accede to it;

the decision was taken by eight votes to six in respect of the proposals concerning South West Africa and South Africa, and by nine votes to five in respect of the proposals concerning other parts of Africa.

In its judgment delivered on July 18, 1966, the Court found that Ethiopia and Liberia could not be considered to have established any legal right or interest appertaining to them in the subject matter of their claims and accordingly decided to reject them. The Court was divided equally on the matter, the decision being reached by the casting vote of the President.

BARCELONA TRACTION, LIGHT AND POWER COMPANY, LIMITED.   Proceedings concerning the Canadian Barcelona Traction Company, bankrupted in Spain in 1948, were instituted by Belgium against Spain in 1958, the application stating that the share capital of the company had, for more than twenty-five years, belonged largely to Belgian nationals. Belgium claimed compensation on the grounds that the manner in which the company had been bankrupted and its assets subsequently disposed of by the Spanish authorities was contrary to international law. After Spain had filed preliminary objections, proceedings were discontinued in 1961 to allow negotiations to take place, and the Court removed the case from its List.

Negotiations failed to produce a settlement, however, and on June 19, 1962, Belgium submitted a new application. It asked the Court to adjudge and declare that Spain is under an obligation to Belgium to make reparation for the damage caused by the conduct of its organs to the Belgian shareholders of Barcelona Traction; and that such reparation should as far as possible annul all the consequences for Belgian nationals of the acts contrary to international law committed by the organs of the Spanish State. The Court was asked to determine the compensation to be paid by Spain to Belgium by reason of all the incidental damage sustained by Belgian nationals, and to declare that, in the event of annulment of the consequences of the acts complained of proving impossible, Spain should be under an obligation to pay compensation to Belgium amounting to 88 per cent of the value of the business at the date of the bankruptcy, provisionally estimated by Belgium at about $90 million, increased by an amount corresponding to all the incidental damage sustained by Belgian nationals.

Spain raised four preliminary objections, two of which were dismissed, and the other two joined to the resumed proceedings on the merits by the Court's judgment of July 24, 1964. In December 1965, after a six-month extension granted at Spain's request, the first Spanish pleading on the merits was filed. The President of the Court, after ascertaining the views of the parties, then fixed November 30, 1966, as the time-limit for the filing of the reply of Belgium and April 30, 1967, for the filing of the rejoinder of Spain, when the case would become ready for hearing.

Advisory Opinions Given by the Court

CONDITIONS OF ADMISSION OF A STATE TO MEMBERSHIP IN THE UNITED NATIONS. The General Assembly, on November 17, 1947, requested the International Court to give an advisory opinion on whether a member of the United Nations was juridically entitled to make its consent to the admission of a new member dependent on conditions not expressly provided in the Charter—in particular, whether it could make its consent subject to the condition that other states be admitted at the same time.

In the interpretation given of Article 4 of the Charter in its advisory opinion of May 28, 1948, the Court declared that the conditions laid down for the admission of states were exhaustive and that if these conditions were fulfilled by a state which was a candidate, the Security Council ought to make the recommendation which would enable the General Assembly to decide upon the admission.

COMPETENCE OF THE GENERAL ASSEMBLY FOR THE ADMISSION OF A STATE TO THE UNITED NATIONS. The preceding opinion given by the Court did not lead to a settlement of the problem in the Security Council. A member of the United Nations then proposed that the word "recommendation" in Article 4 of the Charter should be construed as not necessarily signifying a favourable recommendation. In other words, a state might be admitted by the General Assembly even in the absence of a recommendation, this being interpreted as an unfavourable recommendation. This would, it was suggested, make it possible to escape the effects of the veto.

In the advisory opinion which the Court delivered on this subject on March 3, 1950, it pointed out that the Charter laid down two conditions for the admission of new members: a "recommendation" by the Security Council and a "decision" by the General Assembly. If the latter body had power to decide without a recommendation by the Security Council, the Council would be deprived of an important function assigned to it by the Charter. The absence of a recommendation by the Security Council, as the result of a veto, could not be interpreted as an "unfavourable" recommendation, since the Council itself had interpreted its own decision as meaning that no recommendation had been made.

REPARATION FOR INJURIES SUFFERED IN THE SERVICE OF THE UNITED NATIONS. As a consequence of the assassination of Count Folke Bernadotte and of others serving the United Nations in Palestine, the Assembly, on December 3, 1948, asked the Court whether the United Nations had the capacity to bring an international claim against the state responsible, with a view to obtaining reparation for damage caused to the Organization and to the victim. If this question were answered in the affirmative, it was further asked in what manner the action taken by the United Nations could be reconciled with such rights as might be possessed by the state of which the victim was a national.

In its opinion of April 11, 1949, the Court held that the Organization was intended to exercise functions and rights which could be explained only on the basis of the possession of a large measure of international personality and the capacity to operate upon the international plane. It followed that the Organization had the capacity to bring a claim and to give it the character of an international action for reparation for the damage that had been caused to it. The Court further declared that the Organization could claim reparation not only in respect of damage caused to itself, but also in respect of damage suffered by the victim or persons entitled through him. Although, according to the traditional rule, diplomatic protection had to be exercised by the national state, the Organization should be regarded in international law as possessing the powers which, even if they are not expressly stated in the Charter, are conferred upon the Organization as being essential to the discharge of its functions. The Organization may be required to entrust its agents with important missions in disturbed parts of the world. In such cases, it is necessary that the agents should receive suitable support and protection.

The Court therefore found that the Organization has the capacity to claim appropriate reparation, including also reparation for damage suffered by the victim or by persons entitled through him. The risk of possible competition between the Organization and the victim's national state could be eliminated either by means of a general convention or by a particular agreement in any individual case.

INTERPRETATION OF PEACE TREATIES WITH BULGARIA, HUNGARY AND ROMANIA.   In April 1949, the General Assembly had expressed "deep concern at the grave accusations made against the Governments of Bulgaria, Hungary and Romania regarding the suppression of human rights and fundamental freedoms in those countries" and had drawn the attention of these governments to their obligations under the peace treaties, including the obligation to co-operate in the settlement of all these questions.

In October 1949, the Assembly declared that the refusal of the three governments to co-operate in its efforts to examine the charges brought against them justified its "concern." Confronted by the charges of treaty violations made by certain powers against the three governments, particularly the charge that they had refused to designate their representatives to the treaty commissions for the settlement of disputes —a procedure prescribed in the peace treaties to deal with such disputes—the Assembly put four questions to the Court for an advisory opinion.

The Court was asked if a dispute existed between the three states and certain allied and associated powers in accordance with the provisions of the peace treaties. On March 30, 1950, the Court declared that a dispute did exist. To the further question whether, if a dispute did exist, the three states were obligated to nominate their representatives to the treaty commissions, the Court gave an affirmative answer. It then set a time-limit of thirty days for the three countries to comply with its opinion.

On their failure to nominate their representatives within this limit, the Court, on July 18, 1950, answered the remaining two questions. It decided that the fact that the three countries had not complied with the Court's opinion did not authorize the Secretary-General to appoint the third member of each commission. In view of this, the Court declared, the answer to the fourth question—Will a commission of two members, one appointed by the Secretary-General, and the other by a party to the dispute, be competent to make a definite and binding decision?—was not necessary.

SOUTH WEST AFRICA: INTERNATIONAL STATUS; VOTING PROCEDURE; ADMISSIBILITY OF HEARINGS OF PETITIONERS. South West Africa, administered by South Africa, is the only League of Nations mandate which has not been placed under the international trusteeship system or, alternatively, given its independence. In 1949, owing to the refusal of South Africa to place the territory under trusteeship and its claim that it had no obligations to submit to United Nations supervision of its administration of South West Africa, the General Assembly requested the International Court to give an opinion concerning the status of the territory.

On July 11, 1950, the Court gave its opinion to the effect that the mandate remained in force and that South Africa was obliged to submit to United Nations supervision over the administration of the territory. It found, however, that South Africa was not under legal obligation to place the territory under trusteeship. South Africa continued to maintain that it had no obligation to submit to United Nations supervision, on the ground, among others, that it would no longer be protected by the unanimity principle of the League of Nations.

In 1954, the General Assembly agreed to take decisions on South West Africa by a two-thirds majority and asked the Court to advise whether this was in accordance with the Court's opinion of July 11, 1950. In an advisory opinion handed down on June 7, 1955, the Court ruled in the affirmative.

In response to a further request from the General Assembly in 1955, the Court indicated, in an advisory opinion of June 1, 1956, that the Assembly could legally authorize its Committee on South West Africa to grant hearings to petitioners.

RESERVATIONS TO GENOCIDE CONVENTION. In November 1950, the General Assembly asked the Court a series of questions as to the position of a state which attached reservations to its signature of the multilateral Convention on the Prevention and Punishment of the Crime of Genocide if other states, signatories of the same convention, objected to these reservations.

The Court considered, in its opinion of May 28, 1951, that even if a convention contained no article on the subject of reservations, it did not follow that they were prohibited. The character of the convention, its purpose and its provisions must be taken into account. It was the compatibility of the reservation with the purpose of the convention which must furnish the criterion of the attitude of the state making the reservation, and of the state which objected thereto. The Court did not consider that it was possible to give an absolute answer to the abstract question put to it.

In regard to the effects of the reservation in relations between states, the Court considered that a state could not be bound by a reservation to which it had not consented. Every state was therefore free to decide for itself whether the state which formulated the reservation was or was not a party to the convention. The situation presented real disadvantages, but they could only be remedied by the insertion in the convention of an article on the use of reservations.

A third question referred to the effects of an objection by a state which was not yet a party to the convention, either because it had not signed it or because it had signed, but not ratified it. The Court was of the opinion that, as regards the first case, it would be inconceivable that a state which had not signed the convention should be able to exclude another state from it. In the second case, the situation was different; the objection was valid, but it would not produce an immediate legal effect; it would merely express and proclaim the attitude which a signatory state would assume when it had become a party to the convention. On all the foregoing points, the Court adjudicated only on the specific case referred to it, namely, the Genocide Convention.

EFFECT OF AWARDS OF COMPENSATION MADE BY THE UNITED NATIONS ADMINISTRATIVE TRIBUNAL. The United Nations Administrative Tribunal was established by the General Assembly to hear applications alleging non-observance of contracts of employment of staff members of the Secretariat of the United Nations or of the terms of appointment of such staff members.

In its advisory opinion of July 13, 1954, the Court considered that the General Assembly of the United Nations was not entitled on any grounds to refuse to give effect to an award of compensation made by the United Nations Administrative Tribunal in favour of a staff member of the United Nations whose contract of service had been terminated without his assent. The Tribunal was an independent and truly judicial body pronouncing final judgments without appeal within the limited field of its functions and not merely an advisory or subordinate organ. Its judgments were therefore binding on the United Nations and thus also on the General Assembly.

JUDGMENTS OF THE ADMINISTRATIVE TRIBUNAL OF THE ILO UPON COMPLAINTS MADE AGAINST UNESCO. The Statute of the Administrative Tribunal of the International Labour Organisation (ILO)—the jurisdiction of which had been accepted by the United Nations Educational, Scientific and Cultural Organization for the purpose of settling certain disputes which might arise between it and its staff members—provided that the Tribunal's judgments should be final and without appeal, subject to the right of UNESCO to challenge them on the grounds, *inter alia*, that a decision of the Tribunal confirming its jurisdiction was wrong. The Statute further provided that, in the event of such a challenge, the question of the validity of the decision should be referred to the Court for an advisory opinion, which would be binding.

In a resolution of November 25, 1955, referring to four judgments of ILO's Administrative Tribunal on complaints of former UNESCO staff members, the UNESCO Executive Board put three questions to the Court.

UNESCO alleged that the four judgments given by the Tribunal in favour of staff members were invalid on the ground that the Tribunal had wrongly decided the question of its own jurisdiction. UNESCO contended that the staff members, who had held fixed-term appointments and who had complained of the Director-General's refusal to renew their contracts on expiry, had no legal right to such renewal, and that consequently the Tribunal had no jurisdiction, since it was competent to hear only complaints alleging non-observance of the terms of appointment of officials and of provisions of the staff regulations. It accordingly requested an advisory opinion of the Court.

The Court, on October 23, 1956, decided that an administrative memorandum, which had announced that all holders of fixed-term contracts would, subject to certain conditions, be offered renewals, might reasonably be regarded as binding on the organization and that in establishing the jurisdiction of the Tribunal, it was sufficient that the complaints should appear to have a substantial and not merely an artificial connection with the terms and provisions invoked. The Court was not concerned with the decisions of the Tribunal on the merits. On the issue of jurisdiction, it expressed the opinion that the Tribunal had been competent to hear the complaints in question.

CONSTITUTION OF THE MARITIME SAFETY COMMITTEE OF IMCO. The Inter-Governmental Maritime Consultative Organization (IMCO) comprises, among other organs, an Assembly and a Maritime Safety Committee. Under the terms of Article 28 a, of the Convention establishing IMCO, this Committee consists of fourteen members elected by the Assembly from IMCO members having an important interest in maritime safety, "of which not less than eight shall be the largest ship-owning nations." When on January 15, 1959, the IMCO Assembly, for the first time, proceeded to elect the members of the Committee, it elected neither Liberia nor Panama, although those two states were among the eight members of IMCO which possessed the largest registered tonnage. Subsequently, the Assembly decided to ask the Court whether the Maritime Safety Committee was constituted in accordance with the IMCO Convention.

In its advisory opinion on June 8, 1960, the Court replied to this question in the negative.

CERTAIN EXPENSES OF THE UNITED NATIONS (ARTICLE 17, PARAGRAPH 2, OF THE CHARTER). Article 17, paragraph 2, of the Charter of the United Nations provides that "the expenses of the Organization shall be borne by the Members as apportioned by the General Assembly." On December 20, 1961, the General Assembly adopted a resolution requesting an advisory opinion on whether the expenditures authorized by it relating to United Nations operations in the Congo and to the operations of the United Nations Emergency Force in the Middle East constituted "expenses of the Organization" within the meaning of this Article and paragraph of the Charter. The Court, in its advisory opinion of July 20, 1962, replied in the affirmative that these expenditures were "expenses of the United Nations." The Court pointed out that under Article 17, paragraph 2, of the Charter "the expenses of the Organization" are the amounts paid out to defray the costs of carrying out the purposes of the Organization. After examining the resolutions authorizing the expenditures in question, the Court concluded that they were so incurred. The Court also analysed the principal arguments which had been advanced against the conclusion that these expenditures should be considered as "expenses of the Organization" and found them to be unfounded.

INTERNATIONAL LAW COMMISSION

The International Law Commission has as its object the promotion of the progressive development of international law and its codification. The Statute of the Commission, which, with various later amendments, governs its activities, was originally adopted by the General Assembly on November 21, 1947; the Commission held its first session in 1949.

The Commission consists of twenty-five members (originally fifteen, but increased to twenty-one in 1956 and to twenty-five in 1961), who sit in their personal capacity as experts in international law, and not as representatives of governments. They are elected by the General Assembly for five-year terms.

The Commission normally meets in Geneva for a single session each year. Its records and documents and its annual reports to the General Assembly are published in the *Yearbooks of the International Law Commission.*

When the Commission has chosen a particular topic for work and has reported it to the General Assembly for approval, or when the General Assembly has requested the Commission to work on a particular topic, its usual method of work is as follows. It appoints one of its members as special rapporteur on that topic, and he prepares a draft, usually in the form of draft articles with commentaries, for discussion and adoption by the Commission. After the Commission has provisionally adopted a set of draft articles, it decides to submit them to the governments of member states for comments. Thereafter, the draft articles and commentaries are revised by the Commission in the light of the comments submitted in writing, or made orally in the debates of the General Assembly. When the revision of a set of draft articles has been completed, it is submitted to the General Assembly, which may decide to convoke an international conference to conclude a convention on the topic, or may decide upon some other disposition.

The greater part of the work of the Commission has been referred by the General Assembly to codification conferences, which have adopted multilateral conventions and opened them for signature, ratification and accession by states. This work is described in the section on "Multilateral agreements concluded under the auspices of the United Nations following consideration of the topics by the International Law Commission" (*see page* 458).

Topics which have been considered by the Commission but which have not led, or not yet led, to the conclusion of conventions are dealt with below; reference is also made to any subsequent consideration of these topics in other United Nations organs.

Items Relating to Peace and Security

ARBITRAL PROCEDURE.   Among the topics selected for codification by the Commission at its first session in 1949 was arbitral procedure in the case of international disputes. On the basis of reports submitted by a special rapporteur, the matter was discussed at later sessions and, in 1952, the Commission approved a set of draft articles on the subject. In 1953, the articles, with certain revisions, were presented to the General Assembly, which decided to transmit the text to member governments for whatever comments they deemed appropriate.

In 1955, the Assembly decided to refer the draft back to the Commission to consider the comments of governments and the discussion in the Sixth (Legal) Committee in so far as they might contribute further to the value of the draft. The Commission was asked to report on the matter at the Assembly's 1958 session.

The Commission considered the subject at its 1957 session and, the following year, prepared a model set of rules which it submitted to the Assembly. The Assembly decided to bring the model set of rules to the attention of member states for use in drawing up treaties of arbitration; it also asked governments for their comments, in order to facilitate a review of the matter by the United Nations at an appropriate time.

DRAFT DECLARATION ON RIGHTS AND DUTIES OF STATES. In 1949, on the instructions of the General Assembly, the Commission also prepared a draft declaration on the rights and duties of states, in the form of fourteen articles with commentaries. At its 1949 session, the Assembly commended the draft declaration to the continuing attention of member states and of jurists of all nations; it also invited the suggestions of members on whether any further action should be taken by the Assembly. In view of the scarcity of replies from governments, the Assembly decided in 1951 to postpone further action on the matter.

FORMULATION OF THE NÜRNBERG PRINCIPLES. In 1950, the Commission, as directed by the General Assembly, completed a formulation of the principles of international law recognized in the Charter of the Nürnberg Tribunal and in the judgment of the Tribunal. In the same year, the Assembly decided to send the formulation, which consisted of seven principles with commentaries, to the governments of member states for comments, and requested the Commission, in preparing a draft code of offences against the peace and security of mankind (also requested by the Assembly), to take account of the observations on the formulation which were made in the Assembly or later received from governments.

INTERNATIONAL CRIMINAL JURISDICTION. At the request of the General Assembly, in 1950, the International Law Commission studied the desirability and possibility of establishing an international judicial organ for the trial of genocide and certain other crimes. The Commission concluded that the establishment of an international criminal court was both possible and desirable. It recommended against such a court being set up as a chamber of the International Court of Justice.

In 1951, a special committee of seventeen members, set up by the General Assembly, completed a draft statute for an international criminal court. Under the draft statute, it was proposed that the court should have a permanent structure but should function only on the basis of cases submitted to it. The report of the committee, together with the draft statute, was communicated to governments for their observations. Only a few governments commented on the draft, however, and, in 1952, the Assembly decided to set up a new committee, consisting, again, of seventeen members, which met at United Nations Headquarters in the summer of 1953. The terms of reference of the committee were: (1) to explore the implications and consequences of establishing an international criminal court and of the various methods by which this might be done; (2) to study the relationship between such a court and the United Nations; and (3) to re-examine the draft statute.

The report of the committee, which embodied a number of changes in the 1951 draft statute and alternative texts in respect of several articles, was placed before the Assembly at its 1954 session. The Assembly, however, decided to postpone consideration of the report until it had taken up, in 1956, the report of the special committee on defining aggression, together with the draft code of offences against the peace and security of mankind (*see below*).

In 1956 and 1957, the Assembly postponed discussion of the topic; it was felt that, since the subject was related to the question of defining aggression and to the draft code of offences, consideration should be deferred until the Assembly took up the two related items.

DRAFT CODE OF OFFENCES AGAINST THE PEACE AND SECURITY OF MANKIND, AND THE QUESTION OF DEFINING AGGRESSION. In 1951, the Commission dealt with two interrelated questions which had been referred to it by the General Assembly, namely, the formulation of a draft Code of Offences against the Peace and Security of Mankind, and the Question of Defining Aggression. In connection with the latter question, the General Assembly had referred to the Commission a proposal submitted to the Assembly by the Soviet Union. The Commission did not itself furnish an express definition of aggression, but decided to include acts of aggression in the draft Code of Offences against the Peace and Security of Mankind which it was in the course of preparing. The draft Code listed a series of offences, characterized as "crimes under international law, for which the responsible individuals shall be punishable." The Commission did not propose an instrument for implementing the Code; it thought that, pending establishment of an international criminal court, the Code might be applied by national courts. The Commission considered it impracticable to prescribe a definite penalty for each offence, and left it to the competent tribunal to determine the penalty for any offence under the Code, taking into account the gravity of the particular offence.

At its 1951 session, the Assembly examined the question of defining aggression but decided to postpone consideration of the draft Code. The Assembly came to the conclusion that it was both possible and desirable to achieve a definition of aggression by referring "to the elements which constitute it." At the Assembly's request, the Secretary-General submitted a detailed analysis which covered all aspects of the question.

In December 1952, the Assembly established a fifteen-member special committee which was requested to submit to the Assembly's ninth session, in 1954, draft definitions of aggression or draft statements of the notion of aggression. The special committee met at United Nations Headquarters from August 24 to September 21, 1953. Several texts were presented which aimed at defining aggression, in one form or another. The committee, however, decided unanimously not to put the texts to a vote but to transmit them to the General Assembly and to member states for comments. Comments were received from eleven member governments.

In 1954, the Assembly established another special committee, consisting of nineteen members, and requested it to report to the eleventh session of the Assembly, in 1956. Consideration of the draft Code of Offences against the Peace and Security of Mankind was postponed, owing to the similarity of the problems involved, until the special committee on defining aggression had submitted its report.

The nineteen-member committee met at United Nations Headquarters from October 8 to November 1, 1956. It did not adopt a definition but decided to transmit its report to the Assembly, together with the draft definitions previously submitted to it.

In 1957, the Assembly decided to invite the views of twenty-two states admitted to the United Nations since December 14, 1955, and to renew the request for comments of members which had not previously submitted any. It also decided to refer the replies of governments to a committee composed of member states which had served on the General Committee of the Assembly at its most recent session. The Assembly again deferred consideration of the draft Code until such time as it once more took up the question of defining aggression.

The committee established by the Assembly in 1957 met at Headquarters from April 14 to 24, 1959, to study the comments from governments for the purpose of determining when it would be appropriate for the Assembly to resume consideration of the question. The committee decided that the fourteen replies received did not indicate any change of attitude, and agreed to postpone further consideration of the question until April 1962, unless an absolute majority of its members favoured an earlier meeting in the light of new developments.

The committee met again at United Nations Headquarters in 1962 and in 1965, but on each occasion found itself unable to determine any particular time as appropriate for the Assembly to resume consideration of the question of defining aggression. At its meeting in April 1965, the Committee accordingly decided to adjourn its deliberations until April 1967.

Other Items Considered by the International Law Commission

WAYS AND MEANS OF MAKING THE EVIDENCE OF CUSTOMARY INTERNATIONAL LAW MORE READILY AVAILABLE. At its second session, in 1950, the Commission, as required by its Statute, made suggestions regarding ways and means of making the evidence of customary international law more readily available. In the same year, the General Assembly invited the Secretary-General to consider and report on these suggestions, and on February 1, 1952, it again requested him to report on certain of them. At its seventh session, in 1952, the Assembly authorized the Secretary-General to publish a list of treaty collections and a repertoire of the practice of the Security Council; the former appeared in 1955, and the latter originally in 1954, with supplements issued later. In 1959 and 1962, after further reports by the Secretary-General, the General Assembly decided upon the publication of the *United Nations Juridical Yearbook;* a provisional volume was issued for 1962, and printed volumes are appearing for subsequent years.

RESERVATIONS TO MULTILATERAL CONVENTIONS. In 1951, the Commission reported to the General Assembly on reservations to multilateral conventions. This question arose out of difficulties encountered by the Secretary-General in his practice as depositary of the Genocide Convention. The Secretary-General had followed the rule adopted by the League of Nations, which was that reservations to a clause of a treaty required acceptance by all the parties to the treaty, but this rule was contested by some member states, and in 1950, the Secretary-General had asked the General Assembly for directions on the procedure he should follow. The General Assembly requested an advisory opinion from the International Court of Justice on reservations to the Genocide Convention (*see page* 447), and referred the general question of reservations to multilateral conventions to the Commission, for study both from the point of view of codification and from that of the progressive development of international law. In its report of 1951, the Commission said that the criterion of compatibility with the object and purpose of a convention—applied by the International Court of Justice to the Genocide Convention—would not be suitable for application to multilateral conventions in general; while no single rule uniformly applied could be wholly satisfactory, the rule suitable for application in the majority of cases was that theretofore followed by the Secretary-General. The Assembly, on January 12, 1952, endorsed the Commission's recommendation that clauses on reservations should be inserted in future conventions; stated that the Court's advisory opinion should be followed in regard to the Genocide Convention; and asked the Secretary-General, in respect of future United Nations conventions, to act as depositary for documents containing reservations or objections thereto without passing on the legal effect of such documents, which were to be communicated to all states concerned, to whom it would be left to draw the legal consequences. In 1959, the Secretary-General was asked to follow the same practice with respect to United Nations conventions concluded before, as well as after, the Assembly's decision of 1952.

Extended Participation in General Multilateral Treaties
Concluded under the Auspices of the League of Nations

In 1962, the General Assembly requested the Commission to study the question of participation of new states in certain general multilateral treaties, concluded under the auspices of the League of Nations, which by their terms authorized the Council of the League to invite additional states to become parties but to which states that had not been so invited by the League Council before the dissolution of the League were unable to become parties for want of an invitation.

In its report of 1963, the Commission said that the General Assembly appeared to be entitled, if it so desired, to designate an organ of the United Nations to assume and fulfil the powers which, under the participation clauses of the treaties in question, were formerly exercisable by the Council of the League. The Commission also observed that a number of these treaties might hold no interest to states or might need to be adapted to contemporary conditions.

At its 1963 session, the Assembly decided that it was itself the appropriate organ of the United Nations to exercise the functions of the League Council under twenty-one general multilateral treaties of a technical and non-political character concluded under the auspices of the League of Nations; it also requested the Secretary-General to invite each state which was a member of the United Nations or of a specialized agency or a party to the Statute of the International Court of Justice, or had been designated for this purpose by the Assembly, and which otherwise was not eligible to become a party to the treaties in question, to accede thereto by depositing an instrument of accession with the Secretary-General.

In 1965, the Assembly noted that the Secretary-General had already issued invitations for accession to two treaties which were still in force and were of interest for accession by additional states, and recognized that nine other treaties which it listed in an annex to its resolution might be of interest for accession by additional states. It also drew the attention of parties to the desirability of adapting some of these treaties to contemporary conditions.

Topics Presently under Consideration by the International Law Commission

LAW OF TREATIES. This topic was among those originally selected for codification by the Commission in 1949. After three successive rapporteurs had submitted reports, the Commission decided, in 1961, that its aim would be to prepare draft articles intended to serve as the basis for a convention and that the special rapporteur should be requested to re-examine the work previously done by the Commission in this field.

In 1962, 1963 and 1964, the Commission adopted parts I, II and III of its draft articles on the law of treaties, dealing, respectively, with the conclusion, entry into force and registration of treaties; the invalidity and termination of treaties; and the application, effects, modification and interpretation of treaties. Each part was submitted to governments for their observations. In 1965, the Commission considered the comments received from governments up to that date and re-examined the articles contained in part I. At its twentieth session, in 1965, the General Assembly recommended that the Commission should continue its work on the law of treaties.

SPECIAL MISSIONS. The Vienna Convention on Diplomatic Relations, which was concluded in 1961 on the basis of draft articles prepared by the Commission (see page 462), dealt only with permanent diplomatic missions. In 1963, in accordance with a recommendation adopted at the Vienna Conference and endorsed by the General Assembly, the Commission appointed a special rapporteur to prepare a draft set of articles relating to special missions. In 1964 and 1965, the Commission considered the reports submitted by the special rapporteur and adopted a number of draft articles in which it sought to embody the modern rules of international law concerning special missions. The position of delegates to congresses and conferences was excluded from the scope of these articles. Governments were asked to submit by May 1, 1966, their comments regarding the articles adopted. In December 1965, the General Assembly requested the Commission to continue its work so that a final draft might, if possible, be submitted in 1966.

OTHER ITEMS UNDER CONSIDERATION. In 1962, the Commission appointed a special rapporteur on the subject of relations between states and inter-governmental organizations. It was agreed at the Commission's 1964 session, following the submission of a report by the special rapporteur in 1963, that priority should be given to the question of diplomatic law in its application to this topic. In 1963, special rapporteurs were also appointed for the topics of state responsibility and succession of states and governments.

MULTILATERAL AGREEMENTS CONCLUDED UNDER UNITED NATIONS AUSPICES FOLLOWING CONSIDERATION OF THE TOPICS BY THE INTERNATIONAL LAW COMMISSION

Law of the Sea

WORK OF THE INTERNATIONAL LAW COMMISSION. At its first session in 1949, the Commission included the régime of the high seas and the régime of the territorial sea among topics on which it considered codification was necessary and feasible. Work began on the régime of the high seas with the appointment of a special rapporteur, who presented his first report on the régime of the high seas to the Commission in 1950. In a second report, submitted in 1951, the special rapporteur also dealt with the continental shelf and various related subjects, namely, conservation of the resources of the sea, sedentary fisheries and the contiguous zone. At the same session, the Commission decided to start work on the régime of the territorial sea. In his report on the régime of the territorial sea, the special rapporteur took into account a report of a group of experts, who had met at The Hague in April 1953, on various technical questions related to the topic, as well as comments received from governments giving their views on the delimitation of the territorial sea between two adjacent states.

At successive stages in the preparation of articles on these topics, the draft articles were submitted to governments for their comments and were revised in the light of those comments.

In 1954, the General Assembly asked the Commission to group together systematically all the articles it had adopted concerning the high seas, the territorial sea, the contiguous zone, the continental shelf and the conservation of the living resources of the sea. In 1955, the Commission continued its work in line with these instructions. In its work, the Commission was aided considerably by results achieved by the International Technical Conference on the Conservation of the Living Resources of the Sea, which was held in April and May of that year.

In 1956, the Commission prepared its final report on the Law of the Sea, containing seventy-three draft articles and covering the territorial sea, the high seas, fishing, the contiguous zone and the continental shelf.

This report was submitted to the General Assembly, which, on February 21, 1957, decided to convene an international conference of plenipotentiaries to examine the law of the sea, taking account of not only the legal, but also the technical, biological, economic and political aspects of the problem. The results of its work were to be embodied in one or more international conventions or such other instruments as the conference might deem appropriate.

FIRST UNITED NATIONS CONFERENCE ON THE LAW OF THE SEA. The first United Nations Conference on the Law of the Sea met in Geneva from February 24 to April 27, 1958. Of eighty-six states represented, seventy-nine were members of the United Nations and seven were members of specialized agencies but not of the United Nations. In addition to the set of draft articles drawn up by the Commission, the Conference had before it documentary material prepared by the Secretariat and the specialized agencies, as well as papers by independent experts on the subject.

In view of the wide scope of its work, the Conference established five main committees, each of which, subsequently, submitted draft articles as approved. The Conference agreed to embody these draft articles, some in amended form, in the following four separate draft conventions: the Convention on the Territorial Sea and the Contiguous Zone, the Convention on the High Seas, the Convention on Fishing and the Conservation of the Living Resources of the High Seas, and the Convention on the Continental Shelf.

The Convention on the Territorial Sea and the Contiguous Zone proclaims the juridical character of territorial waters, sets out criteria for delimiting the territorial sea, establishes specific rules for the right of innocent passage of ships through territorial waters and sets forth conditions in which it can be exercised or suspended. The Convention on the High Seas sets out, in general, the conditions under which freedom of the high seas may be exercised. The Convention on Fishing and the Conservation of the Living Resources of the High Seas establishes regulations on conservation, including a procedure for the settlement of disputes by a special commission whose decisions shall be binding.

The Convention on the Continental Shelf deals with the seabed which constitutes the prolongation of a continent. It regulates the exploitation and exploration of resources such as offshore oil or pearl-bearing oysters.

In addition to the four Conventions, the Conference adopted an Optional Protocol of Signature concerning the compulsory settlement of disputes which may arise regarding the Conventions. This provides for compulsory jurisdiction of the International Court or, if the parties so prefer, for submission of the dispute to conciliation or arbitration. The Conference also adopted nine resolutions on various subjects, including the matter of convening a second United Nations Conference on the Law of the Sea.

The final act of the Conference was signed on April 29, 1958. All the Conventions remained open for signature, until October 31, 1958, by members of the United Nations or the specialized agencies and by any other state invited by the General Assembly to become a party; thereafter, the Conventions remained open for accession by such states at any time. Each Convention was to enter into force thirty days after twenty-two ratifications or accessions were received.

The four conventions entered into force on the following dates: the Convention on the High Seas and the Optional Protocol of Signature concerning the Compulsory Settlement of Disputes, September 30, 1962; the Convention on the Continental Shelf, June 10, 1964; the Convention on the Territorial Sea and the Contiguous Zone, September 10, 1965; and the Convention on Fishing and the Conservation of the Living Resources of the High Seas, March 20, 1966.

SECOND UNITED NATIONS CONFERENCE ON THE LAW OF THE SEA. On December 10, 1958, the General Assembly asked the Secretary-General to convene a second United Nations Conference on the Law of the Sea to consider further the questions of the breadth of the territorial sea and fishery limits, questions which had been left unsettled by the first Conference on the Law of the Sea.

Eighty-two states were represented at the Conference, which was held in Geneva from March 16 to April 26, 1960. The Conference failed to adopt any substantive proposal on the two questions before it. It did, however, approve a resolution expressing the need for technical assistance in fishing.

Nationality, including Statelessness

WORK OF THE INTERNATIONAL LAW COMMISSION. One of the topics selected for codification by the International Law Commission at its first session in 1949 was nationality, including statelessness.

At its second session, in 1950, the Commission was asked by the Economic and Social Council to draft a convention regarding the nationality of married women, embodying certain principles recommended by the Commission on the Status of Women. In 1952, the Commission received from its special rapporteur a draft of a convention on the nationality of married persons, but decided that the question could not suitably be considered by it separately but only in the context, and as an integral part, of the whole subject of nationality. The Commission therefore took no further action with respect to the draft. The problem of the nationality of married women continued to receive consideration by other United Nations bodies (see page 368).

Meanwhile, the Commission was informed in 1951 of a request by the Economic and Social Council that it should prepare at the earliest possible date a draft international convention or conventions for the elimination of statelessness. As a result, the Commission, in 1953, prepared two drafts, one on the elimination of future statelessness and the other on the reduction of future statelessness. Both drafts were transmitted to governments for their observations and, in the light of these, the Commission in 1954 redrafted some of the articles. The two draft conventions, each consisting of eighteen articles, aimed, on the one hand, at facilitating acquisition of the nationality of a country by reason of birth within its borders and, on the other hand, at avoiding the loss of nationality except when another nationality was acquired.

UNITED NATIONS CONFERENCE ON THE ELIMINATION OR REDUCTION OF FUTURE STATELESSNESS. On December 4, 1954, the Assembly expressed its desire that an international conference of plenipotentiaries be convened to conclude a convention for the reduction or elimination of future statelessness as soon as at least twenty states had communicated to the Secretary-General their willingness to co-operate in such a conference.

The Conference, which met at Geneva from March 24 to April 18, 1959, adopted provisions aimed at reducing statelessness at birth but failed to reach agreement on how to limit the freedom of states to deprive citizens of their nationality. Consequently, the Conference recommended to the competent organs of the United Nations that it be reconvened at the earliest possible time in order to complete its work.

At its second part, held in New York from August 15 to 28, 1961, the Conference adopted a Convention on the Reduction of Statelessness, which was open for signature from August 30, 1961 until May 31, 1962. The treaty will enter into force two years after the date of the deposit with the Secretary-General of the sixth instrument of ratification or accession. By the end of 1965, the instrument had been signed by five states, but no ratifications or accessions had been received.

Diplomatic Relations

WORK OF THE INTERNATIONAL LAW COMMISSION. In 1952, the Commission undertook the task of codifying the rules of international law governing diplomatic relations.

In 1954, the Commission appointed a special rapporteur who, in 1957, presented a report on the basis of which the Commission drew up a set of draft articles which were later circulated to member governments for their comments. The draft was revised in 1958 in the light of observations by governments and those made in the Assembly's Sixth (Legal) Committee, and the Commission proposed to the Assembly that the text be recommended to member countries with a view to the conclusion of a convention.

UNITED NATIONS CONFERENCE ON DIPLOMATIC INTERCOURSE AND IMMUNITIES. On December 7, 1959, the Assembly endorsed the recommendation of the Commission and decided that an international conference should be convened, not later than the spring of 1961, to formulate a convention on the subject of diplomatic intercourse and immunities. The chapter of the Commission's report, containing forty-five draft articles on diplomatic intercourse and immunities, was referred to the conference by the Assembly.

The United Nations Conference on Diplomatic Intercourse and Immunities met in Vienna from March 2 to April 14, 1961. It was attended by some 320 delegates from eighty-one countries. The Conference adopted the Vienna Convention on Diplomatic Relations, consisting of fifty-three articles and covering most major aspects of permanent diplomatic relations between states. It also approved Optional Protocols concerning acquisition of nationality and the compulsory settlement of disputes.

The final act of the Conference was signed on April 18, 1961, by representatives of seventy-five states. The Convention and Optional Protocols remained open for signature until October 31, 1961, at the Federal Ministry of Foreign Affairs of Austria and subsequently, until March 31, 1962, at United Nations Headquarters. They remain open for accession at any time by all members of the United Nations or of any of its related agencies or parties to the Statute of the International Court, and by any other state invited by the General Assembly to become a party. The Convention and the two Optional Protocols entered into force on April 24, 1964.

Consular Relations

WORK OF THE INTERNATIONAL LAW COMMISSION. In 1955, the Commission decided to initiate work on codification of the rules of international law governing consular relations, and appointed a special rapporteur for the subject. The rapporteur submitted a first report in 1957 and a second one in 1960. At the Commission's 1960 session, a set of sixty-five draft articles was prepared and circulated to member governments for comment. In 1961, the articles were revised in the light of observations by governments and a draft of seventy-one articles was adopted and submitted by the Commission to the General Assembly's sixteenth session later in the year. The Assembly accepted the draft as a satisfactory basis for an international convention and decided that an international conference of plenipotentiaries should be convened in Vienna in 1963.

UNITED NATIONS CONFERENCE ON CONSULAR RELATIONS. The United Nations Conference on Consular Relations, which was attended by delegates of ninety-five countries, met in Vienna from March 4 to April 22, 1963.

The Conference adopted the Vienna Convention on Consular Relations, consisting of seventy-nine articles relating to consular relations, privileges and immunities. It also approved Optional Protocols concerning acquisition of nationality and the compulsory settlement of disputes.

The final act of the Conference was signed on April 24, 1963. The Convention and Optional Protocols remained open for signature until October 31, 1963, at the Federal Ministry of Foreign Affairs of Austria and subsequently, until March 31, 1964, at United Nations Headquarters. They remain open for accession at any time by all members of the United Nations or of any of its related agencies or parties to the Statute of the International Court of Justice, and by any other state invited by the General Assembly to become a party to the Convention and Optional Protocols.

The Convention will enter into force thirty days after twenty-two instruments of ratification or accession are received by the Secretary-General. By December 31, 1965, seventeen countries had ratified or acceded to the Convention. By the same date, eighteen countries had signed and seven had ratified or acceded to the Optional Protocol concerning Acquisition of Nationality; this instrument will come into effect on the same day as the Convention or thirty days after the second instrument of ratification or accession has been deposited with the Secretary-General, whichever date is the later.

The Optional Protocol concerning the Compulsory Settlement of Disputes will also come into effect on the same day as the Convention or thirty days after the second instrument of ratification or accession has been deposited with the Secretary-General, whichever date is the later. It had been signed by thirty-eight states and ratified or acceded to by seven countries as of December 31, 1965.

OTHER LEGAL QUESTIONS

Amendment and Review of the Charter

CHARTER REVIEW. At its first session in 1946, the General Assembly dealt with three items concerned with voting in the Security Council, two of which would have called for a general conference under Article 109 of the Charter. The Assembly, however, concerned itself only with voting in the Council *per se*, not with a possible Charter review conference.

At its eighth session, in 1953, the General Assembly considered three items dealing with a possible review of the Charter. They concerned the publication of documents and preparatory studies in connection with a possible Charter review. A resolution adopted by the Assembly on November 27, 1953, requested the Secretary-General to prepare and circulate among member states during 1954 or shortly thereafter (*a*) a systematic compilation of the documents of the United Nations Conference on International Organization (San Francisco Conference); (*b*) a complete index of the documents of that Conference; and (*c*) a Repertory of the Practice of United Nations Organs, appropriately indexed.

Most of the documentation requested by the General Assembly was prepared by the Secretariat and circulated to member states before and during the tenth session of the Assembly in 1955, and periodic supplements to the Repertory have been issued.

In conformity with Article 109, paragraph 3, of the Charter, the question of convening a general conference for the purpose of reviewing the Charter appeared on the agenda of the tenth session of the General Assembly. On November 21, 1955, the General Assembly established a committee, composed of all the members of the United Nations, to consider, after consultation with the Secretary-General, the question of fixing an appropriate time and place for a conference and to report its recommendations to the Assembly's twelfth session. The Secretary-General was requested to complete and continue the publication programme undertaken pursuant to the Assembly's resolution of November 27, 1953.

The representatives of the USSR and Poland stated that their delegations would not be able to take part in the work of the committee or in any action aimed at reviewing the Charter. On December 16, 1955, the Security Council adopted a resolution in which it expressed its concurrence in the Assembly's decision.

At its 1957, 1959, 1961, 1962, 1963 and 1965 sessions, the Assembly decided, after consideration each time of the report of the committee, that the committee be kept in being and be invited to report with recommendations to the Assembly, and that the publication programme on the Repertory be continued.

AMENDMENTS TO ARTICLES 23, 27, 61 AND 109 OF THE CHARTER. Proposals to enlarge the membership of various United Nations bodies have been made on the grounds that the substantial increase in the membership of the United Nations made such an enlargement necessary.

Between 1956 and 1959, the following three questions were considered: (1) Charter amendment so as to increase the number of non-permanent members of the Security Council and the number of votes required for the Council's decisions; (2) Charter amendment so as to enlarge the eighteen-member Economic and Social Council; and (3) amendment of the Statute of the International Court of Justice so as to increase the number of judges.

In accordance with a resolution adopted by the General Assembly in 1959, the matter of enlarging the membership of the Security Council and the Economic and Social Council was taken up in the Special Political Committee at the fifteenth (1961) session of the Assembly. The discussion revealed widespread agreement on the need to enlarge the two Councils, but the Committee could not agree on how to attain this objective. Consequently, no recommendation was made to the Assembly on the subject.

On July 22, 1963, the Economic and Social Council, after consideration of a resolution of the Economic Commission for Africa on the representation of Africa in the Council, adopted a resolution urging the Assembly, in the light of the additional increase in the membership of the United Nations, to take the necessary action at its eighteenth (1963) session to bring about an appropriate increase in the membership of the Council.

The question of the equitable geographical distribution of members of the Security Council and the Economic and Social Council was considered by the General Assembly at its eighteenth session. On December 17, 1963, the Assembly decided to adopt, in accordance with Article 108 of the Charter of the United Nations, amendments to Articles 23, 27 and 61 of the Charter increasing the membership of the Security Council from eleven to fifteen and the membership of the Economic and Social Council from eighteen to twenty-seven, and, in the case of the Security Council, increasing from seven to nine the number of votes required for adoption of decisions by the Council. In the same resolution, the Assembly further decided the following pattern of election: of the ten non-permanent members of the Security Council, five were to be elected from African and Asian states, one from eastern European states, two from Latin American states and two from western European and other states. Of the nine additional members of the Economic and Social Council, seven were to be elected from African and Asian states, one from Latin American states and one from western European and other states.

In accordance with the provisions of Article 108 of the Charter, the amendments to Articles 23, 27 and 61 came into force on August 31, 1965, when the last of the instruments of ratification of the permanent members of the Security Council was deposited with the Secretary-General. On that date, ninety-five member states had ratified the amendments.

Paragraph 1 of Article 109 of the Charter provides for the calling of a Charter review conference by a two-thirds vote of the members of the General Assembly and by "a vote of any seven members of the Security Council." Paragraph 3 of the same Article provides that if such a conference has not been held before the tenth annual session of the Assembly, the proposal to call such a conference shall be placed on the agenda of that session and the conference shall be held if so decided by a majority vote of the members of the Assembly and "by a vote of any seven members of the Security Council." In view of the coming into force of the amendment to Article 27 increasing from seven to nine the number of votes required for adoption of decisions by the Security Council, the Secretary-General requested, on September 16, 1965, the inclusion in the agenda of the Assembly's twentieth session of an item entitled "Amendment of Article 109 of the Charter of the United Nations."

On December 20, 1965, the General Assembly decided, on the recommendation of the Sixth Committee, to adopt and submit for ratification by member states an amendment to paragraph 1 of Article 109, to the effect that the word "seven" in that paragraph should be replaced by the word "nine." The Assembly also called on all member states to ratify this amendment at the earliest possible date.

Registration and Publication of Treaties and International Agreements

Article 102 of the Charter provides that every treaty and international agreement entered into by any member state after the coming into force of the Charter (October 24, 1945) shall be registered and published by the Secretariat. No party to a treaty or agreement not so registered may invoke it before any United Nations organ.

Recognizing the importance of orderly registration and publication of treaties and international agreements, the General Assembly adopted, on December 14, 1946, detailed regulations to give effect to Article 102 of the Charter. These regulations take into account the desirability of avoiding any breach in the continuity of the system of registration and publication of treaties first introduced under the Covenant of the League of Nations. Accordingly, they do not confine the publication of treaties to those registered in accordance with Article 102 of the Charter, but provide that member states may transmit for filing and recording and publication by the Secretariat treaties and international agreements entered into before October 24, 1945, but which were not included in the League of Nations *Treaty Series*. Similarly, the Secretariat may receive for filing and recording and publication, treaties and international agreements from non-member states concluded by them before or after the entry into force of the Charter and which were not included in the League of Nations *Treaty Series*.

Under the regulations, specialized agencies may also, subject to certain conditions, register or file and record a treaty with the Secretariat, while the United Nations itself registers *ex-officio* international agreements, *inter alia*, when it is a party to such agreements. In order to keep the Register complete, the regulations stipulate that certified statements concerning actions which effect a change in a registered treaty, such as additional ratifications, accessions, prolongations, denunciations and amendments, are also to be registered with the Secretariat.

The texts of the treaties and agreements registered or filed and recorded are published by the Secretariat in the United Nations *Treaty Series* in their original languages; translations in English and French are included.

By the end of 1965, a total of 11,805 treaties and agreements had been registered or filed and recorded, and 4,447 certified statements relating to those treaties and agreements had been registered or filed and recorded.

Principles of International Law
concerning Friendly Relations and Co-operation among States

In 1962, the General Assembly took up for the first time consideration of the item entitled "Principles of international law concerning friendly relations and co-operation among states," in accordance with a decision reached the previous year concerning the future work of the Assembly on the progressive development and codification of international law. At its 1962 session, the Assembly, recognizing the paramount importance of such principles, decided to undertake a study of them with a view to their progressive development and codification, and listed seven principles for study.

In 1963, the Assembly considered four of the principles: the principle that states shall refrain from the threat or use of force in international relations; the principle of the peaceful settlement of disputes; the duty not to intervene in matters within the domestic jurisdiction of a state; and the principle of sovereign equality of states. It decided to refer these four principles to a twenty-seven-member

Special Committee, which was entrusted with the task of drawing up a report on the principles with a view to their progressive development and codification. The Special Committee was also requested to include the question of methods of fact-finding in its deliberations, the feeling having been expressed during the Assembly's discussions that impartial fact-finding by international organizations or pursuant to treaty provisions would represent an important contribution to the peaceful settlement of disputes. The Secretary-General was requested to prepare a study on the relevant aspects of methods of fact-finding, and comments from member states were invited.

The Special Committee met in Mexico City from August 27 to October 2, 1964. In its report to the Assembly, the Committee indicated that it had not been able to reach any consensus on three of the principles referred to it. On the fourth principle, relating to the sovereign equality of states, the Committee adopted a text setting out points of consensus and a list itemizing various proposals and views on which there had been no consensus but for which there had been support. The text on points of consensus contained a statement that all states enjoyed sovereign equality and, as subjects of international law, had equal rights and duties. It then listed the following elements as being included in the principle of sovereign equality: states are juridically equal; each state enjoys the rights inherent in full sovereignty; each state has the duty to respect the personality of other states; the territorial integrity and political independence of the state are inviolable; each state has the right freely to choose and develop its political, social, economic and cultural systems; and each state has the duty to comply fully and in good faith with its international obligations, and to live in peace with other states.

On the question of methods of fact-finding, the Special Committee noted that it had been unable, for lack of time, to formulate conclusions on the question and recommended that, as few states had so far commented on the question, the Assembly should invite member states to do so at an early date.

The Assembly considered the report of the Special Committee in 1965, and undertook a study of the following three additional principles: the duty of states to co-operate with one another in accordance with the Charter; the principle of the equal rights and self-determination of peoples; and the principle that states shall fulfil in good faith the obligations assumed by them in accordance with the Charter. In conjunction with these matters, the Assembly took up an item proposed by Madagascar concerning the observance by member states of the principles relating to the sovereignty of states, their territorial integrity, non-interference in their domestic affairs, the peaceful settlement of disputes and the condemnation of subversive activities. The Assembly decided to reconstitute the Special Committee, increasing its membership to thirty-one, and requested it to prepare a report to the Assembly on the seven principles previously studied by the Assembly with a view to enabling the Assembly to adopt a declaration containing an enunciation of the principles. The item proposed by Madagascar was also referred to the Special Committee.

The question of methods of fact-finding was discussed again by the Assembly in 1965, and the Secretary-General was requested to prepare a further report.

Technical Assistance to Promote the Teaching, Study, Dissemination and Wider Appreciation of International Law

In a resolution adopted on December 20, 1965, the General Assembly adopted a programme of assistance and exchange in the field of international law. Following the recommendations of a Special Committee set up by the Assembly in 1963, the programme is divided into two parts, the first relating to steps to encourage and co-ordinate efforts being made by states and other bodies in the field of international law, and the second dealing with forms of direct assistance which are to be made available to the developing countries. UNESCO is invited to participate in the implementation of the programme.

Actions to be taken to encourage and co-ordinate existing programmes include: the production of a survey on the teaching of international law; the promotion of fellowships offered by states and the exchange of teachers, scholars and experts; the strengthening of library facilities; co-operation with interested organizations; and increased efforts to publicize the legal work of the United Nations. Activities to be undertaken directly by the United Nations under the programme include the following:

(a) organization of regional training and refresher courses for young teachers, post-graduate students and junior governmental officials;

(b) award of fellowships at the request of governments of developing countries to enable the recipients to study the work of the legal organs of the United Nations or other international organizations at their headquarters, or to undertake research on related problems of international law at a recognized university or research institute;

(c) provision of advisory services of experts, at the request of developing countries, covering a wide field—from the establishment or improvement of national programmes for teaching international law to advice on the practical application of rules of international law;

(d) organization of regional seminars to enable leading scholars and senior national officials drawn from the region to discuss international legal problems of either general or regional interest, and legal topics before United Nations organs;

(e) provision of a set of United Nations legal publications to a number of institutions in developing countries; and

(f) preparation of a survey of certain of the principal examples of the codification and progressive development of international law within the framework of the United Nations.

The Assembly's 1965 resolution also called the attention of member states to the existing arrangement whereby they may request assistance in the field of international law related to economic, social and administrative development under the United Nations Development Programme and in connection with development projects under the regular United Nations budget. In addition, the Board of Trustees of the United Nations Institute for Training and Research was requested by the Assembly to consider the ways in which international law may be given its proper place among the activities of the Institute in the light of the report of the Special Committee and of the views expressed on the subject in the Assembly's Sixth Committee.

Under the terms of the resolution, the Secretary-General is requested to invite member states, interested national and international institutions and organizations, and individuals to make voluntary contributions towards the financing of the programme. Provision is to be made for the programme in the regular United Nations budget if voluntary contributions and other sources of funds prove insufficient.

An Advisory Committee, composed of ten member states, was established to advise the Secretary-General on the substantive aspects of the programme and on the implementation of the resolution. The Secretary-General was requested to report to the General Assembly on the implementation of the resolution; the Advisory Committee may also report to it, as appropriate.

Arbitration of Disputes of a Private Law Character in International Trade

In 1953, the International Chamber of Commerce, a non-governmental organization in consultative status to the Economic and Social Council, drew the Council's attention to difficulties in obtaining enforcement of commercial arbitral awards on an international scale. After the Council had considered the matter, a conference of plenipotentiaries was convened to conclude a convention based on a draft convention on the recognition and enforcement of arbitral awards that had been prepared by an *ad hoc* committee of the Council. The conference was also to consider other possible measures for increasing the effectiveness of arbitration in the settlement of private law disputes.

The United Nations Conference on International Commercial Arbitration was held at United Nations Headquarters from May 20 to June 10, 1958. The Conference adopted and opened for signature the Convention on the Recognition and Enforcement of Foreign Arbitral Awards, under which contracting states undertake to recognize and enforce arbitral awards made in the territories of other states, or awards not considered as domestic awards in the state where enforcement of the award is sought. The Convention entered into force on June 7, 1959.

The Conference also adopted a resolution expressing the wish that the United Nations, through its appropriate organs, would take such steps as it deemed feasible to encourage further study of measures for increasing the effectiveness of arbitration in the settlement of private law disputes. In the light of the conclusions reached at the Conference, the Economic and Social Council adopted, on April 17, 1959, a resolution on international commercial arbitration, setting out a broad framework for international co-operation in the promotion of the more effective use of arbitration and recommending what might be done in that connection by the Secretary-General and the regional economic commissions of the United Nations.

In compliance with the Council's resolution, the Secretariat also communicated with a large number of organizations interested in arbitration, and invited suggestions designed to promote more effective use of arbitration as a means of facilitating the continued development of international trade. Among the suggestions received by the Secretariat were proposals for undertaking educational and training programmes in arbitration; the establishment of basic standards of modern arbitration laws as models for domestic legislation; the creation of new national arbitral bodies and regional arbitration centres; and the development of panels of arbitrators. The various suggestions have been examined and kept in view by the Secretariat.

The Economic Commission for Europe (ECE) and the Economic Commission for Asia and the Far East (ECAFE) have been concerned with the arbitration of disputes of a private law nature in international trade for a considerable time. Under the auspices of ECE, a European Convention on International Commercial Arbitration was concluded on April 21, 1961. The Convention, which is primarily designed to meet certain difficulties that may impede the use of arbitration as an effective means of settling European trade disputes, entered into force on January 7, 1964. Also of importance was the preparation of certain optional Arbitration Rules by the *Ad Hoc* Working Group on Arbitration of the ECE Committee on the Development of Trade.

A Centre for the Promotion of Commercial Arbitration was established within the ECAFE Secretariat in 1962, pursuant to the recommendations of a working group of experts which met in Bangkok in January of that year. Since the establishment of the Centre, nearly all the ECAFE Governments have designated institutions and experts in their countries to act as national correspondents of the Centre, and the channels of communication between the Centre and its national correspondents are well established. The over-all purpose of the Centre is the general promotion of arbitral development in the ECAFE region in regard to disputes arising from international trade. A fundamental objective, therefore, is that of informing relevant groups in the various countries of the advantages of and facilities for arbitral settlement through dissemination of information and other measures.

Privileges and Immunities

Article 105 of the Charter provides that the United Nations "shall enjoy, in the territory of each of its members, such privileges and immunities as are necessary for the fulfilment of its purposes." It adds that "representatives of the members of the United Nations and officials of the Organization shall similarly enjoy such privileges and immunities as are necessary for the independent exercise of their functions in connection with the Organization."

Article 105 also authorizes the General Assembly to make recommendations with a view to determining the details of the privileges and immunities to be enjoyed by the Organization, as well as by representatives and officials, or to propose conventions for this purpose. In line with this latter provision, the General Assembly approved, in February 1946, the Convention on the Privileges and Immunities of the United Nations and proposed it for accession by each member of the United Nations. At the end of 1965, ninety-two states were parties to the Convention.

In addition to the Convention, a number of special agreements dealing with privileges and immunities have been concluded with the states in whose territory the United Nations or one of its subsidiary organs has its headquarters or holds meetings. Notable among these are the Agreement of June 26, 1947, between the United Nations and the United States, regarding the Headquarters of the United Nations in New York, and the Interim Arrangement on Privileges and Immunities of the United Nations, concerning the United Nations Office at Geneva, concluded with the Swiss Government on June 11, 1946.

The General Assembly also approved, on November 21, 1947, a Convention on the Privileges and Immunities of the Specialized Agencies.

Reparations for Injury Suffered in the Service of the United Nations

In 1949, the General Assembly authorized the Secretary-General to present claims against governments alleged to be responsible for the injury or death of United Nations agents in the performance of their duties. Since 1950, the Secretary-General has presented claims in certain cases in which he was of the opinion that the circumstances in which United Nations agents were killed or injured appeared to involve the responsibility of certain states.

Reparations for Damage Caused to Third Parties by the United Nations

It has been the policy of the United Nations to accept liability for damage or injury suffered by individuals as the result of acts of United Nations personnel acting in the course of their duties. This policy is based upon recognized general principles of law and is in accordance with the Convention on Privileges and Immunities of the United Nations under which the Organization makes provision for the settlement of disputes or claims of a private law character. In respect of claims arising out of peace-keeping operations, the Organization also takes due account of the general principles set forth in international conventions concerning the protection of life and property of the civilian population during hostilities but does not accept liability for claims of damages which are founded on acts undertaken during military operations or as a result of military necessity.

The Secretary-General has undertaken the settlement of such claims and disputes by direct negotiation with the parties concerned or through the intermediary of interested governments. With regard to peace-keeping operations, where the number of such claims may be numerous, the status agreements concluded with the host governments concerned contain provisions for settlement. In the case of the United Nations Emergency Force (UNEF), for example, the Status Agreement with the Government of Egypt provided for the establishment of a Claims Commission to deal with claims made by Egyptian nationals in respect of any damage alleged to have resulted from an act or omission by a member of the Force relating to his official duties. In practice, however, all such claims have been settled by a process of informal negotiation between the parties directly, or between the UNEF and the Egyptian liaison office, subject to ratification by the claimant concerned.

Similarly, in the case of the United Nations Operations in the Congo (ONUC), the Status Agreement with the Government of the Congo (Leopoldville) contained provisions for the settlement by negotiation of claims presented by citizens and other residents and if necessary for the establishment of arbitral procedures. In the course of the Congo operation, the Secretariat received approximately 2,000 claims from residents in the Congo alleging that they had suffered injury or damage to property by acts of United Nations personnel. The claims were investigated by the competent administrative services of the Secretariat and scrutinized by the Office of Legal Affairs in order to determine the responsibility of the Organization. About 1,400 of the claims were from Belgian nationals and, of these, 581 were accepted as entitled to compensation. The Secretary-General considered that, on practical and legal grounds, it was advantageous for the Organization to settle the Belgian claims through the intermediary of the Belgian Government. Following consultations, the Belgian Government agreed to act as an intermediary, and the Secretary-General concluded an agreement by an exchange of letters with the Belgian Government, effective May 17, 1965, by which the United Nations agreed to pay to the Belgian Government $1,500,000 in final settlement of the claims accepted. Similar arrangements were discussed with governments of other countries with respect to claims by their nationals.

United Nations Administrative Tribunal

The United Nations Administrative Tribunal was established by the General Assembly on November 24, 1949. It is composed of seven members, no two of whom may be nationals of the same state. Three of the members constitute the Tribunal for the consideration of a particular case.

The manner and methods of proceedings of the Tribunal are covered in detail by the Statute adopted at the time of its establishment, as well as the obligations of the Organization in respect of its judgments. Under the procedure established by the General Assembly on November 8, 1955, either party to a case, or the government of any member state, may contest a judgment within thirty days of its publication and request an advisory opinion of the International Court of Justice. Such requests are reviewed in the first instance by a committee of member states whose representatives served on the General Committee of the most recent session of the General Assembly. This committee decides whether there is a substantial basis for submitting the matter to the Court.

The competence of the Tribunal has been extended to several specialized agencies by agreements concluded between the agencies and the United Nations.

Administrative and Budgetary Questions

BUDGET OF THE UNITED NATIONS

The Secretary-General prepares the budget estimates for the Organization. These are reviewed first by the Advisory Committee on Administrative and Budgetary Questions and then by the Assembly's Fifth (Administrative and Budgetary) Committee. The Assembly itself takes final action on the budgetary recommendations of its Fifth Committee.

The regular budget appropriations for the United Nations through 1966 were as follows:

Financial Year	Type of Appropriation	Date of Approval	Amount $	Total Budget (gross) $
1946	Budget	Dec. 14, 1946	19,390,000	19,390,000
1947	Budget	Dec. 14, 1946	27,740,000	
	Supplement	Nov. 20, 1947	876,568	28,616,568
1948	Budget	Nov. 20, 1947	34,825,195	
	Supplement	Dec. 11, 1948	4,460,541	39,285,736
1949	Budget	Dec. 11, 1948	43,487,128	
	Reduction	Dec. 9, 1949	283,048	43,204,080
1950	Budget	Dec. 10, 1949	49,641,773	
	Reduction	Dec. 14, 1950	5,121,000	44,520,773
1951	Budget	Dec. 15, 1950	47,798,600	
	Supplement	Dec. 20, 1951	1,126,900	48,925,500
1952	Budget	Dec. 21, 1951	48,096,780	
	Supplement	Nov. 25, 1952	2,450,880	50,547,660
1953	Budget	Dec. 21, 1952	48,327,700	
	Supplement	Dec. 9, 1953	1,541,750	49,869,450
1954	Budget	Dec. 9, 1953	47,827,110	
	Supplement	Dec. 14, 1954	701,870	48,528,980
1955	Budget	Dec. 17, 1954	46,963,800	
	Supplement	Dec. 16, 1955	3,264,200	50,228,000
1956	Budget	Dec. 16, 1955	48,566,350	
	Supplement	Dec. 7, 1956	2,117,000	50,683,350

Financial Year	Type of Appropriation	Date of Approval	Amount $	Total Budget (gross) $
1957	Budget	Dec. 21, 1956	48,807,650	
	Supplement	Feb. 27, 1957	2,008,050	
	Supplement	Dec. 14, 1957	2,359,000	53,174,700
1958	Budget	Dec. 14, 1957	55,062,850	
	Supplement	Dec. 13, 1958	6,059,050	61,121,900
1959	Budget	Dec. 13, 1958	60,802,120	
	Supplement	Dec. 5, 1959	854,980	61,657,100
1960	Budget	Dec. 5, 1959	63,149,700	
	Supplement	Dec. 20, 1960	2,585,200	65,734,900
1961	Budget	Dec. 20, 1960	72,969,300	
	Reduction	Dec. 18, 1961	1,320,000	71,649,300
1962	Budget	Dec. 20, 1961	82,144,740	
	Supplement	Dec. 20, 1962	3,673,480	85,818,220
1963	Budget	Dec. 20, 1962	93,911,050	
	Reduction	Dec. 11, 1963	1,034,500	92,876,550
1964	Budget	Dec. 17, 1963	101,327,600	
	Supplement	Oct. 17, 1965	1,621,377	102,948,977
1965	Budget	Dec. 21, 1965	108,472,800	108,472,800
1966	Budget	Dec. 21, 1965	121,567,420	
	Reduction	Dec. 16, 1966	486,890	121,080,530

Financing the Budget

United Nations activities are financed either from the regular budget or from separate special accounts, reserve accounts and trust funds. The regular budget provides such expenses as conference costs and Secretariat salaries and for normal "housekeeping" operations, certain technical co-operation programmes, information activities, the International Court of Justice and the United Nations Conference on Trade and Development. Special accounts finance certain peace-keeping operations, such as the United Nations Force in Cyprus and, until June 30, 1964, the United Nations Operation in the Congo. Technical co-operation programmes such as the United Nations Development Programme, as well as the United Nations Children's Fund and aid to certain refugees, are financed from voluntary sources.

The regular budget of the United Nations is financed by contributions from member states on a scale determined periodically by the General Assembly on the recommendation of its Committee on Contributions. In accordance with certain General Assembly decisions on the subject, the Committee is to use capacity-to-pay as the major factor, subject to the principles of a maximum and minimum percentage contribution and to the application of certain other criteria which have been laid down from time to time.

Each year, the United Nations derives income from certain sources, including an assessment on staff salaries and from the sale of United Nations postage stamps and of publications and services to visitors. This income, which amounted to $17,395,409 in 1965, is deducted from the gross budget figure, and member states are assessed on the basis of the net budget.

Pending receipt of assessed contributions, expenditures are financed from a Working Capital Fund, consisting of advances by member states. The Fund is also available for certain other purposes specified in the Assembly's annual resolution on it. For 1966, the level of the Fund was established at $40 million.

The General Assembly in 1957 decided that, in principle, the maximum contribution of any one member state to the ordinary expenses of the United Nations should not exceed 30 per cent of the total. The assessment of the largest contributor—the United States—is currently fixed at 31.91 per cent. The minimum assessment is established at 0.04 per cent. The scale of assessments for members' contributions to the United Nations regular budget for the financial years 1966 and 1967, as adopted in a General Assembly resolution of December 21, 1965, is set out below:

Member State	Per cent	Member State	Per cent
Afghanistan	0.05	Congo (Brazzaville)	0.04
Albania	0.04	Congo (Democratic Republic	
Algeria	0.10	of)	0.05
Argentina	0.92	Costa Rica	0.04
Australia	1.58	Cuba	0.20
Austria	0.53	Cyprus	0.04
Belgium	1.15	Czechoslovakia	1.11
Bolivia	0.04	Dahomey	0.04
Brazil	0.95	Denmark	0.62
Bulgaria	0.17	Dominican Republic	0.04
Burma	0.06	Ecuador	0.05
Burundi	0.04	El Salvador	0.04
Byelorussian SSR	0.52	Ethiopia	0.04
Cambodia	0.04	Finland	0.43
Cameroon	0.04	France	6.09
Canada	3.17	Gabon	0.04
Central African Republic	0.04	Gambia	0.04
Ceylon	0.08	Ghana	0.08
Chad	0.04	Greece	0.25
Chile	0.27	Guatemala	0.04
China	4.25	Guinea	0.04
Colombia	0.23	Haiti	0.04

Member State	Per cent	Member State	Per cent
Honduras	0.04	Pakistan	0.37
Hungary	0.56	Panama	0.04
Iceland	0.04	Paraguay	0.04
India	1.85	Peru	0.09
Iran	0.20	Philippines	0.35
Iraq	0.08	Poland	1.45
Ireland	0.16	Portugal	0.15
Israel	0.17	Romania	0.35
Italy	2.54	Rwanda	0.04
Ivory Coast	0.04	Saudi Arabia	0.07
Jamaica	0.05	Senegal	0.04
Japan	2.77	Sierra Leone	0.04
Jordan	0.04	Singapore	0.04
Kenya	0.04	Somalia	0.04
Kuwait	0.06	South Africa	0.52
Laos	0.04	Spain	0.73
Lebanon	0.05	Sudan	0.06
Liberia	0.04	Sweden	1.26
Libya	0.04	Syria	0.05
Luxembourg	0.05	Thailand	0.14
Madagascar	0.04	Togo	0.04
Malawi	0.04	Trinidad and Tobago	0.04
Malaysia	0.12	Tunisia	0.05
Maldive Islands	0.04	Turkey	0.35
Mali	0.04	Uganda	0.04
Malta	0.04	Ukrainian SSR	1.97
Mauritania	0.04	USSR	14.92
Mexico	0.81	United Arab Republic	0.23
Mongolia	0.04	United Kingdom	7.21
Morocco	0.11	United Republic of Tanzania	0.04
Nepal	0.04	United States	31.91
Netherlands	1.11	Upper Volta	0.04
New Zealand	0.38	Uruguay	0.10
Nicaragua	0.04	Venezuela	0.50
Niger	0.04	Yemen	0.04
Nigeria	0.17	Yugoslavia	0.36
Norway	0.44	Zambia	0.04
		TOTAL	99.82*

* In fixing the total scale of assessments at 99.82 per cent, rather than 100 per cent, for 1966 and 1967, the Committee on Contributions took note of the Secretary-General's expressed hope that Indonesia's withdrawal from the United Nations would be "only a temporary phase," as well as the possibility that more new members would be admitted during the period covered by the scale.

The Assembly, in its 1965 resolution, agreed that states which are not members of the United Nations but which participate in certain of its activities should be called upon to contribute towards the 1965, 1966 and 1967 expenses of such activities on the following basis:

Non-Member State	Per cent	Non-Member State	Per cent
Federal Republic of Germany	7.41	Republic of Korea	0.13
Holy See	0.04	Republic of Viet-Nam	0.08
Liechtenstein	0.04	San Marino	0.04
Monaco	0.04	Switzerland	0.88

Those activities and the countries participating in them are as follows:

International Court of Justice: Liechtenstein, San Marino and Switzerland;

International control of narcotic drugs: Federal Republic of Germany, Liechtenstein, Monaco, Republic of Korea, Republic of Viet-Nam, San Marino and Switzerland;

International Bureau for Declarations of Death of Missing Persons: Federal Republic of Germany;

Economic Commission for Asia and the Far East: Republic of Korea and Republic of Viet-Nam;

Economic Commission for Europe: Federal Republic of Germany;

United Nations Conference on Trade and Development: Federal Republic of Germany, Holy See, Liechtenstein, Monaco, Republic of Korea, Republic of Viet-Nam, San Marino and Switzerland.

United Nations Bond Issue

In an effort to ease the steadily increasing financial difficulties confronting the Organization, the General Assembly, at its sixteenth session in 1961, authorized the Secretary-General to sell up to $200 million worth of United Nations bonds to governments, national banks and approved non-profit institutions or associations. In approving the bond issue, the Assembly stated that in the existing circumstances "extraordinary financial measures" were required but that "such measures should not be deemed a precedent for the future financing" of United Nations expenses.

Final receipts from the bond issue totalled $169,905,679, representing purchases by sixty-four countries. Proceeds were to be utilized for purposes normally related to the Working Capital Fund to provide needed financing for continuing activities, including those relating to the maintenance of international peace and security.

The bonds, issued for a twenty-five-year period, bear an annual interest rate of 2 per cent. According to the Assembly resolution, both interest charges and principal are to be paid by including a sufficient amount in the regular budget of the United Nations each year, starting with the 1963 budget. The resolution also sets forth a 25-year table listing in percentages the annual instalments in which the principal is repayable each year. Percentages range from 3.1 per cent at the end of the first year to 5.1 per cent at the end of the twenty-fifth year.

QUESTIONS RELATING TO THE SECRETARIAT

Geographical Distribution of the Secretariat

The composition of the Secretariat has been under regular review by the General Assembly on the basis of annual reports submitted by the Secretary-General. The main concern has been to ensure a more equitable geographical distribution among the internationally recruited staff. In 1965, the staff of the Secretariat consisted of nationals of some 107 states.

The principle of geographical distribution extends to all appointments of more than one year's duration to posts at the professional level and above, except for staff appointed to posts with special language requirements or recruited specifically for mission service. A specific formula of "desirable ranges" of posts for each nationality applies in the regular Secretariat, which is financed by assessed contributions. In the early years of the Organization, the "desirable range" was calculated on the basis of the ratio of assessed contributions. In 1962, the General Assembly revised the formula by taking into account the factors of membership in the United Nations, population and contributions to the budget. The "desirable ranges" serve as signposts for the Secretary-General in his efforts to achieve a more balanced composition of the Secretariat staff. As at August 31, 1965, there were 1,491 members of the Secretariat occupying posts subject to geographical distribution.

While a large majority of members of the Secretariat staff are recruited for career service, a number are appointed on a fixed-term basis. In recent years, a greater use of fixed-term appointments has been made as a means of accelerating the adjustment of the geographical distribution of the staff. The proportion of staff holding fixed-term appointments increased from 16.6 per cent in 1959 to 29.7 per cent in 1963, and levelled off to 28.1 per cent in 1965. The Secretary-General has aimed at maintaining the ratio at 25 per cent in order to balance the desire to achieve an equitable geographical distribution of staff with considerations of efficiency of operation in the Secretariat.

Secretariat Salaries and Post Adjustments

At its twentieth session, in 1965, the General Assembly adopted a new schedule of post adjustments for United Nations staff in the professional and higher categories and approved a revision of the rates of staff assessments. The changes in salary structure were adopted by the

Assembly on the basis of recommendations by the International Civil Service Advisory Board.

The salary and wage rates for the general service staff and manual workers at Headquarters and Geneva have been set on the basis of the best prevailing conditions of employment in the local area. Periodic adjustments of the rates are made to reflect changes in outside pay scales.

Staff Regulations and Retirement Provisions

The terms of employment of the Secretariat staff are governed by a set of Staff Regulations, which were adopted by the General Assembly in 1952 and amended at subsequent Assembly sessions. These Regulations embody the fundamental conditions of service and the basic rights, duties and obligations of the Secretariat staff. They set out the broad principle of personnel policy for the staffing and administration of the Secretariat. In implementation of the Staff Regulations, the Secretary-General issues, from time to time, Staff Rules and amendments thereto, which are reported to the General Assembly every year.

In 1946, the Assembly adopted a provisional scheme for staff retirement, insurance and related benefits, and two years later, it adopted regulations for the United Nations Joint Staff Pension Fund. These regulations, which took effect on January 23, 1949, have been the subject of amendments at subsequent Assembly sessions, including a major revision adopted at the twentieth session, in 1965, affecting the level of pensionable remuneration and pension benefits.

Staff Assessment and Tax Equalization

In accordance with a General Assembly resolution of November 18, 1948, as amended by a resolution of December 10, 1949, United Nations salaries were established on a gross basis, subject to the deduction from individual salaries, at specified rates, of an assessment comparable to national income taxes.

The Convention on the Privileges and Immunities of the United Nations provides that members of the Secretariat shall be exempt from taxation on the salaries and emoluments paid to them by the United Nations. In cases where a government has not acceded to the Convention and its nationals on the staff have been subject to both staff assessment and national income tax, the United Nations grants relief from this double taxation by reimbursing the staff member in respect of national tax payments.

Until 1956, tax reimbursements were treated as a charge to the regular budget. In order to achieve equal treatment of contributing governments in this respect, the General Assembly, in a resolution of

December 15, 1955, established the Tax Equalization Fund. The resolution provided that all revenues derived from staff assessment, unless otherwise disposed of by specific resolutions of the Assembly, are to be credited to the Fund. The amounts in the Fund are in turn credited to a series of sub-accounts held in the name of each member state, the amount credited to each account being in proportion to the member's percentage contribution to the budget for the financial year concerned. All amounts paid to staff members as relief from double taxation are charged to the account of the member state concerned.

OTHER ADMINISTRATIVE AND BUDGETARY QUESTIONS

United Nations Telecommunication System

In successive decisions of the General Assembly, and by authority of the International Telecommunication Union (itu), the United Nations operates its own radio-telegraph network, linking its main offices.

Establishment of the system was approved in principle by the General Assembly in 1948 and, in December 1950, the Assembly instructed the Secretary-General to proceed with a modified telecommunication scheme. At the Assembly's sixth session in 1951-52, the Secretary-General reported that it had been found possible to establish United Nations links between local telecommunication networks established in various areas.

Under the Headquarters Agreement between the United Nations and the United States (see page 26), the Organization is empowered to set up its own radio-telegraph circuit between Headquarters in New York and the United Nations Office at Geneva. In turn, the United Nations radio station in Geneva is in communication with United Nations radio stations in Jerusalem, Gaza, Karachi, Nicosia, Bangkok, Seoul and Addis Ababa.

In its work of truce observation, the United Nations has found it necessary to establish local radio-telegraph networks. The United Nations Military Observer Group in India and Pakistan, the United Nations Emergency Force in Egypt and the United Nations Truce Supervision Organization in Palestine established such networks, connecting the headquarters of each group with its posts.

Arrangements for the operation of United Nations radio stations have been made between the Organization and the governments of the states concerned, by means of formal and informal agreements.

By Article 26 of the International Telecommunication Convention (Buenos Aires, 1952), the telecommunication operating services of the United Nations are entitled to the rights specified in, and are bound by the obligations of, the Convention and its regulations. In consequence, the United Nations is regarded as an administration in connection with the operation of its telecommunication services. A resolution adopted at Buenos Aires in 1952 declared that the United Nations network should never in normal circumstances compete with existing public channels of communication. Only United Nations traffic is therefore accepted for transmission over the network and, except in case of emergency, traffic of the specialized agencies is carried only when it is connected with and paid for by a United Nations programme.

United Nations Postal Administration

In accordance with a resolution adopted by the General Assembly on November 16, 1950, the United Nations Postal Administration was established on January 1, 1951.

An agreement was signed on March 28, 1951, by Secretary-General Trygve Lie for the United Nations and by Ambassador Warren Austin and Postmaster General Jesse Donaldson for the United States, establishing the postal relationship between the two parties.

Under the terms of this agreement, the United States Post Office Department operates the United Nations Post Office Station on behalf of the United Nations. The United Nations provides the space, custodial services and utilities. The staff and equipment are provided by the United States Post Office Department. Services rendered at this post office are the same as those offered by any United States post office having comparable operations, except that only United Nations postage stamps and postal stationery are used, which are provided free of charge to the post office by the United Nations. The services offered by this post office, however, are not available to the general public.

The United States Post Office Department, in return for its services, retains all revenue from the sale of United Nations postage stamps and postal stationery and is reimbursed by the United Nations for postage applied to all mail dispatched from Headquarters.

The United Nations, through its Postal Administration, engages in the sale of United Nations postage stamps and postal stationery for philatelic purposes. In addition to filling orders received by mail for first day covers, the Postal Administration operates a stamp counter at Headquarters, where visitors may purchase United Nations stamps for both philatelic and postage purposes and where they may dispatch mail bearing United Nations stamps.

United Nations International School

In 1947, an association of Secretariat parents was granted rent-free use of the "Guest House" at United Nations temporary headquarters at Lake Success to operate a nursery school. Two years later, the Association for the United Nations International School, having absorbed the earlier group, opened its first primary class in the same building under a charter from the State of New York.

In 1950, the School took up temporary headquarters in Parkway Village, Queens, and later, in 1958, opened a new branch at 70th Street and First Avenue in Manhattan. Adding a new grade each year, in 1961 the School reached its goal of providing a full programme from elementary through secondary school. Enrolments increased steadily and, in 1965, a site was granted to the School by the City of New York on the East River at 25th Street. Later, an alternative site on First Avenue from 39th to 40th Streets was proposed. A grant of $7.5 million from the Ford Foundation and of $1 million by the Rockefeller brothers was made for construction of a new building for 1,000 students.

From the beginning, the General Assembly has encouraged the development and expansion of the School and has contributed financially to its operation. In 1959, the Assembly decided to contribute, for a period of five years, such continuing financial aid as it might consider necessary. From 1959 to 1964, $295,000 was contributed towards liquidating annual operating deficits and $80,000 to assist the planning for the permanent accommodations of the School. A contribution of $45,000 in 1964-1965 and of $57,000 in 1965-1966 was made towards the annual deficit. This corresponds broadly to the amounts remitted by the School in bursaries and rebates to members of the United Nations.

In December 1965, the General Assembly expressed its gratitude to the City of New York, the Ford Foundation and the Rockefeller family for their generous actions on the School's behalf, and urged the member states which had not yet done so to contribute promptly to the Development Fund of the School, which would make it self-supporting in the future.

The School, with its multinational faculty, is unique in giving to its students from nearly seventy countries an international education in accordance with the principles of the United Nations.

PART THREE

*Inter-Governmental Agencies related
to the United Nations*

Inter-Governmental Agencies related to the United Nations

Much of the United Nations work aimed at improving the economic and social conditions of the people of the world is carried out by specialized inter-governmental agencies. The United Nations Charter provides that the "various specialized agencies, established by inter-governmental agreement and having wide international responsibilities, as defined in their basic instruments, in economic, social, cultural, educational, health and related fields, shall be brought into relationship with the United Nations."

The instruments defining this relationship are the individual agreements between the United Nations and the specialized agencies. These agreements are first negotiated by the Committee on Negotiations with Inter-governmental Agencies, established for this purpose by the Economic and Social Council. They are then approved by the appropriate organ of the specialized agency concerned and submitted for approval to the Council, and by it to the General Assembly. Agreements with thirteen specialized agencies are at present in force.

Although not a specialized agency, the International Atomic Energy Agency (IAEA) is an autonomous inter-governmental organization under the aegis of the United Nations, established to further the peaceful uses of atomic energy.

The agreements between the United Nations and the specialized agencies generally follow a standard pattern. As a rule, they provide for reciprocal representation at meetings; reciprocal inclusion of agenda items when requested; exchange of information and documents; uniformity of personnel arrangements; and co-ordination of statistical services as well as budgetary and financial arrangements. Each specialized agency has agreed to consider any recommendation made to it by the United Nations and to report to the Organization on the action taken to give effect to any such recommendation. In the case of the agreements with the International Bank for Reconstruction and Development (IBRD) and the International Monetary Fund (IMF), the United Nations has agreed to consult with these agencies prior to making any recommendation.

To implement the agreements relating the agencies with the United Nations, to avoid overlapping of activities and, in general, to promote the co-ordination of efforts, an Administrative Committee on Co-ordination (ACC) was established in 1947 by the Economic and Social Council; it reports to the Council periodically. The Committee is composed of the Secretary-General of the United Nations, who acts as Chairman, and the executive heads of the specialized agencies, the Director-General of IAEA, the Administrator and Co-Administrator of the United Nations Development Programme (UNDP), the Executive Director of the World Food Programme, the Executive Director of UNICEF, the Commissioner-General of the United Nations Relief and Works Agency for Palestine Refugees, the United Nations High Commissioner for Refugees, and the Director-General of the General Agreement on Tariffs and Trade (GATT), who participate in the work of ACC as observers.

Consultations in ACC take place on subjects of common interest to the different organizations within the United Nations system and on the United Nations programmes in science and technology, education and training, rural and industrial development, public administration, atomic energy, oceanography, the peaceful uses of outer space, and public information.

In addition to meetings of ACC, *ad hoc* consultations take place between the United Nations and the agencies in order to improve administrative and budgetary co-ordination. Arrangements have been made concerning, among other questions: a joint system of external audit; common collection of contributions; mutual problems affecting the currency of contributions; common financial regulations; a Joint Staff Pension Fund; uniform recruitment policies; personnel regulations, salary, allowance and leave systems; the International Civil Service Advisory Board; and certain common administrative services.

Among the subsidiary bodies of ACC are the Consultative Committee on Administrative Questions (CCAQ) and the Consultative Committee on Public Information (CCPI). CCAQ, established in 1947 and normally meeting once a year, deals with personnel, budgetary and financial questions as well as with administrative questions such as common services, records and other administrative matters. CCPI, established in 1949, seeks to form a common information policy and to co-ordinate the information services involved.

INTERNATIONAL ATOMIC ENERGY AGENCY (IAEA)

The International Atomic Energy Agency (IAEA) had its origin in a proposal made to the United Nations General Assembly on December

8, 1953, by the President of the United States, suggesting the establishment of a world organization devoted exclusively to the peaceful uses of atomic energy. The general lines of that proposal were unanimously endorsed by the General Assembly in a resolution adopted on December 4, 1954.

The Statute of IAEA was approved unanimously on October 26, 1956, at a conference held at United Nations Headquarters, and within three months it had been signed by eighty nations. The Agency legally came into being on July 29, 1957, with the deposit of the necessary ratifications of the Statute.

The Statute conference set up a Preparatory Commission of eighteen states, which first met at United Nations Headquarters and subsequently arranged for the first session of the General Conference, which was held in Vienna from October 1 to 23, 1957.

The functions of IAEA, as set forth in its Statute, are to "seek to accelerate and enlarge the contribution of atomic energy to peace, health and prosperity throughout the world" and to "ensure, so far as it is able, that assistance provided by it or at its request or under its supervision or control, is not used in such a way as to further any military purposes."

To achieve this aim, the Agency: assists research on and practical application of atomic energy for peaceful purposes, including the production of electric power, with special consideration being given to less developed areas; acts as an intermediary between members of the Agency in providing services or supplying materials, equipment or facilities; fosters the exchange of scientific and technical information; encourages the exchange and training of scientists and experts; establishes and administers safeguards to ensure that fissionable and other materials, services, equipment, facilities and information made available by or through the Agency are not used for the furtherance of any military purposes; and establishes, in consultation or in collaboration with the competent organs of the United Nations family concerned, standards of safety for protection of health and minimization of dangers to life and property, and provides for the application of these standards.

Organization

The three organs of the Agency are the General Conference, the Board of Governors and the secretariat.

The General Conference consists of all members, each having one vote. It meets normally once a year and takes its decisions by majority vote, except on financial matters, amendments to the Statute and suspension from membership, which require a two-thirds majority.

The Board of Governors consists of twenty-five members designated or elected on a technological and regional basis. It carries out the statutory functions of the Agency and takes decisions by majority vote, except for certain specific matters, such as the budget, which require a two-thirds majority. The Board meets approximately every third month, and its committees meet frequently.

The staff of the Agency, consisting of about 650 persons, is headed by a Director-General, who carries out his functions subject to the general direction and control of the Board of Governors, with the approval of the General Conference. His term of office is four years. Sigvard Eklund, of Sweden, succeeded Sterling Cole, of the United States, as Director-General on December 1, 1961, and was elected to another four-year term of office in September 1965.

The secretariat is organized into five departments: research and isotopes; safeguards and inspection; technical assistance; technical operations; and administration. IAEA headquarters are in Vienna.

An agreement concerning the Agency's working relationship with the United Nations was approved by the General Conference in October 1957 and by the General Assembly of the United Nations on November 14 of that year. The agreement emphasizes the need for close links between the two organizations.

Relationship agreements have also been concluded with ILO, FAO, UNESCO, WHO, ICAO, WMO, and IMCO, with the European Nuclear Energy Agency of the Organization for European Economic Co-operation, and with the Inter-American Nuclear Energy Commission of the Organization of American States. With FAO, the Agency has set up a Joint Division of Atomic Energy in Agriculture.

Nineteen non-governmental organizations have consultative status with the Agency. In addition, regular working-level relations are maintained with a number of inter-governmental and non-governmental organizations.

Membership

Membership is open to those states, whether or not members of the United Nations or of any of its specialized agencies, which deposit an instrument of acceptance of the Agency's Statute after their membership has been approved by the General Conference upon the recommendation of the Board of Governors. In recommending and approving such membership, the Board of Governors and the General Conference "shall determine that the state is able and willing to carry out the obligations of membership in the Agency, giving due consideration to its ability and willingness to act in accordance with the purposes and principles of the Charter of the United Nations."

As of January 1, 1966, ninety-three countries were members of IAEA.

Budget

The Agency's activities are financed out of the regular budget, based on the assessed contributions of member states; the General Fund, derived from voluntary contributions; and the United Nations Development Programme. The total approved budget for 1966 amounted to $11,222,000, of which $2 million was due to come from voluntary contributions.

Activities

IAEA's activities are designed to promote the development of nuclear power and the use of radioisotopes in medicine, agriculture, hydrology and industry; to spread scientific information and technical skills through fellowships, training courses, conferences and publications; to provide technical assistance; and to deal with legal aspects of nuclear hazards.

CONFERENCES AND TECHNICAL ASSISTANCE. Training of scientific and technical personnel is a prerequisite to peaceful development of atomic energy in many countries. To this end, the Agency provides fellowships, arranges for lectures by visiting professors and holds international and regional training courses. The Agency's International Centre for Theoretical Physics, at Trieste, which began operations in 1964, awards fellowships and has a senior staff of distinguished physicists.

Since 1962, when it had become clear that nuclear energy would soon be an economic means of providing an increasing share of the world's power, IAEA has stepped up its efforts to further nuclear power development. It was responsible for the technical aspects of the third United Nations International Conference on the Peaceful Uses of Atomic Energy, held at Geneva in September 1964. The Agency normally holds ten or twelve major scientific meetings each year, devoted to such subjects as radioisotope sample measurement techniques in medicine and biology, non-destructive testing in nuclear technology, physics and chemistry of fission, nuclear materials management, plasma physics and controlled nuclear fusion, use of isotopes in weed research, radioisotope instruments in industry and geophysics and practices in the treatment of low and intermediate-level wastes.

The Agency provides information and expert advice to countries which are thinking of installing nuclear power or have decided to do so, and has paid particular attention to desalination by means of nuclear energy.

RESEARCH. To promote research, IAEA grants contracts to scientific institutes in member countries and has also placed equipment at the disposal of institutions. It also directs several co-ordinated international programmes of research, for example on the use of isotopes for research in rice cultivation. In 1965, a three-year programme costing $1.3 million was launched in Central America as a stage in a campaign to eliminate the fruit fly by means of radiation.

The Agency's own laboratories take part in these programmes. The laboratory at Seibersdorf, near Vienna, works in the fields of physics, chemistry and radioisotopes in agriculture. At Agency headquarters, there is a laboratory for measuring the radioactivity of the human body and another for the use of radioisotopes in hydrology. In Monaco, a laboratory for oceanographic research operates in conjunction with the Government of Monaco.

IAEA has collaborated with Norway, Finland, Yugoslavia, Pakistan and the Democratic Republic of the Congo in programmes employing research and training reactors. It has held periodic regional study groups on the use of research reactors. A Nuclear Data Unit, to provide a world-wide exchange of reactor information from leading computer centres, was established by the Agency in 1965.

RADIATION SAFETY AND REGULATORY WORK.   The growth in the number of nuclear installations where radiation hazards might arise has led the Agency to concentrate much of its effort on radiation protection, including support of research on the effects of radiation, international meetings of experts and the preparation of internationally valid scientific, technical and legal recommendations.

A special advisory service on radiation protection and disposal of radioactive waste was established in 1965 by IAEA, which has also arranged a number of training courses in this field. The Agency has issued codes and manuals of safe practice, as well as draft model regulations for the safe transport of radioactive materials by land, sea and air. In 1962, as the result of a study by an expert group of the liability problems involved in the use of nuclear ships, a convention on the liability of operators of nuclear ships was adopted by the Diplomatic Conference on Maritime Law, and opened for signature. A convention on civil liability for nuclear damage was adopted in 1963 by an international conference held in Vienna.

SAFEGUARDS.   A revised safeguards system was adopted by the Agency in 1965, with the unanimous support of member states. It was drawn up after a comprehensive review of the system in the light of experience and technological developments. Fourteen Agency officials were designated as inspectors. By the end of 1965, there were forty-six reactors under Agency safeguards in twenty-one countries, and other countries announced their intention of transferring to the Agency responsibility for administering safeguards under various bilateral arrangements.

INTERNATIONAL LABOUR ORGANISATION
(ILO)

The International Labour Organisation (ILO) was established in 1919 as an autonomous institution associated with the League of Nations. Its original Constitution formed part of the Treaty of Versailles. In 1946, ILO became the first specialized agency associated with the United Nations.

ILO was founded to advance the cause of social justice and, in so doing, to contribute to the establishment of universal and lasting peace. The Declaration of Philadelphia, adopted by the International Labour Conference in 1944 and later annexed to the ILO Constitution, reaffirms the principles to which the organization is dedicated. It states that "all human beings, irrespective of race, creed or sex, have the right to pursue both their material well-being and their spiritual development in conditions of freedom and dignity, of economic security and equal opportunity." The ILO's motto, taken from the Declaration of Philadelphia, is: "Poverty anywhere constitutes a danger to prosperity everywhere."

One of the most distinctive features of ILO is its tripartite structure. It is an inter-governmental agency, but employers and workers as well as governments take part in its work, and in the democratic forum of ILO, employers' and workers' delegates have a free voice. They can, and often do, disagree with the governments and with each other.

Organization

The International Labour Conference is the supreme deliberative body of ILO. It meets annually at ILO headquarters in Geneva and is attended by more than 1,000 delegates, technical advisers and observers. Each national delegation is composed of two government delegates, one employers' delegate and one workers' delegate.

The Conference elects the Governing Body of the International Labour Office, adopts the ILO budget, sets international labour standards, in the form of conventions and recommendations, and provides a world forum for the discussion of social and labour questions.

The Governing Body (executive council) normally meets three or four times a year at Geneva. It is composed of twenty-four government members, twelve employers' members and twelve workers' members. Ten of the government members represent "states of chief industrial importance"—Canada, China, France, the Federal Republic of Germany, India, Italy, Japan, the USSR, the United Kingdom and the United States.

The Governing Body elects the Director-General of the International Labour Office and approves the budget for adoption by the Conference. It determines policy and work programmes, decides the Conference agenda, in so far as this is not fixed by the Conference itself, and supervises the work of the Office and of the various ILO committees and other bodies. The Governing Body appoints committees of its own to deal with particular problems. Elections to the Governing Body take place every three years.

The International Labour Office is the organization's secretariat, research centre, operational headquarters and publishing house. It occupies a large building on the banks of the Lake of Geneva and is staffed by about 1,300 officials of some ninety nationalities. The Office has branches in Bonn, Buenos Aires, Cairo, London, Moscow, New Delhi, Ottawa, Paris, Rio de Janeiro, Rome, Tokyo and Washington. It also has offices in Bangkok and Addis Ababa and an area office in Dar-es-Salaam. Liaison with the United Nations Economic Commission for Asia and the Far East and with the United Nations Economic Commission for Africa is the responsibility of the ILO offices in Bangkok and Addis Ababa, respectively.

Together, the Conference, the Governing Body and the Office make up ILO. But ILO also acts through regional conferences, industrial committees and other subsidiary bodies.

The first Director of ILO was Albert Thomas, of France, 1919-1932. His successors were: Harold Butler, of the United Kingdom, 1932-1938; John Winant, of the United States, 1939-1941; and Edward Phelan, of Ireland, 1941-1948, the first to carry the title of Director-General. David A. Morse, of the United States, has held the post of Director-General since 1948.

Membership

The Constitution of ILO provides that a member of the United Nations may become a member of ILO by communicating to the Director-General "its formal acceptance of the obligations of the Constitution of the International Labour Organisation." Countries not members of the United Nations may be admitted to ILO by a two-thirds vote of the International Labour Conference.

As of January 1, 1966, 115 countries were members of ILO.

Budget

The ILO budget, adopted each year by the Conference, is based on contributions from member countries, made according to a scale determined by the Conference. The 1965 gross expenditure budget amounted to $18,684,347.

Activities

One of the primary functions of ILO has always been to raise standards by building up a code of international law and practice. This remains true despite the many new directions into which the organization's activities have extended since the end of the Second World War. Since the establishment of ILO in 1919, the International Labour Conference has adopted a total of some 250 conventions and recommendations. Taken together, these conventions and recommendations form the International Labour Code.

Each convention is a legal instrument regulating some aspect of labour administration, social welfare or human rights; it is conceived as a model for national legislation. Member countries are not bound to ratify conventions even though they may have voted for their adoption, but they are obliged, under the ILO Constitution, to bring all conventions adopted by the Conference to the attention of their legislative authorities. If a convention is ratified, the ratifying country has to report periodically to ILO on its implementation. Similarly, member countries must report from time to time on their position with respect to unratified conventions and also with respect to the recommendations, which, although not subject to ratification, are adopted for the purpose of guiding governments.

TECHNICAL CO-OPERATION. ILO's activities in the important area of technical co-operation have expanded greatly in recent years and now account for more than half of the work of the organization. Before the Second World War, it was not unusual for ILO to send advisory missions to help governments with specific labour or social problems, but the present over-all programme is of unprecedented range and complexity.

Most of ILO's technical assistance programmes, which have been carried out in co-operation with the United Nations Special Fund and Expanded Programme of Technical Assistance (now merged as the United Nations Development Programme), are in Africa, Asia and Latin America; assistance is also extended for projects in the Near and Middle East and Europe and for inter-regional projects.

More than half of ILO technical assistance is in the general field of manpower, including vocational training. The ILO also provides technical assistance in: productivity and management development; co-operation and small industries; social security; occupational safety and health; workers' education; vocational rehabilitation; and labour conditions and administration.

To some extent, the Andean Programme epitomizes the range and variety of ILO operational activity throughout the less developed regions of the world: it is here, on the high plateau of the Andes, that many of the strands come together to form a co-ordinated whole; it is here that, joining forces with the governments concerned and with other organizations of the United Nations family, ILO has set a goal involving nothing less than the ultimate transformation of the way of life of some seven million Indians living in Argentina, Bolivia, Chile, Colombia, Ecuador and Peru. The Andean Programme aims to integrate these peoples into the national life of the countries to which they belong, to give them hope for the future and to enable their governments to put to use the full strength of their untapped human resources. Still one of the largest and most comprehensive multi-agency projects ever attempted, the Andean Programme embraces health, education, agriculture and social services. ILO acts as the co-ordinating agency in co-operation with the United Nations, FAO, WHO and UNESCO. Steps have been taken to transfer executive responsibility for the further implementation of the Programme to the national authorities of the countries concerned and to ensure that all activities covered by the Programme are carried out within the framework of national economic development plans.

When, in 1962, the Andean Programme was reviewed by the ILO's Panel of Consultants on Indigenous and Tribal Populations, it was felt that the experience gained in the Andes could be made to benefit other areas, not only in Latin America but also in the Middle East, Asia and Africa. In pursuance of this recommendation, ILO experts started work on integration schemes for the Indians in the Colombian and Venezuelan parts of the Guajira Peninsula, and, at the beginning of 1965, a mission to Guatemala of experts from the ILO, the FAO and the United Nations prepared the basis for a scheme involving the resettlement of some 500,000 people.

In Africa, at the request of the governments concerned and of the United Nations High Commissioner for Refugees, the ILO assumed in 1964 co-ordinating operational responsibility for integration and zonal development projects for the joint benefit of refugees from Rwanda and the local populations in Burundi and the Kivu Province of the Democratic Republic of the Congo. These projects aim at making the refugees self-supporting through training in agriculture, rural crafts and other skills and integrating them with the local populations through community services in education, public health and social welfare.

EDUCATION AND TRAINING.   The ILO's International Institute for Labour Studies, at Geneva, was established in 1961 to serve as an advanced staff college in social and labour policy. The first course was held in the autumn of 1962 with twenty-nine participants. In 1965, three study courses were held, with a total of seventy participants: the regular study course, an internship study course, and a regional study course held in Ibadan, Nigeria. The subjects taught included characteristics of economic development, the labour force and its employment, labour-management relations, wages in economic development, and social security.

The ILO's International Centre for Advanced Technical and Vocational Training, at Turin, Italy, started operations on October 15, 1965.

The object of the Centre is to provide advanced technical and vocational training at various levels for persons who are considered suitable for more advanced training than any they could obtain in their own countries or regions. In addition to technical training related to particular professions and trades, trainees at the Centre receive instruction in the principles and techniques of supervision and the fundamentals of teaching methods and techniques.

At the end of 1965, there were approximately 150 trainees in attendance at the Centre from some forty countries of Africa, Latin America, Asia and the Near and Middle East.

FOOD AND AGRICULTURE ORGANIZATION
OF THE UNITED NATIONS (FAO)

The United Nations Conference on Food and Agriculture met in the United States at Hot Springs, Virginia, in May 1943 and established an interim commission which drew up a draft constitution. When this document had been accepted by more than twenty governments, the first session of the Food and Agriculture Conference met at Quebec, Canada, and the Food and Agriculture Organization (FAO) came into being on October 16, 1945.

The founder nations of FAO expressed the wish to raise levels of nutrition and standards of living, to improve production and distribution of agricultural products and to better the condition of rural populations.

To help members reach these goals, FAO: provides an intelligence service, including not only facts and figures relating to nutrition, agriculture, forestry and fisheries, but also appraisals and forecasts of production, distribution and consumption in these fields; promotes national and international action to improve production, marketing, processing and distribution of the products of agriculture (including fisheries and forestry), conservation of natural resources, and credit and commodity arrangement policies; and furnishes, on request, technical assistance in any of the above fields.

Organization

FAO works through a Conference, a Council and a staff. The Conference is the policy-making body, in which each member state has one vote. Associate members have the right to attend and to take part in the discussions, but do not have the right to vote. The Conference normally meets biennially.

Between sessions of the Conference, the Council supervises the work of FAO, reviews the world food and agricultural situation and makes recommendations to member governments, and to international bodies, on measures to improve this situation.

The Council is composed of thirty-one member governments elected by the Conference.

The staff, or secretariat, is directed by a Director-General elected by the Conference as the organization's chief executive. Binay Ranjan Sen, of India, was re-elected to a second four-year term of office as Director-General in 1963.

The staff is organized into six departments: programme and budget; technical, comprising animal production and health, forestry and forest products, land and water development, nutrition, and plant production and protection; economic and social affairs; fisheries; public relations and legal affairs; and administration and finance.

FAO's permanent headquarters are in Rome. Regional offices are maintained in Washington, D.C., for North America; Cairo, for the Near East; Bangkok, for Asia and the Far East, with a sub-office at New Delhi; Santiago, Chile, for Latin America, with a sub-office in Mexico City, for northern Latin America and the Caribbean, and in Rio de Janeiro, for eastern Latin America; Accra, for Africa; and Geneva, for Europe. There is a liaison office at United Nations Headquarters.

By the end of 1965, fifty-one member states had set up national FAO committees as points of contact between the organization and governmental and non-governmental agencies.

Membership

Original members of FAO are those nations which are listed in an annex to FAO's Constitution, and which have accepted the Constitution. Additional members are admitted by a vote concurred in by a two-thirds majority of all the members of the Conference, and upon acceptance of FAO's Constitution at the time of admission.

As of January 1, 1966, FAO had 110 states in full membership and four in associate membership.

Budget

The budget is fixed on a biennial basis. The total amount for the 1966-1967 biennium was $49,974,000, to be used in financing FAO's regular programme as an advisory and consultative organization of governments seeking to develop food production throughout the world. FAO receives additional funds to execute certain other programmes, mainly in the field. These include a share (approximately $40-50 million a year) of the funds of the United Nations Development Programme. FAO also carries out field programmes with other international agencies or financed by the assisted countries themselves. For example, FAO provides the staff and UNICEF supplies the funds for its programme to improve the nutrition of the world's children.

Countries wanting expert aid which cannot be covered by normal United Nations aid programme funds often pay the necessary money into a trust fund to finance the FAO programme.

Activities

FREEDOM FROM HUNGER CAMPAIGN. The citizen-supported Freedom from Hunger Campaign was launched by FAO in 1960 to heighten world awareness of the problem of hunger and to create a greater general determination to deal with the problem. It is not primarily a field programme but, inspired by the Campaign, private citizens have collected tens of millions of dollars for field programmes. They are carrying out many of these projects themselves with FAO advice and encouragement, but about $22.8 million worth of projects are being carried out by FAO.

Activities under the Freedom from Hunger Campaign have included land reclamation, land use, irrigation, agricultural education and research, community development, agrarian reform, credit, cooperatives, nutrition and nutrition education, and home economics.

JOINT PROGRAMMES. The joint United Nations/FAO World Food Programme, which formally started operations for an experimental three-year period on January 1, 1963, had by late 1965 backed 115 projects for economic and social development, including feeding programmes, in fifty-five countries, committing more than $60 million, of the total of $94 million pledged by members of the United Nations, or FAO, in cash, commodities and services. A total of seventy countries had subscribed to the Programme, many of them developing countries with limited financial resources.

At the end of 1965, it was agreed to continue the Programme, and countries were invited to pledge up to a target of $275 million in food, cash and services to carry on operations for a further three years. Under the Programme, food may be used in low-income countries as a partial substitute for cash wages paid to workers in development projects, or it may be provided to families, resettled for developmental purposes, until they harvest first crops on their new land. In Honduras, for example, $200,000 worth of food aid paid part of the wages of workers engaged in the control of beetle pest in pine forests in 1964-1965. Supplies under the Programme are also used for emergency relief in cases of disaster, such as earthquakes, floods and volcanic eruptions.

The joint FAO/IAEA Division of Atomic Energy, based in Vienna, came into operation on October 1, 1965. The programmes of the Division concentrate on soil fertility, irrigation and crop production, insect eradication, pest control, pesticide residues and food protection. It is proposed to collaborate closely with other divisions of FAO and the World Health Organization (WHO) and to study the use of radioisotopes for measuring the movement of pesticides within plants and animals, detecting and identifying their metabolism and determining the toxic effects of pesticide residues in human food.

The International Bank for Reconstruction and Development has established jointly with FAO a special division to help evaluate national agricultural development projects for which Bank backing has been sought, and to help carry out these projects. Since its establishment, the new co-operative programme has undertaken a number of missions in various countries for the purpose of identifying programmes suitable for early financing, assisting governments in preparing further projects, assisting the Bank in appraisal of projects and helping review the execution of projects for which financing has already been granted.

An FAO/Industry Co-operative Programme was established in early 1966 to encourage closer working relations between FAO, industry and governments in order to implement development projects and to stimulate economic growth in developing countries. Such implementation includes the mobilization of the managerial ability, technical know-how, scientific experience and capital resources of industry in developing countries. The Programme aims at improving the climate for investment. Participation in the Programme is open to companies engaged in the production and processing of agricultural, forestry and fishery products and the manufacturers of equipment and materials used in this production.

REVIEW OF WORLD FOOD SITUATION.   FAO keeps under constant review the world food and agriculture situation. An FAO publication entitled *The State of Food and Agriculture, 1965* indicates that while the developing countries achieved "impressive gains" over the ten years previous to 1965 in the production of food and the exporting of agricultural products, these advances were in the main wiped out by the rapid growth of population, and the rising volume of trade signified little in the face of falling prices. Preliminary estimates showed that the production of food per person in 1964/65, as compared with the average of the years 1952/53 to 1956/57, rose by 14 per cent in the developed countries but by only 1 per cent in the developing countries.

The FAO report notes that the technical means for coping with the world food situation are available but that the task cannot be accomplished unless, in the words of FAO's Director-General, Dr. B. R. Sen, "the leaders of the nations are alive to the issues at stake, and are prepared to devote a large share of the world's resources to meet the looming crisis." It was, he thought, a considerable achievement that it had been possible to cope with the population explosion without widespread starvation resulting from it, but it was imperative that mankind should accept collective responsibility for the elimination of hunger and malnutrition.

While keeping under constant review the world food and agriculture situation, FAO has been giving increased attention to practical activities such as agricultural planning and marketing. Many new developments in the international trade of commodities require active participation by FAO, which also has to contribute appropriate studies and reports. Work on the statistics of hunger has been stepped up, particularly with reference to future world food requirements.

During 1965, work was started on an Indicative World Plan which will provide guidelines to governments on desirable levels of development of their agricultural production, consumption and trade. It will also point up the difference between the continuation of present trends and the realistic requirements of future world population.

AGRICULTURE.   FAO's Land and Water Development Division is concerned with the co-ordinated development of resources. The Division's work ranges from such purely physical matters as hydrology, soils, geology and civil engineering—factors which are basic to irrigation development—to farm management, and includes soil surveying, the use of fertilizers and the development, adaptation and application of farm machinery.

The Plant Production and Protection Division's field activities include participation in projects of the United Nations Development Programme and UNICEF, as well as Freedom from Hunger Campaign projects. FAO's seed-exchange service dispatches many thousands of seed samples and supervises micro-seed projects being financed under the joint FAO/UNESCO Gift Coupon Scheme. FAO also tests varieties of wheat and barley and aids development work in these and other crops.

The Animal Production and Health Division works to reduce

livestock diseases such as foot-and-mouth disease and rinderpest. Another important part of the Division's work is fostering the expansion of quarantine services. It has also launched research programmes into the mineral deficiencies of livestock in Latin America and, through its joint programme with the Danish Government for training dairy technicians, has held training seminars in the Middle East, Latin America and the Far East.

FISHERIES. The Fisheries Department administers United Nations Development Programme projects for the development of the world's fisheries. Records of the world fish catch each year are reported by the Fishery Statistics Section. Through the Fisheries Biology Branch, FAO has called for a reduction of whaling catches and for carrying out a survey to appraise the residual stocks and establishing whaling quotas, backed by an international inspection system, to prevent possible extinction of the species.

FORESTRY. FAO issues a series of regional studies of timber trends and prospects as part of an appraisal of world wood resources and requirements. It has also issued, in 1965, a study indicating that more than eleven million acres of quick-growing trees have been planted throughout the world during the past twenty years to meet the growing demand for wood. Emphasis in recent years has been on the development of raw material resources for the production of pulp and paper. A new field of concern has been the conservation and management of wildlife, particularly in Africa.

NUTRITION. FAO extends assistance to countries in the establishment of nutrition services and in nutrition education and for school feeding programmes, and also provides advice to member countries on the revision of food laws and regulations. The "Codex Alimentarius" is a joint FAO/WHO programme aimed at the establishment of international food standards to facilitate international trade in food products and also to protect consumers against frauds and adulterations. Other FAO activities include the strengthening and expanding of home economics and extension programmes in Latin America, the Caribbean, the Near East, Asia and the Far East, and Africa.

UNITED NATIONS EDUCATIONAL, SCIENTIFIC AND CULTURAL ORGANIZATION (UNESCO)

A conference for the establishment of an educational, scientific and cultural organization of the United Nations met in London from November 1 to 16, 1945, and drew up the Constitution of UNESCO. It also established a Preparatory Educational, Scientific and Cultural Commission, to function until the organization came into being on November 4, 1946, when the UNESCO Constitution was formally accepted by twenty of its signatories.

The purpose of UNESCO, as defined in its Constitution, is to "contribute to peace and security by promoting collaboration among the nations through education, science and culture in order to further universal respect for justice, for the rule of law, and for the human rights and fundamental freedoms for all."

UNESCO's assignment is, therefore, to stimulate educational, scientific and cultural progress, and to encourage international co-operation in these fields by assisting member states and serving as a clearinghouse to make pertinent material readily available to them.

Organization

UNESCO works through a General Conference, an Executive Board and a secretariat.

The General Conference, consisting of representatives from each member state, convenes every two years to formulate policies and to approve the programme and budget for the next two years.

The Executive Board is elected by the General Conference to oversee the programme. This Board, made up of thirty members who are responsible to their governments, meets two or three times a year.

The Secretariat is responsible for executing the programme. It is headed by a Director-General proposed by the Executive Board and appointed by the Conference. The first Director-General was Julian Huxley, of the United Kingdom, 1946-1948. He was succeeded by Jaime Torres Bodet, of Mexico, 1948-1952; Luther H. Evans, of the United States, 1953-1958; Vittorino Veronese, of Italy, 1958-1961; and, since 1961, René Maheu, of France. John W. Taylor, of the United States, served as Acting Director-General on an interim appointment from November 1952 to July 1953.

National commissions, composed of representatives of the government and of non-governmental organizations in each of the member states, link UNESCO with the educational, scientific and cultural life in each country and assist in carrying out UNESCO's programme. UNESCO headquarters are in Paris.

Membership

Membership in the United Nations carries with it the right to membership in UNESCO. States not members of the United Nations may be admitted to membership of UNESCO, upon recommendation of the Executive Board, by a two-thirds majority vote of the General Conference, provided that the Economic and Social Council of the United Nations has not recommended the rejection of their application for membership.

As of January 1, 1966, UNESCO had 120 member states and three associate members. Associate members enjoy the same rights in the organization as full members, except that they cannot vote at the General Conference or hold office on the Executive Board.

Budget

A budget of $49 million was approved for UNESCO's activities for the two years 1965 and 1966. In addition, for this same period, the organization was allocated nearly $52 million for technical assistance activities under the United Nations Development Programme.

Activities

UNESCO's programme is carried out in member states only at the request of governments, and with their co-operation. UNESCO can only make recommendations; no nation is bound to follow them.

UNESCO's programme has two main aspects: permanent activities of general interest to all member states, such as the exchange of information and documentation, assistance to international non-governmental organizations and the preparation of international conventions; and special activities designed to deal with specific problems in particular states.

This programme is broken down into six main areas of activity: education, natural science, social and human sciences, culture, mass communication and international exchanges.

EDUCATION.   With an estimated 700 million people, or about two-fifths of the world's adult population, illiterate, UNESCO's programmes give special attention to literacy work and to linking this work with over-all economic and social development plans in member states. In 1965, UNESCO helped to promote a world congress, held at Teheran, on the eradication of illiteracy. Plans have been made for launching pilot literacy projects in a number of selected countries in all regions of the world, financed by the United Nations Development Programme with UNESCO acting as executive agency.

Continued importance has been accorded to educational planning through the International Institute of Educational Planning, in Paris. Co-operation between UNESCO and the World Bank in educational planning and financing has also resulted in aid missions to a number of member states in Africa, Asia and Latin America.

After some years of study, a report on how the professional, social and economic status of teachers could be improved has been issued jointly by UNESCO and the International Labour Office. This is to be proposed as an international instrument.

Aid is being continued to UNESCO's three large-scale regional programmes in Africa, Asia and Latin America in the form of help to member states in the improvement of teacher training and curriculum adaptation; in developing new teaching techniques, including audiovisual aids, particularly for the study of science and modern languages; and in educational planning. The major share of this aid continues to go to the newly independent states of Africa. Under these regional programmes, it is hoped that an over-all goal of universal primary education will be reached by 1980.

In Africa, UNESCO assists its regional education, information and research centre at Accra, Ghana; a textbook production unit at Yaoundé, Cameroon; and a pilot project for the application of new methods and techniques in education at Dakar, Senegal.

In Asia, three of UNESCO's main concerns continue to be its regional office for education in Asia, at Bangkok, and its centres for training educational planners and administrators at New Delhi, and teacher educators at Quezon City.

In Latin America, with the completion of a ten-year major project on the extension and improvement of primary education, stress is now being laid on the development of secondary and higher education, with assistance given to various Latin American universities for the training of educational specialists and research workers.

In the Arab states, UNESCO's main assistance is directed towards an advanced training centre at Beirut and a regional centre for education and community development near Cairo. UNESCO also is aiding Arab refugees, in collaboration with UNRWA.

School buildings are also of concern to UNESCO and support continues for the three regional school construction bureaus in Khartoum, Bangkok and Mexico City.

The Educational Clearing House at UNESCO headquarters in Paris collects data from all member states on curricula, education statistics, and fellowships, scholarships and teaching posts. The Clearing House also assembles material for UNESCO's *World Survey on Education*, four volumes of which have been issued.

NATURAL SCIENCES.   Following a decision of its General Conference in 1964, UNESCO now accords science the same priority as education in its programme. In science, it is working towards three major objectives: the development of the basic structure of science in its member states; the fostering of international co-operation for the advancement of scientific research and documentation; and the application of science and technology to development.

Regional activities relating to this programme are carried out by the four UNESCO science co-operation offices in Latin America, the Middle East, South Asia and South-east Asia and by a regional centre for science and technology in Africa.

As part of its programme to encourage international scientific co-operation, UNESCO launched an International Hydrological Decade on January 1, 1965. In a world where water shortages are no longer confined to desert and near-desert areas, research is being focussed, during the Hydrological Decade, on establishing a scientific inventory of the world's resources in water so that it can be rationally managed. This is part of an over-all programme of research related to natural resources.

Co-operation in seismology and earthquake engineering has also been stimulated. A UNESCO survey of the world's major seismic zones led to recommendations for better scientific observatories and improved building codes to protect the populations of these regions. UNESCO now offers a service of reconnaissance missions to study the effects of severe earthquakes.

In the marine sciences, the Inter-governmental Oceanographic Commission set up by UNESCO co-ordinates research work on the high seas. One of its projects, the six-year International Indian Ocean Expedition, was completed at the end of 1965; forty vessels from fifteen countries took part in the expedition. An international co-operative investigation of the Tropical Atlantic has been completed, and a co-operative study of the Kuroshio Current in the Northwest Pacific is being carried out. The Commission is also focussing oceanographic research on such topics as marine pollution and the effect on the weather of changes in the ocean.

Another main theme in UNESCO's science programme is that of laying the foundations for research and its applications. These activities begin with science teaching for children—notably through pilot projects destined to acquaint teachers with modern ways of teaching chemistry, physics and biology—and continue through an international network of postgraduate courses in leading universities for scientists from developing countries.

Under the United Nations Development Programme, aid is given to institutes of technology and schools of engineering in Asia, Latin America, Africa and the Arab world. These programmes also involve research for development, as illustrated by a project in Tunisia on irrigation with brackish water and a mathematical model study of the Mekong River Delta.

SOCIAL SCIENCES.   UNESCO is continuing to facilitate international co-operation among social scientists and the exchange of information and documentation, and is also encouraging the organization of teaching and development of research in countries where the social sciences are not yet fully used. An international survey is being made of main trends in psychology, linguistics, social and cultural anthropology, demography, sociology and economics.

At the same time, UNESCO's department of social sciences is concentrating on several of the major problems affecting the evolution of present-day societies: universal respect for human rights, with emphasis on the struggle against race prejudice; the economic and social problems of newly independent countries; and the economic and social consequences of disarmament.

An analysis office on the role of education, science, technology and information in economic development, and a statistical office are operated for the benefit of UNESCO's other departments and its member states.

CULTURE. UNESCO's programme is concentrated on the three major successive phases of cultural life: creation of original works; protection of existing works; and dissemination and international appreciation of cultures.

UNESCO encourages artistic creation by offering its aid to such organizations as the International Theatre Institute, the International Music Council and the Pen Club. Through symposia and studies, it has undertaken a broad survey of the influence of new information media, particularly films and television, on literature and art.

Because libraries and museums have the double role of preserving culture and making it accessible, UNESCO has consistently aided their development and the improvement of their facilities. The success of the international campaign to save the monuments of Nubia drew world attention to the need to protect mankind's common cultural heritage.

A ten-year major project on the mutual appreciation of Eastern and Western cultural values has produced studies, teaching material, exchanges of professors and students, translations of literary works and the organization of travelling art exhibits.

MASS COMMUNICATION. UNESCO's work in the field of mass communication is aimed towards a freer flow of information and towards stimulating the distribution of information to increase mutual understanding among peoples.

UNESCO's department of mass communication, emphasizing educational uses of the various information media, works to expand press, radio, film and television services in the developing countries of the world, chiefly in Africa. There is, for example, a six-year pilot project in Dakar, Senegal, on experimental television programmes for adult education.

Educational radio broadcasts have been established in numerous countries, ranging from dawn broadcasts into the Andes, to the Radio Rural Forum in India, which broadcasts to tribal populations in eighty-two dialects. Many countries in Asia, Africa and Latin America benefit from work on the use of audio-visual aids in education.

The possibilities and the problems inherent in the new field of satellite communications have also been studied by UNESCO.

UNESCO operates two institutes for higher studies in journalism, one at the University of Strasbourg, in France, and the other at the University of Quito, in Ecuador, and courses in basic journalistic training have been set up at universities in Dakar, Senegal, and Manila, the Philippines.

Among the many publications of the organization, *The* UNESCO *Courier* is perhaps the best known. Published in eight languages—English, French, Spanish, Russian, German, Italian, Arabic and Japanese—it is distributed in more than 120 countries and has a circulation of over 500,000.

INTERNATIONAL EXCHANGES.   The promotion of travel abroad for educational, scientific and cultural purposes is an essential element in UNESCO's work to develop greater international understanding and a more effective sharing of knowledge and skills among its member states. UNESCO provides information and advice on exchange programmes through the operation of the Educational Clearing House (*described under* "Education" *above*) and through its publications. One of these is *Study Abroad*, a biennial review containing information on opportunities for study abroad through fellowships, scholarships and educational exchanges. Another is *Vacations Abroad*, an annual guide to short-term educational opportunities such as vacation courses, study tours and work camps.

The UNESCO *Handbook of International Exchanges* provides information on the aims, programmes and activities of national and international organizations and on inter-governmental agreements concerning international relations and exchanges in the fields of education, science, culture and mass communication.

UNESCO also publishes *Teachers for Africa*, a booklet aimed at helping African countries recruit teachers abroad. It awards and administers international fellowships under its regular programme and the United Nations Development Programme.

TECHNICAL ASSISTANCE.   By the end of 1965, UNESCO was responsible for over 1,000 specialists working in the field either as experts assigned to individual countries under the United Nations Development Programme and UNESCO's own programme of participation in the activities of member states, or in UNESCO regional offices. The main fields in which UNESCO provides experts and advisers to member states are: the extension and modernization of educational facilities at all levels, teacher training, the fight against illiteracy, the improvement of science teaching, the training of scientists and engineers, assistance to scientific research and technical documentation services, and the development of social science teaching and mass communication facilities.

WORLD HEALTH ORGANIZATION (WHO)

The founding of the World Health Organization (WHO) goes back to a proposal, made at the United Nations Conference on International Organization in San Francisco in 1945, which envisaged the creation of a specialized institution in the field of health.

In June and July 1946, at an international health conference held in New York, representatives of sixty-four countries drafted and signed the Constitution of WHO and established an interim commission composed of representatives of eighteen governments. The commission carried on the most urgent health work previously undertaken by such bodies as the League of Nations Health Organization, the Office International d'Hygiène Publique and UNRRA, and prepared for the establishment of WHO as a permanent organization.

The WHO Constitution came into force on April 7, 1948, after twenty-six members of the United Nations had ratified it. Throughout the world, April 7 of each year is celebrated as World Health Day.

The objective of WHO is "the attainment by all peoples of the highest possible level of health," and health, as defined in the WHO Constitution, is "a state of complete physical, mental and social well-being and not merely the absence of disease or infirmity." WHO, accordingly, has a wide range of functions, including the following: to act as the directing and co-ordinating authority on international health work; to stimulate and advance work to eradicate epidemic, endemic and other diseases; to promote improved standards of teaching and training in the health, medical and related professions; to establish, and to stimulate the establishment of, international standards for biological, pharmaceutical and similar products, and to standardize diagnostic procedures; and to foster activities in the field of mental health, especially those activities affecting the harmony of human relations.

WHO runs a number of world-wide services, such as the notification of quarantinable diseases; assists member countries, on request, to improve their health services; and stimulates medical research in a variety of ways.

Organization

The main organs of WHO are the World Health Assembly, the Executive Board, six regional committees and the secretariat.

The World Health Assembly, the supreme governing body, meets each year and is composed of delegations of the organization's member states. It determines the policies and programmes of WHO and votes the budget.

The Executive Board, a technical and non-political organ, is made up of twenty-four persons designated by as many member states elected by the World Health Assembly. It meets at least twice a year to prepare the work of the Assembly and to give effect to its decisions.

WHO's headquarters are in Geneva, but the activities of the organization have been largely decentralized to six regional organizations, each having a regional committee composed of government representatives of the countries in the region and a regional office. WHO has regional offices at New Delhi, for South-east Asia; Alexandria, for the Eastern Mediterranean; Manila, for the Western Pacific; Washington, for the Americas (Pan American Sanitary Bureau); Brazzaville, for Africa; and Copenhagen, for Europe.

The secretariat, under the Director-General, Dr. M. G. Candau of Brazil, comprises the technical and administrative personnel of the organization; current work is entrusted to a staff of about 3,000 from more than eighty different countries working at WHO's headquarters, in regional offices and in field projects throughout the world.

Membership

Membership in WHO is open to all states. Members of the United Nations join WHO by accepting its Constitution; other states become WHO members when the World Health Assembly has approved their application by a simple majority vote. Territories which are not responsible for the conduct of their international relations may become associate members.

As of January 1, 1966, WHO had 122 member states and three associate members.

Budget

The regular budget of WHO is made up of the annual contributions of member states; for 1966, it exceeded $42 million. Added to this was an estimated $9.5 million from the United Nations Development Programme and about $3 million from WHO's voluntary fund for health promotion, which receives contributions from public and private sources. Activities of the Pan American Health Organization (PAHO) are integrated with those of WHO and were financed in 1966 out of a (PAHO) budget of about $12 million.

Activities

CONTROL OF COMMUNICABLE DISEASES. Since the eighth World Health Assembly, held in Mexico City in 1955, WHO has been engaged in a world-wide campaign to root out malaria, a disease to which more than 1,400 million people were exposed. By the end of 1965, over 55 per cent of the population living in the world's original malarious areas had been freed from the threat of the disease.

In many countries, a double attack on the tubercle bacillus is being pursued with WHO assistance by using powerful new drugs and by continuing large-scale BCG vaccination campaigns to prevent tuberculosis. In combination, these two actions offer the possibility of eliminating tuberculosis as a major public health problem in most countries. WHO helped to develop a heat-stable freeze-dried BCG vaccine giving consistently better results than the earlier fluid vaccine.

There has been an impressive decline in the number of cases of yaws—a crippling infection, widespread in the tropics—as a result of vigorous mass campaigns assisted by WHO in which more than 38 million people were treated with penicillin in forty countries. The stage is now one of surveillance to prevent recrudescence of the disease, while laboratory studies continue in order to improve various diagnostic tests.

In 1965, the World Health Assembly decided that smallpox eradication was to be a major objective of WHO and called for a ten-year plan to completely eradicate the disease. Twelve countries have achieved eradication of smallpox since 1959.

Over 400 million people are probably infected with trachoma, and in areas where practically the whole population has this eye disease, 1 per cent of adults are totally blind and 4 per cent suffer from loss of vision rendering them economically dependent. WHO continues to support trachoma research and to give practical assistance to governments for control programmes.

Bilharziasis is a disease transmitted through contact with water. It is caused by a tiny parasite that spends part of its life cycle in a water snail host. The disease is particularly common in irrigated areas of warm countries. WHO surveys have confirmed that the disease is on the increase and is appearing in countries hitherto considered free of it. In field and laboratory trials in eight countries, a number of molluscicides are being tested for efficacy against the snail host. Good results have been obtained with a new drug tested with WHO assistance, and studies are continuing on the effects of long-term administration of the drug.

Many of the deformities and disabilities caused by leprosy can be prevented by early diagnosis and treatment, yet not more than one-fifth of the world's estimated ten million leprosy sufferers are receiving treatment of any kind. WHO gives advice on the organization of up-to-date leprosy services and the application of existing knowledge to treatment and rehabilitation.

ENVIRONMENTAL HEALTH.   In its efforts to improve community water supply, WHO has provided teams of experts to advise countries on the technical aspects of water-supply programmes and has continued to help train the various types of specialized personnel needed for the construction, operation and maintenance of public water supplies.

A study has been undertaken on international standardization of methods and instruments for measuring air pollution, and an illustrated monograph on various aspects of air pollution has been published by WHO.

The development and evaluation of new insecticides suitable for use in disease-control programmes are of great importance for the success of malaria eradication and the control of other insect-borne diseases. WHO has set up a scheme of collaboration between the chemical industry and independent research institutes for this purpose and for undertaking basic research into the nature of insect resistance to insecticides.

PUBLIC HEALTH SERVICES.   WHO is advising governments on the planning of public health services, sometimes as independent programmes but often as part of wider schemes of social and economic development. In many large development programmes at community level in a number of countries, work on health, education, agricultural improvement and other aspects of economic and social development is co-ordinated.

New international sanitary regulations codifying health measures applicable to ground, sea and air travel were formulated by WHO in 1951 and became effective on October 1, 1952, replacing all the health conventions previously in force. WHO administers these regulations and maintains a world-wide system of reception and distribution of notifications of quarantinable diseases, including a network of broadcasting stations relaying daily radio-telegraph broadcasts from Geneva.

RESEARCH.   WHO's work in the field of veterinary public health is mainly concentrated on four animal diseases transmissible to man: brucellosis or Malta fever, rabies, leptospirosis and hydatidosis, with emphasis on the search for better preventive methods. WHO is also pursuing comparative studies of cancer and heart diseases in animals because they may give clues to the causes of these diseases in man. Arterial lesions in swine, the effect of "social" stress on cardiovascular diseases in birds, and the effect of diet, growth and sex on these diseases in turkeys are among the factors studied in this programme.

An International Agency for Research on Cancer was established by the eighteenth World Health Assembly in 1965. Located in Lyons, France, the Agency will serve as the means for governments and WHO to stimulate and support all phases of cancer research.

WHO is also promoting research concerning the hitherto little known factors that give rise to the major cardiovascular diseases. A study of heart disease based on autopsy material is going forward under WHO auspices in several countries.

A ten-year programme of research in social psychiatry and the epidemiology of mental disorders has been started with the aim of obtaining comparable information on the distribution of mental disorders, the factors affecting their development in different social and cultural settings and the effect of treatment. Other work includes advice to governments on mental health activities as part of the public health programme, and on the organization of services for persons affected by mental deficiency, alcoholism and drug dependence.

EDUCATION AND TRAINING.   Shortages of health personnel, whether of doctors, nurses, sanitary engineers, laboratory technicians or others, are to be found in every country. WHO helps develop schools for the health professions, provides teaching staff and awards about 3,000 fellowships a year for study abroad.

WHO is giving increasing help to enable countries to meet the pressing demand for more and better trained nursing and midwifery personnel and to improve their nursing education programmes. The organization also assists in setting up post-basic and post-graduate nursing courses in many countries.

WHO is also much concerned with the training of staff for mother and child health services, with surveying children's health needs and controlling children's diseases, and with the problem of premature babies. Many programmes are run in co-operation with UNICEF.

A programme for the development of protein-rich food is being continued and reinforced in collaboration with FAO and UNICEF, and a survey of the existing facilities for training workers in nutrition has been undertaken by FAO and WHO in Africa, Latin America and South-east Asia. WHO is collaborating closely in the World Food Programme and gives advice on the health aspects of many related projects.

BIOLOGY AND PHARMACOLOGY.   International laboratories make samples of internationally standardized biological substances available to laboratories all over the world. Because these substances—

hormones, vitamins and antibiotics, among others—are too complex for their potency to be measured by ordinary chemical or physical means, experimental comparison with a recognized standard is needed. Who has adopted international standards for about seventy such substances, continuing the work in this field which was started by the League of Nations.

The safety of drugs has become a major problem with the increase in the production and variety of these substances all over the world, often without proper check. Who is running an inter-governmental information service on adverse drug reactions which should permit stoppage of any drug suddenly revealed as dangerous. Quality control of drugs is another problem, and who has included specifications for the identity and purity of 555 pharmaceutical preparations in the second edition of the *International Pharmacopoeia*.

The control of narcotic drugs, which is governed by international treaties, is one of the oldest examples of international co-operation in the social and economic fields. Who is required to advise the other international organs concerned on those drugs which are liable to produce addiction. It also does much work in the field of the treatment and rehabilitation of addicts and in the prevention of drug addiction.

INTERNATIONAL BANK FOR RECONSTRUCTION AND DEVELOPMENT (WORLD BANK, OR IBRD)

The International Bank for Reconstruction and Development (World Bank, or IBRD) was founded at the Bretton Woods Monetary and Financial Conference in July 1944 and began operations in June 1946. The Bank is an international co-operative organization associated with the United Nations as a specialized agency. Its aim is to assist the economic development of its member countries and thus raise the standards of living of the peoples of the world. It makes loans for productive purposes to member governments and to government agencies or private enterprises under governmental guarantee.

Organization

All powers of the Bank are vested in the Board of Governors, which meets annually. The Board consists of one Governor and one Alternate appointed by each member.

The Board of Governors has delegated most of its powers to

twenty Executive Directors, who meet at least once a month at the Bank's headquarters. Five of the Directors are appointed by the five members having the largest number of shares of capital stock; the others are elected by the remaining members. The Executive Directors function as a Board, and each Director is entitled to cast as a unit the aggregate number of votes of the member or members which he represents.

The President of the Bank is selected by the Executive Directors and also serves as their Chairman. Subject to the general direction of the Executive Directors on questions of policy, he is responsible for conducting the business of the Bank.

The Presidents of the Bank have been Eugene Meyer (June 18 to December 18, 1946); John J. McCloy (March 17, 1947 to June 30, 1949); Eugene R. Black (July 1, 1949 to December 31, 1962); and George D. Woods (since January 1, 1963).

The headquarters of the Bank are in Washington, D.C. Small offices are also maintained in Paris, New York and London.

Membership

As of January 1, 1966, the Bank had 103 members.

Administrative Budget

The administrative expenses of the Bank are paid out of the Bank's income and are controlled through an administrative budget approved by the Executive Directors. For the fiscal year ending June 30, 1966, the administrative budget of the Bank amounted to approximately $27.8 million.

Capital of the Bank

The authorized capital of the Bank is $24,000 million. As of December 31, 1965, capital subscriptions of the Bank's 103 members totalled $21,605 million.

Only one-tenth of the subscribed capital is actually paid in. Most of the paid-in subscriptions are in national currencies and may be lent only with the consent of the member concerned. The remaining 90 per cent of the Bank's capital is not available for lending but is subject to call only if required to meet outstanding obligations of the Bank.

By December 31, 1965, funds available to the Bank for lending from subscriptions amounted to $1,779 million. Most of the Bank's lending funds, which now total nearly $8,100 million, have therefore come from other sources, mainly from borrowing in the capital markets of the world.

Activities

BORROWING OPERATIONS.   The Bank has been very active in selling its bonds in the world's capital markets. By December 31, 1965, the Bank's outstanding funded debt amounted to $2,727 million, of which $1,994 million was repayable in United States dollars, $390 million in Deutsche marks, $187 million in Swiss francs, $46 million in pounds sterling, $40 million in Canadian dollars, $36 million in Netherlands guilders, $24 million in Italian lire and $10 million in Belgian francs.

In addition to its direct borrowing, the Bank sells parts of its loans. By December 31, 1965, the Bank had sold $1,940 million of its loans, of which all but $69 million were sold without the Bank's guarantee.

LENDING OPERATIONS.   As of December 31, 1965, the Bank had made 446 loans, totalling $9,312 million, in seventy-seven countries or territories. Asia and the Middle East had received a total of $3,140 million; the Western Hemisphere, $2,400 million; Europe, $2,031 million; Africa, $1,220 million; and Australasia, $520 million. India is the Bank's largest single borrower, with loans totalling $972 million.

Excluding $497 million lent in 1947 for reconstruction in Europe, total lending, divided by purpose, was approximately as follows: $3,179 million for transport; $3,159 million for electric power; $1,433 million for industry; $712 million for agriculture and forestry; $205 million for general development purposes; $88 million for telecommunications; $31 million for water supply; and $9 million for education.

Under its Articles of Agreement, the Bank is restricted to making loans for productive purposes which will assist in the reconstruction or development of its member states, where funds are not obtainable in the private market on reasonable terms. Loans are long-term—ten to thirty-five years—and can be made only to member states or their political subdivisions, or to private enterprises located in the territories of members. Loans to borrowers other than governments must be guaranteed by the government in whose territory the project is located. Proceeds of loans are not tied to a particular source of supply; borrowers are free to use the proceeds to make purchases in any member country, or in Switzerland, which has established, by agreement, a special relationship with the Bank.

In order to ensure that its loans are sound and that they conform to the Articles of Agreement, the Bank applies businesslike banking practices to its investigations of loan applications. In addition, all loan agreements specify the purposes for which the loan is made and, in most cases, the goods and services that may be purchased with the proceeds. Disbursements under the Bank's normal project loans are made only as expenditures are incurred for specified goods and services. The borrower is required to furnish evidence that the goods or services to be financed are covered by the loan agreement, that they are reasonable in cost and of proper quality and that shipment is being made. The Bank also maintains supervision over the end-use of items purchased with its funds through actual inspection of projects and through periodic reports from engineers and others concerned with the progress of a project.

The rate of interest charged by the Bank is related to the rate which it would itself have to pay to borrow money at the time the loan is made and the ability of member countries to raise funds in the capital markets of the world. The standard rate is 5 and one-half per cent. In February 1965, the Bank decided that countries able to cover the bulk of their external capital needs from private market sources should be charged rates of interest roughly comparable to those they pay when borrowing in the market, but in no case more than 1 per cent above the standard rate.

TECHNICAL ASSISTANCE AND TRAINING. The Bank also renders to its member governments technical assistance in a wide variety of ways, ranging from full-scale economic surveys of their development potential to regional investigation or advice on particular projects. Resident advisers have, on request, been stationed in many countries. Field missions of the Bank have been set up both in West and East Africa to help African countries identify and prepare projects for presentation to the Bank and its affiliate, the International Development Association.

The Bank finances and organizes numerous studies of a pre-investment nature. These studies range in purpose from a sector study designed to aid in the formulation of an investment programme in a major field, such as power or transport, to a project study to determine the feasibility of a particular project, such as a bridge or port facility. In another area of pre-investment assistance, the Bank, acting as executing agency, carries out a number of surveys financed by the United Nations Development Programme.

The Economic Development Institute, the Bank's staff college, provides senior officials from less developed countries with training in economic management. Until 1962, the Institute offered only a six-month general course, given once each year. Since then, several new courses have been added to provide for special needs not fully met previously, and courses are now being offered in Spanish and French for nationals of Spanish and French-speaking countries. Courses in project evaluation have been added for officials who formulate, appraise and select development projects. To meet regional training needs, the Institute has conducted project evaluation courses in India and Pakistan. By the end of 1965, over 500 senior officials from more than ninety countries had participated in the various courses conducted by the Institute.

The Bank has organized consultative groups of capital-providing countries and international agencies to co-ordinate the flow of finance and technical assistance to a number of countries, in addition to consortia of aid-pledging countries and institutions for India and Pakistan.

SETTLEMENT OF INVESTMENT DISPUTES.   To help encourage a freer flow of private capital to the developing countries, the Executive Directors of the Bank have prepared and submitted to member governments the text of a Convention on the Settlement of Investment Disputes between States and Nationals of Other States. The Convention will enter into force thirty days after it has been signed and ratified by twenty governments.

INTERNATIONAL FINANCE CORPORATION
(IFC)

The International Finance Corporation (IFC) was established in 1956 as an affiliate of the World Bank. The purpose of the Corporation is to further economic development by encouraging the growth of productive private enterprise in member countries, particularly in the less developed areas, thus supplementing the activities of the World Bank.

Organization

While IFC is an affiliate of the World Bank, with headquarters in Washington, D.C., it is a separate legal entity and has its own funds and staff. The World Bank, however, provides a wide range of administrative and other services for IFC. Membership in IFC is open to all governments which are members of the Bank. The Governors and Executive Directors of the World Bank representing governments which are also members of IFC hold identical positions for IFC. The President of the World Bank is also the President of IFC and serves as Chairman of IFC's Board of Directors.

The annual meetings of the Board of Governors of IFC are held in conjunction with those of the World Bank and the International Development Association.

IFC acts for the World Bank group of institutions in the technical and financial appraisal, preparation and supervision of manufacturing and mining projects.

Membership

Membership in IFC is open to all governments which are members of the World Bank. By January 1, 1966, eighty countries had become members of IFC.

Resources

IFC's authorized capital is $110 million, of which approximately $99.3 million has been paid in by its member governments.

An amendment to IFC's Articles of Agreement to permit the Corporation to borrow from the Bank took effect on September 1, 1965, and an amendment to the Bank's Articles permitting it to make loans to IFC up to four times the Corporation's unimpaired subscribed capital and surplus came into force on December 17, 1965. As a result, approximately $400 million was added to IFC's potential resources for lending to private enterprises without government guarantee, enabling the Corporation to participate in larger projects and to make loan and equity commitments to a larger number of individual enterprises.

Activities

The Corporation has established four main methods of operation to assist private enterprise in developing countries: direct investment in industrial companies, with the participation of domestic or foreign private investors and entrepreneurs; assistance to privately owned development finance companies; stand-by and underwriting commitments; and the sale of investments from portfolio to other financial institutions. The Corporation does not seek or accept governmental guarantees of its investments.

Any enterprise in which IFC invests must be designed to make an effective contribution to the economic development of the country in which it is located. The amount required must be justified by the contribution which the investment is expected to make. A project or venture in which IFC participates must also have a sound capital structure, capable and experienced management and the prospect of profitable operation. IFC must have assurance not only that private investors will put up a considerable portion of the capital required but also that sufficient private investment funds for the venture are not available on reasonable terms without IFC participation.

IFC takes the lead in the World Bank family to encourage the establishment and expansion of development finance companies. These companies are designed to fill a gap in national capital markets by providing long-term equity and loan finance to the private productive sector of the economy. They finance existing enterprises in the process of expansion and modernization and also play a promotional role in identifying investment opportunities, financing new companies and attracting foreign capital. By December 1965, IFC had a share interest in sixteen development finance companies in fourteen countries.

From the beginning of its operations in July 1956 to December 31, 1965, the Corporation had undertaken 112 investment commitments totalling $150 million in thirty-four countries.

During the same period, sales of and participation in IFC investments and underwriting commitments totalled approximately $6.3 million. These transactions raised the total amount of investments sold to $31.9 million.

Acquisition by others of securities covered by stand-by and underwriting commitments totalled $0.4 million.

Gross earnings for the year ending December 31, 1965 totalled $6.3 million; after deduction of administrative expenses of $2.8 million, net income for the calendar year came to $3.5 million. Accumulated net income, which was transferred to a reserve against losses, totalled $25.9 million as of December 31, 1965.

INTERNATIONAL DEVELOPMENT ASSOCIATION (IDA)

The International Development Association (IDA) was established in September 1960, as an affiliate of the World Bank, to promote economic development in the less developed areas of the world included within its membership. IDA provides finance on terms which are more flexible and bear less heavily on the balance of payments of recipient countries than do conventional loans. IDA has its own funds, but its directors, officers and staff are those of the Bank, serving *ex officio* with the Association. While the terms of IDA credits are much more lenient than those of the Bank, IDA uses the same high standards of project planning and execution when considering a credit operation.

Membership

Membership is open to all member countries of the World Bank. By January 1, 1966, ninety-six countries had joined IDA.

Resources

IDA's resources come mainly from subscriptions and contributions of its members. The initial subscriptions of all members are proportioned to their subscriptions to the capital stock of the Bank. However, under the Association's Articles of Agreement, members of IDA are divided into two groups: Part I, or high income, countries; and Part II, or developing, countries. A Part I country pays its entire subscription in convertible currency, all of which may be used by IDA for its lending, while a Part II country pays only 10 per cent in convertible funds and the remainder in its own currency, which may not be used by IDA without the member's consent. All Part II countries and the dependent and associated territories of Part I countries are eligible to receive IDA credits.

IDA is authorized to accept supplementary contributions and is required to maintain a regular review of the adequacy of its resources. In 1963, the Executive Directors proposed that IDA resources be replenished through supplementary contributions by its economically advanced members. Accordingly, eighteen countries—Australia, Austria, Belgium, Canada, Denmark, Finland, France, Germany, Italy, Japan, Kuwait, Luxembourg, the Netherlands, Norway, South Africa, Sweden, the United Kingdom and the United States—provided supplementary resources of about $750 million for commitment through June 30, 1966. Sweden made four special contributions amounting to $18 million, and the Bank itself contributed $125 million from its net income for the 1964 and 1965 fiscal years. In addition, Part II countries released a total of $5 million equivalent of their local currency subscriptions for use by IDA. At the end of 1965, paid-in and prospective resources of the Association amounted to $1,676 million.

Credit Operations

By December 31, 1965, IDA had extended seventy-nine development credits totalling $1,192.5 million in thirty countries. Forty-four of the credits, totalling $899 million, went to countries in Asia and the Middle East. Africa received a total of $127.7 million; the Western Hemisphere, $100.4 million; and Turkey, $65.7 million.

Transportation was the principal economic sector assisted by IDA lending, accounting for $464 million. Credits totalling $221.4 million were made to assist industrial development and $215.8 million to assist agriculture and forestry. The balance of IDA lending was distributed as follows: electric power, $96.7 million; telecommunications, $75 million; water supply, $62.5 million; and education, $57.1 million. All IDA credits have been for terms of fifty years, free of interest. Amortization is to begin after a ten-year period of grace; thereafter, 1 per cent of the principal is repayable annually for ten years, and 3 per cent is repayable annually for the final thirty years. A service charge of three-quarters of 1 per cent per annum, payable on the amounts withdrawn and outstanding, is being made to meet IDA's administrative costs.

INTERNATIONAL MONETARY FUND (FUND, OR IMF)

The Articles of Agreement for the International Monetary Fund (IMF) were drawn up by the United Nations Monetary and Financial Conference, which met at Bretton Woods, New Hampshire, in July 1944. The Conference was attended by representatives of forty-four nations. The Articles of Agreement came into force on December 27, 1945, and the inaugural meeting of the Fund's Board of Governors was held, in conjunction with that of the Board of Governors of the International Bank for Reconstruction and Development, in Savannah, Georgia, in March 1946.

The Fund was established to promote international co-operation on monetary problems through a permanent institution which provides the machinery for consultation and collaboration. Its main purposes are: to facilitate, as primary objectives of economic policy, the expansion and balanced growth of international trade, contributing thereby to the promotion and maintenance of high levels of employment and real income and to the development of the productive resources of all members; to promote exchange stability, to maintain orderly exchange arrangements among members and to avoid competitive exchange depreciation; and to give confidence to members by making the Fund's resources available to them under adequate safeguards.

Organization

The Fund works through a Board of Governors, a Board of Executive Directors, a Managing Director and a staff.

All powers of the Fund are vested in the Board of Governors, which consists of one Governor and one Alternate appointed by each member. Voting power of the Governors is related to the size of the quota of the member nations they represent.

The Board of Executive Directors is responsible for the conduct of the general operations of the Fund and exercises the powers delegated to it by the Board of Governors. Five Executive Directors are appointed by members having the largest quotas, and the others, at present fifteen, are elected by the Governors representing the remaining members. Each appointed Director casts all the votes of the country which appointed him, and each elected Director casts as a unit all the votes of the countries which elected him.

The Executive Directors appoint a Managing Director, who must not be a Governor or an Executive Director. The Managing Director is the Chairman of the Board of Executive Directors and chief of the operating staff.

The first Managing Director was Camille Gutt, of Belgium, 1946-1951. He was succeeded by Ivar Rooth, of Sweden, 1951-1956. Per Jacobsson, of Sweden, was Managing Director from December 1956 until his death in May 1963. His successor is Pierre-Paul Schweitzer, of France, appointed in June 1963.

The headquarters of the Fund are in Washington, D.C.

Membership

As of January 1, 1966, the Fund had 103 members.

Resources

As of December 31, 1965, assets of the Fund included, in round figures, $2,668.9 million in gold, $13,546.3 million in various national currencies and $938.4 million in subscriptions receivable. Total quotas were $15,976.6 million. The subscriptions of members are equal to their quotas. Each member must pay in gold 25 per cent of its subscription or 10 per cent of its net official gold and dollar holdings, whichever is less. The balance is paid in the member's own currency.

Under an arrangement concluded in 1962, ten major industrial nations stand ready to lend the Fund up to $6,000 million in their respective currencies should this be necessary to forestall or cope with a threat to the international monetary system.

Administrative Budget

The Fund's total administrative expenditure for the fiscal year ended April 30, 1965, was $13,011,474. Total income for the same period was $47,749,062. The Fund's income is derived principally from charges on its transactions and income from certain short-term investments.

Activities

At the end of 1965, twenty-seven countries had eliminated exchange restrictions in accordance with Article VIII of the Fund's Articles of Agreement. Annual consultations with those members maintaining restrictions under Article XIV are required by the Fund's Articles of Agreement.

The Fund began active exchange operations on March 1, 1947; by December 31, 1965, it had concluded exchange transactions with fifty-six of its members. These countries purchased United States and Canadian dollars, pounds sterling, Deutsche marks, Belgian and French francs, Australian pounds, Mexican pesos, Argentine pesos, Italian lire, Danish and Swedish kronor, Japanese yen, Austrian schillings, Spanish pesetas and Netherlands guilders, aggregating $11,500 million, in exchange for an equivalent amount of their own currencies. Total repayments for the period March 1, 1947 to December 31, 1965, amounted to nearly $5,800 million.

The Fund maintains an extensive programme of technical assistance to many parts of the world. It also provides studies, reports and publications on international economic and financial subjects.

INTERNATIONAL CIVIL AVIATION
ORGANIZATION (ICAO)

A convention providing for the establishment of an international civil aviation organization was drawn up by the International Civil Aviation Conference held in Chicago from November 1 to December 7, 1944. The International Civil Aviation Organization (ICAO) came into being on April 4, 1947, thirty days after the convention had been ratified by the required twenty-six states. Under an agreement drawn up by the Chicago Conference, a provisional international civil aviation organization operated from June 6, 1945, until the formal establishment of ICAO.

The Chicago Convention superseded the provisions of two earlier agreements, namely, the Paris Convention of 1919, which established the International Commission for Air Navigation to set up standards on technical matters, and the Pan American Convention on Commercial Aviation, drawn up at Havana in 1928.

The aims and objectives of ICAO are to develop the principles and techniques of international air navigation, and to foster the planning and development of international air transport so as to: ensure the safe and orderly growth of international civil aviation throughout the world; encourage the arts of aircraft design and operation for peaceful purposes; encourage the development of airways, airports and air navigation facilities for international civil aviation; meet the needs of the peoples of the world for safe, regular, efficient and economical air transport; prevent economic waste caused by unreasonable competition; ensure that the rights of contracting states are fully respected and that every contracting state has a fair opportunity to operate international airlines; avoid discrimination between contracting states; promote safety of flight in international air navigation; and promote generally the development of all aspects of international civil aeronautics.

Organization

ICAO operates through an Assembly, a Council and a secretariat, and also through a number of commissions and committees.

The Assembly consists of all the member states of ICAO, each of which has one vote. It is convened by the Council at least once every three years. The Assembly decides on ICAO policy, votes on the budget and deals with any questions not specifically referred to the Council.

The Council, composed of twenty-seven states elected by the Assembly, carries out the directives of the Assembly. It elects its President, appoints the Secretary-General and administers the finances of the organization. It creates standards for international air navigation and collects, examines and publishes information concerning air navigation. It may also act, if so requested by the countries concerned, as a tribunal for the settlement of any dispute arising among member states relating to international civil aviation. The Council is assisted in its work by an Air Navigation Commission and by four committees: air transport, legal, joint support of air navigation services, and finance.

The Secretary-General of ICAO appoints the staff of the secretariat and supervises and directs its activities. B. T. Twigt, of the Netherlands, was appointed Secretary-General in March 1964 for a three-year term beginning in August 1964.

ICAO headquarters are in Montreal, Canada. The organization maintains six field offices which serve as liaison between ICAO and its various member states: the North American and Caribbean office in Mexico City; the South American office in Lima; the European office in Paris; the Middle East and East African office in Cairo; the Far East and Pacific office in Bangkok; and the African office in Dakar.

Membership

States which have ratified or adhered to the Convention on International Civil Aviation become member states of ICAO. As of January 1, 1966, 110 states were members.

Budget

ICAO's net budget for 1966 amounted to $6,048,000.

Activities

Since its establishment, ICAO has sought to bring about concerted action by the nations of the world in the organization and maintenance of facilities and services necessary for international air transport. Patterns for meteorological services, traffic control, communications, radio beacons and other facilities for safe international flight have been developed.

Regional air navigation meetings have been held covering all the major international flying areas of the world as classified by ICAO: North Atlantic, European, Mediterranean, Caribbean, Middle East, South American-South Atlantic, Pacific, Africa-Indian Ocean and South-east Asia. These meetings examined existing facilities for airports, navigational aids, communications, air traffic control, meteorology, operations, and search and rescue and determined what additional facilities and operating procedures were needed to make flying in these regions safer, more economical and more regular. One such meeting resulted in member states agreeing to maintain ocean weather stations at specific points in the North Atlantic. In addition to meteorological information, these stations provide navigation aids, communications facilities, and search and rescue facilities throughout the region. Twenty-six nations are involved in the scheme, which provides for nine stations to be manned by twenty-one ships.

ICAO has also brought about the co-operative maintenance of other air navigation and meteorological facilities required by aircraft flying over sparsely populated regions or regions of uncertain sovereignty. Two agreements relating to the maintenance and financing of air navigation services in Iceland and in Greenland and the Faroe Islands are now in effect; both agreements have the participation of seventeen member states of ICAO. The two agreements include also the joint financing of a submarine cable system across the North Atlantic via Greenland and Iceland designed to substantially improve aeronautical communications services.

The continuous development of aviation technology and the introduction of new and different types of aircraft on the world's air routes have created problems which ICAO must solve. For many years, the needs of jet aircraft received first place in the organization's planning; now the likelihood that supersonic transports will be available for commercial operation in a few years makes it necessary to ensure that services and facilities for these aircraft will be available when the time for commercial introduction comes. In this respect, the greatest urgency is that of providing the trained men to operate these services; all over the world—even in the most developed countries—these men are in short supply, and ICAO is devoting much of its efforts to increasing the number available.

STANDARDS AND RECOMMENDED PRACTICES. To ensure the highest practicable degree of uniformity in international civil aviation regulations, the ICAO Council has adopted fifteen sets of standards and recommended practices. These are constantly reviewed, and amendments are made when necessary. All are in effect, as annexes to the ICAO Convention, in the territories of ICAO's member states. Standards have been established for: personnel licensing, rules of the air, meteorology, aeronautical charts, dimensional units to be used in air-ground communications, operation of aircraft in international commercial air transport, aircraft nationality and registration marks, airworthiness of aircraft, facilitation, aeronautical telecommunications, air traffic services, search and rescue, aircraft accident inquiry, aerodromes and aeronautical information services.

If a state is unable to put a standard into effect in its territory, it must notify ICAO of the differences between its own practices and those established by the international standard. The Council must in turn notify all other members of ICAO of these differences. Notification to ICAO of non-compliance with recommended practices is, however, unnecessary.

INTERNATIONAL AIR LAW CONVENTIONS. The principal achievements of ICAO in the legal field are four international air law conventions, and a protocol of amendment to a convention which has been in existence since 1929. They are: the Convention on the International Recognition of Rights in Aircraft, adopted by the ICAO Assembly in Geneva in June 1948; the Convention on Damage Caused by Foreign Aircraft to Third Parties on the Surface, adopted at a diplomatic conference in Rome in September 1952; the Convention, supplementary to the Warsaw Convention, for the Unification of Certain Rules for the International Carriage by Air Performed by a Person Other than the Contracting Carrier, approved at a diplomatic conference in Guadalajara, Mexico, in September 1961; and the Tokyo Convention of 1963, which provides among other things for the jurisdiction of various states in case of offences and acts committed on board aircraft. A protocol of amendment to the Warsaw Convention of 1929 concerning the liability of the air carrier to passengers and cargo was adopted by a diplomatic conference held at The Hague in September 1955.

Agreements, arrangements and modifications thereof concluded between states or between states and airlines are registered with ICAO. National aviation laws and regulations are also filed by ICAO.

AIR TRANSPORT. In air transport, much of ICAO's activity is of a continuing or long-term nature, such as follow-up work in the facilitation field and the production of statistical digests.

ICAO's basic aim in the field of facilitation is to achieve—to the maximum degree consistent with the public interest—free and unimpeded passage of aircraft and of the crews, passengers, baggage, cargo and mail that they carry on international flights. ICAO has set down international standards specifying the maximum formalities and documentation requirements which any state may impose; it has also, with the publication of the *Aims and Objectives of ICAO in the Field of Facilitation,* provided a guide to contracting states for future planning in this field.

One of the mandatory functions of the ICAO Council is to request, collect, examine and publish statistical information, which states are obligated to file. The information relates to the advancement of air navigation and the operation of international air services, including information about the cost of operation and details of subsidies paid to airlines from public funds.

One of the most important tasks in the field of air transport economics is the preparation of economic studies which are designed to serve states and their air carriers as basic planning documents. In recent years, the subjects which have been studied include: economic implications of the introduction of jet aircraft; air freight; inclusive tour services; air transport in Africa, prepared jointly with ECA; and aerial work. A review of the economic situation of air transport, with particular reference to supersonic transports, was published just prior to the fifteenth session of the ICAO Assembly in June 1965, and served as a basis for discussion at that Assembly. ICAO is preparing regional forecasts of future civil aviation developments.

TECHNICAL ASSISTANCE. Because the developing countries are very often unable to build roads or railroads, aircraft may be used to fill the transportation gap. For this reason, ICAO has been active in the technical co-operation field and has participated in the Expanded Programme of Technical Assistance and in the work of the United Nations Special Fund, the two programmes which were merged in 1965 as the United Nations Development Programme.

ICAO's technical assistance activities come mainly under five categories: ground facilities and services required by civil aviation;

services required to assure safety in flight; economics of air transport; organization and administration of civil aviation; and air law and regulations. Assistance is given by ICAO through the provision of experts, fellowships and equipment. Because many civil aviation problems lend themselves to regional rather than national solutions, much of ICAO's technical assistance work has been carried out in the form of regional or inter-regional projects.

During the early years of the United Nations Expanded Programme of Technical Assistance, a large number of ICAO-equipped and operated training schools were set up in developing countries to give basic training in aviation trades, such as air-traffic control, radio communications, meteorology, airport management, and air-frame and engine maintenance. More recently has come the establishment of large-scale civil aviation training centres which can more effectively meet the particular needs of various countries within a given area for both basic and advanced training.

Problems of training for flight safety are more complex than the training of ground staff. For several years, ICAO had a regional flight safety project consisting of a pilot examiner and an airworthiness expert who assisted governments, particularly in the Middle East, in setting up their own flight safety organizations and who actually carried out the duties of flight safety inspectors on behalf of the governments they assisted.

UNIVERSAL POSTAL UNION (UPU)

The first attempt to arrive at agreement on general principles governing international postal exchanges was made at an international postal conference held in Paris in 1863 and attended by representatives of fifteen American and European countries. The conference adopted resolutions with the purpose of securing greater uniformity in postal relations which hitherto had been regulated by numerous bilateral agreements.

Eleven years later, the first International Postal Congress met in Berne, Switzerland, with delegates from twenty-two countries participating. The Congress adopted the Berne Treaty, which was signed on October 9, 1874, and came into force on July 1, 1875; it formally established the General Postal Union. The second International Postal Congress, held in Paris in 1878, changed the name of the General Postal Union to the Universal Postal Union (UPU).

Under an Agreement signed in Paris on July 4, 1947, between the

UPU and the United Nations, the UPU was recognized by the United Nations as the specialized agency responsible for international postal services.

The aim of the UPU is to secure the organization and improvement of postal services and thus to promote the development of international collaboration in the cultural, social and economic spheres. To this end, the members of UPU form a single postal territory for the reciprocal exchange of correspondence.

Organization

The principal organs of UPU are the Universal Postal Congress, the Executive Council, the Consultative Committee for Postal Studies and the International Bureau.

The Universal Postal Congress, which usually meets at five-year intervals, reviews the Acts of the UPU, including the subsidiary agreements, and fixes the place of meeting of the following Congress.

The Executive Council, which normally holds one session a year at Berne, consists of twenty-seven members elected by the Congress on an equitable geographical basis. The Council ensures the continuity of the work of UPU in the interval between Congresses. For this purpose, it maintains close contact with postal administrations, exercises certain control over the activities of the International Bureau, ensures working relations with the United Nations and other international organizations, promotes the development of postal technical assistance, and makes studies and submits proposals to the Congress.

The Consultative Committee for Postal Studies, established in 1957, is open to all UPU members. It is charged with carrying out studies and issuing advice on technical, operational and economic questions of concern to postal administrations. A twenty-six-member Management Council, meeting once a year, co-ordinates and determines the execution of the Committee's programme.

The International Bureau of UPU, which is its permanent secretariat with headquarters in Berne, serves postal administrations as an organ for liaison, information and consultation. It also acts as a clearing-house for the settlement of accounts relative to the international postal service. The Swiss Government exercises general supervision over the Bureau in some fields.

Dr. Edouard Weber, of Switzerland, was succeeded as Director-General by Michel Rahi, of the United Arab Republic.

Membership

As of January 1, 1966, there were 127 UPU members.

Budget

Each Congress fixes the maximum figure for the ordinary annual expenses of the Union. These expenses, as well as extraordinary charges, are met in common by all the members of UPU, who are divided, for this purpose, into seven classes, of which each contributes a set proportion. In the case of new members, the Swiss Government determines, in agreement with the government of the member concerned, the class to which it will belong.

The fifteenth Universal Postal Congress, held in Vienna in 1964, fixed a financial ceiling of about $1,230,000 for the annual ordinary expenses of UPU.

The Swiss Government supervises the expenses of the International Bureau and advances the necessary funds.

Activities

The basic activity of the Union is to make provisions for the various international postal services carried out by the postal administrations of its members. The Universal Postal Convention and other legislation of the UPU allow international postal exchanges to be made under principles and practices which are largely standardized.

The fifteenth Universal Postal Congress, held in Vienna in 1964, adopted a new form for the basic Acts of the Union which are now largely comparable in structure with those of the other specialized agencies. The new basic Acts, which entered into force on January 1, 1966, are as follows: Constitution of the Universal Postal Union; General Regulations of the Universal Postal Union; Universal Postal Convention, and detailed regulations for implementing the Convention.

The Constitution, containing the organic provisions of an essential, permanent and general nature, constitutes the basic act of the organization and is completed by the General Regulations. The Convention and its detailed regulations contain the common rules of the international postal service and, in particular, form the basis for provision of the letter post. The Universal Postal Convention regulates the letter mail services—letters, postcards, printed papers, small packets and air mail—and also fixes the basic charges, weight limits and dimensions for articles of correspondence. Implementation of the Constitution, the General Regulations and the Convention is obligatory for all members.

Eight other postal services—for example, postal parcels, money orders and insured letters and boxes—are regulated by special agreements binding only those members of UPU which have acceded to them.

The Congress, also in 1964, revised some postal charges, taking into account the rise in general transport rates since 1957.

The Executive Council has begun work on the numerous studies entrusted to it by the Congress. Within an investigation of the general postage rate structure, the Council will examine the question of appropriately classifying punched cards and photographic films.

To allow a wider examination of the air-mail conveyance question, it was decided to reconstitute the International Air Transport Association-UPU Contact Committee.

The first meeting of the Customs Co-operation Council-UPU Contact Committee took place in Paris in 1965. This body aims at the simplification and acceleration of customs treatment of mails as part of a general attempt to improve and harmonize the working of customs, in order to facilitate the development of international trade.

UPU's participation in the technical co-operation programme of the United Nations began in 1963. At present, a substantial number of postal officials from developing countries are undergoing training in advanced countries, and some experts in fields connected with postal services are on missions in countries requiring their help.

INTERNATIONAL TELECOMMUNICATION
UNION (ITU)

A convention establishing an International Telegraph Union was signed in Paris, on May 17, 1865, by the plenipotentiaries of twenty founding states: Austria, Baden, Bavaria, Belgium, Denmark, France, Greece, Hanover, Italy, the Netherlands, Norway, Portugal, Prussia, Russia, Saxony, Spain, Sweden, Switzerland, Turkey and Wurttemberg. In 1885, in Berlin, the first regulations relating to international telephone services were inserted in the Telegraph Regulations annexed to this Convention.

At the first International Radiotelegraph Conference, held in Berlin, twenty-seven states signed the International Radiotelegraph Convention of November 3, 1906.

In 1932, the International Telegraph Convention and the International Radiotelegraph Convention were merged to form the International Telecommunication Convention, which was signed in Madrid on December 9, 1932. Under this Convention, which came into force on January 1, 1934, the International Telecommunication Union (ITU) succeeded the International Telegraph Union.

In 1947, at international conferences held in the United States, ITU readjusted its organizational structure, adopted measures designed to take account of certain advances that had been made in the techniques of telecommunication and entered into an agreement with the United Nations whereby, among other provisions, ITU was recognized as the specialized agency for telecommunications. A new Convention was adopted containing provisions to give effect to the substantial changes made.

ITU was governed from January 1949 until December 1953 by the 1947 Convention; a revised Convention, adopted by the Buenos Aires Plenipotentiary Conference in 1952, entered into force on January 1, 1954; currently, the Geneva Convention which entered into force on January 1, 1961, governs ITU. A new Convention, adopted by the Montreux Plenipotentiary Conference in 1965, entered into force on January 1, 1967.

ITU's three main purposes are: to maintain and extend international co-operation for the improvement and rational use of telecommunications; to promote the development and most efficient operation of technical facilities in order to increase their usefulness and, as far as possible, to make them generally available to the public; and to harmonize the actions of nations in the attainment of these common ends.

The term "telecommunication" is defined by international agreement as any transmission, emission or reception of signs, signals, writing, images and sounds or intelligence of any nature by wire, radio, optical or other electromagnetic systems. The term "radiocommunication" is defined as any telecommunication by means of radio waves.

ITU has six main functions: it makes allocation of the radio-frequency spectrum and registers radio-frequency assignments to avoid harmful interference between radio stations of different countries; it co-ordinates efforts to eliminate harmful interference between radio stations; it seeks to establish the lowest possible charges for telecommunications; it fosters the creation, development and improvement of telecommunications in newly independent or developing countries, especially by its participation in the appropriate programmes of the United Nations; it promotes the adoption of measures for ensuring the safety of life through the co-operation of telecommunication services; and it undertakes studies, issues recommendations and opinions and collects and publishes information for the benefit of its members and associate members.

Organization

The organization of ITU consists of a Plenipotentiary Conference, which is the supreme organ of ITU; Administrative Conferences; an Administrative Council; and four permanent organs: a General Secretariat, an International Frequency Registration Board (IFRB), an

International Telegraph and Telephone Consultative Committee (CCITT) and an International Radio Consultative Committee (CCIR).

The Plenipotentiary Conference, at which all members and associate members have the right to be represented, normally meets at a date and place fixed by the preceding Conference. Each member has one vote in the Conference, which determines general policies, considers the report of the Administrative Council, establishes the basis for the budget and determines a fiscal limit for expenditure until the next Conference. It approves the accounts; elects the Administrative Council, the Secretary-General and the Deputy Secretary-General; revises the Convention if it considers this necessary; and enters into or revises agreements with other international organizations.

There are two ordinary Administrative Conferences, one dealing with telegraph and telephone and the other with radio regulations. Extraordinary and special administrative conferences may also be held.

The Administrative Council, which was increased from twenty-five to twenty-nine members by the Montreux Plenipotentiary Conference in 1965, supervises ITU's administrative functions between sessions of the Plenipotentiary Conference, reviews and approves the annual budget and co-ordinates the work of ITU with other international organizations. It meets annually at ITU headquarters in Geneva.

The General Secretariat, with a staff of about 175 persons, is headed by the Secretary-General. Gerald C. Gross, of the United States, retired from this post on December 31, 1965, and was succeeded by Dr. M. B. Sarwate, of India. Following Dr. Sarwate's death in early 1967, Mohammed Ezzedine Mili, of Tunisia, became Secretary-General *ad interim*.

Membership

As of January 1, 1966 there were 129 members of ITU.

Budget

The expenses of ITU are borne by all members and associate members, each of them choosing the class of contribution in which it wishes to be included and paying in advance its annual contributory share of the budget calculated on the basis of the budgetary provisions.

A revised budget of $4,601,180 for 1965 was adopted at the Administrative Council's twentieth session.

Activities

One of the most important duties of the General Secretariat is to collect, collate, publish and keep up to date the numerous documents essential for the day-to-day operation of telecommunication services. It is also responsible for the secretarial arrangements of conferences and meetings of ITU. It maintains relations, both by correspondence and by meetings, with the United Nations, the specialized agencies and other international organizations. With it are deposited instruments of ratification of the Convention and instruments of accession.

STUDIES OF THE INTERNATIONAL CONSULTATIVE COMMITTEES. The two international consultative committees—the CCITT and the CCIR—work through study groups composed of experts from governmental telecommunication administrations and recognized private operating agencies. They work by correspondence, by meetings or in plenary assemblies.

Study groups of the International Telegraph and Telephone Consultative Committee (CCITT) are concerned with: telegraph and telephone operations and tariffs; general tariff principles; maintenance of the international network; protection against electro-magnetic disturbances; protection of cable sheaths and poles; definitions, vocabulary and symbols; telegraph apparatus, transmissions and switching; telephone switching and transmission performance; semi-automatic and automatic telephone networks; facsimile; transmission systems; telephone circuits; and data transmission.

For establishing a plan to develop the international network, there are a joint CCITT/CCIR world-wide plan committee and four regional plan committees—for Africa, Asia, Europe and Latin America.

The secretariat of CCITT prepares a number of special publications in connection with telegraphy and telephony; some of these publications are drafted for the technical information of the new and developing countries.

Study groups of the International Radio Consultative Committee (CCIR) are concerned with: transmitters; receivers; fixed service systems; space systems and radioastronomy; propagation, including the effects of the earth and the troposphere; ionospheric propagation; standard frequencies and time signals; international monitoring; radio-relay systems; broadcasting, including tropical broadcasting; television; mobile services; and vocabulary. There is also a joint CCIR-CCITT study group for television transmission. Another study group investigates the technical problems of telecommunication with and between points in space.

A number of special publications in the radio field are prepared by the secretariat.

INTERNATIONAL FREQUENCY REGISTRATION BOARD. The International Frequency Registration Board (IFRB) consists of eleven independent radio experts (five as from January 1, 1967), all from different countries, elected by the preceding Administrative Radio Conference and working full time at the Union's headquarters in Geneva. They elect a Chairman and a Vice-Chairman for each year from among their own number.

The Board's main task is to decide whether radio frequencies which countries assign to their radio stations, and which they have notified to the Board, are in accordance with the Convention and the Radio Regulations and will not cause harmful interference to other stations. If the Board's finding in a particular case is favourable, the frequency is recorded in the huge Master International Frequency Register kept by the IFRB and thus obtains formal international recognition and protection. An average of more than 1,700 frequency assignment, or change of assignment, notices from countries arrive at the IFRB each week. Another important task of the IFRB is to work out seasonal high-frequency broadcasting schedules.

The data recorded in the IFRB's Master International Frequency Register are published from time to time in international frequency lists. The IFRB also prepares for publication a monthly summary of monitoring information showing the precision with which radio stations keep to their assigned frequency, their strength of reception and observed times of operation.

The IFRB provides technical advice to members of the ITU to enable them to operate effectively as many radio channels as possible in the overcrowded parts of the radio spectrum where there is liable to be harmful interference between stations. In addition, the IFRB investigates cases of harmful interference reported to it and makes recommendations to the countries concerned on how best to solve their particular problem.

TECHNICAL ASSISTANCE.   ITU's technical assistance activities —carried out under the United Nations Expanded Programme of Technical Assistance and the United Nations Special Fund, which were merged in 1965 to form the United Nations Development Programme—have included the assignment of experts to countries in Africa, Asia, the Far East, the Caribbean and Central and Latin America, the awarding of fellowships and the provision of telecommunications equipment for training purposes or to help experts carry out their missions. Most of the technical assistance projects in which ITU has served as executing agency have been in the telecommunications training field.

SPACE TELECOMMUNICATIONS.   ITU's various organs have been actively engaged in studies covering space telecommunication technique and regulations, both before and since the Extraordinary Administrative Radio Conference on Space Radiocommunications, held in October 1963, which allocated about 15 per cent of the entire radio frequency spectrum (over 6000 Mc/s) for outer space.

WORLD METEOROLOGICAL ORGANIZATION (WMO)

International co-operation in meteorology was first established by an international conference, held in 1853 in Brussels, which dealt with a programme for collecting meteorological observations made by ships at sea.

In 1878, at a conference held in Utrecht, the Netherlands, the International Meteorological Organization (IMO) was established. The members of IMO were the directors of the meteorological services of various countries and territories throughout the world. Thus, IMO was not formally a governmental organization. Nevertheless, it pursued ambitious programmes of perfecting and standardizing meteorological activities, especially services to maritime navigation, agriculture and, increasingly, aviation.

The establishment of the United Nations provided a new framework for international collaboration in various areas, including technical and scientific fields. Consequently, the Conference of Directors of the national meteorological services, which met in Washington in 1947, adopted the World Meteorological Convention, thus establishing a new organization. In 1951, the World Meteorological Organization (WMO) commenced activity, the former organization having been dissolved.

As stated in the preamble to its Convention, WMO was established "with a view to co-ordinating, standardizing and improving world meteorological activities and to encouraging an efficient exchange of meteorological information between countries in the aid of human activities."

The purposes of WMO are: to facilitate international co-operation in the establishment of networks of stations and centres to provide meteorological services and observations; to promote the establishment and maintenance of systems for the rapid exchange of weather information; to promote standardization of meteorological observations and ensure the uniform publication of observations and statistics; to further the application of meteorology to aviation, shipping, agriculture and other human activities; and to encourage research and training in meteorology.

Organization

WMO is headed by a President and two Vice-Presidents. It works through a World Meteorological Congress, an Executive Committee and regional associations and technical commissions set up by the Congress, and through a permanent secretariat in Geneva headed by a Secretary-General.

The World Meteorological Congress, which is composed of all WMO members, meets at least once every four years. It adopts technical regulations covering meteorological practices and procedures and determines the general policies for the fulfilment of the purposes of WMO.

The Executive Committee, which meets at least once a year, prepares studies and recommendations for the Congress, supervises the implementation of Congress resolutions and regulations and informs and offers advice to members on technical matters. The Executive Committee also approves the annual financial appropriations of the organization within the over-all budget approved by the Congress. The Committee is composed of twenty-one directors of national meteorological services.

The members of WMO are grouped into six regional associations; their task is to co-ordinate meteorological activity within their respective regions and to examine from the regional point of view questions referred to them by the Executive Committee. The six regions are: Africa, Asia, South America, North and Central America, the south-west Pacific and Europe.

The technical commissions are composed of experts nominated by members. The commissions are responsible for studying the applications of meteorology and the special technical branches which are related to the study and observation of the weather. Technical commissions have been established for agricultural meteorology, maritime meteorology, aeronautical meteorology, hydrometeorology, synoptic meteorology, aerology, climatology and instruments and methods of observation.

The secretariat of WMO, with a staff of about 150, carries out the duties allocated to it in the Convention and the regulations of the organization. Among its general functions are the following: to serve as the administrative, documentary and information centre of WMO; to make technical studies as directed by the Congress and the Executive Committee; to organize and perform secretarial duties at sessions of the Congress and the Executive Committee; to prepare, edit, publish and distribute the publications of WMO; to maintain liaison and collaborate with the secretariats of other international organizations; and to act as the channel for communications, notifications and invitations between WMO, its members, the constituent bodies of WMO and other international organizations.

The President of WMO is Alf Nyberg, of Sweden; the First Vice-President, L. de Azcárraga, of Spain; and the Second Vice-President, Academician E. K. Fedorov, of the Soviet Union. The Secretary-General is D. A. Davies, of the United Kingdom.

WMO headquarters are in Geneva.

Membership

Members of WMO are states and territories maintaining their own meteorological services. As of January 1, 1966 there were 126 members of WMO—114 states and twelve territories.

Budget

WMO's expenditures are apportioned among its members in the proportion determined by the Congress. Its budget for the four-year financial period 1964-1967 was $5,524,000, plus a regular budget fund for meteorological development of $1.5 million.

Activities

INTERNATIONAL EXCHANGE OF WEATHER REPORTS.   One of the most essential and permanent tasks of WMO is to arrange for the international exchange of weather reports. At regular intervals, by day and by night, observers at weather stations throughout the world make meteorological observations at exactly the same time. The methods and practices followed—and even the order in which readings are made—are based on internationally agreed decisions and are practically uniform everywhere.

Every day, about 8,000 stations, 3,000 transport and reconnaissance aircraft and 4,000 ships transmit 100,000 weather observations for the surface of the earth and 10,000 observations relating to the upper air. The technical regulations containing the international rules which govern this work were adopted by WMO in 1955 and have been kept up to date.

Practically all weather information obtained from the sea is provided by voluntary observers on merchant ships, which are supplied with instruments by the meteorological services and report regularly by radio to selected coastal stations. In return, meteorological services, co-operating according to an international scheme developed by WMO, provide shipping with weather forecasts.

There are about 4,000 observing ships on the oceans, as well as thirteen stationary ocean weather ships. An international list of the voluntary observing ships recruited from about thirty different countries is issued each year by WMO. It indicates the call-sign, route and instruments used by each of the ships.

The international exchange of weather information by means of telecommunications, such as radiotelephony and radiotelegraphy, requires constant examination and review. Teletype networks and facsimile broadcasts are being introduced to replace the slower and less dependable wireless broadcasts in the Morse code. Agreements on plans of broadcasts and networks, hours of observation and of transmission, and so on, fall within the province of WMO and are part of its routine duties. In dealing with several aspects of its telecommunication problems, WMO works in close co-operation with the International Telecommunication Union.

Together with the International Civil Aviation Organization (ICAO), WMO has standardized internationally the meteorological services provided to civil aviation all over the world.

The developing requirements of aviation resulting from the introduction of jet aircraft and the planned introduction of supersonic aircraft into commercial aviation have determined the activities of WMO in this field during recent years. Training seminars on high-level forecasting have been organized jointly with ICAO in Cairo, Nicosia and Bangkok to train meteorologists in new techniques.

USE OF ARTIFICIAL SATELLITES.   The use of satellites for meteorological purposes was initiated in 1960, and several experimental meteorological satellites have been launched since then. Cloud pictures and photographs of snow cover over the earth's surface and of the distribution of ice on rivers and oceans obtained from satellites constitute a major contribution to research in meteorology and to weather forecasting. Scientific measurements obtained from the satellites, such as infra-red radiation measurements, are also of great value. The satellites will not, of course, replace the present world-wide network of meteorological stations. One of their main tasks will be to fill in the "blanks" on the weather chart over oceans, deserts and polar regions. They will also give valuable supplementary information in areas where surface observations are available.

In order to benefit all nations and to develop forecasting capabilities, the 1963 World Meteorological Congress recommended the establishment of a "World Weather Watch" based on meteorological satellites and a system of world and regional centres. WMO has also initiated an international programme for research in meteorology in the light of developments in outer space, indicating priorities which appear especially important from the international point of view. Activities in this field are all directed towards ensuring that all nations may benefit from this extraordinary new tool for weather observations and research.

METEOROLOGY AND ATOMIC ENERGY.   At the request of the United Nations General Assembly, WMO studied the question of whether regular observations of atmospheric radioactivity could be incorporated into the existing system of meteorological reporting. A plan for the incorporation of such data was submitted to the Assembly in 1962 and implemented the following year.

WMO advises the United Nations Scientific Committee on the Effects of Atomic Radiation regarding the meteorological factors influencing the atmospheric transport and removal of radioactive particles. The use of radioactive isotopes as a measuring technique in meteorology and hydrometeorological observations is also being studied and promoted by WMO. Together with the International Atomic Energy Agency (IAEA), WMO is engaged in a project to promote research on the water cycle—rain, run-off, rivers, oceans and evaporation— through the use of hydrogen and oxygen isotopes.

TECHNICAL CO-OPERATION.   All those who work under the changing skies—the farmer, the aviator and the sailor, for example— realize how their lives depend on the weather, but not so well known is the importance of the knowledge of weather in the economic life of a country. Sudden disasters resulting from storms and floods retard economic advancement. Rainfall observations and river-stage and river- flow observations are a vital need for designing hydroelectric and irrigation schemes and other water use and control projects. The existence of a national weather service and its proper functioning are of great importance to the development of a country's economy.

Many countries wishing to establish meteorological services or to improve or increase the application of meteorology and hydrology to their projects of economic development have requested technical assistance from WMO. To this end, WMO organizes expert missions and grants fellowships. It has also participated in the United Nations Expanded Programme of Technical Assistance and served as executing agency of the United Nations Special Fund, the two programmes that were merged in 1965 to form the United Nations Development Programme. Most of the projects in which WMO serves as executing agency concern the establishment of networks of meteorological and hydrological stations to provide the data necessary for the expansion of irrigated land and hydroelectric power supply.

WATER RESOURCE DEVELOPMENT.   The help of the meteorologist and the hydrologist is needed to control the vast quantities of water flowing down the rivers into the sea, to prevent floods and to harness rivers so that electric energy and water may be provided for irrigation and industry.

WMO deals with those aspects of the water resource development programme of the United Nations which fall within the common ground between meteorology and hydrology. A technical commission for hydrological meteorology was created in 1959 and held its first session in Washington, D.C., in April 1961. Under joint projects with the United Nations Economic Commissions for Asia and the Far East and for Latin America, WMO is endeavouring to remedy the lack of hydrological data in those regions.

CLIMATIC ATLASES.   A World Climatic Atlas is being developed
by WMO to meet the needs of scientists, engineers, economists and
others. The only existing climatic atlas on a world scale dates back to
1898.
    Detailed specifications regarding national and regional climatic
atlases have been approved and adopted by WMO. A regional climatic
atlas is under preparation for Africa, and WMO working groups have
started the study of similar maps for Europe and South America.
Geographical societies and commercial publishers are being informed
of the WMO specifications to promote uniformity in the preparation of
climatic maps all over the world.

INTER-GOVERNMENTAL MARITIME
CONSULTATIVE ORGANIZATION (IMCO)

A Convention setting up the Inter-Governmental Maritime Consultative Organization (IMCO) was prepared by the United Nations Maritime Conference held in Geneva in 1948. The Convention could not
become operative until it had been accepted by twenty-one states, including seven with at least one million gross tons of shipping each.
This happened when, on March 17, 1958, Japan became the twenty-
first state (and also the eighth with over one million tons of shipping)
to accept the Convention.
    Four meetings of a preparatory committee, held at Geneva, Lake
Success, New York and London in 1948, 1958 and 1959, paved the
way for the first IMCO Assembly in London in January 1959, and IMCO
started its work.
    The aims of IMCO are to facilitate co-operation and exchange of
information among governments on technical matters affecting shipping and, with special responsibility for the safety of life at sea, to
assure that the highest possible standards of maritime safety and of
efficient navigation are achieved. IMCO is responsible for convening,
where necessary, international conferences on shipping matters and for
drafting international maritime conventions or agreements.

Organization

The policy-making body of IMCO is the Assembly, in which all IMCO
member states are represented. The Assembly decides upon the work
programme, votes the budget, approves financial regulations, elects
the IMCO Council and approves appointment of the Secretary-General.

The Assembly normally meets at IMCO headquarters in London. Regular sessions are held every two years.

The Council, which is IMCO's governing body between Assembly sessions, consists of representatives of sixteen member states elected by the Assembly for a term of two years. The Council normally meets twice a year.

The third main organ of IMCO is the Maritime Safety Committee, consisting of representatives of fourteen member states. It is elected by the Assembly for a term of four years.

In 1964 and 1965, the Assembly approved amendments to the IMCO Convention expanding membership of the Council and the Maritime Safety Committee. These amendments will become operative twelve months after their acceptance by two-thirds of IMCO's member states.

The secretariat of IMCO is composed of the Secretary-General, Jean Roullier, of France; the Deputy Secretary-General, Colin Goad, of the United Kingdom, who is also Secretary of the Maritime Safety Committee; and a small staff.

Membership

As of January 1, 1966, sixty states were members of IMCO.

Budget

All member states contribute to the budget of IMCO on an agreed scale of assessments. A budget of $1,744,492 for 1966/67 was voted by the fourth IMCO Assembly in 1965.

Activities

CONVENTIONS AND AGREEMENTS.   Maritime safety has been the subject of numerous inter-governmental agreements, the most important of which are the International Convention for the Safety of Life at Sea, which was revised in 1960 at a Conference organized by IMCO, and the International Convention for the Prevention of Pollution of the Sea by Oil, which was revised at an IMCO Conference in 1962. IMCO carries out administrative duties in respect of both conventions and of the Regulations for Preventing Collisions at Sea.

An International Maritime Dangerous Goods Code and the major part of its annexes were approved by the fourth IMCO Assembly in 1965 for distribution to IMCO member states and states which took part in the 1960 Safety Conference, with a recommendation that they be adopted or be used as a basis for national regulations.

A conference convened by IMCO in the spring of 1965, and attended by sixty-eight states and a number of international organizations, drew up the Convention on Facilitation of International Maritime Traffic and its five-section technical annex. The Conference also approved a number of resolutions which lay the foundations for a continuing programme of facilitation.

The International Code of Signals, which was drawn up in 1931, has been revised and is being widely distributed. The date for its entry into force, as approved by the fourth IMCO Assembly in 1965, is January 1, 1968, ITU concurrence on certain portions being expected in the interim. Should it not be possible to obtain such concurrence by that date, every effort will be made to bring the Code into force as soon thereafter as possible. The Code is being prepared in nine languages—English, French, German, Greek, Italian, Japanese, Norwegian, Russian and Spanish. The IMCO Assembly recommended that the Code be carried by as many categories of ships as possible.

The Code of Safe Practice for Bulk Cargoes other than grain was approved by the fourth IMCO Assembly in 1965 for distribution to IMCO member states and states which took part in the 1960 Safety Conference, and for general sale. The strength of grain fittings is currently being studied.

STUDIES OF SPECIFIC PROBLEMS.   Subdivision and stability problems are studied by a sub-committee, established by the Maritime Safety Committee, and three subordinate bodies. Subdivision studies are aimed at reviewing the criteria, embodied in the 1960 Safety Convention, for watertight subdivision and damage stability of passenger ships and determining whether it is possible and practicable to extend subdivision requirements to cargo ships. Stability studies aim at establishing international intact stability requirements for passenger, cargo and fishing vessels. A memorandum of practical advice to fishermen for avoiding a reduction of stability during fishing operations was issued in 1964.

IMCO's Sub-Committee on Oil Pollution provides a forum where national experience and knowledge can be pooled and utilized at the international level. A subsidiary working group is considering certain specific technical problems, such as the "load-on-top" system of tanker operation, in the light of the provisions of the International Convention for Prevention of Pollution of the Sea by Oil, and the development and testing of oily-water separators with a view to establishing international performance and testing specifications. A two-volume report on oil pollution throughout the world and the measures taken to combat it was issued in 1965.

A sub-committee is continuing studies on a universal system of tonnage measurement for ships, to be achieved either by unification or simplication of existing systems or by developing an entirely new system based on new concepts. When finally completed, the universal system will be proposed for international agreement at a conference convened for the purpose.

A sub-committee and associated working group have begun studies on fire test procedures, internationally applicable requirements for tanker lifeboats, safety measures for tankers and protection of existing passenger ships from fire.

GENERAL AGREEMENT ON TARIFFS
AND TRADE (GATT)

In 1946, the United Nations Economic and Social Council decided to convene an international conference on trade and employment, and it established a Preparatory Committee to prepare a draft convention for an international trade organization. A draft charter, adopted by the Preparatory Committee in August 1947, formed the basis for the work of the United Nations Conference on Trade and Employment, which was held in Havana from November 1947 to March 1948 and which drew up a charter, known as the Havana Charter, for an International Trade Organization.

While the Charter for the International Trade Organization was being worked out, the governments that formed the Preparatory Committee agreed to sponsor negotiations aimed at lowering customs tariffs and reducing other trade restrictions among themselves, without waiting for the International Trade Organization itself to come into being. Thus the first tariff negotiating conference was held at Geneva in 1947, side by side with the labours of the Committee which was preparing the Havana Charter. The tariff concessions resulting from these negotiations were embodied in a multilateral treaty called the General Agreement on Tariffs and Trade (GATT), which included a set of rules designed to prevent the tariff concessions from being frustrated by other protective devices. The Agreement was signed on October 30, 1947, at Geneva, and came into force on January 1, 1948. Originally, the GATT was accepted by twenty-three countries.

GATT was intended as a stop-gap arrangement pending the entry into force of the Havana Charter and the creation of the International Trade Organization, which would have been a specialized agency of the United Nations. But, as a result of the lack of acceptances of the Havana Charter, it became evident by the end of 1950 that the attempt to establish the International Trade Organization would be postponed indefinitely. Thus, GATT has stood alone since 1948 as the only international instrument which lays down rules of conduct for trade, and which has been accepted by a high proportion of the leading trading nations.

Main Principles

The General Agreement is a multilateral trade treaty embodying reciprocal rights and obligations. Although the text of the General Agreement is complicated, it contains, in essence, four fundamental principles.

The first principle is that trade should be conducted on the basis of non-discrimination. In particular, all contracting parties are bound by the most-favoured-nation clause in the application of import and export duties and charges and in their administration.

The second general principle is that protection shall be afforded to domestic industries exclusively through the customs tariff and not through other commercial measures. The use of import quotas as a means of protection is thus prohibited. Import quotas may be used for certain other purposes—notably to redress a country's balance of payments—but the circumstances in which import quotas may be used are very carefully defined, and there are elaborate procedures for consultations.

The third principle, inherent throughout the Agreement, is the concept of consultation aimed at avoiding damage to the trading interests of contracting parties.

Finally, GATT provides a framework within which negotiations can be held for the reduction of tariffs and other barriers to trade and a structure for embodying the results of such negotiations in a legal instrument.

The sum total of the detailed rules constitutes a code which contracting parties to the General Agreement have agreed upon to govern their trading relationships.

Secretariat

The secretariat, with a staff of about 180, is located in Geneva. The Director-General is Eric Wyndham White, of the United Kingdom.

Membership

As of January 1, 1966, there were sixty-seven contracting parties to GATT, and a further thirteen countries participated in the work of GATT under special arrangements.

Budget

Governments participate financially in accordance with a scale of contributions which is assessed on each country's share in the total trade of the contracting parties and participating governments. The contributions assessed for 1966 totalled $2,233,000.

Activities

Under the terms of GATT, the contracting parties are required to meet from time to time to give effect to provisions requiring joint action. By the end of 1965, twenty-two regular sessions had been held. The sessions are broadly concerned with items arising out of the operation of GATT, or matters put on the agenda by member governments for discussion in the GATT forum.

A Council of Representatives has been established to undertake work, both of an urgent and of a routine character, between the regular sessions of the contracting parties.

REDUCTION OF TARIFFS AND OTHER TRADE BARRIERS.   The reduction of tariffs is laid down in the General Agreement as one of the principal means of attaining its broad objectives. There have been five main tariff negotiating conferences under GATT: in 1947, at Geneva; in 1949, at Annecy, France; in 1951, at Torquay, England; and in 1956 and again in 1960-1962, at Geneva. As a result of these conferences, the tariff rates for tens of thousands of items entering into world commerce have been reduced, or "bound" against increase.

The sixth negotiating conference, known as the "Kennedy Round," was inaugurated in Geneva in 1964. Based on directives laid down by ministers, this negotiation looked towards the reduction of tariff and non-tariff barriers to trade on a far more comprehensive basis than in any negotiations held hitherto under GATT. The ministers, when laying down directives, emphasized that in the negotiations every effort should be made to reduce barriers to exports of less-developed countries and that the developed countries could not expect to receive reciprocity from the less-developed countries.

TRADE PROBLEMS OF DEVELOPING COUNTRIES.   The efforts of GATT directed towards the expansion of trade have been increasingly focussed on specific trade and development problems of developing countries. This trend also reflects the growing importance of these countries in GATT. Of the twenty-three countries which signed the General Agreement in 1947, ten were developing countries. At the beginning of 1966, of the sixty-seven contracting parties, forty-four were developing countries. A further twelve developing countries have other forms of membership. It is thus clear that these countries have a vital interest in the way in which the problems they face in trade and development are dealt with in GATT.

GATT has staged an intensive campaign to expand the export earnings of the less-developed countries, at first through the Trade Expansion Programme and, later, through the seven-point Action Programme. In 1965, an important step was taken to add additional articles, contained in a new Part IV, to the GATT, in which are set out the objectives and commitments of GATT members as regards trade and development. At the same time, the contracting parties established the Committee on Trade and Development to supervise the implementation of the new Part IV and, in effect, all of GATT's operations specifically designed to benefit the trade and development of less-developed countries.

In 1964, the International Trade Centre was established, within the GATT secretariat, in order to provide trade information and trade advisory services for the benefit of developing countries. The Centre is designed to provide these countries with information on export markets and marketing and to help them develop the techniques of export promotion and train the personnel required to apply them.

GATT conducts training courses, at its Geneva headquarters, on GATT operations and on commercial policy for officials from developing countries who have been granted fellowships by the United Nations technical assistance authorities. Up to the end of 1965, more than 140 officials from over fifty countries and territories had attended these courses.

REMOVAL OF QUANTITATIVE RESTRICTIONS ON IMPORTS. The general prohibition on the use of quantitative restrictions on imports, together with the rule of non-discrimination, is one of the basic principles of the General Agreement. The main exception allows a contracting party to apply import restrictions for the purpose of safeguarding its balance of payments and monetary reserves and, in certain circumstances, to use such restrictions in a discriminatory way. Countries applying import restrictions on balance-of-payments grounds are required to consult with the organization at regular intervals (once a year for an industrialized country and once every two years for a less-developed country); countries introducing new restrictions or substantially intensifying existing restrictions are required to consult; and any country which considers that another country is applying restrictions inconsistently with the provisions of the Agreement and that its trade is adversely affected has the right to bring the matter up for discussion and to ask for redress. The general purpose of such consultations is to afford an opportunity for the exchange of views on the problems facing the countries resorting to restrictions as well as the difficulties which are created for exporting countries. On financial questions arising in any consultation of this nature, the contracting parties rely on the advice of the International Monetary Fund. Over the years, a considerable number of consultations have been held. They have had a large part in ensuring that restrictions have been relaxed or removed as rapidly as improvements in the balance of payments of individual countries permitted.

REGIONAL TRADE ARRANGEMENTS. The General Agreement contains special rules relating to the setting up of customs unions and free-trade areas. These rules are designed to ensure that such forms of economic integration shall, in effect, lead to the reduction and elimination of barriers within the area without raising new barriers to trade with the outside world, and to ensure that a grouping of this kind is a movement towards liberalism and not an attempt to create new preferential arrangements. Thus, in recent years, the contracting parties have given special attention to the effects on international trade of the European Economic Community, the European Free Trade Association, the Latin American Free Trade Association and other regional arrangements. Trade aspects of the treaties establishing these integrated groups have been thoroughly examined, and the development of these groupings is kept under review.

SETTLEMENT OF TRADE DISPUTES. Among the matters which are referred to the sessions of the contracting parties are the trade disputes which have been brought up under the procedures of Article XXII or Article XXIII, procedures which enable complaints to be made that benefits under the Agreement are being nullified or impaired. A contracting party which considers that a benefit which should accrue to it is being nullified or impaired or that the attainment of any objective of the Agreement is being impeded may seek consultations with the parties concerned. If, after consultations, no satisfactory adjustment is reached, a complaint may be lodged, and the contracting parties are then required to carry out prompt investigations, to make recommendations or to give rulings. In recent years, the practice has grown of submitting such differences—if not settled at the stage of consultations—to a group of experts chosen from countries which have no direct interest in the matter. These panels of conciliation, as they are called, have had a marked success in assisting the disputants to reach agreement.

Over the years, large and small countries have been involved in these applications, both as complainants and as defendants. Complaints by Chile against Australia, by Norway against Germany, by the United Kingdom and France against Greece and by India against Pakistan have been successfully dealt with. A French tax on imports and exports, which was intended to provide a social assurance fund for agricultural workers, was the subject of complaint as an infringement of the GATT. In due course, the tax was suppressed. Other complaints successfully dealt with have included the suppression of a discriminatory tax levied on imports by the Belgian authorities and the lessening of restrictions on American coal imported into Germany. In another type of case, following a complaint by Czechoslovakia, trade between that country and Peru, which had been stopped by the Peruvian Government, was restored. In 1957, Brazil took steps to settle a long-standing complaint regarding the discrimination in internal taxation between certain domestic and foreign products. In 1962, Uruguay brought up cases against a number of contracting parties concerning their import restrictions and other barriers affecting Uruguay's export interests. The contracting parties which maintained restrictions unjustifiable under the terms of GATT were urged to remove them and in due course Uruguay reported that good progress had been made.

Appendices

Appendices

CHARTER OF THE UNITED NATIONS

Preamble

WE THE PEOPLES
OF THE UNITED NATIONS
DETERMINED

to save succeeding generations from the scourge of war, which twice in our lifetime has brought untold sorrow to mankind, and

to reaffirm faith in fundamental human rights, in the dignity and worth of the human person, in the equal rights of men and women and of nations large and small, and

to establish conditions under which justice and respect for the obligations arising from treaties and other sources of international law can be maintained, and

to promote social progress and better standards of life in larger freedom,

AND FOR THESE ENDS

to practice tolerance and live together in peace with one another as good neighbors, and

to unite our strength to maintain international peace and security, and

to ensure, by the acceptance of principles and the institution of methods, that armed force shall not be used, save in the common interest, and

to employ international machinery for the promotion of the economic and social advancement of all peoples,

HAVE RESOLVED TO
COMBINE OUR EFFORTS TO
ACCOMPLISH THESE AIMS

Accordingly, our respective Governments, through representatives assembled in the city of San Francisco, who have exhibited their full powers found to be in good and due form, have agreed to the present Charter of the United Nations and do hereby establish an international organization to be known as the United Nations.

The Charter of the United Nations was adopted at San Francisco on June 25, 1945, and was signed the following day. It came into force on October 24, 1945, when a majority of the signatories had ratified it.

Amendments to Articles 23, 27 and 61 of the Charter were approved by the United Nations General Assembly on December 17, 1963, at the Assembly's eighteenth session, and came into force on August 31, 1965.

CHAPTER I

PURPOSES AND PRINCIPLES

Article 1

The Purposes of the United Nations are:

1. To maintain international peace and security, and to that end: to take effective collective measures for the prevention and removal of threats to the peace, and for the suppression of acts of aggression or other breaches of the peace, and to bring about by peaceful means, and in conformity with the principles of justice and international law, adjustment or settlement of international disputes or situations which might lead to a breach of the peace;

2. To develop friendly relations among nations based on respect for the principle of equal rights and self-determination of peoples, and to take other appropriate measures to strengthen universal peace;

3. To achieve international cooperation in solving international problems of an economic, social, cultural, or humanitarian character, and in promoting and encouraging respect for human rights and for fundamental freedoms for all without distinction as to race, sex, language, or religion; and

4. To be a center for harmonizing the actions of nations in the attainment of these common ends.

Article 2

The Organization and its Members, in pursuit of the Purposes stated in Article 1, shall act in accordance with the following Principles.

1. The Organization is based on the principle of the sovereign equality of all its Members.

2. All Members, in order to ensure to all of them the rights and benefits resulting from membership, shall fulfill in good faith the obligations assumed by them in accordance with the present Charter.

3. All Members shall settle their international disputes by peaceful means in such a manner that international peace and security, and justice, are not endangered.

4. All Members shall refrain in their international relations from the threat or use of force against the territorial integrity or political independence of any state, or in any other manner inconsistent with the Purposes of the United Nations.

5. All Members shall give the United Nations every assistance in any action it takes in accordance with the present Charter, and shall refrain from giving assistance to any state against which the United Nations is taking preventive or enforcement action.

6. The Organization shall ensure that states which are not Members of the United Nations act in accordance with these Principles so far as may be necessary for the maintenance of international peace and security.

7. Nothing contained in the present Charter shall authorize the United Nations to intervene in matters which are essentially within the domestic jurisdiction of any state or shall require the Members to submit such matters to settlement under the present Charter; but this principle shall not prejudice the application of enforcement measures under Chapter VII.

CHAPTER II
MEMBERSHIP

Article 3

The original Members of the United Nations shall be the states which, having participated in the United Nations Conference on International Organization at San Francisco, or having previously signed the Declaration by United Nations of January 1, 1942, sign the present Charter and ratify it in accordance with Article 110.

Article 4

1. Membership in the United Nations is open to all other peace-loving states which accept the obligations contained in the present Charter and, in the judgment of the Organization, are able and willing to carry out these obligations.

2. The admission of any such state to membership in the United Nations will be effected by a decision of the General Assembly upon the recommendation of the Security Council.

Article 5

A Member of the United Nations against which preventive or enforcement action has been taken by the Security Council may be suspended from the exercise of the rights and privileges of membership by the General Assembly upon the recommendation of the Security Council. The exercise of these rights and privileges may be restored by the Security Council.

Article 6

A Member of the United Nations which has persistently violated the Principles contained in the present Charter may be expelled from the Organization by the General Assembly upon the recommendation of the Security Council.

CHAPTER III
ORGANS

Article 7

1. There are established as the principal organs of the United Na-

tions: a General Assembly, a Security Council, an Economic and Social Council, a Trusteeship Council, an International Court of Justice, and a Secretariat.

2. Such subsidiary organs as may be found necessary may be established in accordance with the present Charter.

Article 8

The United Nations shall place no restrictions on the eligibility of men and women to participate in any capacity and under conditions of equality in its principal and subsidiary organs.

CHAPTER IV
THE GENERAL ASSEMBLY

Composition

Article 9

1. The General Assembly shall consist of all the Members of the United Nations.

2. Each member shall have not more than five representatives in the General Assembly.

Functions and Powers

Article 10

The General Assembly may discuss any questions or any matters within the scope of the present Charter or relating to the powers and functions of any organs provided for in the present Charter, and, except as provided in Article 12, may make recommendations to the Members of the United Nations or to the Security Council or to both on any such questions or matters.

Article 11

1. The General Assembly may consider the general principles of co-

operation in the maintenance of international peace and security, including the principles governing disarmament and the regulation of armaments, and may make recommendations with regard to such principles to the Members or to the Security Council or to both.

2. The General Assembly may discuss any questions relating to the maintenance of international peace and security brought before it by any Member of the United Nations, or by the Security Council, or by a state which is not a Member of the United Nations in accordance with Article 35, paragraph 2, and, except as provided in Article 12, may make recommendations with regard to any such questions to the state or states concerned or to the Security Council or to both. Any such question on which action is necessary shall be referred to the Security Council by the General Assembly either before or after discussion.

3. The General Assembly may call the attention of the Security Council to situations which are likely to endanger international peace and security.

4. The powers of the General Assembly set forth in this Article shall not limit the general scope of Article 10.

Article 12

1. While the Security Council is exercising in respect of any dispute or situation the functions assigned to it in the present Charter, the General Assembly shall not make any recommendation with regard to that dispute or situation unless the Security Council so requests.

2. The Secretary-General, with the consent of the Security Council, shall notify the General Assembly at each session of any matters relative to the maintenance of international peace and security which are being dealt with by the Security Council and shall similarly notify the General Assembly, or the Members of the United Nations if the General Assembly is not in session, immediately the Security Council ceases to deal with such matters.

Article 13

1. The General Assembly shall initiate studies and make recommendations for the purpose of:

a. promoting international cooperation in the political field and encouraging the progressive development of international law and its codification;

b. promoting international cooperation in the economic, social, cultural, educational, and health fields, and assisting in the realization of human rights and fundamental freedoms for all without distinction as to race, sex, language, or religion.

2. The further responsibilities, functions and powers of the General Assembly with respect to matters mentioned in paragraph 1(b) above are set forth in Chapters IX and X.

Article 14

Subject to the provisions of Article 12, the General Assembly may recommend measures for the peaceful adjustment of any situation, regardless of origin, which it deems likely to impair the general welfare or friendly relations among nations, including situations resulting from a violation of the provisions of the present Charter setting forth the Purposes and Principles of the United Nations.

Article 15

1. The General Assembly shall receive and consider annual and special reports from the Security Council; these reports shall include an

account of the measures that the Security Council has decided upon or taken to maintain international peace and security.

2. The General Assembly shall receive and consider reports from the other organs of the United Nations.

Article 16

The General Assembly shall perform such functions with respect to the international trusteeship system as are assigned to it under Chapters XII and XIII, including the approval of the trusteeship agreements for areas not designated as strategic.

Article 17

1. The General Assembly shall consider and approve the budget of the Organization.

2. The expenses of the Organization shall be borne by the Members as apportioned by the General Assembly.

3. The General Assembly shall consider and approve any financial and budgetary arrangements with specialized agencies referred to in Article 57 and shall examine the administrative budgets of such specialized agencies with a view to making recommendations to the agencies concerned.

Voting

Article 18

1. Each member of the General Assembly shall have one vote.

2. Decisions of the General Assembly on important questions shall be made by a two-thirds majority of the members present and voting. These questions shall include: recommendations with respect to the maintenance of international peace and security, the election of the non-permanent members of the Security Council, the election of the members of the Economic and Social Council, the election of members of the Trusteeship Council in accordance with paragraph 1(c) of Article 86, the admission of new Members to the United Nations, the suspension of the rights and privileges of membership, the expulsion of Members, questions relating to the operation of the trusteeship system, and budgetary questions.

3. Decisions on other questions, including the determination of additional categories of questions to be decided by a two-thirds majority, shall be made by a majority of the members present and voting.

Article 19

A Member of the United Nations which is in arrears in the payment of its financial contributions to the Organization shall have no vote in the General Assembly if the amount of its arrears equals or exceeds the amount of the contributions due from it for the preceding two full years. The General Assembly may, nevertheless, permit such a Member to vote if it is satisfied that the failure to pay is due to conditions beyond the control of the Member.

Procedure

Article 20

The General Assembly shall meet in regular annual sessions and in such special sessions as occasion may require. Special sessions shall be convoked by the Secretary-General at the request of the Security Council or of a majority of the Members of the United Nations.

Article 21

The General Assembly shall adopt its own rules of procedure. It shall elect its President for each session.

Article 22

The General Assembly may establish such subsidiary organs as it deems necessary for the performance of its functions.

CHAPTER V
THE SECURITY COUNCIL

Composition

Article 23 *

1. The Security Council shall consist of fifteen Members of the United Nations. The Republic of China, France, the Union of Soviet Socialist Republics, the United Kingdom of Great Britain and Northern Ireland, and the United States of America shall be permanent members of the Security Council. The General Assembly shall elect ten other Members of the United Nations to be non-permanent members of the Security Council, due regard being specially paid, in the first instance to the contribution of Members of the United Nations to the maintenance of international peace and security and to the other purposes of the Organization, and also to equitable geographical distribution.

2. The non-permanent members of the Security Council shall be elected for a term of two years. In the first election of the non-permanent members after the increase of the membership of the Security Council from eleven to fifteen, two of the four additional members shall be chosen for a term of one year. A retiring member shall not be eligible for immediate re-election.

3. Each member of the Security Council shall have one representative.

Functions and Powers

Article 24

1. In order to ensure prompt and effective action by the United Nations, its Members confer on the Security Council primary responsibility for the maintenance of international peace and security, and agree that in carrying out its duties under this responsibility the Security Council acts on their behalf.

2. In discharging these duties the Security Council shall act in accordance with the Purposes and Principles of the United Nations. The specific powers granted to the Security Council for the discharge of these duties are laid down in Chapters VI, VII, VIII, and XII.

3. The Security Council shall submit annual and, when necessary,

---

* As amended. The original text of Article 23 reads as follows:

1. The Security Council shall consist of eleven Members of the United Nations. The Republic of China, France, the Union of Soviet Socialist Republics, the United Kingdom of Great Britain and Northern Ireland, and the United States of America shall be permanent members of the Security Council. The General Assembly shall elect six other Members of the United Nations to be non-permanent members of the Security Council, due regard being specially paid, in the first instance to the contribution of Members of the United Nations to the maintenance of international peace and security and to the other purposes of the Organization, and also to equitable geographical distribution.

2. The non-permanent members of the Security Council shall be elected for a term of two years. In the first election of the non-permanent members, however, three shall be chosen for a term of one year. A retiring member shall not be eligible for immediate re-election.

3. Each member of the Security Council shall have one representative.

special reports to the General Assembly for its consideration.

Article 25

The Members of the United Nations agree to accept and carry out the decisions of the Security Council in accordance with the present Charter.

Article 26

In order to promote the establishment and maintenance of international peace and security with the least diversion for armaments of the world's human and economic resources, the Security Council shall be responsible for formulating, with the assistance of the Military Staff Committee referred to in Article 47, plans to be submitted to the Members of the United Nations for the establishment of a system for the regulation of armaments.

Voting

Article 27 *

1. Each member of the Security Council shall have one vote.

2. Decisions of the Security Council on procedural matters shall be made by an affirmative vote of nine members.

3. Decisions of the Security Council on all other matters shall be made by an affirmative vote of nine members including the concurring votes of the permanent members; provided that, in decisions under Chapter VI, and under paragraph 3 of Article 52, a party to a dispute shall abstain from voting.

Procedure

Article 28

1. The Security Council shall be so organized as to be able to function continuously. Each member of the Security Council shall for this purpose be represented at all times at the seat of the Organization.

2. The Security Council shall hold periodic meetings at which each of its members may, if it so desires, be represented by a member of the government or by some other specially designated representative.

3. The Security Council may hold meetings at such places other than the seat of the Organization as in its judgment will best facilitate its work.

Article 29

The Security Council may establish such subsidiary organs as it deems necessary for the performance of its functions.

Article 30

The Security Council shall adopt its own rules of procedure, including the method of selecting its President.

Article 31

Any Member of the United Nations which is not a member of the Security Council may participate, without vote, in the discussion of any question brought before the Security Council whenever the latter

---

* As amended. The original text of Article 27 reads as follows:
    1. Each member of the Security Council shall have one vote.
    2. Decisions of the Security Council on procedural matters shall be made by an affirmative vote of seven members.
    3. Decisions of the Security Council on all other matters shall be made by an affirmative vote of seven members including the concurring votes of the permanent members; provided that, in decisions under Chapter VI, and under paragraph 3 of Article 52, a party to a dispute shall abstain from voting.

considers that the interests of that Member are specially affected.

Article 32

Any Member of the United Nations which is not a member of the Security Council or any state which is not a Member of the United Nations, if it is a party to a dispute under consideration by the Security Council, shall be invited to participate, without vote, in the discussion relating to the dispute. The Security Council shall lay down such conditions as it deems just for the participation of a state which is not a Member of the United Nations.

CHAPTER VI
PACIFIC SETTLEMENT OF DISPUTES

Article 33

1. The parties to any dispute, the continuance of which is likely to endanger the maintenance of international peace and security, shall, first of all, seek a solution by negotiation, enquiry, mediation, conciliation, arbitration, judicial settlement, resort to regional agencies or arrangements, or other peaceful means of their own choice.

2. The Security Council shall, when it deems necessary, call upon the parties to settle their dispute by such means.

Article 34

The Security Council may investigate any dispute, or any situation which might lead to international friction or give rise to a dispute, in order to determine whether the continuance of the dispute or situation is likely to endanger the maintenance of international peace and security.

Article 35

1. Any Member of the United Nations may bring any dispute, or any situation of the nature referred to in Article 34, to the attention of the Security Council or of the General Assembly.

2. A state which is not a Member of the United Nations may bring to the attention of the Security Council or of the General Assembly any dispute to which it is a party if it accepts in advance, for the purposes of the dispute, the obligations of pacific settlement provided in the present Charter.

3. The proceedings of the General Assembly in respect of matters brought to its attention under this Article will be subject to the provisions of Articles 11 and 12.

Article 36

1. The Security Council may, at any stage of a dispute of the nature referred to in Article 33 or of a situation of like nature, recommend appropriate procedures or methods of adjustment.

2. The Security Council should take into consideration any procedures for the settlement of the dispute which have already been adopted by the parties.

3. In making recommendations under this Article the Security Council should also take into consideration that legal disputes should as a general rule be referred by the parties to the International Court of Justice in accordance with the provisions of the Statute of the Court.

Article 37

1. Should the parties to a dispute of the nature referred to in Article 33 fail to settle it by the means indicated in that Article, they shall refer it to the Security Council.

2. If the Security Council deems that the continuance of the dispute is in fact likely to endanger the maintenance of international peace and security, it shall decide whether to take action under Article 36 or to recommend such terms of settlement as it may consider appropriate.

Article 38

Without prejudice to the provisions of Articles 33 to 37, the Security Council may, if all the parties to any dispute so request, make recommendations to the parties with a view to a pacific settlement of the dispute.

CHAPTER VII

ACTION WITH RESPECT TO THREATS TO THE PEACE, BREACHES OF THE PEACE, AND ACTS OF AGGRESSION

Article 39

The Security Council shall determine the existence of any threat to the peace, breach of the peace, or act of aggression and shall make recommendations, or decide what measures shall be taken in accordance with Articles 41 and 42, to maintain or restore international peace and security.

Article 40

In order to prevent an aggravation of the situation, the Security Council may, before making the recommendations or deciding upon the measures provided for in Article 39, call upon the parties concerned to comply with such provisional measures as it deems necessary or desirable. Such provisional measures shall be without prejudice to the rights, claims, or position of the parties con-

cerned. The Security Council shall duly take account of failure to comply with such provisional measures.

Article 41

The Security Council may decide what measures not involving the use of armed force are to be employed to give effect to its decisions, and it may call upon the Members of the United Nations to apply such measures. These may include complete or partial interruption of economic relations and of rail, sea, air, postal, telegraphic, radio, and other means of communication, and the severance of diplomatic relations.

Article 42

Should the Security Council consider that measures provided for in Article 41 would be inadequate or have proved to be inadequate, it may take such action by air, sea, or land forces as may be necessary to maintain or restore international peace and security. Such action may include demonstrations, blockade, and other operations by air, sea, or land forces of Members of the United Nations.

Article 43

1. All Members of the United Nations, in order to contribute to the maintenance of international peace and security, undertake to make available to the Security Council, on its call and in accordance with a special agreement or agreements, armed forces, assistance, and facilities, including rights of passage, necessary for the purpose of maintaining international peace and security.

2. Such agreement or agreements shall govern the numbers and types of forces, their degree of readiness and general location, and the nature of the facilities and assistance to be provided.

3. The agreement or agreements shall be negotiated as soon as possible on the initiative of the Security Council. They shall be concluded between the Security Council and Members or between the Security Council and groups of Members and shall be subject to ratification by the signatory states in accordance with their respective constitutional processes.

Article 44

When the Security Council has decided to use force it shall, before calling upon a Member not represented on it to provide armed forces in fulfillment of the obligations assumed under Article 43, invite that Member, if the Member so desires, to participate in the decisions of the Security Council concerning the employment of contingents of that Member's armed forces.

Article 45

In order to enable the United Nations to take urgent military measures, Members shall hold immediately available national air-force contingents for combined international enforcement action. The strength and degree of readiness of these contingents and plans for their combined action shall be determined, within the limits laid down in the special agreement or agreements referred to in Article 43, by the Security Council with the assistance of the Military Staff Committee.

Article 46

Plans for the application of armed force shall be made by the Security Council with the assistance of the Military Staff Committee.

Article 47

1. There shall be established a Military Staff Committee to advise and assist the Security Council on all questions relating to the Security Council's military requirements for the maintenance of international peace and security, the employment and command of forces placed at its disposal, the regulation of armaments, and possible disarmament.

2. The Military Staff Committee shall consist of the Chiefs of Staff of the permanent members of the Security Council or their representatives. Any Member of the United Nations not permanently represented on the Committee shall be invited by the Committee to be associated with it when the efficient discharge of the Committee's responsibilities requires the participation of that Member in its work.

3. The Military Staff Committee shall be responsible under the Security Council for the strategic direction of any armed forces placed at the disposal of the Security Council. Questions relating to the command of such forces shall be worked out subsequently.

4. The Military Staff Committee, with the authorization of the Security Council and after consultation with appropriate regional agencies, may establish regional subcommittees.

Article 48

1. The action required to carry out the decisions of the Security Council for the maintenance of international peace and security shall be taken by all the Members of the United Nations or by some of them, as the Security Council may determine.

2. Such decisions shall be carried out by the Members of the United Nations directly and through their action in the appropriate international agencies of which they are members.

Article 49

The Members of the United Nations shall join in affording mutual assistance in carrying out the measures decided upon by the Security Council.

Article 50

If preventive or enforcement measures against any state are taken by the Security Council, any other state, whether a Member of the United Nations or not, which finds itself confronted with special economic problems arising from the carrying out of those measures shall have the right to consult the Security Council with regard to a solution of those problems.

Article 51

Nothing in the present Charter shall impair the inherent right of individual or collective self-defense if an armed attack occurs against a Member of the United Nations, until the Security Council has taken measures necessary to maintain international peace and security. Measures taken by Members in the exercise of this right of self-defense shall be immediately reported to the Security Council and shall not in any way affect the authority and responsibility of the Security Council under the present Charter to take at any time such action as it deems necessary in order to maintain or restore international peace and security.

CHAPTER VIII
REGIONAL ARRANGEMENTS

Article 52

1. Nothing in the present Charter precludes the existence of regional arrangements or agencies for dealing with such matters relating to the maintenance of international peace and security as are appropriate for regional action, provided that such arrangements or agencies and their activities are consistent with the Purposes and Principles of the United Nations.

2. The Members of the United Nations entering into such arrangements or constituting such agencies shall make every effort to achieve pacific settlement of local disputes through such regional arrangements or by such regional agencies before referring them to the Security Council.

3. The Security Council shall encourage the development of pacific settlement of local disputes through such regional arrangements or by such regional agencies either on the initiative of the states concerned or by reference from the Security Council.

4. This Article in no way impairs the application of Articles 34 and 35.

Article 53

1. The Security Council shall, where appropriate, utilize such regional arrangements or agencies for enforcement action under its authority. But no enforcement action shall be taken under regional arrangements or by regional agencies without the authorization of the Security Council, with the exception of measures against any enemy state, as defined in paragraph 2 of this Article, provided for pursuant to Article 107 or in regional arrangements directed against renewal of aggressive policy on the part of any such state, until such time as the Organization may, on request of the Governments concerned, be charged with the responsibility for preventing further aggression by such a state.

2. The term enemy state as used in paragraph 1 of this Article applies to any state which during the Second World War has been an enemy of any signatory of the present Charter.

Article 54

The Security Council shall at all times be kept fully informed of activities undertaken or in contemplation under regional arrangements or by regional agencies for the maintenance of international peace and security.

CHAPTER IX
INTERNATIONAL ECONOMIC AND SOCIAL CO-OPERATION

Article 55

With a view to the creation of conditions of stability and well-being which are necessary for peaceful and friendly relations among nations based on respect for the principle of equal rights and self-determination of peoples, the United Nations shall promote:

a. higher standards of living, full employment, and conditions of economic and social progress and development;

b. solutions of international economic, social, health, and related problems; and international cultural and educational co-operation; and

c. universal respect for, and observance of, human rights and fundamental freedoms for all without distinction as to race, sex, language, or religion.

Article 56

All Members pledge themselves to take joint and separate action in co-operation with the Organization for the achievement of the purposes set forth in Article 55.

Article 57

1. The various specialized agencies, established by intergovernmental agreement and having wide international responsibilities, as defined in their basic instruments, in economic, social, cultural, educational, health, and related fields, shall be brought into relationship with the United Nations in accordance with the provisions of Article 63.

2. Such agencies thus brought into relationship with the United Nations are hereinafter referred to as specialized agencies.

Article 58

The Organization shall make recommendations for the coordination of the policies and activities of the specialized agencies.

Article 59

The Organization shall, where appropriate, initiate negotiations among the states concerned for the creation of any new specialized agencies required for the accomplishment of the purposes set forth in Article 55.

Article 60

Responsibility for the discharge of the functions of the Organization set forth in this Chapter shall be vested in the General Assembly and, under the authority of the General Assembly, in the Economic and Social Council, which shall have for this purpose the powers set forth in Chapter X.

CHAPTER X
THE ECONOMIC AND SOCIAL COUNCIL

Composition

Article 61 °

1. The Economic and Social Council shall consist of twenty-seven Members of the United Nations elected by the General Assembly.

2. Subject to the provisions of paragraph 3, nine members of the Economic and Social Council shall be elected each year for a term of three years. A retiring member shall be eligible for immediate re-election.

3. At the first election after the increase in the membership of the Economic and Social Council from eighteen to twenty-seven members, in addition to the members elected in place of the six members whose term of office expires at the end of that year, nine additional members shall be elected. Of these nine additional members, the term of office of three members so elected shall expire at the end of one year, and of three other members at the end of two years, in accordance with arrangements made by the General Assembly.

4. Each member of the Economic and Social Council shall have one representative.

Functions and Powers

Article 62

1. The Economic and Social Council may make or initiate studies and reports with respect to international economic, social, cultural, educational, health, and related matters and may make recommendations with respect to any such matters to the General Assembly, to the Members of the United Nations, and to the specialized agencies concerned.

2. It may make recommendations for the purpose of promoting respect for, and observance of, human rights and fundamental freedoms for all.

3. It may prepare draft conventions for submission to the General Assembly, with respect to matters falling within its competence.

4. It may call, in accordance with the rules prescribed by the United Nations, international conferences on matters falling within its competence.

Article 63

1. The Economic and Social Council may enter into agreements with any of the agencies referred to in Article 57, defining the terms on which the agency concerned shall be brought into relationship with the United Nations. Such agreements shall be subject to approval by the General Assembly.

° As amended. The original text of Article 27 reads as follows:
  1. The Economic and Social Council shall consist of eighteen Members of the United Nations elected by the General Assembly.
  2. Subject to the provisions of paragraph 3, six members of the Economic and Social Council shall be elected each year for a term of three years. A retiring member shall be eligible for immediate re-election.
  3. At the first election, eighteen members of the Economic and Social Council shall be chosen. The term of office of six members so chosen shall expire at the end of one year, and of six other members at the end of two years, in accordance with arrangements made by the General Assembly.
  4. Each member of the Economic and Social Council shall have one representative.

2. It may coordinate the activities of the specialized agencies through consultation with and recommendations to such agencies and through recommendations to the General Assembly and to the Members of the United Nations.

Article 64

1. The Economic and Social Council may take appropriate steps to obtain regular reports from the specialized agencies. It may make arrangements with the Members of the United Nations and with the specialized agencies to obtain reports on the steps taken to give effect to its own recommendations and to recommendations on matters falling within its competence made by the General Assembly.
2. It may communicate its observations on these reports to the General Assembly.

Article 65

The Economic and Social Council may furnish information to the Security Council and shall assist the Security Council upon its request.

Article 66

1. The Economic and Social Council shall perform such functions as fall within its competence in connection with the carrying out of the recommendations of the General Assembly.
2. It may, with the approval of the General Assembly, perform services at the request of Members of the United Nations and at the request of specialized agencies.
3. It shall perform such other functions as are specified elsewhere in the present Charter or as may be

assigned to it by the General Assembly.

Voting

Article 67

1. Each member of the Economic and Social Council shall have one vote.
2. Decisions of the Economic and Social Council shall be made by a majority of the members present and voting.

Procedure

Article 68

The Economic and Social Council shall set up commissions in economic and social fields and for the promotion of human rights, and such other commissions as may be required for the performance of its functions.

Article 69

The Economic and Social Council shall invite any Member of the United Nations to participate, without vote, in its deliberations on any matter of particular concern to that Member.

Article 70

The Economic and Social Council may make arrangements for representatives of the specialized agencies to participate, without vote, in its deliberations and in those of the commissions established by it, and for its representatives to participate in the deliberations of the specialized agencies.

Article 71

The Economic and Social Council may make suitable arrangements for consultation with non-governmental organizations which are concerned with matters within its competence. Such arrangements may be made with international organizations and, where appropriate, with national organizations after consultation with the Member of the United Nations concerned.

Article 72

1. The Economic and Social Council shall adopt its own rules of procedure, including the method of selecting its President.
2. The Economic and Social Council shall meet as required in accordance with its rules, which shall include provision for the convening of meetings on the request of a majority of its members.

CHAPTER XI

DECLARATION REGARDING NON-SELF-GOVERNING TERRITORIES

Article 73

Members of the United Nations which have or assume responsibilities for the administration of territories whose peoples have not yet attained a full measure of self-government recognize the principle that the interests of the inhabitants of these territories are paramount, and accept as a sacred trust the obligation to promote to the utmost, within the system of international peace and security established by the present Charter, the well-being of the inhabitants of these territories, and, to this end:

    a. to ensure, with due respect for the culture of the peoples concerned, their political, economic, social, and educational advancement, their just treatment, and their protection against abuses;

    b. to develop self-government, to take due account of the political aspirations of the peoples, and to assist them in the progressive development of their free political institutions, according to the particular circumstances of each territory and its peoples and their varying stages of advancement;

    c. to further international peace and security;

    d. to promote constructive measures of development, to encourage research, and to cooperate with one another and, when and where appropriate, with specialized international bodies with a view to the practical achievement of the social, economic, and scientific purposes set forth in this Article; and

    e. to transmit regularly to the Secretary-General for information purposes, subject to such limitation as security and constitutional considerations may require, statistical and other information of a technical nature relating to economic, social, and educational conditions in the territories for which they are respectively responsible other than those territories to which Chapter XII and XIII apply.

Article 74

Members of the United Nations also agree that their policy in respect of the territories to which this Chapter applies, no less than in respect of their metropolitan areas, must be based on the general principle of good-neighborliness, due account being taken of the interests and well-being of the rest of the world, in social, economic, and commercial matters.

Chapter XII
INTERNATIONAL TRUSTEESHIP SYSTEM

Article 75

The United Nations shall establish under its authority an international trusteeship system for the administration and supervision of such territories as may be placed thereunder by subsequent individual agreements. These territories are hereinafter referred to as trust territories.

Article 76

The basic objectives of the trusteeship system, in accordance with the Purposes of the United Nations laid down in Article 1 of the present Charter, shall be:

a. to further international peace and security;

b. to promote the political, economic, social, and educational advancement of the inhabitants of the trust territories, and their progressive development towards self-government or independence as may be appropriate to the particular circumstances of each territory and its peoples and the freely expressed wishes of the peoples concerned, and as may be provided by the terms of each trusteeship agreement;

c. to encourage respect for human rights and for fundamental freedoms for all without distinction as to race, sex, language, or religion, and to encourage recognition of the interdependence of the peoples of the world; and

d. to ensure equal treatment in social, economic, and commercial matters for all Members of the United Nations and their nationals, and also equal treatment for the latter in the administration of justice, without prejudice to the attainment of the foregoing objectives and subject to the provisions of Article 80.

Article 77

1. The trusteeship system shall apply to such territories in the following categories as may be placed thereunder by means of trusteeship agreements:

a. territories now held under mandate;

b. territories which may be detached from enemy states as a result of the Second World War; and

c. territories voluntarily placed under the system by states responsible for their administration.

2. It will be a matter for subsequent agreement as to which territories in the foregoing categories will be brought under the trusteeship system and upon what terms.

Article 78

The trusteeship system shall not apply to territories which have become Members of the United Nations, relationship among which shall be based on respect for the principle of sovereign equality.

Article 79

The terms of trusteeship for each territory to be placed under the trusteeship system, including any alteration or amendment, shall be agreed upon by the states directly concerned, including the mandatory power in the case of territories held under mandate by a Member of the United Nations, and shall be approved as provided for in Articles 83 and 85.

Article 80

1. Except as may be agreed upon in individual trusteeship agree-

ments, made under Articles 77, 79, and 81, placing each territory under the trusteeship system, and until such agreements have been concluded, nothing in this Chapter shall be construed in or of itself to alter in any manner the rights whatsoever of any states or any peoples or the terms of existing international instruments to which Members of the United Nations may respectively be parties.

2. Paragraph 1 of this Article shall not be interpreted as giving grounds for delay or postponement of the negotiation and conclusion of agreements for placing mandated and other territories under the trusteeship system as provided for in Article 77.

Article 81

The trusteeship agreement shall in each case include the terms under which the trust territory will be administered and designate the authority which will exercise the administration of the trust territory. Such authority, hereinafter called the administering authority, may be one or more states or the Organization itself.

Article 82

There may be designated, in any trusteeship agreement, a strategic area or areas which may include part or all of the trust territory to which the agreement applies, without prejudice to any special agreement or agreements made under Article 43.

Article 83

1. All functions of the United Nations relating to strategic areas, including the approval of the terms of the trusteeship agreements and of their alteration or amendment, shall be exercised by the Security Council.

2. The basic objectives set forth in Article 76 shall be applicable to the people of each strategic area.

3. The Security Council shall, subject to the provisions of the trusteeship agreements and without prejudice to security considerations, avail itself of the assistance of the Trusteeship Council to perform those functions of the United Nations under the trusteeship system relating to political, economic, social, and educational matters in the strategic areas.

Article 84

It shall be the duty of the administering authority to ensure that the trust territory shall play its part in the maintenance of international peace and security. To this end the administering authority may make use of volunteer forces, facilities, and assistance from the trust territory in carrying out the obligations towards the Security Council undertaken in this regard by the administering authority, as well as for local defense and the maintenance of law and order within the trust territory.

Article 85

1. The functions of the United Nations with regard to trusteeship agreements for all areas not designated as strategic, including the approval of the terms of the trusteeship agreements and of their alteration or amendment, shall be exercised by the General Assembly.

2. The Trusteeship Council, operating under the authority of the General Assembly, shall assist the General Assembly in carrying out these functions.

CHAPTER XIII
THE TRUSTEESHIP COUNCIL

Composition

Article 86

1. The Trusteeship Council shall consist of the following Members of the United Nations:

a. those Members administering trust territories;

b. such of those Members mentioned by name in Article 23 as are not administering trust territories; and

c. as many other Members elected for three-year terms by the General Assembly as may be necessary to ensure that the total number of members of the Trusteeship Council is equally divided between those Members of the United Nations which administer trust territories and those which do not.

2. Each member of the Trusteeship Council shall designate one specially qualified person to represent it therein.

Functions and Powers

Article 87

The General Assembly and, under its authority, the Trusteeship Council, in carrying out their functions, may:

a. consider reports submitted by the administering authority;

b. accept petitions and examine them in consultation with the administering authority;

c. provide for periodic visits to the respective trust territories at times agreed upon with the administering authority; and

d. take these and other actions in conformity with the terms of the trusteeship agreements.

Article 88

The Trusteeship Council shall formulate a questionnaire on the political, economic, social, and educational advancement of the inhabitants of each trust territory, and the administering authority for each trust territory within the competence of the General Assembly shall make an annual report to the General Assembly upon the basis of such questionnaire.

Voting

Article 89

1. Each member of the Trusteeship Council shall have one vote.

2. Decisions of the Trusteeship Council shall be made by a majority of the members present and voting.

Procedure

Article 90

1. The Trusteeship Council shall adopt its own rules of procedure, including the method of selecting its President.

2. The Trusteeship Council shall meet as required in accordance with its rules, which shall include provision for the convening of meetings on the request of a majority of its members.

Article 91

The Trusteeship Council shall, when appropriate, avail itself of the assistance of the Economic and Social Council and of the specialized agencies in regard to matters with which they are respectively concerned.

CHAPTER XIV
THE INTERNATIONAL COURT OF JUSTICE

Article 92

The International Court of Justice shall be the principal judicial organ of the United Nations. It shall function in accordance with the annexed Statute, which is based upon the Statute of the Permanent Court of International Justice and forms an integral part of the present Charter.

Article 93

1. All Members of the United Nations are *ipso facto* parties to the Statute of the International Court of Justice.

2. A state which is not a Member of the United Nations may become a party to the Statute of the International Court of Justice on conditions to be determined in each case by the General Assembly upon the recommendation of the Security Council.

Article 94

1. Each Member of the United Nations undertakes to comply with the decision of the International Court of Justice in any case to which it is a party.

2. If any party to a case fails to perform the obligations incumbent upon it under a judgment rendered by the Court, the other party may have recourse to the Security Council, which may, if it deems necessary, make recommendations or decide upon measures to be taken to give effect to the judgment.

Article 95

Nothing in the present Charter shall prevent Members of the United Nations from entrusting the solution of their differences to other tribunals by virtue of agreements already in existence or which may be concluded in the future.

Article 96

1. The General Assembly or the Security Council may request the International Court of Justice to give an advisory opinion on any legal question.

2. Other organs of the United Nations and specialized agencies, which may at any time be so authorized by the General Assembly, may also request advisory opinions of the Court on legal questions arising within the scope of their activities.

CHAPTER XV
THE SECRETARIAT

Article 97

The Secretariat shall comprise a Secretary-General and such staff as the Organization may require. The Secretary-General shall be appointed by the General Assembly upon the recommendation of the Security Council. He shall be the chief administrative officer of the Organization.

Article 98

The Secretary-General shall act in that capacity in all meetings of the General Assembly, of the Security Council, of the Economic and Social Council, and of the Trusteeship Council, and shall perform such other functions as are entrusted to him by these organs. The Secretary-General shall make an annual report to the General Assembly on the work of the Organization.

Article 99

The Secretary-General may bring to the attention of the Security Council any matter which in his opinion may threaten the maintenance of international peace and security.

Article 100

1. In the performance of their duties the Secretary-General and the staff shall not seek or receive instructions from any government or from any other authority external to the Organization. They shall refrain from any action which might reflect on their position as international officials responsible only to the Organization.

2. Each Member of the United Nations undertakes to respect the exclusively international character of the responsibilities of the Secretary-General and the staff and not to seek to influence them in the discharge of their responsibilities.

Article 101

1. The staff shall be appointed by the Secretary-General under regulations established by the General Assembly.

2. Appropriate staffs shall be permanently assigned to the Economic and Social Council, the Trusteeship Council, and, as required, to other organs of the United Nations. These staffs shall form a part of the Secretariat.

3. The paramount consideration in the employment of the staff and in the determination of the conditions of service shall be the necessity of securing the highest standards of efficiency, competence, and integrity.

Due regard shall be paid to the importance of recruiting the staff on as wide a geographical basis as possible.

Chapter XVI
MISCELLANEOUS PROVISIONS

Article 102

1. Every treaty and every international agreement entered into by any Member of the United Nations after the present Charter comes into force shall as soon as possible be registered with the Secretariat and published by it.

2. No party to any such treaty or international agreement which has not been registered in accordance with the provisions of paragraph 1 of this Article may invoke that treaty or agreement before any organ of the United Nations.

Article 103

In the event of a conflict between the obligations of the Members of the United Nations under the present Charter and their obligations under any other international agreement, their obligations under the present Charter shall prevail.

Article 104

The Organization shall enjoy in the territory of each of its Members such legal capacity as may be necessary for the exercise of its functions and the fulfillment of its purposes.

Article 105

1. The Organization shall enjoy in the territory of each of its Members such privileges and immunities as are necessary for the fulfillment of its purposes.

2. Representatives of the Members of the United Nations and officials of the Organization shall similarly enjoy such privileges and immunities as are necessary for the independent exercise of their functions in connection with the Organization.

3. The General Assembly may make recommendations with a view to determining the details of the application of paragraphs 1 and 2 of this Article or may propose conventions to the Members of the United Nations for this purpose.

Chapter XVII
TRANSITIONAL SECURITY ARRANGEMENTS

Article 106

Pending the coming into force of such special agreements referred to in Article 43 as in the opinion of the Security Council enable it to begin the exercise of its responsibilities under Article 42, the parties to the Four-Nation Declaration, signed at Moscow, October 30, 1943, and France, shall, in accordance with the provisions of paragraph 5 of that Declaration, consult with one another and as occasion requires with other Members of the United Nations with a view to such joint action on behalf of the Organization as may be necessary for the purpose of maintaining international peace and security.

Article 107

Nothing in the present Charter shall invalidate or preclude action, in relation to any state which during the Second World War has been an enemy of any signatory to the present Charter, taken or authorized as a result of that war by the Governments having responsibility for such action.

Chapter XVIII
AMENDMENTS

Article 108

Amendments to the present Charter shall come into force for all Members of the United Nations when they have been adopted by a vote of two thirds of the members of the General Assembly and ratified in accordance with their respective constitutional processes by two thirds of the Members of the United Nations, including all the permanent members of the Security Council.

Article 109

1. A General Conference of the Members of the United Nations for the purpose of reviewing the present Charter may be held at a date and place to be fixed by a two-thirds vote of the members of the General Assembly and by a vote of any seven members of the Security Council. Each Member of the United Nations shall have one vote in the conference.

2. Any alteration of the present Charter recommended by a two-thirds vote of the conference shall take effect when ratified in accordance with their respective constitutional processes by two thirds of the Members of the United Nations including all the permanent members of the Security Council.

3. If such a conference has not been held before the tenth annual session of the General Assembly following the coming into force of the present Charter, the proposal to call such a conference shall be placed on the agenda of that session of the

General Assembly, and the conference shall be held if so decided by a majority vote of the members of the General Assembly and by a vote of any seven members of the Security Council.

Chapter XIX
RATIFICATION AND SIGNATURE

Article 110

1. The present Charter shall be ratified by the signatory states in accordance with their respective constitutional processes.

2. The ratifications shall be deposited with the Government of the United States of America, which shall notify all the signatory states of each deposit as well as the Secretary-General of the Organization when he has been appointed.

3. The present Charter shall come into force upon the deposit of ratifications by the Republic of China, France, the Union of Soviet Socialist Republics, the United Kingdom of Great Britain and Northern Ireland, and the United States of America, and by a majority of the other signatory states. A protocol of the ratifications deposited shall thereupon be drawn up by the Government of the United States of America which shall communicate copies thereof to all the signatory states.

4. The states signatory to the present Charter which ratify it after it has come into force will become original Members of the United Nations on the date of the deposit of their respective ratifications.

Article 111

The present Charter, of which the Chinese, French, Russian, English, and Spanish texts are equally authentic, shall remain deposited in the archives of the Government of the United States of America. Duly certified copies thereof shall be transmitted by that Government to the Governments of the other signatory states.

IN FAITH WHEREOF the representatives of the Governments of the United Nations have signed the present Charter.

DONE at the city of San Francisco the twenty-sixth day of June, one thousand nine hundred and forty-five.

STATUTE OF THE INTERNATIONAL COURT OF JUSTICE

Article 1

THE INTERNATIONAL COURT OF JUSTICE established by the Charter of the United Nations as the principal judicial organ of the United Nations shall be constituted and shall function in accordance with the provisions of the present Statute.

CHAPTER I

ORGANIZATION OF THE COURT

Article 2

The Court shall be composed of a body of independent judges, elected regardless of their nationality from among persons of high moral character, who possess the qualifications required in their respective countries for appointment to the highest judicial offices, or are jurisconsults of recognized competence in international law.

Article 3

1. The Court shall consist of fifteen members, no two of whom may be nationals of the same state.

2. A person who for the purposes of membership in the Court could be regarded as a national of more than one state shall be deemed to be a national of the one in which he ordinarily exercises civil and political rights.

Article 4

1. The members of the Court shall be elected by the General Assembly and by the Security Council from a list of persons nominated by the national groups in the Permanent Court of Arbitration, in accordance with the following provisions.

2. In the case of Members of the United Nations not represented in the Permanent Court of Arbitration, candidates shall be nominated by national groups appointed for this purpose by their governments under the same conditions as those prescribed for members of the Permanent Court of Arbitration by Article 44 of the Convention of The Hague of 1907 for the pacific settlement of international disputes.

3. The conditions under which a state which is a party to the present Statute but is not a Member of the United Nations may participate in electing the members of the Court shall, in the absence of a special agreement, be laid down by the General Assembly upon recommendation of the Security Council.

Article 5

1. At least three months before the date of the election, the Secretary-General of the United Nations shall address a written request to the members of the Permanent Court of Arbitration belonging to the states which are parties to the present Statute, and to the members of the national groups appointed under Article 4, paragraph 2, inviting them to undertake, within a given time, by national groups, the nomination of persons in a position to accept the duties of a member of the Court.

2. No group may nominate more than four persons, not more than two of whom shall be of their own nationality. In no case may the number of candidates nominated by

a group be more than double the number of seats to be filled.

Article 6

Before making these nominations, each national group is recommended to consult its highest court of justice, its legal faculties and schools of law, and its national academies and national sections of international academies devoted to the study of law.

Article 7

1. The Secretary-General shall prepare a list in alphabetical order of all the persons thus nominated. Save as provided in Article 12, paragraph 2, these shall be the only persons eligible.

2. The Secretary-General shall submit this list to the General Assembly and to the Security Council.

Article 8

The General Assembly and the Security Council shall proceed independently of one another to elect the members of the Court.

Article 9

At every election, the electors shall bear in mind not only that the persons to be elected should individually possess the qualifications required, but also that in the body as a whole the representation of the main forms of civilization and of the principal legal systems of the world should be assured.

Article 10

1. Those candidates who obtain an absolute majority of votes in the General Assembly and in the Security Council shall be considered as elected.

2. Any vote of the Security Council, whether for the election of judges or for the appointment of members of the conference envisaged in Article 12, shall be taken without any distinction between permanent and non-permanent members of the Security Council.

3. In the event of more than one national of the same state obtaining an absolute majority of the votes both of the General Assembly and of the Security Council, the eldest of these only shall be considered as elected.

Article 11

If, after the first meeting held for the purpose of the election, one or more seats remain to be filled, a second and, if necessary, a third meeting shall take place.

Article 12

1. If, after the third meeting, one or more seats still remain unfilled, a joint conference consisting of six members, three appointed by the General Assembly and three by the Security Council, may be formed at any time at the request of either the General Assembly or the Security Council, for the purpose of choosing by the vote of an absolute majority one name for each seat still vacant, to submit to the General Assembly and the Security Council for their respective acceptance.

2. If the joint conference is unanimously agreed upon any person who fulfills the required conditions, he may be included in its list, even though he was not included in the list of nominations referred to in Article 7.

3. If the joint conference is satisfied that it will not be successful in procuring an election, those members of the Court who have already been elected shall, within a period

to be fixed by the Security Council, proceed to fill the vacant seats by selection from among those candidates who have obtained votes either in the General Assembly or in the Security Council.

4. In the event of an equality of votes among the judges, the eldest judge shall have a casting vote.

Article 13

1. The members of the Court shall be elected for nine years and may be re-elected; provided, however, that of the judges elected at the first election, the terms of five judges shall expire at the end of three years and the terms of five more judges shall expire at the end of six years.

2. The judges whose terms are to expire at the end of the above-mentioned initial periods of three and six years shall be chosen by lot to be drawn by the Secretary-General immediately after the first election has been completed.

3. The members of the Court shall continue to discharge their duties until their places have been filled. Though replaced, they shall finish any cases which they may have begun.

4. In the case of the resignation of a member of the Court, the resignation shall be addressed to the President of the Court for transmission to the Secretary-General. This last notification makes the place vacant.

Article 14

Vacancies shall be filled by the same method as that laid down for the first election, subject to the following provision: the Secretary-General shall, within one month of the occurrence of the vacancy, proceed to issue the invitations provided for in Article 5, and the date of the election shall be fixed by the Security Council.

Article 15

A member of the Court elected to replace a member whose term of office has not expired shall hold office for the remainder of his predecessor's term.

Article 16

1. No member of the Court may exercise any political or administrative function, or engage in any other occupation of a professional nature.

2. Any doubt on this point shall be settled by the decision of the Court.

Article 17

1. No member of the Court may act as agent, counsel, or advocate in any case.

2. No member may participate in the decision of any case in which he has previously taken part as agent, counsel, or advocate for one of the parties, or as a member of a national or international court, or of a commission of enquiry, or in any other capacity.

3. Any doubt on this point shall be settled by the decision of the Court.

Article 18

1. No member of the Court can be dismissed unless, in the unanimous opinion of the other members, he has ceased to fulfill the required conditions.

2. Formal notification thereof shall be made to the Secretary-General by the Registrar.

3. This notification makes the place vacant.

Article 19

The members of the Court, when engaged on the business of the Court, shall enjoy diplomatic privileges and immunities.

Article 20

Every member of the Court shall, before taking up his duties, make a solemn declaration in open court that he will exercise his powers impartially and conscientiously.

Article 21

1. The Court shall elect its President and Vice-President for three years; they may be re-elected.
2. The Court shall appoint its Registrar and may provide for the appointment of such other officers as may be necessary.

Article 22

1. The seat of the Court shall be established at The Hague. This, however, shall not prevent the Court from sitting and exercising its functions elsewhere whenever the Court considers it desirable.
2. The President and the Registrar shall reside at the seat of the Court.

Article 23

1. The Court shall remain permanently in session, except during the judicial vacations, the dates and duration of which shall be fixed by the Court.
2. Members of the Court are entitled to periodic leave, the dates and duration of which shall be fixed by the Court, having in mind the distance between The Hague and the home of each judge.
3. Members of the Court shall be bound, unless they are on leave or prevented from attending by illness or other serious reasons duly explained to the President, to hold themselves permanently at the disposal of the Court.

Article 24

1. If, for some special reason, a member of the Court considers that he should not take part in the decision of a particular case, he shall so inform the President.
2. If the President considers that for some special reason one of the members of the Court should not sit in a particular case, he shall give him notice accordingly.
3. If in any such case the member of the Court and the President disagree, the matter shall be settled by the decision of the Court.

Article 25

1. The full Court shall sit except when it is expressly provided otherwise in the present Statute.
2. Subject to the condition that the number of judges available to constitute the Court is not thereby reduced below eleven, the Rules of the Court may provide for allowing one or more judges, according to circumstances and in rotation, to be dispensed from sitting.
3. A quorum of nine judges shall suffice to constitute the Court.

Article 26

1. The Court may from time to time form one or more chambers, composed of three or more judges as the Court may determine, for dealing with particular categories of cases; for example, labor cases and cases relating to transit and communications.
2. The Court may at any time form a chamber for dealing with

a particular case. The number of judges to constitute such a chamber shall be determined by the Court with the approval of the parties.

3. Cases shall be heard and determined by the chambers provided for in this Article if the parties so request.

Article 27

A judgment given by any of the chambers provided for in Articles 26 and 29 shall be considered as rendered by the Court.

Article 28

The chambers provided for in Articles 26 and 29 may, with the consent of the parties, sit and exercise their functions elsewhere than at The Hague.

Article 29

With a view to the speedy dispatch of business, the Court shall form annually a chamber composed of five judges which, at the request of the parties, may hear and determine cases by summary procedure. In addition, two judges shall be selected for the purpose of replacing judges who find it impossible to sit.

Article 30

1. The Court shall frame rules for carrying out its functions. In particular, it shall lay down rules of procedure.

2. The Rules of the Court may provide for assessors to sit with the Court or with any of its chambers, without the right to vote.

Article 31

1. Judges of the nationality of each of the parties shall retain their right to sit in the case before the Court.

2. If the Court includes upon the Bench a judge of the nationality of one of the parties, any other party may choose a person to sit as judge. Such person shall be chosen preferably from among those persons who have been nominated as candidates as provided in Articles 4 and 5.

3. If the Court includes upon the Bench no judge of the nationality of the parties, each of these parties may proceed to choose a judge as provided in paragraph 2 of this Article.

4. The provisions of this Article shall apply to the case of Articles 26 and 29. In such cases, the President shall request one or, if necessary, two of the members of the Court forming the chamber to give place to the members of the Court of the nationality of the parties concerned, and, failing such, or if they are unable to be present, to the judges specially chosen by the parties.

5. Should there be several parties in the same interest, they shall, for the purpose of the preceding provisions, be reckoned as one party only. Any doubt upon this point shall be settled by the decision of the Court.

6. Judges chosen as laid down in paragraphs 2, 3, and 4 of this Article shall fulfill the conditions required by Articles 2, 17 (paragraph 2), 20, and 24 of the present Statute. They shall take part in the decision on terms of complete equality with their colleagues.

Article 32

1. Each member of the Court shall receive an annual salary.

2. The President shall receive a special annual allowance.

3. The Vice-President shall receive a special allowance for every day on which he acts as President.

4. The judges chosen under Article 31, other than members of the Court, shall receive compensation for each day on which they exercise their functions.

5. These salaries, allowances, and compensation shall be fixed by the General Assembly. They may not be decreased during the term of office.

6. The salary of the Registrar shall be fixed by the General Assembly on the proposal of the Court.

7. Regulations made by the General Assembly shall fix the conditions under which retirement pensions may be given to members of the Court and to the Registrar, and the conditions under which members of the Court and the Registrar shall have their traveling expenses refunded.

8. The above salaries, allowances, and compensation shall be free of all taxation.

Article 33

The expenses of the Court shall be borne by the United Nations in such a manner as shall be decided by the General Assembly.

CHAPTER II
COMPETENCE OF THE COURT

Article 34

1. Only states may be parties in cases before the Court.

2. The Court, subject to and in conformity with its Rules, may request of public international organizations information relevant to cases before it, and shall receive such information presented by such organizations on their own initiative.

3. Whenever the construction of the constituent instrument of a public international organization or of an international convention adopted thereunder is in question in a case before the Court, the Registrar shall so notify the public international organization concerned and shall communicate to it copies of all the written proceedings.

Article 35

1. The Court shall be open to the states parties to the present Statute.

2. The conditions under which the Court shall be open to other states shall, subject to the special provisions contained in treaties in force, be laid down by the Security Council, but in no case shall such conditions place the parties in a position of inequality before the Court.

3. When a state which is not a Member of the United Nations is a party to a case, the Court shall fix the amount which that party is to contribute towards the expenses of the Court. This provision shall not apply if such state is bearing a share of the expenses of the Court.

Article 36

1. The jurisdiction of the Court comprises all cases which the parties refer to it and all matters specially provided for in the Charter of the United Nations or in treaties and conventions in force.

2. The states parties to the present Statute may at any time declare that they recognize as compulsory *ipso facto* and without special agreement, in relation to any other state accepting the same obligation, the jurisdiction of the Court in all legal disputes concerning:

    a. the interpretation of a treaty;

    b. any question of international law;

    c. the existence of any fact which, if established, would constitute a breach of an international obligation;

d. the nature or extent of the reparation to be made for the breach of an international obligation.

3. The declarations referred to above may be made unconditionally or on condition of reciprocity on the part of several or certain states, or for a certain time.

4. Such declarations shall be deposited with the Secretary-General of the United Nations, who shall transmit copies thereof to the parties to the Statute and to the Registrar of the Court.

5. Declarations made under Article 36 of the Statute of the Permanent Court of International Justice and which are still in force shall be deemed, as between the parties to the present Statute, to be acceptances of the compulsory jurisdiction of the International Court of Justice for the period which they still have to run and in accordance with their terms.

6. In the event of a dispute as to whether the Court has jurisdiction, the matter shall be settled by the decision of the Court.

Article 37

Whenever a treaty or convention in force provides for reference of a matter to a tribunal to have been instituted by the League of Nations, or to the Permanent Court of International Justice, the matter shall, as between the parties to the present Statute, be referred to the International Court of Justice.

Article 38

1. The Court, whose function is to decide in accordance with inter-national law such disputes as are submitted to it, shall apply:

a. international conventions, whether general or particular, establishing rules expressly recognized by the contesting states;

b. international custom, as evidence of a general practice accepted as law;

c. the general principles of law recognized by civilized nations;

d. subject to the provisions of Article 59, judicial decisions and the teachings of the most highly qualified publicists of the various nations, as subsidiary means for the determination of rules of law.

2. This provision shall not prejudice the power of the Court to decide a case *ex aequo et bono,* if the parties agree thereto.

CHAPTER III
PROCEDURE

Article 39

1. The official languages of the Court shall be French and English. If the parties agree that the case shall be conducted in French, the judgment shall be delivered in French. If the parties agree that the case shall be conducted in English, the judgment shall be delivered in English.

2. In the absence of an agreement as to which language shall be employed, each party may, in the pleadings, use the language which it prefers; the decision of the Court shall be given in French and English. In this case the Court shall at the same time determine which of the two texts shall be considered as authoritative.

3. The Court shall, at the request of any party, authorize a language other than French or English to be used by that party.

Article 40

1. Cases are brought before the Court, as the case may be, either by the notification of the special agreement or by a written application addressed to the Registrar. In either case the subject of the dispute and the parties shall be indicated.

2. The Registrar shall forthwith communicate the application to all concerned.

3. He shall also notify the Members of the United Nations through the Secretary-General, and also any other states entitled to appear before the Court.

Article 41

1. The Court shall have the power to indicate, if it considers that circumstances so require, any provisional measures which ought to be taken to preserve the respective rights of either party.

2. Pending the final decision, notice of the measures suggested shall forthwith be given to the parties and to the Security Council.

Article 42

1. The parties shall be represented by agents.

2. They may have the assistance of counsel or advocates before the Court.

3. The agents, counsel, and advocates of parties before the Court shall enjoy the privileges and immunities necessary to the independent exercise of their duties.

Article 43

1. The procedure shall consist of two parts: written and oral.

2. The written proceedings shall consist of the communication to the Court and to the parties of memorials, counter-memorials and, if necessary, replies; also all papers and documents in support.

3. These communications shall be made through the Registrar, in the order and within the time fixed by the Court.

4. A certified copy of every document produced by one party shall be communicated to the other party.

5. The oral proceedings shall consist of the hearing by the Court of witnesses, experts, agents, counsel, and advocates.

Article 44

1. For the service of all notices upon persons other than the agents, counsel, and advocates, the Court shall apply direct to the government of the state upon whose territory the notice has to be served.

2. The same provision shall apply whenever steps are to be taken to procure evidence on the spot.

Article 45

The hearing shall be under the control of the President or, if he is unable to preside, of the Vice-President; if neither is able to preside, the senior judge present shall preside.

Article 46

The hearing in Court shall be public, unless the Court shall decide otherwise, or unless the parties demand that the public be not admitted.

Article 47

1. Minutes shall be made at each hearing and signed by the Registrar and the President.

2. These minutes alone shall be authentic.

Article 48

The Court shall make orders for the conduct of the case, shall decide the form and time in which each party must conclude its arguments, and make all arrangements connected with the taking of evidence.

Article 49

The Court may, even before the hearing begins, call upon the agents to produce any document or to supply any explanations. Formal note shall be taken of any refusal.

Article 50

The Court may, at any time, entrust any individual, body, bureau, commission, or other organization that it may select, with the task of carrying out an enquiry or giving an expert opinion.

Article 51

During the hearing any relevant questions are to be put to the witnesses and experts under the conditions laid down by the Court in the rules of procedure referred to in Article 30.

Article 52

After the Court has received the proofs and evidence within the time specified for the purpose, it may refuse to accept any further oral or written evidence that one party may desire to present unless the other side consents.

Article 53

1. Whenever one of the parties does not appear before the Court, or fails to defend its case, the other party may call upon the Court to decide in favor of its claim.

2. The Court must, before doing so, satisfy itself, not only that it has jurisdiction in accordance with Articles 36 and 37, but also that the claim is well founded in fact and law.

Article 54

1. When, subject to the control of the Court, the agents, counsel, and advocates have completed their presentation of the case, the President shall declare the hearing closed.

2. The Court shall withdraw to consider the judgment.

3. The deliberations of the Court shall take place in private and remain secret.

Article 55

1. All questions shall be decided by a majority of the judges present.

2. In the event of an equality of votes, the President or the judge who acts in his place shall have a casting vote.

Article 56

1. The judgment shall state the reasons on which it is based.

2. It shall contain the names of the judges who have taken part in the decision.

Article 57

If the judgment does not represent in whole or in part the unanimous opinion of the judges, any judge shall be entitled to deliver a separate opinion.

Article 58

The judgment shall be signed by the President and by the Registrar. It shall be read in open court, due notice having been given to the agents.

Article 59

The decision of the Court has no binding force except between the parties and in respect of that particular case.

Article 60

The judgment is final and without appeal. In the event of dispute as to the meaning or scope of the judgment, the Court shall construe it upon the request of any party.

Article 61

1. An application for revision of a judgment may be made only when it is based upon the discovery of some fact of such a nature as to be a decisive factor, which fact was, when the judgment was given, unknown to the Court and also to the party claiming revision, always provided that such ignorance was not due to negligence.

2. The proceedings for revision shall be opened by a judgment of the Court expressly recording the existence of the new fact, recognizing that it has such a character as to lay the case open to revision, and declaring the application admissible on this ground.

3. The Court may require previous compliance with the terms of the judgment before it admits proceedings in revision.

4. The application for revision must be made at latest within six months of the discovery of the new fact.

5. No application for revision may be made after the lapse of ten years from the date of the judgment.

Article 62

1. Should a state consider that it has an interest of a legal nature which may be affected by the decision in the case, it may submit a request to the Court to be permitted to intervene.

2. It shall be for the Court to decide upon this request.

Article 63

1. Whenever the construction of a convention to which states other than those concerned in the case are parties is in question, the Registrar shall notify all such states forthwith.

2. Every state so notified has the right to intervene in the proceedings; but if it uses this right, the construction given by the judgment will be equally binding upon it.

Article 64

Unless otherwise decided by the Court, each party shall bear its own costs.

CHAPTER IV
ADVISORY OPINIONS

Article 65

1. The Court may give an advisory opinion on any legal question at the request of whatever body may be authorized by or in accordance with the Charter of the United Nations to make such a request.

2. Questions upon which the advisory opinion of the Court is asked shall be laid before the Court by means of a written request containing an exact statement of the question upon which an opinion is required, and accompanied by all documents likely to throw light upon the question.

Article 66

1. The Registrar shall forthwith give notice of the request for an advisory opinion to all states entitled to appear before the Court.

2. The Registrar shall also, by means of a special and direct com-

munication, notify any state entitled to appear before the Court or international organization considered by the Court, or, should it not be sitting, by the President, as likely to be able to furnish information on the question, that the Court will be prepared to receive, within a time limit to be fixed by the President, written statements, or to hear, at a public sitting to be held for the purpose, oral statements relating to the question.

3. Should any such state entitled to appear before the Court have failed to receive the special communication referred to in paragraph 2 of this Article, such state may express a desire to submit a written statement or to be heard; and the Court will decide.

4. States and organizations having presented written or oral statements or both shall be permitted to comment on the statements made by other states or organizations in the form, to the extent, and within the time limits which the Court, or, should it not be sitting, the President, shall decide in each particular case. Accordingly, the Registrar shall in due time communicate any such written statements to states and organizations having submitted similar statements.

Article 67

The Court shall deliver its advisory opinions in open court, notice having been given to the Secretary-General and to the representatives of Members of the United Nations, of other states and of international organizations immediately concerned.

Article 68

In the exercise of its advisory functions the Court shall further be guided by the provisions of the present Statute which apply in contentious cases to the extent to which it recognizes them to be applicable.

Chapter V
AMENDMENT

Article 69

Amendments to the present Statute shall be effected by the same procedure as is provided by the Charter of the United Nations for amendments to that Charter, subject however to any provisions which the General Assembly upon recommendation of the Security Council may adopt concerning the participation of states which are parties to the present Statute but are not Members of the United Nations.

Article 70

The Court shall have power to propose such amendments to the present Statute as it may deem necessary, through written communications to the Secretary-General, for consideration in conformity with the provisions of Article 69.

UNIVERSAL DECLARATION OF HUMAN RIGHTS

Preamble

Whereas recognition of the inherent dignity and of the equal and inalienable rights of all members of the human family is the foundation of freedom, justice and peace in the world,

Whereas disregard and contempt for human rights have resulted in barbarous acts which have outraged the conscience of mankind, and the advent of a world in which human beings shall enjoy freedom of speech and belief and freedom from fear and want has been proclaimed as the highest aspiration of the common people,

Whereas it is essential, if man is not to be compelled to have recourse, as a last resort, to rebellion against tyranny and oppression, that human rights should be protected by the rule of law,

Whereas it is essential to promote the development of friendly relations between nations,

Whereas the peoples of the United Nations have in the Charter reaffirmed their faith in fundamental human rights, in the dignity and worth of the human person and in the equal rights of men and women and have determined to promote

social progress and better standards of life in larger freedom,

Whereas Member States have pledged themselves to achieve, in co-operation with the United Nations, the promotion of universal respect for and observance of human rights and fundamental freedoms,

Whereas a common understanding of these rights and freedoms is of the greatest importance for the full realization of this pledge,

Now, Therefore,

THE GENERAL ASSEMBLY

proclaims

THIS UNIVERSAL DECLARATION OF HUMAN RIGHTS as a common standard of achievement for all peoples and all nations, to the end that every individual and every organ of society, keeping this Declaration constantly in mind, shall strive by teaching and education to promote respect for these rights and freedoms and by progressive measures, national and international, to secure their universal and effective recognition and observance, both among the peoples of Member States themselves and among the peoples of territories under their jurisdiction.

The Universal Declaration of Human Rights was adopted by the United Nations General Assembly on December 10, 1948.

The rights embodied in the Declaration have been set forth in two covenants—the International Covenant on Civil and Political Rights and the International Covenant on Economic, Social and Cultural Rights—which were adopted by the General Assembly on December 16, 1966.

Article 1. All human beings are born free and equal in dignity and rights. They are endowed with reason and conscience and should act towards one another in a spirit of brotherhood.

Article 2. Everyone is entitled to all the rights and freedoms set forth in this Declaration, without distinction of any kind, such as race, colour, sex, language, religion, political or other opinion, national or social origin, property, birth or other status. Furthermore, no distinction shall be made on the basis of the political, jurisdictional or international status of the country or territory to which a person belongs, whether it be independent, trust, non-self-governing or under any other limitation of sovereignty.

Article 3. Everyone has the right to life, liberty and security of person.

Article 4. No one shall be held in slavery or servitude; slavery and the slave trade shall be prohibited in all their forms.

Article 5. No one shall be subjected to torture or to cruel, inhuman or degrading treatment or punishment.

Article 6. Everyone has the right to recognition everywhere as a person before the law.

Article 7. All are equal before the law and are entitled without any discrimination to equal protection of the law. All are entitled to equal protection against any discrimination in violation of this Declaration and against any incitement to such discrimination.

Article 8. Everyone has the right to an effective remedy by the competent national tribunals for acts violating the fundamental rights granted him by the constitution or by law.

Article 9. No one shall be subjected to arbitrary arrest, detention or exile.

Article 10. Everyone is entitled in full equality to a fair and public hearing by an independent and impartial tribunal, in the determination of his rights and obligations and of any criminal charge against him.

Article 11. (1) Everyone charged with a penal offence has the right to be presumed innocent until proved guilty according to law in a public trial at which he has had all the guarantees necessary for his defence.

(2) No one shall be held guilty of any penal offence on account of any act or omission which did not constitute a penal offence, under national or international law, at the time when it was committed. Nor shall a heavier penalty be imposed than the one that was applicable at the time the penal offence was committed.

Article 12. No one shall be subjected to arbitrary interference with his privacy, family, home or correspondence, nor to attacks upon his honour and reputation. Everyone has the right to the protection of the law against such interference or attacks.

Article 13. (1) Everyone has the right to freedom of movement and residence within the borders of each state.

(2) Everyone has the right to leave any country, including his own, and to return to his country.

Article 14. (1) Everyone has the right to seek and to enjoy in other countries asylum from persecution.

(2) This right may not be invoked in the case of prosecutions genuinely arising from non-political crimes or from acts contrary to the purposes and principles of the United Nations.

Article 15. (1) Everyone has the right to a nationality.

(2) No one shall be arbitrarily deprived of his nationality nor denied the right to change his nationality.

Article 16. (1) Men and women of full age, without any limitation due to race, nationality or religion, have the right to marry and to found a family. They are entitled to equal rights as to marriage, during marriage and at its dissolution.

(2) Marriage shall be entered into only with the free and full consent of the intending spouses.

(3) The family is the natural and fundamental group unit of society and is entitled to protection by society and the State.

Article 17. (1) Everyone has the right to own property alone as well as in association with others.

(2) No one shall be arbitrarily deprived of his property.

Article 18. Everyone has the right to freedom of thought, conscience and religion; this right includes freedom to change his religion or belief, and freedom, either alone or in community with others and in public or private, to manifest his religion or belief in teaching, practice, worship and observance.

Article 19. Everyone has the right to freedom of opinion and expression; this right includes freedom to hold opinions without interference and to seek, receive and impart information and ideas through any media and regardless of frontiers.

Article 20. (1) Everyone has the right to freedom of peaceful assembly and association.

(2) No one may be compelled to belong to an association.

Article 21. (1) Everyone has the right to take part in the government of his country, directly or through freely chosen representatives.

(2) Everyone has the right of equal access to public service in his country.

(3) The will of the people shall be the basis of the authority of government; this will shall be expressed in periodic and genuine elections which shall be by universal and equal suffrage and shall be held by secret vote or by equivalent free voting procedures.

Article 22. Everyone, as a member of society, has the right to social security and is entitled to realization, through national effort and international co-operation and in accordance with the organization and resources of each State, of the economic, social and cultural rights indispensable for his dignity and the free development of his personality.

Article 23. (1) Everyone has the right to work, to free choice of employment, to just and favourable conditions of work and to protection against unemployment.

(2) Everyone, without any discrimination, has the right to equal pay for equal work.

(3) Everyone who works has the right to just and favourable remuneration ensuring for himself and his family an existence worthy of human dignity, and supplemented, if necessary, by other means of social protection.

(4) Everyone has the right to form and to join trade unions for the protection of his interests.

Article 24. Everyone has the right to rest and leisure, including reasonable limitation of working hours and periodic holidays with pay.

Article 25. (1) Everyone has the right to a standard of living adequate for the health and well-being of himself and of his family, including food, clothing, housing and medical care and necessary social services, and the right to security in the event of unemployment, sickness, disability, widowhood, old age or other lack of livelihood in circumstances beyond his control.

(2) Motherhood and childhood are entitled to special care and assistance. All children, whether born in or out of wedlock, shall enjoy the same social protection.

Article 26. (1) Everyone has the right to education. Education shall be free, at least in the elementary and fundamental stages. Elementary education shall be compulsory. Technical and professional education shall be made generally available and higher education shall be equally accessible to all on the basis of merit.

(2) Education shall be directed to the full development of the human personality and to the strengthening of respect for human rights and fundamental freedoms. It shall promote understanding, tolerance and friendship among all nations, racial or religious groups, and shall further the activities of the United Nations for the maintenance of peace.

(3) Parents have a prior right to choose the kind of education that shall be given to their children.

Article 27. (1) Everyone has the right freely to participate in the cultural life of the community, to enjoy the arts and to share in scientific advancement and its benefits.

(2) Everyone has the right to the protection of the moral and material interests resulting from any scientific, literary or artistic production of which he is the author.

Article 28. Everyone is entitled to a social and international order in which the rights and freedoms set forth in this Declaration can be fully realized.

Article 29. (1) Everyone has duties to the community in which alone the free and full development of his personality is possible.

(2) In the exercise of his rights and freedoms, everyone shall be subject

only to such limitations as are determined by law solely for the purpose of securing due recognition and respect for the rights and freedoms of others and of meeting the just requirements of morality, public order and the general welfare in a democratic society.

(3) These rights and freedoms may in no case be exercised contrary to the purposes and principles of the United Nations.

Article 30. Nothing in this Declaration may be interpreted as implying for any State, group or person any right to engage in any activity or to perform any act aimed at the destruction of any of the rights and freedoms set forth herein.

UNITED NATIONS INFORMATION CENTRES AND SERVICES

[Countries not specified under *"Services to"*
are covered by Headquarters]

Accra—United Nations Information Centre, Liberia and Maxwell Roads (Post Office Box 2339), Accra, Ghana.
Services to: Gambia, Ghana, Guinea, Sierra Leone.

Addis Ababa—United Nations Information Service, Economic Commission for Africa, Africa Hall (Post Office Box 3001), Addis Ababa, Ethiopia.
Services to: Ethiopia.

Algiers—United Nations Information Centre, 19 Avenue Claude Debussy (Post Office Box 803), Algiers, Algeria.
Services to: Algeria.

Asunción—United Nations Information Centre, Calle Coronel Bogado 871 (Post Office Box 1107), Asunción, Paraguay.
Services to: Paraguay.

Athens—United Nations Information Centre, 36 Am lia Avenue, Athens 119, Greece.
Services to: Cyprus, Greece, Israel, Turkey.

Baghdad—United Nations Information Centre, 27J2/1 Abu Nouwas Street, Bataween (Post Office Box 2048 Alwiyah), Baghdad, Iraq.
Services to: Iraq.

Bangkok—United Nations Information Service, Economic Commission for Asia and the Far East, Sala Santitham, Bangkok, Thailand.
Services to: Cambodia, Laos, Malaysia, Thailand, Viet-Nam.

Beirut—United Nations Information Centre, United Nations Building, Bir Hassan (Post Office Box 4656), Beirut, Lebanon.
Services to: Jordan, Kuwait, Lebanon, Syria.

Belgrade—United Nations Information Centre, Svetozara Markovica 58 (Post Office Box 157), Belgrade, Yugoslavia.
Services to: Albania, Yugoslavia.

Bogotá—United Nations Information Centre, Calle 19, No. 7-30, 7° Piso (Post Office Box 6567), Bogotá, Colombia.
Services to: Colombia, Ecuador, Venezuela.

Buenos Aires—United Nations Information Centre, Charcas 684, 3er Piso, Buenos Aires, Argentina.
Services to: Argentina, Uruguay.

Bujumbura—United Nations Information Centre, Avenue de la Poste and Place Jungers (Post Office Box 1490), Bujumbura, Burundi.
Services to: Burundi, Rwanda.

CAIRO—United Nations Information Centre, Sharia Osoris, Imm. Tagher, Garden City (Post Office Box 262), Cairo, United Arab Republic.
Services to: Saudi Arabia, United Arab Republic, Yemen.

COLOMBO—United Nations Information Centre, 204 Buller's Road (Post Office Box 1505), Colombo, Ceylon.
Services to: Ceylon.

COPENHAGEN—United Nations Information Centre, 37 H. C. Andersen's Boulevard, Copenhagen V, Denmark.
Services to: Denmark, Finland, Iceland, Norway, Sweden.

DAKAR—United Nations Information Centre, 2 Avenue Roume (Post Office Box 154), Dakar, Senegal.
Services to: Senegal.

DAR ES SALAAM—United Nations Information Centre, Matasalamat Building (Post Office Box 9224), Dar es Salaam, United Republic of Tanzania.
Services to: Kenya, Malawi, United Republic of Tanzania, Zambia.

GENEVA—United Nations Information Service, United Nations Office at Geneva, Palais des Nations, Geneva, Switzerland.
Services to: Austria, Bulgaria, Germany, Hungary, Poland, Romania, Switzerland.

KABUL—United Nations Information Centre, Shah Mahmoud Ghazi Square (Post Office Box 5), Kabul, Afghanistan.
Services to: Afghanistan.

KARACHI—United Nations Information Centre, Havelock Road (Post Office Box 349, G.P.O.), Karachi 1, Pakistan.
Services to: Pakistan.

KATHMANDU—United Nations Information Centre, Kingsway Road (Post Office Box 107), Kathmandu, Nepal.
Services to: Nepal.

KHARTOUM—United Nations Information Centre, House No. 7, Block 5 R.F.E., Gordon Avenue (Post Office Box 1992), Khartoum, Sudan.
Services to: Sudan.

KINSHASA (formerly Leopoldville)—United Nations Information Centre, Royal Hotel, Boulevard du trente juin (Post Office Box 7248), Kinshasa, Democratic Republic of the Congo.
Services to: Democratic Republic of the Congo.

LAGOS—United Nations Information Centre, 17 Kingsway Road, Ikoyi (Post Office Box 1068), Lagos, Nigeria.
Services to: Nigeria.

LA PAZ—United Nations Information Centre, Avenida Arce No. 2419 (Post Office Box 686), La Paz, Bolivia.
Services to: Bolivia.

LIMA—United Nations Information Centre, Edificio Pacifico, 2do. Piso, Plaza Washington 125 (Post Office Box 4480), Lima, Peru.
Services to: Peru.

LOMÉ—United Nations Information Centre, 18, Ancien Boulevard Circulaire (Post Office Box 911), Lomé, Togo.
Services to: Togo.

LONDON—United Nations Information Centre, 14/15 Stratford Place, London W.1., England.
Services to: Ireland, Netherlands, United Kingdom.

MANILA—United Nations Information Centre, WHO Building, Taft Avenue/Corner Isaac Peral (Post Office Box 2149), Manila, Philippines.
Services to: Philippines.

MEXICO CITY—United Nations Information Centre, Hamburgo 63, 3er Piso, Mexico 6, D.F., Mexico.
Services to: Cuba, Dominican Republic, Mexico.

MONROVIA—United Nations Information Centre, ULRC Building (Post Office Box 274), Monrovia, Liberia.
Services to: Liberia.

MOSCOW—United Nations Information Centre, No. 4/16 Ulitsa, Lunacharskogo 1, Moscow, USSR.
Services to: Byelorussian SSR, Ukrainian SSR, USSR.

NEW DELHI—United Nations Information Service, 21 Curzon Road, New Delhi, India.
Services to: India.

PARIS—United Nations Information Centre, 26 Avenue de Ségur, Paris 7, France.
Services to: Belgium, France, Luxembourg.

PORT MORESBY—United Nations Information Centre, Hunter Street, Port Moresby, Papua and New Guinea.
Services to: Papua and New Guinea.

PORT OF SPAIN—United Nations Information Centre, 19 Keate Street (Post Office Box 812), Port of Spain, Trinidad and Tobago.
Services to: Barbados, Guyana, Jamaica, Trinidad and Tobago, Caribbean area.

PRAGUE—United Nations Information Centre, Panska 5, Prague 1, Czechoslovakia.
Services to: Czechoslovakia.

RABAT—United Nations Information Centre, 2 rue Lieutenant Revel (Post Office Box 524), Rabat, Morocco.
Services to: Morocco.

RANGOON—United Nations Information Centre, 24 B Manawhari Road, Rangoon, Burma.
Services to: Burma.

RIO DE JANEIRO—United Nations Information Centre, Rua Mexico 11, Sala 1502 (Post Office Box 1750), Rio de Janeiro, Brazil.
Services to: Brazil.

ROME—United Nations Information Centre, Palazzetto Venezia, Piazza San Marco 50, Rome, Italy.
Services to: Italy.

SAN SALVADOR—United Nations Information Centre, Avenida Roosevelt 2818 (Post Office Box 1114), San Salvador, El Salvador.
Services to: British Honduras, Costa Rica, El Salvador, Guatemala, Honduras, Nicaragua, Panama.

SANTIAGO—United Nations Information Service, Economic Commission for Latin America, Edificio Naciones Unidas, Avenida Dag Hammarskjöld, Santiago, Chile.
Services to: Chile.

SYDNEY—United Nations Information Centre, 44 Martin Place (Post Office Box 4030, G.P.O.), Sydney, Australia.
Services to: Australia, New Zealand.

TANANARIVE—United Nations Information Centre, 26 rue de Liège (Post Office Box 1348), Tananarive, Madagascar.
Services to: Madagascar.

TEHERAN—United Nations Information Centre, Kh. Takhte-Jamshid, 12 Kh. Bandar Pahlavi (Post Office Box 1555), Teheran, Iran.
Services to: Iran.

TOKYO—United Nations Information Centre, Room 411/412, New Ohtemachi Building, 4, 2-Chome, Ohtemachi, Chiyoda-ku, Tokyo, Japan.
Services to: Japan.

TUNIS—United Nations Information Centre, 61 Boulevard Bab Benat (Post Office Box 863), Tunis, Tunisia.
Services to: Libya, Tunisia.

WASHINGTON—United Nations Information Centre, Suite 714, 1028 Connecticut Avenue, N.W., Washington, D.C., 20006, U.S.A.

YAOUNDÉ—United Nations Information Centre (Post Office Box 836), Yaoundé, Cameroon.
Services to: Cameroon.

Index

Abbreviations used in Index

Index

66-16122—16M—March 1968